SWEET BRIAR COLLEGE

W9-AFL-288

Date Due

131
324
R

LIBRARY OF
Western Union College
LE MARS, IOWA

Vol. No. 4905

328
R

WITHDRAWN FROM
WESTMAR LIBRARY

Patent Office

THE PATENT OFFICE is the popular name for the seat of the Department of the Interior of which the Patent Office is a bureau. It is of the Doric style of Greek architecture and stands on the ground set aside by L'Enfant, the French engineer who planned Washington, for "a national church." Its construction has been piecemeal, following the growth of patent business. In 1867 it was finished at a cost of $2,347,011.65.

A COMPILATION

OF THE

MESSAGES AND PAPERS

OF THE

PRESIDENTS

1789 - 1902

WITHDRAWN FROM
WESTMAR LIBRARY

BY

JAMES D. RICHARDSON.

A REPRESENTATIVE FROM THE STATE OF TENNESSEE

VOLUME V

PUBLISHED BY

BUREAU OF NATIONAL LITERATURE AND ART

1904

353.035
R523
1904
v.5

J
81
.896
1904

Copyright 1897,
BY
JAMES D. RICHARDSON

62267

Prefatory Note

This volume, the fifth of the series, comprises a period of twelve years. It includes the four years' term of the Taylor-Fillmore Administration and the full terms of Presidents Pierce and Buchanan. This brings the history down to March 4, 1861, the beginning of the late war between the States. These twelve years form an important and eventful epoch in the affairs of our country, as they immediately precede the war and cover the official utterances of the Executives during this period. Some of the more important events and incidents of these twelve years are the Bulwer-Clayton treaty with Great Britain for a joint occupancy of the proposed ship canal through Central America; the compromise measures of 1850; the admission of California, Minnesota, Oregon, and Kansas as States; the Gadsden purchase, by which the United States acquired 45,535 square miles of territory, being portions of Arizona and New Mexico; the Kansas-Nebraska legislation; the famous Dred Scott decision; the John Brown insurrection, and the disruption of the Democratic party in the national campaign of 1860.

This volume contains several veto messages which are interesting. By President Pierce, vetoes of "An act making a grant of public lands to the several States for the benefit of indigent insane persons;" of six acts relating to internal improvements; of an act for a subsidy for ocean mails, and of an act for the ascertainment and allowance of French spoliation claims. By President Buchanan, vetoes of an act granting lands for agricultural purposes; of two acts relating to internal improvements, and of a homestead act.

Interesting reading is furnished in the protests of President Buchanan against the action of the House of Representatives in ordering the appointment of a committee to investigate the conduct of the President.

The careful reader will find in this volume errors which the compiler could not correct. For instance, on page 410 certain figures are given from a report of the Postmaster-General, which when added do not produce the total given. The error may arise from the failure to make the proper addition, or it may be that the total is correct and that the figures first given are incorrect. The original message contains the same error. Similar errors occur elsewhere in the compilation. These matters are, however, trivial and perhaps need not have been mentioned.

JAMES D. RICHARDSON.

JULY 4, 1897.

Zachary Taylor

March 5, 1849, to July 9, 1850

HOME AT BATON ROUGE, LOUISIANA, OF

ZACHARY TAYLOR

With official portrait engraved from copy of original in steel

ZACHARY TAYLOR.

Zachary Taylor

ZACHARY TAYLOR was born in Orange County, Va., November 24, 1784. He was the third son of Richard Taylor, a colonel in the War of the Revolution, who was conspicuous for his zeal and courage. In 1785 his father removed to Kentucky, then a sparsely occupied county of Virginia, and made his home near the present city of Louisville, where he died. Zachary had but little opportunity for attending school in this new settlement, but was surrounded during all the years of his childhood and early manhood by conditions and circumstances well adapted to form the character illustrated by his eventful career. In 1808 he was appointed a lieutenant in the Seventh Infantry, and in 1810 was promoted to the grade of captain in the same regiment. The same year was married to Miss Margaret Smith, of Maryland. For meritorious conduct in defending Fort Harrison, on the Wabash River, against the Indians received the brevet of major. In 1814 commanded in a campaign against hostile Indians and their British allies on Rock River. Was made lieutenant-colonel of the First Infantry in 1819, and in 1832 became full colonel of that regiment, with headquarters at Fort Crawford, Prairie du Chien. Was occupied with his regiment fighting the Indians in the Black Hawk and other campaigns until 1836, when he was transferred to Florida for service in the Seminole War. For gallant conduct there the next year received the brevet of brigadier-general, and in 1838 was appointed to the chief command in Florida. In 1840 was assigned to command the southern division of the western department of the Army. About this time he made his family home at Baton Rouge, La. In 1845 was ordered to the defense of Texas, which had been annexed to the United States. He went to Corpus Christi, and on March 8, 1846, advanced, and after some fighting, in which he routed and drove the enemy across the Rio Grande, on May 18 occupied Matamoras. He remained there for a short period, obtaining reenforcements. In September fought the enemy at Monterey and captured that town. The following February fought and won the battle of Buena Vista. In the meantime, besides engagements less important, he had won the victories of Palo Alto and Resaca de la Palma, which created great enthusiasm throughout the Union. The terms of capitulation granted by him to the enemy at Monterey were not approved by the Government at Washington. Soon after the battles of Palo Alto and Resaca de la Palma he received the rank of brevet major-general, and on June 27, 1846, was appointed major-general and was commander in chief of all the American forces in Mexico until Major-General Scott was ordered there in 1846. The latter part of November returned to his home in Louisiana. Upon his return to the United States he was received wherever he went with popular demonstrations. Was nominated for President by the national convention of the Whig party at Philadelphia on June 7, 1848, on the fourth ballot, defeating General Scott, Mr. Clay, and Mr. Webster. At the election on November 7 the Whig ticket (Taylor and Fillmore) was successful, receiving 163 electoral votes, while the Democratic candidates (Cass and Butler) each received 127 votes. He was inaugurated March 5, 1849, and died in Washington City July 9, 1850. Was buried in Cave Hill Cemetery, Louisville, Ky.

INAUGURAL ADDRESS.

Elected by the American people to the highest office known to our laws, I appear here to take the oath prescribed by the Constitution, and, in compliance with a time-honored custom, to address those who are now assembled.

The confidence and respect shown by my countrymen in calling me to be the Chief Magistrate of a Republic holding a high rank among the nations of the earth have inspired me with feelings of the most profound gratitude; but when I reflect that the acceptance of the office which their partiality has bestowed imposes the discharge of the most arduous duties and involves the weightiest obligations, I am conscious that the position which I have been called to fill, though sufficient to satisfy the loftiest ambition, is surrounded by fearful responsibilities. Happily, however, in the performance of my new duties I shall not be without able cooperation. The legislative and judicial branches of the Government present prominent examples of distinguished civil attainments and matured experience, and it shall be my endeavor to call to my assistance in the Executive Departments individuals whose talents, integrity, and purity of character will furnish ample guaranties for the faithful and honorable performance of the trusts to be committed to their charge. With such aids and an honest purpose to do whatever is right, I hope to execute diligently, impartially, and for the best interests of the country the manifold duties devolved upon me.

In the discharge of these duties my guide will be the Constitution, which I this day swear to "preserve, protect, and defend." For the interpretation of that instrument I shall look to the decisions of the judicial tribunals established by its authority and to the practice of the Government under the earlier Presidents, who had so large a share in its formation. To the example of those illustrious patriots I shall always defer with reverence, and especially to his example who was by so many titles "the Father of his Country."

To command the Army and Navy of the United States; with the advice and consent of the Senate, to make treaties and to appoint ambassadors and other officers; to give to Congress information of the state of the Union and recommend such measures as he shall judge to be necessary; and to take care that the laws shall be faithfully executed—these are the most important functions intrusted to the President by the Constitution, and it may be expected that I shall briefly indicate the principles which will control me in their execution.

Chosen by the body of the people under the assurance that my Administration would be devoted to the welfare of the whole country, and not to the support of any particular section or merely local interest, I this day renew the declarations I have heretofore made and proclaim my fixed determination to maintain to the extent of my ability the Government in its original purity and to adopt as the basis of my public policy those great republican doctrines which constitute the strength of our national existence.

In reference to the Army and Navy, lately employed with so much distinction on active service, care shall be taken to insure the highest condition of efficiency, and in furtherance of that object the military and naval schools, sustained by the liberality of Congress, shall receive the special attention of the Executive.

As American freemen we can not but sympathize in all efforts to extend the blessings of civil and political liberty, but at the same time we are warned by the admonitions of history and the voice of our own beloved Washington to abstain from entangling alliances with foreign nations. In all disputes between conflicting governments it is our interest not less than our duty to remain strictly neutral, while our geographical position, the genius of our institutions and our people, the advancing spirit of civilization, and, above all, the dictates of religion direct us to the cultivation of peaceful and friendly relations with all other powers. It is to be hoped that no international question can now arise which a government confident in its own strength and resolved to protect its own just rights may not settle by wise negotiation; and it eminently becomes a government like our own, founded on the morality and intelligence of its citizens and upheld by their affections, to exhaust every resort of honorable diplomacy before appealing to arms. In the conduct of our foreign relations I shall conform to these views, as I believe them essential to the best interests and the true honor of the country.

The appointing power vested in the President imposes delicate and onerous duties. So far as it is possible to be informed, I shall make honesty, capacity, and fidelity indispensable prerequisites to the bestowal of office, and the absence of either of these qualities shall be deemed sufficient cause for removal.

It shall be my study to recommend such constitutional measures to Congress as may be necessary and proper to secure encouragement and protection to the great interests of agriculture, commerce, and manufactures, to improve our rivers and harbors, to provide for the speedy extinguishment of the public debt, to enforce a strict accountability on the part of all officers of the Government and the utmost economy in all public expenditures; but it is for the wisdom of Congress itself, in which all legislative powers are vested by the Constitution, to regulate these and other matters of domestic policy. I shall look with confidence to the enlightened patriotism of that body to adopt such measures of conciliation as may harmonize conflicting interests and tend to perpetuate that Union which should be the paramount object of our hopes and affections. In any action calculated to promote an object so near the heart of everyone who truly loves his country I will zealously unite with the coordinate branches of the Government.

In conclusion I congratulate you, my fellow-citizens, upon the high state of prosperity to which the goodness of Divine Providence has conducted our common country. Let us invoke a continuance of the same protecting care which has led us from small beginnings to the eminence we this day occupy, and let us seek to deserve that continuance by prudence and moderation in our councils, by well-directed attempts to assuage the bitterness which too often marks unavoidable differences of opinion, by the promulgation and practice of just and liberal principles, and by an enlarged patriotism, which shall acknowledge no limits but those of our own widespread Republic.

MARCH 5, 1849.

SPECIAL MESSAGES.

WASHINGTON, *March 13, 1849.*

To the Senate of the United States:

I herewith communicate to the Senate, in confidence, a report and accompanying papers* from the Secretary of State, in answer to its resolution of the 12th instant.

Z. TAYLOR.

---

*Instructions to United States minister at London relative to further extension of reciprocity and equality in the laws of navigation, and contemplating the opening of the coasting trade of the United States to the vessels of other nations.

WASHINGTON, *March 20, 1849.*

To the Senate of the United States:

In answer to the resolution of the Senate of yesterday, passed in executive session, requesting a communication of certain papers relative to the amendments made by the Senate to the treaty of Guadalupe Hidalgo, I transmit a report from the Secretary of State and the documents by which it was accompanied. It is desirable that the latter should be returned to the Department of State.

Z. TAYLOR.

WASHINGTON, *March 22, 1849.*

To the Senate of the United States:

In compliance with the request contained in the resolution of the Senate yesterday, adopted in executive session, calling for certain papers in relation to the amendments made by the Senate in the treaty of Guadalupe Hidalgo, I transmit a report from the Secretary of State and the documents by which it was accompanied.

Z. TAYLOR.

PROCLAMATION.

BY THE PRESIDENT OF THE UNITED STATES.

A PROCLAMATION.

There is reason to believe that an armed expedition is about to be fitted out in the United States with an intention to invade the island of Cuba or some of the Provinces of Mexico. The best information which the Executive has been able to obtain points to the island of Cuba as the object of this expedition. It is the duty of this Government to observe the faith of treaties and to prevent any aggression by our citizens upon the territories of friendly nations. I have therefore thought it necessary and proper to issue this my proclamation to warn all citizens of the United States who shall connect themselves with an enterprise so grossly in violation of our laws and our treaty obligations that they will thereby subject themselves to the heavy penalties denounced against them by our acts of Congress and will forfeit their claim to the protection of their country. No such persons must expect the interference of this Government in any form on their behalf, no matter to what extremities they may be reduced in consequence of their conduct. An enterprise to invade the territories of a friendly nation, set on foot and prosecuted within the limits of the United States, is in the highest degree criminal, as tending to endanger the peace and compromit the honor of this nation; and therefore I exhort all good citizens, as they regard our national reputation, as they respect their own laws and the laws of nations, as they value the blessings of peace and the welfare of their country, to discountenance and prevent by all lawful means any such enterprise; and I call upon every officer of this Government, civil or military, to use all efforts in his power to arrest for trial and punishment every such offender against the laws providing for the performance of our sacred obligations to friendly powers.

Given under my hand the 11th day of August, A. D. 1849, and the seventy-fourth of the Independence of the United States.

Z. TAYLOR.

By the President:

J. M. CLAYTON,
Secretary of State.

EXECUTIVE ORDER.

GENERAL ORDERS, No. 34.

WAR DEPARTMENT,
ADJUTANT-GENERAL'S OFFICE,
Washington, June 19, 1849.

I. The following orders of the President of the United States and Secretary of War communicate to the Army the death of the late ex-President, James K. Polk:

WASHINGTON, *June 19, 1849.*

The President with deep regret announces to the American people the death of James K. Polk, late President of the United States, which occurred at Nashville on the 15th instant.

A nation is suddenly called upon to mourn the loss of one the recollection of whose long services in its councils will be forever preserved on the tablets of history.

As a mark of respect to the memory of a citizen who has been distinguished by the highest honors which his country could bestow, it is ordered that the Executive Mansion and the several Departments at Washington be immediately placed in mourning and all business be suspended during to-morrow.

It is further ordered that the War and Navy Departments cause suitable military and naval honors to be paid on this occasion to the memory of the illustrious dead.

Z. TAYLOR.

WAR DEPARTMENT, *June 19, 1849.*

The President of the United States with deep regret announces to the Army the death of James K. Polk, our distinguished and honored fellow-citizen.

He died at Nashville the 15th instant, having but recently left the theater of his high public duties at this capital and retired to his home amid the congratulations of his fellow-citizens. He died in the prime of life, after having received and enjoyed the highest honors of the Republic.

His Administration was eventful. No branch of the Government will be more intimately associated with it in history than the Army and its glorious achievements. Accordingly, the President orders that appropriate military honors shall be paid to his memory by the Army of the United States.

The Adjutant-General will give the necessary instructions for carrying into effect the foregoing orders.

G. W. CRAWFORD,
Secretary of War.

II. On the day succeeding the arrival of this general order at each military post the troops will be paraded at 10 o'clock a. m. and the order read to them, after which all labors for the day will cease.

The national flag will be displayed at half-staff.

At dawn of day thirteen guns will be fired, and afterwards at intervals of thirty minutes between the rising and setting sun a single gun, and at the close of the day a national salute of thirty guns.

The officers of the Army will wear crape on the left arm and on their swords and the colors of the several regiments will be put in mourning for the period of six months.

By order:

R. JONES, *Adjutant-General.*

FIRST ANNUAL MESSAGE.

WASHINGTON, *December 4, 1849.*

Fellow-Citizens of the Senate and House of Representatives:

Sixty years have elapsed since the establishment of this Government, and the Congress of the United States again assembles to legislate for an empire of freemen. The predictions of evil prophets, who formerly pretended to foretell the downfall of our institutions, are now remembered only to be derided, and the United States of America at this moment present to the world the most stable and permanent Government on earth.

Such is the result of the labors of those who have gone before us. Upon Congress will eminently depend the future maintenance of our system of free government and the transmission of it unimpaired to posterity.

We are at peace with all the other nations of the world, and seek to maintain our cherished relations of amity with them. During the past year we have been blessed by a kind Providence with an abundance of the fruits of the earth, and although the destroying angel for a time visited extensive portions of our territory with the ravages of a dreadful pestilence, yet the Almighty has at length deigned to stay his hand and to restore the inestimable blessing of general health to a people who have acknowledged His power, deprecated His wrath, and implored His merciful protection.

While enjoying the benefits of amicable intercourse with foreign nations, we have not been insensible to the distractions and wars which have prevailed in other quarters of the world. It is a proper theme of thanksgiving to Him who rules the destinies of nations that we have been able to maintain amidst all these contests an independent and neutral position toward all belligerent powers.

Our relations with Great Britain are of the most friendly character. In consequence of the recent alteration of the British navigation acts, British vessels, from British and other foreign ports, will under our existing laws, after the 1st day of January next, be admitted to entry in our ports with cargoes of the growth, manufacture, or production of any part of the world on the same terms as to duties, imposts, and charges as vessels of the United States with their cargoes, and our vessels will be admitted to the same advantages in British ports, entering therein on the same terms as British vessels. Should no order in council disturb this legislative arrangement, the late act of the British Parliament, by which Great Britain is brought within the terms proposed by the act of Congress of the 1st of March, 1817, it is hoped will be productive of benefit to both countries.

A slight interruption of diplomatic intercourse which occurred between this Government and France, I am happy to say, has been terminated, and our minister there has been received. It is therefore unnecessary to refer now to the circumstances which led to that interruption. I need not express to you the sincere satisfaction with which we shall welcome the arrival of another envoy extraordinary and minister plenipotentiary from a sister Republic to which we have so long been, and still remain, bound by the strongest ties of amity.

Shortly after I had entered upon the discharge of the Executive duties I was apprised that a war steamer belonging to the German Empire was being fitted out in the harbor of New York with the aid of some of our naval officers, rendered under the permission of the late Secretary of the Navy. This permission was granted during an armistice between that Empire and the Kingdom of Denmark, which had been engaged in the Schleswig-Holstein war. Apprehensive that this act of intervention on our part might be viewed as a violation of our neutral obligations incurred by the treaty with Denmark and of the provisions of the act of Congress of the 20th of April, 1818, I directed that no further aid should be rendered by any agent or officer of the Navy; and I instructed the Secretary of State to apprise the minister of the German Empire accredited to this

Government of my determination to execute the law of the United States and to maintain the faith of treaties with all nations. The correspondence which ensued between the Department of State and the minister of the German Empire is herewith laid before you. The execution of the law and the observance of the treaty were deemed by me to be due to the honor of the country, as well as to the sacred obligations of the Constitution. I shall not fail to pursue the same course should a similar case arise with any other nation. Having avowed the opinion on taking the oath of office that in disputes between conflicting foreign governments it is our interest not less than our duty to remain strictly neutral, I shall not abandon it. You will perceive from the correspondence submitted to you in connection with this subject that the course adopted in this case has been properly regarded by the belligerent powers interested in the matter.

Although a minister of the United States to the German Empire was appointed by my predecessor in August, 1848, and has for a long time been in attendance at Frankfort-on-the-Main, and although a minister appointed to represent that Empire was received and accredited here, yet no such government as that of the German Empire has been definitively constituted. Mr. Donelson, our representative at Frankfort, remained there several months in the expectation that a union of the German States under one constitution or form of government might at length be organized. It is believed by those well acquainted with the existing relations between Prussia and the States of Germany that no such union can be permanently established without her cooperation. In the event of the formation of such a union and the organization of a central power in Germany of which she should form a part, it would become necessary to withdraw our minister at Berlin; but while Prussia exists as an independent kingdom and diplomatic relations are maintained with her there can be no necessity for the continuance of the mission to Frankfort. I have therefore recalled Mr. Donelson and directed the archives of the legation at Frankfort to be transferred to the American legation at Berlin.

Having been apprised that a considerable number of adventurers were engaged in fitting out a military expedition within the United States against a foreign country, and believing from the best information I could obtain that it was destined to invade the island of Cuba, I deemed it due to the friendly relations existing between the United States and Spain, to the treaty between the two nations, to the laws of the United States, and, above all, to the American honor to exert the lawful authority of this Government in suppressing the expedition and preventing the invasion. To this end I issued a proclamation enjoining it upon the officers of the United States, civil and military, to use all lawful means within their power. A copy of that proclamation is herewith submitted. The expedition has been suppressed. So long as the act of Congress of the 20th of April, 1818, which owes its existence to the law of nations and to the policy of Washington himself, shall remain on our statute books, I hold it to be the duty of the Executive faithfully to obey its injunctions.

While this expedition was in progress I was informed that a foreigner who claimed our protection had been clandestinely and, as was supposed, forcibly carried off in a vessel from New Orleans to the island of Cuba. I immediately caused such steps to be taken as I thought necessary, in case the information I had received should prove correct, to vindicate the honor of the country and the right of every person seeking an asylum on our soil to the protection of our laws. The person alleged to have been abducted was promptly restored, and the circumstances of the case are now about to undergo investigation before a judicial tribunal. I would respectfully suggest that although the crime charged to have been committed in this case is held odious, as being in conflict with our opinions on the subject of national sovereignty and personal freedom, there is no prohibition of it or punishment for it provided in any act of Congress. The expediency of supplying this defect in our criminal code is therefore recommended to your consideration.

I have scrupulously avoided any interference in the wars and contentions which have recently distracted Europe. During the late conflict between Austria and Hungary there seemed to be a prospect that the latter might become an independent nation. However faint that prospect at the time appeared, I thought it my duty, in accordance with the general sentiment of the American people, who deeply sympathized with the Magyar patriots, to stand prepared, upon the contingency of the establishment by her of a permanent government, to be the first to welcome independent Hungary into the family of nations. For this purpose I invested an agent then in Europe with power to declare our willingness promptly to recognize her independence in the event of her ability to sustain it. The powerful intervention of Russia in the contest extinguished the hopes of the struggling Magyars. The United States did not at any time interfere in the contest, but the feelings of the nation were strongly enlisted in the cause, and by the sufferings of a brave people, who had made a gallant, though unsuccessful, effort to be free.

Our claims upon Portugal have been during the past year prosecuted with renewed vigor, and it has been my object to employ every effort of honorable diplomacy to procure their adjustment. Our late chargé d'affaires at Lisbon, the Hon. George W. Hopkins, made able and energetic, but unsuccessful, efforts to settle these unpleasant matters of controversy and to obtain indemnity for the wrongs which were the subjects of complaint. Our present chargé d'affaires at that Court will also bring to the prosecution of these claims ability and zeal. The revolutionary and distracted condition of Portugal in past times has been represented as one of the leading causes of her delay in indemnifying our suffering citizens.

But I must now say it is matter of profound regret that these claims have not yet been settled. The omission of Portugal to do justice to the American claimants has now assumed a character so grave and serious that I shall shortly make it the subject of a special message to Congress, with a view to such ultimate action as its wisdom and patriotism may suggest.

With Russia, Austria, Prussia, Sweden, Denmark, Belgium, the Netherlands, and the Italian States we still maintain our accustomed amicable relations.

During the recent revolutions in the Papal States our chargé d'affaires at Rome has been unable to present his letter of credence, which, indeed, he was directed by my predecessor to withhold until he should receive further orders. Such was the unsettled condition of things in those States that it was not deemed expedient to give him any instructions on the subject of presenting his credential letter different from those with which he had been furnished by the late Administration until the 25th of June last, when, in consequence of the want of accurate information of the exact state of things at that distance from us, he was instructed to exercise his own discretion in presenting himself to the then existing Government if in his judgment sufficiently stable, or, if not, to await further events. Since that period Rome has undergone another revolution, and he abides the establishment of a government sufficiently permanent to justify him in opening diplomatic intercourse with it.

With the Republic of Mexico it is our true policy to cultivate the most friendly relations. Since the ratification of the treaty of Guadalupe Hidalgo nothing has occurred of a serious character to disturb them. A faithful observance of the treaty and a sincere respect for her rights can not fail to secure the lasting confidence and friendship of that Republic. The message of my predecessor to the House of Representatives of the 8th of February last, communicating, in compliance with a resolution of that body, a copy of a paper called a protocol, signed at Queretaro on the 30th of May, 1848, by the commissioners of the United States and the minister of foreign affairs of the Mexican Government, having been a subject of correspondence between the Department of State and the envoy extraordinary and minister plenipotentiary of that Republic accredited to this Government, a transcript of that correspondence is herewith submitted.

The commissioner on the part of the United States for marking the boundary between the two Republics, though delayed in reaching San Diego by unforeseen obstacles, arrived at that place within a short period after the time required by the treaty, and was there joined by the commissioner on the part of Mexico. They entered upon their duties, and at the date of the latest intelligence from that quarter some progress had been made in the survey. The expenses incident to the organization of the commission and to its conveyance to the point where its operations were to begin have so much reduced the fund appropriated by Congress that a further sum, to cover the charges which must be incurred during the present fiscal year, will be necessary. The great length of frontier along which the boundary extends, the nature of the adjacent territory, and the difficulty of obtaining supplies except at or near the extremes of the line render it also indispensable that a liberal provision should be made to meet the necessary charges during the fiscal year ending on the 30th of June, 1851. I accordingly recommend this subject to your attention.

In the adjustment of the claims of American citizens on Mexico, provided for by the late treaty, the employment of counsel on the part of the Government may become important for the purpose of assisting the commissioners in protecting the interests of the United States. I recommend this subject to the early and favorable consideration of Congress.

Complaints have been made in regard to the inefficiency of the means provided by the Government of New Granada for transporting the United States mail across the Isthmus of Panama, pursuant to our postal convention with that Republic of the 6th of March, 1844. Our chargé d'affaires at Bogota has been directed to make such representations to the Government of New Granada as will, it is hoped, lead to a prompt removal of this cause of complaint.

The sanguinary civil war with which the Republic of Venezuela has for some time past been ravaged has been brought to a close. In its progress the rights of some of our citizens resident or trading there have been violated. The restoration of order will afford the Venezuelan Government an opportunity to examine and redress these grievances and others of longer standing which our representatives at Caracas have hitherto ineffectually urged upon the attention of that Government.

The extension of the coast of the United States on the Pacific and the unexampled rapidity with which the inhabitants of California especially are increasing in numbers have imparted new consequence to our relations with the other countries whose territories border upon that ocean. It is probable that the intercourse between those countries and our possessions in that quarter, particularly with the Republic of Chili, will become extensive and mutually advantageous in proportion as California and Oregon shall increase in population and wealth. It is desirable, therefore, that this Government should do everything in its power to foster and strengthen its relations with those States, and that the spirit of amity between us should be mutual and cordial.

I recommend the observance of the same course toward all other American States. The United States stand as the great American power, to which, as their natural ally and friend, they will always be disposed first to look for mediation and assistance in the event of any collision between them and any European nation. As such we may often kindly mediate in their behalf without entangling ourselves in foreign wars or unnecessary controversies. Whenever the faith of our treaties with any of them shall require our interference, we must necessarily interpose.

A convention has been negotiated with Brazil providing for the satisfaction of American claims on that Government, and it will be submitted to the Senate. Since the last session of Congress we have received an envoy extraordinary and minister plenipotentiary from that Empire, and our relations with it are founded upon the most amicable understanding.

Your attention is earnestly invited to an amendment of our existing laws relating to the African slave trade with a view to the effectual suppression of that barbarous traffic. It is not to be denied that this trade is still in part carried on by means of vessels built in the United States and owned or navigated by some of our citizens. The correspondence between the Department of State and the minister and consul of the United States at Rio de Janeiro, which has from time to time been laid before Congress, represents that it is a customary device to evade the penalties of our laws by means of sea letters. Vessels sold in Brazil, when provided with such papers by the consul, instead of returning to the United States for a new register proceed at once to the coast of Africa for the purpose of obtaining cargoes of slaves. Much additional information of the same character has recently been transmitted to the Department of State. It has not been considered the policy of our laws to subject an American citizen who in a foreign country purchases a vessel built in the United States to the inconvenience of sending her home for a new register before permitting her to proceed on a voyage. Any alteration of the laws which might have a tendency to impede the free transfer of property in vessels between our citizens, or the free navigation of those vessels between different parts of the world when employed in lawful commerce, should be well and cautiously considered; but I trust that your wisdom will devise a method by which our general policy in this respect may be preserved, and at the same time the abuse of our flag by means of sea letters, in the manner indicated, may be prevented.

Having ascertained that there is no prospect of the reunion of the five States of Central America which formerly composed the Republic of that name, we have separately negotiated with some of them treaties of amity and commerce, which will be laid before the Senate.

A contract having been concluded with the State of Nicaragua by a company composed of American citizens for the purpose of constructing a ship canal through the territory of that State to connect the Atlantic and Pacific oceans, I have directed the negotiation of a treaty with Nicaragua pledging both Governments to protect those who shall engage in and perfect the work. All other nations are invited by the State of Nicaragua to enter into the same treaty stipulations with her; and the benefit to be derived by each from such an arrangement will be the protection of this great interoceanic communication against any power which might seek to obstruct it or to monopolize its advantages. All States entering into such a treaty will enjoy the right of passage through the canal on payment of the same tolls. The work, if constructed under these guaranties, will become a bond of peace instead of a subject of contention and strife between the nations of the earth. Should the great maritime States of Europe consent to this arrangement (and we have no reason to suppose that a proposition so fair and honorable will be opposed by any), the energies of their people and ours will cooperate in promoting the success of the enterprise. I do not recommend any appropriation from the National Treasury for this purpose, nor do I believe that such an appropriation is necessary. Private enterprise, if properly protected, will complete the work should it prove to be feasible. The parties who have procured the charter from Nicaragua for its construction desire no assistance from this Government beyond its protection; and they profess that, having examined the proposed line of communication, they will be ready to commence the undertaking whenever that protection shall be extended to them. Should there appear to be reason, on examining the whole evidence, to entertain a serious doubt of the practicability of constructing such a canal, that doubt could be speedily solved by an actual exploration of the route.

Should such a work be constructed under the common protection of all nations, for equal benefits to all, it would be neither just nor expedient that any great maritime state should command the communication. The territory through which the canal may be opened ought to be freed from the claims of any foreign power. No such power should occupy a position that would enable it hereafter to exercise so controlling an influence over the commerce of the world or to obstruct a highway which ought to be dedicated to the common uses of mankind.

The routes across the Isthmus at Tehuantepec and Panama are also worthy of our serious consideration. They did not fail to engage the attention of my predecessor. The negotiator of the treaty of Guadalupe Hidalgo was instructed to offer a very large sum of money for the right of transit across the Isthmus of Tehuantepec. The Mexican Government did not accede to the proposition for the purchase of the right of way, probably because it had already contracted with private individuals for the construction of a passage from the Guasacualco River to Tehuantepec. I shall not renew any proposition to purchase for money a right which ought to be equally secured to all nations on payment of a reasonable toll to the owners of the improvement, who would doubtless be well contented with that compensation and the guaranties of the maritime states of the world in separate treaties negotiated with Mexico, binding her and them to protect those who should construct the work. Such guaranties would do more to secure the completion of the communication through the territory of Mexico than any other reasonable consideration that could be offered; and as Mexico herself would be the greatest gainer by the opening of this communication between the Gulf and the Pacific Ocean, it is presumed that she would not hesitate to yield her aid in the manner proposed to accomplish an improvement so important to her own best interests.

We have reason to hope that the proposed railroad across the Isthmus at Panama will be successfully constructed under the protection of the late treaty with New Granada, ratified and exchanged by my predecessor on the 10th day of June, 1848, which guarantees the perfect neutrality of the Isthmus and the rights of sovereignty and property of New Granada over that territory, "with a view that the free transit from ocean to ocean may not be interrupted or embarrassed" during the existence of the treaty. It is our policy to encourage every practicable route across the isthmus which connects North and South America, either by railroad or canal, which the energy and enterprise of our citizens may induce them to complete, and I consider it obligatory upon me to adopt that policy, especially in consequence of the absolute necessity of facilitating intercourse with our possessions on the Pacific.

The position of the Sandwich Islands with reference to the territory of the United States on the Pacific, the success of our persevering and benevolent citizens who have repaired to that remote quarter in Christianizing the natives and inducing them to adopt a system of government and laws suited to their capacity and wants, and the use made by our numerous whale ships of the harbors of the islands as places of resort for obtaining refreshments and repairs all combine to render their destiny peculiarly interesting to us. It is our duty to encourage the authorities of those islands in their efforts to improve and elevate the moral and political condition of the inhabitants, and we should make reasonable allowances for the difficulties inseparable from this task. We desire that the islands may maintain their independence and that other nations should concur with us in this sentiment. We could in no event be indifferent to their passing under the dominion of any other power. The principal commercial states have in this a common interest, and it is to be hoped that no one of them will attempt to interpose obstacles to the entire independence of the islands.

The receipts into the Treasury for the fiscal year ending on the 30th of June last were, in cash, $48,830,097.50, and in Treasury notes funded $10,833,000, making an aggregate of $59,663,097.50; and the expenditures for the same time were, in cash, $46,798,667.82, and in Treasury notes funded $10,833,000, making an aggregate of $57,631,667.82.

The accounts and estimates which will be submitted to Congress in the report of the Secretary of the Treasury show that there will probably be a deficit occasioned by the expenses of the Mexican War and treaty on the 1st day of July next of $5,828,121.66, and on the 1st day of July, 1851, of $10,547,092.73, making in the whole a probable deficit to be provided for of $16,375,214.39. The extraordinary expenses of the war with Mexico and the purchase of California and New Mexico exceed in amount this deficit, together with the loans heretofore made for those

LIBRARY OF
Western Union College
LE MARS, IOWA

Vol. No.

objects. I therefore recommend that authority be given to borrow whatever sum may be necessary to cover that deficit. I recommend the observance of strict economy in the appropriation and expenditure of public money.

I recommend a revision of the existing tariff and its adjustment on a basis which may augment the revenue. I do not doubt the right or duty of Congress to encourage domestic industry, which is the great source of national as well as individual wealth and prosperity. I look to the wisdom and patriotism of Congress for the adoption of a system which may place home labor at last on a sure and permanent footing and by due encouragement of manufactures give a new and increased stimulus to agriculture and promote the development of our vast resources and the extension of our commerce. Believing that to the attainment of these ends, as well as the necessary augmentation of the revenue and the prevention of frauds, a system of specific duties is best adapted, I strongly recommend to Congress the adoption of that system, fixing the duties at rates high enough to afford substantial and sufficient encouragement to our own industry and at the same time so adjusted as to insure stability.

The question of the continuance of the subtreasury system is respectfully submitted to the wisdom of Congress. If continued, important modifications of it appear to be indispensable.

For further details and views on the above and other matters connected with commerce, the finances, and revenue I refer to the report of the Secretary of the Treasury.

No direct aid has been given by the General Government to the improvement of agriculture except by the expenditure of small sums for the collection and publication of agricultural statistics and for some chemical analyses, which have been thus far paid for out of the patent fund. This aid is, in my opinion, wholly inadequate. To give to this leading branch of American industry the encouragement which it merits, I respectfully recommend the establishment of an agricultural bureau, to be connected with the Department of the Interior. To elevate the social condition of the agriculturist, to increase his prosperity, and to extend his means of usefulness to his country, by multiplying his sources of information, should be the study of every statesman and a primary object with every legislator.

No civil government having been provided by Congress for California, the people of that Territory, impelled by the necessities of their political condition, recently met in convention for the purpose of forming a constitution and State government, which the latest advices give me reason to suppose has been accomplished; and it is believed they will shortly apply for the admission of California into the Union as a sovereign State. Should such be the case, and should their constitution be conformable to the requisitions of the Constitution of the United States, I recommend their application to the favorable consideration of Congress.

The people of New Mexico will also, it is believed, at no very distant period present themselves for admission into the Union. Preparatory to the admission of California and New Mexico the people of each will have instituted for themselves a republican form of government, "laying its foundation in such principles and organizing its powers in such form as to them shall seem most likely to effect their safety and happiness." By awaiting their action all causes of uneasiness may be avoided and confidence and kind feeling preserved. With a view of maintaining the harmony and tranquillity so dear to all, we should abstain from the introduction of those exciting topics of a sectional character which have hitherto produced painful apprehensions in the public mind; and I repeat the solemn warning of the first and most illustrious of my predecessors against furnishing "any ground for characterizing parties by geographical discriminations."

A collector has been appointed at San Francisco under the act of Congress extending the revenue laws over California, and measures have been taken to organize the custom-houses at that and the other ports mentioned in that act at the earliest period practicable. The collector proceeded overland, and advices have not yet been received of his arrival at San Francisco. Meanwhile, it is understood that the customs have continued to be collected there by officers acting under the military authority, as they were during the Administration of my predecessor. It will, I think, be expedient to confirm the collections thus made, and direct the avails (after such allowances as Congress may think fit to authorize) to be expended within the Territory or to be paid into the Treasury for the purpose of meeting appropriations for the improvement of its rivers and harbors.

A party engaged on the coast survey was dispatched to Oregon in January last. According to the latest advices, they had not left California; and directions have been given to them, as soon as they shall have fixed on the sites of the two light-houses and the buoys authorized to be constructed and placed in Oregon, to proceed without delay to make reconnoissances of the most important points on the coast of California, and especially to examine and determine on sites for light-houses on that coast, the speedy erection of which is urgently demanded by our rapidly increasing commerce.

I have transferred the Indian agencies from upper Missouri and Council Bluffs to Santa Fe and Salt Lake, and have caused to be appointed subagents in the valleys of the Gila, the Sacramento, and the San Joaquin rivers. Still further legal provisions will be necessary for the effective and successful extension of our system of Indian intercourse over the new territories.

I recommend the establishment of a branch mint in California, as it will, in my opinion, afford important facilities to those engaged in mining, as well as to the Government in the disposition of the mineral lands.

I also recommend that commissions be organized by Congress to examine and decide upon the validity of the present subsisting land titles in California and New Mexico, and that provision be made for the establishment of offices of surveyor-general in New Mexico, California, and Oregon and for the surveying and bringing into market the public lands in those Territories. Those lands, remote in position and difficult of access, ought to be disposed of on terms liberal to all, but especially favorable to the early emigrants.

In order that the situation and character of the principal mineral deposits in California may be ascertained, I recommend that a geological and mineralogical exploration be connected with the linear surveys, and that the mineral lands be divided into small lots suitable for mining and be disposed of by sale or lease, so as to give our citizens an opportunity of procuring a permanent right of property in the soil. This would seem to be as important to the success of mining as of agricultural pursuits.

The great mineral wealth of California and the advantages which its ports and harbors and those of Oregon afford to commerce, especially with the islands of the Pacific and Indian oceans and the populous regions of eastern Asia, make it certain that there will arise in a few years large and prosperous communities on our western coast. It therefore becomes important that a line of communication, the best and most expeditious which the nature of the country will admit, should be opened within the territory of the United States from the navigable waters of the Atlantic or the Gulf of Mexico to the Pacific. Opinion, as elicited and expressed by two large and respectable conventions lately assembled at St. Louis and Memphis, points to a railroad as that which, if practicable, will best meet the wishes and wants of the country. But while this, if in successful operation, would be a work of great national importance and of a value to the country which it would be difficult to estimate, it ought also to be regarded as an undertaking of vast magnitude and expense, and one which must, if it be indeed practicable, encounter many difficulties in its construction and use. Therefore, to avoid failure and disappointment; to enable Congress to judge whether in the condition of the country through which it must pass the work be feasible, and, if it be found so, whether it should be undertaken as a national improvement or left to individual enterprise, and in the latter alternative what aid, if any, ought to be extended to it by the Government, I recommend as a preliminary measure a careful reconnoissance of the several proposed routes by a scientific corps and a report as to the practicability of making such a road, with an estimate of the cost of its construction and support.

For further views on these and other matters connected with the duties of the home department I refer you to the report of the Secretary of the Interior.

I recommend early appropriations for continuing the river and harbor improvements which have been already begun, and also for the construction of those for which estimates have been made, as well as for examinations and estimates preparatory to the commencement of such others as the wants of the country, and especially the advance of our population over new districts and the extension of commerce, may render necessary. An estimate of the amount which can be advantageously expended within the next fiscal year under the direction of the Bureau of Topographical Engineers accompanies the report of the Secretary of War, to which I respectfully invite the attention of Congress.

The cession of territory made by the late treaty with Mexico has greatly extended our exposed frontier and rendered its defense more difficult. That treaty has also brought us under obligations to Mexico, to comply with which a military force is requisite. But our military establishment is not materially changed as to its efficiency from the condition in which it stood before the commencement of the Mexican War. Some addition to it will therefore be necessary, and I recommend to the favorable consideration of Congress an increase of the several corps of the Army at our distant Western posts, as proposed in the accompanying report of the Secretary of War.

Great embarrassment has resulted from the effect upon rank in the Army heretofore given to brevet and staff commissions. The views of the Secretary of War on this subject are deemed important, and if carried into effect will, it is believed, promote the harmony of the service. The plan proposed for retiring disabled officers and providing an asylum for such of the rank and file as from age, wounds, and other infirmities occasioned by service have become unfit to perform their respective duties is recommended as a means of increasing the efficiency of the Army and as an act of justice due from a grateful country to the faithful soldier.

The accompanying report of the Secretary of the Navy presents a full and satisfactory account of the condition and operations of the naval service during the past year. Our citizens engaged in the legitimate pursuits of commerce have enjoyed its benefits. Wherever our national vessels have gone they have been received with respect, our officers have been treated with kindness and courtesy, and they have on all occasions pursued a course of strict neutrality, in accordance with the policy of our Government.

The naval force at present in commission is as large as is admissible with the number of men authorized by Congress to be employed.

I invite your attention to the recommendation of the Secretary of the Navy on the subject of a reorganization of the Navy in its various grades of officers, and the establishing of a retired list for such of the officers as are disqualified for active and effective service. Should Congress adopt some such measure as is recommended, it will greatly increase the efficiency of the Navy and reduce its expenditures.

I also ask your attention to the views expressed by him in reference to the employment of war steamers and in regard to the contracts for the transportation of the United States mails and the operation of the system upon the prosperity of the Navy.

By an act of Congress passed August 14, 1848, provision was made for extending post-office and mail accommodations to California and Oregon. Exertions have been made to execute that law, but the limited provisions of the act, the inadequacy of the means it authorizes, the ill adaptation of our post-office laws to the situation of that country, and the measure of compensation for services allowed by those laws, compared with the prices of labor and rents in California, render those exertions in a great degree ineffectual. More particular and efficient provision by law is required on this subject.

The act of 1845 reducing postage has now, by its operation during four years, produced results fully showing that the income from such reduced postage is sufficient to sustain the whole expense of the service of the Post-Office Department, not including the cost of transportation in mail steamers on the lines from New York to Chagres and from Panama to Astoria, which have not been considered by Congress as properly belonging to the mail service.

It is submitted to the wisdom of Congress whether a further reduction of postage should not now be made, more particularly on the letter correspondence. This should be relieved from the unjust burden of transporting and delivering the franked matter of Congress, for which public service provision should be made from the Treasury. I confidently believe that a change may safely be made reducing all single-letter postage to the uniform rate of 5 cents, regardless of distance, without thereby imposing any greater tax on the Treasury than would constitute a very moderate compensation for this public service; and I therefore respectfully recommend such a reduction. Should Congress prefer to abolish the franking privilege entirely, it seems probable that no demand on the Treasury would result from the proposed reduction of postage. Whether any further diminution should now be made, or the result of the reduction to 5 cents, which I have recommended, should be first tested, is submitted to your decision.

Since the commencement of the last session of Congress a postal treaty with Great Britain has been received and ratified, and such relations have been formed by the post-office departments of the two countries in pursuance of that treaty as to carry its provisions into full operation. The attempt to extend this same arrangement through England to France has not been equally successful, but the purpose has not been abandoned.

For a particular statement of the condition of the Post-Office Department and other matters connected with that branch of the public service I refer you to the report of the Postmaster-General.

By the act of the 3d of March, 1849, a board was constituted to make arrangements for taking the Seventh Census, composed of the Secretary of State, the Attorney-General, and the Postmaster-General; and it was made the duty of this board " to prepare and cause to be printed such forms and schedules as might be necessary for the full enumeration of the inhabitants of the United States, and also proper forms and schedules for collecting in statistical tables, under proper heads, such information as to mines, agriculture, commerce, manufactures, education, and other topics as would exhibit a full view of the pursuits, industry, education, and resources of the country." The duties enjoined upon the census board thus established having been performed, it now rests with Congress to enact a law for carrying into effect the provision of the Constitution which requires an actual enumeration of the people of the United States within the ensuing year.

Among the duties assigned by the Constitution to the General Government is one of local and limited application, but not on that account the less obligatory. I allude to the trust committed to Congress as the exclusive legislator and sole guardian of the interests of the District of Columbia. I beg to commend these interests to your kind attention. As the national metropolis the city of Washington must be an object of general interest; and founded, as it was, under the auspices of him whose immortal name it bears, its claims to the fostering care of Congress present themselves with additional strength. Whatever can contribute to its prosperity must enlist the feelings of its constitutional guardians and command their favorable consideration.

Our Government is one of limited powers, and its successful administration eminently depends on the confinement of each of its coordinate branches within its own appropriate sphere. The first section of the Constitution ordains that—

All legislative powers herein granted shall be vested in a Congress of the United States, which shall consist of a Senate and House of Representatives.

The Executive has authority to recommend (not to dictate) measures to Congress. Having performed that duty, the executive department of the Government can not rightfully control the decision of Congress on any subject of legislation until that decision shall have been officially submitted to the President for approval. The check provided by the Constitution in the clause conferring the qualified veto will never be exercised by me except in the cases contemplated by the fathers of the Republic. I view it as an extreme measure, to be resorted to only in extraordinary cases, as where it may become necessary to defend the executive against the encroachments of the legislative power or to prevent hasty and inconsiderate or unconstitutional legislation. By cautiously confining this remedy within the sphere prescribed to it in the cotemporaneous expositions of the framers of the Constitution, the will of the people, legitimately expressed on all subjects of legislation through their constitutional organs, the Senators and Representatives of the United States, will have its full effect. As indispensable to the preservation of our system of self-government, the independence of the representatives of the States and the people is guaranteed by the Constitution, and they owe no responsibility to any human power but their constituents. By holding the representative responsible only to the people, and exempting him from all other influences, we elevate the character of the constituent and quicken his sense of responsibility to his country. It is under these circumstances only that the elector can feel that in the choice of the lawmaker he is himself truly a component part of the sovereign power of the nation. With equal care we should study to defend the rights of the executive and judicial departments. Our Government can only be preserved in its purity by the suppression and entire elimination of every claim or tendency of one coordinate branch to encroachment upon another. With the strict observance of this rule and the other injunctions of the Constitution, with a sedulous inculcation of that respect and love for the Union of the States which our fathers cherished and enjoined upon their children, and with the aid of that overruling Providence which has so long and so kindly guarded our liberties and institutions, we may reasonably expect to transmit them, with their innumerable blessings, to the remotest posterity.

But attachment to the Union of the States should be habitually fostered in every American heart. For more than half a century, during which kingdoms and empires have fallen, this Union has stood unshaken. The patriots who formed it have long since descended to the grave; yet still it remains, the proudest monument to their memory and the object of affection and admiration with everyone worthy to bear the American name. In my judgment its dissolution would be the greatest of calamities, and to avert that should be the study of every American. Upon its preservation must depend our own happiness and that of countless generations to come. Whatever dangers may threaten it, I shall stand by it and maintain it in its integrity to the full extent of the obligations imposed and the powers conferred upon me by the Constitution.

Z. TAYLOR.

SPECIAL MESSAGES.

WASHINGTON, *December 17, 1849.*

To the Senate of the United States:

I transmit to the Senate, for its consideration with a view to ratification, a convention between the United States and His Majesty the Emperor of Brazil, signed at Rio de Janeiro on the 27th of January last, providing for the adjustment of claims of citizens of the United States on the Brazilian Government. A copy of a dispatch from Mr. Tod, the United States minister at Rio de Janeiro, relative to the convention is also herewith communicated. As it is understood that the Emperor's ratification is ready to be exchanged for that of the United States, and as the period limited for the exchange will expire on the 27th of next month, it is desirable that the decision of the Senate in regard to the instrument should be known as soon as may be convenient.

                                        Z. TAYLOR.

WASHINGTON, *December 21, 1849.*

To the Senate of the United States:

I transmit to the Senate, for its consideration with a view to ratification, a treaty between the United States and His Majesty the King of the Hawaiian Islands, yesterday concluded and signed in this city on the part of the respective Governments by the Secretary of State of the United States and by James Jackson Jarves, His Hawaiian Majesty's special commissioner.

                                        Z. TAYLOR.

WASHINGTON, *December 27, 1849.*

To the Senate and House of Representatives:

In consequence of the unexpected delay in proceeding to business, I deem it necessary to invite the immediate attention of Congress to so much of the report of the Secretary of the Treasury as relates to the appropriations required for the expenses of collecting the revenue for the second half of the current fiscal year.

                                        Z. TAYLOR.

WASHINGTON, *January 4, 1850.*

To the Senate and House of Representatives of the United States:

I herewith submit to you copies of a correspondence with the lady of Sir John Franklin, relative to the well-known expedition under his command to the arctic regions for the discovery of a northwest passage. On the receipt of her first letter imploring the aid of the American Government in a search for the missing ships engaged in an enterprise which interested all civilized nations, I anxiously sought the means of affording that assistance, but was prevented from accomplishing the object I had in view in consequence of the want of vessels suitable to encounter the perils of a proper exploration, the lateness of the season, and the want of an appropriation by Congress to enable me to furnish and equip an efficient squadron for that object. All that I could do in compliance with a request which I was deeply anxious to gratify was to cause the advertisements of reward promulged by the British Government and the best information I could obtain as to the means of finding the vessels under the command of Sir John Franklin to be widely circulated among our whalers and seafaring men whose spirit of enterprise might lead them to the inhospitable regions where that heroic officer and his brave followers, who periled their lives in the cause of science and for the benefit of the world, were supposed to be imprisoned among the icebergs or wrecked upon a desert shore.

Congress being now in session, the propriety and expediency of an appropriation for fitting out an expedition to proceed in search of the missing ships, with their officers and crews, is respectfully submitted to your consideration.

Z. TAYLOR.

EXECUTIVE OFFICE, *January 14, 1850.*

The PRESIDENT OF THE SENATE OF THE UNITED STATES.

SIR: I transmit herewith, to be laid before the Senate for its constitutional action thereon, a treaty concluded with the half-breeds of the Dacotah or Sioux Indians for lands reserved for them in the treaty of July 15, 1830, with the Sioux and other Indians, with accompanying papers.

Z. TAYLOR.

WASHINGTON, *January 14, 1850.*

To the Senate of the United States:

I herewith transmit reports from the Secretary of State and the Secretary of the Navy, containing the information called for by the resolution of the Senate of the 7th instant, in relation to the abduction* of Rey, *alias* Garcia, from New Orleans.

Z. TAYLOR.

WASHINGTON, *January 14, 1850.*

To the Senate of the United States:

I transmit to the Senate, for their consideration, a copy of a correspondence between the Department of State and the chargé d'affaires of Austria near this Government, on the subject of the convention for the extension of certain stipulations contained in the treaty of commerce and navigation of August 27, 1829, between the United States and Austria, concluded and signed on the 8th of May, 1848, and submitted to the Senate on the same day by my predecessor.

Z. TAYLOR.

WASHINGTON, *January 23, 1850.*

To the Senate of the United States:

I transmit to the Senate, in answer to a resolution of that body passed on the 17th instant, the accompanying reports of heads of Departments, which contain all the official information in the possession of the Executive asked for by the resolution.

*By the Spanish consul at New Orleans.

On coming into office I found the military commandant of the Department of California exercising the functions of civil governor in that Territory, and left, as I was, to act under the treaty of Guadalupe Hidalgo, without the aid of any legislative provision establishing a government in that Territory, I thought it best not to disturb that arrangement, made under my predecessor, until Congress should take some action on that subject. I therefore did not interfere with the powers of the military commandant, who continued to exercise the functions of civil governor as before; but I made no such appointment, conferred no such authority, and have allowed no increased compensation to the commandant for his services.

With a view to the faithful execution of the treaty so far as lay in the power of the Executive, and to enable Congress to act at the present session with as full knowledge and as little difficulty as possible on all matters of interest in these Territories, I sent the Hon. Thomas Butler King as bearer of dispatches to California, and certain officers to California and New Mexico, whose duties are particularly defined in the accompanying letters of instruction addressed to them severally by the proper Departments.

I did not hesitate to express to the people of those Territories my desire that each Territory should, if prepared to comply with the requisitions of the Constitution of the United States, form a plan of a State constitution and submit the same to Congress with a prayer for admission into the Union as a State, but I did not anticipate, suggest, or authorize the establishment of any such government without the assent of Congress, nor did I authorize any Government agent or officer to interfere with or exercise any influence or control over the election of delegates or over any convention in making or modifying their domestic institutions or any of the provisions of their proposed constitution. On the contrary, the instructions given by my orders were that all measures of domestic policy adopted by the people of California must originate solely with themselves; that while the Executive of the United States was desirous to protect them in the formation of any government republican in its character, to be at the proper time submitted to Congress, yet it was to be distinctly understood that the plan of such a government must at the same time be the result of their own deliberate choice and originate with themselves, without the interference of the Executive.

I am unable to give any information as to laws passed by any supposed government in California or of any census taken in either of the Territories mentioned in the resolution, as I have no information on those subjects.

As already stated, I have not disturbed the arrangements which I found had existed under my predecessor.

In advising an early application by the people of these Territories for admission as States I was actuated principally by an earnest desire to afford to the wisdom and patriotism of Congress the opportunity of avoiding occasions of bitter and angry dissensions among the people of the United States.

Under the Constitution every State has the right of establishing and from time to time altering its municipal laws and domestic institutions independently of every other State and of the General Government, subject only to the prohibitions and guaranties expressly set forth in the Constitution of the United States. The subjects thus left exclusively to the respective States were not designed or expected to become topics of national agitation. Still, as under the Constitution Congress has power to make all needful rules and regulations respecting the Territories of the United States, every new acquisition of territory has led to discussions on the question whether the system of involuntary servitude which prevails in many of the States should or should not be prohibited in that territory. The periods of excitement from this cause which have heretofore occurred have been safely passed, but during the interval, of whatever length, which may elapse before the admission of the Territories ceded by Mexico as States it appears probable that similar excitement will prevail to an undue extent.

Under these circumstances I thought, and still think, that it was my duty to endeavor to put it in the power of Congress, by the admission of California and New Mexico as States, to remove all occasion for the unnecessary agitation of the public mind.

It is understood that the people of the western part of California have formed a plan of a State constitution and will soon submit the same to the judgment of Congress and apply for admission as a State. This course on their part, though in accordance with, was not adopted exclusively in consequence of, any expression of my wishes, inasmuch as measures tending to this end had been promoted by the officers sent there by my predecessor, and were already in active progress of execution before any communication from me reached California. If the proposed constitution shall, when submitted to Congress, be found to be in compliance with the requisitions of the Constitution of the United States, I earnestly recommend that it may receive the sanction of Congress.

The part of California not included in the proposed State of that name is believed to be uninhabited, except in a settlement of our countrymen in the vicinity of Salt Lake.

A claim has been advanced by the State of Texas to a very large portion of the most populous district of the Territory commonly designated by the name of New Mexico. If the people of New Mexico had formed a plan of a State government for that Territory as ceded by the treaty of Guadalupe Hidalgo, and had been admitted by Congress as a State, our Constitution would have afforded the means of obtaining an adjustment of the question of boundary with Texas by a judicial decision. At present, however, no judicial tribunal has the power of deciding that question, and it remains for Congress to devise some mode for its adjustment. Meanwhile I submit to Congress the question whether it would be expedient before such adjustment to establish a Territorial government, which by including the district so claimed would practically decide the question adversely to the State of Texas, or by excluding it would decide it in her favor. In my opinion such a course would not be expedient, especially as the people of this Territory still enjoy the benefit and protection of their municipal laws originally derived from Mexico and have a military force stationed there to protect them against the Indians. It is undoubtedly true that the property, lives, liberties, and religion of the people of New Mexico are better protected than they ever were before the treaty of cession.

Should Congress, when California shall present herself for incorporation into the Union, annex a condition to her admission as a State affecting her domestic institutions contrary to the wishes of her people, and even compel her temporarily to comply with it, yet the State could change her constitution at any time after admission when to her it should seem expedient. Any attempt to deny to the people of the State the right of self-government in a matter which peculiarly affects themselves will infallibly be regarded by them as an invasion of their rights, and, upon the principles laid down in our own Declaration of Independence, they will certainly be sustained by the great mass of the American people. To assert that they are a conquered people and must as a State submit to the will of their conquerors in this regard will meet with no cordial response among American freemen. Great numbers of them are native citizens of the United States, not inferior to the rest of our countrymen in intelligence and patriotism, and no language of menace to restrain them in the exercise of an undoubted right, substantially guaranteed to them by the treaty of cession itself, shall ever be uttered by me or encouraged and sustained by persons acting under my authority. It is to be expected that in the residue of the territory ceded to us by Mexico the people residing there will at the time of their incorporation into the Union as a State settle all questions of domestic policy to suit themselves.

No material inconvenience will result from the want for a short period of a government established by Congress over that part of the territory which lies eastward of the new State of California; and the reasons for my opinion that New Mexico will at no very distant period ask for admission into the Union are founded on unofficial information which, I suppose, is common to all who have cared to make inquiries on that subject.

Seeing, then, that the question which now excites such painful sensations in the country will in the end certainly be settled by the silent effect of causes independent of the action of Congress, I again submit to your wisdom the policy recommended in my annual message of awaiting the salutary operation of those causes, believing that we shall thus avoid the creation of geographical parties and secure the harmony of feeling so necessary to the beneficial action of our political system.   Connected, as the Union is, with the remembrance of past happiness, the sense of present blessings, and the hope of future peace and prosperity, every dictate of wisdom, every feeling of duty, and every emotion of patriotism tend to inspire fidelity and devotion to it and admonish us cautiously to avoid any unnecessary controversy which can either endanger it or impair its strength, the chief element of which is to be found in the regard and affection of the people for each other.

Z. TAYLOR.

[A similar message, dated January 21, 1850, was sent to the House of Representatives, in answer to a resolution of that body.]

WASHINGTON, *January 23, 1850.*

To the Senate of the United States:

I transmit to the Senate a copy of the convention between the United States and His Majesty the Emperor of Brazil, providing for the satisfaction of claims of citizens of the United States against the Brazilian Government, signed at Rio de Janeiro on the 27th of January last, and the ratifications of which were exchanged in this city on the 18th instant.   It is desirable that Congress should prescribe the mode in which the claims referred to are to be adjusted and the money stipulated to be paid by Brazil shall be distributed amongst the claimants.   Extracts from dispatches of the minister of the United States at Rio de Janeiro and a copy of a letter from an agent of claimants there are also herewith communicated, to which your attention is invited.   I have authorized our minister to demand, receive, and give acquittances for the amount payable by Brazil, and have caused him to be instructed to remit the same to the Treasury of the United States.

Z. TAYLOR.

[The same message was sent to the House of Representatives.]

WASHINGTON, *January 30, 1850.*

To the Senate of the United States:

In reply to the resolution of the Senate of the 7th instant, requesting of me all the official correspondence since the 4th of March last between this Government and its military authorities at Santa Fe or with the authorities of the State of Texas relating to the boundary or occupation of Texas, and the reasons why the judicial authority of Texas has not been recognized by the military authority at Santa Fe, I herewith submit the accompanying reports, which contain the information called for by the resolution.

I have not been informed of any acts of interference by the military forces stationed at Santa Fe with the judicial authority of Texas established or sought to be established there.   I have received no communication from the governor of Texas on any of the matters referred to in the resolution. And I concur in the opinion expressed by my predecessor in the letter addressed by the late Secretary of State to the governor of Texas on the 12th day of February, 1847, that the boundary between the State of Texas and the Territory of New Mexico "is a subject which more properly belongs to the legislative than to the executive branch of the Government."

Z. TAYLOR.

WASHINGTON, *February 6, 1850.*

To the Senate of the United States:

In reply to the resolution of the Senate of the 28th ultimo, I have to state that the resolution of the Senate of the 2d of March, 1849, respecting James W. Schaumburg, was in April of that year submitted for the opinion of the Attorney-General upon questions arising in the case. No opinion had been given by him when it became necessary, prior to the meeting of the Senate, to prepare the nominations for promotions in the Army. The nomination of Lieutenant Ewell was then decided upon, after due consideration was given to the resolution of the Senate of the 2d of March, 1849.

I herewith submit a report from the Secretary of War, showing the grounds upon which the decision above referred to was made.

Z. TAYLOR.

WASHINGTON, *February 13, 1850.*

To the Senate of the United States:

I have received a resolution of the Senate of the 28th ultimo, requesting the President of the United States "to cause to be laid before the Senate, in open session if in his opinion consistent with the public interest, otherwise in executive session, copies of all instructions and communications of the late Secretary of State to our late chargé d'affaires to Guatemala and all dispatches and communications from said chargé d'affaires to the Department of State, including any conventions or treaties he may have concluded with either of the States composing the late Republic of Central America; and also all correspondence between our said chargé d'affaires and the Government or representatives of either of said States; and also all instructions and communications from the present Secretary of State to our late chargé d'affaires or our present chargé d'affaires to either of said States and all dispatches or communications from our chargé d'affaires to the Department of State, including any conventions or treaties he may have concluded with either of said States; and also all correspondence between the Department of State and either of said chargés d'affaires touching the so-called Kingdom of the Mosquitos and the right of way from the Atlantic to the Pacific through Lake Nicaragua."

The information called for by this resolution will be cheerfully communicated to the Senate as soon as it shall be found to be compatible with the public interest.

Z. TAYLOR.

WASHINGTON, *February 13, 1850.*

To the House of Representatives of the United States:

I have received a resolution of the House of Representatives of the 24th ultimo, requesting the President of the United States "to communicate to that body (provided the publication thereof be not prejudicial to the public interest) all such information as may be within the knowledge of the executive department relative to the alleged extraordinary proceedings of the English Government in the forcible seizure and occupation of the island of Tigre, in the State of Nicaragua, Central America; also all facts, circumstances, or communications within the knowledge of the Executive relative to any seizure, occupation, or attempted seizure or occupation, by the English Government of any port, river, town, territory, or island belonging to or claimed by any of the States of Central America; also that he be requested to communicate to this House, if not incompatible with the public interest, all treaties not heretofore published which may have been negotiated with any of the States of Central America by any person acting by authority from the late Administration or under the auspices of the present Executive." The information called for by this resolution will be cheerfully communicated to the House as soon as it shall be found compatible with the public interest.

Z. TAYLOR.

WASHINGTON, *February 13, 1850.*

To the House of Representatives of the United States:

I transmit herewith to the House of Representatives, for the information of that body, an authenticated copy of the constitution of the State of California, received by me from General Riley.

Z. TAYLOR.

WASHINGTON, *February 13, 1850.*

To the Senate of the United States:

I transmit herewith to the Senate, for the information of that body, an authenticated copy of the constitution of California, received by me from the Hon. William M. Gwyn.

Z. TAYLOR.

WASHINGTON, *March 1, 1850.*

To the Senate of the United States:

In reply to the resolution of the Senate of the 12th ultimo, requesting the President of the United States "to inform the Senate of the amount of prize money paid into the Treasury in conformity with the eighteenth section of the act of March 3, 1849," etc., I transmit herewith a report from the Secretary of the Navy, with accompanying documents.

Z. TAYLOR.

WASHINGTON, *March 4, 1850.*

To the Senate and House of Representatives of the United States:

I herewith transmit to Congress copies of a recent correspondence between the Department of State and the British minister at Washington, relating to subjects* which seem to require the consideration of the legislative rather than the executive branch of the Government.

Z. TAYLOR.

WASHINGTON, *March 6, 1850.*

To the Senate of the United States:

In answer to the inquiries contained in the resolution of the Senate of the 4th instant, in relation to the appointment of postmasters by the Postmaster-General, I send to the Senate herewith the letter of the Postmaster-General furnishing the desired information.

Z. TAYLOR.

MARCH 8, 1850.

To the Senate of the United States:

The Postmaster-General has this day communicated to me the letter herewith transmitted, in addition to his communication by me sent to the Senate on the 6th instant, in relation to the inquiries contained in the resolution of the Senate as to the appointment of postmasters.

Z. TAYLOR.

WASHINGTON, *March 19, 1850.*

To the Senate of the United States:

I transmit herewith, for the consideration and constitutional action of the Senate, a communication from the Secretary of the Interior, covering two treaties with Indians of New Mexico, one negotiated with the Navajo tribe on the 9th of September last by Colonel John Washington, of the Army, and J. S. Calhoun, United States Indian agent at Santa Fe, and the other with the Utah tribe, negotiated by J. S. Calhoun on the 13th of December last.

Z. TAYLOR.

WASHINGTON, *March 19, 1850.*

To the Senate of the United States:

I herewith transmit to the Senate, for their advice in regard to its ratification, "a general treaty of amity, navigation, and commerce" between

*Navigation laws and tariff on British productions.

the United States of America and the State of Nicaragua, concluded at Leon by E. George Squier, chargé d'affaires of the United States, on their part, and Señor Zepeda, on the part of the Republic of Nicaragua.

I also transmit, for the advice of the Senate in regard to its ratification, "a general treaty of amity, navigation, and commerce" negotiated by Mr. Squier with the Republic of San Salvador.

I also transmit to the Senate a copy of the instructions to and correspondence with the said chargé d'affaires relating to those treaties.

I also transmit, for the advice of the Senate in regard to its ratification, "a general treaty of peace, amity, commerce, and navigation" negotiated by Elijah Hise, our late chargé d'affaires, with the State of Guatemala.

I also transmit, for the information of the Senate, a copy of a treaty negotiated by Mr. Hise with the Government of Nicaragua on the 21st of June last, accompanied by copies of his instructions from and correspondence with the Department of State.

On the 12th day of November, 1847, Señor Buétrago, secretary of state and of the affairs of war and foreign relations and domestic administration of the Supreme Government of the State of Nicaragua, addressed a letter from the Government House at Leon to Mr. Buchanan, then Secretary of State of the United States, asking the friendly offices of this Government to prevent an attack upon the town of San Juan de Nicaragua, then contemplated by the British authorities as the allies of the Mosquito King. That letter, a translation of which is herewith sent, distinctly charges that—

The object of the British in taking this key of the continent is not to protect the small tribe of the Mosquitos, but to establish their own empire over the Atlantic extremity of the line, by which a canal connecting the two oceans is most practicable, insuring to them the preponderance on the American continent, as well as their direct relations with Asia, the East Indies, and other important countries in the world.

No answer appears to have been returned to this letter.

A communication was received by my predecessor from Don José Guerrero, President and Supreme Director of the State of Nicaragua, dated the 15th day of December, 1847, expressing his desire to establish relations of amity and commerce with the United States, a translation of which is herewith inclosed. In this the President of Nicaragua says:

My desire was carried to the utmost on seeing in your message at the opening of the Twenty-ninth Congress of your Republic a sincere profession of political faith in all respects conformable with the principles professed by these States, determined, as they are, to sustain with firmness the continental cause, the rights of Americans in general, and the noninterference of European powers in their concerns.

This letter announces the critical situation in which Nicaragua was placed and charges upon the Court of St. James a "well-known design to establish colonies on the coast of Nicaragua and to render itself master of the interoceanic canal, for which so many facilities are presented by the isthmus in that State." No reply was made to this letter.

The British ships of war *Alarm* and *Vixen* arrived at San Juan de Nicaragua on the 8th day of February, 1848, and on the 12th of that month the British forces, consisting of 260 officers and men, attacked and captured the post of Serapaqui, garrisoned, according to the British statements, by about 200 soldiers, after a sharp action of one hour and forty minutes.

On the 7th day of March, 1848, articles of agreement were concluded by Captain Locke, on the part of Great Britain, with the commissioners of the State of Nicaragua in the island of Cuba, in the Lake of Nicaragua, a copy of which will be found in the correspondence relating to the Mosquito Territory presented to and published by the House of Commons of Great Britain on the 3d day of July, 1848, herewith submitted. A copy of the same document will also be found accompanying the note of the minister for foreign affairs of Nicaragua to the Secretary of State of the United States under date the 17th March, 1848.

By the third article of the agreement it is provided that Nicaragua "shall not disturb the inhabitants of San Juan, understanding that any such act will be considered by Great Britain as a declaration of open hostilities." By the sixth article it is provided that these articles of agreement will not "hinder Nicaragua from soliciting by means of a commissioner to Her Britannic Majesty a final arrangement of these affairs."

The communication from Señor Sebastian Salinas, the secretary of foreign affairs of the State of Nicaragua, to Mr. Buchanan, the Secretary of State of the United States, dated 17th March, 1848, a translation of which is herewith submitted, recites the aggressions of Great Britain and the seizure of a part of the Nicaraguan territory in the name of the Mosquito King. No answer appears to have been given to this letter.

On the 28th day of October, 1847, Joseph W. Livingston was appointed by this Government consul of the United States for the port of San Juan de Nicaragua. On the 16th day of December, 1847, after having received his exequatur from the Nicaraguan Government, he addressed a letter to Mr. Buchanan, Secretary of State, a copy of which is herewith submitted, representing that he had been informed that the English Government would take possession of San Juan de Nicaragua in January, 1848.

In another letter, dated the 8th of April, 1848, Mr. Livingston states that "at the request of the minister for foreign affairs of Nicaragua he transmits a package of papers containing the correspondence relative to the occupation of the port of San Juan by British forces in the name of the Mosquito nation."

On the 3d day of June, 1848, Elijah Hise, being appointed chargé d'affaires of the United States to Guatemala, received his instructions, a copy of which is herewith submitted. In these instructions the following passages occur:

The independence as well as the interests of the nations on this continent require that they should maintain the American system of policy entirely distinct from that which prevails in Europe. To suffer any interference on the part of the European Governments with the domestic concerns of the American Republics and to permit them to establish new colonies upon this continent would be to jeopard their independence and to ruin their interests. These truths ought everywhere throughout this continent to be impressed on the public mind. But what can the United States do to resist such European interference whilst the Spanish American Republics continue to weaken themselves by division and civil war and deprive themselves of the ability of doing anything for their own protection?

This last significant inquiry seems plainly to intimate that the United States could do nothing to arrest British aggression while the Spanish American Republics continue to weaken themselves by division and civil war and deprive themselves of the ability of doing anything for their protection.

These instructions, which also state the dissolution of the Central American Republic, formerly composed of the five States of Nicaragua, Costa Rica, Honduras, San Salvador, and Guatemala, and their continued separation, authorize Mr. Hise to conclude treaties of commerce with the Republics of Guatemala and San Salvador, but conclude with saying that it was not deemed advisable to empower Mr. Hise to conclude a treaty with either Nicaragua, Honduras, or Costa Rica until more full and statistical information should have been communicated by him to the Department in regard to those States than that which it possesses.

The States of Nicaragua, Costa Rica, and Honduras are the only Central American States whose consent or cooperation would in any event be necessary for the construction of the ship canal contemplated between the Pacific and Atlantic oceans by the way of Lake Nicaragua.

In pursuance of the sixth article of the agreement of the 7th of March, 1848, between the forces of Great Britain and the authorities of Nicaragua, Señor Francisco Castillon was appointed commissioner from Nicaragua to Great Britain, and on the 5th day of November, 1848, while at Washington on his way to London, addressed a letter to the Secretary of State, a translation of which is herewith submitted, asking this Government to instruct its minister plenipotentiary residing in London to sustain the right of Nicaragua to her territory claimed by Mosquito, and especially to the port of San Juan, expressing the hope of Nicaragua "that the Government of the Union, firmly adhering to its principle of resisting all foreign intervention in America, would not hesitate to order such steps to be taken as might be effective before things reached a point in which the intervention of the United States would prove of no avail."

To this letter also no answer appears to have been returned, and no instructions were given to our minister in London in pursuance of the request contained in it.

On the 3d day of March, 1847, Christopher Hempstead was appointed consul at Belize, and an application was then made for his exequatur through our minister in London, Mr. Bancroft. Lord Palmerston referred Mr. Bancroft's application for an exequatur for Mr. Hempstead to the colonial office. The exequatur was granted, and Mr. Hempstead, in a letter to the Department of State bearing date the 12th day of February, 1848, a copy of which is herewith submitted, acknowledged the receipt of his exequatur from Her Britannic Majesty, by virtue of which he has discharged his consular functions. Thus far this Government has recognized the existence of a British colony at Belize, within the territory of Honduras. I have recalled the consul, and have appointed no one to supply his place.

On the 26th day of May, 1848, Mr. Hempstead represented in a letter to the Department of State that the Indians had "applied to Her Majesty's superintendent at Belize for protection, and had desired him to take possession of the territory which they occupied and take them under his protection as British subjects;" and he added that in the event of the success of their application "the British Government would then have possession of the entire coast from Cape Conte to San Juan de Nicaragua." In another letter, dated the 29th day of July, 1848, he wrote:

I have not a doubt but the designs of Her Majesty's officers here and on the Mosquito shore are to obtain territory on this continent.

The receipt of this letter was regularly acknowledged on the 29th day of August, 1848.

When I came into office I found the British Government in possession of the port of San Juan, which it had taken by force of arms after we had taken possession of California and while we were engaged in the negotiation of a treaty for the cession of it, and that no official remonstrance had been made by this Government against the aggression, nor any attempt to resist it. Efforts were then being made by certain private citizens of the United States to procure from the State of Nicaragua by contract the right to cut the proposed ship canal by the way of the river San Juan and the lakes of Nicaragua and Managua to Realejo, on the Pacific Ocean. A company of American citizens entered into such a contract with the State of Nicaragua. Viewing the canal as a matter of great importance to the people of the United States, I resolved to adopt the policy of protecting the work and binding the Government of Nicaragua, through whose territory it would pass, also to protect it. The instructions to E. George Squier, appointed by me chargé d'affaires to Guatemala on the 2d day of April, 1849, are herewith submitted, as fully indicating the views which governed me in directing a treaty to be made with Nicaragua. I considered the interference of the British Government on this continent in seizing the port of San Juan, which commanded the route believed to be the most eligible for the canal across the Isthmus, and occupying it at the very moment when it was known, as I believe, to Great Britain that we were engaged in the negotiation for the purchase of California, as an unfortunate coincidence, and one calculated to lead to the inference that she entertained designs by no means in harmony with the interests of the United States.

Seeing that Mr. Hise had been positively instructed to make no treaty, not even a treaty of commerce, with Nicaragua, Costa Rica, or Honduras, I had no suspicion that he would attempt to act in opposition to his instructions, and in September last I was for the first time informed that he had actually negotiated two treaties with the State of Nicaragua, the one a treaty of commerce, the other a treaty for the construction of the proposed ship canal, which treaties he brought with him on his return home. He also negotiated a treaty of commerce with Honduras; and in each of these treaties it is recited that he had full powers for the purpose. He had no such powers, and the whole proceeding on his part with reference to those States was not only unauthorized by instructions, but in opposition to those he had received from my predecessor and after the date of his letter of recall and the appointment of his successor. But I have no evidence that Mr. Hise, whose letter of recall (a copy of which is herewith submitted) bears date the 2d day of May, 1849, had received that letter on the 21st day of June, when he negotiated the treaty with Nicaragua. The difficulty of communicating with him was so great that I have reason to believe he had not received it. He did not acknowledge it.

The twelfth article of the treaty negotiated by Mr. Hise in effect guarantees the perfect independence of the State of Nicaragua and her sovereignty over her alleged limits from the Caribbean Sea to the Pacific Ocean, pledging the naval and military power of the United States to support it. This treaty authorizes the chartering of a corporation by this Government to cut a canal outside of the limits of the United States, and gives to us the exclusive right to fortify and command it. I have not approved it, nor have I now submitted it for ratification; not merely because of the facts already mentioned, but because on the 31st day of December last Señor Edwardo Carcache, on being accredited to this Government as chargé d'affaires from the State of Nicaragua, in a note to the Secretary of State, a translation of which is herewith sent, declared that he was ''only empowered to exchange ratifications of the treaty concluded with Mr. Squier, and that the special convention concluded at Guatemala by Mr. Hise, the chargé d'affaires of the United States, and Señor Selva, the commissioner of Nicaragua, had been, as was publicly and universally known, disapproved by his Government.''

We have no precedent in our history to justify such a treaty as that negotiated by Mr. Hise since the guaranties we gave to France of her American possessions. The treaty negotiated with New Granada on the 12th day of December, 1846, did not guarantee the sovereignty of New Granada on the whole of her territory, but only over ''the single Province of the Isthmus of Panama,'' immediately adjoining the line of the railroad, the neutrality of which was deemed necessary by the President and Senate to the construction and security of the work.

The thirty-fifth article of the treaty with Nicaragua, negotiated by Mr. Squier, which is submitted for your advice in regard to its ratification, distinctly recognizes the rights of sovereignty and property which the State of Nicaragua possesses in and over the line of the canal therein provided for. If the Senate doubt on that subject, it will be clearly wrong to involve us in a controversy with England by adopting the treaty; but after the best consideration which I have been able to give to the subject my own judgment is convinced that the claims of Nicaragua are just, and that as our commerce and intercourse with the Pacific require the opening of this communication from ocean to ocean it is our duty to ourselves to assert their justice.

This treaty is not intended to secure to the United States any monopoly or exclusive advantage in the use of the canal. Its object is to guarantee protection to American citizens and others who shall construct the canal, and to defend it when completed against unjust confiscations or obstructions, and to deny the advantages of navigation through it to those nations only which shall refuse to enter into the same guaranties. A copy of the contract of the canal company is herewith transmitted, from which, as well as from the treaty, it will be perceived that the same benefits are offered to all nations in the same terms.

The message of my predecessor to the Senate of the 10th February, 1847, transmitting for ratification the treaty with New Granada, contains in general the principles by which I have been actuated in directing the negotiation with Nicaragua. The only difference between the two cases consists in this: In that of Nicaragua the British Government has seized upon part of her territory and was in possession of it when we negotiated the treaty with her. But that possession was taken after our occupation of California, when the effect of it was to obstruct or control the most eligible route for a ship communication to the territories acquired by us on the Pacific. In the case of New Granada, her possession was undisturbed at the time of the treaty, though the British possession in the right of the Mosquito King was then extended into the territories claimed by New Granada as far as Boca del Toro. The professed objects of both the treaties are to open communications across the Isthmus to all nations and to invite their guaranties on the same terms. Neither of them proposes to guarantee territory to a foreign nation in which the United States will not have a common interest with that nation. Neither of them constitutes an alliance for any political object, but for a purely commercial purpose, in which all the navigating nations of the world have a common interest. Nicaragua, like New Granada, is a power which will not excite the jealousy of any nation.

As there is nothing narrow, selfish, illiberal, or exclusive in the views of the United States as set forth in this treaty, as it is indispensable to the successful completion of the contemplated canal to secure protection to it from the local authorities and this Government, and as I have no doubt that the British pretension to the port of San Juan in right of the Mosquito King is without just foundation in any public law ever before recognized in any other instance by Americans or Englishmen as applicable to Indian titles on this continent, I shall ratify this treaty in case the Senate shall advise that course. Its principal defect is taken from the treaty with New Granada, the negotiator having made it liable to be abrogated on notice after twenty years. Both treaties should have been perpetual or limited only by the duration of the improvements they were intended to protect. The instructions to our chargé d'affaires, it will be seen, prescribe no limitation for the continuance of the treaty with Nicaragua. Should the Senate approve of principle of the treaty, an amendment in this respect is deemed advisable; and it will be well to invite by another amendment the protection of other nations, by expressly offering them in the treaty what is now offered by implication only—the same advantages which we propose for ourselves on the same conditions upon which we shall have acquired them. The policy of this treaty is not novel, nor does it originate from any suggestion either of my immediate predecessor or myself. On the 3d day of March, 1835, the following resolution, referred to by the late President in his message to the Senate relative to the treaty with New Granada, was adopted in executive session by the Senate without division:

Resolved, That the President of the United States be respectfully requested to consider the expediency of opening negotiations with the Governments of Central America and New Granada for the purpose of effectually protecting, by suitable treaty stipulations with them, such individuals or companies as may undertake to open a communication between the Atlantic and Pacific oceans by the construction of a ship canal across the isthmus which connects North and South America, and of securing forever by such stipulations the free and equal rights of navigating such a canal to all such nations on the payment of such reasonable tolls as may be established to compensate the capitalists who may engage in such undertaking and complete the work.

President Jackson accorded with the policy suggested in this resolution, and in pursuance of it sent Charles Biddle as agent to negotiate with the Governments of Central America and New Granada. The result is fully set forth in the report of a select committee of the House of Representatives of the 20th of February, 1849, upon a joint resolution of Congress to authorize the survey of certain routes for a canal or railroad between the Atlantic and Pacific oceans. The policy indicated in the resolution of the 3d March, 1835, then adopted by the President and Senate, is that now proposed for the consideration and sanction of the Senate. So far as my knowledge extends, such has ever been the liberal policy of the leading statesmen of this country, and by no one has it been more earnestly recommended than by my lamented predecessor.

Z. TAYLOR.

WASHINGTON, *March 26, 1850.*

To the House of Representatives of the United States:

I herewith transmit, for the information of Congress, a copy of the report* of Thomas Butler King, esq., appointed bearer of dispatches and special agent to California, made in pursuance of instructions issued from the Department of State on the 3d day of April last.

Z. TAYLOR.

WASHINGTON, *March 28, 1850.*

To the Senate of the United States:

In compliance with a resolution of the Senate of the 22d instant, requesting the President of the United States to communicate to that body a copy of the instructions given to the agent of the United States who was employed to visit Hungary during the recent war between that country and Austria, and of the correspondence by and with such agent, so far as the publication of the same may be consistent with the public interest, I herewith transmit to the Senate a copy of the instructions to A. Dudley Mann, esq., relating to Hungary, he having been appointed by me special agent to that country on the 18th day of June last, together with a copy of the correspondence with our late chargé d'affaires to Austria referred to in those instructions and of other papers disclosing the policy of this Government in reference to Hungary and her people. I also transmit, in compliance with the resolution of the Senate, but in a separate packet, a copy of the correspondence of Mr. Mann with the Department of State. The latter I have caused to be marked *"executive"*—the information contained in it being such as will be found on examination most appropriately to belong to the Senate in the exercise of its executive functions. The publication of this correspondence of the agent sent by me to Hungary is a matter referred entirely to the judgment and discretion of the Senate.

It will be seen by the documents now transmitted that no minister or agent was accredited by the Government of Hungary to this Government at any period since I came into office, nor was any communication ever received by this Government from the minister of foreign affairs of Hungary or any other executive officer authorized to act in her behalf.

My purpose, as freely avowed in this correspondence, was to have acknowledged the independence of Hungary had she succeeded in establishing a government *de facto* on a basis sufficiently permanent in its character to have justified me in doing so according to the usages and settled principles of this Government; and although she is now fallen and many of her gallant patriots are in exile or in chains, I am free still to declare that had she been successful in the maintenance of such a government as we could have recognized we should have been the first to welcome her into the family of nations.

Z. TAYLOR.

*On California affairs.

WASHINGTON, *April 3, 1850.*

To the Senate and House of Representatives of the United States:

I transmit a translation of a note, under date the 20th of last month, addressed to the Secretary of State by the minister of the Mexican Republic accredited to this Government, expressing the views of that Government with reference to the control of the wild Indians of the United States on the frontier of Mexico, as stipulated for in the eleventh article of the treaty of Guadalupe Hidalgo.

Z. TAYLOR.

WASHINGTON, *April 22, 1850.*

To the Senate of the United States:

I herewith transmit to the Senate, for their advice with regard to its ratification, a convention between the United States and Great Britain, concluded at Washington on the 19th instant by John M. Clayton, Secretary of State, on the part of the United States, and by the Right Hon. Sir Henry Lytton Bulwer, on the part of Great Britain.

This treaty has been negotiated in accordance with the general views expressed in my message to Congress in December last. Its object is to establish a commercial alliance with all great maritime states for the protection of a contemplated ship canal through the territory of Nicaragua to connect the Atlantic and Pacific oceans, and at the same time to insure the same protection to the contemplated railways or canals by the Tehuantepec and Panama routes, as well as to every other interoceanic communication which may be adopted to shorten the transit to or from our territories on the Pacific.

It will be seen that this treaty does not propose to take money from the public Treasury to effect any object contemplated by it. It yields protection to the capitalists who may undertake to construct any canal or railway across the Isthmus, commencing in the southern part of Mexico and terminating in the territory of New Granada. It gives no preference to any one route over another, but proposes the same measure of protection for all which ingenuity and enterprise can construct. Should this treaty be ratified, it will secure in future the liberation of all Central America from any kind of foreign aggression.

At the time negotiations were opened with Nicaragua for the construction of a canal through her territory I found Great Britain in possession of nearly half of Central America, as the ally and protector of the Mosquito King. It has been my object in negotiating this treaty not only to secure the passage across the Isthmus to the Government and citizens of the United States by the construction of a great highway dedicated to the use of all nations on equal terms, but to maintain the independence and sovereignty of all the Central American Republics. The Senate will judge how far these objects have been effected.

If there be any who would desire to seize and annex any portion of the territories of these weak sister republics to the American Union, or to extend our dominion over them, I do not concur in their policy; and I wish it to be understood in reference to that subject that I adopt the views entertained, so far as I know, by all my predecessors.

The principles by which I have been regulated in the negotiation of this treaty are in accordance with the sentiments well expressed by my immediate predecessor on the 10th of February, 1847, when he communicated to the Senate the treaty with New Granada for the protection of the railroad at Panama. It is in accordance with the whole spirit of the resolution of the Senate of the 3d of March, 1835, referred to by President Polk, and with the policy adopted by President Jackson immediately after the passage of that resolution, who dispatched an agent to Central America and New Granada "to open negotiations with those Governments for the purpose of effectually protecting, by suitable treaty stipulations with them, such individuals or companies as might undertake to open a communication between the Atlantic and Pacific oceans by the construction of a ship canal across the isthmus which connects North and South America, and of securing forever by such stipulations the free and equal right of navigating such canal to all such nations on the payment of such reasonable tolls as might be established to compensate the capitalists who should engage in such undertaking and complete the work."

I also communicate herewith a copy of the correspondence between the American Secretary of State and the British plenipotentiary at the time of concluding the treaty. Whatever honor may be due to the party first proposing such a treaty justly belongs to the United States. My predecessor, in his message of the 10th of February, 1847, referring to the treaty with New Granada for the protection of the Panama Railroad, observes that—

Should the proposition thus tendered be rejected we may deprive the United States of the just influence which its acceptance might secure to them, and confer the glory and benefits of being the first among the nations in concluding such an arrangement upon the Government either of Great Britain or France. That either of these Governments would embrace the offer can not be doubted, because there does not appear to be any other effectual means of securing to all nations the advantages of this important passage but the guaranty of great commercial powers that the Isthmus shall be neutral territory. The interests of the world at stake are so important that the security of this passage between the two oceans can not be suffered to depend upon the wars and revolutions which may arise among different nations.

Should the Senate in its wisdom see fit to confirm this treaty, and the treaty heretofore submitted by me for their advice in regard to its ratification, negotiated with the State of Nicaragua on the 3d day of September last, it will be necessary to amend one or both of them, so that both treaties may stand in conformity with each other in their spirit and intention. The Senate will discover by examining them both that this is a task of no great difficulty.

I have good reason to believe that France and Russia stand ready to accede to this treaty, and that no other great maritime state will refuse its accession to an arrangement so well calculated to diffuse the blessings of peace, commerce, and civilization, and so honorable to all nations which may enter into the engagement.

Z. TAYLOR.

WASHINGTON, *May 6, 1850.*

To the Senate of the United States:

I transmit to the Senate, for its consideration with a view to ratification, a consular convention between the United States and the Republic of New Granada, signed in this city on the 4th of this month by the Secretary of State on the part of the United States, and by Señor Don Rafael Rivas, chargé d'affaires of New Granada, on the part of that Republic.

Z. TAYLOR.

WASHINGTON, *May 7, 1850.*

To the House of Representatives of the United States:

I herewith transmit to the House of Representatives copies of a correspondence between the Department of State and the British legation in this city, relative to the reciprocal admission of the natural products of the United States and Canada free of duty into the territories of both countries. It will be seen by the accompanying documents that the late Secretary of the Treasury recommended, in his correspondence with the Committee on Commerce in the House of Representatives, reciprocal free trade in the natural products of the United States and Canada; that in March and June, 1849, a correspondence was opened between the British chargé d'affaires then residing in Washington and the Secretary of State upon the subject of a commercial convention or treaty to carry out the views of Her Majesty's Government in relation thereto, and that the proposition for such a convention or treaty was declined on the part of the American Government for reasons which are fully set forth in the note of the Secretary of State to Mr. Crampton of the 26th of June last. During the negotiations connected with this correspondence, not considering the markets of Canada as an equivalent for those of the United States, I directed the Secretary of State to inquire what other benefits of trade and commerce would be yielded by the British authorities in connection with such a measure, and particularly whether the free navigation of the St. Lawrence would be conceded to us. That subject has accordingly been presented to the British Government, and the result was communicated by Her Majesty's minister in Washington on the 27th of March last in reply to a note from the Secretary of State of the 26th of that month. From these papers it will be perceived that the navigation of the St. Lawrence and of the canals connecting it with the Western lakes will be opened

Article IX.

The ratifications of this Convention shall be exchanged at Washington, within six months from this day, or sooner, if possible.

In faith whereof, we, the respective Plenipotentiaries, have signed this Convention, and have hereunto affixed our Seals.

Done, at Washington, the nineteenth day of April, Anno Domini, one thousand eight hundred and fifty.

FINAL PAGE OF CLAYTON–BULWER TREATY, RATIFIED IN
PRESIDENT TAYLOR'S ADMINISTRATION.

to the citizens of the United States in the event that the bill referred to in the correspondence, providing for the admission of their natural products, should become a law. The whole subject is now submitted to the consideration of Congress, and especially whether the concession proposed by Great Britain is an equivalent for the reciprocity desired by her.

Z. TAYLOR.

WASHINGTON, *May 8, 1850.*

To the Senate of the United States:

With reference to the convention between the United States and Her Britannic Majesty relative to interoceanic communication by the way of Nicaragua, recently submitted to the Senate, I transmit a copy of a note, under date the 29th ultimo, addressed to the Secretary of State by Sir Henry L. Bulwer, Her Britannic Majesty's minister here, and of Mr. Clayton's reply, under date the 30th ultimo. Intelligence received from the chargé d'affaires of the United States in Central America and from other quarters having led to an apprehension that Mr. Chatfield, Her Britannic Majesty's minister in that country, had concluded a treaty with the Government of Costa Rica placing that State under the protection of the British Government, I deemed it my duty to cause inquiries upon the subject to be addressed to Her Majesty's Government through Sir Henry L. Bulwer. The note of that functionary communicates the answer to those inquiries, and may be deemed satisfactory, both from the denial of the fact that any such treaty has been concluded and from its positive disavowal on behalf of the British Government of the policy intended to be subserved by such treaties.

Z. TAYLOR.

WASHINGTON, *May 18, 1850.*

To the House of Representatives of the United States:

I herewith transmit to the House of Representatives a report of the Secretary of State, with accompanying papers,* in answer to its resolution of the 28th of March last.

Z. TAYLOR.

WASHINGTON, *May 20, 1850.*

To the Senate of the United States:

I transmit herewith reports from the Secretary of the Interior and Secretary of War, in reply to the resolution of the Senate of the 30th ultimo, calling for information in relation to the hostilities and outrages committed during the past year by the Seminole Indians in Florida, the steps taken for their removal west of the Mississippi, the area now occupied by them, etc.

Z. TAYLOR.

*Communications from the United States consul at Vienna.

WASHINGTON, *May 22, 1850*.

To the Senate of the United States:

I herewith transmit to the Senate reports of the several heads of Departments, to whom were referred the resolutions of the Senate of the 9th instant, "requesting the President of the United States to furnish to the Senate copies of all correspondence between any of the Executive Departments and General Persifor F. Smith and Brigadier-General B. Riley, or either of them, relative to affairs in California, which had not been communicated to the Senate; and also all information existing in any of the Executive Departments respecting the transactions of the convention in California by which the project of a State government was prepared, and particularly a copy of the journals of said convention and of such of the ordinances adopted by it as may in any way have been communicated to any of the said Departments; and likewise to inform the Senate if the surrender of General Riley to the jurisdiction and civil authority of the government made by the aforesaid convention was by order of the Executive of the United States, and, if not, whether the proclamation of General Riley recognizing the said State government and submitting to its jurisdiction has received the sanction of the Executive; and also that he furnish to the Senate whatever intelligence may have been received in the executive department respecting the condition of civil affairs in the Oregon Territory."

The reports, with the official correspondence accompanying them, it is believed, embrace all the information in the Departments called for by the resolutions.

Z. TAYLOR.

WASHINGTON, *May 24, 1850*.

To the Senate of the United States:

In the month of January last I nominated Thomas Sewall to be consul of the United States for the port of Santiago de Cuba, to which office he had been appointed by me during the recess of the Senate. The Spanish Government having refused to recognize Mr. Sewall as consul for that port, I now withdraw that nomination and nominate William N. Adams to fill the vacancy thus occasioned.

Z. TAYLOR.

WASHINGTON, *May 29, 1850*.

To the Senate of the United States:

I transmit to the Senate a copy of a dispatch from the minister of the United States at London, together with the memorial and other documents addressed to the Senate and House of Representatives of the United States by Count de Bronno Bronski which accompanied it, relative to an improved breed of silkworms which he desires to have introduced into this country.

Z. TAYLOR.

WASHINGTON, *June 3, 1850.*

To the Senate of the United States:

I transmit to the Senate herewith reports from the several heads of Departments, which contain all the information in possession of the Executive relative to the subject of the resolution of the 23d instant [ultimo].

No information has been received establishing the existence of any revolutionary movement in the island of Cuba among the inhabitants of that island. The correspondence submitted discloses, however, the fact that repeated attempts have been made under the direction of foreigners enjoying the hospitality of this country to get up armed expeditions in the United States for the purpose of invading Cuba. It will be seen by that correspondence that this Government has been faithful in the discharge of its treaty obligations with Spain and in the execution of the acts of Congress which have for their object the maintenance in this regard of the peace and honor of this country.

Z. TAYLOR

WASHINGTON, *June 10, 1850.*

To the Senate of the United States:

I submit herewith, in reply to a resolution of the Senate of the 3d instant, calling for "copies of the instructions given and orders issued in relation to the assemblage of persons on Round Island, coast of Mississippi, during the summer of 1849, and of the correspondence between the President or heads of Departments and the governor of Mississippi and the officers, naval or military, of the United States in reference to the observation, investment, and dispersion of said assemblage upon said island," a report from the Secretary of the Navy and accompanying documents, which contain all the information on the subject not heretofore communicated to the Senate.

Z. TAYLOR.

WASHINGTON, *June 13, 1850.*

To the House of Representatives of the United States:

I transmit to the House of Representatives a copy of a dispatch addressed by the minister of the United States at Paris to the Secretary of State, with a translation of the documents which accompanied it, relative to the memorial of Pierre Piron, a citizen of the French Republic, who, it will be perceived, presents a just claim to pecuniary remuneration from this Government on account of services rendered to citizens of the United States.

Z. TAYLOR.

WASHINGTON, *June 17, 1850.*

To the Senate of the United States:

I have received a copy of the resolution of the Senate of the 11th June instant, requesting me "to inform the Senate whether any orders have

been issued to any military officer or officers at Santa Fe to hold possession against the authority of Texas, or in any way to embarrass or prevent the exercise of her jurisdiction over that country, and to furnish the
Senate with copies of any correspondence which may have taken place
between the War Department and the military stationed at Santa Fe since
the date of my last communication to the Senate on that subject.''

In reply to that resolution I state that no such orders have been given.

I herewith present to the Senate copies of all the correspondence referred
to in the resolution.   All the other orders relating to the subject-matter
of the resolution have been heretofore communicated to the Senate.

I have already, in a former message, referred to the fact that the boundary between Texas and New Mexico is disputed.   I have now to state
that information has been recently received that a certain Robert S.
Neighbors, styling himself commissioner of the State of Texas, has proceeded to Santa Fe with a view of organizing counties in that district
under the authority of Texas.   While I have no power to decide the
question of boundary, and no desire to interfere with it, as a question of
title, I have to observe that the possession of the territory into which it
appears that Mr. Neighbors has thus gone was actually acquired by the
United States from Mexico, and has since been held by the United States,
and, in my opinion, ought so to remain until the question of boundary
shall have been determined by some competent authority.   Meanwhile, I
think there is no reason for seriously apprehending that Texas will practically interfere with the possession of the United States.

Z. TAYLOR.

WASHINGTON, *June 26, 1850.*

To the House of Representatives of the United States:

I herewith transmit a report of the Secretary of War, communicating
the information, as far as it can be furnished, required by the resolution
of the House of Representatives of the 17th instant, respecting the amount
of money collected from customs in California from the conclusion of the
war until the collector appointed under the act of March 3, 1849, entered
upon his duties, the objects for which said money has been expended,
and the authority under which the collections and disbursements were
made.

Z. TAYLOR.

WASHINGTON, *June 27, 1850.*

To the Senate of the United States:

In compliance with the resolution of the Senate of the 3d instant,
requesting information in regard to the indemnity stipulated to be paid
by the Government of Peru to the Government of the United States pursuant to the modified convention of the 17th of March, 1841, I transmit

a report from the Secretary of State and the documents by which it was accompanied. The sums paid by that Government under the convention are mentioned in the letters of Messrs. E. McCall & Co., of Lima, who were appointed by my predecessor the agents to receive the installments as they might fall due.

Z. TAYLOR.

WASHINGTON, *July 1, 1850.*

To the House of Representatives of the United States:

In reply to the resolution of the House of Representatives of the 17th ultimo, in regard to the number of vessels, guns, and men constituting the African squadron, the annual expenses of that squadron, etc., I submit herewith a report from the Secretary of the Navy, with accompanying documents.

Z. TAYLOR.

WASHINGTON, *July 1, 1850.*

To the Senate of the United States:

I herewith transmit a report from the Secretary of War, prepared in answer to a resolution of the Senate of the 27th ultimo, requesting information of the proceedings of the Executive in regard to the appointment of the officer now commanding in New Mexico, the orders and instructions given to and correspondence with him, and upon other subjects mentioned in the resolution.

Z. TAYLOR.

WASHINGTON, *July 2, 1850.*

To the Senate of the United States:

In the month of March last I nominated William McNeir to be a justice of the peace in and for the county of Washington, in the District of Columbia, and on the 24th day of June the Senate advised and consented to the nomination. Since then I have learned from the late mayor of the city of Washington, upon whose recommendation the nomination was made, that the person whom he intended to recommend for that office was George McNeir, whom I now nominate to be a justice of the peace in and for the county of Washington, in the District of Columbia.

In the month of February last I nominated Benjamin Riddells as consul of the United States for Chihuahua, and on the 10th day of June last the Senate advised and consented to that nomination. I have since learned that the persons recommending the appointment of Mr. Riddells by the prænomen of Benjamin intended to recommend Bennet Riddells, whom I now nominate to be consul of the United States for Chihuahua in order to correct the mistake thus inadvertently made.

Z. TAYLOR.

PROCLAMATIONS.

ZACHARY TAYLOR, PRESIDENT OF THE UNITED STATES OF AMERICA.

To all whom it may concern:

An exequatur having been granted to Señor Carlos de España, bearing date the 29th October, 1846, recognizing him as the consul of Her Catholic Majesty at the port of New Orleans and declaring him free to exercise and enjoy such functions, powers, and privileges as are allowed to the consuls of the most favored nations in the United States:

These are now to declare that I do no longer recognize the said Carlos de España as consul of Her Catholic Majesty in any part of the United States, nor permit him to exercise and enjoy any of the functions, powers, or privileges allowed to the consuls of Spain; and I do hereby wholly revoke and annul the said exequatur heretofore given, and do declare the same to be absolutely null and void from this day forward.

In testimony whereof I have caused these letters to be made patent and the seal of the United States of America to be hereunto affixed.

[SEAL.]   Given under my hand this 4th day of January, A. D. 1850, and of the Independence of the United States the seventy-fourth.

Z. TAYLOR.

By the President:

JOHN M. CLAYTON, *Secretary of State.*

BY THE PRESIDENT OF THE UNITED STATES.

A PROCLAMATION.

Whereas by an act of the Congress of the United States of the 14th of August, 1848, entitled ''An act to establish the Territorial government of Oregon,'' the President of the United States is authorized to establish such ports of delivery in the collection district created by that act, not exceeding two in number (one of which shall be located on Pugets Sound), as he may deem proper:

Now, therefore, I, Zachary Taylor, President of the United States of America, do hereby declare and proclaim the ports of Nesqually (on Pugets Sound) and Portland, in the collection district of Oregon, in the Territory of Oregon, to be constituted ports of delivery, with all the privileges authorized by law to such ports.

In witness whereof I have hereunto set my hand and caused the seal of the United States to be affixed.

[SEAL.]   Done at the city of Washington, this 10th day of January, A. D. 1850, and of the Independence of the United States the seventy-fourth.

Z. TAYLOR.

By the President:

J. M. CLAYTON, *Secretary of State.*

In witness whereof, I have hereunto set my hand, and caused the seal of the United States to be affixed. Done at the City of Washington, this fifth day of July, in the year of our Lord one thousand eight hundred and fifty, and of the Independence of the United States the seventy-fifth.

Z. Taylor.

By the President.

Jn. M. Clayton — Secretary of State.

SIGNATURE OF PRESIDENT TAYLOR ON A STATE DOCUMENT.

DEATH OF PRESIDENT TAYLOR.

ANNOUNCEMENT TO MR. FILLMORE.

[From official records in the State Department.]

DEPARTMENT OF STATE,
Washington, July 9, 1850.

MILLARD FILLMORE,
President of the United States.

SIR: The melancholy and most painful duty devolves on us to announce to you that Zachary Taylor, late President of the United States, is no more. He died at the President's mansion this evening at half-past 10 o'clock.

We have the honor to be, etc.,

JOHN M. CLAYTON,
Secretary of State.

GEO. W. CRAWFORD,
Secretary of War.

W. M. MEREDITH,
Secretary of the Treasury.

WM. BALLARD PRESTON,
Secretary of the Navy.

T. EWING,
Secretary of the Interior.

J. COLLAMER,
Postmaster-General.

[The announcement as published in the Daily National Intelligencer of July 11, 1850, contains also the signature of Reverdy Johnson, Attorney-General.]

REPLY OF MR. FILLMORE.

[From official records in the State Department.]

WASHINGTON, *July 9, 1850.*

To the Hons. JOHN M. CLAYTON, Secretary of State; W. M. MEREDITH, Secretary of the Treasury; T. EWING, Secretary of the Interior; GEO. W. CRAWFORD, Secretary of War; WM. BALLARD PRESTON, Secretary of the Navy; J. COLLAMER, Postmaster-General; REVERDY JOHNSON, Attorney-General.

GENTLEMEN: I have just received your note conveying the melancholy and painful intelligence of the decease of Zachary Taylor, late President of the United States. I have no language to express the emotions of my heart. The shock is so sudden and unexpected that I am overwhelmed with grief.

I shall avail myself of the earliest moment to communicate this sad intelligence to Congress, and shall appoint a time and place for taking the oath of office prescribed to the President of the United States. You are requested to be present and witness the ceremony.

I am, gentlemen, etc.,

MILLARD FILLMORE.

COMMUNICATION TO THE SENATE FROM MR. FILLMORE.

[From Senate Journal, Thirty-first Congress, first session, p. 443.]

WASHINGTON, *July 10, 1850.*

To the Senate of the United States:

In consequence of the lamented death of Zachary Taylor, late President of the United States, I shall no longer occupy the chair of the Senate, and I have thought that a formal communication to the Senate to that effect, through your Secretary, might enable you the more promptly to proceed to the choice of a presiding officer.

MILLARD FILLMORE.

ANNOUNCEMENT TO CONGRESS.

[From Senate Journal, Thirty-first Congress, first session, p. 443.]

WASHINGTON, *July 10, 1850.*

Fellow-Citizens of the Senate and House of Representatives:

I have to perform the melancholy duty of announcing to you that it has pleased Almighty God to remove from this life Zachary Taylor, late President of the United States. He deceased last evening at the hour of half-past 10 o'clock, in the midst of his family and surrounded by affectionate friends, calmly and in the full possession of all his faculties. Among his last words were these, which he uttered with emphatic distinctness:

I have always done my duty. I am ready to die. My only regret is for the friends I leave behind me.

Having announced to you, fellow-citizens, this most afflicting bereavement, and assuring you that it has penetrated no heart with deeper grief than mine, it remains for me to say that I propose this day at 12 o'clock, in the Hall of the House of Representatives, in the presence of both Houses of Congress, to take the oath prescribed by the Constitution, to enable me to enter on the execution of the office which this event has devolved on me.

MILLARD FILLMORE.

ANNOUNCEMENT TO REPRESENTATIVES OF THE UNITED STATES ABROAD.

[From official records in the State Department.]

CIRCULAR.

DEPARTMENT OF STATE, *Washington, July 10, 1850.*

SIR: It has become my most painful duty to announce to you the decease of Zachary Taylor, late President of the United States.

This afflicting event took place on the 9th instant at the Executive Mansion in this city, at thirty minutes after 10 o'clock in the evening.

I am, sir, respectfully, your obedient servant,

JOHN M. CLAYTON.

ANNOUNCEMENT TO REPRESENTATIVES OF FOREIGN GOVERNMENTS IN THE UNITED STATES.

[From official records in the State Department.]

CIRCULAR.

DEPARTMENT OF STATE, *Washington, July 10, 1850.*

SIR: It is my great misfortune to be obliged to inform you of an event not less afflicting to the people of the United States than distressing to my own feelings and the feelings of all those connected with the Government.

The President, Zachary Taylor, departed this life yesterday at half-past 10 o'clock in the evening.

You are respectfully invited to attend the funeral ceremonies, which will take place on Saturday next, and with the particular arrangements for which you will be made acquainted in due time.

Not doubting your sympathy and condolence with the Government and people of the country on this bereavement, I have the honor to be, sir, with high consideration, your obedient servant,

JOHN M. CLAYTON.

ANNOUNCEMENT TO THE ARMY.

[From official records in the War Department.]

GENERAL ORDERS, No. 21.

WAR DEPARTMENT, ADJUTANT-GENERAL'S OFFICE,
Washington, July 11, 1850.

I. The following order of the President of the United States announces to the Army the lamented death of the illustrious General Zachary Taylor, late President of the United States:

WAR DEPARTMENT, *July 11, 1850.*

The President of the United States with profound sorrow announces to the Army, the Navy, and Marine Corps the death of Zachary Taylor, late President of the United States. He died at the Executive Mansion on the night of the 9th instant at half-past 10 o'clock.

His last public appearance was in participating in the ceremonies of our national anniversary at the base of the monument now rearing to the memory of Washington. His last official act was to affix his signature to the convention recently concluded between the United States and Great Britain.

The vigor of a constitution strong by nature and confirmed by active and temperate habits had in later years become impaired by the arduous toils and exposures of his military life.

Solely engrossed in maintaining the honor and advancing the glory of his country, in a career of forty years in the Army of the United States he rendered himself signal and illustrious. An unbroken current of success and victory, terminated by an achievement unsurpassed in our annals, left nothing to be accomplished for his military fame.

His conduct and courage gave him this career of unexampled fortune, and with the crowning virtues of moderation and humanity under all circumstances, and especially in the moment of victory, revealed to his countrymen those great and good qualities which induced them unsolicited to call him from his high military command to the highest civil office of honor and trust in the Republic; not that he desired to be first, but that he was felt to be worthiest.

The simplicity of his character, the singleness of his purpose, the elevation and patriotism of his principles, his moral courage, his justice, magnanimity and benevolence, his wisdom, moderation, and power of command, while they have endeared him to the heart of the nation, add to the deep sense of the national calamity in the loss of a Chief Magistrate whom death itself could not appall in the consciousness of "having always done his duty."

The officers of the Army, of the Navy, and Marine Corps will, as a manifestation of their respect for the exalted character and eminent public services of the illustrious dead, and of their sense of the calamity the country has sustained by this afflicting dispensation of Providence, wear crape on the left arm and upon the hilt of the sword for six months.

It is further directed that funeral honors be paid at each of the military posts according to general regulations, and at navy-yards and on board all public vessels in commission, by firing thirty minute guns, commencing at meridian, on the day after the receipt of this order, and by wearing their flags at half-mast.

By order of the President:

GEORGE W. CRAWFORD,
Secretary of War.

II. The day after the receipt of this general order at each military post the troops will be paraded at 10 o'clock a. m. and the order read to them, after which all labors for the day will cease.

The national flag will be displayed at half-staff.

At dawn of day thirteen guns will be fired, and afterwards at intervals of thirty minutes between the rising and setting sun a single gun, and at the close of the day a national salute of thirty guns.

The officers of the Army will wear the badge of mourning on the left arm and on their swords and the colors of the several regiments will be put in mourning for the period of six months.

By order:

R. JONES,
Adjutant-General.

[The Secretary of the Navy made the same announcement to the Navy as that portion of the above signed by the Secretary of War.]

ORDER OF THE PRESIDENT.

[From the Daily National Intelligencer, July 12, 1850.]

WASHINGTON, *July 10, 1850.*

In consequence of the death of the President of the United States, I direct that the several Executive Departments be closed until after the funeral of the illustrious deceased, and that they, as well as the Executive Mansion, be placed in mourning, and that the several officers of the Government wear the usual badge of mourning for the term of six months.

MILLARD FILLMORE.

ACTION OF CONGRESS.

[From Senate Journal, Thirty-first Congress, first session, p. 445.]

RESOLUTION OF THE SENATE.

Whereas it has pleased Divine Providence to remove from this life Zachary Taylor, late President of the United States, the Senate, sharing in the general sorrow which this melancholy event must produce, is desirous of manifesting its sensibility on this occasion: Therefore

Resolved, That a committee consisting of Messrs. Webster, Cass, and King be appointed on the part of the Senate to meet such committee as may be appointed on the part of the House of Representatives to consider and report what measures it may be deemed proper to adopt to show the respect and affection of Congress for the memory of the illustrious deceased and to make the necessary arrangements for his funeral.

[From House Journal, Thirty-first Congress, first session, p. 1121.]

RESOLUTION OF THE HOUSE OF REPRESENTATIVES.

Whereas it has pleased Divine Providence to remove from this life Zachary Taylor, late President of the United States, the House of Representatives, sharing in the general sorrow which this melancholy event must produce, is desirous of manifesting its sensibility on the occasion: Therefore

Resolved, That a committee consisting of thirteen members be appointed on the part of this House to meet such committee as may be appointed on the part of the Senate to consider and report what measures it may be deemed proper to adopt in order to show the respect and affection of Congress for the memory of the illustrious deceased and to make the necessary arrangements for his funeral.

[The committee consisted of Messrs. Conrad, of Louisiana; McDowell, of Virginia; Winthrop, of Massachusetts; Bissell, of Illinois; Duer, of New York; Orr, of South Carolina; Breck, of Kentucky; Strong, of Pennsylvania; Vinton, of Ohio; Cabell, of Florida; Kerr, of Maryland; Stanly, of North Carolina; Littlefield, of Maine.]

OFFICIAL ARRANGEMENTS FOR THE FUNERAL.

[From the Daily National Intelligencer, July 13, 1850.]

WASHINGTON, *July 11, 1850.*

The Committee of Arrangements of the two Houses of Congress, having consulted with the family of the deceased, have concluded that the funeral of the late President be solemnized on Saturday, the 13th of July, at 12 o'clock; the religious services to be performed by the Rev. Dr. Pyne at the Executive Mansion, according to the usage of the Episcopal Church, in which church the deceased most usually worshiped; the body to be afterwards taken from the President's house to the Congress Burying Ground, accompanied by a military escort and civic procession, and deposited in the receiving tomb.

The military arrangements to be under the direction of Major-General Scott, the General Commanding in Chief of the Army of the United States, and Major-General Walter Jones, of the militia of the District of Columbia.

Commodore Warrington, the senior naval officer now in the city, to have the direction of the naval arrangements.

The marshal of the District of Columbia to have the direction of the civic procession.

All the members of the diplomatic corps, all officers of Government, the clergy of the District and elsewhere, all associations and fraternities, and citizens generally are invited to attend.

And it is respectfully recommended to the officers of the Government that they wear the usual badge of mourning.

ORDER OF THE PROCESSION.

FUNERAL ESCORT.

(In column of march.)

Composed of such corps of the Army and the militia as may be ordered or as may report themselves for duty on the occasion.

CIVIC PROCESSION.

The United States marshal of the District of Columbia and his aids.
The mayors of Washington and Georgetown.
The Committee of Arrangements of the two Houses of Congress.
The chaplains of the two Houses of Congress and the officiating clergyman of the occasion.
Attending physicians to the late President.

Pallbearers.—Hon. Henry Clay, Hon. T. H. Benton, Hon. Lewis Cass, Hon. Daniel Webster, Hon. J. M. Berrien, Hon. Truman Smith, Hon. R. C. Winthrop, Hon. Linn Boyd, Hon. James McDowell, Hon. S. F. Vinton, Hon. Hugh White, Hon. Isaac E. Holmes, G. W. P. Custis, esq., Hon. R. J. Walker, Chief Justice Cranch, Joseph Gales, esq., Major-General Jesup, Major-General Gibson, Commodore Ballard, Brigadier-General Henderson.

The horse used by General Taylor in the late war.

Family and relatives of the late President.

The President of the United States and the heads of Departments.

The Sergeant-at-Arms of the Senate.

The Senate of the United States, preceded by the President *pro tempore* and Secretary.

The Sergeant-at-Arms of the House of Representatives.

The House of Representatives, preceded by their Speaker and Clerk.

The Chief Justice and associate justices of the Supreme Court of the United States and its officers.

The diplomatic corps.

Governors of States and Territories.

Ex-members of Congress.

Members of State legislatures.

District judges of the United States.

Judges of the circuit and criminal courts of the District of Columbia, with the members of the bar and officers of the courts.

The judges of the several States.

The Comptroller of the Treasury, Auditors, Treasurer, Register, Solicitor, and Commissioners of Land Office, Pensions, Indian Affairs, Patents, and Public Buildings.

The clerks, etc., of the several Departments, preceded by their respective chief clerks, and all other civil officers of the Government.

Clergy of the District of Columbia and elsewhere.

Officers and soldiers of the Revolution.

Corporate authorities of Washington.

Corporate authorities of Georgetown.

Officers and soldiers who served in the War of 1812 and in the late war.

Presidents, professors, and students of the colleges of the District of Columbia.

Such societies and fraternities as may wish to join the procession, to report to the marshal of the District, who will assign them their respective positions.

Citizens and strangers.

The procession will move from the President's house at 1 o'clock precisely, or on the conclusion of the religious services.

DANIEL WEBSTER,
Chairman of the Committee on the part of the Senate.

CHAS. M. CONRAD,
Chairman of the Committee on the part of the House of Representatives.

[From official records in the War Department.]

GENERAL ORDERS, NO. 22.

WAR DEPARTMENT, ADJUTANT-GENERAL'S OFFICE,
Washington, July 11, 1850.

The joint committees of the Congress of the United States having designated the General in Chief, Major-General Scott, to take charge of the military arrangements for the funeral ceremonies of the late President of the United States, the Secretary of War directs that the Commanding General of the Army give the necessary orders and instructions accordingly. The military arrangements will conform to the directions found in the reports of the special committees of the Senate and House of Representatives.

By order of the Secretary of War:

R. JONES, *Adjutant-General.*

GENERAL ORDERS.

HEADQUARTERS OF THE ARMY,
ADJUTANT-GENERAL'S OFFICE,
Washington, July 12, 1850.

The Major-General Commanding the Army of the United States, having been charged by the joint committees of Congress with the military preparations for the funeral honors to be paid to the illustrious statesman, soldier, and citizen, Zachary Taylor, late President of the United States, directs the following order of arrangement:

ORDER OF THE MILITARY PROCESSION.

FUNERAL ESCORT.

(In column of march.)

Infantry.—Maryland volunteers; volunteer troops from other States; battalion of volunteers from the District of Columbia.

Firing party (to be commanded by an officer of the Army).—Two companies of volunteers from Washington; two companies of volunteers from Baltimore; battalion of United States marines; battalion of United States artillery, as infantry; troop of United States light artillery.

Dismounted officers of volunteers, Marine Corps, Navy, and Army, in the order named.

Mounted officers of volunteers, Marine Corps, Navy, and Army, in the order named.

Major-General Walter Jones, commanding the militia; aids-de-camp.

Major-General Winfield Scott, commanding the Army; aids-de-camp.

The troops will be formed in line in the Avenue, north of the President's mansion, precisely at 11 o'clock a. m., Saturday, the 13th instant, with the right (Brevet Major Sedgwick's troop of light artillery) resting opposite the War Department.

The procession will move at 1 o'clock p. m., when minute guns will be fired by detachments of artillery stationed near St. John's church, the City Hall, and the Capitol, respectively.

On arriving on the north front of the Congressional Burial Ground the escort will be formed in two lines, the first consisting of the firing party, facing the cemetery and 30 paces from it; the second composed of the rest of the infantry, 20 paces in rear; the battery of artillery to take position on the rising ground 100 paces in rear of the second line.

At sunrise to-morrow (the 13th instant) a Federal salute will be fired from the military stations in the vicinity of Washington, minute guns between the hours of 1 and 3, and a national salute at the setting of the sun.

The usual badge of mourning will be worn on the left arm and on the hilt of the sword.

The Adjutant-General of the Army is charged with the details of the military arrangements of the day, aided by the Assistant Adjutants-General on duty at Washington, by Brevet Lieutenant-Colonel Swords, of the staff, and Lieutenant W. T. Sherman, Third Artillery.

The United States marshal of the District of Columbia having been charged with the direction of the civic procession, the military will co-operate in the general order of arrangements.

By command of Major-General Scott:

R. JONES,
Adjutant-General.

[From the Daily National Intelligencer, July 12, 1850.]

GENERAL ORDER.

The major-general, zealous to execute the honorable commission in which the joint committees of Congress have associated him with the General in Chief of the Army, deems it proper and conducive to the end in view to make the best preparation in his power for carrying into effect the field arrangements of the military movements in the procession of the funeral of the late President, arrangements which must necessarily await the arrival of the General in Chief. For that purpose he thinks it expedient to appoint a general rendezvous where all the corps and companies of militia, including all who may march from any of the States with those of this District, may assemble at an early hour in the morning of Saturday, the 13th instant, and there receive final orders for being formed and posted. They are therefore requested to take notice that such rendezvous is in front of the City Hall. The corps and companies from the States are requested to repair to this general rendezvous immediately on arrival; those of the District not later than 9 o'clock a. m. The commandants of corps and companies are expected to report, immediately on arriving at the rendezvous, to the major-general or such staff officer as may be detailed for the purpose, the strength of their respective commands.

All officers not on duty in their respective corps or companies are requested to appear in full uniform and mounted. The post intended for them is in the personal suite of the General in Chief. The major-general knows of no more honorable or more interesting post that he could assign them in time of peace than that of following the lead of the renowned Scott in the procession of the funeral of the renowned Taylor.

WALTER JONES,
Major-General Militia District of Columbia.

RESOLUTION OF CONDOLENCE BY CONGRESS.

[From original in the State Department.]

A RESOLUTION expressing the condolence of Congress for Mrs. Margaret S. Taylor.

Resolved by the Senate and House of Representatives of the United States of America in Congress assembled, That the President of the United States be requested to transmit a copy of the proceedings of the two Houses on the 10th instant in relation to the death of the late President of the United States to Mrs. Margaret S. Taylor, and to assure her of the profound respect of the two Houses of Congress for her person and character and of their sincere condolence on the late afflicting dispensation of Providence.

Millard Fillmore

July 10, 1850, to March 4, 1853

OLD HOME AT BUFFALO, NEW YORK, OF

MILLARD FILLMORE

With official portrait engraved from copy of original in steel

MILLARD FILLMORE

Millard Fillmore

MILLARD FILLMORE was born February 7, 1800, in the township of
Locke (now Summerhill), Cayuga County, N. Y. He was the second son
of Nathaniel Fillmore and Phœbe Millard. His ancestors served with
distinction in the French and Revolutionary wars. He attended the
primitive schools in the neighborhood three months in the year, devoting
the other nine to working on his father's farm. His father, having formed
a distaste for farming, was desirous that his sons should follow other occupations. Accordingly, Millard, after serving an apprenticeship for a
few months, began in 1815 the business of carding and dressing cloth.
Was afterwards a school-teacher. In 1819 decided to become a lawyer,
and in 1823, although he had not completed the usual course required,
was admitted as an attorney by the court of common pleas of Erie County.
February 5, 1826, was married to Miss Abigail Powers, daughter of a
clergyman. In 1827 was admitted as an attorney and two years later
as counselor before the supreme court. In 1830 removed to Buffalo and
became a successful lawyer. His political career began and ended with
the birth and extinction of the Whig party. Was elected to the legislature of his State in 1828, and served three terms; while there he was distinguished by his advocacy of the act to abolish imprisonment for debt,
which passed in 1831. In 1832 was elected to Congress, and after serving one term retired till 1836, when he was reelected, and again returned
in 1838 and 1840, declining a renomination in 1842. Was the author of
the tariff of 1842. He retired from Congress in 1843. Was an unsuccessful candidate for Vice-President before the Whig convention at Baltimore in 1844. Was nominated by acclamation for governor of New York
in the following September, but was defeated by Silas Wright. In 1847
was elected comptroller of the State. In 1848 was nominated by the
Whigs for Vice-President on the ticket with General Taylor and was
elected in the following November. He presided as Vice-President with
strict impartiality during exciting debates in the Senate. By the death
of President Taylor became President July 10, 1850. Was a candidate
for President at the Whig convention in 1852, but General Scott received
the nomination. Three weeks after the close of his Administration his
wife died. Afterwards married Caroline C. McIntosh, who survived him.
In 1856, while in Rome, he was nominated for the Presidency by the

American (Whig) party, but was defeated by Mr. Buchanan. After his retirement from office he resided in Buffalo the remainder of his life. He established the Buffalo Historical Society. Was called upon to welcome distinguished visitors to his city, and frequently presided over conventions and other public meetings, but held no office after retiring from the Presidency. He again visited Europe in 1866. Died at Buffalo, N. Y., March 8, 1874, and was buried in that city in Forest Lawn Cemetery.

SPECIAL MESSAGES.

WASHINGTON, *July 10, 1850.*

Fellow-Citizens of the Senate and House of Representatives:

A great man has fallen among us, and a whole country is called to an occasion of unexpected, deep, and general mourning.

I recommend to the two Houses of Congress to adopt such measures as in their discretion may seem proper to perform with due solemnities the funeral obsequies of Zachary Taylor, late President of the United States, and thereby to signify the great and affectionate regard of the American people for the memory of one whose life has been devoted to the public service, whose career in arms has not been surpassed in usefulness or brilliancy, who has been so recently raised by the unsolicited voice of the people to the highest civil authority in the Government, which he administered with so much honor and advantage to his country, and by whose sudden death so many hopes of future usefulness have been blighted forever.

To you, Senators and Representatives of a nation in tears, I can say nothing which can alleviate the sorrow with which you are oppressed. I appeal to you to aid me, under the trying circumstances which surround me, in the discharge of the duties from which, however much I may be oppressed by them, I dare not shrink; and I rely upon Him who holds in His hands the destinies of nations to endow me with the requisite strength for the task and to avert from our country the evils apprehended from the heavy calamity which has befallen us.

I shall most readily concur in whatever measures the wisdom of the two Houses may suggest as befitting this deeply melancholy occasion.

MILLARD FILLMORE.

WASHINGTON, *July 15, 1850.*

To the Senate of the United States:

I transmit to the Senate, for its consideration with a view to ratification, a treaty between the United States and the Republic of Peru, signed in this city on the 13th instant by the plenipotentiaries of the parties.

A report from the Secretary of State relative to the treaty, and the documents therein referred to, are also herewith transmitted.

MILLARD FILLMORE.

WASHINGTON, *July 17, 1850.*

To the Senate of the United States:

In further answer to a resolution of the Senate of the 27th ultimo, in reference to a proclamation issued by the military officer commanding in New Mexico and other matters, I herewith transmit a report from the Secretary of War, communicating information not received at the Department until after the date of his report of the 1st instant on this subject.

MILLARD FILLMORE.

WASHINGTON, *July 17, 1850.*

To the Senate of the United States:

In answer to a resolution of the Senate of the 1st instant, requesting the President to furnish the Senate with "the report and map of Lieutenant J. D. Webster, Corps of Topographical Engineers, of a survey of the Gulf coast at the mouth of the Rio Grande and its vicinity," and in compliance therewith, I transmit herewith a report from the Secretary of War, accompanied by the report and map above referred to.

MILLARD FILLMORE.

WASHINGTON, *July 18, 1850.*

To the House of Representatives of the United States:

I herewith transmit to the House of Representatives, in compliance with the request contained in their resolution of the 24th day of January last, the information asked for by that resolution, relating to certain proceedings of the British Government in the forcible seizure and occupation of the island of Tigre; also all the "facts, circumstances, and communications within the knowledge of the Executive relative to any seizure or occupation, or attempted seizure or occupation, by the British Government of any port, river, town, territory, or island belonging to or claimed by any of the States of Central America."

The resolution of the House speaks of the island of Tigre, in the State of Nicaragua. I am not aware of the existence of any such island in that State, and presume that the resolution refers to the island of the same name in the Gulf of Fonseca, in the State of Honduras.

The concluding part of the resolution, requesting the President to communicate to the House all treaties not heretofore published which may have been negotiated with any of the States of Central America "by any person acting by authority of the late Administration or under the auspices of the present Administration," so far as it has reference to treaties negotiated with any of those States by instructions from this Government, can not be complied with, inasmuch as those treaties have not been acted upon by the Senate of the United States, and are now in the possession of that body, to whom by the Constitution they are directed to be transmitted for advice in regard to their ratification.

But as its communication is not liable to the same objection, I transmit for the information of the House a copy of a treaty in regard to a ship canal across the Isthmus, negotiated by Elijah Hise, our late chargé d'affaires in Guatemala, with the Government of Nicaragua on the 21st day of June, 1849, accompanied by copies of his instructions from and correspondence with the Department of State.

I shall cheerfully comply with the request of the House of Representatives to lay before them the treaties negotiated with the States of Central America, now before the Senate, whenever it shall be compatible with the public interest to make the communication. For the present I communicate herewith a copy of the treaty with Great Britain and of the correspondence between the American Secretary of State and the British plenipotentiary at the time it was concluded. The ratifications of it were exchanged at Washington on the 4th day of July instant.

I also transmit the report of the Secretary of State, to whom the resolution of the House was referred, and who conducted the negotiations relative to Central America, under the direction of my lamented predecessor.

MILLARD FILLMORE.

WASHINGTON, *July 20, 1850.*

To the Senate of the United States:

I herewith transmit to the Senate, with a view to its ratification, a convention between the United States and the Mexican Republic for the extradition of fugitives from justice. This convention was negotiated under the directions of my predecessor, and was signed this day by John M. Clayton, Secretary of State, on the part of the United States, and by Señor Don Luis de la Rosa, envoy extraordinary and minister plenipotentiary of Mexico, on the part of that Republic. The length of the boundary line between the two countries, extending, as it does, from the Pacific to the Gulf, renders such a convention indispensable to the maintenance of good order and the amicable relations now so happily subsisting between the sister Republics.

MILLARD FILLMORE.

WASHINGTON, *July 23, 1850.*

To the Senate of the United States:

I lay before the Senate, for their consideration and advice as to its ratification, a treaty concluded in the city of Washington on the 1st day of

April, 1850, by and between Ardavan S. Loughery, commissioner on the part of the United States, and delegates of the Wyandott tribe of Indians.

I also lay before the Senate a letter from the Secretary of the Interior and the papers therein referred to.
MILLARD FILLMORE.

WASHINGTON, July 30, 1850.

To the Senate of the United States:

I herewith transmit to the Senate, in answer to its resolution of the 5th instant, requesting the President to communicate to that body "any information, if any has been received by the Government, showing that an American vessel has been recently stopped upon the high seas and searched by a British ship of war," the accompanying copies of papers. The Government has no knowledge of any alleged stopping or searching on the high seas of American vessels by British ships of war except in the cases therein mentioned. The circumstances of these cases will appear by the inclosed correspondence, taken from the files of the Navy Department. No remonstrance or complaint by the owners of these vessels has been presented to the Government of the United States.
MILLARD FILLMORE.

WASHINGTON, August 2, 1850.

To the Senate of the United States:

I have the honor to transmit herewith a report of the Secretary of War, in answer to a resolution of the Senate passed on the 8th of July last, calling for information in relation to the removal of Fort Polk, etc. The documents accompanying the report contain all the information required by the resolution.
MILLARD FILLMORE.

WASHINGTON, August 6, 1850.

To the Senate and House of Representatives:

I herewith transmit to the two Houses of Congress a letter from his excellency the governor of Texas, dated on the 14th day of June last, addressed to the late President of the United States, which, not having been answered by him, came to my hands on his death; and I also transmit a copy of the answer which I have felt it to be my duty to cause to be made to that communication.

Congress will perceive that the governor of Texas officially states that by authority of the legislature of that State he dispatched a special commissioner with full power and instructions to extend the civil jurisdiction of the State over the unorganized counties of El Paso, Worth, Presidio, and Santa Fe, situated on its northwestern limits.

He proceeds to say that the commissioner had reported to him in an official form that the military officers employed in the service of the United States stationed at Santa Fe interposed adversely with the inhabitants to the fulfillment of his object in favor of the establishment of a separate State government east of the Rio Grande, and within the rightful limits of the State of Texas. These four counties, which Texas thus proposes to establish and organize as being within her own jurisdiction, extend over the whole of the territory east of the Rio Grande, which has heretofore been regarded as an essential and integral part of the department of New Mexico, and actually governed and possessed by her people until conquered and severed from the Republic of Mexico by the American arms.

The legislature of Texas has been called together by her governor for the purpose, as is understood, of maintaining her claim to the territory east of the Rio Grande and of establishing over it her own jurisdiction and her own laws by force.

These proceedings of Texas may well arrest the attention of all branches of the Government of the United States, and I rejoice that they occur while the Congress is yet in session. It is, I fear, far from being impossible that, in consequence of these proceedings of Texas, a crisis may be brought on which shall summon the two Houses of Congress, and still more emphatically the executive government, to an immediate readiness for the performance of their respective duties.

By the Constitution of the United States the President is constituted Commander in Chief of the Army and Navy, and of the militia of the several States when called into the actual service of the United States. The Constitution declares also that he shall take care that the laws be faithfully executed and that he shall from time to time give to the Congress information of the state of the Union.

Congress has power by the Constitution to provide for calling forth the militia to execute the laws of the Union, and suitable and appropriate acts of Congress have been passed as well for providing for calling forth the militia as for placing other suitable and efficient means in the hands of the President to enable him to discharge the constitutional functions of his office.

The second section of the act of the 28th of February, 1795, declares that whenever the laws of the United States shall be opposed or their execution obstructed in any State by combinations too powerful to be suppressed by the ordinary course of judicial proceedings or the power vested in the marshals, the President may call forth the militia, as far as may be necessary, to suppress such combinations and to cause the laws to be duly executed.

By the act of March 3, 1807, it is provided that in all cases of obstruction to the laws either of the United States or any individual State or Territory, where it is lawful for the President to call forth the militia for the purpose of causing the laws to be duly executed, it shall be lawful for him to employ for the same purposes such part of the land or naval force of the United States as shall be judged necessary.

These several enactments are now in full force, so that if the laws of the United States are opposed or obstructed in any State or Territory by combinations too powerful to be suppressed by the judicial or civil authorities it becomes a case in which it is the duty of the President either to call out the militia or to employ the military and naval force of the United States, or to do both if in his judgment the exigency of the occasion shall so require, for the purpose of suppressing such combinations. The constitutional duty of the President is plain and peremptory and the authority vested in him by law for its performance clear and ample.

Texas is a State, authorized to maintain her own laws so far as they are not repugnant to the Constitution, laws, and treaties of the United States; to suppress insurrections against her authority, and to punish those who may commit treason against the State according to the forms provided by her own constitution and her own laws.

But all this power is local and confined entirely within the limits of Texas herself. She can possibly confer no authority which can be lawfully exercised beyond her own boundaries.

All this is plain, and hardly needs argument or elucidation. If Texas militia, therefore, march into any one of the other States or into any Territory of the United States, there to execute or enforce any law of Texas, they become at that moment trespassers; they are no longer under the protection of any lawful authority, and are to be regarded merely as intruders; and if within such State or Territory they obstruct any law of the United States, either by power of arms or mere power of numbers, constituting such a combination as is too powerful to be suppressed by the civil authority, the President of the United States has no option left to him, but is bound to obey the solemn injunction of the Constitution and exercise the high powers vested in him by that instrument and by the acts of Congress.

Or if any civil posse, armed or unarmed, enter into any Territory of the United States, under the protection of the laws thereof, with intent to seize individuals, to be carried elsewhere for trial for alleged offenses, and this posse be too powerful to be resisted by the local civil authorities, such seizure or attempt to seize is to be prevented or resisted by the authority of the United States.

The grave and important question now arises whether there be in the Territory of New Mexico any existing law of the United States opposition to which or the obstruction of which would constitute a case calling for the interposition of the authority vested in the President.

The Constitution of the United States declares that—

This Constitution, and the laws of the United States which shall be made in pursuance thereof, and all treaties made, or which shall be made, under the authority of the United States. shall be the supreme law of the land.

If, therefore, New Mexico be a Territory of the United States, and if any treaty stipulation be in force therein, such treaty stipulation is the supreme law of the land, and is to be maintained and upheld accordingly.

In the letter to the governor of Texas my reasons are given for believing that New Mexico is now a Territory of the United States, with the same extent and the same boundaries which belonged to it while in the actual possession of the Republic of Mexico, and before the late war. In the early part of that war both California and New Mexico were conquered by the arms of the United States, and were in the military possession of the United States at the date of the treaty of peace.

By that treaty the title by conquest was confirmed and these territories, provinces, or departments separated from Mexico forever, and by the same treaty certain important rights and securities were solemnly guaranteed to the inhabitants residing therein.

By the fifth article of the treaty it is declared that—

The boundary line between the two Republics shall commence in the Gulf of Mexico 3 leagues from land, opposite the mouth of the Rio Grande, otherwise called Rio Bravo del Norte, or opposite the mouth of its deepest branch if it should have more than one branch emptying directly into the sea; from thence up the middle of that river, following the deepest channel where it has more than one, to the point where it strikes the southern boundary of New Mexico; thence westwardly, along the whole southern boundary of New Mexico (which runs north of the town called Paso) to its western termination; thence northward along the western line of New Mexico until it intersects the first branch of the river Gila (or, if it should not intersect any branch of that river, then to the point on the said line nearest to such branch, and thence in a direct line to the same); thence down the middle of the said branch and of the said river until it empties into the Rio Colorado; thence across the Rio Colorado, following the division line between Upper and Lower California, to the Pacific Ocean.

The eighth article of the treaty is in the following terms:

Mexicans now established in territories previously belonging to Mexico, and which remain for the future within the limits of the United States as defined by the present treaty, shall be free to continue where they now reside or to remove at any time to the Mexican Republic, retaining the property which they possess in the said territories, or disposing thereof and removing the proceeds wherever they please without their being subjected on this account to any contribution, tax, or charge whatever.

Those who shall prefer to remain in the said territories may either retain the title and rights of Mexican citizens or acquire those of citizens of the United States; but they shall be under the obligation to make their election within one year from the date of the exchange of ratifications of this treaty; and those who shall remain in the said territories after the expiration of that year without having declared their intention to retain the character of Mexicans shall be considered to have elected to become citizens of the United States.

In the said territories property of every kind now belonging to Mexicans not established there shall be inviolably respected. The present owners, the heirs of these, and all Mexicans who may hereafter acquire said property by contract shall enjoy with respect to it guaranties equally ample as if the same belonged to citizens of the United States.

The ninth article of the treaty is in these words:

The Mexicans who, in the territories aforesaid, shall not preserve the character of citizens of the Mexican Republic, conformably with what is stipulated in the preceding article, shall be incorporated into the Union of the United States and be admitted at the proper time (to be judged of by the Congress of the United States) to the enjoyment of all the rights of citizens of the United States according to the principles of the Constitution, and in the meantime shall be maintained and protected in the free enjoyment of their liberty and property and secured in the free exercise of their religion without restriction.

It is plain, therefore, on the face of these treaty stipulations that all Mexicans established in territories north or east of the line of demarcation already mentioned come within the protection of the ninth article, and that the treaty, being a part of the supreme law of the land, does extend over all such Mexicans, and assures to them perfect security in the free enjoyment of their liberty and property, as well as in the free exercise of their religion; and this supreme law of the land, being thus in actual force over this territory, is to be maintained until it shall be displaced or superseded by other legal provisions; and if it be obstructed or resisted by combinations too powerful to be suppressed by the civil authority the case is one which comes within the provisions of law and which obliges the President to enforce those provisions. Neither the Constitution nor the laws nor my duty nor my oath of office leave me any alternative or any choice in my mode of action.

The executive government of the United States has no power or authority to determine what was the true line of boundary between Mexico and the United States before the treaty of Guadalupe Hidalgo, nor has it any such power now, since the question has become a question between the State of Texas and the United States. So far as this boundary is doubtful, that doubt can only be removed by some act of Congress, to which the assent of the State of Texas may be necessary, or by some appropriate mode of legal adjudication; but in the meantime, if disturbances or collisions arise or should be threatened, it is absolutely incumbent on the executive government, however painful the duty, to take care that the laws be faithfully maintained; and he can regard only the actual state of things as it existed at the date of the treaty, and is bound to protect all inhabitants who were then established and who now remain north and east of the line of demarcation in the full enjoyment of their liberty and property, according to the provisions of the ninth article of the treaty. In other words, all must be now regarded as New Mexico which was possessed and occupied as New Mexico by citizens of Mexico at the date of the treaty until a definite line of boundary shall be established by competent authority.

This assertion of duty to protect the people of New Mexico from threatened violence, or from seizure to be carried into Texas for trial for alleged offenses against Texan laws, does not at all include any claim of power on the part of the Executive to establish any civil or military government within that Territory. *That power* belongs exclusively to the legislative department, and Congress is the sole judge of the time and manner of creating or authorizing any such government.

The duty of the Executive extends only to the execution of laws and the maintenance of treaties already in force and the protection of all the people of the United States in the enjoyment of the rights which those treaties and laws guarantee.

It is exceedingly desirable that no occasion should arise for the exercise of the powers thus vested in the President by the Constitution and the laws. With whatever mildness those powers might be executed, or however clear the case of necessity, yet consequences might, nevertheless, follow of which no human sagacity can foresee either the evils or the end.

Having thus laid before Congress the communication of his excellency the governor of Texas and the answer thereto, and having made such observations as I have thought the occasion called for respecting constitutional obligations which may arise in the further progress of things and may devolve on me to be performed, I hope I shall not be regarded as stepping aside from the line of my duty, notwithstanding that I am aware that the subject is now before both Houses, if I express my deep and earnest conviction of the importance of an immediate decision or arrangement or settlement of the question of boundary between Texas and the Territory of New Mexico. All considerations of justice, general expediency, and domestic tranquillity call for this. It seems to be in its character and by position the first, or one of the first, of the questions growing out of the acquisition of California and New Mexico, and now requiring decision.

No government can be established for New Mexico, either State or Territorial, until it shall be first ascertained what New Mexico is, and what are her limits and boundaries. These can not be fixed or known till the line of division between her and Texas shall be ascertained and established; and numerous and weighty reasons conspire, in my judgment, to show that this divisional line should be established by Congress with the assent of the government of Texas. In the first place, this seems by far the most prompt mode of proceeding by which the end can be accomplished. If judicial proceedings were resorted to, such proceedings would necessarily be slow, and years would pass by, in all probability, before the controversy could be ended. So great a delay in this case is to be avoided if possible. Such delay would be every way inconvenient, and might be the occasion of disturbances and collisions. For the same reason I would, with the utmost deference to the wisdom of Congress, express a doubt of the expediency of the appointment of commissioners, and of an examination, estimate, and an award of indemnity to be made by them. This would be but a species of arbitration, which might last as long as a suit at law.

So far as I am able to comprehend the case, the general facts are now all known, and Congress is as capable of deciding on it justly and properly now as it probably would be after the report of the commissioners. If the claim of title on the part of Texas appears to Congress to be well founded in whole or in part, it is in the competency of Congress to offer her an indemnity for the surrender of that claim. In a case like this, surrounded, as it is, by many cogent considerations, all calling for amicable adjustment and immediate settlement, the Government of the United States would be justified, in my opinion, in allowing an indemnity to Texas, not unreasonable or extravagant, but fair, liberal, and awarded in a just spirit of accommodation.

I think no event would be hailed with more gratification by the people of the United States than the amicable adjustment of questions of difficulty which have now for a long time agitated the country and occupied, to the exclusion of other subjects, the time and attention of Congress.

Having thus freely communicated the results of my own reflections on the most advisable mode of adjusting the boundary question, I shall nevertheless cheerfully acquiesce in any other mode which the wisdom of Congress may devise. And in conclusion I repeat my conviction that every consideration of the public interest manifests the necessity of a provision by Congress for the settlement of this boundary question before the present session be brought to a close. The settlement of other questions connected with the same subject within the same period is greatly to be desired, but the adjustment of this appears to me to be in the highest degree important. In the train of such an adjustment we may well hope that there will follow a return of harmony and good will, an increased attachment to the Union, and the general satisfaction of the country.

MILLARD FILLMORE.

WASHINGTON, *August 8, 1850.*

To the Senate and House of Representatives:

It has been suggested that the language in the first paragraph of my message to the two Houses of Congress of the 6th instant may convey the idea that Governor Bell's letter to my predecessor was received by him before his death. It was addressed to him, but appears, in point of fact, to have been sent to me from the post-office after his death.

I make this communication to accompany the message and prevent misapprehension.

MILLARD FILLMORE.

WASHINGTON, *August 10, 1850.*

To the Senate of the United States:

I transmit herewith a communication from the Department of the Interior and the papers which accompanied it, being the first part of the results of investigations by Henry R. Schoolcraft, esq., under the provisions of an act of Congress approved March 3, 1847, requiring the Secretary of War "to collect and digest such statistics and materials as may illustrate the history, the present condition, and future prospects of the Indian tribes of the United States."

MILLARD FILLMORE.

WASHINGTON, *August 24, 1850.*

To the Senate of the United States:

I have the honor to transmit herewith a report submitted by the Secretary of the Treasury, to whom was referred the resolution of the Senate of the 31st July last, requesting to be furnished with certain information in relation to the commerce, etc., of the district of Brazos Santiago, in Texas.

MILLARD FILLMORE.

WASHINGTON, *August 26, 1850.*

To the Senate of the United States:

I have the honor to inclose herewith a letter just received from the Secretary of War, transmitting a communication from the Colonel of the Corps of Topographical Engineers, with accompanying papers, which he requests may be taken as a supplement to the "report and map of Lieutenant J. D. Webster, Corps of Topographical Engineers, of a survey of the Gulf coast at the mouth of the Rio Grande and its vicinity," called for by a resolution of the Senate of the 1st of July last.

MILLARD FILLMORE.

WASHINGTON, *September 2, 1850.*

To the Senate of the United States:

I have the honor herewith to transmit to your honorable body a report from the Secretary of the Navy, accompanied by copies of the correspondence relating to the resignation of Edward C. Anderson, a lieutenant in the Navy, in answer to a resolution of the Senate of August 28, 1850, adopted in executive session.

MILLARD FILLMORE.

WASHINGTON, *September 9, 1850.*

To the Senate of the United States:

In answer to a resolution of the Senate of the 5th instant, I have the honor herewith to transmit to the Senate a letter from the Secretary of State, accompanied by a copy of the report of the commissioner to China made in pursuance of the provisions of the act to carry into effect certain provisions of the treaties between the United States and China and the Ottoman Porte, giving certain judicial powers, etc.

MILLARD FILLMORE.

WASHINGTON, *September 9, 1850.*

To the Senate of the United States:

In compliance with the request of the Hon. Manuel Alvarez, acting governor, etc., I have the honor to transmit to the Senate herewith a copy of the constitution recently adopted by the inhabitants of New Mexico, together with a digest of the votes for and against it.

Congress having just passed a bill providing a Territorial government for New Mexico, I do not deem it advisable to submit any recommendation on the subject of a State government.

MILLARD FILLMORE.

WASHINGTON, *September 12, 1850.*

The SPEAKER OF THE HOUSE OF REPRESENTATIVES.

SIR: In answer to a resolution of the House of Representatives adopted September 2, 1850, calling upon me to communicate the full and exact cost of each of the lines of mail steamers now in service, etc., I have the honor to transmit herewith reports from the Secretary of the Navy and Postmaster-General, containing the desired information.

MILLARD FILLMORE.

WASHINGTON, *September 16, 1850.*

To the Senate of the United States:

In answer to a resolution of the Senate of the 9th instant, adopted in executive session, asking information in reference to the nomination of John Howard Payne as consul to Tunis, I have the honor to transmit a report from the Secretary of State, giving the desired information.

MILLARD FILLMORE.

WASHINGTON, *September 23, 1850.*

To the Senate and House of Representatives:

Having been informed that it is the wish of the family and relatives of the late lamented President of the United States that his remains should be removed to the State of Kentucky, and being desirous of manifesting the most sincere and profound respect for the character of the deceased, in which I doubt not Congress will fully concur, I have felt it to be my duty to make known to you the wishes of the family, that you might previous to your adjournment adopt such proceedings and take such order on the subject as in your wisdom may seem meet and proper on the occasion.

MILLARD FILLMORE.

[The remains of the late President of the United States were removed from Washington to Louisville, Ky., October 25, 1850.]

WASHINGTON, *September 27, 1850.*

To the Senate of the United States:

I herewith transmit to the Senate, in answer to their resolution of the 23d instant, a report from the Secretary of State, with the papers * therein referred to.

MILLARD FILLMORE.

WASHINGTON, *September 28, 1850.*

To the Senate of the United States:

In answer to your resolution of the 24th instant, expressing an opinion adverse to the alleged resignation of Lieutenant Anderson, of the Navy, I have the honor herewith to transmit a report from the Secretary of the Navy, accompanied by the correspondence in reference to such resignation.

Regarding the opinion of the Senate in this matter with the most profound respect, I have given to the subject the most anxious consideration, and submitted the question to the deliberation of my Cabinet, and after a careful examination of the whole correspondence they are unanimously of opinion that Lieutenant Anderson tendered his resignation, which was duly accepted, and that he was therefore rightfully dropped from the Register. I concur fully in this opinion. With these convictions I feel compelled to adhere to the decision of my lamented predecessor, and can only regret that I have the misfortune in this instance to differ from those for whom, individually and collectively, I entertain the highest respect.

MILLARD FILLMORE.

PROCLAMATION.

BY THE PRESIDENT OF THE UNITED STATES OF AMERICA.

A PROCLAMATION.

Whereas by an act of the Congress of the United States of the 24th of May, 1828, entitled "An act in addition to an act entitled 'An act concerning discriminating duties of tonnage and impost' and to equalize the duties on Prussian vessels and their cargoes," it is provided that upon satisfactory evidence being given to the President of the United States by the government of any foreign nation that no discriminating duties of tonnage or impost are imposed or levied in the ports of the said nation upon vessels wholly belonging to citizens of the United States, or upon the produce, manufactures, or merchandise imported in the same from the United States or from any foreign country, the President is thereby authorized to issue his proclamation declaring that the foreign discriminating duties of tonnage and impost within the United States

---

* Communications from the United States minister to Turkey relative to the Hungarian exiles.

are and shall be suspended and discontinued so far as respects the vessels of the said foreign nation and the produce, manufactures, or merchandise imported into the United States in the same from the said foreign nation or from any other foreign country, the said suspension to take effect from the time of such notification being given to the President of the United States and to continue so long as the reciprocal exemption of vessels belonging to citizens of the United States and their cargoes, as aforesaid, shall be continued, and no longer; and

Whereas satisfactory evidence has lately been received by me from the Government of the Republic of Chile, through an official communication of Señor Don Manuel Carvallo, accredited to this Government as envoy extraordinary and minister plenipotentiary of that Republic, under date of the 31st of October, 1850, that no other or higher duties of tonnage and impost are imposed or levied in the ports of Chile upon vessels wholly belonging to citizens of the United States and upon the produce, manufactures, or merchandise imported in the same from the United States and from any foreign country whatever than are levied on Chilean ships and their cargoes in the same ports and under like circumstances:

Now, therefore, I, Millard Fillmore, President of the United States of America, do hereby declare and proclaim that so much of the several acts imposing discriminating duties of tonnage and impost within the United States are and shall be suspended and discontinued so far as respects the vessels of Chile and the produce, manufactures, and merchandise imported into the United States in the same from Chile and from any other foreign country whatever, the said suspension to take effect from the day above mentioned and to continue thenceforward so long as the reciprocal exemption of the vessels of the United States and the produce, manufactures, and merchandise imported into Chile in the same, as aforesaid, shall be continued on the part of the Government of Chile.

Given under my hand, at the city of Washington, this 1st day of November, A. D. 1850, and the seventy-fifth of the Independence of the United States.

MILLARD FILLMORE.

By the President:

W. S. DERRICK, *Acting Secretary of State.*

FIRST ANNUAL MESSAGE.

WASHINGTON, *December 2, 1850.*

Fellow-Citizens of the Senate and of the House of Representatives:

Being suddenly called in the midst of the last session of Congress by a painful dispensation of Divine Providence to the responsible station which I now hold, I contented myself with such communications to the Legislature as the exigency of the moment seemed to require. The country was shrouded in mourning for the loss of its venerable Chief Magistrate and all hearts were penetrated with grief. Neither the time nor the occasion appeared to require or to justify on my part any general expression of political opinions or any announcement of the principles which would govern me in the discharge of the duties to the performance of which I had been so unexpectedly called. I trust, therefore, that it may not be deemed inappropriate if I avail myself of this opportunity of the reassembling of Congress to make known my sentiments in a general manner in regard to the policy which ought to be pursued by the Government both in its intercourse with foreign nations and its management and administration of internal affairs.

Nations, like individuals in a state of nature, are equal and independent, possessing certain rights and owing certain duties to each other, arising from their necessary and unavoidable relations; which rights and duties there is no common human authority to protect and enforce. Still, they are rights and duties, binding in morals, in conscience, and in honor, although there is no tribunal to which an injured party can appeal but the disinterested judgment of mankind, and ultimately the arbitrament of the sword.

Among the acknowledged rights of nations is that which each possesses of establishing that form of government which it may deem most conducive to the happiness and prosperity of its own citizens, of changing that form as circumstances may require, and of managing its internal affairs according to its own will. The people of the United States claim this right for themselves, and they readily concede it to others. Hence it becomes an imperative duty not to interfere in the government or internal policy of other nations; and although we may sympathize with the unfortunate or the oppressed everywhere in their struggles for freedom, our principles forbid us from taking any part in such foreign contests. We make no wars to promote or to prevent successions to thrones, to maintain any theory of a balance of power, or to suppress the actual government which any country chooses to establish for itself. We instigate no revolutions, nor suffer any hostile military expeditions to be fitted out in the United States to invade the territory or provinces of a friendly nation. The great law of morality ought to have a national as well as a personal and individual application. We should act toward other nations as we wish them to act toward us, and justice and conscience should form the rule of conduct between governments, instead of mere power, self-interest, or the desire of aggrandizement. To maintain a strict neutrality in foreign wars, to cultivate friendly relations, to reciprocate every noble and generous act, and to perform punctually and scrupulously every treaty obligation—these are the duties which we owe to other states, and by the performance of which we best entitle ourselves to like treatment from them; or, if that, in any case, be refused, we can enforce our own rights with justice and a clear conscience.

In our domestic policy the Constitution will be my guide, and in questions of doubt I shall look for its interpretation to the judicial decisions of that tribunal which was established to expound it and to the usage of the Government, sanctioned by the acquiescence of the country. I regard all its provisions as equally binding. In all its parts it is the will of the people expressed in the most solemn form, and the constituted authorities are but agents to carry that will into effect. Every power which it has granted is to be exercised for the public good; but no pretense of utility, no honest conviction, even, of what might be expedient, can justify the assumption of any power not granted. The powers conferred upon the Government and their distribution to the several departments are as clearly expressed in that sacred instrument as the imperfection of human language will allow, and I deem it my first duty not to question its wisdom, add to its provisions, evade its requirements, or nullify its commands.

Upon you, fellow-citizens, as the representatives of the States and the people, is wisely devolved the legislative power. I shall comply with my duty in laying before you from time to time any information calculated to enable you to discharge your high and responsible trust for the benefit of our common constituents.

My opinions will be frankly expressed upon the leading subjects of legislation; and if—which I do not anticipate—any act should pass the two Houses of Congress which should appear to me unconstitutional, or an encroachment on the just powers of other departments, or with provisions hastily adopted and likely to produce consequences injurious and unforeseen, I should not shrink from the duty of returning it to you, with my reasons, for your further consideration. Beyond the due performance of these constitutional obligations, both my respect for the Legislature and my sense of propriety will restrain me from any attempt to control or influence your proceedings. With you is the power, the honor, and the responsibility of the legislation of the country.

The Government of the United States is a limited Government. It is confined to the exercise of powers expressly granted and such others as may be necessary for carrying those powers into effect; and it is at all times an especial duty to guard against any infringement on the just rights of the States. Over the objects and subjects intrusted to Congress its legislative authority is supreme. But here that authority ceases, and every citizen who truly loves the Constitution and desires the continuance of its existence and its blessings will resolutely and firmly resist any interference in those domestic affairs which the Constitution has clearly and unequivocally left to the exclusive authority of the States. And every such citizen will also deprecate useless irritation among the several members of the Union and all reproach and crimination tending to alienate one portion of the country from another. The beauty of our system of government consists, and its safety and durability must consist, in avoiding mutual collisions and encroachments and in the regular separate action of all, while each is revolving in its own distinct orbit.

The Constitution has made it the duty of the President to take care that the laws be faithfully executed. In a government like ours, in which all laws are passed by a majority of the representatives of the people, and these representatives are chosen for such short periods that any injurious or obnoxious law can very soon be repealed, it would appear unlikely that any great numbers should be found ready to resist the execution of the laws. But it must be borne in mind that the country is extensive; that there may be local interests or prejudices rendering a law odious in one part which is not so in another, and that the thoughtless and inconsiderate, misled by their passions or their imaginations, may be induced madly to resist such laws as they disapprove. Such persons should recollect that without law there can be no real practical liberty; that when law is trampled under foot tyranny rules, whether it appears in the form of a military despotism or of popular violence. The law is the only sure protection of the weak and the only efficient restraint upon the strong. When impartially and faithfully administered, none is beneath its protection and none above its control. You, gentlemen, and the country may be assured that to the utmost of my ability and to the extent of the power vested in me I shall at all times and in all places take care that the laws be faithfully executed. In the discharge of this duty, solemnly imposed upon me by the Constitution and by my oath of office, I shall shrink from no responsibility, and shall endeavor to meet events as they may arise with firmness, as well as with prudence and discretion.

The appointing power is one of the most delicate with which the Executive is invested. I regard it as a sacred trust, to be exercised with the sole view of advancing the prosperity and happiness of the people. It shall be my effort to elevate the standard of official employment by selecting for places of importance individuals fitted for the posts to which they are assigned by their known integrity, talents, and virtues. In so extensive a country, with so great a population, and where few persons appointed to office can be known to the appointing power, mistakes will sometimes unavoidably happen and unfortunate appointments be made notwithstanding the greatest care. In such cases the power of removal may be properly exercised; and neglect of duty or malfeasance in office will be no more tolerated in individuals appointed by myself than in those appointed by others.

I am happy in being able to say that no unfavorable change in our foreign relations has taken place since the message at the opening of the last session of Congress. We are at peace with all nations and we enjoy in an eminent degree the blessings of that peace in a prosperous and growing commerce and in all the forms of amicable national intercourse. The unexampled growth of the country, the present amount of its population, and its ample means of self-protection assure for it the respect of all nations, while it is trusted that its character for justice and a regard to the rights of other States will cause that respect to be readily and cheerfully paid.

A convention was negotiated between the United States and Great Britain in April last for facilitating and protecting the construction of a ship canal between the Atlantic and Pacific oceans and for other purposes. The instrument has since been ratified by the contracting parties, the exchange of ratifications has been effected, and proclamation thereof has been duly made.

In addition to the stipulations contained in this convention, two other objects remain to be accomplished between the contracting powers:

First. The designation and establishment of a free port at each end of the canal.

Second. An agreement fixing the distance from the shore within which belligerent maritime operations shall not be carried on.

On these points there is little doubt that the two Governments will come to an understanding.

The company of citizens of the United States who have acquired from the State of Nicaragua the privilege of constructing a ship canal between the two oceans through the territory of that State have made progress in their preliminary arrangements. The treaty between the United States and Great Britain of the 19th of April last, above referred to, being now in operation, it is to be hoped that the guaranties which it offers will be sufficient to secure the completion of the work with all practicable expedition. It is obvious that this result would be indefinitely postponed if any other than peaceful measures for the purpose of harmonizing conflicting claims to territory in that quarter should be adopted. It will consequently be my endeavor to cause any further negotiations on the part of this Government which may be requisite for this purpose to be so conducted as to bring them to a speedy and successful close.

Some unavoidable delay has occurred, arising from distance and the difficulty of intercourse between this Government and that of Nicaragua, but as intelligence has just been received of the appointment of an envoy extraordinary and minister plenipotentiary of that Government to reside at Washington, whose arrival may soon be expected, it is hoped that no further impediments will be experienced in the prompt transaction of business between the two Governments.

Citizens of the United States have undertaken the connection of the two oceans by means of a railroad across the Isthmus of Tehuantepec, under grants of the Mexican Government to a citizen of that Republic. It is understood that a thorough survey of the course of the communication is in preparation, and there is every reason to expect that it will be prosecuted with characteristic energy, especially when that Government shall have consented to such stipulations with the Government of the United States as may be necessary to impart a feeling of security to those who may embark their property in the enterprise. Negotiations are pending for the accomplishment of that object, and a hope is confidently entertained that when the Government of Mexico shall become duly sensible of the advantages which that country can not fail to derive from the work, and learn that the Government of the United States desires that the right of sovereignty of Mexico in the Isthmus shall remain unimpaired, the stipulations referred to will be agreed to with alacrity.

By the last advices from Mexico it would appear, however, that that Government entertains strong objections to some of the stipulations which the parties concerned in the project of the railroad deem necessary for their protection and security. Further consideration, it is to be hoped, or some modification of terms, may yet reconcile the differences existing between the two Governments in this respect.

Fresh instructions have recently been given to the minister of the United States in Mexico, who is prosecuting the subject with promptitude and ability.

Although the negotiations with Portugal for the payment of claims of citizens of the United States against that Government have not yet resulted in a formal treaty, yet a proposition, made by the Government of Portugal for the final adjustment and payment of those claims, has recently been accepted on the part of the United States. It gives me pleasure to say that Mr. Clay, to whom the negotiation on the part of the United States had been intrusted, discharged the duties of his appointment with ability and discretion, acting always within the instructions of his Government.

It is expected that a regular convention will be immediately negotiated for carrying the agreement between the two Governments into effect.

The commissioner appointed under the act of Congress for carrying into effect the convention with Brazil of the 27th of January, 1849, has entered upon the performance of the duties imposed upon him by that act. It is hoped that those duties may be completed within the time which it prescribes. The documents, however, which the Imperial Government, by the third article of the convention, stipulates to furnish to the Government of the United States have not yet been received. As it is presumed that those documents will be essential for the correct disposition of the claims, it may become necessary for Congress to extend the period limited for the duration of the commission. The sum stipulated by the fourth article of the convention to be paid to this Government has been received.

The collection in the ports of the United States of discriminating duties upon the vessels of Chili and their cargoes has been suspended, pursuant to the provisions of the act of Congress of the 24th of May, 1828. It is to be hoped that this measure will impart a fresh impulse to the commerce between the two countries, which of late, and especially since our acquisition of California, has, to the mutual advantage of the parties, been much augmented.

Peruvian guano has become so desirable an article to the agricultural interest of the United States that it is the duty of the Government to employ all the means properly in its power for the purpose of causing that article to be imported into the country at a reasonable price. Nothing will be omitted on my part toward accomplishing this desirable end. I am persuaded that in removing any restraints on this traffic the Peruvian Government will promote its own best interests, while it will afford a proof of a friendly disposition toward this country, which will be duly appreciated.

The treaty between the United States and His Majesty the King of the Hawaiian Islands, which has recently been made public, will, it is believed, have a beneficial effect upon the relations between the two countries.

The relations between those parts of the island of St. Domingo which were formerly colonies of Spain and France, respectively, are still in an unsettled condition. The proximity of that island to the United States and the delicate questions involved in the existing controversy there render it desirable that it should be permanently and speedily adjusted. The interests of humanity and of general commerce also demand this; and as intimations of the same sentiment have been received from other governments, it is hoped that some plan may soon be devised to effect the object in a manner likely to give general satisfaction. The Government of the United States will not fail, by the exercise of all proper friendly offices, to do all in its power to put an end to the destructive war which has raged between the different parts of the island and to secure to them both the benefits of peace and commerce.

I refer you to the report of the Secretary of the Treasury for a detailed statement of the finances.

The total receipts into the Treasury for the year ending 30th of June last were $47,421,748.90.

The total expenditures during the same period were $43,002,168.90.

The public debt has been reduced since the last annual report from the Treasury Department $495,276.79.

By the nineteenth section of the act of 28th January, 1847, the proceeds of the sales of the public lands were pledged for the interest and principal of the public debt. The great amount of those lands subsequently granted by Congress for military bounties will, it is believed, very nearly supply the public demand for several years to come, and but little reliance can, therefore, be placed on that hitherto fruitful source of revenue. Aside from the permanent annual expenditures, which have necessarily largely increased, a portion of the public debt, amounting to $8,075,986.59, must be provided for within the next two fiscal years. It is most desirable that these accruing demands should be met without resorting to new loans.

All experience has demonstrated the wisdom and policy of raising a large portion of revenue for the support of Government from duties on goods imported. The power to lay these duties is unquestionable, and its chief object, of course, is to replenish the Treasury. But if in doing this an incidental advantage may be gained by encouraging the industry of our own citizens, it is our duty to avail ourselves of that advantage.

A duty laid upon an article which can not be produced in this country, such as tea or coffee, adds to the cost of the article, and is chiefly or wholly paid by the consumer. But a duty laid upon an article which may be produced here stimulates the skill and industry of our own country to produce the same article, which is brought into the market in competition with the foreign article, and the importer is thus compelled to reduce his price to that at which the domestic article can be sold, thereby throwing a part of the duty upon the producer of the foreign article. The continuance of this process creates the skill and invites the capital which finally enable us to produce the article much cheaper than it could have been procured from abroad, thereby benefiting both the producer and the consumer at home. The consequence of this is that the artisan and the agriculturist are brought together, each affords a ready market for the produce of the other, the whole country becomes prosperous, and the ability to produce every necessary of life renders us independent in war as well as in peace.

A high tariff can never be permanent. It will cause dissatisfaction, and will be changed. It excludes competition, and thereby invites the investment of capital in manufactures to such excess that when changed it brings distress, bankruptcy, and ruin upon all who have been misled by its faithless protection. What the manufacturer wants is uniformity and permanency, that he may feel a confidence that he is not to be ruined by sudden changes. But to make a tariff uniform and permanent it is not only necessary that the laws should not be altered, but that the duty should not fluctuate. To effect this all duties should be specific wherever the nature of the article is such as to admit of it. *Ad valorem* duties fluctuate with the price and offer strong temptations to fraud and perjury. Specific duties, on the contrary, are equal and uniform in all ports and at all times, and offer a strong inducement to the importer to bring the best article, as he pays no more duty upon that than upon one of inferior quality. I therefore strongly recommend a modification of the present tariff, which has prostrated some of our most important and necessary manufactures, and that specific duties be imposed sufficient to raise the requisite revenue, making such discriminations in favor of the industrial pursuits of our own country as to encourage home production without excluding foreign competition. It is also important that an unfortunate provision in the present tariff, which imposes a much higher duty upon the raw material that enters into our manufactures than upon the manufactured article, should be remedied.

The papers accompanying the report of the Secretary of the Treasury will disclose frauds attempted upon the revenue, in variety and amount so great as to justify the conclusion that it is impossible under any system of *ad valorem* duties levied upon the foreign cost or value of the article to secure an honest observance and an effectual administration of the laws. The fraudulent devices to evade the law which have been detected by the vigilance of the appraisers leave no room to doubt that similar impositions not discovered, to a large amount, have been successfully practiced since the enactment of the law now in force. This state of things has already had a prejudicial influence upon those engaged in foreign commerce. It has a tendency to drive the honest trader from the business of importing and to throw that important branch of employment into the hands of unscrupulous and dishonest men, who are alike regardless of law and the obligations of an oath. By these means the plain intentions of Congress, as expressed in the law, are daily defeated. Every motive of policy and duty, therefore, impels me to ask the earnest attention of Congress to this subject. If Congress should deem it unwise to attempt any important changes in the system of levying duties at this session, it will become indispensable to the protection of the revenue that such remedies as in the judgment of Congress may mitigate the evils complained of should be at once applied.

As before stated, specific duties would, in my opinion, afford the most perfect remedy for this evil; but if you should not concur in this view, then, as a partial remedy, I beg leave respectfully to recommend that instead of taking the invoice of the article abroad as a means of determining its value here, the correctness of which invoice it is in many cases impossible to verify, the law be so changed as to require a home valuation or appraisal, to be regulated in such manner as to give, as far as practicable, uniformity in the several ports.

There being no mint in California, I am informed that the laborers in the mines are compelled to dispose of their gold dust at a large discount. This appears to me to be a heavy and unjust tax upon the labor of those employed in extracting this precious metal, and I doubt not you will be disposed at the earliest period possible to relieve them from it by the establishment of a mint. In the meantime, as an assayer's office is established there, I would respectfully submit for your consideration the propriety of authorizing gold bullion which has been assayed and stamped to be received in payment of Government dues. I can not conceive that the Treasury would suffer any loss by such a provision, which will at once raise bullion to its par value, and thereby save (if I am rightly informed) many millions of dollars to the laborers which are now paid in brokerage to convert this precious metal into available funds. This discount upon their hard earnings is a heavy tax, and every effort should be made by the Government to relieve them from so great a burden.

More than three-fourths of our population are engaged in the cultivation of the soil. The commercial, manufacturing, and navigating interests are all to a great extent dependent on the agricultural. It is therefore the most important interest of the nation, and has a just claim to the fostering care and protection of the Government so far as they can be extended consistently with the provisions of the Constitution. As this can not be done by the ordinary modes of legislation, I respectfully recommend the establishment of an agricultural bureau, to be charged with the duty of giving to this leading branch of American industry the encouragement which it so well deserves. In view of the immense mineral resources of our country, provision should also be made for the employment of a competent mineralogist and chemist, who should be required, under the direction of the head of the bureau, to collect specimens of the various minerals of our country and to ascertain by careful analysis their respective elements and properties and their adaptation to useful purposes. He should also be required to examine and report upon the qualities of different soils and the manures best calculated to improve their productiveness. By publishing the results of such experiments, with suitable explanations, and by the collection and distribution of rare seeds and plants, with instructions as to the best system of cultivation, much may be done to promote this great national interest.

In compliance with the act of Congress passed on the 23d of May, 1850, providing, among other things, for taking the Seventh Census, a superintendent was appointed and all other measures adopted which were deemed necessary to insure the prompt and faithful performance of that duty. The appropriation already made will, it is believed, be sufficient to defray the whole expense of the work, but further legislation may be necessary in regard to the compensation of some of the marshals of the Territories. It will also be proper to make provision by law at an early day for the publication of such abstracts of the returns as the public interests may require.

The unprecedented growth of our territories on the Pacific in wealth and population and the consequent increase of their social and commercial relations with the Atlantic States seem to render it the duty of the Government to use all its constitutional power to improve the means of intercourse with them. The importance of opening "a line of communication, the best and most expeditious of which the nature of the country will admit," between the Valley of the Mississippi and the Pacific was brought to your notice by my predecessor in his annual message; and as the reasons which he presented in favor of the measure still exist in full force, I beg leave to call your attention to them and to repeat the recommendations then made by him.

The uncertainty which exists in regard to the validity of land titles in California is a subject which demands your early consideration. Large bodies of land in that State are claimed under grants said to have been made by authority of the Spanish and Mexican Governments. Many of these have not been perfected, others have been revoked, and some are believed to be fraudulent. But until they shall have been judicially investigated they will continue to retard the settlement and improvement of the country. I therefore respectfully recommend that provision be made by law for the appointment of commissioners to examine all such claims with a view to their final adjustment.

I also beg leave to call your attention to the propriety of extending at an early day our system of land laws, with such modifications as may be necessary, over the State of California and the Territories of Utah and New Mexico. The mineral lands of California will, of course, form an exception to any general system which may be adopted. Various methods of disposing of them have been suggested. I was at first inclined to favor the system of leasing, as it seemed to promise the largest revenue to the Government and to afford the best security against monopolies; but further reflection and our experience in leasing the lead mines and selling lands upon credit have brought my mind to the conclusion that there would be great difficulty in collecting the rents, and that the relation of debtor and creditor between the citizens and the Government would be attended with many mischievous consequences. I therefore recommend that instead of retaining the mineral lands under the permanent control of the Government they be divided into small parcels and sold, under such restrictions as to quantity and time as will insure the best price and guard most effectually against combinations of capitalists to obtain monopolies.

The annexation of Texas and the acquisition of California and New Mexico have given increased importance to our Indian relations. The various tribes brought under our jurisdiction by these enlargements of our boundaries are estimated to embrace a population of 124,000.

Texas and New Mexico are surrounded by powerful tribes of Indians, who are a source of constant terror and annoyance to the inhabitants. Separating into small predatory bands, and always mounted, they overrun the country, devastating farms, destroying crops, driving off whole herds of cattle, and occasionally murdering the inhabitants or carrying them into captivity. The great roads leading into the country are infested with them, whereby traveling is rendered extremely dangerous and immigration is almost entirely arrested. The Mexican frontier, which by the eleventh article of the treaty of Guadalupe Hidalgo we are bound to protect against the Indians within our border, is exposed to these incursions equally with our own. The military force stationed in that country, although forming a large proportion of the Army, is represented as entirely inadequate to our own protection and the fulfillment of our treaty stipulations with Mexico. The principal deficiency is in cavalry, and I recommend that Congress should, at as early a period as practicable, provide for the raising of one or more regiments of mounted men.

For further suggestions on this subject and others connected with our domestic interests and the defense of our frontier, I refer you to the reports of the Secretary of the Interior and of the Secretary of War.

I commend also to your favorable consideration the suggestion contained in the last-mentioned report and in the letter of the General in Chief relative to the establishment of an asylum for the relief of disabled and destitute soldiers. This subject appeals so strongly to your sympathies that it would be superfluous in me to say anything more than barely to express my cordial approbation of the proposed object.

The Navy continues to give protection to our commerce and other national interests in the different quarters of the globe, and, with the exception of a single steamer on the Northern lakes, the vessels in commission are distributed in six different squadrons.

The report of the head of that Department will exhibit the services of these squadrons and of the several vessels employed in each during the past year. It is a source of gratification that, while they have been constantly prepared for any hostile emergency, they have everywhere met with the respect and courtesy due as well to the dignity as to the peaceful dispositions and just purposes of the nation.

The two brigantines accepted by the Government from a generous citizen of New York and placed under the command of an officer of the Navy to proceed to the Arctic Seas in quest of the British commander Sir John Franklin and his companions, in compliance with the act of Congress approved in May last, had when last heard from penetrated into a high northern latitude; but the success of this noble and humane enterprise is yet uncertain.

I invite your attention to the view of our present naval establishment and resources presented in the report of the Secretary of the Navy, and the suggestions therein made for its improvement, together with the naval policy recommended for the security of our Pacific Coast and the protection and extension of our commerce with eastern Asia. Our facilities for a larger participation in the trade of the East, by means of our recent settlements on the shores of the Pacific, are too obvious to be overlooked or disregarded.

The questions in relation to rank in the Army and Navy and relative rank between officers of the two branches of the service, presented to the Executive by certain resolutions of the House of Representatives at the last session of Congress, have been submitted to a board of officers in each branch of the service, and their report may be expected at an early day.

I also earnestly recommend the enactment of a law authorizing officers of the Army and Navy to be retired from the service when incompetent for its vigorous and active duties, taking care to make suitable provision for those who have faithfully served their country and awarding distinctions by retaining in appropriate commands those who have been particularly conspicuous for gallantry and good conduct. While the obligation of the country to maintain and honor those who, to the exclusion of other pursuits, have devoted themselves to its arduous service is acknowledged, this obligation should not be permitted to interfere with the efficiency of the service itself.

I am gratified in being able to state that the estimates of expenditure for the Navy in the ensuing year are less by more than $1,000,000 than those of the present, excepting the appropriation which may become necessary for the construction of a dock on the coast of the Pacific, propositions for which are now being considered and on which a special report may be expected early in your present session.

There is an evident justness in the suggestion of the same report that appropriations for the naval service proper should be separated from those for fixed and permanent objects, such as building docks and navy-yards and the fixtures attached, and from the extraordinary objects under the care of the Department which, however important, are not essentially naval.

A revision of the code for the government of the Navy seems to require the immediate consideration of Congress. Its system of crimes and punishments had undergone no change for half a century until the last session, though its defects have been often and ably pointed out; and the abolition of a particular species of corporal punishment, which then took place, without providing any substitute, has left the service in a state of defectiveness which calls for prompt correction. I therefore recommend that the whole subject be revised without delay and such a system established for the enforcement of discipline as shall be at once humane and effectual.

The accompanying report of the Postmaster-General presents a satisfactory view of the operations and condition of that Department.

At the close of the last fiscal year the length of the inland mail routes in the United States (not embracing the service in Oregon and California) was 178,672 miles, the annual transportation thereon 46,541,423 miles, and the annual cost of such transportation $2,724,426.

The increase of the annual transportation over that of the preceding year was 3,997,354 miles and the increase in cost was $342,440.

The number of post-offices in the United States on the 1st day of July last was 18,417, being an increase of 1,670 during the preceding year.

The gross revenues of the Department for the fiscal year ending June 30, 1850, amounted to $5,552,971.48, including the annual appropriation of $200,000 for the franked matter of the Departments and excluding the foreign postages collected for and payable to the British Government.

The expenditures for the same period were $5,212,953.43, leaving a balance of revenue over expenditures of $340,018.05.

I am happy to find that the fiscal condition of the Department is such as to justify the Postmaster-General in recommending the reduction of our inland letter postage to 3 cents the single letter when prepaid and 5 cents when not prepaid. He also recommends that the prepaid rate shall be reduced to 2 cents whenever the revenues of the Department, after the reduction, shall exceed its expenditures by more than 5 per cent for two consecutive years; that the postage upon California and other letters sent by our ocean steamers shall be much reduced, and that the rates of postage on newspapers, pamphlets, periodicals, and other printed matter shall be modified and some reduction thereon made.

It can not be doubted that the proposed reductions will for the present diminish the revenues of the Department. It is believed that the deficiency, after the surplus already accumulated shall be exhausted, may be almost wholly met either by abolishing the existing privileges of sending free matter through the mails or by paying out of the Treasury to the Post-Office Department a sum equivalent to the postage of which it is deprived by such privileges. The last is supposed to be the preferable mode, and will, if not entirely, so nearly supply that deficiency as to make any further appropriation that may be found necessary so inconsiderable as to form no obstacle to the proposed reductions.

I entertain no doubt of the authority of Congress to make appropriations for leading objects in that class of public works comprising what are usually called works of internal improvement. This authority I suppose to be derived chiefly from the power of regulating commerce with foreign nations and among the States and the power of laying and collecting imposts. Where commerce is to be carried on and imposts collected there must be ports and harbors as well as wharves and custom-houses. If ships laden with valuable cargoes approach the shore or sail along the coast, light-houses are necessary at suitable points for the protection of life and property. Other facilities and securities for commerce and navigation are hardly less important; and those clauses of the Constitution, therefore, to which I have referred have received from the origin of the Government a liberal and beneficial construction. Not only have light-houses, buoys, and beacons been established and floating lights maintained, but harbors have been cleared and improved, piers constructed, and even breakwaters for the safety of shipping and sea walls to protect harbors from being filled up and rendered useless by the action of the ocean, have been erected at very great expense. And this construction of the Constitution appears the more reasonable from the consideration that if these works, of such evident importance and utility, are not to be accomplished by Congress they can not be accomplished at all. By the adoption of the Constitution the several States voluntarily parted with the power of collecting duties of imposts in their own ports, and it is not to be expected that they should raise money by internal taxation, direct or indirect, for the benefit of that commerce the revenues derived from which do not, either in whole or in part, go into their own treasuries. Nor do I perceive any difference between the power of Congress to make appropriations for objects of this kind on the ocean and the power to make appropriations for similar objects on lakes and rivers, wherever they are large enough to bear on their waters an extensive traffic. The magnificent Mississippi and its tributaries and the vast lakes of the North and Northwest appear to me to fall within the exercise of the power as justly and as clearly as the ocean and the Gulf of Mexico. It is a mistake to regard expenditures judiciously made for these objects as expenditures for local purposes. The position or sight of the work is necessarily local, but its utility is general. A ship canal around the Falls of St. Mary of less than a mile in length, though local in its construction, would yet be national in its purpose and its benefits, as it would remove the only obstruction to a navigation of more than 1,000 miles, affecting several States, as well as our commercial relations with Canada. So, too, the breakwater at the mouth of the Delaware is erected, not for the exclusive benefit of the States bordering on the bay and river of that name, but for that of the whole coastwise navigation of the United States and, to a considerable extent, also of foreign commerce. If a ship be lost on the bar at the entrance of a Southern port for want of sufficient depth of water, it is very likely to be a Northern ship; and if a steamboat be sunk in any part of the Mississippi on account of its channel not having been properly cleared of obstructions, it may be a boat belonging to either of eight or ten States. I may add, as somewhat remarkable, that among all the thirty-one States there is none that is not to a greater or less extent bounded on the ocean, or the Gulf of Mexico, or one of the Great Lakes, or some navigable river.

In fulfilling our constitutional duties, fellow-citizens, on this subject, as in carrying into effect all other powers conferred by the Constitution, we should consider ourselves as deliberating and acting for one and the same country, and bear constantly in mind that our regard and our duty are due not to a particular part only, but to the whole.

I therefore recommend that appropriations be made for completing such works as have been already begun and for commencing such others as may seem to the wisdom of Congress to be of public and general importance.

The difficulties and delays incident to the settlement of private claims by Congress amount in many cases to a denial of justice. There is reason to apprehend that many unfortunate creditors of the Government have thereby been unavoidably ruined. Congress has so much business of a public character that it is impossible it should give much attention to mere private claims, and their accumulation is now so great that many claimants must despair of ever being able to obtain a hearing. It may well be doubted whether Congress, from the nature of its organization, is properly constituted to decide upon such cases. It is impossible that each member should examine the merits of every claim on which he is compelled to vote, and it is preposterous to ask a judge to decide a case which he has never heard. Such decisions may, and frequently must, do injustice either to the claimant or the Government, and I perceive no better remedy for this growing evil than the establishment of some tribunal to adjudicate upon such claims. I beg leave, therefore, most respectfully to recommend that provision be made by law for the appointment of a commission to settle all private claims against the United States; and as an *ex parte* hearing must in all contested cases be very unsatisfactory, I also recommend the appointment of a solicitor, whose duty it shall be to represent the Government before such commission and protect it against all illegal, fraudulent, or unjust claims which may be presented for their adjudication.

This District, which has neither voice nor vote in your deliberations, looks to you for protection and aid, and I commend all its wants to your favorable consideration, with a full confidence that you will meet them not only with justice, but with liberality. It should be borne in mind that in this city, laid out by Washington and consecrated by his name, is located the Capitol of our nation, the emblem of our Union and the symbol of our greatness. Here also are situated all the public buildings necessary for the use of the Government, and all these are exempt from taxation. It should be the pride of Americans to render this place attractive to the people of the whole Republic and convenient and safe for the transaction of the public business and the preservation of the public records. The Government should therefore bear a liberal proportion of the burdens of all necessary and useful improvements. And as nothing could contribute more to the health, comfort, and safety of the city and the security of the public buildings and records than an abundant supply of pure water, I respectfully recommend that you make such provisions for obtaining the same as in your wisdom you may deem proper.

The act, passed at your last session, making certain propositions to Texas for settling the disputed boundary between that State and the Territory of New Mexico was, immediately on its passage, transmitted by express to the governor of Texas, to be laid by him before the general assembly for its agreement thereto. Its receipt was duly acknowledged, but no official information has yet been received of the action of the general assembly thereon. It may, however, be very soon expected, as, by the terms of the propositions submitted they were to have been acted upon on or before the first day of the present month.

It was hardly to have been expected that the series of measures passed at your last session with the view of healing the sectional differences which had sprung from the slavery and territorial questions should at once have realized their beneficent purpose. All mutual concession in the nature of a compromise must necessarily be unwelcome to men of extreme opinions. And though without such concessions our Constitution could not have been formed, and can not be permanently sustained, yet we have seen them made the subject of bitter controversy in both sections of the Republic. It required many months of discussion and deliberation to secure the concurrence of a majority of Congress in their favor. It would be strange if they had been received with immediate approbation by people and States prejudiced and heated by the exciting controversies of their representatives. I believe those measures to have been required by the circumstances and condition of the country. I believe they were necessary to allay asperities and animosities that were rapidly alienating one section of the country from another and destroying those fraternal sentiments which are the strongest supports of the Constitution. They were adopted in the spirit of conciliation and for the purpose of conciliation. I believe that a great majority of our fellow-citizens sympathize in that spirit and that purpose, and in the main approve and are prepared in all respects to sustain these enactments. I can not doubt that the American people, bound together by kindred blood and common traditions, still cherish a paramount regard for the Union of their fathers, and that they are ready to rebuke any attempt to violate its integrity, to disturb the compromises on which it is based, or to resist the laws which have been enacted under its authority.

The series of measures to which I have alluded are regarded by me as a settlement in principle and substance—a final settlement of the dangerous and exciting subjects which they embraced. Most of these subjects, indeed, are beyond your reach, as the legislation which disposed of them was in its character final and irrevocable. It may be presumed from the opposition which they all encountered that none of those measures was free from imperfections, but in their mutual dependence and connection they formed a system of compromise the most conciliatory and best for the entire country that could be obtained from conflicting sectional interests and opinions.

For this reason I recommend your adherence to the adjustment established by those measures until time and experience shall demonstrate the necessity of further legislation to guard against evasion or abuse.

By that adjustment we have been rescued from the wide and boundless agitation that surrounded us, and have a firm, distinct, and legal ground to rest upon. And the occasion, I trust, will justify me in exhorting my countrymen to rally upon and maintain that ground as the best, if not the only, means of restoring peace and quiet to the country and maintaining inviolate the integrity of the Union.

And now, fellow-citizens, I can not bring this communication to a close without invoking you to join me in humble and devout thanks to the Great Ruler of Nations for the multiplied blessings which He has graciously bestowed upon us. His hand, so often visible in our preservation, has stayed the pestilence, saved us from foreign wars and domestic disturbances, and scattered plenty throughout the land.

Our liberties, religious and civil, have been maintained, the fountains of knowledge have all been kept open, and means of happiness widely spread and generally enjoyed greater than have fallen to the lot of any other nation.   And while deeply penetrated with gratitude for the past, let us hope that His all-wise providence will so guide our counsels as that they shall result in giving satisfaction to our constituents, securing the peace of the country, and adding new strength to the united Government under which we live.   MILLARD FILLMORE.

SPECIAL MESSAGES.

WASHINGTON, *December 9, 1850.*

To the House of Representatives:

I communicate to the House of Representatives a translation of a note of the 5th instant addressed to the Secretary of State by the minister of the Mexican Republic accredited to this Government, relative to a subject* to which the attention of Congress was invited in my message at the opening of the present session.   MILLARD FILLMORE.

[The same message was sent to the Senate.]

WASHINGTON, *December 12, 1850.*

To the Senate of the United States:

I herewith transmit a report of the Secretary of State, with accompanying documents, relating to the African slave trade, in answer to the resolution of the Senate of the 28th of August last.

MILLARD FILLMORE.

WASHINGTON, *December 13, 1850.*

To the Senate and House of Representatives:

I have the pleasure of announcing to Congress the agreement on the part of Texas to the propositions offered to that State by the act of Congress approved on the 9th day of September last, entitled ''An act proposing to the State of Texas the establishment of her northern and western boundaries, the relinquishment by the said State of all territory claimed by her exterior to said boundaries and of all her claims upon the United States, and to establish a Territorial government for New Mexico.''

By the terms of that act it was required that the agreement of Texas to the propositions contained in it should be given on or before the 1st day of December, 1850.   An authenticated transcript of a law passed

*Incursions of Indians of the United States upon the population of the Mexican frontier.

by the legislature of Texas on the 25th day of November, agreeing to and accepting the propositions contained in the act of Congress, has been received. This law, after reciting the provisions of the act of Congress, proceeds to enact and declare as follows, viz:

Therefore, first. *Be it enacted by the legislature of the State of Texas,* That the State of Texas hereby agrees to and accepts said propositions; and it is hereby declared that the said State shall be bound by the terms thereof according to their true import and meaning.

Second. That the governor of this State be, and is hereby, requested to cause a copy of this act, authenticated under the seal of the State, to be furnished to the President of the United States by mail as early as practicable, and also a copy thereof, certified in like manner, to be transmitted to each of the Senators and Representatives of Texas in Congress. And that this act take effect from and after its passage.

C. G. KEENAN,
Speaker of the House of Representatives.

JOHN A. GREER,
President of the Senate.

Approved, November 25, 1850.

P. H. BELL.

From the common sources of public information it would appear that a very remarkable degree of unanimity prevailed, not only in the legislature, but among the people of Texas, in respect to the agreement of the State to that which had been proposed by Congress.

I can not refrain from congratulating Congress and the country on the success of this great and leading measure of conciliation and peace. The difficulties felt and the dangers apprehended from the vast acquisitions of territory under the late treaty with Mexico seem now happily overcome by the wisdom of Congress. Within that territory there already exists one State, respectable for the amount of her population, distinguished for singular activity and enterprise, and remarkable in many respects from her condition and history. This new State has come into the Union with manifestations not to be mistaken of her attachment to that Constitution and that Government which now embrace her and her interests within their protecting and beneficent control.

Over the residue of the acquired territories regular Territorial governments are now established in the manner which has been most usual in the history of this Government. Various other acts of Congress may undoubtedly be requisite for the benefit as well as for the proper government of these so distant parts of the country. But the same legislative wisdom which has triumphed over the principal difficulties and accomplished the main end may safely be relied on for whatever measures may yet be found necessary to perfect its work, so that the acquisition of these vast regions to the United States may rather strengthen than weaken the Constitution, which is over us all, and the Union, which affords such ample daily proofs of its inestimable value.

MILLARD FILLMORE.

WASHINGTON, *December 17, 1850.*

To the Senate of the United States:

I herewith transmit a letter from the Secretary of War, communicating a report of a board of officers to which, in pursuance of a resolution of the Senate passed on the 30th of September last, were submitted the questions proposed therein, relative to the expediency and necessity of creating additional grades of commissioned officers in the Army and of enacting provisions authorizing officers of the Army to exercise civil functions in emergencies to be enumerated and restraining them from usurping the powers of civil functionaries.

MILLARD FILLMORE.

WASHINGTON, *December 30, 1850.*

To the Senate of the United States:

I herewith transmit to the Senate, in reply to their resolution of the 26th instant, a report from the Secretary of State, with accompanying papers.*

MILLARD FILLMORE.

WASHINGTON, *January 3, 1851.*

To the House of Representatives:

By a resolution passed by the House of Representatives on the 24th day of July, 1850, the President was requested to cause to be prepared and communicated to the House certain opinions of the Attorneys-General therein specified. On inquiry I learned that the force employed in the Attorney-General's Office was not sufficient to perform this work; consequently, I employed Benjamin F. Hall, esq., a counselor at law, on the 9th day of September last, to execute it, and requested him to commence it immediately. I informed him that I was not authorized to give any other assurances as to compensation than that it rested with Congress to provide and fix it. I believe Mr. Hall to be in all respects competent and well fitted for the task which he has undertaken, and diligent in the performance of it; and it appears to me that the most just mode of compensation will be to make a per diem allowance of $8 per day for the time actually employed, to be paid on the certificate of the Attorney-General.

I also transmit herewith a portion of the manuscript prepared in pursuance of said resolution, with a letter from Mr. Hall to me indicating the mode in which he thinks the work should be prepared and printed, which appears to me worthy of consideration and adoption by the House.

MILLARD FILLMORE.

*Correspondence with the Austrian chargé d'affaires respecting the appointment or proceedings of the agent sent to examine and report upon the condition and prospects of the Hungarian people during their struggle for independence.

RIDICULE OF JENNY LIND'S POPULARITY IN 1850.

WASHINGTON, *January 10, 1851.*

To the Senate of the United States:

I have the honor herewith to transmit to the Senate a communication from the Secretary of the Navy on the subject of the discipline of the Navy, suggesting such amendments of the law as may be necessary in consequence of the recent act abolishing flogging; to which I respectfully invite the immediate attention of Congress.

MILLARD FILLMORE.

WASHINGTON, *January 14, 1851.*

To the House of Representatives of the United States:

In compliance with the resolution of the House of Representatives adopted July 18, 1850, requesting the President to communicate his views on sundry questions of rank, precedence, and command among officers of the Army and officers of the Navy, respectively, and of relative rank between officers of the Army and Navy when brought into cooperation, I caused to be convened a board of intelligent and experienced officers in each branch of the service to consider the matters involved in said resolutions and to report their opinion for my advice and information.

Their reports have been made, and I have the honor herewith to submit copies of them, together with bills drafted substantially in accordance therewith, on the subject of rank in each branch of the service.

The subject is one of great interest, and it is highly important that it should be settled by legislative authority and with as little delay as possible consistently with its proper examination.

The points on which it will be perceived that the two boards disagree in regard to relative rank between officers of the Army and Navy are not esteemed of very great practical importance, and the adoption of the rule proposed by either would be acceptable to the Executive.

But even if a decision on these shall be suspended, it is hoped that the bills which are designed to regulate rank, precedence, and command in the Army and Navy as separate branches of service may receive the sanction of Congress, with such amendments as may be deemed appropriate, in the course of the present session.

MILLARD FILLMORE.

WASHINGTON, *February 3, 1851.*

To the Senate of the United States:

I transmit to the Senate a report from the Secretary of State, with accompanying papers,* in answer to their resolution of the 30th ultimo.

MILLARD FILLMORE.

*Correspondence relative to the possessory rights of the British Hudsons Bay Company in Oregon.

WASHINGTON, *February 12, 1851.*

To the Senate of the United States:

I transmit herewith a report from the Secretary of State, with accompanying documents,* in answer to the Senate's resolution of the 1st instant.

MILLARD FILLMORE.

WASHINGTON, *February 13, 1851.*

To the Senate of the United States:

I herewith communicate to the Senate, for its consideration, a general convention between the United States and the Swiss Confederation, concluded and signed at Berne on the 25th day of November last by Mr. A. Dudley Mann on the part of the United States and by Messrs. Druey and Frey-Hérosée on the part of the Swiss Confederation. I communicate at the same time a copy of the instructions under which Mr. Mann acted and his dispatch of the 30th November last, explanatory of the articles of the convention.

In submitting this convention to the consideration of the Senate I feel it my duty to invite its special attention to the first and fifth articles. These articles appear to contain provisions quite objectionable, if, indeed, they can be considered as properly embraced in the treaty-making power. The second clause of the first article is in these words:

In the United States of America citizens of Switzerland shall be received and treated in each State upon the same footing and upon the same conditions as citizens of the United States born in or belonging to other States of the Union.

It is well known that according to the Constitution of the United States a citizen of one State may hold lands in any other State; and States have, sometimes by general, sometimes by special, laws, removed the disabilities attaching to foreigners not naturalized in regard to the holding of land. But this is not supposed to be a power properly to be exercised by the President and Senate in concluding and ratifying a treaty with a foreign state. The authority naturally belongs to the State within whose limits the land may lie. The naturalization of foreigners is provided for by the laws of the United States, in pursuance of the provision of the Constitution; but when, under the operation of these laws, foreigners become citizens of the United States, all would seem to be done which it is in the power of this Government to do to enable foreigners to hold land. The clause referred to, therefore, appears to me inadmissible.

The fourth clause of the same article provides, among other things, that citizens of Switzerland may, within the United States, acquire, possess, and alienate personal and real estate, and the fifth article grants them the power of disposing of their real estate, which, perhaps, would

* Correspondence with Spain relative to the claim of the owners of the schooner *Amistad* for compensation on account of the liberation of negroes on board said vessel.

be no otherwise objectionable, if it stood by itself, than as it would seem to imply a power to hold that of which they are permitted to dispose.

These objections, perhaps, may be removed by striking out the second clause of the first article and the words "and real" in the fourth clause. An amendment similar to the last here suggested was made by the Senate in the convention between the United States and the King of Bavaria, the ratification of which, as amended, the Senate advised and consented to on the 15th day of March, 1845.

But there is another and a decisive objection, arising from the last clause in the first article. That clause is in these words:

On account of the tenor of the federal constitution of Switzerland, Christians alone are entitled to the enjoyment of the privileges guaranteed by the present article in the Swiss Cantons. But said Cantons are not prohibited from extending the same privileges to citizens of the United States of other religious persuasions.

It appears from this that Christians alone are, in some of the Swiss Cantons, entitled to the enjoyment of privileges guaranteed by the first article, although the Cantons themselves are not prohibited from extending the same privileges to citizens of the United States of other religious persuasions.

It is quite certain that neither by law, nor by treaty, nor by any other official proceeding is it competent for the Government of the United States to establish any distinction between its citizens founded on differences in religious beliefs. Any benefit or privilege conferred by law or treaty on one must be common to all, and we are not at liberty, on a question of such vital interest and plain constitutional duty, to consider whether the particular case is one in which substantial inconvenience or injustice might ensue. It is enough that an inequality would be sanctioned hostile to the institutions of the United States and inconsistent with the Constitution and the laws.

Nor can the Government of the United States rely on the individual Cantons of Switzerland for extending the same privileges to other citizens of the United States as this article extends to Christians. It is indispensable not only that every privilege granted to any of the citizens of the United States should be granted to all, but also that the grant of such privilege should stand upon the same stipulation and assurance by the whole Swiss Confederation as those of other articles of the convention.

There have been instances, especially some of recent occurrence, in which the Executive has transmitted treaties to the Senate with suggestions of amendment, and I have therefore thought it not improper to send the present convention to the Senate, inviting its attention to such amendments as appeared to me to be important, although I have entertained considerable doubt whether it would not be better to send back the convention for correction in the objectionable particulars before laying it before the Senate for ratification.

MILLARD FILLMORE.

62267

WASHINGTON, *February 13, 1851.*

To the Senate of the United States:

In answer to the resolution of the Senate of the 10th instant, calling for information relative to a contract alleged to have been made by Mr. I. D. Marks with the Mexican Government, I transmit a report from the Secretary of State and the documents* which accompanied it.

MILLARD FILLMORE.

WASHINGTON, *February 13, 1851.*

To the Senate of the United States:

In compliance with the resolution of the Senate of the 28th of January, 1851, I have the honor to transmit herewith reports from the Secretary of State and Secretary of the Treasury, giving the required correspondence in the case of the British ship *Albion*, seized in Oregon for an alleged violation of the revenue laws.   MILLARD FILLMORE.

WASHINGTON, *February 15, 1851.*

To the Senate of the United States:

In addition to the information heretofore communicated, I now transmit to the Senate a report from the Secretary of State, with accompanying papers,† in answer to their resolution of the 28th ultimo.

MILLARD FILLMORE.

WASHINGTON, *February 15, 1851.*

To the Senate of the United States:

I herewith transmit to the Senate a report ‡ from the Secretary of State, in answer to their resolution of the 10th instant.

MILLARD FILLMORE.

WASHINGTON, *February 18, 1851.*

The PRESIDENT OF THE SENATE:

In addition to the papers already transmitted to the Senate in compliance with its resolution of the 28th ultimo, I have the honor herewith to transmit an additional report § from the Secretary of the Treasury.

MILLARD FILLMORE.

---

* Relating to drafts upon the Treasury of the United States by Mexico on account of indemnity due that Government in pursuance of the treaty of Guadalupe Hidalgo.

† Additional correspondence relative to the seizure of the British ship *Albion*.

‡ Relating to taxation by New Granada on United States citizens when *in transitu* across the Isthmus of Panama, and to the United States mail service at said Isthmus.

§ Relating to the seizure of the British ship *Albion*.

EXECUTIVE DEPARTMENT, *February 19, 1851.*

To the Senate of the United States:

I have received the resolution of the Senate of the 18th instant, requesting me to lay before that body, if not incompatible with the public interest, any information I may possess in regard to an alleged recent case of a forcible resistance to the execution of the laws of the United States in the city of Boston, and to communicate to the Senate, under the above conditions, what means I have adopted to meet the occurrence, and whether in my opinion any additional legislation is necessary to meet the exigency of the case and to more vigorously execute existing laws.

The public newspapers contain an affidavit of Patrick Riley, a deputy marshal for the district of Massachusetts, setting forth the circumstances of the case, a copy of which affidavit is herewith communicated. Private and unofficial communications concur in establishing the main facts of this account, but no satisfactory official information has as yet been received; and in some important respects the accuracy of the account has been denied by persons whom it implicates. Nothing could be more unexpected than that such a gross violation of law, such a high-handed contempt of the authority of the United States, should be perpetrated by a band of lawless confederates at noonday in the city of Boston, and in the very temple of justice. I regard this flagitious proceeding as being a surprise not unattended by some degree of negligence; nor do I doubt that if any such act of violence had been apprehended thousands of the good citizens of Boston would have presented themselves voluntarily and promptly to prevent it. But the danger does not seem to have been timely made known or duly appreciated by those who were concerned in the execution of the process. In a community distinguished for its love of order and respect for the laws, among a people whose sentiment is liberty and law, and not liberty without law nor above the law, such an outrage could only be the result of sudden violence, unhappily too much unprepared for to be successfully resisted. It would be melancholy indeed if we were obliged to regard this outbreak against the constitutional and legal authority of the Government as proceeding from the general feeling of the people in a spot which is proverbially called "the Cradle of American Liberty." Such, undoubtedly, is not the fact. It violates without question the general sentiment of the people of Boston and of a vast majority of the whole people of Massachusetts, as much as it violates the law, defies the authority of the Government, and disgraces those concerned in it, their aiders and abettors.

It is, nevertheless, my duty to lay before the Senate, in answer to its resolution, some important facts and considerations connected with the subject.

A resolution of Congress of September 23, 1789, declared:

That it be recommended to the legislatures of the several States to pass laws making it expressly the duty of the keepers of their jails to receive and safe keep therein all prisoners committed under the authority of the United States until they shall be discharged by the course of the laws thereof, under the like penalties as in the case of prisoners committed under the authority of such States respectively; the United States to pay for the use and keeping of such jails at the rate of 50 cents per month for each prisoner that shall, under their authority, be committed thereto during the time such prisoner shall be therein confined, and also to support such of said prisoners as shall be committed for offenses.

A further resolution of Congress, of the 3d of March, 1791, provides that—

Whereas Congress did, by a resolution of the 23d day of September, 1789, recommend to the several States to pass laws making it expressly the duty of the keepers of their jails to receive and safe keep therein all prisoners committed under the authority of the United States: In order, therefore, to insure the administration of justice—

Resolved by the Senate and House of Representatives of the United States of America in Congress assembled, That in case any State shall not have complied with the said recommendation the marshal in such State, under the direction of the judge of the district, be authorized to hire a convenient place to serve as a temporary jail, and to make the necessary provision for the safe-keeping of prisoners committed under the authority of the United States until permanent provision shall be made by law for that purpose; and the said marshal shall be allowed his reasonable expenses incurred for the above purposes, to be paid out of the Treasury of the United States.

And a resolution of Congress of March 3, 1821, provides that—

Where any State or States, having complied with the recommendation of Congress in the resolution of the 23d day of September, 1789, shall have withdrawn, or shall hereafter withdraw, either in whole or in part, the use of their jails for prisoners committed under the authority of the United States, the marshal in such State or States, under the direction of the judge of the district, shall be, and hereby is, authorized and required to hire a convenient place to serve as a temporary jail, and to make the necessary provision for the safe-keeping of prisoners committed under the authority of the United States until permanent provision shall be made by law for that purpose; and the said marshal shall be allowed his reasonable expenses incurred for the above purposes, to be paid out of the Treasury of the United States.

These various provisions of the law remain unrepealed.

By the law of Massachusetts, as that law stood before the act of the legislature of that State of the 24th of March, 1843, the common jails in the respective counties were to be used for the detention of any persons detained or committed by the authority of the courts of the United States, as well as by the courts and magistrates of the State. But these provisions were abrogated and repealed by the act of the legislature of Massachusetts of the 24th of March, 1843.

That act declares that—

No judge of any court of record of this Commonwealth and no justice of the peace shall hereafter take cognizance or grant a certificate in cases that may arise under the third section of an act of Congress passed February 12, 1793, and entitled "An act respecting fugitives from justice and persons escaping from the service of their masters," to any person who claims any other person as a fugitive slave within the jurisdiction of the Commonwealth.

And it further declares that—

No sheriff, deputy sheriff, coroner, constable, jailer, or other officer of this Commonwealth shall hereafter arrest or detain, or aid in the arrest or detention or imprisonment, in any jail or other building belonging to this Commonwealth, or to any county, city, or town thereof, of any person for the reason that he is claimed as a fugitive slave.

And it further declares that—

Any justice of the peace, sheriff, deputy sheriff, coroner, constable, or jailer who shall offend against the provisions of this law by in any way acting, directly or indirectly, under the power conferred by the third section of the act of Congress aforementioned shall forfeit a sum not exceeding $1,000 for every such offense to the use of the county where said offense is committed, or shall be subject to imprisonment not exceeding one year in the county jail.

This law, it is obvious, had two objects. The first was to make it a penal offense in all officers and magistrates of the Commonwealth to exercise the powers conferred on them by the act of Congress of the 12th of February, 1793, entitled "An act respecting fugitives from justice and persons escaping from the service of their masters," and which powers they were fully competent to perform up to the time of this inhibition and penal enactment; second, to refuse the use of the jails of the State for the detention of any person claimed as a fugitive slave.

It is deeply to be lamented that the purpose of these enactments is quite apparent. It was to prevent, as far as the legislature of the State could prevent, the laws of Congress passed for the purpose of carrying into effect that article of the Constitution of the United States which declares that "no person held to service or labor in one State, under the laws thereof, escaping into another, shall in consequence of any law or regulation therein be discharged from such service or labor, but shall be delivered up on claim of the party to whom such service or labor may be due" from being carried into effect. But these acts of State legislation, although they may cause embarrassment and create expense, can not derogate either from the duty or the authority of Congress to carry out fully and fairly the plain and imperative constitutional provision for the delivery of persons bound to labor in one State and escaping into another to the party to whom such labor may be due. It is quite clear that by the resolution of Congress of March 3, 1821, the marshal of the United States in any State in which the use of the jails of the State has been withdrawn, in whole or in part, from the purpose of the detention of persons committed under the authority of the United States is not only empowered, but expressly required, under the direction of the judge of the district, to hire a convenient place for the safe-keeping of prisoners committed under authority of the United States. It will be seen from papers accompanying this communication that the attention of the marshal of Massachusetts was distinctly called to this provision of the law by a letter from the Secretary of the Navy of the date of October 28 last.

There is no official information that the marshal has provided any such place for the confinement of his prisoners. If he has not, it is to be regretted that this power was not exercised by the marshal under the direction of the district judge immediately on the passage of the act of the legislature of Massachusetts of the 24th of March, 1843, and especially that it was not exercised on the passage of the fugitive-slave law of the last session, or when the attention of the marshal was afterwards particularly drawn to it.

It is true that the escape from the deputy marshals in this case was not owing to the want of a prison or place of confinement, but still it is not easy to see how the prisoner could have been safely and conveniently detained during an adjournment of the hearing for some days without such place of confinement. If it shall appear that no such place has been obtained, directions to the marshal will be given to lose no time in the discharge of this duty.

I transmit to the Senate the copy of a proclamation issued by me on the 18th instant in relation to these unexpected and deplorable occurrences in Boston, together with copies of instructions from the Departments of War and Navy relative to the general subject. And I communicate also copies of telegraphic dispatches transmitted from the Department of State to the district attorney and marshal of the United States for the district of Massachusetts and their answers thereto.

In regard to the last branch of the inquiry made by the resolution of the Senate, I have to observe that the Constitution declares that "the President shall take care that the laws be faithfully executed," and that "he shall be Commander in Chief of the Army and Navy of the United States, and of the militia of the several States when called into the actual service of the United States," and that "Congress shall have power to provide for calling forth the militia to execute the laws of the Union, suppress insurrections, and repel invasions." From which it appears that the Army and Navy are by the Constitution placed under the control of the Executive; and probably no legislation of Congress could add to or diminish the power thus given but by increasing or diminishing or abolishing altogether the Army and Navy. But not so with the militia. The President can not call the militia into service, even to execute the laws or repel invasions, but by the authority of acts of Congress passed for that purpose. But when the militia are called into service in the manner prescribed by law, then the Constitution itself gives the command to the President. Acting on this principle, Congress, by the act of February 28, 1795, authorized the President to call forth the militia to repel invasion and "suppress insurrections against a State government, and to suppress combinations against the laws of the United States, and cause the laws to be faithfully executed." But the act proceeds to declare that whenever it may be necessary, in the judgment of the President, to use the military force thereby directed to be called forth, the

President shall forthwith, by proclamation, command such insurgents to disperse and retire peaceably to their respective abodes within a limited time. These words are broad enough to require a proclamation in all cases where militia are called out under that act, whether to repel invasion or suppress an insurrection or to aid in executing the laws. This section has consequently created some doubt whether the militia could be called forth to aid in executing the laws without a previous proclamation. But yet the proclamation seems to be in words directed only against insurgents, and to require them to disperse, thereby implying not only an insurrection, but an organized, or at least an embodied, force. Such a proclamation in aid of the civil authority would often defeat the whole object by giving such notice to persons intended to be arrested that they would be enabled to fly or secrete themselves. The force may be wanted sometimes to make the arrest, and also sometimes to protect the officer after it is made, and to prevent a rescue. I would therefore suggest that this section be modified by declaring that nothing therein contained shall be construed to require any previous proclamation when the militia are called forth, either to repel invasion, to execute the laws, or suppress combinations against them, and that the President may make such call and place such militia under the control of any civil officer of the United States to aid him in executing the laws or suppressing such combinations; and while so employed they shall be paid by and subsisted at the expense of the United States.

Congress, not probably adverting to the difference between the militia and the Regular Army, by the act of March 3, 1807, authorized the President to use the land and naval forces of the United States for the same purposes for which he might call forth the militia, and subject to the same proclamation. But the power of the President under the Constitution, as Commander of the Army and Navy, is general, and his duty to see the laws faithfully executed is general and positive; and the act of 1807 ought not to be construed as evincing any disposition in Congress to limit or restrain this constitutional authority. For greater certainty, however, it may be well that Congress should modify or explain this act in regard to its provisions for the employment of the Army and Navy of the United States, as well as that in regard to calling forth the militia. It is supposed not to be doubtful that all citizens, whether enrolled in the militia or not, may be summoned as members of the *posse comitatus*, either by the marshal or a commissioner according to law, and that it is their duty to obey such summons. But perhaps it may be doubted whether the marshal or a commissioner can summon as the *posse comitatus* an organized militia force, acting under its own appropriate officers, without the consent of such officers. This point may deserve the consideration of Congress.

I use this occasion to repeat the assurance that so far as depends on me the laws shall be faithfully executed and all forcible opposition to them suppressed; and to this end I am prepared to exercise, whenever it may become necessary, the power constitutionally vested in me to the fullest extent. I am fully persuaded that the great majority of the people of this country are warmly and strongly attached to the Constitution, the preservation of the Union, the just support of the Government, and the maintenance of the authority of law. I am persuaded that their earnest wishes and the line of my constitutional duty entirely concur, and I doubt not firmness, moderation, and prudence, strengthened and animated by the general opinion of the people, will prevent the repetition of occurrences disturbing the public peace and reprobated by all good men.

MILLARD FILLMORE.

WASHINGTON, *February 25, 1851.*

To the Senate of the United States:

I transmit to the Senate, for its consideration with a view to ratification, a convention between the United States and the Mexican Republic for the protection of a transit way across the Isthmus of Tehuantepec, signed in the City of Mexico on the 25th ultimo.

Accompanying the treaty is a letter from Mr. P. A. Hargous, the present proprietor and holder of the privileges granted by Mexico, signifying his assent to and acceptance of the terms of its provisions. There is also an abstract of title to him from the original grantee and copies of the several powers and conveyances by which that title is derived to him. It may be well that these papers should be returned to be deposited among the archives of the Department of State.

The additional article of the treaty makes an unnecessary reference to the eleventh, twelfth, and thirteenth articles of the treaty of the 22d of June last, because the eleventh, twelfth, and thirteenth articles of the present treaty contain exactly the same provisions as those contained in the same articles of that treaty, as will appear from the copy of the treaty of the 22d of June last, herewith communicated.

MILLARD FILLMORE.

WASHINGTON, *February 26, 1851.*

To the Senate of the United States:

I herewith communicate to the Senate, for its consideration, a convention for the adjustment of certain claims of citizens of the United States against Her Most Faithful Majesty's Government,* concluded and signed this day in the city of Washington by the respective plenipotentiaries.

MILLARD FILLMORE

* Portugal.

WASHINGTON, *February 27, 1851.*

To the Senate of the United States:

I transmit herewith a report of the Secretary of State, with accompanying documents,* in compliance with the resolution of the Senate of the 17th ultimo.

MILLARD FILLMORE.

WASHINGTON, *February 28, 1851.*

To the Senate of the United States:

In answer to the resolution of the Senate of the 16th ultimo, requesting information touching the difficulties between the British authorities and San Salvador, I transmit a report from the Secretary of State and the documents which accompanied it.

MILLARD FILLMORE.

WASHINGTON, *March 1, 1851.*

Hon. HOWELL COBB,
  Speaker of the House of Representatives:

I have the honor herewith to transmit to the House of Representatives manuscript No. 2 of the opinions of the Attorneys-General, prepared in pursuance of its resolution.

MILLARD FILLMORE.

WASHINGTON, *March 3, 1851.*

To the Senate of the United States:

In answer to the resolution of the Senate of the 26th ultimo, calling for information respecting a forcible abduction of any citizen of the United States from the Territory of New Mexico and his conveyance within the limits of the Mexican Republic, I transmit a report from the Secretary of State and the documents which accompanied it.

MILLARD FILLMORE.

PROCLAMATIONS.

BY THE PRESIDENT OF THE UNITED STATES OF AMERICA.

A PROCLAMATION.

Whereas by an act of the Congress of the United States of the 9th of September, 1850, entitled "An act proposing to the State of Texas the establishment of her northern and western boundaries, the relinquishment by the said State of all territory claimed by her exterior to said boundaries and of all her claims upon the United States, and to establish a Territorial government for New Mexico," it was provided that the

* Correspondence relative to prisoners captured by Spanish authorities at or near the island of Contoy, and to projected expeditions to Cuba.

following propositions should be, and the same were thereby, offered to the State of Texas, which, when agreed to by the said State in an act passed by the general assembly, should be binding and obligatory upon the United States and upon the said State of Texas, provided the said agreement by the said general assembly should be given on or before the 1st day of December, 1850, namely:

"First. The State of Texas will agree that her boundary on the north shall commence at the point at which the meridian of 100° west from Greenwich is intersected by the parallel of 36° 30' north latitude, and shall run from said point due west to the meridian of 103° west from Greenwich; thence her boundary shall run due south to the thirty-second degree of north latitude; thence on the said parallel of 32° of north latitude to the Rio Bravo del Norte, and thence with the channel of said river to the Gulf of Mexico.

"Second. The State of Texas cedes to the United States all her claim to territory exterior to the limits and boundaries which she agrees to establish by the first article of this agreement.

"Third. The State of Texas relinquishes all claim upon the United States for liability of the debts of Texas and for compensation or indemnity for the surrender to the United States of her ships, forts, arsenals, custom-houses, custom-house revenue, arms and munitions of war, and public buildings with their sites, which became the property of the United States at the time of the annexation.

"Fourth. The United States, in consideration of said establishment of boundaries, cession of claim to territory, and relinquishment of claims, will pay to the State of Texas the sum of $10,000,000 in a stock bearing 5 per cent interest, and redeemable at the end of fourteen years, the interest payable half-yearly at the Treasury of the United States.

"Fifth. Immediately after the President of the United States shall have been furnished with an authentic copy of the act of the general assembly of Texas accepting these propositions, he shall cause the stock to be issued in favor of the State of Texas, as provided for in the fourth article of this agreement: *Provided also*, That no more than $5,000,000 of said stock shall be issued until the creditors of the State holding bonds and other certificates of stock of Texas for which duties on imports were specially pledged shall first file at the Treasury of the United States releases of all claim against the United States for or on account of said bonds or certificates in such form as shall be prescribed by the Secretary of the Treasury and approved by the President of the United States: *Provided*, That nothing herein contained shall be construed to impair or qualify anything contained in the third article of the second section of the 'Joint resolution for annexing Texas to the United States,' approved March 1, 1845, either as regards the number of States that may hereafter be formed out of the State of Texas or otherwise;" and

Whereas it was further provided by the eighteenth section of the same act of Congress "that the provisions of this act be, and they are hereby, suspended until the boundary between the United States and the State of Texas shall be adjusted, and when such adjustment shall have been effected the President of the United States shall issue his proclamation declaring this act to be in full force and operation;" and

Whereas the legislature of the State of Texas, by an act approved the 25th of November last, entitled "An act accepting the propositions made by the United States to the State of Texas in an act of the Congress of the United States approved the 9th day of September, A. D. 1850, and entitled 'An act proposing to the State of Texas the establishment of her northern and western boundaries, the relinquishment by the said State of all territory claimed by her exterior to said boundaries and of all her claims upon the United States, and to establish a Territorial government for New Mexico,'" of which act a copy, authenticated under the seal of the State, has been furnished to the President, enacts "that the State of Texas hereby agrees to and accepts said propositions, and it is hereby declared that the said State shall be bound by the terms thereof, according to their true import and meaning:"

Now, therefore, I, Millard Fillmore, President of the United States of America, do hereby declare and proclaim that the said act of the Congress of the United States of the 9th of September last is in full force and operation.

Given under my hand, at the city of Washington, this 13th day of December, A. D. 1850, and the seventy-fifth of the Independence of these United States.

[SEAL.]

MILLARD FILLMORE.

By the President:
DANL. WEBSTER,
Secretary of State.

BY THE PRESIDENT OF THE UNITED STATES.

A PROCLAMATION.

Whereas information has been received that sundry lawless persons, principally persons of color, combined and confederated together for the purpose of opposing by force the execution of the laws of the United States, did, at Boston, in Massachusetts, on the 15th of this month, make a violent assault on the marshal or deputy marshals of the United States for the district of Massachusetts, in the court-house, and did overcome the said officers, and did by force rescue from their custody a person arrested as a fugitive slave, and then and there a prisoner lawfully holden by the said marshal or deputy marshals of the United States, and other scandalous outrages did commit in violation of law:

Now, therefore, to the end that the authority of the laws may be maintained and those concerned in violating them brought to immediate and condign punishment, I have issued this my proclamation, calling on all well-disposed citizens to rally to the support of the laws of their country, and requiring and commanding all officers, civil and military, and all other persons, civil or military, who shall be found within the vicinity of this outrage, to be aiding and assisting by all means in their power in quelling this and other such combinations and assisting the marshal and his deputies in recapturing the above-mentioned prisoner; and I do especially direct that prosecutions be commenced against all persons who shall have made themselves aiders or abettors in or to this flagitious offense; and I do further command that the district attorney of the United States and all other persons concerned in the administration or execution of the laws of the United States cause the foregoing offenders and all such as aided, abetted, or assisted them or shall be found to have harbored or concealed such fugitive contrary to law to be immediately arrested and proceeded with according to law.

Given under my hand and the seal of the United States this 18th day of February, 1851.

[SEAL.]   MILLARD FILLMORE.

DANL. WEBSTER,
      Secretary of State.

[From Executive Journal of the Senate, Vol. VIII, p. 299.]

WASHINGTON, *March 3, 1851.*

To the Senators of the United States, respectively.

SIR: Whereas divers and weighty causes connected with executive business necessary to be transacted create an extraordinary occasion requiring that the Senate be convened, you are therefore requested, as a member of that body, to attend a meeting thereof to be holden at the Capitol, in the city of Washington, on the 4th day of March instant.

MILLARD FILLMORE.

SPECIAL MESSAGES.

WASHINGTON, *March 4, 1851.*

To the Senate of the United States:

Sundry nominations having been made during the last session of the Senate which were not finally disposed of, I hereby nominate anew each person so nominated at the last session whose nomination was not finally acted on before the termination of that session to the same office for which he was nominated as aforesaid.

MILLARD FILLMORE.

A Proclamation:
by the
President of the United States.

Whereas information has been received, that sundry lawless persons, principally persons of color, combined and confederated together, for the purpose of opposing by force, the execution of the Laws of the United States, did, at Boston, in Massachusetts, on the 15th of this month, make a violent assault on the Marshal or Deputy Marshals of the United States, for the District of Massachusetts, in the Court House, and did overcome the said Officers, and did, by force, rescue from their custody, a person arrested as a fugitive slave, and, then and there, a prisoner lawfully holden by the said Marshal, or Deputy Marshals of the United States, and other scandalous outrages did commit, in violation of law; Now Therefore, to the end, that the

PRESIDENT FILLMORE'S FUGITIVE SLAVE PROCLAMATION.

found to *have* harbor or conceal such fugitive, contrary
to law, to be immediately arrested and proceeded
with according to law.

Given under my hand and
the Seal of the United States, this
18 B day of February, 1851.

Millard Fillmore

Secretary of State —

LAST PAGE OF FILLMORE'S FUGITIVE SLAVE
PROCLAMATION.

WASHINGTON, *March 10, 1851.*

To the Senate of the United States:

I transmit herewith a report of the Secretary of State, with the accompanying documents,* in compliance with the resolution of the Senate of the 8th instant.

MILLARD FILLMORE.

PROCLAMATIONS.

BY THE PRESIDENT OF THE UNITED STATES.

A PROCLAMATION.

Whereas there is reason to believe that a military expedition is about to be fitted out in the United States with intention to invade the island of Cuba, a colony of Spain, with which this country is at peace; and

Whereas it is believed that this expedition is instigated and set on foot chiefly by foreigners who dare to make our shores the scene of their guilty and hostile preparations against a friendly power and seek by falsehood and misrepresentation to seduce our own citizens, especially the young and inconsiderate, into their wicked schemes—an ungrateful return for the benefits conferred upon them by this people in permitting them to make our country an asylum from oppression and in flagrant abuse of the hospitality thus extended to them; and

Whereas such expeditions can only be regarded as adventures for plunder and robbery, and must meet the condemnation of the civilized world, whilst they are derogatory to the character of our country, in violation of the laws of nations, and expressly prohibited by our own. Our statutes declare ''that if any person shall, within the territory or jurisdiction of the United States, begin or set on foot or provide or prepare the means for any military expedition or enterprise to be carried on from thence against the territory or dominions of any foreign prince or state or of any colony, district, or people with whom the United States are at peace, every person so offending shall be deemed guilty of a high misdemeanor and shall be fined not exceeding $3,000 and imprisoned not more than three years:''

Now, therefore, I have issued this my proclamation, warning all persons who shall connect themselves with any such enterprise or expedition in violation of our laws and national obligations that they will thereby subject themselves to the heavy penalties denounced against such offenses and will forfeit their claim to the protection of this Government or any interference on their behalf, no matter to what extremities they may be reduced in consequence of their illegal conduct. And therefore I exhort all good citizens, as they regard our national reputation, as they respect

* Correspondence with the United States minister at Constantinople respecting the liberation of Kossuth and his companions.

their own laws and the laws of nations, as they value the blessings of peace and the welfare of their country, to discountenance and by all lawful means prevent any such enterprise; and I call upon every officer of this Government, civil or military, to use all efforts in his power to arrest for trial and punishment every such offender against the laws of the country.

Given under my hand the 25th day of April, A. D. 1851, and the seventy-fifth of the Independence of the United States.

[SEAL.]   MILLARD FILLMORE.

By the President:

   W. S. DERRICK,
      Acting Secretary of State.

BY THE PRESIDENT OF THE UNITED STATES.

A PROCLAMATION.

Whereas there is reason to believe that a military expedition is about to be fitted out in the United States for the purpose of invading the Mexican Republic, with which this country is at peace; and

Whereas there is reason to apprehend that a portion of the people of this country, regardless of their duties as good citizens, are concerned in or may be seduced to take part in the same; and

Whereas such enterprises tend to degrade the character of the United States in the opinion of the civilized world and are expressly prohibited by law:

Now, therefore, I have issued this my proclamation, warning all persons who shall connect themselves with any such enterprise in violation of the laws and national obligations of the United States that they will thereby subject themselves to the heavy penalties denounced against such offenses; that if they should be captured within the jurisdiction of the Mexican authorities they must expect to be tried and punished according to the laws of Mexico and will have no right to claim the interposition of this Government in their behalf.

I therefore exhort all well-disposed citizens who have at heart the reputation of their country and are animated with a just regard for its laws, its peace, and its welfare to discountenance and by all lawful means prevent any such enterprise; and I call upon every officer of this Government, civil or military, to be vigilant in arresting for trial and punishment every such offender.

Given under my hand the 22d day of October, A. D. 1851, and the seventy-sixth of the Independence of the United States.

                                             MILLARD FILLMORE.
By the President:

   J. J. CRITTENDEN,
      Acting Secretary of State.

SECOND ANNUAL MESSAGE.

WASHINGTON, *December 2, 1851.*

Fellow-Citizens of the Senate and of the House of Representatives:

I congratulate you and our common constituency upon the favorable auspices under which you meet for your first session. Our country is at peace with all the world. The agitation which for a time threatened to disturb the fraternal relations which make us one people is fast subsiding, and a year of general prosperity and health has crowned the nation with unusual blessings. None can look back to the dangers which are passed or forward to the bright prospect before us without feeling a thrill of gratification, at the same time that he must be impressed with a grateful sense of our profound obligations to a beneficent Providence, whose paternal care is so manifest in the happiness of this highly favored land.

Since the close of the last Congress certain Cubans and other foreigners resident in the United States, who were more or less concerned in the previous invasion of Cuba, instead of being discouraged by its failure have again abused the hospitality of this country by making it the scene of the equipment of another military expedition against that possession of Her Catholic Majesty, in which they were countenanced, aided, and joined by citizens of the United States. On receiving intelligence that such designs were entertained, I lost no time in issuing such instructions to the proper officers of the United States as seemed to be called for by the occasion. By the proclamation a copy of which is herewith submitted I also warned those who might be in danger of being inveigled into this scheme of its unlawful character and of the penalties which they would incur. For some time there was reason to hope that these measures had sufficed to prevent any such attempt. This hope, however, proved to be delusive. Very early in the morning of the 3d of August a steamer called the *Pampero* departed from New Orleans for Cuba, having on board upward of 400 armed men with evident intentions to make war upon the authorities of the island. This expedition was set on foot in palpable violation of the laws of the United States. Its leader was a Spaniard, and several of the chief officers and some others engaged in it were foreigners. The persons composing it, however, were mostly citizens of the United States.

Before the expedition set out, and probably before it was organized, a slight insurrectionary movement, which appears to have been soon suppressed, had taken place in the eastern quarter of Cuba. The importance of this movement was, unfortunately, so much exaggerated in the accounts of it published in this country that these adventurers seem to have been led to believe that the Creole population of the island not only desired to throw off the authority of the mother country, but had resolved upon that step and had begun a well-concerted enterprise for effecting it. The persons engaged in the expedition were generally young and ill informed. The steamer in which they embarked left New Orleans stealthily and without a clearance. After touching at Key West, she proceeded to the coast of Cuba, and on the night between the 11th and 12th of August landed the persons on board at Playtas, within about 20 leagues of Havana.

The main body of them proceeded to and took possession of an inland village 6 leagues distant, leaving others to follow in charge of the baggage as soon as the means of transportation could be obtained. The latter, having taken up their line of march to connect themselves with the main body, and having proceeded about 4 leagues into the country, were attacked on the morning of the 13th by a body of Spanish troops, and a bloody conflict ensued, after which they retreated to the place of disembarkation, where about 50 of them obtained boats and reembarked therein. They were, however, intercepted among the keys near the shore by a Spanish steamer cruising on the coast, captured and carried to Havana, and after being examined before a military court were sentenced to be publicly executed, and the sentence was carried into effect on the 16th of August.

On receiving information of what had occurred Commodore Foxhall A. Parker was instructed to proceed in the steam frigate *Saranac* to Havana and inquire into the charges against the persons executed, the circumstances under which they were taken, and whatsoever referred to their trial and sentence. Copies of the instructions from the Department of State to him and of his letters to that Department are herewith submitted.

According to the record of the examination, the prisoners all admitted the offenses charged against them, of being hostile invaders of the island. At the time of their trial and execution the main body of the invaders was still in the field making war upon the Spanish authorities and Spanish subjects. After the lapse of some days, being overcome by the Spanish troops, they dispersed on the 24th of August. Lopez, their leader, was captured some days after, and executed on the 1st of September. Many of his remaining followers were killed or died of hunger and fatigue, and the rest were made prisoners. Of these none appear to have been tried or executed. Several of them were pardoned upon application of their friends and others, and the rest, about 160 in number, were sent to Spain. Of the final disposition made of these we have no official information.

Such is the melancholy result of this illegal and ill-fated expedition. Thus thoughtless young men have been induced by false and fraudulent representations to violate the law of their country through rash and unfounded expectations of assisting to accomplish political revolutions in other states, and have lost their lives in the undertaking. Too severe a judgment can hardly be passed by the indignant sense of the community upon those who, being better informed themselves, have yet led away the ardor of youth and an ill-directed love of political liberty. The correspondence between this Government and that of Spain relating to this transaction is herewith communicated.

Although these offenders against the laws have forfeited the protection of their country, yet the Government may, so far as consistent with its obligations to other countries and its fixed purpose to maintain and enforce the laws, entertain sympathy for their unoffending families and friends, as well as a feeling of compassion for themselves. Accordingly, no proper effort has been spared and none will be spared to procure the release of such citizens of the United States engaged in this unlawful enterprise as are now in confinement in Spain; but it is to be hoped that such interposition with the Government of that country may not be considered as affording any ground of expectation that the Government of the United States will hereafter feel itself under any obligation of duty to intercede for the liberation or pardon of such persons as are flagrant offenders against the law of nations and the laws of the United States. These laws must be executed. If we desire to maintain our respectability among the nations of the earth, it behooves us to enforce steadily and sternly the neutrality acts passed by Congress and to follow as far as may be the violation of those acts with condign punishment.

But what gives a peculiar criminality to this invasion of Cuba is that, under the lead of Spanish subjects and with the aid of citizens of the United States, it had its origin with many in motives of cupidity. Money was advanced by individuals, probably in considerable amounts, to purchase Cuban bonds, as they have been called, issued by Lopez, sold, doubtless, at a very large discount, and for the payment of which the public lands and public property of Cuba, of whatever kind, and the fiscal resources of the people and government of that island, from whatever source to be derived, were pledged, as well as the good faith of the government expected to be established. All these means of payment, it is evident, were only to be obtained by a process of bloodshed, war, and revolution. None will deny that those who set on foot military expeditions against foreign states by means like these are far more culpable than the ignorant and the necessitous whom they induce to go forth as the ostensible parties in the proceeding. These originators of the invasion of Cuba seem to have determined with coolness and system upon an undertaking which should disgrace their country, violate its laws, and put to hazard the lives of ill-informed and deluded men. You will consider whether further legislation be necessary to prevent the perpetration of such offenses in future.

No individuals have a right to hazard the peace of the country or to

violate its laws upon vague notions of altering or reforming governments in other states. This principle is not only reasonable in itself
and in accordance with public law, but is ingrafted into the codes of
other nations as well as our own. But while such are the sentiments
of this Government, it may be added that every independent nation
must be presumed to be able to defend its possessions against unauthorized individuals banded together to attack them. The Government
of the United States at all times since its establishment has abstained
and has sought to restrain the citizens of the country from entering into
controversies between other powers, and to observe all the duties of
neutrality. At an early period of the Government, in the Administration of Washington, several laws were passed for this purpose. The
main provisions of these laws were reenacted by the act of April, 1818,
by which, amongst other things, it was declared that—

> If any person shall, within the territory or jurisdiction of the United States, begin,
> or set on foot, or provide or prepare the means for, any military expedition or enter-
> prise to be carried on from thence against the territory or dominions of any foreign
> prince or state, or of any colony, district, or people, with whom the United States
> are at peace, every person so offending shall be deemed guilty of a high misdemeanor,
> and shall be fined not exceeding $3,000 and imprisoned not more than three years.

And this law has been executed and enforced to the full extent of the
power of the Government from that day to this.

In proclaiming and adhering to the doctrine of neutrality and nonintervention, the United States have not followed the lead of other civilized
nations; they have taken the lead themselves and have been followed by
others. This was admitted by one of the most eminent of modern British
statesmen, who said in Parliament, while a minister of the Crown, "that if
he wished for a guide in a system of neutrality he should take that laid
down by America in the days of Washington and the secretaryship of
Jefferson;" and we see, in fact, that the act of Congress of 1818 was followed the succeeding year by an act of the Parliament of England substantially the same in its general provisions. Up to that time there had
been no similar law in England, except certain highly penal statutes
passed in the reign of George II, prohibiting English subjects from enlist-
ing in foreign service, the avowed object of which statutes was that
foreign armies, raised for the purpose of restoring the house of Stuart to
the throne, should not be strengthened by recruits from England herself.

All must see that difficulties may arise in carrying the laws referred
to into execution in a country now having 3,000 or 4,000 miles of seacoast, with an infinite number of ports and harbors and small inlets, from
some of which unlawful expeditions may suddenly set forth, without the
knowledge of Government, against the possessions of foreign states.

"Friendly relations with all, but entangling alliances with none," has
long been a maxim with us. Our true mission is not to propagate our
opinions or impose upon other countries our form of government by arti-

fice or force, but to teach by example and show by our success, moderation, and justice the blessings of self-government and the advantages of free institutions. Let every people choose for itself and make and alter its political institutions to suit its own condition and convenience. But while we avow and maintain this neutral policy ourselves, we are anxious to see the same forbearance on the part of other nations whose forms of government are different from our own. The deep interest which we feel in the spread of liberal principles and the establishment of free governments and the sympathy with which we witness every struggle against oppression forbid that we should be indifferent to a case in which the strong arm of a foreign power is invoked to stifle public sentiment and repress the spirit of freedom in any country.

The Governments of Great Britain and France have issued orders to their naval commanders on the West India station to prevent, by force if necessary, the landing of adventurers from any nation on the island of Cuba with hostile intent. The copy of a memorandum of a conversation on this subject between the chargé d'affaires of Her Britannic Majesty and the Acting Secretary of State and of a subsequent note of the former to the Department of State are herewith submitted, together with a copy of a note of the Acting Secretary of State to the minister of the French Republic and of the reply of the latter on the same subject. These papers will acquaint you with the grounds of this interposition of two leading commercial powers of Europe, and with the apprehensions, which this Government could not fail to entertain, that such interposition, if carried into effect, might lead to abuses in derogation of the maritime rights of the United States. The maritime rights of the United States are founded on a firm, secure, and well-defined basis; they stand upon the ground of national independence and public law, and will be maintained in all their full and just extent. The principle which this Government has heretofore solemnly announced it still adheres to, and will maintain under all circumstances and at all hazards. That principle is that in every regularly documented merchant vessel the crew who navigate it and those on board of it will find their protection in the flag which is over them. No American ship can be allowed to be visited or searched for the purpose of ascertaining the character of individuals on board, nor can there be allowed any watch by the vessels of any foreign nation over American vessels on the coast of the United States or the seas adjacent thereto. It will be seen by the last communication from the British chargé d'affaires to the Department of State that he is authorized to assure the Secretary of State that every care will be taken that in executing the preventive measures against the expeditions which the United States Government itself has denounced as not being entitled to the protection of any government no interference shall take place with the lawful commerce of any nation.

In addition to the correspondence on this subject herewith submitted, official information has been received at the Department of State of assurances by the French Government that in the orders given to the French naval forces they were expressly instructed, in any operations they might engage in, to respect the flag of the United States wherever it might appear, and to commit no act of hostility upon any vessel or armament under its protection.

Ministers and consuls of foreign nations are the means and agents of communication between us and those nations, and it is of the utmost importance that while residing in the country they should feel a perfect security so long as they faithfully discharge their respective duties and are guilty of no violation of our laws. This is the admitted law of nations and no country has a deeper interest in maintaining it than the United States. Our commerce spreads over every sea and visits every clime, and our ministers and consuls are appointed to protect the interests of that commerce as well as to guard the peace of the country and maintain the honor of its flag. But how can they discharge these duties unless they be themselves protected? And if protected it must be by the laws of the country in which they reside. And what is due to our own public functionaries residing in foreign nations is exactly the measure of what is due to the functionaries of other governments residing here. As in war the bearers of flags of truce are sacred, or else wars would be interminable, so in peace ambassadors, public ministers, and consuls, charged with friendly national intercourse, are objects of especial respect and protection, each according to the rights belonging to his rank and station. In view of these important principles, it is with deep mortification and regret I announce to you that during the excitement growing out of the executions at Havana the office of Her Catholic Majesty's consul at New Orleans was assailed by a mob, his property destroyed, the Spanish flag found in the office carried off and torn in pieces, and he himself induced to flee for his personal safety, which he supposed to be in danger. On receiving intelligence of these events I forthwith directed the attorney of the United States residing at New Orleans to inquire into the facts and the extent of the pecuniary loss sustained by the consul, with the intention of laying them before you, that you might make provision for such indemnity to him as a just regard for the honor of the nation and the respect which is due to a friendly power might, in your judgment, seem to require. The correspondence upon this subject between the Secretary of State and Her Catholic Majesty's minister plenipotentiary is herewith transmitted.

The occurrence at New Orleans has led me to give my attention to the state of our laws in regard to foreign ambassadors, ministers, and consuls. I think the legislation of the country is deficient in not providing sufficiently either for the protection or the punishment of consuls. I therefore recommend the subject to the consideration of Congress.

Your attention is again invited to the question of reciprocal trade between the United States and Canada and other British possessions near our frontier. Overtures for a convention upon this subject have been received from Her Britannic Majesty's minister plenipotentiary, but it seems to be in many respects preferable that the matter should be regulated by reciprocal legislation. Documents are laid before you showing the terms which the British Government is willing to offer and the measures which it may adopt if some arrangement upon this subject shall not be made.

From the accompanying copy of a note from the British legation at Washington and the reply of the Department of State thereto it will appear that Her Britannic Majesty's Government is desirous that a part of the boundary line between Oregon and the British possessions should be authoritatively marked out, and that an intention was expressed to apply to Congress for an appropriation to defray the expense thereof on the part of the United States. Your attention to this subject is accordingly invited and a proper appropriation recommended.

A convention for the adjustment of claims of citizens of the United States against Portugal has been concluded and the ratifications have been exchanged. The first installment of the amount to be paid by Portugal fell due on the 30th of September last and has been paid.

The President of the French Republic, according to the provisions of the convention, has been selected as arbiter in the case of the *General Armstrong*, and has signified that he accepts the trust and the high satisfaction he feels in acting as the common friend of two nations with which France is united by sentiments of sincere and lasting amity.

The Turkish Government has expressed its thanks for the kind reception given to the Sultan's agent, Amin Bey, on the occasion of his recent visit to the United States. On the 28th of February last a dispatch was addressed by the Secretary of State to Mr. Marsh, the American minister at Constantinople, instructing him to ask of the Turkish Government permission for the Hungarians then imprisoned within the dominions of the Sublime Porte to remove to this country. On the 3d of March last both Houses of Congress passed a resolution requesting the President to authorize the employment of a public vessel to convey to this country Louis Kossuth and his associates in captivity.

The instruction above referred to was complied with, and the Turkish Government having released Governor Kossuth and his companions from prison, on the 10th of September last they embarked on board of the United States steam frigate *Mississippi*, which was selected to carry into effect the resolution of Congress. Governor Kossuth left the *Mississippi* at Gibraltar for the purpose of making a visit to England, and may shortly be expected in New York. By communications to the Department of State he has expressed his grateful acknowledgments for the interposition of this Government in behalf of himself and his associates. This country has been justly regarded as a safe asylum for those whom political events have exiled from their own homes in Europe, and it is recommended to Congress to consider in what manner Governor Kossuth and his companions, brought hither by its authority, shall be received and treated.

It is earnestly to be hoped that the differences which have for some time past been pending between the Government of the French Republic and that of the Sandwich Islands may be peaceably and durably adjusted so as to secure the independence of those islands. Long before the events which have of late imparted so much importance to the possessions of the United States on the Pacific we acknowledged the independence of the Hawaiian Government. This Government was first in taking that step, and several of the leading powers of Europe immediately followed. We were influenced in this measure by the existing and prospective importance of the islands as a place of refuge and refreshment for our vessels engaged in the whale fishery, and by the consideration that they lie in the course of the great trade which must at no distant day be carried on between the western coast of North America and eastern Asia.

We were also influenced by a desire that those islands should not pass under the control of any other great maritime state, but should remain in an independent condition, and so be accessible and useful to the commerce of all nations. I need not say that the importance of these considerations has been greatly enhanced by the sudden and vast development which the interests of the United States have attained in California and Oregon, and the policy heretofore adopted in regard to those islands will be steadily pursued.

It is gratifying, not only to those who consider the commercial interests of nations, but also to all who favor the progress of knowledge and the diffusion of religion, to see a community emerge from a savage state and attain such a degree of civilization in those distant seas.

It is much to be deplored that the internal tranquillity of the Mexican Republic should again be seriously disturbed, for since the peace between that Republic and the United States it had enjoyed such comparative repose that the most favorable anticipations for the future might with a degree of confidence have been indulged. These, however, have been thwarted by the recent outbreak in the State of Tamaulipas, on the right bank of the Rio Bravo. Having received information that persons from the United States had taken part in the insurrection, and apprehending that their example might be followed by others, I caused orders to be issued for the purpose of preventing any hostile expeditions against Mexico from being set on foot in violation of the laws of the United States. I likewise issued a proclamation upon the subject, a copy of which is herewith laid before you. This appeared to be rendered imperative by the obligations of treaties and the general duties of good neighborhood.

In my last annual message I informed Congress that citizens of the

United States had undertaken the connection of the two oceans by means of a railroad across the Isthmus of Tehuantepec, under a grant of the Mexican Government to a citizen of that Republic, and that this enterprise would probably be prosecuted with energy whenever Mexico should consent to such stipulations with the Government of the United States as should impart a feeling of security to those who should invest their property in the enterprise.

A convention between the two Governments for the accomplishment of that end has been ratified by this Government, and only awaits the decision of the Congress and the Executive of that Republic.

Some unexpected difficulties and delays have arisen in the ratification of that convention by Mexico, but it is to be presumed that her decision will be governed by just and enlightened views, as well of the general importance of the object as of her own interests and obligations.

In negotiating upon this important subject this Government has had in view one, and only one, object. That object has been, and is, the construction or attainment of a passage from ocean to ocean, the shortest and the best for travelers and merchandise, and equally open to all the world. It has sought to obtain no territorial acquisition, nor any advantages peculiar to itself; and it would see with the greatest regret that Mexico should oppose any obstacle to the accomplishment of an enterprise which promises so much convenience to the whole commercial world and such eminent advantages to Mexico herself. Impressed with these sentiments and these convictions, the Government will continue to exert all proper efforts to bring about the necessary arrangement with the Republic of Mexico for the speedy completion of the work.

For some months past the Republic of Nicaragua has been the theater of one of those civil convulsions from which the cause of free institutions and the general prosperity and social progress of the States of Central America have so often and so severely suffered. Until quiet shall have been restored and a government apparently stable shall have been organized, no advance can prudently be made in disposing of the questions pending between the two countries.

I am happy to announce that an interoceanic communication from the mouth of the St. John to the Pacific has been so far accomplished as that passengers have actually traversed it and merchandise has been transported over it, and when the canal shall have been completed according to the original plan the means of communication will be further improved. It is understood that a considerable part of the railroad across the Isthmus of Panama has been completed, and that the mail and passengers will in future be conveyed thereon.

Whichever of the several routes between the two oceans may ultimately prove most eligible for travelers to and from the different States on the Atlantic and Gulf of Mexico and our coast on the Pacific, there is little reason to doubt that all of them will be useful to the public, and will liberally reward that individual enterprise by which alone they have been or are expected to be carried into effect.

Peace has been concluded between the contending parties in the island of St. Domingo, and, it is hoped, upon a durable basis. Such is the extent of our commercial relations with that island that the United States can not fail to feel a strong interest in its tranquillity.

The office of commissioner to China remains unfilled. Several persons have been appointed, and the place has been offered to others, all of whom have declined its acceptance on the ground of the inadequacy of the compensation. The annual allowance by law is $6,000, and there is no provision for any outfit. I earnestly recommend the consideration of this subject to Congress. Our commerce with China is highly important, and is becoming more and more so in consequence of the increasing intercourse between our ports on the Pacific Coast and eastern Asia. China is understood to be a country in which living is very expensive, and I know of no reason why the American commissioner sent thither should not be placed, in regard to compensation, on an equal footing with ministers who represent this country at the Courts of Europe.

By reference to the report of the Secretary of the Treasury it will be seen that the aggregate receipts for the last fiscal year amounted to $52,312,979.87, which, with the balance in the Treasury on the 1st July, 1850, gave as the available means for the year the sum of $58,917,-524.36.

The total expenditures for the same period were $48,005,878.68. The total imports for the year ending June 30, 1851, were $215,725,995, of which there were in specie $4,967,901. The exports for the same period were $217,517,130, of which there were of domestic products $178,546,555; foreign goods reexported, $9,738,695; specie, $29,231,880.

Since the 1st of December last the payments in cash on account of the public debt, exclusive of interest, have amounted to $7,501,456.56, which, however, includes the sum of $3,242,400, paid under the twelfth article of the treaty with Mexico, and the further sum of $2,591,213.45, being the amount of awards to American citizens under the late treaty with Mexico, for which the issue of stock was authorized, but which was paid in cash from the Treasury.

The public debt on the 20th ultimo, exclusive of the stock authorized to be issued to Texas by the act of 9th September, 1850, was $62,560,-395.26.

The receipts for the next fiscal year are estimated at $51,800,000, which, with the probable unappropriated balance in the Treasury on the 30th June next, will give as the probable available means for that year the sum of $63,258,743.09.

It has been deemed proper, in view of the large expenditures consequent upon the acquisition of territory from Mexico, that the estimates for the next fiscal year should be laid before Congress in such manner as to distinguish the expenditures so required from the otherwise ordinary demands upon the Treasury.

The total expenditures for the next fiscal year are estimated at $42,-892,299.19, of which there is required for the ordinary purposes of the Government, other than those consequent upon the acquisition of our new territories, and deducting the payments on account of the public debt, the sum of $33,343,198.08, and for the purposes connected, directly or indirectly, with those territories and in the fulfillment of the obligations of the Government contracted in consequence of their acquisition the sum of $9,549,101.11.

If the views of the Secretary of the Treasury in reference to the expenditures required for these territories shall be met by corresponding action on the part of Congress, and appropriations made in accordance therewith, there will be an estimated unappropriated balance in the Treasury on the 30th June, 1853, of $20,366,443.90 wherewith to meet that portion of the public debt due on the 1st of July following, amounting to $6,237,931.35, as well as any appropriations which may be made beyond the estimates.

In thus referring to the estimated expenditures on account of our newly acquired territories, I may express the hope that Congress will concur with me in the desire that a liberal course of policy may be pursued toward them, and that every obligation, express or implied, entered into in consequence of their acquisition shall be fulfilled by the most liberal appropriations for that purpose.

The values of our domestic exports for the last fiscal year, as compared with those of the previous year, exhibit an increase of $43,646,322. At first view this condition of our trade with foreign nations would seem to present the most flattering hopes of its future prosperity. An examination of the details of our exports, however, will show that the increased value of our exports for the last fiscal year is to be found in the high price of cotton which prevailed during the first half of that year, which price has since declined about one-half.

The value of our exports of breadstuffs and provisions, which it was supposed the incentive of a low tariff and large importations from abroad would have greatly augmented, has fallen from $68,701,921 in 1847 to $26,051,373 in 1850 and to $21,948,653 in 1851, with a strong probability, amounting almost to a certainty, of a still further reduction in the current year.

The aggregate values of rice exported during the last fiscal year, as compared with the previous year, also exhibit a decrease, amounting to $460,917, which, with a decline in the values of the exports of tobacco for the same period, make an aggregate decrease in these two articles of $1,156,751.

The policy which dictated a low rate of duties on foreign merchandise, it was thought by those who promoted and established it, would tend to benefit the farming population of this country by increasing the demand and raising the price of agricultural products in foreign markets.

The foregoing facts, however, seem to show incontestably that no such result has followed the adoption of this policy. On the contrary, notwithstanding the repeal of the restrictive corn laws in England, the foreign demand for the products of the American farmer has steadily declined, since the short crops and consequent famine in a portion of Europe have been happily replaced by full crops and comparative abundance of food.

It will be seen by recurring to the commercial statistics for the past year that the value of our domestic exports has been increased in the single item of raw cotton by $40,000,000 over the value of that export for the year preceding. This is not due to any increased general demand for that article, but to the short crop of the preceding year, which created an increased demand and an augmented price for the crop of last year. Should the cotton crop now going forward to market be only equal in quantity to that of the year preceding and be sold at the present prices, then there would be a falling off in the value of our exports for the present fiscal year of at least $40,000,000 compared with the amount exported for the year ending 30th June, 1851.

The production of gold in California for the past year seems to promise a large supply of that metal from that quarter for some time to come. This large annual increase of the currency of the world must be attended with its usual results. These have been already partially disclosed in the enhancement of prices and a rising spirit of speculation and adventure, tending to overtrading, as well at home as abroad. Unless some salutary check shall be given to these tendencies it is to be feared that importations of foreign goods beyond a healthy demand in this country will lead to a sudden drain of the precious metals from us, bringing with it, as it has done in former times, the most disastrous consequences to the business and capital of the American people.

The exports of specie to liquidate our foreign debt during the past fiscal year have been $24,263,979 over the amount of specie imported. The exports of specie during the first quarter of the present fiscal year have been $14,651,827. Should specie continue to be exported at this rate for the remaining three quarters of this year, it will drain from our metallic currency during the year ending 30th June, 1852, the enormous amount of $58,607,308.

In the present prosperous condition of the national finances it will become the duty of Congress to consider the best mode of paying off the public debt. If the present and anticipated surplus in the Treasury should not be absorbed by appropriations of an extraordinary character, this surplus should be employed in such way and under such restrictions as Congress may enact in extinguishing the outstanding debt of the nation.

By reference to the act of Congress approved 9th September, 1850, it will be seen that, in consideration of certain concessions by the State of Texas, it is provided that—

The United States shall pay to the State of Texas the sum of $10,000,000 in a stock bearing 5 per cent interest and redeemable at the end of fourteen years, the interest payable half-yearly at the Treasury of the United States.

In the same section of the law it is further provided—

That no more than five millions of said stock shall be issued until the creditors of the State holding bonds and other certificates of stock of Texas, *for which duties on imports were specially* pledged, shall first file at the Treasury of the United States releases of all claims against the United States for or on account of said bonds or certificates, in such form as shall be prescribed by the Secretary of the Treasury and approved by the President of the United States.

The form of release thus provided for has been prescribed by the Secretary of the Treasury and approved. It has been published in all the leading newspapers in the commercial cities of the United States, and all persons holding claims of the kind specified in the foregoing proviso were required to file their releases (in the form thus prescribed) in the Treasury of the United States on or before the 1st day of October, 1851. Although this publication has been continued from the 25th day of March, 1851, yet up to the 1st of October last comparatively few releases had been filed by the creditors of Texas.

The authorities of the State of Texas, at the request of the Secretary of the Treasury, have furnished a schedule of the public debt of that State created prior to her admission into the Union, with a copy of the laws under which each class was contracted.

I have, from the documents furnished by the State of Texas, determined the classes of claims which in my judgment fall within the provisions of the act of Congress of the 9th of September, 1850.

On being officially informed of the acceptance by Texas of the propositions contained in the act referred to I caused the stock to be prepared, and the five millions which are to be issued unconditionally, bearing an interest of 5 per cent from the 1st day of January, 1851, have been for some time ready to be delivered to the State of Texas. The authorities of Texas up to the present time have not authorized anyone to receive this stock, and it remains in the Treasury Department subject to the order of Texas.

The releases required by law to be deposited in the Treasury not having been filed there, the remaining five millions have not been issued. This last amount of the stock will be withheld from Texas until the conditions upon which it is to be delivered shall be complied with by the creditors of that State, unless Congress shall otherwise direct by a modification of the law.

In my last annual message, to which I respectfully refer, I stated briefly the reasons which induced me to recommend a modification of the present tariff by converting the *ad valorem* into a specific duty wherever the article imported was of such a character as to permit it, and that such a discrimination should be made in favor of the industrial pursuits of our own country as to encourage home production without excluding foreign competition.

The numerous frauds which continue to be practiced upon the revenue by false invoices and undervaluations constitute an unanswerable reason for adopting specific instead of *ad valorem* duties in all cases where the nature of the commodity does not forbid it. A striking illustration of these frauds will be exhibited in the report of the Secretary of the Treasury, showing the custom-house valuation of articles imported under a former law, subject to specific duties, when there was no inducement to undervaluation, and the custom-house valuations of the same articles under the present system of *ad valorem* duties, so greatly reduced as to leave no doubt of the existence of the most flagrant abuses under the existing laws. This practical evasion of the present law, combined with the languishing condition of some of the great interests of the country, caused by overimportations and consequent depressed prices, and with the failure in obtaining a foreign market for our increasing surplus of breadstuffs and provisions, has induced me again to recommend a modification of the existing tariff.

The report of the Secretary of the Interior, which accompanies this communication, will present a condensed statement of the operations of that important Department of the Government.

It will be seen that the cash sales of the public lands exceed those of the preceding year, and that there is reason to anticipate a still further increase, notwithstanding the large donations which have been made to many of the States and the liberal grants to individuals as a reward for military services. This fact furnishes very gratifying evidence of the growing wealth and prosperity of our country.

Suitable measures have been adopted for commencing the survey of the public lands in California and Oregon. Surveying parties have been organized and some progress has been made in establishing the principal base and meridian lines. But further legislation and additional appropriations will be necessary before the proper subdivisions can be made and the general land system extended over those remote parts of our territory.

On the 3d of March last an act was passed providing for the appointment of three commissioners to settle private land claims in California. Three persons were immediately appointed, all of whom, however, declined accepting the office in consequence of the inadequacy of the compensation. Others were promptly selected, who for the same reason also declined, and it was not until late in the season that the services of suitable persons could be secured. A majority of the commissioners convened in this city on the 10th of September last, when detailed instructions were given to them in regard to their duties. Their first meeting for the transaction of business will be held in San Francisco on the 8th day of the present month.

I have thought it proper to refer to these facts, not only to explain the causes of the delay in filling the commission, but to call your attention to the propriety of increasing the compensation of the commissioners. The office is one of great labor and responsibility, and the compensation should be such as to command men of a high order of talents and the most unquestionable integrity.

The proper disposal of the mineral lands of California is a subject surrounded by great difficulties. In my last annual message I recommended the survey and sale of them in small parcels under such restrictions as would effectually guard against monopoly and speculation; but upon further information, and in deference to the opinions of persons familiar with the subject, I am inclined to change that recommendation and to advise that they be permitted to remain as at present, a common field, open to the enterprise and industry of all our citizens, until further experience shall have developed the best policy to be ultimately adopted in regard to them. It is safer to suffer the inconveniences that now exist for a short period than by premature legislation to fasten on the country a system founded in error, which may place the whole subject beyond the future control of Congress.

The agricultural lands should, however, be surveyed and brought into market with as little delay as possible, that the titles may become settled and the inhabitants stimulated to make permanent improvements and enter on the ordinary pursuits of life. To effect these objects it is desirable that the necessary provision be made by law for the establishment of land offices in California and Oregon and for the efficient prosecution of the surveys at an early day.

Some difficulties have occurred in organizing the Territorial governments of New Mexico and Utah, and when more accurate information shall be obtained of the causes a further communication will be made on that subject.

In my last annual communication to Congress I recommended the establishment of an agricultural bureau, and I take this occasion again to invoke your favorable consideration of the subject.

Agriculture may justly be regarded as the great interest of our people. Four-fifths of our active population are employed in the cultivation of the soil, and the rapid expansion of our settlements over new territory is daily adding to the number of those engaged in that vocation. Justice and sound policy, therefore, alike require that the Government should use all the means authorized by the Constitution to promote the interests and welfare of that important class of our fellow-citizens. And yet it is a singular fact that whilst the manufacturing and commercial interests have engaged the attention of Congress during a large portion of every session and our statutes abound in provisions for their protection and encouragement, little has yet been done directly for the advancement of agriculture. It is time that this reproach to our legislation should be removed, and I sincerely hope that the present Congress will not close their labors without adopting efficient means to supply the omissions of those who have preceded them.

An agricultural bureau, charged with the duty of collecting and disseminating correct information as to the best modes of cultivation and of the most effectual means of preserving and restoring the fertility of the soil and of procuring and distributing seeds and plants and other vegetable productions, with instructions in regard to the soil, climate, and treatment best adapted to their growth, could not fail to be, in the language of Washington in his last annual message to Congress, a "very cheap instrument of immense national benefit."

Regarding the act of Congress approved 28th September, 1850, granting bounty lands to persons who had been engaged in the military service of the country, as a great measure of national justice and munificence, an anxious desire has been felt by the officers intrusted with its immediate execution to give prompt effect to its provisions. All the means within their control were therefore brought into requisition to expedite the adjudication of claims, and I am gratified to be able to state that near 100,000 applications have been considered and about 70,000 warrants issued within the short space of nine months. If adequate provision be made by law to carry into effect the recommendations of the Department, it is confidently expected that before the close of the next fiscal year all who are entitled to the benefits of the act will have received their warrants.

The Secretary of the Interior has suggested in his report various amendments of the laws relating to pensions and bounty lands for the purpose of more effectually guarding against abuses and frauds on the Government, to all of which I invite your particular attention.

The large accessions to our Indian population consequent upon the acquisition of New Mexico and California and the extension of our settlements into Utah and Oregon have given increased interest and importance to our relations with the aboriginal race.

No material change has taken place within the last year in the condition and prospects of the Indian tribes who reside in the Northwestern Territory and west of the Mississippi River. We are at peace with all of them, and it will be a source of pleasure to you to learn that they are gradually advancing in civilization and the pursuits of social life.

Along the Mexican frontier and in California and Oregon there have been occasional manifestations of unfriendly feeling and some depredations committed. I am satisfied, however, that they resulted more from the destitute and starving condition of the Indians than from any settled hostility toward the whites. As the settlements of our citizens progress toward them, the game, upon which they mainly rely for subsistence, is driven off or destroyed, and the only alternative left to them is starvation or plunder. It becomes us to consider, in view of this condition of things, whether justice and humanity, as well as an enlightened economy, do not require that instead of seeking to punish them for offenses which are the result of our own policy toward them we should not provide for their immediate wants and encourage them to engage in agriculture and to rely on their labor instead of the chase for the means of support.

Various important treaties have been negotiated with different tribes during the year, by which their title to large and valuable tracts of country has been extinguished, all of which will at the proper time be submitted to the Senate for ratification.

The joint commission under the treaty of Guadalupe Hidalgo has been actively engaged in running and marking the boundary line between the United States and Mexico. It was stated in the last annual report of the Secretary of the Interior that the initial point on the Pacific and the point of junction of the Gila with the Colorado River had been determined and the intervening line, about 150 miles in length, run and marked by temporary monuments. Since that time a monument of marble has been erected at the initial point, and permanent landmarks of iron have been placed at suitable distances along the line.

The initial point on the Rio Grande has also been fixed by the commissioners, at latitude 32° 22', and at the date of the last communication the survey of the line had been made thence westward about 150 miles to the neighborhood of the copper mines.

The commission on our part was at first organized on a scale which experience proved to be unwieldy and attended with unnecessary expense. Orders have therefore been issued for the reduction of the number of persons employed within the smallest limits consistent with the safety of those engaged in the service and the prompt and efficient execution of their important duties.

Returns have been received from all the officers engaged in taking the census in the States and Territories except California. The superintendent employed to make the enumeration in that State has not yet made his full report, from causes, as he alleges, beyond his control. This failure is much to be regretted, as it has prevented the Secretary of the Interior from making the decennial apportionment of Representatives among the States, as required by the act approved May 23, 1850. It is hoped, however, that the returns will soon be received, and no time will then be lost in making the necessary apportionment and in transmitting the certificates required by law.

The Superintendent of the Seventh Census is diligently employed, under the direction of the Secretary of the Interior, in classifying and arranging in tabular form all the statistical information derived from the returns of the marshals, and it is believed that when the work shall be completed it will exhibit a more perfect view of the population, wealth, occupations, and social condition of a great country than has ever been presented to the world. The value of such a work as the basis of enlightened legislation can hardly be overestimated, and I earnestly hope that Congress will lose no time in making the appropriations necessary to complete the classifications and to publish the results in a style worthy of the subject and of our national character.

The want of a uniform fee bill, prescribing the compensation to be allowed district attorneys, clerks, marshals, and commissioners in civil and criminal cases, is the cause of much vexation, injustice, and complaint. I would recommend a thorough revision of the laws on the whole subject and the adoption of a tariff of fees which, as far as practicable, should be uniform, and prescribe a specific compensation for every service which the officer may be required to perform. This subject will be fully presented in the report of the Secretary of the Interior.

In my last annual message I gave briefly my reasons for believing that you possessed the constitutional power to improve the harbors of our Great Lakes and seacoast and the navigation of our principal rivers, and recommended that appropriations should be made for completing such works as had already been commenced and for commencing such others as might seem to the wisdom of Congress to be of public and general importance. Without repeating the reasons then urged, I deem it my duty again to call your attention to this important subject. The works on many of the harbors were left in an unfinished state, and consequently exposed to the action of the elements, which is fast destroying them. Great numbers of lives and vast amounts of property are annually lost for want of safe and convenient harbors on the Lakes. None but those who have been exposed to that dangerous navigation can fully appreciate the importance of this subject. The whole Northwest appeals to you for relief, and I trust their appeal will receive due consideration at your hands.

The same is in a measure true in regard to some of the harbors and inlets on the seacoast.

The unobstructed navigation of our large rivers is of equal importance. Our settlements are now extending to the sources of the great rivers which empty into and form a part of the Mississippi, and the value of the public lands in those regions would be greatly enhanced by freeing the navigation of those waters from obstructions. In view, therefore, of this great interest, I deem it my duty again to urge upon Congress to make such appropriations for these improvements as they may deem necessary.

The surveys of the Delta of the Mississippi, with a view to the prevention of the overflows that have proved so disastrous to that region of country, have been nearly completed, and the reports thereof are now in course of preparation and will shortly be laid before you.

The protection of our southwestern frontier and of the adjacent Mexican States against the Indian tribes within our border has claimed my earnest and constant attention. Congress having failed at the last session to adopt my recommendation that an additional regiment of mounted men specially adapted to that service should be raised, all that remained to be done was to make the best use of the means at my disposal. Accordingly, all the troops adapted to that service that could properly be spared from other quarters have been concentrated on that frontier and officers of high reputation selected to command them. A new arrangement of the military posts has also been made, whereby the troops are brought nearer to the Mexican frontier and to the tribes they are intended to overawe.

Sufficient time has not yet elapsed to realize all the benefits that are expected to result from these arrangements, but I have every reason to hope that they will effectually check their marauding expeditions. The nature of the country, which furnishes little for the support of an army and abounds in places of refuge and concealment, is remarkably well adapted to this predatory warfare, and we can scarcely hope that any military force, combined with the greatest vigilance, can entirely suppress it.

By the treaty of Guadalupe Hidalgo we are bound to protect the territory of Mexico against the incursions of the savage tribes within our border "with equal diligence and energy" as if the same were made within our territory or against our citizens. I have endeavored to comply as far as possible with this provision of the treaty. Orders have been given to the officers commanding on that frontier to consider the Mexican territory and its inhabitants as equally with our own entitled to their protection, and to make all their plans and arrangements with a view to the attainment of this object. Instructions have also been given to the Indian commissioners and agents among these tribes in all treaties to make the clauses designed for the protection of our own citizens apply also to those of Mexico. I have no reason to doubt that these instructions have been fully carried into effect; nevertheless, it is probable that in spite of all our efforts some of the neighboring States of Mexico may have suffered, as our own have, from depredations by the Indians.

To the difficulties of defending our own territory, as above mentioned, are superadded, in defending that of Mexico, those that arise from its remoteness, from the fact that we have no right to station our troops within her limits and that there is no efficient military force on the Mexican side to cooperate with our own. So long as this shall continue to be the case the number and activity of our troops will rather increase than diminish the evil, as the Indians will naturally turn toward that country where they encounter the least resistance. Yet these troops are necessary to subdue them and to compel them to make and observe treaties. Until this shall have been done neither country will enjoy any security from their attacks.

The Indians in California, who had previously appeared of a peaceable character and disposed to cultivate the friendship of the whites, have recently committed several acts of hostility. As a large portion of the reenforcements sent to the Mexican frontier were drawn from the Pacific, the military force now stationed there is considered entirely inadequate to its defense. It can not be increased, however, without an increase of the Army, and I again recommend that measure as indispensable to the protection of the frontier.

I invite your attention to the suggestions on this subject and on others connected with his Department in the report of the Secretary of War.

The appropriations for the support of the Army during the current fiscal year ending 30th June next were reduced far below the estimate submitted by the Department. The consequence of this reduction is a considerable deficiency, to which I invite your early attention.

The expenditures of that Department for the year ending 30th June last were $9,060,268.58. The estimates for the year commencing 1st July next and ending June 30, 1853, are $7,898,775.83, showing a reduction of $1,161,492.75.

The board of commissioners to whom the management of the affairs of the military asylum created by the act of 3d March last was intrusted have selected a site for the establishment of an asylum in the vicinity of this city, which has been approved by me subject to the production of a satisfactory title.

The report of the Secretary of the Navy will exhibit the condition of the public service under the supervision of that Department. Our naval force afloat during the present year has been actively and usefully employed in giving protection to our widely extended and increasing commerce and interests in the various quarters of the globe, and our flag has everywhere afforded the security and received the respect inspired by the justice and liberality of our intercourse and the dignity and power of the nation.

The expedition commanded by Lieutenant De Haven, dispatched in search of the British commander Sir John Franklin and his companions in the Arctic Seas, returned to New York in the month of October, after having undergone great peril and suffering from an unknown and dangerous navigation and the rigors of a northern climate, without any satisfactory information of the objects of their search, but with new contributions to science and navigation from the unfrequented polar regions. The officers and men of the expedition having been all volunteers for this service and having so conducted it as to meet the entire approbation of the Government, it is suggested, as an act of grace and generosity, that the same allowance of extra pay and emoluments be extended to them that were made to the officers and men of like rating in the late exploring expedition to the South Seas.

I earnestly recommend to your attention the necessity of reorganizing the naval establishment, apportioning and fixing the number of officers in each grade, providing some mode of promotion to the higher grades of the Navy having reference to merit and capacity rather than seniority or date of entry into the service, and for retiring from the effective list upon reduced pay those who may be incompetent to the performance of active duty. As a measure of economy, as well as of efficiency, in this arm of the service, the provision last mentioned is eminently worthy of your consideration.

The determination of the questions of relative rank between the sea officers and civil officers of the Navy, and between officers of the Army and Navy, in the various grades of each, will also merit your attention. The failure to provide any substitute when corporal punishment was abolished for offenses in the Navy has occasioned the convening of numerous courts-martial upon the arrival of vessels in port, and is believed to have had an injurious effect upon the discipline and efficiency of the service. To moderate punishment from one grade to another is among the humane reforms of the age, but to abolish one of severity, which applied so generally to offenses on shipboard, and provide nothing in its stead is to suppose a progress of improvement in every individual among seamen which is not assumed by the Legislature in respect to any other class of men. It is hoped that Congress, in the ample opportunity afforded by the present session, will thoroughly investigate this important subject, and establish such modes of determining guilt and such gradations of punishment as are consistent with humanity and the personal rights of individuals, and at the same time shall insure the most energetic and efficient performance of duty and the suppression of crime in our ships of war.

The stone dock in the navy-yard at New York, which was ten years in process of construction, has been so far finished as to be surrendered up to the authorities of the yard. The dry dock at Philadelphia is reported as completed, and is expected soon to be tested and delivered over to the agents of the Government. That at Portsmouth, N. H., is also nearly ready for delivery; and a contract has been concluded, agreeably to the act of Congress at its last session, for a floating sectional dock on the Bay of San Francisco. I invite your attention to the recommendation of the Department touching the establishment of a navy-yard in conjunction with this dock on the Pacific. Such a station is highly necessary to the convenience and effectiveness of our fleet in that ocean, which must be expected to increase with the growth of commerce and the rapid extension of our whale fisheries over its waters.

The Naval Academy at Annapolis, under a revised and improved system of regulations, now affords opportunities of education and instruction to the pupils quite equal, it is believed, for professional improvement, to those enjoyed by the cadets in the Military Academy. A large class of acting midshipmen was received at the commencement of the last academic term, and a practice ship has been attached to the institution to afford the amplest means for regular instruction in seamanship, as well as for cruises during the vacations of three or four months in each year.

The advantages of science in nautical affairs have rarely been more strikingly illustrated than in the fact, stated in the report of the Navy Department, that by means of the wind and current charts projected and prepared by Lieutenant Maury, the Superintendent of the Naval Observ-atory, the passage from the Atlantic to the Pacific ports of our country has been shortened by about forty days.

The estimates for the support of the Navy and Marine Corps the ensuing fiscal year will be found to be $5,856,472.19, the estimates for the current year being $5,900,621.

The estimates for special objects under the control of this Department amount to $2,684,220.89, against $2,210,980 for the present year, the increase being occasioned by the additional mail service on the Pacific Coast and the construction of the dock in California, authorized at the last session of Congress, and some slight additions under the head of improvements and repairs in navy-yards, buildings, and machinery.

I deem it of much importance to a just economy and a correct understanding of naval expenditures that there should be an entire separation of the appropriations for the support of the naval service proper from those for permanent improvements at navy-yards and stations and from ocean steam mail service and other special objects assigned to the supervision of this Department.

The report of the Postmaster-General, herewith communicated, presents an interesting view of the progress, operations, and condition of his Department.

At the close of the last fiscal year the length of mail routes within the United States was 196,290 miles, the annual transportation thereon 53,-272,252 miles, and the annual cost of such transportation $3,421,754.

The length of the foreign mail routes is estimated at 18,349 miles and the annual transportation thereon at 615,206 miles. The annual cost of this service is $1,472,187, of which $448,937 are paid by the Post-Office Department and $1,023,250 are paid through the Navy Department.

The annual transportation within the United States, excluding the service in California and Oregon, which is now for the first time reported and embraced in the tabular statements of the Department, exceeds that of the preceding year 6,162,855 miles, at an increased cost of $547,110.

The whole number of post-offices in the United States on the 30th day of June last was 19,796. There were 1,698 post-offices established and 256 discontinued during the year.

The gross revenues of the Department for the fiscal year, including the appropriations for the franked matter of Congress, of the Departments, and officers of Government, and excluding the foreign postages collected for and payable to the British post-office, amounted to $6,727,-866.78.

The expenditures for the same period, excluding $20,599.49, paid under an award of the Auditor, in pursuance of a resolution of the last Congress, for mail service on the Ohio and Mississippi rivers in 1832 and 1833, and the amount paid to the British post-office for foreign postages collected for and payable to that office, amounted to $6,024,566.79, leaving a balance of revenue over the proper expenditures of the year of $703,299.99.

The receipts for postages during the year, excluding the foreign postages collected for and payable to the British post-office, amounted to $6,345,747.21, being an increase of $997,610.79, or 18.65 per cent, over the like receipts for the preceding year.

The reduction of postage under the act of March last did not take effect until the commencement of the present fiscal year. The accounts for the first quarter under the operation of the reduced rates will not be settled before January next, and no reliable estimate of the receipts for the present year can yet be made. It is believed, however, that they will fall far short of those of the last year. The surplus of the revenues now on hand is, however, so large that no further appropriation from the Treasury in aid of the revenues of the Department is required for the current fiscal year, but an additional appropriation for the year ending June 30, 1853, will probably be found necessary when the receipts of the first two quarters of the fiscal year are fully ascertained.

In his last annual report the Postmaster-General recommended a reduction of postage to rates which he deemed as low as could be prudently adopted unless Congress was prepared to appropriate from the Treasury for the support of the Department a sum more than equivalent to the mail services performed by it for the Government. The recommendations of the Postmaster-General in respect to letter postage, except on letters from and to California and Oregon, were substantially adopted by the last Congress. He now recommends adherence to the present letter rates and advises against a further reduction until justified by the revenue of the Department.

He also recommends that the rates of postage on printed matter be so revised as to render them more simple and more uniform in their operation upon all classes of printed matter. I submit the recommendations of the report to your favorable consideration.

The public statutes of the United States have now been accumulating for more than sixty years, and, interspersed with private acts, are scattered through numerous volumes, and, from the cost of the whole, have become almost inaccessible to the great mass of the community. They also exhibit much of the incongruity and imperfection of hasty legislation. As it seems to be generally conceded that there is no "common law" of the United States to supply the defects of their legislation, it is most important that that legislation should be as perfect as possible, defining every power intended to be conferred, every crime intended to be made punishable, and prescribing the punishment to be inflicted. In addition to some particular cases spoken of more at length, the whole criminal code is now lamentably defective. Some offenses are imperfectly described and others are entirely omitted, so that flagrant crimes may be committed with impunity. The scale of punishment is not in all cases graduated according to the degree and nature of the offense, and is often rendered more unequal by the different modes of imprisonment or penitentiary confinement in the different States.

Many laws of a permanent character have been introduced into appropriation bills, and it is often difficult to determine whether the particular clause expires with the temporary act of which it is a part or continues in force. It has also frequently happened that enactments and provisions of law have been introduced into bills with the title or general subject of which they have little or no connection or relation. In this mode of legislation so many enactments have been heaped upon each other, and often with but little consideration, that in many instances it is difficult to search out and determine what is the law.

The Government of the United States is emphatically a government of written laws. The statutes should therefore, as far as practicable, not only be made accessible to all, but be expressed in language so plain and simple as to be understood by all and arranged in such method as to give perspicuity to every subject. Many of the States have revised their public acts with great and manifest benefit, and I recommend that provision be made by law for the appointment of a commission to revise the public statutes of the United States, arranging them in order, supplying deficiencies, correcting incongruities, simplifying their language, and reporting them to Congress for its action.

An act of Congress approved 30th September, 1850, contained a provision for the extension of the Capitol according to such plan as might be approved by the President, and appropriated $100,000 to be expended under his direction by such architect as he should appoint to execute the same. On examining the various plans which had been submitted by different architects in pursuance of an advertisement by a committee of the Senate no one was found to be entirely satisfactory, and it was therefore deemed advisable to combine and adopt the advantages of several.

The great object to be accomplished was to make such an addition as would afford ample and convenient halls for the deliberations of the two Houses of Congress, with sufficient accommodations for spectators and suitable apartments for the committees and officers of the two branches of the Legislature. It was also desirable not to mar the harmony and beauty of the present structure, which, as a specimen of architecture, is so universally admired. Keeping these objects in view, I concluded to make the addition by wings, detached from the present building, yet connected with it by corridors. This mode of enlargement will leave the present Capitol uninjured and afford great advantages for ventilation and the admission of light, and will enable the work to progress without interrupting the deliberations of Congress. To carry this plan into effect I have appointed an experienced and competent architect. The corner stone was laid on the 4th day of July last with suitable ceremonies, since which time the work has advanced with commendable rapidity, and the foundations of both wings are now nearly complete.

I again commend to your favorable regard the interests of the District of Columbia, and deem it only necessary to remind you that although its inhabitants have no voice in the choice of Representatives in Congress, they are not the less entitled to a just and liberal consideration in your legislation. My opinions on this subject were more fully expressed in my last annual communication.

Other subjects were brought to the attention of Congress in my last annual message, to which I would respectfully refer. But there was one of more than ordinary interest, to which I again invite your special attention. I allude to the recommendation for the appointment of a commission to settle private claims against the United States. Justice to individuals, as well as to the Government, imperatively demands that some more convenient and expeditious mode than an appeal to Congress should be adopted.

It is deeply to be regretted that in several instances officers of the Government, in attempting to execute the law for the return of fugitives from labor, have been openly resisted and their efforts frustrated and defeated by lawless and violent mobs; that in one case such resistance resulted in the death of an estimable citizen, and in others serious injury ensued to those officers and to individuals who were using their endeavors to sustain the laws. Prosecutions have been instituted against the alleged offenders so far as they could be identified, and are still pending. I have regarded it as my duty in these cases to give all aid legally in my power to the enforcement of the laws, and I shall continue to do so wherever and whenever their execution may be resisted.

The act of Congress for the return of fugitives from labor is one required and demanded by the express words of the Constitution.

The Constitution declares that—

No person held to service or labor in one State, under the laws thereof, escaping into another, shall, in consequence of any law or regulation therein, be discharged from such service or labor, but shall be delivered up on claim of the party to whom such service or labor may be due.

This constitutional provision is equally obligatory upon the legislative, the executive, and judicial departments of the Government, and upon every citizen of the United States.

Congress, however, must from necessity first act upon the subject by prescribing the proceedings necessary to ascertain that the person is a fugitive and the means to be used for his restoration to the claimant. This was done by an act passed during the first term of President Washington, which was amended by that enacted by the last Congress, and it now remains for the executive and judicial departments to take care that these laws be faithfully executed. This injunction of the Constitution is as peremptory and as binding as any other; it stands exactly on the same foundation as that clause which provides for the return of fugitives from justice, or that which declares that no bill of attainder or *ex post facto* law shall be passed, or that which provides for an equality of taxation according to the census, or the clause declaring that all duties shall be uniform throughout the United States, or the important provision that the trial of all crimes shall be by jury. These several articles and clauses of the Constitution, all resting on the same authority, must stand or fall together. Some objections have been urged against the details of the act for the return of fugitives from labor, but it is worthy of remark that the main opposition is aimed against the Constitution itself, and proceeds from persons and classes of persons many of whom declare their wish to see that Constitution overturned. They avow their hostility to any law which shall give full and practical effect to this requirement of the Constitution. Fortunately, the number of these persons is comparatively small, and is believed to be daily diminishing; but the issue which they present is one which involves the supremacy and even the existence of the Constitution.

Cases have heretofore arisen in which individuals have denied the binding authority of acts of Congress, and even States have proposed to nullify such acts upon the ground that the Constitution was the supreme law of the land, and that those acts of Congress were repugnant to that instrument; but nullification is now aimed not so much against particular laws as being inconsistent with the Constitution as against the Constitution itself, and it is not to be disguised that a spirit exists, and has been actively at work, to rend asunder this Union, which is our cherished inheritance from our Revolutionary fathers.

In my last annual message I stated that I considered the series of measures which had been adopted at the previous session in reference to the agitation growing out of the Territorial and slavery questions as a final settlement in principle and substance of the dangerous and exciting subjects which they embraced, and I recommended adherence to the adjustment established by those measures until time and experience should demonstrate the necessity of further legislation to guard against evasion or abuse. I was not induced to make this recommendation because I thought those measures perfect, for no human legislation can be perfect. Wide differences and jarring opinions can only be reconciled by yielding something on all sides, and this result had been reached after an angry conflict of many months, in which one part of the country was arrayed against another, and violent convulsion seemed to be imminent. Looking at the interests of the whole country, I felt it to be my duty to seize upon this compromise as the best that could be obtained amid conflicting interests and to insist upon it as a final settlement, to be adhered to by all who value the peace and welfare of the country. A year has now elapsed since that recommendation was made. To that recommendation I still adhere, and I congratulate you and the country upon the general acquiescence in these measures of peace which has been exhibited in all parts of the Republic. And not only is there this general acquiescence in these measures, but the spirit of conciliation which has been manifested in regard to them in all parts of the country has removed doubts and uncertainties in the minds of thousands of good men concerning the durability of our popular institutions and given renewed assurance that our liberty and our Union may subsist together for the benefit of this and all succeeding generations.

MILLARD FILLMORE.

SPECIAL MESSAGES.

WASHINGTON, December 12, 1851.

To the Senate of the United States:

I transmit to the Senate, for its consideration with a view to ratification, a treaty of friendship, commerce, and navigation between the United States and the Republic of Costa Rica, signed in this city on the 10th day of July last.

MILLARD FILLMORE.

WASHINGTON, December 15, 1851.

To the Senate of the United States:

I transmit to the Senate a report* of the Secretary of State, in answer to their resolution of the 8th of March last.

MILLARD FILLMORE.

WASHINGTON, December 15, 1851.

To the Senate of the United States:

I have received a resolution of the Senate, adopted on the 12th instant, in the following terms:

Resolved, That the President of the United States be requested to communicate to the Senate, if not inconsistent with the public interest, any information the Executive may have received respecting the firing into and seizure of the American steamship *Prometheus* by a British vessel of war in November last near Greytown, on the Mosquito Coast, and also what measures have been taken by the Executive to ascertain the state of the facts and to vindicate the honor of the country.

*Relating to the free navigation of the St. Lawrence, St. John, and other large rivers, and to the free enjoyment of the British North American fisheries by United States citizens.

In answer to this request I submit to the Senate the accompanying extracts from a communication addressed to the Department of State by Mr. Joseph L. White, as counsel of the American, Atlantic and Pacific Ship Canal Company, dated 2d instant.

This communication is the principal source of the information received by the Executive in relation to the subject alluded to, and is presumed to be essentially correct in its statement of the facts. Upon receiving this communication instructions such as the occasion seemed to demand were immediately dispatched to the minister of the United States in London. Sufficient time has not elapsed for the return of any answer to this dispatch from him, and in my judgment it would at the present moment be inconsistent with the public interest to communicate those instructions. A communication, however, of all the correspondence will be made to the Senate at the earliest moment at which a proper regard to the public interest will permit.

At the same time instructions were given to Commodore Parker, commanding the Home Squadron, a copy of which, so far as they relate to the case of the *Prometheus*, is herewith transmitted to the Senate.

MILLARD FILLMORE.

WASHINGTON, *December 16, 1851.*

To the Senate of the United States:

In answer to the resolution of the Senate of the 9th instant, requesting information in regard to the imprisonment of John S. Thrasher at Havana, I transmit a report from the Secretary of State and the documents which accompanied it.

MILLARD FILLMORE.

WASHINGTON, *December 16, 1851.*

To the Senate of the United States:

In answer to the resolution of the Senate of the 8th instant, requesting the communication of a dispatch* addressed to the Department of State by Mr. Niles, late chargé d'affaires of the United States at Turin, I transmit a report from the Secretary of State, which is accompanied by a copy of the dispatch.

MILLARD FILLMORE.

WASHINGTON, *December 23, 1851.*

To the House of Representatives:

I transmit to the House of Representatives a report from the Secretary of State, in answer to the first part† of a resolution of the 15th Decem-

---

* On the subject of a ship canal between the Atlantic and Pacific oceans.

† Relating to the conclusion of a treaty between Spain, France, and Great Britain in respect to the island of Cuba.

ber, 1851, and also a report from the Secretary of the Navy, in answer to the remaining part* of the same resolution.

MILLARD FILLMORE.

WASHINGTON, *December 23, 1851.*

To the House of Representatives:

In answer to a resolution of the House of Representatives of the 15th instant, requesting information in regard to the imprisonment, trial, and sentence of John S. Thrasher in the island of Cuba, I transmit a report from the Secretary of State and the documents which accompanied it.

MILLARD FILLMORE.

WASHINGTON, *December 29, 1851.*

To the Senate and House of Representatives:

I transmit herewith a copy of a letter of the 26th instant, addressed to the Secretary of State by the contractors for paying the next install-ment due to Mexico pursuant to the treaty of Guadalupe Hidalgo, repre-senting the necessity of an immediate appropriation by Congress of the money necessary for that purpose. MILLARD FILLMORE.

WASHINGTON, *January 2, 1852.*

To the House of Representatives:

As a further answer to the resolution of the House of Representatives of the 15th ultimo, calling for information respecting the imprisonment, trial, and sentence of John S. Thrasher in the island of Cuba, I transmit another report from the Secretary of State.

MILLARD FILLMORE.

WASHINGTON, *January 2, 1852.*

To the House of Representatives of the United States:

I transmit to the House of Representatives a copy of the resolution adopted by the Legislative Council of Canada, together with the copy of the note by which the resolution was communicated to this Government, expressing the satisfaction of that Council at receiving intelligence of certain donations in aid of the reconstruction of the library of the Cana-dian Parliament. MILLARD FILLMORE.

[The same message, dated January 6, 1852, was sent to the Senate.]

*Pertaining to the relative strength of the British, French, and United States squadrons in the West India seas, and whether additional appropriations are necessary to increase the United States force on that station.

WASHINGTON, *January 3, 1852.*

To the Senate of the United States:

I nominate Elisha Whittlesey and Elias S. Terry to be commissioners under the seventeenth article of the treaty concluded with the Cherokee tribe of Indians at New Echota on the 29th day of December, 1835, to adjudicate the claim of David Taylor for 640 acres of land, which has been duly appraised in accordance with the terms of the ninth article of said treaty, but not paid for. The facts of the case will more fully appear in the accompanying papers from the Department of the Interior.

MILLARD FILLMORE.

WASHINGTON, *January 5, 1852.*

To the House of Representatives:

I transmit to the House of Representatives a report of the Secretary of State, relative to the persons belonging to the expedition of Lopez who were taken prisoners in Cuba and afterwards sent to Spain, and who have now been pardoned and released by Her Catholic Majesty. The appropriation the expediency of which is suggested in the report I cordially commend to the consideration of Congress, with the single additional suggestion that to be available it should be promptly made.

MILLARD FILLMORE.

[The same message was sent to the Senate.]

WASHINGTON, *January 9, 1852.*

To the House of Representatives:

In answer to a resolution of the House of Representatives of the 15th ultimo, requesting information in regard to the Territory of Utah, I transmit a report from the Secretary of State, to whom the resolution was referred.

MILLARD FILLMORE.

WASHINGTON, *January 12, 1852.*

To the House of Representatives:

In answer to the resolution of the House of Representatives of the 5th instant, I herewith transmit to it a report and accompanying papers* from the Secretary of State.

MILLARD FILLMORE.

WASHINGTON, *January 16, 1852.*

To the House of Representatives:

I transmit a copy of a letter which has been addressed to me by the secretary of the Territory of Utah since my recent message to the House

---

*Relating to a circular issued by the secretary of state for the British colonial department relative to the employment in the British West India colonies of free blacks and liberated slaves from the United States.

of Representatives in answer to its resolution requesting information in regard to the affairs of that Territory.

MILLARD FILLMORE.

WASHINGTON, *January 19, 1852.*

To the Senate and House of Representatives of the United States:

I transmit to Congress a report from the Secretary of State, accompanied by a letter to him from the contractors for paying the installment of Mexican indemnity due on the 31st May next, and respectfully invite attention to the subject.

MILLARD FILLMORE.

WASHINGTON, *January 20, 1852.*

To the Senate and House of Representatives of the United States:

I communicate to both Houses of Congress a report from the Department of State, containing copies of the correspondence which has taken place between that Department and the minister of the United States in Paris respecting the political occurrences which have recently taken place in France.

MILLARD FILLMORE.

WASHINGTON, *January 22, 1852.*

To the Senate of the United States:

In compliance with a resolution of the Senate passed March 13, 1851, I herewith transmit a report of the Secretary of War, containing information in regard to the claims of citizens of California for services rendered and for money and for property furnished in 1846 and 1847 in the conquest of that country.

MILLARD FILLMORE.

WASHINGTON, *January 23, 1852.*

To the House of Representatives:

I transmit a report from the Secretary of State and the documents which accompanied it, upon the subject of a resolution of the House of Representatives of yesterday, relative to the Mexican indemnity.

MILLARD FILLMORE.

WASHINGTON, *January 28, 1852.*

To the House of Representatives:

In answer to the resolution of the House of Representatives of the 15th ultimo, requesting information respecting the seizure and confiscation of the bark *Georgiana*, of Maine, and brig *Susan Loud*, of Massachusetts,* I transmit a report from the Secretary of State and the documents which accompanied it.

MILLARD FILLMORE.

_____
* By the Spanish or Cuban authorities.

WASHINGTON, *January 28, 1852.*

To the House of Representatives:

In answer to the resolution of the House of Representatives of the 7th August, 1850, and the 17th December, 1851, requesting information touching the claims of citizens of the United States on the Government of Portugal, I transmit a report from the Secretary of State and the documents which accompanied the same.

MILLARD FILLMORE.

WASHINGTON, *February 9, 1852.*

To the Senate of the United States:

I transmit to the Senate, for its consideration with a view to ratification, a treaty of friendship, commerce, and navigation between the United States and the Republic of Peru, concluded and signed at Lima on the 26th day of July last.

A copy of a dispatch of Mr. J. R. Clay, the chargé d'affaires of the United States at Lima, to the Secretary of State, bearing date the 6th December last, is also transmitted for the information of the Senate.

MILLARD FILLMORE.

WASHINGTON, *February 10, 1852.*

To the Senate and House of Representatives:

I transmit to Congress a copy of the instruction dispatched from the Department of State to the minister of the United States at London respecting the attack on the United States steamer *Prometheus* in the harbor of San Juan de Nicaragua by the British brig of war *Express*, and also a copy of the dispatches of Mr. Lawrence to that Department and of his correspondence with Her Britannic Majesty's principal secretary of state for foreign affairs on the same subject.

MILLARD FILLMORE.

EXECUTIVE CHAMBER,
Washington City, February 10, 1852.

To the Senate and House of Representatives of the United States:

I transmit herewith a report from the Secretary of the Interior, containing a report from Thomas U. Walter, architect for the extension of the Capitol.

MILLARD FILLMORE.

WASHINGTON, *February 12, 1852.*

To the House of Representatives:

In answer to the resolution of the House of Representatives of the 26th of December last, requesting information in regard to the seizure of the brig *Arve** at Jeremie, in the island of St. Domingo, I transmit a report from the Secretary of State and the documents by which it was accompanied.

MILLARD FILLMORE.

WASHINGTON, *February 12, 1852.*
To the Senate of the United States:

In compliance with the resolution of the Senate of the 26th ultimo, requesting information upon the subject of the mission of Mr. Balistier, late consul at Singapore, to eastern Asia, I transmit a report from the Secretary of State and the documents which accompanied it.

MILLARD FILLMORE.

WASHINGTON, *February 13, 1852.*
To the Senate of the United States:

I transmit herewith, for the constitutional action of the Senate, treaties recently concluded with certain Indian tribes at Traverse des Sioux, Mendota, Pembina, and Fort Laramie, together with communications from the Department of the Interior and other documents connected therewith.

MILLARD FILLMORE.

WASHINGTON, *February 14, 1852.*
To the House of Representatives:

I communicate to the House of Representatives herewith a report to me, dated the 13th instant, from the Secretary of the Interior, respecting the delay and difficulty in making the apportionment among the several States of the Representatives in the Thirty-third Congress, as required by the act of 23d May, 1850, in consequence of the want of full returns of the population of the State of California, and suggesting the necessity for remedial legislation.

The subject is one of much importance, and I earnestly commend it to the early consideration of Congress.

MILLARD FILLMORE.

[The same message was sent to the Senate.]

WASHINGTON, *February 16, 1852.*
To the Senate and House of Representatives of the United States:

I transmit to Congress a letter addressed to the Secretary of State by the commissioner of the United States under the convention with Brazil, setting forth the obstacles which have impeded the conclusion of the business of that commission.

MILLARD FILLMORE.

* By Haytien authorities.

WASHINGTON, *February 16, 1852*

To the Senate of the United States:

I herewith communicate to the Senate, for its consideration with a view to ratification, a treaty of commerce and navigation concluded by the minister resident of the United States at Constantinople with the chargé d'affaires of the Shah of Persia at the same place. The treaty is in the Persian and French languages, but is accompanied by an English translation. A copy of the correspondence between the Department of State and the legation of the United States at Constantinople on the subject is also herewith communicated.   MILLARD FILLMORE.

WASHINGTON, *February 18, 1852.*

To the House of Representatives:

In answer to the resolution of the House of Representatives requesting the official correspondence respecting an alleged misunderstanding between Captain Long, of the Navy of the United States, and Louis Kossuth, I transmit reports from the Secretaries of State and of the Navy and the papers which accompanied them.

MILLARD FILLMORE.

WASHINGTON, *March 1, 1852.*

To the Senate and House of Representatives of the United States:

In compliance with the provisions of the act of Congress of the 11th August, 1848, I transmit to that body the copy of a dispatch from the commissioner *ad interim* of the United States at Canton, together with the copy of certain rules and regulations for masters, officers, and seamen of vessels of the United States of America at the free ports of China, which accompanied said dispatch, and which are submitted for the revision of Congress.   MILLARD FILLMORE.

WASHINGTON, *March 4, 1852.*

To the House of Representatives of the United States:

In compliance with the resolution of the House of Representatives of the 17th ultimo, I transmit herewith a report from the Secretary of the Navy and a report from the Solicitor of the Treasury Department in relation to the accounts of Prosper M. Wetmore, late navy agent in the city of New York.   MILLARD FILLMORE.

WASHINGTON, *March 4, 1852.*

To the Senate and House of Representatives of the United States:

I transmit to Congress a letter addressed to me by the governor of the Territory of Minnesota, with the statements to which it refers, of the disbursements up to the 1st of January last of the money appropriated by the act approved June 11, 1850, for the erection of public buildings in that Territory.

MILLARD FILLMORE.

WASHINGTON, *March 4, 1852.*

To the Senate and House of Representatives of the United States:

I transmit to Congress a dispatch addressed to the Secretary of State by the minister of the United States at Mexico, and the papers therein referred to, relative to the cemetery which has been constructed in the neighborhood of that city as a place of sepulture for the remains of the officers and soldiers of the United States who died or were killed in that vicinity during the late war, and for such citizens of the United States as may hereafter die there. A copy of the report of the agent who was sent for the purpose of superintending the work is also herewith transmitted. It will be seen that a sum of $2,500 or $3,000, in addition to the amount appropriated by the act of Congress approved September 28, 1850, is represented to be necessary to carry the objects of that appropriation into full effect. I accordingly recommend that provision therefor may be made.

MILLARD FILLMORE.

WASHINGTON, *March 25, 1852.*

To the House of Representatives:

As a further answer to the resolution of the House of Representatives of the 5th of January last, requesting information in regard to a circular of Her Britannic Majesty's secretary of state for colonial affairs in respect to the encouragement of the emigration of colored laborers from the United States to the British West India islands, I transmit another dispatch addressed to the Department of State by the minister of the United States at London.

MILLARD FILLMORE.

WASHINGTON, *March 26, 1852.*

To the Senate and House of Representatives of the United States:

At the close of the commission to adjudicate upon the claims of citizens of the United States under the treaty of Guadalupe Hidalgo I directed a list to be made of papers which had been presented to that commission, and, pursuant to the act of Congress approved 3d March, 1849, the papers themselves to be carefully arranged and deposited for safe-keeping in the Department of State. I deemed all this necessary as well for the interest of the claimants as to secure the Government against fraudulent claims which might be preferred hereafter. A few days since I was surprised to learn that some of these papers had been fraudulently abstracted by one of the claimants, and upon the case being made known to me by the Secretary of State I referred it to the Attorney-General for the purpose of ascertaining what punishment could be inflicted upon the person who had been guilty of this offense.

I now communicate to you his opinion and that of the attorney of the United States for this District, by which you will perceive that it is doubtful whether there be any law for punishing the very grave offense of fraudulently abstracting or mutilating the papers and public documents in the several Departments of this Government. It appears to me that the protection of the public records and papers requires that such acts should be made penal and a suitable punishment inflicted upon the offender, and I therefore bring the subject to your consideration, to enable you to act upon it should you concur with me in this opinion.

MILLARD FILLMORE.

WASHINGTON, *March 26, 1852.*

To the House of Representatives:

In compliance with the resolution of the House of Representatives of the 18th instant, I transmit a copy of the correspondence with John P. Gaines, governor of the Territory of Oregon, relative to the seat of government of said Territory.

MILLARD FILLMORE.

WASHINGTON, *March 29, 1852.*

To the Senate of the United States:

In compliance with the resolution of the Senate of the 24th instant, relating to the extension of the Capitol, I have the honor to submit herewith a report from the Secretary of the Interior, which furnishes, it is believed, the required information.

MILLARD FILLMORE.

WASHINGTON CITY, *March 29, 1852.*

To the Senate of the United States:

I have the resolution of your honorable body adopted in executive session March 24, 1852, by which I am requested to return to the Senate the resolution advising and consenting to the appointment of George C. Laurason as collector of the customs for the district of New Orleans, provided a commission had not been issued to him, and in reply thereto I would respectfully state that prior to the receipt of said resolution I had signed the commission to Mr. Laurason and transmitted it to the Secretary of the Treasury, to whom your resolution was immediately referred; and I have the honor now to transmit his reply, by which it will be seen that the commission, after having been duly executed, was sent to the First Comptroller, where it still remains. I suppose, according to the doctrine laid down in the case of Marbury *v.* Madison (1 Cranch R., 137), the appointment must be deemed complete, and nothing short of the removal of Mr. Laurason can enable me again to submit his nomination to the consideration of the Senate; but as the commission has not been technically issued to Mr. Laurason, I deem it most respectful to comply with your request by returning the copy of the resolution which notified me that the Senate advised and consented to his appointment.

MILLARD FILLMORE.

WASHINGTON CITY, *April 6, 1852.*

To the House of Representatives:

In compliance with the resolution of the House of the 31st ultimo, I have the honor herewith to transmit a report from the Secretary of War, accompanied by the original manuscript report of Captain Thomas J. Crane, dated February 3, 1844, on the best mode of improving the navigation of the Ohio River at the Falls of Louisville, together with the original maps accompanying the same.

MILLARD FILLMORE.

WASHINGTON, *April 8, 1852.*

To the Senate of the United States:

I herewith transmit to the Senate, in reply to their resolution of the 4th ultimo, a report from the Secretary of State, with accompanying papers.*

MILLARD FILLMORE.*

WASHINGTON, *April 19, 1852.*

To the Senate and House of Representatives of the United States:

I invite the attention of Congress to the state of affairs in the Territory of Oregon, growing out of a conflict of opinion among the authorities of that Territory in regard to a proper construction of the acts of Congress approved the 14th August, 1848, and 11th June, 1850, the former entitled "An act to establish a Territorial government of Oregon," and the latter entitled "An act to make further appropriations for public buildings in the Territories of Minnesota and Oregon." In order to enable Congress to understand the controversy and apply such remedy with a view to adjust it as may be deemed expedient, I transmit—

1. An act of the legislative assembly of that Territory, passed February 1, 1851, entitled "An act to provide for the selection of places for the location and erection of public buildings of the Territory of Oregon."

2. Governor Gaines's message to the legislative assembly of the 3d February, 1851.

3. The opinion of the Attorney-General of the United States of 23d

*Relating to the relations between the United States and Japan.

April, in regard to the act of the legislative assembly of the 1st February, 1851.

4. The opinion of the supreme court of Oregon, pronounced on the 9th December, 1851.

5. A letter of Judge Pratt of the 15th December, 1851, dissenting from that opinion.

6. Governor Gaines's letter to the President of the 1st January, 1852.

7. Report of the Attorney-General of the United States on that letter, dated 22d March, 1852.

If it should be the sense of Congress that the seat of government of Oregon has not already been established by the local authorities pursuant to the law of the United States for the organization of that Territory, or, if so established, should be deemed objectionable, in order to appease the strife upon the subject which seems to have arisen in that Territory I recommend that the seat of government be either permanently or temporarily ordained by act of Congress, and that that body should in the same manner express its approval or disapproval of such laws as may have been enacted in the Territory at the place alleged to be its seat of government, and which may be so enacted until intelligence of the decision of Congress shall reach there.

MILLARD FILLMORE.

WASHINGTON, *May 1, 1852.*

To the Senate of the United States:

I transmit to the Senate, for their consideration and advice with regard to its ratification, a convention between the United States and the Free and Hanseatic Republics of Hamburg, Bremen, and Lubeck, signed in this city by their respective plenipotentiaries on the 30th day of April, A. D. 1852, for the mutual extension of the jurisdiction of consuls. A copy of a note from the special plenipotentiary of Hamburg, Bremen, and Lubeck accompanies the convention.

MILLARD FILLMORE.

WASHINGTON, *May 5, 1852.*

To the Senate of the United States:

On the 3d of March, 1849, a general convention of peace, amity, commerce, and navigation between the United States and the Republic of Guatemala, by Elijah Hise, the chargé d'affaires of the United States to that Republic, on the part of this Government, and by Señor Don Jose Mariano Rodriguez, minister for foreign affairs, on the part of the Government of Guatemala. This convention was approved by the Senate on the 24th of September, 1850, and by a resolution of the 27th of that month that body authorized the ratification of this Government to be exchanged for the ratification of the Government of Guatemala at any time prior to the 1st of April, 1851. I accordingly ratified the convention on the 14th of November, 1850, but there was then no person in this country authorized to effect the exchange of ratifications on the part of the Guatemalan Government, and the United States had no diplomatic representative there. When, however, in the summer of 1851, Mr. J. Bozman Kerr proceeded to Nicaragua as the chargé d'affaires of the United States, he was empowered and instructed, when he should have concluded the business, which it was presumed would not have detained him long, in Nicaragua, to repair to Guatemala and effect the exchange on the part of this Government. Circumstances, however, have hitherto prevented him from accomplishing this object. Meanwhile Señor Don Felipe Molina has been received as chargé d'affaires of Guatemala here, and has been empowered to effect the exchange on the part of that Government.

I accordingly recommend that the Senate authorize a further extension of the period for exchanging the ratifications, in order that the convention may go into operation. It is presumed that if this recommendation should be adopted a few weeks from the date of the decision of the Senate upon the subject would be necessary to complete the preparations for carrying it into effect.   MILLARD FILLMORE.

WASHINGTON, *May 29, 1852.*

To the Senate of the United States:

The resolution of the Senate of the 6th instant, requesting the "papers and proofs on file in any of the Executive Departments touching the claim of Samuel A. Belden & Co., of Brownsville, Tex., against the Mexican Government for injuries inflicted upon said Belden & Co., as alleged by them in violation of the treaty of Guadalupe Hidalgo," was referred to the heads of those Departments, and the documents herewith transmitted have been reported to me from the Department of State as comprising all on the files of that Department called for by the resolution, with the exception of those of a diplomatic character. As the claim referred to is a subject of negotiation with the Mexican Government, it is not deemed expedient at this juncture to make public the documents which have been reserved. According to the reports of the Secretary of the Treasury, of the Secretary of the Interior, of the Secretary of War, of the Secretary of the Navy, and of the Postmaster-General, there are no papers in their respective Departments relative to the claim of Messrs. Belden & Co.

MILLARD FILLMORE.

WASHINGTON, *June 1, 1852.*

To the Senate of the United States:

I communicate to the Senate herewith, for its constitutional action thereon, eighteen treaties negotiated with Indian tribes in California, as described in the accompanying letter of the Secretary of the Interior, dated the 22d ultimo, with a copy of the report of the superintendent of Indian affairs for the State of California and other correspondence in relation thereto.

MILLARD FILLMORE.

WASHINGTON, *June 11, 1852.*

To the Senate of the United States:

I transmit to the Senate, for its consideration with a view to ratification, a convention between the United States and the Sultan of Borneo, signed at Bruni on the 23d of June, 1850. A copy of two dispatches to this department from Mr. Balestier, who concluded the convention on the part of this Government, one dated the 22d of April and the other the 24th June, 1851, is also transmitted for the information of the Senate. As the period limited for the exchange of the ratifications, which is to be effected at Bruni, will expire on the 23d instant, I recommend that if the Senate should approve the convention authority may be given to perform that ceremony within a year from that date. The instrument would have been submitted to the Senate in season for the ratification to be exchanged within the stipulated time had not Mr. Balestier's arrival with it in the United States been unavoidably delayed.

MILLARD FILLMORE.

WASHINGTON, *June 11, 1852.*

To the Senate and House of Representatives:

I transmit to Congress a report from the Secretary of State, on the subject of the disorders on the Rio Grande frontier, and recommend the legislation which it suggests, in order that the duties and obligations of this Government occasioned thereby may be more effectually discharged and the peace and security of the inhabitants of the United States in that quarter more efficiently maintained.

MILLARD FILLMORE.

WASHINGTON, *June 14, 1852.*

To the Senate and House of Representatives:

I transmit herewith, for your consideration, a report from the Secretary of State, accompanied by a communication from His Excellency Señor Don A. Calderon de la Barca, envoy extraordinary and minister plenipotentiary of Her Catholic Majesty, claiming indemnity for those Spanish subjects in New Orleans who sustained injury from the unlawful violence of the mob in that city consequent upon hearing the news of the execution of those persons who unlawfully invaded Cuba in August, 1851. My own views of the national liability upon this subject were expressed in the note of the Secretary of State to Mr. Calderon of the 13th November, 1851, and I do not understand that Her Catholic Majesty's minister controverts the correctness of the position there taken. He, however, insists that the thirteenth article of the treaty of 1795 promises indemnity for such injuries sustained within one year after the commencement of war between the two nations, and although he admits this is not within the letter of the treaty, yet he conceives that, as between two friendly nations, it is within the spirit of it.

This view of the case is at his request submitted for your consideration, but whether you may deem it correct or not, there is, perhaps, one ground upon which this indemnity, which can not be large in amount, may be granted without establishing a dangerous precedent, and the granting of which would commend itself to the generous feelings of the entire country, and that is this: The Queen of Spain, with a magnanimity worthy of all commendation, in a case where we had no legal right to solicit the favor, granted a free pardon to all the persons who had so unjustifiably invaded her dominions and murdered her subjects in Cuba, in violation of her own laws as well as those of the United States and the public law of nations. Such an act of mercy, which restored many misguided and unfortunate youth of this country to their parents and friends, seems to me to merit some corresponding act of magnanimity and generosity on the part of the Government of this country, and I think that there can be none more appropriate than to grant an indemnity to those Spanish subjects who were resident among us and who suffered by the violence of the mob, not on account of any fault which they themselves had committed, but because they were the subjects of the Queen of Spain. Such an act would tend to confirm that friendship which has so long existed between the two nations and to perpetuate it as a blessing to both, and I therefore recommend it to your favorable consideration.

MILLARD FILLMORE.

WASHINGTON, *June 22, 1852.*

To the Senate of the United States:

I transmit herewith a report from the Secretary of State, with the accompanying documents,* in compliance with the Senate's resolution of the 29th of April last. MILLARD FILLMORE.

WASHINGTON, *June 22, 1852.*

To the Senate of the United States:

I transmit to the Senate, for its consideration with a view to ratification, a convention for the mutual delivery of criminals fugitives from justice in certain cases between the United States on the one part and Prussia and other States of the Germanic Confederation on the other part, signed in this city on the 16th instant.

MILLARD FILLMORE.

---

* Correspondence of the American chargé at Vienna on the subject of the apprehension and imprisonment by the Austrian authorities of Rev. Charles L. Brace, an American citizen.

WASHINGTON, *June 23, 1852.*

To the Senate of the United States:

I transmit herewith a report from the Secretary of State, with the accompanying documents,* in compliance with the Senate's resolution of the 3d instant.

MILLARD FILLMORE.

WASHINGTON, *June 26, 1852.*

To the Senate of the United States:

I transmit and commend to the consideration of the Senate a report from the Secretary of State, touching the convention between the United States and the Mexican Republic for the mutual extradition of fugitives from justice in certain cases, which convention I submitted to the Senate soon after I entered upon the office of President of the United States.

MILLARD FILLMORE.

DEPARTMENT OF STATE,
Washington, June 26, 1852.

The PRESIDENT OF THE UNITED STATES:

It was understood that at the close of the Administration of your predecessor an extradition treaty was concluded in this city between the United States and the Mexican Republic, which, however, was submitted to the Senate by yourself, but before I entered upon my present office.

It is presumed that as the treaty has not been returned to this Department the Senate has made no decision in regard to it.

The necessity for a compact upon that subject between the two Governments, whose territories, being conterminous, afford great facilities for wrongdoers in the one to screen themselves from punishment by seeking refuge in the other, would at all times be obvious, but at the present juncture may be considered as urgent.

I would consequently suggest that the attention of the Senate be respectfully invited to the matter, in order that if the treaty before them should be deemed objectionable another, embodying such amendments as may be supposed to be necessary, may be proposed to the Mexican Government.

Respectfully submitted.

DANL. WEBSTER.

WASHINGTON, *June 26, 1852.*

To the Senate of the United States:

I have received and taken into respectful consideration the resolution of the Senate of yesterday, adopted in executive session, requesting information in regard to supposed negotiations between the United States and Great Britain and between the United States and the Republics of Nicaragua and Costa Rica, respectively. Any information which may be in the possession of the Executive on these subjects shall in due time be laid before the Senate, but it is apprehended that it would not comport with the public interests to communicate it under existing circumstances.

MILLARD FILLMORE.

*Correspondence relative to the withdrawal of Mr. Hülsemann, chargé d'affaires from Austria to the United States.

WASHINGTON, *June 26, 1852.*

To the Senate of the United States:

I have received the resolution of the Senate of the 11th instant, passed in executive session, making inquiry respecting supposed propositions of the King of the Sandwich Islands to convey the sovereignty of those islands to the United States and requesting all official information in my possession touching the subject.

This request has been taken into the most respectful consideration, but the conclusion at which I have arrived is that the public interest would not be promoted, but, on the contrary, might under circumstances of possible occurrence, be seriously endangered if it were now to be complied with.

MILLARD FILLMORE.

WASHINGTON CITY, *July 1, 1852.*

To the Senate of the United States:

On the 26th ultimo I received a resolution of the Senate, passed in executive session, in the following words:

Resolved, That the President of the United States be requested to inform the Senate, if not in his opinion incompatible with the public interest, whether any convention or compact has been entered into on the part of the United States and the Government of Great Britain whereby the two Governments jointly recommend or advise the Republics of Costa Rica and Nicaragua, or either of those Republics, and the Mosquito Indians, inhabiting the Mosquito Coast, in Central America, on matters affecting their several and respective boundaries, or whereby any recommendation or advice is given to either of said Republics or said Indians respecting the territorial rights thereafter to be enjoyed or observed by them respectively, or in any other manner affecting or regulating the relations hereafter to be maintained between said Republics themselves, or either of them, and the said Indians concerning their territorial boundaries or other matters thereto appertaining. And if there be any such convention or compact, then that the President be requested to communicate the same, or a copy thereof, to the Senate, and to inform the Senate whether the same was made at the request or invitation of either of said Republics or of said Indians, or with their privity, approbation, or consent. And that the President be further requested to communicate to the Senate copies of all correspondence between the Executive and Great Britain, or with either of said Republics of Central America, touching said convention, and of all documents connected therewith. And if such convention or compact has been made, that the President be further requested to inform the Senate whether the same has been formally communicated to the respective Governments of Nicaragua and Costa Rica and the Mosquito Indians on the part of the Governments of Great Britain and the United States, and in what form such communications have been made to them, and that he lay before the Senate copies of any instructions that have been given to the representatives or agents of the United States at Nicaragua and Costa Rica touching such convention and the matters therein contained, with copies of like instructions to any naval officer of the United States relating to or in any manner concerning the said convention or its communication to said Republics or said Indians.

On the same day I returned the following answer to that resolution:

I have received and taken into respectful consideration the resolution of the Senate of yesterday, adopted in executive session, requesting information in regard to supposed negotiations between the United States and Great Britain and between the United States and the Republics of Nicaragua and Costa Rica, respectively. Any information which may be in the possession of the Executive on these subjects shall in due time be laid before the Senate, but it is apprehended that it would not comport with the public interests to communicate it under existing circumstances.

Great was my surprise to observe this morning in one of the public journals a statement of what purports to be a proposition, jointly signed by Her Britannic Majesty's minister here and the Secretary of State, for the adjustment of certain claims to territory between Nicaragua, Costa Rica, and the Mosquito Indians. I have caused immediate inquiry to be made into the origin of this highly improper publication, and shall omit no proper or legal means for bringing it to light. Whether it shall turn out to have been caused by unfaithfulness or breach of duty in any officer of this Government, high or low, or by a violation of diplomatic confidence, the appropriate remedy will be immediately applied, as being due not only to this Government, but to other governments. And I hold this communication to be especially proper to be made immediately by me to the Senate, after what has transpired on this subject, that the Senate may be perfectly assured that no information asked by it has been withheld and at the same time permitted to be published to the world.

This publication can not be considered otherwise than as a breach of official duty by some officer of the Government or a gross violation of the confidence necessary always to be reposed in the representatives of other nations. An occurrence of this kind can not but weaken the faith so desirable to be preserved between different governments and to injure the negotiations now pending, and it merits the severest reprobation.

MILLARD FILLMORE.

WASHINGTON CITY, *July 2, 1852.*

To the Senate of the United States:

I herewith transmit, for the advice and consent of the Senate, a treaty recently negotiated with the Chickasaw Nation of Indians.

The nature and objects of the treaty are fully explained by the report of Mr. Harper, who negotiated it in behalf of the United States.

MILLARD FILLMORE.

WASHINGTON, *July 2, 1852.*

To the Senate and House of Representatives:

By an act of Congress approved on the 10th day of February, 1852, an appropriation of $6,000 was made for the relief of *American citizens* then lately imprisoned and pardoned by the Queen of Spain, intended to provide for the return of such of the Cuban prisoners as were citizens of the United States who had been transported to Spain and there pardoned by the Spanish Government. It will be observed that no provision was made for such foreigners or aliens as were engaged in the Cuban expedition, and who had shared the fate of American citizens, for whose relief the said act was intended to provide. I now transmit a report from the First Comptroller, with accompanying papers, from which it will be perceived that fifteen foreigners were connected with that expedition, who were also pardoned by the Queen of Spain, and have been transported to the United States under a contract made with our consul, at an expense of $1,013.34, for the payment of which no provision has been made by law. The consul having evidently acted with good intentions, the claim is submitted for the consideration of Congress.

MILLARD FILLMORE.

WASHINGTON, *July 13, 1852.*

To the House of Representatives:

In answer to the resolution of the House of Representatives requesting information relative to the policy of the Government in regard to the island of Cuba, I transmit a report from the Department of State and the documents by which it was accompanied.

MILLARD FILLMORE.

EXECUTIVE MANSION,
Washington City, July 26, 1852.

To the Senate of the United States:

In obedience to your resolution adopted in executive session June 11, 1852, I have the honor herewith to communicate a report* from the Secretary of the Interior, containing the information called for by that resolution. MILLARD FILLMORE.

WASHINGTON, *July 27, 1852.*

To the Senate.of the United States:

In answer to the resolution of the Senate of the 19th instant, requesting the correspondence between the Government of the United States and that of the Mexican Republic respecting a right of way across the Isthmus of Tehuantepec, I transmit a report from the Department of State and the documents by which it was accompanied.

MILLARD FILLMORE.

WASHINGTON, *July 29, 1852.*

To the Senate of the United States:

In compliance with the resolution of the Senate of the 27th instant, I transmit the copy of the notes† of Mr. Luis de la Rosa and Mr. J. M. Gonzales de la Vega, which it requests.

MILLARD FILLMORE.

---

* Relating to the boundary line between the United States and Mexico.
† Upon the subject of the American and Mexican boundary commission.

WASHINGTON, *July 31, 1852.*

To the Senate of the United States:

I communicate to the Senate herewith, for its constitutional action thereon, nineteen treaties negotiated by commissioners on the part of the United States with various tribes of Indians in the Territory of Oregon, accompanied by a letter to me from the Secretary of the Interior and certain documents having reference thereto.

MILLARD FILLMORE.

WASHINGTON, *August 2, 1852.*

To the Senate of the United States:

In answer to the resolution of the Senate of the 23d ultimo, requesting information in regard to the fisheries on the coasts of the British possessions in North America, I transmit a report from the Acting Secretary of State and the documents by which it was accompanied. Commodore M. C. Perry, with the United States steam frigate *Mississippi* under his command, has been dispatched to that quarter for the purpose of protecting the rights of American fishermen under the convention of 1818.

MILLARD FILLMORE.

WASHINGTON, *August 9, 1852.*

To the House of Representatives of the United States:

I transmit a report from the Acting Secretary of State and the documents by which it was accompanied, in answer to a resolution of the House of Representatives of the 22d ultimo, on the subject of the fisheries, and state for the information of that House that the United States steam frigate *Mississippi* has been dispatched to the fishing grounds on the coasts of the British possessions in North America for the purpose of protecting the rights of American fishermen under the convention between the United States and Great Britain of the 20th of October, 1818.

MILLARD FILLMORE.

WASHINGTON, *August 10, 1852.*

To the Senate of the United States:

I transmit a copy of the certificate of the exchange of the ratifications of the general convention of peace, amity, commerce, and navigation between the United States and the Republic of San Salvador, signed at Leon, in Nicaragua, on the 2d of January, 1850. It will be seen that the exchange was not effected until the 2d of June last, but that it was stipulated that the convention was not to be binding upon either of the parties thereto until the Senate of the United States should have duly sanctioned the exchange.

The Senate by its resolution of the 27th of September, 1850, authorized the exchange to take place at any time prior to the 1st of April, 1851.

Mr. Kerr, the chargé d'affaires of the United States to Nicaragua, however, who was authorized to make the exchange on the part of this Government, was unavoidably detained in that Republic, in consequence of which the exchange could not be effected within the period referred to.

The expediency of sanctioning the exchange which has been made by Mr. Kerr, and of authorizing the convention to go into effect, is accordingly submitted to the consideration of the Senate.

MILLARD FILLMORE.

WASHINGTON, *August 12, 1852.*

To the Senate of the United States:

In answer to the resolution of the Senate dated the 20th ultimo, requesting information in regard to controversies between the consul of the United States at Acapulco and the Mexican authorities, I transmit a report from the Secretary of State and the documents by which it was accompanied.

MILLARD FILLMORE.

WASHINGTON, *August 13, 1852.*

To the Senate of the United States: ●

I transmit a report from the Secretary of State upon the subject of the relations between the United States and the Republics of Nicaragua and Costa Rica, in Central America, which has been delayed longer than I desired in consequence of the ill health of the Secretary of State.

MILLARD FILLMORE.

WASHINGTON, *August 14, 1852.*

To the Senate of the United States:

I have received a resolution from your honorable body of the 6th instant, appearing to have been adopted in open legislative session, requesting me "to inform the Senate, if not incompatible with the public interests, whether any propositions have been made by the King of the Sandwich Islands to transfer the sovereignty of these islands to the United States, and to communicate to the Senate all the official information on that subject in my possession;" in reply to which I have to state that on or about the 12th day of June last I received a similar resolution from the Senate adopted in executive or secret session, to which I returned an answer stating that in my opinion a communication of the information requested at that juncture would not comport with the public interest. Nothing has since transpired to change my views on that subject, and I therefore feel constrained again to decline giving the information asked.

MILLARD FILLMORE.

WASHINGTON, *August 21, 1852.*

To the Senate of the United States:

In answer to the resolution of the Senate of the 9th instant, requesting information touching the Lobos Islands, I transmit a report from the Secretary of State and the documents by which it was accompanied. The instructions to the squadron of the United States called for by the resolution will be communicated on an early future occasion.

MILLARD FILLMORE.

WASHINGTON, *August 27, 1852.*

To the Senate of the United States:

In answer to the resolution of the Senate of the 14th ultimo, requesting a copy of the correspondence of Mr. R. M. Walsh while he was employed as a special agent of this Government in the island of St. Domingo, I transmit a report from the Secretary of State and the documents by which it was accompanied.

MILLARD FILLMORE.

WASHINGTON, *August 27, 1852.*

To the Senate of the United States:

I transmit a further report from the Secretary of State relative to the Lobos Islands. This report is accompanied by a copy of the orders of the Navy Department to Commodore McCauley, requested by the resolution of the Senate of the 9th instant.

MILLARD FILLMORE.

WASHINGTON, *August 27, 1852.*

To the Senate of the United States:

As it is not deemed advisable that the instruction to Mr. R. M. Walsh,* a copy of which is herewith transmitted, should be published at this time, I communicate it confidentially to the Senate in executive session.

MILLARD FILLMORE.

WASHINGTON, *August 27, 1852.*

To the Senate of the United States:

I transmit to the Senate, for its consideration with a view to ratification, a supplementary convention relative to commerce and navigation between the United States and the Netherlands, signed in this city on the 26th instant.

MILLARD FILLMORE.

* Special agent of the United States in the island of St. Domingo.

WASHINGTON, *August 27, 1852.*

To the Senate of the United States:

I transmit to the Senate, for its consideration with a view to ratification, a convention between the United States and Belgium for regulating the right of inheriting and acquiring property, signed in this city on the 25th instant.

MILLARD FILLMORE.

WASHINGTON, *August 31, 1852.*

To the Senate of the United States:

In answer to the resolution of the Senate of the 21st instant, requesting information in respect to foreign postal arrangements, and especially cheap ocean postage, I transmit a report of the Secretary of State and the documents by which it was accompanied.

MILLARD FILLMORE.

EXECUTIVE ORDERS.

WASHINGTON CITY,
May 17, 1852.

The SECRETARY OF WAR.

MY DEAR SIR: I have just issued an authority to Hugh Maxwell, collector at New York, under the eighth section of the act of April 20, 1818, to arrest any unlawful expedition that may be attempted to be fitted out within his district, and I have given him power to call upon any military and naval officers that may be there to aid him in the execution of this duty; and I will thank you to issue the necessary instructions to the proper military officer in that district.

I am, your obedient servant,

MILLARD FILLMORE.

WASHINGTON CITY,
Tuesday, June 29, 1852—12.30 o'clock p. m.

SIR:* The tolling bells announce the death of the Hon. Henry Clay. Though this event has been long anticipated, yet the painful bereavement could never be fully realized. I am sure all hearts are too sad at this moment to attend to business, and I therefore respectfully suggest that your Department be closed for the remainder of the day.

I have the honor to be, your obedient servant,

MILLARD FILLMORE.

* Addressed to the heads of the several Executive Departments.

WASHINGTON, *September 13, 1852.*

General JOS. G. TOTTEN.

SIR: I have to acknowledge the receipt of your favor of the 11th instant and to say that I shall be pleased if you will cause the necessary surveys, projects, and estimates for determining the best means of affording the cities of Washington and Georgetown an unfailing and abundant supply of good and wholesome water to be made as soon as possible.

I am, very respectfully, your obedient servant,

MILLARD FILLMORE.

[From the Daily National Intelligencer, October 26, 1852.]

EXECUTIVE MANSION,
Washington, Monday Morning, October 25, 1852.

The ACTING SECRETARY OF STATE and the SECRETARIES OF THE TREASURY, INTERIOR, WAR, NAVY, the ATTORNEY-GENERAL and POSTMASTER-GENERAL.

GENTLEMEN: The painful intelligence received yesterday enforces upon me the sad duty of announcing to the Executive Departments the death of the Secretary of State. Daniel Webster died at Marshfield, in Massachusetts, on Sunday, the 24th of October, between 2 and 3 o'clock in the morning.

Whilst this irreparable loss brings its natural sorrow to every American heart and will be heard far beyond our borders with mournful respect wherever civilization has nurtured men who find in transcendent intellect and faithful, patriotic service a theme for praise, it will visit with still more poignant emotion his colleagues in the Administration, with whom his relations have been so intimate and so cordial.

The fame of our illustrious statesman belongs to his country, the admiration of it to the world. The record of his wisdom will inform future generations not less than its utterance has enlightened the present. He has bequeathed to posterity the richest fruits of the experience and judgment of a great mind conversant with the greatest national concerns. In these his memory will endure as long as our country shall continue to be the home and guardian of freemen.

The people will share with the Executive Departments in the common grief which bewails his departure from amongst us.

In the expression of individual regret at this afflicting event the Executive Departments of the Government will be careful to manifest every observance of honor which custom has established as appropriate to the memory of one so eminent as a public functionary and so distinguished as a citizen.

The Acting Secretary of State will communicate this sad intelligence to the diplomatic corps near this Government and, through our ministers abroad, to foreign governments.

The members of the Cabinet are requested, as a further testimony of respect for the deceased, to wear the usual badges of mourning for thirty days.

I am, gentlemen, your obedient servant,

MILLARD FILLMORE.

THIRD ANNUAL MESSAGE.

WASHINGTON, *December 6, 1852.*

Fellow-Citizens of the Senate and of the House of Representatives:

The brief space which has elapsed since the close of your last session has been marked by no extraordinary political event. The quadrennial election of Chief Magistrate has passed off with less than the usual excitement. However individuals and parties may have been disappointed in the result, it is, nevertheless, a subject of national congratulation that the choice has been effected by the independent suffrages of a free people, undisturbed by those influences which in other countries have too often affected the purity of popular elections.

Our grateful thanks are due to an all-merciful Providence, not only for staying the pestilence which in different forms has desolated some of our cities, but for crowning the labors of the husbandman with an abundant harvest and the nation generally with the blessings of peace and prosperity.

Within a few weeks the public mind has been deeply affected by the death of Daniel Webster, filling at his decease the office of Secretary of State. His associates in the executive government have sincerely sympathized with his family and the public generally on this mournful occasion. His commanding talents, his great political and professional eminence, his well-tried patriotism, and his long and faithful services in the most important public trusts have caused his death to be lamented throughout the country and have earned for him a lasting place in our history.

In the course of the last summer considerable anxiety was caused for a short time by an official intimation from the Government of Great Britain that orders had been given for the protection of the fisheries upon the coasts of the British Provinces in North America against the alleged encroachments of the fishing vessels of the United States and France. The shortness of this notice and the season of the year seemed to make it a matter of urgent importance. It was at first apprehended that an increased naval force had been ordered to the fishing grounds to carry into effect the British interpretation of those provisions in the convention of 1818 in reference to the true intent of which the two Governments differ. It was soon discovered that such was not the design of Great Britain, and satisfactory explanations of the real objects of the measure have been given both here and in London.

The unadjusted difference, however, between the two Governments as to the interpretation of the first article of the convention of 1818 is still a matter of importance. American fishing vessels, within nine or ten years, have been excluded from waters to which they had free access for twenty-five years after the negotiation of the treaty. In 1845 this exclusion was relaxed so far as concerns the Bay of Fundy, but the just and liberal intention of the home Government, in compliance with what we think the true construction of the convention, to open all the other outer bays to our fishermen was abandoned in consequence of the opposition of the colonies. Notwithstanding this, the United States have, since the Bay of Fundy was reopened to our fishermen in 1845, pursued the most liberal course toward the colonial fishing interests. By the revenue law of 1846 the duties on colonial fish entering our ports were very greatly reduced, and by the warehousing act it is allowed to be entered in bond without payment of duty. In this way colonial fish has acquired the monopoly of the export trade in our market and is entering to some extent into the home consumption. These facts were among those which increased the sensibility of our fishing interest at the movement in question.

These circumstances and the incidents above alluded to have led me to think the moment favorable for a reconsideration of the entire subject of the fisheries on the coasts of the British Provinces, with a view to place them upon a more liberal footing of reciprocal privilege. A willingness to meet us in some arrangement of this kind is understood to exist on the part of Great Britain, with a desire on her part to include in one comprehensive settlement as well this subject as the commercial intercourse between the United States and the British Provinces. I have thought that, whatever arrangements may be made on these two subjects, it is expedient that they should be embraced in separate conventions. The illness and death of the late Secretary of State prevented the commencement of the contemplated negotiation. Pains have been taken to collect the information required for the details of such an arrangement. The subject is attended with considerable difficulty. If it is found practicable to come to an agreement mutually acceptable to the two parties, conventions may be concluded in the course of the present winter. The control of Congress over all the provisions of such an arrangement affecting the revenue will of course be reserved.

The affairs of Cuba formed a prominent topic in my last annual message. They remain in an uneasy condition, and a feeling of alarm and irritation on the part of the Cuban authorities appears to exist. This feeling has interfered with the regular commercial intercourse between the United States and the island and led to some acts of which we have a right to complain. But the Captain-General of Cuba is clothed with no power to treat with foreign governments, nor is he in any degree under the control of the Spanish minister at Washington. Any communication which he may hold with an agent of a foreign power is informal and matter of courtesy. Anxious to put an end to the existing inconveniences (which seemed to rest on a misconception), I directed the newly appointed minister to Mexico to visit Havana on his way to Vera Cruz. He was respectfully received by the Captain-General, who conferred with him freely on the recent occurrences, but no permanent arrangement was effected.

In the meantime the refusal of the Captain-General to allow passengers and the mail to be landed in certain cases, for a reason which does not furnish, in the opinion of this Government, even a good presumptive ground for such prohibition, has been made the subject of a serious remonstrance at Madrid, and I have no reason to doubt that due respect will be paid by the Government of Her Catholic Majesty to the representations which our minister has been instructed to make on the subject.

It is but justice to the Captain-General to add that his conduct toward the steamers employed to carry the mails of the United States to Havana has, with the exceptions above alluded to, been marked with kindness and liberality, and indicates no general purpose of interfering with the commercial correspondence and intercourse between the island and this country.

Early in the present year official notes were received from the ministers of France and England inviting the Government of the United States to become a party with Great Britain and France to a tripartite convention, in virtue of which the three powers should severally and collectively disclaim now and for the future all intention to obtain possession of the island of Cuba, and should bind themselves to discountenance all attempts to that effect on the part of any power or individual whatever. This invitation has been respectfully declined, for reasons which it would occupy too much space in this communication to state in detail, but which led me to think that the proposed measure would be of doubtful constitutionality, impolitic, and unavailing. I have, however, in common with several of my predecessors, directed the ministers of France and England to be assured that the United States entertain no designs against Cuba, but that, on the contrary, I should regard its incorporation into the Union at the present time as fraught with serious peril.

Were this island comparatively destitute of inhabitants or occupied by a kindred race, I should regard it, if voluntarily ceded by Spain, as a most desirable acquisition. But under existing circumstances I should look upon its incorporation into our Union as a very hazardous measure. It would bring into the Confederacy a population of a different national stock, speaking a different language, and not likely to harmonize with the other members. It would probably affect in a prejudicial manner the industrial interests of the South, and it might revive those conflicts of opinion between the different sections of the country which lately shook the Union to its center, and which have been so happily compromised.

The rejection by the Mexican Congress of the convention which had been concluded between that Republic and the United States for the protection of a transit way across the Isthmus of Tehuantepec and of the interests of those citizens of the United States who had become proprietors of the rights which Mexico had conferred on one of her own citizens in regard to that transit has thrown a serious obstacle in the way of the attainment of a very desirable national object. I am still willing to hope that the differences on the subject which exist, or may hereafter arise, between the Governments will be amicably adjusted. This subject, however, has already engaged the attention of the Senate of the United States, and requires no further comment in this communication.

The settlement of the question respecting the port of San Juan de Nicaragua and of the controversy between the Republics of Costa Rica and Nicaragua in regard to their boundaries was considered indispensable to the commencement of the ship canal between the two oceans, which was the subject of the convention between the United States and Great Britain of the 19th of April, 1850. Accordingly, a proposition for the same purposes, addressed to the two Governments in that quarter and to the Mosquito Indians, was agreed to in April last by the Secretary of State and the minister of Her Britannic Majesty. Besides the wish to aid in reconciling the differences of the two Republics, I engaged in the negotiation from a desire to place the great work of a ship canal between the two oceans under one jurisdiction and to establish the important port of San Juan de Nicaragua under the government of a civilized power. The proposition in question was assented to by Costa Rica and the Mosquito Indians. It has not proved equally acceptable to Nicaragua, but it is to be hoped that the further negotiations on the subject which are in train will be carried on in that spirit of conciliation and compromise which ought always to prevail on such occasions, and that they will lead to a satisfactory result.

I have the satisfaction to inform you that the executive government of Venezuela has acknowledged some claims of citizens of the United States which have for many years past been urged by our chargé d'affaires at Caracas. It is hoped that the same sense of justice will actuate the Congress of that Republic in providing the means for their payment.

The recent revolution in Buenos Ayres and the Confederated States having opened the prospect of an improved state of things in that quarter, the Governments of Great Britain and France determined to negotiate with the chief of the new confederacy for the free access of their commerce to the extensive countries watered by the tributaries of the La Plata; and they gave a friendly notice of this purpose to the United States, that we might, if we thought proper, pursue the same course. In compliance with this invitation, our minister at Rio Janeiro and our chargé d'affaires at Buenos Ayres have been fully authorized to conclude treaties with the newly organized confederation or the States composing it. The delays which have taken place in the formation of the new government have as yet prevented the execution of those instructions, but there is every reason to hope that these vast countries will be eventually opened to our commerce.

A treaty of commerce has been concluded between the United States and the Oriental Republic of Uruguay, which will be laid before the Senate. Should this convention go into operation, it will open to the commercial enterprise of our citizens a country of great extent and unsurpassed in natural resources, but from which foreign nations have hitherto been almost wholly excluded.

The correspondence of the late Secretary of State with the Peruvian chargé d'affaires relative to the Lobos Islands was communicated to Congress toward the close of the last session. Since that time, on further investigation of the subject, the doubts which had been entertained of the title of Peru to those islands have been removed, and I have deemed it just that the temporary wrong which had been unintentionally done her from want of information should be repaired by an unreserved acknowledgment of her sovereignty.

I have the satisfaction to inform you that the course pursued by Peru has been creditable to the liberality of her Government. Before it was known by her that her title would be acknowledged at Washington, her minister of foreign affairs had authorized our chargé d'affaires at Lima to announce to the American vessels which had gone to the Lobos for guano that the Peruvian Government was willing to freight them on its own account. This intention has been carried into effect by the Peruvian minister here by an arrangement which is believed to be advantageous to the parties in interest.

Our settlements on the shores of the Pacific have already given a great extension, and in some respects a new direction, to our commerce in that ocean. A direct and rapidly increasing intercourse has sprung up with eastern Asia. The waters of the Northern Pacific, even into the Arctic Sea, have of late years been frequented by our whalemen. The application of steam to the general purposes of navigation is becoming daily more common, and makes it desirable to obtain fuel and other necessary supplies at convenient points on the route between Asia and our Pacific shores. Our unfortunate countrymen who from time to time suffer shipwreck on the coasts of the eastern seas are entitled to protection. Besides these specific objects, the general prosperity of our States on the Pacific requires that an attempt should be made to open the opposite regions of Asia to a mutually beneficial intercourse. It is obvious that this attempt could be made by no power to so great advantage as by the United States, whose constitutional system excludes every idea of distant colonial dependencies. I have accordingly been led to order an appropriate naval force to Japan, under the command of a discreet and intelligent officer of the highest rank known to our service. He is instructed to endeavor to obtain from the Government of that country some relaxation of the inhospitable and antisocial system which it has pursued for about two centuries. He has been directed particularly to remonstrate in the strongest language against the cruel treatment to which our shipwrecked mariners have often been subjected and to insist that they shall be treated with humanity. He is instructed, however, at the same time, to give that Government the amplest assurances that the objects of the United States are such, and such only, as I have indicated, and that the expedition is friendly and peaceful. Notwithstanding the jealousy with which the Governments of eastern Asia regard all overtures from foreigners, I am not without hopes of a beneficial result of the expedition. Should it be crowned with success, the advantages will not be confined to the United States, but, as in the case of China, will be equally enjoyed by all the other maritime powers. I have much satisfaction in stating that in all the steps preparatory to this expedition the Government of the United States has been materially aided by the good offices of the King of the Netherlands, the only European power having any commercial relations with Japan.

In passing from this survey of our foreign relations, I invite the attention of Congress to the condition of that Department of the Government to which this branch of the public business is intrusted. Our intercourse with foreign powers has of late years greatly increased, both in consequence of our own growth and the introduction of many new states into the family of nations. In this way the Department of State has become overburdened. It has by the recent establishment of the Department of the Interior been relieved of some portion of the domestic business. If the residue of the business of that kind—such as the distribution of Congressional documents, the keeping, publishing, and distribution of the laws of the United States, the execution of the copyright law, the subject of reprieves and pardons, and some other subjects relating to interior administration—should be transferred from the Department of State, it would unquestionably be for the benefit of the public service. I would also suggest that the building appropriated to the State Department is not fireproof; that there is reason to think there are defects in its construction, and that the archives of the Government in charge of the Department, with the precious collections of the manuscript papers of Washington, Jefferson, Hamilton, Madison, and Monroe, are exposed to destruction by fire. A similar remark may be made of the buildings appropriated to the War and Navy Departments.

The condition of the Treasury is exhibited in the annual report from that Department.

The cash receipts into the Treasury for the fiscal year ending the 30th June last, exclusive of trust funds, were $49,728,386.89, and the expend-

itures for the same period, likewise exclusive of trust funds, were $46,-
007,896.20, of which $9,455,815.83 was on account of the principal and
interest of the public debt, including the last installment of the indemnity
to Mexico under the treaty of Guadalupe Hidalgo, leaving a balance of
$14,632,136.37 in the Treasury on the 1st day of July last. Since this
latter period further purchases of the principal of the public debt have
been made to the extent of $2,456,547.49, and the surplus in the Treas-
ury will continue to be applied to that object whenever the stock can be
procured within the limits as to price authorized by law.

The value of foreign merchandise imported during the last fiscal year
was $207,240,101, and the value of domestic productions exported was
$149,861,911, besides $17,204,026 of foreign merchandise exported, making the aggregate of the entire exports $167,065,937. Exclusive of the
above, there was exported $42,507,285 in specie, and imported from for-
eign ports $5,262,643.

In my first annual message to Congress I called your attention to what
seemed to me some defects in the present tariff, and recommended such
modifications as in my judgment were best adapted to remedy its evils
and promote the prosperity of the country. Nothing has since occurred
to change my views on this important question.

Without repeating the arguments contained in my former message in
favor of discriminating protective duties, I deem it my duty to call your
attention to one or two other considerations affecting this subject. The
first is the effect of large importations of foreign goods upon our currency. Most of the gold of California, as fast as it is coined, finds its
way directly to Europe in payment for goods purchased. In the second
place, as our manufacturing establishments are broken down by competition with foreigners, the capital invested in them is lost, thousands of
honest and industrious citizens are thrown out of employment, and the
farmer, to that extent, is deprived of a home market for the sale of his
surplus produce. In the third place, the destruction of our manufactures
leaves the foreigner without competition in our market, and he consequently raises the price of the article sent here for sale, as is now seen in
the increased cost of iron imported from England. The prosperity and
wealth of every nation must depend upon its productive industry. The
farmer is stimulated to exertion by finding a ready market for his surplus products, and benefited by being able to exchange them without
loss of time or expense of transportation for the manufactures which his
comfort or convenience requires. This is always done to the best advantage where a portion of the community in which he lives is engaged in
other pursuits. But most manufactures require an amount of capital and
a practical skill which can not be commanded unless they be protected for
a time from ruinous competition from abroad. Hence the necessity of
laying those duties upon imported goods which the Constitution authorizes for revenue in such a manner as to protect and encourage the labor

of our own citizens. Duties, however, should not be fixed at a rate so high as to exclude the foreign article, but should be so graduated as to enable the domestic manufacturer fairly to compete with the foreigner in our own markets, and by this competition to reduce the price of the manufactured article to the consumer to the lowest rate at which it can be produced. This policy would place the mechanic by the side of the farmer, create a mutual interchange of their respective commodities, and thus stimulate the industry of the whole country and render us independent of foreign nations for the supplies required by the habits or necessities of the people.

Another question, wholly independent of protection, presents itself, and that is, whether the duties levied should be upon the value of the article at the place of shipment, or, where it is practicable, a specific duty, graduated according to quantity, as ascertained by weight or measure. All our duties are at present *ad valorem*. A certain percentage is levied on the price of the goods at the port of shipment in a foreign country. Most commercial nations have found it indispensable, for the purpose of preventing fraud and perjury, to make the duties specific whenever the article is of such a uniform value in weight or measure as to justify such a duty. Legislation should never encourage dishonesty or crime. It is impossible that the revenue officers at the port where the goods are entered and the duties paid should know with certainty what they cost in the foreign country. Yet the law requires that they should levy the duty according to such cost. They are therefore compelled to resort to very unsatisfactory evidence to ascertain what that cost was. They take the invoice of the importer, attested by his oath, as the best evidence of which the nature of the case admits. But everyone must see that the invoice may be fabricated and the oath by which it is supported false, by reason of which the dishonest importer pays a part only of the duties which are paid by the honest one, and thus indirectly receives from the Treasury of the United States a reward for his fraud and perjury. The reports of the Secretary of the Treasury heretofore made on this subject show conclusively that these frauds have been practiced to a great extent. The tendency is to destroy that high moral character for which our merchants have long been distinguished, to defraud the Government of its revenue, to break down the honest importer by a dishonest competition, and, finally, to transfer the business of importation to foreign and irresponsible agents, to the great detriment of our own citizens. I therefore again most earnestly recommend the adoption of specific duties wherever it is practicable, or a home valuation, to prevent these frauds.

I would also again call your attention to the fact that the present tariff in some cases imposes a higher duty upon the raw material imported than upon the article manufactured from it, the consequence of which is that the duty operates to the encouragement of the foreigner and the discouragement of our own citizens.

For full and detailed information in regard to the general condition of our Indian affairs, I respectfully refer you to the report of the Secretary of the Interior and the accompanying documents.

The Senate not having thought proper to ratify the treaties which have been negotiated with the tribes of Indians in California and Oregon, our relations with them have been left in a very unsatisfactory condition.

In other parts of our territory particular districts of country have been set apart for the exclusive occupation of the Indians, and their right to the lands within those limits has been acknowledged and respected. But in California and Oregon there has been no recognition by the Government of the exclusive right of the Indians to any part of the country. They are therefore mere tenants at sufferance, and liable to be driven from place to place at the pleasure of the whites.

The treaties which have been rejected proposed to remedy this evil by allotting to the different tribes districts of country suitable to their habits of life and sufficient for their support. This provision, more than any other, it is believed, led to their rejection; and as no substitute for it has been adopted by Congress, it has not been deemed advisable to attempt to enter into new treaties of a permanent character, although no effort has been spared by temporary arrangements to preserve friendly relations with them.

If it be the desire of Congress to remove them from the country altogether, or to assign to them particular districts more remote from the settlements of the whites, it will be proper to set apart by law the territory which they are to occupy and to provide the means necessary for removing them to it. Justice alike to our own citizens and to the Indians requires the prompt action of Congress on this subject.

The amendments proposed by the Senate to the treaties which were negotiated with the Sioux Indians of Minnesota have been submitted to the tribes who were parties to them, and have received their assent. A large tract of valuable territory has thus been opened for settlement and cultivation, and all danger of collision with these powerful and warlike bands has been happily removed.

The removal of the remnant of the tribe of Seminole Indians from Florida has long been a cherished object of the Government, and it is one to which my attention has been steadily directed. Admonished by past experience of the difficulty and cost of the attempt to remove them by military force, resort has been had to conciliatory measures. By the invitation of the Commissioner of Indian Affairs, several of the principal chiefs recently visited Washington, and whilst here acknowledged in writing the obligation of their tribe to remove with the least possible delay. Late advices from the special agent of the Government represent that they adhere to their promise, and that a council of their people has been called to make their preliminary arrangements. A general emigration may therefore be confidently expected at an early day.

The report from the General Land Office shows increased activity in its operations. The survey of the northern boundary of Iowa has been completed with unexampled dispatch. Within the last year 9,522,953 acres of public land have been surveyed and 8,032,463 acres brought into market.

	Acres.
In the last fiscal year there were sold	1,553,071
Located with bounty-land warrants	3,201,314
Located with other certificates	115,682
Making a total of	4,870,067
In addition there were—	
Reported under swamp-land grants	5,219,188
For internal improvements, railroads, etc	3,025,920
Making an aggregate of	13,115,175

Being an increase of the amount sold and located under land warrants of 569,220 acres over the previous year.

The whole amount thus sold, located under land warrants, reported under swamp-land grants, and selected for internal improvements exceeds that of the previous year by 3,342,372 acres; and the sales would without doubt have been much larger but for the extensive reservations for railroads in Missouri, Mississippi, and Alabama.

	Acres.
For the quarter ending 30th September, 1852, there were sold	243,255
Located with bounty-land warrants	1,387,116
Located with other certificates	15,649
Reported under swamp-land grants	2,485,233
Making an aggregate for the quarter of	4,131,253

Much the larger portion of the labor of arranging and classifying the returns of the last census has been finished, and it will now devolve upon Congress to make the necessary provision for the publication of the results in such form as shall be deemed best. The apportionment of representation on the basis of the new census has been made by the Secretary of the Interior in conformity with the provisions of law relating to that subject, and the recent elections have been made in accordance with it.

I commend to your favorable regard the suggestion contained in the report of the Secretary of the Interior that provision be made by law for the publication and distribution, periodically, of an analytical digest of all the patents which have been or may hereafter be granted for useful inventions and discoveries, with such descriptions and illustrations as may be necessary to present an intelligible view of their nature and operation. The cost of such publication could easily be defrayed out of the patent fund, and I am persuaded that it could be applied to no object more acceptable to inventors and beneficial to the public at large.

An appropriation of $100,000 having been made at the last session for the purchase of a suitable site and for the erection, furnishing, and fitting up of an asylum for the insane of the District of Columbia and of the Army and Navy of the United States, the proper measures have been adopted to carry this beneficent purpose into effect.

By the latest advices from the Mexican boundary commission it appears that the survey of the river Gila from its confluence with the Colorado to its supposed intersection with the western line of New Mexico has been completed. The survey of the Rio Grande has also been finished from the point agreed on by the commissioners as "the point where it strikes the southern boundary of New Mexico" to a point 135 miles below Eagle Pass, which is about two-thirds of the distance along the course of the river to its mouth.

The appropriation which was made at the last session of Congress for the continuation of the survey is subject to the following proviso:

Provided, That no part of this appropriation shall be used or expended until it shall be made satisfactorily to appear to the President of the United States that the southern boundary of New Mexico is not established by the commissioner and surveyor of the United States farther north of the town called "Paso" than the same is laid down in Disturnell's map, which is added to the treaty.

My attention was drawn to this subject by a report from the Department of the Interior, which reviewed all the facts of the case and submitted for my decision the question whether under existing circumstances any part of the appropriation could be lawfully used or expended for the further prosecution of the work. After a careful consideration of the subject I came to the conclusion that it could not, and so informed the head of that Department. Orders were immediately issued by him to the commissioner and surveyor to make no further requisitions on the Department, as they could not be paid, and to discontinue all operations on the southern line of New Mexico. But as the Department had no exact information as to the amount of provisions and money which remained unexpended in the hands of the commissioner and surveyor, it was left discretionary with them to continue the survey down the Rio Grande as far as the means at their disposal would enable them or at once to disband the commission. A special messenger has since arrived from the officer in charge of the survey on the river with information that the funds subject to his control were exhausted and that the officers and others employed in the service were destitute alike of the means of prosecuting the work and of returning to their homes.

The object of the proviso was doubtless to arrest the survey of the southern and western lines of New Mexico, in regard to which different opinions have been expressed; for it is hardly to be supposed that there could be any objection to that part of the line which extends along the channel of the Rio Grande. But the terms of the law are so broad as to forbid the use of any part of the money for the prosecution of the work, or even for the payment to the officers and agents of the arrearages of pay which are justly due to them.

I earnestly invite your prompt attention to this subject, and recommend a modification of the terms of the proviso, so as to enable the Department to use as much of the appropriation as will be necessary to discharge the existing obligations of the Government and to complete the survey of the Rio Grande to its mouth.

It will also be proper to make further provision by law for the fulfillment of our treaty with Mexico for running and marking the residue of the boundary line between the two countries.

Permit me to invite your particular attention to the interests of the District of Columbia, which are confided by the Constitution to your peculiar care.

Among the measures which seem to me of the greatest importance to its prosperity are the introduction of a copious supply of water into the city of Washington and the construction of suitable bridges across the Potomac to replace those which were destroyed by high water in the early part of the present year.

At the last session of Congress an appropriation was made to defray the cost of the surveys necessary for determining the best means of affording an unfailing supply of good and wholesome water. Some progress has been made in the survey, and as soon as it is completed the result will be laid before you.

Further appropriations will also be necessary for grading and paving the streets and avenues and inclosing and embellishing the public grounds within the city of Washington.

I commend all these objects, together with the charitable institutions of the District, to your favorable regard.

Every effort has been made to protect our frontier and that of the adjoining Mexican States from the incursions of the Indian tribes. Of about 11,000 men of which the Army is composed, nearly 8,000 are employed in the defense of the newly acquired territory (including Texas) and of emigrants proceeding thereto. I am gratified to say that these efforts have been unusually successful. With the exception of some partial outbreaks in California and Oregon and occasional depredations on a portion of the Rio Grande, owing, it is believed, to the disturbed state of that border region, the inroads of the Indians have been effectually restrained.

Experience has shown, however, that whenever the two races are brought into contact collisions will inevitably occur. To prevent these collisions the United States have generally set apart portions of their territory for the exclusive occupation of the Indian tribes. A difficulty occurs, however, in the application of this policy to Texas. By the terms of the compact by which that State was admitted into the Union she retained the ownership of all the vacant lands within her limits. The government of that State, it is understood, has assigned no portion of her territory to the Indians, but as fast as her settlements advance lays it off into counties and proceeds to survey and sell it. This policy manifestly tends not only to alarm and irritate the Indians, but to compel them to resort to plunder for subsistence. It also deprives this

Government of that influence and control over them without which no durable peace can ever exist between them and the whites. I trust, therefore, that a due regard for her own interests, apart from considerations of humanity and justice, will induce that State to assign a small portion of her vast domain for the provisional occupancy of the small remnants of tribes within her borders, subject, of course, to her ownership and eventual jurisdiction. If she should fail to do this, the fulfillment of our treaty stipulations with Mexico and our duty to the Indians themselves will, it is feared, become a subject of serious embarrassment to the Government. It is hoped, however, that a timely and just provision by Texas may avert this evil.

No appropriations for fortifications were made at the two last sessions of Congress. The cause of this omission is probably to be found in a growing belief that the system of fortifications adopted in 1816, and heretofore acted on, requires revision.

The subject certainly deserves full and careful investigation, but it should not be delayed longer than can be avoided. In the meantime there are certain works which have been commenced, some of them nearly completed, designed to protect our principal seaports from Boston to New Orleans and a few other important points. In regard to the necessity for these works, it is believed that little difference of opinion exists among military men. I therefore recommend that the appropriations necessary to prosecute them be made.

I invite your attention to the remarks on this subject and on others connected with his Department contained in the accompanying report of the Secretary of War.

Measures have been taken to carry into effect the law of the last session making provision for the improvement of certain rivers and harbors, and it is believed that the arrangements made for that purpose will combine efficiency with economy. Owing chiefly to the advanced season when the act was passed, little has yet been done in regard to many of the works beyond making the necessary preparations. With respect to a few of the improvements, the sums already appropriated will suffice to complete them; but most of them will require additional appropriations. I trust that these appropriations will be made, and that this wise and beneficent policy, so auspiciously resumed, will be continued. Great care should be taken, however, to commence no work which is not of sufficient importance to the commerce of the country to be viewed as national in its character. But works which have been commenced should not be discontinued until completed, as otherwise the sums expended will in most cases be lost.

The report from the Navy Department will inform you of the prosperous condition of the branch of the public service committed to its charge. It presents to your consideration many topics and suggestions of which I ask your approval. It exhibits an unusual degree of activity in the operations of the Department during the past year. The preparations for the Japan expedition, to which I have already alluded; the arrangements made for the exploration and survey of the China Seas, the Northern Pacific, and Behrings Straits; the incipient measures taken toward a reconnoissance of the continent of Africa eastward of Liberia; the preparation for an early examination of the tributaries of the river La Plata, which a recent decree of the provisional chief of the Argentine Confederation has opened to navigation—all these enterprises and the means by which they are proposed to be accomplished have commanded my full approbation, and I have no doubt will be productive of most useful results.

Two officers of the Navy were heretofore instructed to explore the whole extent of the Amazon River from the confines of Peru to its mouth. The return of one of them has placed in the possession of the Government an interesting and valuable account of the character and resources of a country abounding in the materials of commerce, and which if opened to the industry of the world will prove an inexhaustible fund of wealth. The report of this exploration will be communicated to you as soon as it is completed.

Among other subjects offered to your notice by the Secretary of the Navy, I select for special commendation, in view of its connection with the interests of the Navy, the plan submitted by him for the establishment of a permanent corps of seamen and the suggestions he has presented for the reorganization of the Naval Academy.

In reference to the first of these, I take occasion to say that I think it will greatly improve the efficiency of the service, and that I regard it as still more entitled to favor for the salutary influence it must exert upon the naval discipline, now greatly disturbed by the increasing spirit of insubordination resulting from our present system. The plan proposed for the organization of the seamen furnishes a judicious substitute for the law of September, 1850, abolishing corporal punishment, and satisfactorily sustains the policy of that act under conditions well adapted to maintain the authority of command and the order and security of our ships. It is believed that any change which proposes permanently to dispense with this mode of punishment should be preceded by a system of enlistment which shall supply the Navy with seamen of the most meritorious class, whose good deportment and pride of character may preclude all occasion for a resort to penalties of a harsh or degrading nature. The safety of a ship and her crew is often dependent upon immediate obedience to a command, and the authority to enforce it must be equally ready. The arrest of a refractory seaman in such moments not only deprives the ship of indispensable aid, but imposes a necessity for double service on others, whose fidelity to their duties may be relied upon in such an emergency. The exposure to this increased and arduous labor since the passage of the act of 1850 has already had, to a most observable and injurious extent, the effect of preventing the enlistment of the best seamen in the Navy. The plan now suggested is designed to promote a condition of service in which this objection will no longer exist. The details of this plan may be established in great part, if not altogether, by the Executive under the authority of existing laws, but I have thought it proper, in accordance with the suggestion of the Secretary of the Navy, to submit it to your approval.

The establishment of a corps of apprentices for the Navy, or boys to be enlisted until they become of age, and to be employed under such regulations as the Navy Department may devise, as proposed in the report, I cordially approve and commend to your consideration; and I also concur in the suggestion that this system for the early training of seamen may be most usefully ingrafted upon the service of our merchant marine.

The other proposition of the report to which I have referred—the reorganization of the Naval Academy—I recommend to your attention as a project worthy of your encouragement and support. The valuable services already rendered by this institution entitle it to the continuance of your fostering care.

Your attention is respectfully called to the report of the Postmaster-General for the detailed operation of his Department during the last fiscal year, from which it will be seen that the receipts from postages for that time were less by $1,431,696 than for the preceding fiscal year, being a decrease of about 23 per cent.

This diminution is attributable to the reduction in the rates of postage made by the act of March 3, 1851, which reduction took effect at the commencement of the last fiscal year.

Although in its operation during the last year the act referred to has not fulfilled the predictions of its friends by increasing the correspondence of the country in proportion to the reduction of postage, I should, nevertheless, question the policy of returning to higher rates. Experience warrants the expectation that as the community becomes accustomed to cheap postage correspondence will increase. It is believed that from this cause and from the rapid growth of the country in population and business the receipts of the Department must ultimately exceed its expenses, and that the country may safely rely upon the continuance of the present cheap rate of postage.

In former messages I have, among other things, respectfully recommended to the consideration of Congress the propriety and necessity of further legislation for the protection and punishment of foreign consuls residing in the United States; to revive, with certain modifications, the act of 10th March, 1838, to restrain unlawful military expeditions against the inhabitants of conterminous states or territories; for the preservation and protection from mutilation or theft of the papers, records, and archives of the nation; for authorizing the surplus revenue to be applied to the payment of the public debt in advance of the time when it will become due; for the establishment of land offices for the sale of the public lands in California and the Territory of Oregon; for the construction of a road from the Mississippi Valley to the Pacific Ocean; for the establishment of a bureau of agriculture for the promotion of that interest, perhaps the most important in the country; for the prevention of frauds upon the Government in applications for pensions and bounty lands; for the establishment of a uniform fee bill, prescribing a specific compensation for every service required of clerks, district attorneys, and marshals; for authorizing an additional regiment of mounted men for the defense of our frontiers against the Indians and for fulfilling our treaty stipulations with Mexico to defend her citizens against the Indians "with equal diligence and energy as our own;" for determining the relative rank between the naval and civil officers in our public ships and between the officers of the Army and Navy in the various grades of each; for reorganizing the naval establishment by fixing the number of officers in each grade, and providing for a retired list upon reduced pay of those unfit for active duty; for prescribing and regulating punishments in the Navy; for the appointment of a commission to revise the public statutes of the United States by arranging them in order, supplying deficiencies, correcting incongruities, simplifying their language, and reporting them to Congress for its final action; and for the establishment of a commission to adjudicate and settle private claims against the United States. I am not aware, however, that any of these subjects have been finally acted upon by Congress. Without repeating the reasons for legislation on these subjects which have been assigned in former messages, I respectfully recommend them again to your favorable consideration.

I think it due to the several Executive Departments of this Government to bear testimony to the efficiency and integrity with which they are conducted. With all the careful superintendence which it is possible for the heads of those Departments to exercise, still the due administration and guardianship of the public money must very much depend on the vigilance, intelligence, and fidelity of the subordinate officers and clerks, and especially on those intrusted with the settlement and adjustment of claims and accounts. I am gratified to believe that they have generally performed their duties faithfully and well. They are appointed to guard the approaches to the public Treasury, and they occupy positions that expose them to all the temptations and seductions which the cupidity of peculators and fraudulent claimants can prompt them to employ. It will be but a wise precaution to protect the Government against that source of mischief and corruption, as far as it can be done, by the enactment of all proper legal penalties. The laws in this respect are supposed to be defective, and I therefore deem it my duty to call your attention to the subject and to recommend that provision be made by law for the punishment not only of those who shall accept bribes, but also of those who shall either promise, give, or offer to give to any of those officers or clerks a bribe or reward touching or relating to any matter of their official action or duty.

It has been the uniform policy of this Government, from its foundation to the present day, to abstain from all interference in the domestic affairs of other nations. The consequence has been that while the nations of Europe have been engaged in desolating wars our country has pursued its peaceful course to unexampled prosperity and happiness. The wars in which we have been compelled to engage in defense of the rights and honor of the country have been, fortunately, of short duration. During the terrific contest of nation against nation which succeeded the French Revolution we were enabled by the wisdom and firmness of President Washington to maintain our neutrality. While other nations were drawn into this wide-sweeping whirlpool, we sat quiet and unmoved upon our own shores. While the flower of their numerous armies was wasted by disease or perished by hundreds of thousands upon the battle-field, the youth of this favored land were permitted to enjoy the blessings of peace beneath the paternal roof. While the States of Europe incurred enormous debts, under the burden of which their subjects still groan, and which must absorb no small part of the product of the honest industry of those countries for generations to come, the United States have once been enabled to exhibit the proud spectacle of a nation free from public debt, and if permitted to pursue our prosperous way for a few years longer in peace we may do the same again.

But it is now said by some that this policy must be changed. Europe is no longer separated from us by a voyage of months, but steam navigation has brought her within a few days' sail of our shores. We see more of her movements and take a deeper interest in her controversies. Although no one proposes that we should join the fraternity of potentates who have for ages lavished the blood and treasure of their subjects in maintaining "the balance of power," yet it is said that we ought to interfere between contending sovereigns and their subjects for the purpose of overthrowing the monarchies of Europe and establishing in their place republican institutions. It is alleged that we have heretofore pursued a different course from a sense of our weakness, but that now our conscious strength dictates a change of policy, and that it is consequently our duty to mingle in these contests and aid those who are struggling for liberty.

This is a most seductive but dangerous appeal to the generous sympathies of freemen. Enjoying, as we do, the blessings of a free Government, there is no man who has an American heart that would not rejoice to see these blessings extended to all other nations. We can not witness the struggle between the oppressed and his oppressor anywhere without the deepest sympathy for the former and the most anxious desire for his triumph. Nevertheless, is it prudent or is it wise to involve ourselves in these foreign wars? Is it indeed true that we have heretofore refrained from doing so merely from the degrading motive of a conscious weakness? For the honor of the patriots who have gone before us, I can not admit it. Men of the Revolution, who drew the sword against the oppressions of the mother country and pledged to Heaven "their lives, their fortunes, and their sacred honor" to maintain their freedom, could never have been actuated by so unworthy a motive. They knew no weakness or fear where right or duty pointed the way, and it is a libel upon their fair fame for us, while we enjoy the blessings for which they so nobly fought and bled, to insinuate it. The truth is that the course which they pursued was dictated by a stern sense of international justice, by a statesmanlike prudence and a far-seeing wisdom, looking not merely to the present necessities but to the permanent safety and interest of the country. They knew that the world is governed less by sympathy than by reason and force; that it was not possible for this nation to become a "propagandist" of free principles without arraying against it the combined powers of Europe, and that the result was more likely to be the overthrow of republican liberty here than its establishment there. History has been written in vain for those who can doubt this. France had no sooner established a republican form of government than she manifested a desire to force its blessings on all the world. Her own historian informs us that, hearing of some petty acts of tyranny in a neighboring principality, "the National Convention declared that she would afford succor and fraternity to all nations who wished to recover their liberty, and she gave it in charge to the executive power to give orders to the generals of the French armies to aid all citizens who might have been or should be oppressed in the cause of liberty." Here was the false step which led to her subsequent misfortunes. She soon found herself involved in war with all the rest of Europe. In less than ten years her Government was changed from a republic to an empire, and finally, after shedding rivers of blood, foreign powers restored her exiled dynasty and exhausted Europe sought peace and repose in the unquestioned ascendency of monarchical principles. Let us learn wisdom from her example. Let us remember that revolutions do not always establish freedom. Our own free institutions were not the offspring of our Revolution. They existed before. They were planted in the free charters of self-government under which the English colonies grew up, and our Revolution only freed us from the dominion of a foreign power whose government was at variance with those institutions. But European nations have had no such training for self-government, and every effort to establish it by bloody revolutions has been, and must without that preparation continue to be, a failure. Liberty unregulated by law degenerates into anarchy, which soon becomes the most horrid of all despotisms. Our policy is wisely to govern ourselves, and thereby to set such an example of national justice, prosperity, and true glory as shall teach to all nations the blessings of self-government and the unparalleled enterprise and success of a free people.

We live in an age of progress, and ours is emphatically a country of progress. Within the last half century the number of States in this Union has nearly doubled, the population has almost quadrupled, and our boundaries have been extended from the Mississippi to the Pacific. Our territory is checkered over with railroads and furrowed with canals. The inventive talent of our country is excited to the highest pitch, and the numerous applications for patents for valuable improvements distinguish this age and this people from all others. The genius of one American has enabled our commerce to move against wind and tide and that of another has annihilated distance in the transmission of intelligence. The whole country is full of enterprise. Our common schools are diffusing intelligence among the people and our industry is fast accumulating the comforts and luxuries of life. This is in part owing to our peculiar position, to our fertile soil and comparatively sparse population; but much of it is also owing to the popular institutions under which we live, to the freedom which every man feels to engage in any useful pursuit according to his taste or inclination, and to the entire confidence that his person and property will be protected by the laws. But whatever may be the cause of this unparalleled growth in population, intelligence, and wealth, one thing is clear—that the Government must keep pace with the progress of the people. It must participate in their spirit of enterprise, and while it exacts obedience to the laws and restrains all unauthorized invasions of the rights of neighboring states, it should foster and protect home industry and lend its powerful strength to the improvement of such means of intercommunication as are necessary to promote our internal commerce and strengthen the ties which bind us together as a people.

It is not strange, however much it may be regretted, that such an exuberance of enterprise should cause some individuals to mistake change for progress and the invasion of the rights of others for national prowess and glory. The former are constantly agitating for some change in the organic law, or urging new and untried theories of human rights. The latter are ever ready to engage in any wild crusade against a neighboring people, regardless of the justice of the enterprise and without looking at the fatal consequences to ourselves and to the cause of popular government. Such expeditions, however, are often stimulated by mercenary individuals, who expect to share the plunder or profit of the enterprise without exposing themselves to danger, and are led on by some irresponsible foreigner, who abuses the hospitality of our own Government by seducing the young and ignorant to join in his scheme of personal ambition or revenge under the false and delusive pretense of extending the area of freedom. These reprehensible aggressions but retard the true progress of our nation and tarnish its fair fame. They should therefore receive the indignant frowns of every good citizen who sincerely loves his country and takes a pride in its prosperity and honor.

Our Constitution, though not perfect, is doubtless the best that ever was formed. Therefore let every proposition to change it be well weighed and, if found beneficial, cautiously adopted. Every patriot will rejoice to see its authority so exerted as to advance the prosperity and honor of the nation, whilst he will watch with jealousy any attempt to mutilate this charter of our liberties or pervert its powers to acts of aggression or injustice. Thus shall conservatism and progress blend their harmonious action in preserving the form and spirit of the Constitution and at the same time carry forward the great improvements of the country with a rapidity and energy which freemen only can display.

In closing this my last annual communication, permit me, fellow-citizens, to congratulate you on the prosperous condition of our beloved country. Abroad its relations with all foreign powers are friendly, its rights are respected, and its high place in the family of nations cheerfully recognized. At home we enjoy an amount of happiness, public and private, which has probably never fallen to the lot of any other people. Besides affording to our own citizens a degree of prosperity of which on so large a scale I know of no other instance, our country is annually affording a refuge and a home to multitudes, altogether without example, from the Old World.

We owe these blessings, under Heaven, to the happy Constitution and Government which were bequeathed to us by our fathers, and which it is our sacred duty to transmit in all their integrity to our children. We must all consider it a great distinction and privilege to have been chosen by the people to bear a part in the administration of such a Government. Called by an unexpected dispensation to its highest trust at a season of embarrassment and alarm, I entered upon its arduous duties with extreme diffidence. I claim only to have discharged them to the best of an humble ability, with a single eye to the public good, and it is with devout gratitude in retiring from office that I leave the country in a state of peace and prosperity.   MILLARD FILLMORE.

SPECIAL MESSAGES.

WASHINGTON, *December 7, 1852.*

To the Senate of the United States:

I transmit to the Senate, for its consideration with a view to ratification, a treaty of friendship, commerce, and navigation, between the United States and the Oriental Republic of Uruguay, signed at Montevideo on the 28th of August last.

MILLARD FILLMORE.

WASHINGTON, *December 8, 1852.*

To the Senate of the United States:

I transmit to the Senate, for its consideration with a view to ratification, an additional article, signed in this city on the 16th ultimo, to the convention for the mutual delivery of criminals fugitives from justice in certain cases between the United States on the one part and Prussia and other States of the Germanic Confederation on the other part, concluded on the 15th of June, 1852. MILLARD FILLMORE.

WASHINGTON, *January 4, 1853.*

To the Senate of the United States:

In answer to the resolution of the Senate of the 30th ultimo, requesting information in regard to the establishment of a new British colony in Central America, I transmit a report from the Secretary of State and the documents by which it was accompanied.

MILLARD FILLMORE.

WASHINGTON, *January 4, 1853.*

To the Senate of the United States:

In answer to the Senate's resolution of the 3d instant, calling for information relative to a proposed tripartite convention on the subject of the island of Cuba, I transmit to the Senate a report from the Secretary of State and the papers which accompanied it.

MILLARD FILLMORE.

WASHINGTON, *January 12, 1853.*

To the Senate of the United States:

In pursuance of the eleventh article of the treaty with the Chickasaw Indians signed on the 20th day of October, 1832, I herewith transmit a recommendation from the Secretary of the Treasury for the investment of a portion of the funds belonging to said nation, for the purpose of obtaining the advice and consent of the Senate to make the investment as therein recommended. MILLARD FILLMORE.

WASHINGTON, *January 12, 1853.*

To the Senate of the United States:

In reply to the resolution of your honorable body of the 5th instant, I herewith communicate a report of the Secretary of the Interior giving the information* required. MILLARD FILLMORE.

*Relating to the Mexican boundary commission.

To the Senate of the United States:

In answer to the resolution of the Senate dated the 13th ultimo, requesting further information in regard to the imprisonment of the United States consul and of other American citizens in the castle at Acapulco, I transmit a report from the Secretary of State and the documents by which it is accompanied.

JANUARY 17, 1853.

MILLARD FILLMORE.

WASHINGTON, *January 17, 1853.*

To the Senate and House of Representatives:

I transmit herewith a communication lately received at the Department of State from the minister of Her Most Catholic Majesty, accompanied by a letter of instructions from the Spanish Government relative to the case of the *Amistad.* In Mr. Calderon's communication reference is had to former letters addressed by him to the Department of State on the same subject, copies of which are herewith transmitted, and an earnest wish is expressed that a final settlement of this long-pending claim should be made. The tone of the letter of instructions from Mr. Manuel Bertran de Lis is somewhat more peremptory than could be wished, but this circumstance will not, probably, prevent Congress from giving his suggestions the attention to which they may be entitled.

The claim of the Spanish Government on behalf of its subjects interested in the *Amistad* was the subject of discussion during the Administration of President Tyler between the Spanish minister and Mr. Webster, then Secretary of State. In an elaborate letter of the latter, addressed to the Chevalier d'Argais on the 1st of September, 1841, the opinion is confidently maintained that the claim is unfounded. The Administration of President Polk took a different view of the matter. The justice of the claim was recognized in a letter from the Department of State to the Spanish minister of the 19th of March, 1847, and in his annual message of the same year the President recommended its payment.

Under these circumstances the attention of Congress is again invited to the subject. Respect to the Spanish Government demands that its urgent representation should be candidly and impartially weighed. If Congress should be of opinion that the claim is just, every consideration points to the propriety of its prompt recognition and payment, and if the two Houses should come to the opposite conclusion it is equally desirable that the result should be announced without unnecessary delay.

MILLARD FILLMORE.

WASHINGTON, *January 18, 1853.*

To the Senate and House of Representatives of the United States:

I have the honor herewith to transmit a report from the Secretary of the Interior, from which it appears that the efforts of that Department to induce the Indians remaining in Florida to migrate to the country assigned to their tribe west of the Mississippi have been entirely unsuccessful. The only alternative that now remains is either to compel them by force to comply with the treaty made with the tribe in May, 1832, by which they agreed to migrate within three years from that date, or allow the arrangement made with them in 1842, referred to in the Secretary's report, by which they were permitted to remain in the temporary occupancy of a portion of the peninsula until the Government should see fit to remove them, to continue.

It can not be denied that the withholding so large a portion of her territory from settlement is a source of injury to the State of Florida; and although, ever since the arrangement above referred to, the Indians have manifested a desire to remain at peace with the whites, the presence of a people who may at any time and upon any real or fancied provocation be driven to acts of hostility is a source of constant anxiety and alarm to the inhabitants on that border.

There can be no doubt, also, that the welfare of the Indians would be promoted by their removal from a territory where frequent collisions between them and their more powerful neighbors are daily becoming more inevitable.

On the other hand, there is every reason to believe that any manifestation of a design to remove them by force or to take possession of the territory allotted to them would be immediately retaliated by acts of cruelty on the defenseless inhabitants.

The number of Indians now remaining in the State is, it is true, very inconsiderable (not exceeding, it is believed, 500), but owing to the extent of the country occupied by them and its adaptation to their peculiar mode of warfare, a force very disproportioned to their numbers would be necessary to capture them, or even to protect the white settlements from their incursions. The military force now stationed in that State would be inadequate to these objects, and if it should be determined to enforce their removal or to survey the territory allotted to them some addition to it would be necessary, as the Government has but a small force available for that service. Additional appropriations for the support of the Army would also, in that event, be necessary.

For these reasons I have deemed it proper to submit the whole matter to Congress, for such action as they may deem best.

MILLARD FILLMORE.

WASHINGTON, *January 19, 1853.*

To the House of Representatives:

In answer to the resolution of the House of Representatives of the 27th ultimo, requesting information relative to the claims on Spain in the cases of the bark *Georgiana* and the brig *Susan Loud*, I transmit a report from the Secretary of State, to whom the resolution was referred.

MILLARD FILLMORE.

WASHINGTON, *January 21, 1853*.

To the Senate of the United States:

In compliance with the resolution of the Senate of the 10th instant, requesting certain correspondence relative to Central America, I transmit a report from the Secretary of State and the documents by which it was accompanied.

MILLARD FILLMORE.

WASHINGTON, *January 24, 1853*.

To the House of Representatives of the United States:

In obedience to a resolution of your honorable body of December 27, 1852, in reference to claims of custom-house officers for additional pay, I have the honor herewith to transmit a report from the Secretary of the Treasury giving the desired information; and in answer to the seventh interrogatory, asking "whether in my opinion further legislation is necessary or advisable either to protect the Treasury from unjust claims or to secure to the claimants their just rights," I would state that in my opinion no further legislation is necessary to effect either object. My views on this subject will be more fully seen on reference to an opinion given by me to the Secretary of the Treasury, a copy of which is annexed to his report.

MILLARD FILLMORE.

WASHINGTON, *January 24, 1853*.

To the Senate of the United States:

In answer to the resolution of the Senate of the 14th instant, relative to the award of the Emperor Louis Napoleon, of France, in the case of the brig *General Armstrong*, I transmit a report from the Secretary of State and the documents by which it was accompanied.

MILLARD FILLMORE.

WASHINGTON, *January 27, 1853*.

To the Senate of the United States:

In answer to the resolution of the Senate of the 13th instant, requesting a copy of correspondence and other documents relative to Nicaragua, Costa Rica, and the territory claimed by the Mosquito Indians, I transmit a report of the Secretary of State, to whom the resolution was referred.

MILLARD FILLMORE.

WASHINGTON, *January 27, 1853.*

To the House of Representatives:

Since my last message to your honorable body, communicating a report from the Treasury Department, in answer to your resolution of the 3d instant [27th ultimo?], in reference to the compensation of weighers and gaugers, further communications on that subject have been received from New Orleans, which have just been reported to me by the Secretary of the Treasury and which I deem it my duty to communicate to the House.

MILLARD FILLMORE.

WASHINGTON, *February 3, 1853.*

To the Senate of the United States:

I transmit herewith to the Senate in a new draft the convention with the Swiss Confederation, originally negotiated at Berne and concluded in that city on the 25th of November, 1850. On the 7th of March, 1851, it was considered by the Senate of the United States, whose assent was given to it with certain amendments, as will appear from the Journal of the Senate of that day. The convention was sent back to Switzerland with these alterations, which were taken into consideration by the Government of that Confederation, whose action in the premises will be learned by a letter from its President of the 5th of July, 1852.

The modifications which the Government of the Swiss Confederation are desirous of introducing into the amendments made by the Senate of the United States and the articles affected by them are not inconsistent with the object and spirit of those amendments, and appear to me to proceed upon a reasonable principle of compromise.

I have thought it expedient, in submitting them to the Senate with a view to their advice and consent to the ratification of the treaty in its present form, to have the entire instrument taken into a continuous draft, as well the portions—by far the greater part—already assented to by the Senate as the modifications proposed by the Government of the Swiss Confederation in reference to these amendments. In preparing the new draft a few slight alterations have been made in the modifications proposed by the Swiss Government.

Should the convention receive the approbation of the Senate in its present form, it will be immediately transmitted to Switzerland for ratification by the Swiss Confederation.

The delays which have taken place in the negotiation of this treaty have been principally caused by the want of a resident diplomatic agent of the United States at Berne, and are among the reasons for which an appropriation for a chargé d'affaires to that Government has recently, by my direction, been recommended in a letter from the Department of State to the chairman of the Committee on Foreign Relations of the Senate.

MILLARD FILLMORE.

WASHINGTON, *February 3, 1853.*

To the Senate of the United States:

In compliance with the resolution of the Senate of the 11th ultimo, asking for information with regard to the execution of the postal convention between the United States and Great Britain, I transmit a report from the Secretary of State and the documents which accompanied it.

MILLARD FILLMORE.

WASHINGTON, *February 7, 1853.*

To the Senate and House of Representatives:

Having in my message to Congress at the opening of the session adverted to the pending negotiations between this Government and that of Great Britain relative to the fisheries and commercial reciprocity with the British American Provinces, I transmit for the information of Congress the accompanying report from the Department of State on the present state of the negotiations, and I respectfully invite the attention of the two Houses to the suggestion in the latter part of the report.

MILLARD FILLMORE.

WASHINGTON, *February 9, 1853.*

To the Senate and House of Representatives:

I herewith transmit a communication from the Secretary of the Navy, accompanied by the first part of Lieutenant Herndon's report of the exploration of the valley of the Amazon and its tributaries, made by him in connection with Lieutenant Lardner Gibbon, under instructions from the Navy Department.

MILLARD FILLMORE.

WASHINGTON, *February 14, 1853.*

To the Senate of the United States:

I herewith communicate to the Senate, for its consideration with a view to ratification, a convention on the subject of the extradition of fugitives from justice between the United States and Belgium, concluded and signed in this city on the 11th instant by the respective plenipotentiaries.

MILLARD FILLMORE.

WASHINGTON, *February 18, 1853.*

To the Senate and House of Representatives:

I transmit a report from the Secretary of State, embodying the substance of recent communications made by the minister of Her Britannic Majesty to the Department of State on the subject of the interoceanic canal by the Nicaragua route, which formed the chief object of the treaty between the United States and Great Britain of the 19th April, 1850, and the relations of Great Britain to the protectorate of Mosquito, which she expresses herself desirous of relinquishing on terms consistent with her honorable engagements to the Indians of that name.

In consequence of these communications and other considerations stated in the report, it is deemed advisable by the Department that our diplomatic relations with the States of Central America should be placed on a higher and more efficient footing, and this measure meets my approbation. The whole subject is one of so much delicacy and importance that I should have preferred, so near the close of my Administration, not to make it the subject of an Executive communication. But inasmuch as the measure proposed can not, even if deemed expedient by my successor, take effect for near a twelvemonth unless an appropriation is made by this Congress, I have thought it my duty to submit the report of the Department to the two Houses. The importance of the measure seemed to require an exposition somewhat in detail of the grounds on which it is recommended.

MILLARD FILLMORE.

WASHINGTON, *February 18, 1853.*

To the Senate of the United States:

I transmit to the Senate, with the view to its ratification, a convention which was yesterday concluded between the United States and Great Britain for the establishment of international copyright.

MILLARD FILLMORE.

WASHINGTON, *February 19, 1853.*

To the Senate of the United States:

In answer to the resolution of the Senate of the 14th instant, relative to the fisheries on the coasts of Florida, I transmit herewith a report from the Secretary of State and the documents which accompanied it.

MILLARD FILLMORE.

WASHINGTON, *February 21, 1853.*

To the Senate of the United States:

In compliance with your resolution of the 19th of February instant, I herewith communicate a report from the Secretary of War, containing the report of Lieutenant Meigs, of the Engineer Corps, on the surveys, projects, and estimates for supplying the cities of Washington and Georgetown with an unfailing and abundant supply of water.

MILLARD FILLMORE.

WASHINGTON, *February 21, 1853.*

To the Senate of the United States:

I have the honor to transmit herewith a report from the Secretary of the Treasury of the 21st instant, in reference to the reinvestment of certain moneys belonging to the Chickasaw Nation of Indians which will come into the Treasury during the succeeding vacation of the Senate, and I respectfully concur in the recommendation made by the Secretary.

MILLARD FILLMORE.

WASHINGTON, *February 23, 1853.*

To the Senate of the United States:

I transmit to the Senate, for advice and consent with a view to ratification, a convention between the United States and Her Britannic Majesty for the adjustment of certain claims of citizens of the United States on the British Government and of British subjects on the Government of the United States, signed in London on the 8th instant. Although it is stipulated by the terms of the first article of the convention that the commissioner on the part of this Government shall be appointed by the President of the United States, it is not understood that this stipulation was intended to dispense with the concurrence of the Senate in such appointment.

MILLARD FILLMORE.

WASHINGTON, *February 25, 1853.*

To the Senate of the United States:

I transmit to the Senate, for its consideration with a view to ratification, a consular convention concluded in this city on the 23d instant between the United States and His Majesty the Emperor of the French.

MILLARD FILLMORE.

WASHINGTON, *February 26, 1853.*

To the Senate of the United States:

I transmit a copy of a proclamation of yesterday, which I deemed it advisable to issue, relative to an extraordinary session of the Senate on the 4th of March next.

MILLARD FILLMORE.

WASHINGTON, *February 28, 1853.*

To the Senate of the United States:

In answer to the resolution of the Senate of the 17th January last, requesting information in regard to the fisheries on the coasts of the British North American Provinces, I transmit a report from the Secretary of State and the documents which accompanied it.

MILLARD FILLMORE.

WASHINGTON, *February 28, 1853.*

To the Senate of the United States:

I herewith transmit, for the consideration and advice of the Senate, a treaty recently entered into with the Apache Indians in New Mexico by Colonel Sumner and Mr. Greiner, acting on behalf of the United States, together with the letter of Colonel Sumner on the subject of the treaty and reports thereon from the Commissioner of Indian Affairs and the Secretary of the Interior.

MILLARD FILLMORE.

PROCLAMATION.

BY THE PRESIDENT OF THE UNITED STATES OF AMERICA.

A PROCLAMATION.

The attention of the President having been called to the proceedings of Congress at the close of its session on the 4th of March, 1851, from which it appears that the constitutional term of that body was held not to have expired until 12 o'clock at noon of that day, and a notice having been issued, agreeably to former usage, to convene the Senate at 11 o'clock a. m. on the 4th of March next, it is apparent that such call is in conflict with the decision aforesaid:

Now, therefore, as well for the purpose of removing all doubt as to the legality of such call as of establishing a precedent of what is deemed a proper mode of convening the Senate, I, Millard Fillmore, President of the United States, have considered it to be my duty to issue this my proclamation, revoking said call and hereby declaring that an extraordinary occasion requires the Senate of the United States to convene for the transaction of business at the Capitol, in the city of Washington, on Friday, the 4th day of March next, at 12 o'clock at noon of that day, of which all who shall at that time be entitled to act as members of that body are hereby required to take notice.

Given under my hand and the seal of the United States, at Washington, this 25th day of February, A. D. 1853, and of the Independence of the United States the seventy-seventh.

[SEAL.]

MILLARD FILLMORE.

By the President:

EDWARD EVERETT,
Secretary of State.

Franklin Pierce

March 4, 1853, to March 4, 1857

HOME AT CONCORD, NEW HAMPSHIRE, OF

FRANKLIN PIERCE

With official portrait engraved from copy of original in steel

PIERCE

Franklin Pierce

FRANKLIN PIERCE was born in Hillsboro, N. H., November 23, 1804. Was the fourth son of Benjamin and Anna Pierce. His father was a citizen of Massachusetts; was a soldier in the War of the Revolution, attaining the rank of captain and brevet major. After peace was declared he removed from Massachusetts to New Hampshire and located near what is now Hillsboro. His first wife was Elizabeth Andrews, who died at an early age. His second wife, the mother of Franklin Pierce, was Anna Kendrick, of Amherst, N. H. He was sheriff of his county, a member of the State legislature and of the governor's council, and was twice chosen governor of his State (as a Democrat), first in 1827 and again in 1829. For many years he was declared to be "the most influential man in New Hampshire." He died in 1839. Franklin was given an academic education in well-known institutions at Hancock, Francestown, and Exeter, and in 1820 was sent to Bowdoin College. His college mates there were John P. Hale, his future political rival; Professor Calvin E. Stowe; Sergeant S. Prentiss, the distinguished orator; Henry W. Longfellow, and Nathaniel Hawthorne, his future biographer and lifelong friend. He graduated in 1824, being third in his class. After taking his degree he began the study of law at Portsmouth in the office of Levi Woodbury, where he remained about a year. Afterwards spent two years in the law school at Northampton, Mass., and in the office of Judge Edmund Parker, at Amherst, N. H. In 1827 was admitted to the bar and began practice in his native town. Espoused the cause of Andrew Jackson with ardor, and in 1829 was elected to represent his native town in the legislature, where by three subsequent elections he served four years, the last two as speaker. In 1833 was elected to represent his native district in the lower House of Congress, where he remained four years; served on the Judiciary and other important committees. His first important speech in the House was delivered in 1834 upon the necessity of economy and of watchfulness against frauds in the payment of Revolutionary claims. In 1834 married Miss Jane Means Appleton, daughter of Rev. Jesse Appleton, president of Bowdoin College. In 1837 was elected to the United States Senate. On account of ill health of his wife, deeming it best for her to return to New Hampshire, on June 28, 1842, resigned his seat, and returning to his home resumed the practice of the law. In 1838 he changed his residence from Hillsboro to Concord. In 1845 declined an appointment to the United States Senate to fill a vacancy. Also declined the nomination for governor, tendered by the Democratic State convention, and in 1845 an appointment to the office of Attorney-General of the United States, tendered by President Polk. In 1846, when the war with Mexico began, he enlisted as a private in a volunteer company organized at Concord; was soon afterwards commissioned colonel of the Ninth Regiment of Infantry; March 3, 1847, was commissioned brigadier-general in the Volunteer Army, and on March 27 embarked for Mexico, arriving at Vera Cruz June 28. August 6, 1847, joined General Scott with his brigade at Puebla, and soon set out for the capture of the City of Mexico. Took part in the battle of Contreras September 19, 1847, in which engagement he was severely injured by being thrown from his horse. The next day, not having recovered, he undertook to accompany his brigade in action against the enemy, when he fainted. He persisted in remaining on duty in the subsequent operations of the Army. His conduct and services were spoken of in high terms by his superior officers, Generals Scott, Worth, and Pillow. Before the battle of Molino del Rey was appointed one of the American commissioners in the effort for peace, a truce being declared for that purpose. The effort failed and the fighting was renewed. Participated in the battle of Molino del Rey and continued on duty till peace was declared. Resigned his commission in March, 1848, and returned to his home. The same month the legislature of his State voted him a sword of honor in appreciation of his services in the war. Resumed his law practice and was highly successful. In 1850 was a member of the constitutional convention which met at Concord to amend the constitution of New Hampshire, and was chosen to preside over its deliberations; he favored the removal of the religious-test clause in the old constitution, by which Roman Catholics were disqualified from holding office in the State, and also the abolition of any "property qualification;" he carried these amendments through the convention, but the people defeated them at the election. In January, 1852, the Democratic State convention of New Hampshire declared for him for President, but in a letter January 12 he positively refused to permit the delegation to present his name. The national convention of the party met at Baltimore June 1, 1852. On the fourth day he was nominated for President, and was elected in November, receiving 254 electoral votes, while his opponent, General Scott, received only 42. Was inaugurated March 4, 1853. In 1856 was voted for by his friends in the national Democratic convention for renomination, but was unsuccessful. Upon the expiration of his term as President he retired to his home at Concord, where he resided the remainder of his life. Died October 8, 1869, and was buried at Concord.

INAUGURAL ADDRESS.

My COUNTRYMEN: It is a relief to feel that no heart but my own can know the personal regret and bitter sorrow over which I have been borne to a position so suitable for others rather than desirable for myself.

The circumstances under which I have been called for a limited period to preside over the destinies of the Republic fill me with a profound sense of responsibility, but with nothing like shrinking apprehension. I repair to the post assigned me not as to one sought, but in obedience to the unsolicited expression of your will, answerable only for a fearless, faithful, and diligent exercise of my best powers. I ought to be, and am, truly grateful for the rare manifestation of the nation's confidence; but this, so far from lightening my obligations, only adds to their weight. You have summoned me in my weakness; you must sustain me by your strength. When looking for the fulfillment of reasonable requirements, you will not be unmindful of the great changes which have occurred, even within the last quarter of a century, and the consequent augmentation and complexity of duties imposed in the administration both of your home and foreign affairs.

Whether the elements of inherent force in the Republic have kept pace with its unparalleled progression in territory, population, and wealth has been the subject of earnest thought and discussion on both sides of the ocean. Less than sixty-four years ago the Father of his Country made "the" then "recent accession of the important State of North Carolina to the Constitution of the United States" one of the subjects of his special congratulation. At that moment, however, when the agitation consequent upon the Revolutionary struggle had hardly subsided, when we were just emerging from the weakness and embarrassments of the Confederation, there was an evident consciousness of vigor equal to the great mission so wisely and bravely fulfilled by our fathers. It was not a presumptuous assurance, but a calm faith, springing from a clear view of the sources of power in a government constituted like ours. It is no paradox to say that although comparatively weak the new-born nation was intrinsically strong. Inconsiderable in population and apparent resources, it was upheld by a broad and intelligent comprehension of rights and an all-pervading purpose to maintain them, stronger than armaments. It came from the furnace of the Revolution, tempered to the necessities of the times. The thoughts of the men of that day were as practical as their sentiments were patriotic. They wasted no portion of their energies upon idle and delusive speculations, but with a firm and fearless step advanced beyond the governmental landmarks which had hitherto circumscribed the limits of human freedom and planted their standard, where it has stood against dangers which have threatened from abroad, and internal agitation, which has at times fearfully menaced at home. They proved themselves equal to the solution of the great problem, to understand which their minds had been illuminated by the dawning lights of the Revolution. The object sought was not a thing dreamed of; it was a thing realized. They had exhibited not only the power to achieve, but, what all history affirms to be so much more unusual, the capacity to maintain. The oppressed throughout the world from that day to the present have turned their eyes hitherward, not to find those lights extinguished or to fear lest they should wane, but to be constantly cheered by their steady and increasing radiance.

In this our country has, in my judgment, thus far fulfilled its highest duty to suffering humanity. It has spoken and will continue to speak, not only by its words, but by its acts, the language of sympathy, encouragement, and hope to those who earnestly listen to tones which pronounce for the largest rational liberty. But after all, the most animating encouragement and potent appeal for freedom will be its own history—its trials and its triumphs. Preeminently, the power of our advocacy reposes in our example; but no example, be it remembered, can be powerful for lasting good, whatever apparent advantages may be gained, which is not based upon eternal principles of right and justice. Our fathers decided for themselves, both upon the hour to declare and the hour to strike. They were their own judges of the circumstances under which it became them to pledge to each other "their lives, their fortunes, and their sacred honor" for the acquisition of the priceless inheritance transmitted to us. The energy with which that great conflict was opened and, under the guidance of a manifest and beneficent Providence, the uncomplaining endurance with which it was prosecuted to its consummation were only surpassed by the wisdom and patriotic spirit of concession which characterized all the counsels of the early fathers.

One of the most impressive evidences of that wisdom is to be found in the fact that the actual working of our system has dispelled a degree of solicitude which at the outset disturbed bold hearts and far-reaching intellects. The apprehension of dangers from extended territory, multiplied States, accumulated wealth, and augmented population has proved to be unfounded. The stars upon your banner have become nearly threefold their original number; your densely populated possessions skirt the shores of the two great oceans; and yet this vast increase of people and territory has not only shown itself compatible with the harmonious action of the States and Federal Government in their respective constitutional spheres, but has afforded an additional guaranty of the strength and integrity of both.

With an experience thus suggestive and cheering, the policy of my Administration will not be controlled by any timid forebodings of evil from expansion. Indeed, it is not to be disguised that our attitude as a nation and our position on the globe render the acquisition of certain possessions not within our jurisdiction eminently important for our protection, if not in the future essential for the preservation of the rights of commerce and the peace of the world. Should they be obtained, it will be through no grasping spirit, but with a view to obvious national interest and security, and in a manner entirely consistent with the strictest observance of national faith. We have nothing in our history or position to invite aggression; we have everything to beckon us to the cultivation of relations of peace and amity with all nations. Purposes, therefore, at once just and pacific will be significantly marked in the conduct of our foreign affairs. I intend that my Administration shall leave no blot upon our fair record, and trust I may safely give the assurance that no act within the legitimate scope of my constitutional control will be tolerated on the part of any portion of our citizens which can not challenge a ready justification before the tribunal of the civilized world. An Administration would be unworthy of confidence at home or respect abroad should it cease to be influenced by the conviction that no apparent advantage can be purchased at a price so dear as that of national wrong or dishonor. It is not your privilege as a nation to speak of a distant past. The striking incidents of your history, replete with instruction and furnishing abundant grounds for hopeful confidence, are comprised in a period comparatively brief. But if your past is limited, your future is boundless. Its obligations throng the unexplored pathway of advancement, and will be limitless as duration. Hence a sound and comprehensive policy should embrace not less the distant future than the urgent present.

The great objects of our pursuit as a people are best to be attained by peace, and are entirely consistent with the tranquillity and interests of the rest of mankind. With the neighboring nations upon our continent we should cultivate kindly and fraternal relations. We can desire nothing in regard to them so much as to see them consolidate their strength and pursue the paths of prosperity and happiness. If in the course of their growth we should open new channels of trade and create additional facilities for friendly intercourse, the benefits realized will be equal and mutual. Of the complicated European systems of national polity we have heretofore been independent. From their wars, their tumults, and anxieties we have been, happily, almost entirely exempt. Whilst these are confined to the nations which gave them existence, and within their legitimate jurisdiction, they can not affect us except as they appeal to our sympathies in the cause of human freedom and universal advancement. But the vast interests of commerce are common to all mankind, and the advantages of trade and international intercourse must always present a noble field for the moral influence of a great people.

With these views firmly and honestly carried out, we have a right to expect, and shall under all circumstances require, prompt reciprocity. The rights which belong to us as a nation are not alone to be regarded, but those which pertain to every citizen in his individual capacity, at home and abroad, must be sacredly maintained. So long as he can discern every star in its place upon that ensign, without wealth to purchase for him preferment or title to secure for him place, it will be his privilege, and must be his acknowledged right, to stand unabashed even in the presence of princes, with a proud consciousness that he is himself one of a nation of sovereigns and that he can not in legitimate pursuit wander so far from home that the agent whom he shall leave behind in the place which I now occupy will not see that no rude hand of power or tyrannical passion is laid upon him with impunity. He must realize that upon every sea and on every soil where our enterprise may rightfully seek the protection of our flag American citizenship is an inviolable panoply for the security of American rights. And in this connection it can hardly be necessary to reaffirm a principle which should now be regarded as fundamental. The rights, security, and repose of this Confederacy reject the idea of interference or colonization on this side of the ocean by any foreign power beyond present jurisdiction as utterly inadmissible.

The opportunities of observation furnished by my brief experience as a soldier confirmed in my own mind the opinion, entertained and acted upon by others from the formation of the Government, that the maintenance of large standing armies in our country would be not only dangerous, but unnecessary. They also illustrated the importance—I might well say the absolute necessity—of the military science and practical skill furnished in such an eminent degree by the institution which has made your Army what it is, under the discipline and instruction of officers not more distinguished for their solid attainments, gallantry, and devotion to the public service than for unobtrusive bearing and high moral tone. The Army as organized must be the nucleus around which in every time of need the strength of your military power, the sure bulwark of your defense—a national militia—may be readily formed into a well-disciplined and efficient organization. And the skill and self-devotion of the Navy assure you that you may take the performance of the past as a pledge for the future, and may confidently expect that the flag which has waved its untarnished folds over every sea will still float in undiminished honor. But these, like many other subjects, will be appropriately brought at a future time to the attention of the coordinate branches of the Government, to which I shall always look with profound respect and with trustful confidence that they will accord to me the aid and support which I shall so much need and which their experience and wisdom will readily suggest.

In the administration of domestic affairs you expect a devoted integrity in the public service and an observance of rigid economy in all departments, so marked as never justly to be questioned. If this reasonable expectation be not realized, I frankly confess that one of your leading hopes is doomed to disappointment, and that my efforts in a very important particular must result in a humiliating failure. Offices can be properly regarded only in the light of aids for the accomplishment of these objects, and as occupancy can confer no prerogative nor importunate desire for preferment any claim, the public interest imperatively demands that they be considered with sole reference to the duties to be performed. Good citizens may well claim the protection of good laws and the benign influence of good government, but a claim for office is what the people of a republic should never recognize. No reasonable man of any party will expect the Administration to be so regardless of its responsibility and of the obvious elements of success as to retain persons known to be under the influence of political hostility and partisan prejudice in positions which will require not only severe labor, but cordial cooperation. Having no implied engagements to ratify, no rewards to bestow, no resentments to remember, and no personal wishes to consult in selections for official station, I shall fulfill this difficult and delicate trust, admitting no motive as worthy either of my character or position which does not contemplate an efficient discharge of duty and the best interests of my country. I acknowledge my obligations to the masses of my countrymen, and to them alone. Higher objects than personal aggrandizement gave direction and energy to their exertions in the late canvass, and they shall not be disappointed. They require at my hands diligence, integrity, and capacity wherever there are duties to be performed. Without these qualities in their public servants, more stringent laws for the prevention or punishment of fraud, negligence, and peculation will be vain. With them they will be unnecessary.

But these are not the only points to which you look for vigilant watchfulness. The dangers of a concentration of all power in the general government of a confederacy so vast as ours are too obvious to be disregarded. You have a right, therefore, to expect your agents in every department to regard strictly the limits imposed upon them by the Constitution of the United States. The great scheme of our constitutional liberty rests upon a proper distribution of power between the State and Federal authorities, and experience has shown that the harmony and happiness of our people must depend upon a just discrimination between the separate rights and responsibilities of the States and your common rights and obligations under the General Government; and here, in my opinion, are the considerations which should form the true basis of future concord in regard to the questions which have most seriously disturbed public tranquillity. If the Federal Government will confine itself to the exercise of powers clearly granted by the Constitution, it can hardly happen that its action upon any question should endanger the institutions of the States or interfere with their right to manage matters strictly domestic according to the will of their own people.

In expressing briefly my views upon an important subject which has recently agitated the nation to almost a fearful degree, I am moved by no other impulse than a most earnest desire for the perpetuation of that Union which has made us what we are, showering upon us blessings and conferring a power and influence which our fathers could hardly have anticipated, even with their most sanguine hopes directed to a far-off future. The sentiments I now announce were not unknown before the expression of the voice which called me here. My own position upon this subject was clear and unequivocal, upon the record of my words and my acts, and it is only recurred to at this time because silence might perhaps be misconstrued. With the Union my best and dearest earthly hopes are entwined. Without it what are we individually or collectively? What becomes of the noblest field ever opened for the advancement of our race in religion, in government, in the arts, and in all that dignifies and adorns mankind? From that radiant constellation which both illumines our own way and points out to struggling nations their course, let but a single star be lost, and, if there be not utter darkness, the luster of the whole is dimmed. Do my countrymen need any assurance that such a catastrophe is not to overtake them while I possess the power to stay it? It is with me an earnest and vital belief that as the Union has been the source, under Providence, of our prosperity to this time, so it is the surest pledge of a continuance of the blessings we have enjoyed, and which we are sacredly bound to transmit undiminished to our children. The field of calm and free discussion in our country is open, and will always be so, but never has been and never can be traversed for good in a spirit of sectionalism and uncharitableness. The founders of the Republic dealt with things as they were presented to them, in a spirit of self-sacrificing patriotism, and, as time has proved, with a comprehensive wisdom which it will always be safe for us to consult. Every measure tending to strengthen the fraternal feelings of all the members of our Union has had my heartfelt approbation. To every theory of society or government, whether the offspring of feverish ambition or of morbid enthusiasm, calculated to dissolve the bonds of law and affection which unite us, I shall interpose a ready and stern resistance. I believe that involuntary servitude, as it exists in different States of this Confederacy, is recognized by the Constitution. I believe that it stands like any other admitted right, and that the States where it exists are entitled to efficient remedies to enforce the constitutional provisions. I hold that the laws of 1850, commonly called the "compromise measures," are strictly constitutional and to be unhesitatingly carried into effect. I believe that the constituted authorities of this Republic are bound to regard the rights of the South in this respect as they would view any other legal and constitutional right, and that the laws to enforce them should be respected and obeyed, not with a reluctance encouraged by abstract opinions as to their propriety in a different state of society, but cheerfully and according to the decisions of the tribunal to which their exposition belongs. Such have been, and are, my convictions, and upon them I shall act. I fervently hope that the question is at rest, and that no sectional or ambitious or fanatical excitement may again threaten the durability of our institutions or obscure the light of our prosperity.

But let not the foundation of our hope rest upon man's wisdom. It will not be sufficient that sectional prejudices find no place in the public deliberations. It will not be sufficient that the rash counsels of human passion are rejected. It must be felt that there is no national security but in the nation's humble, acknowledged dependence upon God and His overruling providence.

We have been carried in safety through a perilous crisis. Wise counsels, like those which gave us the Constitution, prevailed to uphold it. Let the period be remembered as an admonition, and not as an encouragement, in any section of the Union, to make experiments where experiments are fraught with such fearful hazard. Let it be impressed upon all hearts that, beautiful as our fabric is, no earthly power or wisdom could ever reunite its broken fragments. Standing, as I do, almost within view of the green slopes of Monticello, and, as it were, within reach of the tomb of Washington, with all the cherished memories of the past gathering around me like so many eloquent voices of exhortation from heaven, I can express no better hope for my country than that the kind Providence which smiled upon our fathers may enable their children to preserve the blessings they have inherited.

MARCH 4, 1853.

SPECIAL MESSAGES.

WASHINGTON, *March 21, 1853.*

To the Senate of the United States:

In answer to the resolution of the Senate of the 17th instant, respecting certain propositions to Nicaragua and Costa Rica relative to the settlement of the territorial controversies between the States and Governments bordering on the river San Juan, I transmit a report from the Secretary of State and the documents by which it was accompanied.

FRANKLIN PIERCE.

WASHINGTON, *March 21, 1853.*

To the Senate:

The eleventh article of the treaty with the Chickasaw Indians of the 20th October, 1832, provides that certain moneys arising from the sales of the lands ceded by that treaty shall be laid out under the direction of the President of the United States, by and with the advice and consent of the Senate, in such safe and valuable stock as he may approve of, for the benefit of the Chickasaw Nation.

The report of the Secretary of the Treasury of the 15th instant, herewith transmitted, shows that the sum of $58,100 5 per cent stock, created under the act of 3d March, 1843, now stands on the books of the

Treasury in the name of the Secretary of the Treasury, as trustee for the Chickasaw national fund. This stock, by the terms of its issue, is redeemable on the 1st July next, when interest thereon will cease. It therefore becomes my duty to lay before the Senate the subject of reinvesting this amount under the same trust.

The second section of the act of 11th September, 1841 (the first section of which repeals the provisions of the act of 7th July, 1838, directing the investment of the Smithsonian fund in the stocks of the States), enacts that "all other funds held in trust by the United States, and the annual interest accruing thereon, when not otherwise required by treaty, shall in like manner be invested in stocks of the United States bearing a like rate of interest."

I submit to the Senate whether it will advise and consent that the Secretary of the Treasury be authorized, under my direction, to reinvest the above-mentioned sum of $58,100 in stocks of the United States under the same trust.

FRANKLIN PIERCE.

WASHINGTON, *March 21, 1853.*
To the Senate of the United States:

In answer to the resolution of the Senate of the 18th of January last, calling for further correspondence touching the revolution in France of December, 1851, I transmit a report from the Secretary of State and the documents by which it was accompanied.

FRANKLIN PIERCE.

EXECUTIVE CHAMBER, *March 25, 1853.*
To the Senate of the United States:

I nominate Mrs. Mary Berard to be deputy postmaster at "West Point," N. Y., the commissions for said office having exceeded $1,000 for the year ending the 30th June, 1852. Mrs. B. has held said office since the 12th of May, 1848, under an appointment of the Post-Office Department.

FRANKLIN PIERCE.

EXECUTIVE ORDERS.

EXECUTIVE OFFICE, *March 23, 1853.*

Believing that the public interests involved in the erection of the wings of the United States Capitol will be promoted by the exercise of a general supervision and control of the whole work by a skillful and competent officer of the Corps of Engineers or of the Topographical Corps, and as the officers of those corps are more immediately amenable to the Secretary of War, I hereby direct that the jurisdiction heretofore exercised over the said work by the Department of the Interior be transferred to the War Department, and request that the Secretary of War will designate to the President a suitable officer to take charge of the same. FRANKLIN PIERCE.

BY THE PRESIDENT OF THE UNITED STATES.

WASHINGTON, *April 20, 1853.*

The President has, with deep sorrow, received information that the Vice-President of the United States, William R. King, died on the 18th instant at his residence in Alabama.

In testimony of respect for eminent station, exalted character, and, higher and above all station, for a career of public service and devotion to this Union which for duration and usefulness is almost without a parallel in the history of the Republic, the labors of the various Departments will be suspended.

The Secretaries of War and Navy will issue orders that appropriate military and naval honors be rendered to the memory of one to whom such a tribute will not be formal, but heartfelt from a people the deceased has so faithfully served.

The public offices will be closed to-morrow and badges of mourning be placed on the Executive Mansion and all the Executive Departments at Washington. FRANKLIN PIERCE.

GENERAL ORDERS, NO. 11.

WAR DEPARTMENT,
ADJUTANT-GENERAL'S OFFICE,
Washington, April 20, 1853.

I. The following order announces to the Army the death of William Rufus King, late Vice-President of the United States:

WAR DEPARTMENT,
Washington, April 20, 1853.

With deep sorrow the President announces to the Army the death of William Rufus King, Vice-President of the United States, who died on the evening of Monday, the 18th instant, at his residence in Dallas County, Ala.

Called into the service of his country at a period in life when but few are prepared to enter upon its realities, his long career of public usefulness at home and abroad has always been honored by the public confidence, and was closed in the second office within the gift of the people.

From sympathy with his relatives and the American people for their loss and from respect for his distinguished public services, the President directs that appropriate honors to his memory be paid by the Army.

JEFFERSON DAVIS,
Secretary of War.

II. On the day next succeeding the receipt of this order at each military post the troops will be paraded at 10 o'clock a. m. and this order read to them.

The national flag will be displayed at half-staff.

At dawn of day thirteen guns will be fired. Commencing at 12 o'clock m. seventeen minute guns will be fired and at the close of the day the national salute of thirty-one guns.

The usual badge of mourning will be worn by officers of the Army and the colors of the several regiments will be put in mourning for the period of three months.

By order:

S. COOPER,
Adjutant-General.

[From the Daily National Intelligencer, April 21, 1853.]

GENERAL ORDER.

NAVY DEPARTMENT,
April 20, 1853.

With deep sorrow the President announces to the officers of the Navy and Marine Corps the death of William Rufus King, Vice-President of the United States, who died on the evening of Monday, the 18th instant, at his residence in Alabama.

Called into the service of his country at a period of life when but few are prepared to enter upon its realities, his long career of public usefulness at home and abroad has always been honored by the public confidence, and was closed in the second office within the gift of the people.

From sympathy with his relatives and the American people for their loss and from respect for his distinguished public services, the President directs that appropriate honors be paid to his memory at each of the navy-yards and naval stations and on board all the public vessels in commission on the day after this order is received by firing at dawn of day thirteen guns, at 12 o'clock m. seventeen minute guns, and at the close of the day the national salute, by carrying their flags at half-mast one day, and by the officers wearing crape on the left arm for three months.

J. C. DOBBIN,
Secretary of the Navy.

FIRST ANNUAL MESSAGE.

WASHINGTON, D. C., *December 5, 1853.*

Fellow-Citizens of the Senate and of the House of Representatives:

The interest with which the people of the Republic anticipate the assembling of Congress and the fulfillment on that occasion of the duty imposed upon a new President is one of the best evidences of their capacity to realize the hopes of the founders of a political system at once complex and symmetrical. While the different branches of the Government are to a certain extent independent of each other, the duties of all alike have direct reference to the source of power. Fortunately, under this system no man is so high and none so humble in the scale of public station as to escape from the scrutiny or to be exempt from the responsibility which all official functions imply.

Upon the justice and intelligence of the masses, in a government thus organized, is the sole reliance of the confederacy and the only security for honest and earnest devotion to its interests against the usurpations and encroachments of power on the one hand and the assaults of personal ambition on the other.

The interest of which I have spoken is inseparable from an inquiring, self-governing community, but stimulated, doubtless, at the present time by the unsettled condition of our relations with several foreign powers, by the new obligations resulting from a sudden extension of the field of enterprise, by the spirit with which that field has been entered and the amazing energy with which its resources for meeting the demands of humanity have been developed.

Although disease, assuming at one time the characteristics of a widespread and devastating pestilence, has left its sad traces upon some portions of our country, we have still the most abundant cause for reverent thankfulness to God for an accumulation of signal mercies showered upon us as a nation. It is well that a consciousness of rapid advancement and increasing strength be habitually associated with an abiding sense of dependence upon Him who holds in His hands the destiny of men and of nations.

Recognizing the wisdom of the broad principle of absolute religious toleration proclaimed in our fundamental law, and rejoicing in the benign influence which it has exerted upon our social and political condition, I should shrink from a clear duty did I fail to express my deepest conviction that we can place no secure reliance upon any apparent progress if it be not sustained by national integrity, resting upon the great truths affirmed and illustrated by divine revelation. In the midst of our sorrow for the afflicted and suffering, it has been consoling to see how promptly disaster made true neighbors of districts and cities separated widely from each other, and cheering to watch the strength of that common bond of brotherhood which unites all hearts, in all parts of this Union, when danger threatens from abroad or calamity impends over us at home.

Our diplomatic relations with foreign powers have undergone no essential change since the adjournment of the last Congress. With some of them questions of a disturbing character are still pending, but there are good reasons to believe that these may all be amicably adjusted.

For some years past Great Britain has so construed the first article of the convention of the 20th of April, 1818, in regard to the fisheries on the northeastern coast, as to exclude our citizens from some of the fishing grounds to which they freely resorted for nearly a quarter of a century subsequent to the date of that treaty. The United States have never acquiesced in this construction, but have always claimed for their fishermen all the rights which they had so long enjoyed without molestation. With a view to remove all difficulties on the subject, to extend the rights of our fishermen beyond the limits fixed by the convention of 1818, and to regulate trade between the United States and the British North American Provinces, a negotiation has been opened with a fair prospect of a favorable result. To protect our fishermen in the enjoyment of their rights and prevent collision between them and British fishermen, I deemed it expedient to station a naval force in that quarter during the fishing season.

Embarrassing questions have also arisen between the two Governments in regard to Central America. Great Britain has proposed to settle them by an amicable arrangement, and our minister at London is instructed to enter into negotiations on that subject.

A commission for adjusting the claims of our citizens against Great Britain and those of British subjects against the United States, organized under the convention of the 8th of February last, is now sitting in London for the transaction of business.

It is in many respects desirable that the boundary line between the United States and the British Provinces in the northwest, as designated in the convention of the 15th of June, 1846, and especially that part which separates the Territory of Washington from the British possessions on the north, should be traced and marked. I therefore present the subject to your notice.

With France our relations continue on the most friendly footing. The extensive commerce between the United States and that country might, it is conceived, be released from some unnecessary restrictions to the mutual advantage of both parties. With a view to this object, some progress has been made in negotiating a treaty of commerce and navigation.

Independently of our valuable trade with Spain, we have important political relations with her growing out of our neighborhood to the islands of Cuba and Porto Rico. I am happy to announce that since the last Congress no attempts have been made by unauthorized expeditions within the United States against either of those colonies. Should any movement be manifested within our limits, all the means at my command will be vigorously exerted to repress it. Several annoying occurrences have taken place at Havana, or in the vicinity of the island of Cuba, between our citizens and the Spanish authorities. Considering the proximity of that island to our shores, lying, as it does, in the track of trade between some of our principal cities, and the suspicious vigilance with which foreign intercourse, particularly that with the United States, is there guarded, a repetition of such occurrences may well be apprehended.

As no diplomatic intercourse is allowed between our consul at Havana and the Captain-General of Cuba, ready explanations can not be made or prompt redress afforded where injury has resulted. All complaint on the part of our citizens under the present arrangement must be, in the first place, presented to this Government and then referred to Spain. Spain again refers it to her local authorities in Cuba for investigation, and postpones an answer till she has heard from those authorities. To avoid these irritating and vexatious delays, a proposition has been made to provide for a direct appeal for redress to the Captain-General by our consul in behalf of our injured fellow-citizens. Hitherto the Government of Spain has declined to enter into any such arrangement. This course on her part is deeply regretted, for without some arrangement of this kind the good understanding between the two countries may be exposed to occasional interruption. Our minister at Madrid is instructed to renew the proposition and to press it again upon the consideration of Her Catholic Majesty's Government.

For several years Spain has been calling the attention of this Government to a claim for losses by some of her subjects in the case of the schooner *Amistad*. This claim is believed to rest on the obligations imposed by our existing treaty with that country. Its justice was admitted in our diplomatic correspondence with the Spanish Government as early as March, 1847, and one of my predecessors, in his annual message of that year, recommended that provision should be made for its payment. In January last it was again submitted to Congress by the Executive. It has received a favorable consideration by committees of both branches, but as yet there has been no final action upon it. I conceive that good faith requires its prompt adjustment, and I present it to your early and favorable consideration.

Martin Koszta, a Hungarian by birth, came to this country in 1850, and declared his intention in due form of law to become a citizen of the United States. After remaining here nearly two years he visited Turkey. While at Smyrna he was forcibly seized, taken on board an Austrian brig of war then lying in the harbor of that place, and there confined in irons, with the avowed design to take him into the dominions of Austria. Our consul at Smyrna and legation at Constantinople interposed for his release, but their efforts were ineffectual. While thus in prison Commander Ingraham, with the United States ship of war *St. Louis*, arrived at Smyrna, and after inquiring into the circumstances of the case came to the conclusion that Koszta was entitled to the protection of this Government, and took energetic and prompt measures for his release. Under an arrangement between the agents of the United States and of Austria, he was transferred to the custody of the French consul-general at Smyrna, there to remain until he should be disposed of by the mutual agreement of the consuls of the respective Governments at that place. Pursuant to that agreement, he has been released, and is now in the United States. The Emperor of Austria has made the conduct of our officers who took part in this transaction a subject of grave complaint. Regarding Koszta as still his subject, and claiming a right to seize him within the limits of the Turkish Empire, he has demanded of this Government its consent to the surrender of the prisoner, a disavowal of the acts of its agents, and satisfaction for the alleged outrage. After a careful consideration of the case I came to the conclusion that Koszta was seized without legal authority at Smyrna; that he was wrongfully detained on board of the Austrian brig of war; that at the time of his seizure he was clothed with the nationality of the United States, and that the acts of our officers, under the circumstances of the case, were justifiable, and their conduct has been fully approved by me, and a compliance with the several demands of the Emperor of Austria has been declined.

For a more full account of this transaction and my views in regard to it I refer to the correspondence between the chargé d'affaires of Austria and the Secretary of State, which is herewith transmitted. The principles and policy therein maintained on the part of the United States will, whenever a proper occasion occurs, be applied and enforced.

The condition of China at this time renders it probable that some important changes will occur in that vast Empire which will lead to a more unrestricted intercourse with it. The commissioner to that country who has been recently appointed is instructed to avail himself of all occasions to open and extend our commercial relations, not only with the Empire of China, but with other Asiatic nations.

In 1852 an expedition was sent to Japan, under the command of Commodore Perry, for the purpose of opening commercial intercourse with that Empire. Intelligence has been received of his arrival there and of his having made known to the Emperor of Japan the object of his visit. But it is not yet ascertained how far the Emperor will be disposed to abandon his restrictive policy and open that populous country to a commercial intercourse with the United States.

It has been my earnest desire to maintain friendly intercourse with the Governments upon this continent and to aid them in preserving good understanding among themselves. With Mexico a dispute has arisen as to the true boundary line between our Territory of New Mexico and the

Mexican State of Chihuahua. A former commissioner of the United States, employed in running that line pursuant to the treaty of Guadalupe Hidalgo, made a serious mistake in determining the initial point on the Rio Grande; but inasmuch as his decision was clearly a departure from the directions for tracing the boundary contained in that treaty, and was not concurred in by the surveyor appointed on the part of the United States, whose concurrence was necessary to give validity to that decision, this Government is not concluded thereby; but that of Mexico takes a different view of the subject.

There are also other questions of considerable magnitude pending between the two Republics. Our minister in Mexico has ample instructions to adjust them. Negotiations have been opened, but sufficient progress has not been made therein to enable me to speak of the probable result. Impressed with the importance of maintaining amicable relations with that Republic and of yielding with liberality to all her just claims, it is reasonable to expect that an arrangement mutually satisfactory to both countries may be concluded and a lasting friendship between them confirmed and perpetuated.

Congress having provided for a full mission to the States of Central America, a minister was sent thither in July last. As yet he has had time to visit only one of these States (Nicaragua), where he was received in the most friendly manner. It is hoped that his presence and good offices will have a benign effect in composing the dissensions which prevail among them, and in establishing still more intimate and friendly relations between them respectively and between each of them and the United States.

Considering the vast regions of this continent and the number of states which would be made accessible by the free navigation of the river Amazon, particular attention has been given to this subject. Brazil, through whose territories it passes into the ocean, has hitherto persisted in a policy so restricted in regard to the use of this river as to obstruct and nearly exclude foreign commercial intercourse with the States which lie upon its tributaries and upper branches. Our minister to that country is instructed to obtain a relaxation of that policy and to use his efforts to induce the Brazilian Government to open to common use, under proper safeguards, this great natural highway for international trade. Several of the South American States are deeply interested in this attempt to secure the free navigation of the Amazon, and it is reasonable to expect their cooperation in the measure. As the advantages of free commercial intercourse among nations are better understood, more liberal views are generally entertained as to the common rights of all to the free use of those means which nature has provided for international communication. To these more liberal and enlightened views it is hoped that Brazil will conform her policy and remove all unnecessary restrictions upon the free use of a river which traverses so many states and so large a part of the continent. I am happy to inform you that the Republic of

Paraguay and the Argentine Confederation have yielded to the liberal policy still resisted by Brazil in regard to the navigable rivers within their respective territories. Treaties embracing this subject, among others, have been negotiated with these Governments, which will be submitted to the Senate at the present session.

A new branch of commerce, important to the agricultural interests of the United States, has within a few years past been opened with Peru. Notwithstanding the inexhaustible deposits of guano upon the islands of that country, considerable difficulties are experienced in obtaining the requisite supply. Measures have been taken to remove these difficulties and to secure a more abundant importation of the article. Unfortunately, there has been a serious collision between our citizens who have resorted to the Chincha Islands for it and the Peruvian authorities stationed there. Redress for the outrages committed by the latter was promptly demanded by our minister at Lima. This subject is now under consideration, and there is reason to believe that Peru is disposed to offer adequate indemnity to the aggrieved parties.

We are thus not only at peace with all foreign countries, but, in regard to political affairs, are exempt from any cause of serious disquietude in our domestic relations.

The controversies which have agitated the country heretofore are passing away with the causes which produced them and the passions which they had awakened; or, if any trace of them remains, it may be reasonably hoped that it will only be perceived in the zealous rivalry of all good citizens to testify their respect for the rights of the States, their devotion to the Union, and their common determination that each one of the States, its institutions, its welfare, and its domestic peace, shall be held alike secure under the sacred ægis of the Constitution.

This new league of amity and of mutual confidence and support into which the people of the Republic have entered happily affords inducement and opportunity for the adoption of a more comprehensive and unembarrassed line of policy and action as to the great material interests of the country, whether regarded in themselves or in connection with the powers of the civilized world.

The United States have continued gradually and steadily to expand through acquisitions of territory, which, how much soever some of them may have been questioned, are now universally seen and admitted to have been wise in policy, just in character, and a great element in the advancement of our country, and with it of the human race, in freedom, in prosperity, and in happiness. The thirteen States have grown to be thirty-one, with relations reaching to Europe on the one side and on the other to the distant realms of Asia.

I am deeply sensible of the immense responsibility which the present magnitude of the Republic and the diversity and multiplicity of its interests devolves upon me, the alleviation of which, so far as relates to the immediate conduct of the public business, is, first, in my reliance on the wisdom and patriotism of the two Houses of Congress, and, secondly, in the directions afforded me by the principles of public polity affirmed by our fathers of the epoch of 1798, sanctioned by long experience, and consecrated anew by the overwhelming voice of the people of the United States.

Recurring to these principles, which constitute the organic basis of union, we perceive that vast as are the functions and the duties of the Federal Government, vested in or intrusted to its three great departments—the legislative, executive, and judicial—yet the substantive power, the popular force, and the large capacities for social and material development exist in the respective States, which, all being of themselves well-constituted republics, as they preceded so they alone are capable of maintaining and perpetuating the American Union. The Federal Government has its appropriate line of action in the specific and limited powers conferred on it by the Constitution, chiefly as to those things in which the States have a common interest in their relations to one another and to foreign governments, while the great mass of interests which belong to cultivated men—the ordinary business of life, the springs of industry, all the diversified personal and domestic affairs of society—rest securely upon the general reserved powers of the people of the several States. There is the effective democracy of the nation, and there the vital essence of its being and its greatness.

Of the practical consequences which flow from the nature of the Federal Government, the primary one is the duty of administering with integrity and fidelity the high trust reposed in it by the Constitution, especially in the application of the public funds as drawn by taxation from the people and appropriated to specific objects by Congress.

Happily, I have no occasion to suggest any radical changes in the financial policy of the Government. Ours is almost, if not absolutely, the solitary power of Christendom having a surplus revenue drawn immediately from imposts on commerce, and therefore measured by the spontaneous enterprise and national prosperity of the country, with such indirect relation to agriculture, manufactures, and the products of the earth and sea as to violate no constitutional doctrine and yet vigorously promote the general welfare. Neither as to the sources of the public treasure nor as to the manner of keeping and managing it does any grave controversy now prevail, there being a general acquiescence in the wisdom of the present system.

The report of the Secretary of the Treasury will exhibit in detail the state of the public finances and the condition of the various branches of the public service administered by that Department of the Government.

The revenue of the country, levied almost insensibly to the taxpayer, goes on from year to year, increasing beyond either the interests or the prospective wants of the Government.

At the close of the fiscal year ending June 30, 1852, there remained in the Treasury a balance of $14,632,136. The public revenue for the fiscal year ending June 30, 1853, amounted to $58,931,865 from customs and to $2,405,708 from public lands and other miscellaneous sources, amounting together to $61,337,574, while the public expenditures for the same period, exclusive of payments on account of the public debt, amounted to $43,554,262, leaving a balance of $32,425,447 of receipts above expenditures.

This fact of increasing surplus in the Treasury became the subject of anxious consideration at a very early period of my Administration, and the path of duty in regard to it seemed to me obvious and clear, namely: First, to apply the surplus revenue to the discharge of the public debt so far as it could judiciously be done, and, secondly, to devise means for the gradual reduction of the revenue to the standard of the public exigencies.

Of these objects the first has been in the course of accomplishment in a manner and to a degree highly satisfactory. The amount of the public debt of all classes was on the 4th of March, 1853, $69,190,037, payments on account of which have been made since that period to the amount of $12,703,329, leaving unpaid and in continuous course of liquidation the sum of $56,486,708. These payments, although made at the market price of the respective classes of stocks, have been effected readily and to the general advantage of the Treasury, and have at the same time proved of signal utility in the relief they have incidentally afforded to the money market and to the industrial and commercial pursuits of the country.

The second of the above-mentioned objects, that of the reduction of the tariff, is of great importance, and the plan suggested by the Secretary of the Treasury, which is to reduce the duties on certain articles and to add to the free list many articles now taxed, and especially such as enter into manufactures and are not largely, or at all, produced in the country, is commended to your candid and careful consideration.

You will find in the report of the Secretary of the Treasury, also, abundant proof of the entire adequacy of the present fiscal system to meet all the requirements of the public service, and that, while properly administered, it operates to the advantage of the community in ordinary business relations.

I respectfully ask your attention to sundry suggestions of improvements in the settlement of accounts, especially as regards the large sums of outstanding arrears due to the Government, and of other reforms in the administrative action of his Department which are indicated by the Secretary; as also to the progress made in the construction of marine hospitals, custom-houses, and of a new mint in California and assay office in the city of New York, heretofore provided for by Congress, and also to the eminently successful progress of the Coast Survey and of the Light-House Board.

Among the objects meriting your attention will be important recommendations from the Secretaries of War and Navy. I am fully satisfied that the Navy of the United States is not in a condition of strength and efficiency commensurate with the magnitude of our commercial and other interests, and commend to your especial attention the suggestions on this subject made by the Secretary of the Navy. I respectfully submit that the Army, which under our system must always be regarded with the highest interest as a nucleus around which the volunteer forces of the nation gather in the hour of danger, requires augmentation, or modification, to adapt it to the present extended limits and frontier relations of the country and the condition of the Indian tribes in the interior of the continent, the necessity of which will appear in the communications of the Secretaries of War and the Interior.

In the administration of the Post-Office Department for the fiscal year ending June 30, 1853, the gross expenditure was $7,982,756, and the gross receipts during the same period $5,942,734, showing that the current revenue failed to meet the current expenses of the Department by the sum of $2,042,032. The causes which, under the present postal system and laws, led inevitably to this result are fully explained by the report of the Postmaster-General, one great cause being the enormous rates the Department has been compelled to pay for mail service rendered by railroad companies.

The exhibit in the report of the Postmaster-General of the income and expenditures by mail steamers will be found peculiarly interesting and of a character to demand the immediate action of Congress.

Numerous and flagrant frauds upon the Pension Bureau have been brought to light within the last year, and in some instances merited punishments inflicted; but, unfortunately, in others guilty parties have escaped, not through the want of sufficient evidence to warrant a conviction, but in consequence of the provisions of limitation in the existing laws.

From the nature of these claims, the remoteness of the tribunals to pass upon them, and the mode in which the proof is of necessity furnished, temptations to crime have been greatly stimulated by the obvious difficulties of detection. The defects in the law upon this subject are so apparent and so fatal to the ends of justice that your early action relating to it is most desirable.

During the last fiscal year 9,819,411 acres of the public lands have been surveyed and 10,363,891 acres brought into market. Within the same period the sales by public purchase and private entry amounted to 1,083,-495 acres; located under military bounty-land warrants, 6,142,360 acres; located under other certificates, 9,427 acres; ceded to the States as swamp lands, 16,684,253 acres; selected for railroad and other objects under acts of Congress, 1,427,457 acres; total amount of lands disposed of within the fiscal year, 25,346,992 acres, which is an increase in quantity sold and located under land warrants and grants of 12,231,818 acres over the fiscal year immediately preceding. The quantity of land sold during the second and third quarters of 1852 was 334,451 acres; the amount received therefor was $623,687. The quantity sold the second and third quarters of the year 1853 was 1,609,919 acres, and the amount received therefor $2,226,876.

The whole number of land warrants issued under existing laws prior to the 30th of September last was 266,042, of which there were outstanding at that date 66,947. The quantity of land required to satisfy these outstanding warrants is 4,778,120 acres.

Warrants have been issued to 30th of September last under the act of 11th February, 1847, calling for 12,879,280 acres, under acts of September 28, 1850, and March 22, 1852, calling for 12,505,360 acres, making a total of 25,384,640 acres.

It is believed that experience has verified the wisdom and justice of the present system with regard to the public domain in most essential particulars.

You will perceive from the report of the Secretary of the Interior that opinions which have often been expressed in relation to the operation of the land system as not being a source of revenue to the Federal Treasury were erroneous. The net profits from the sale of the public lands to June 30, 1853, amounted to the sum of $53,289,465.

I recommend the extension of the land system over the Territories of Utah and New Mexico, with such modifications as their peculiarities may require.

Regarding our public domain as chiefly valuable to provide homes for the industrious and enterprising, I am not prepared to recommend any essential change in the land system, except by modifications in favor of the actual settler and an extension of the preemption principle in certain cases, for reasons and on grounds which will be fully developed in the reports to be laid before you.

Congress, representing the proprietors of the territorial domain and charged especially with power to dispose of territory belonging to the United States, has for a long course of years, beginning with the Administration of Mr. Jefferson, exercised the power to construct roads within the Territories, and there are so many and obvious distinctions between this exercise of power and that of making roads within the States that the former has never been considered subject to such objections as apply to the latter; and such may now be considered the settled construction of the power of the Federal Government upon the subject.

Numerous applications have been and no doubt will continue to be made for grants of land in aid of the construction of railways. It is not believed to be within the intent and meaning of the Constitution that the power to dispose of the public domain should be used otherwise than might be expected from a prudent proprietor, and therefore that grants of land to aid in the construction of roads should be restricted to cases where it would be for the interest of a proprietor under like circumstances thus to contribute to the construction of these works. For the practical operation of such grants thus far in advancing the interests of the States in which the works are located, and at the same time the substantial interests of all the other States, by enhancing the value and promoting the rapid sale of the public domain, I refer you to the report of the Secretary of the Interior. A careful examination, however, will show that this experience is the result of a just discrimination and will be far from affording encouragement to a reckless or indiscriminate extension of the principle.

I commend to your favorable consideration the men of genius of our country who by their inventions and discoveries in science and arts have contributed largely to the improvements of the age without, in many instances, securing for themselves anything like an adequate reward. For many interesting details upon this subject I refer you to the appropriate reports, and especially urge upon your early attention the apparently slight, but really important, modifications of existing laws therein suggested.

The liberal spirit which has so long marked the action of Congress in relation to the District of Columbia will, I have no doubt, continue to be manifested.

The erection of an asylum for the insane of the District of Columbia and of the Army and Navy of the United States has been somewhat retarded by the great demand for materials and labor during the past summer, but full preparation for the reception of patients before the return of another winter is anticipated; and there is the best reason to believe, from the plan and contemplated arrangements which have been devised, with the large experience furnished within the last few years in relation to the nature and treatment of the disease, that it will prove an asylum indeed to this most helpless and afflicted class of sufferers and stand as a noble monument of wisdom and mercy.

Under the acts of Congress of August 31, 1852, and of March 3, 1853, designed to secure for the cities of Washington and Georgetown an abundant supply of good and wholesome water, it became my duty to examine the report and plans of the engineer who had charge of the surveys under the act first named. The best, if not the only, plan calculated to secure permanently the object sought was that which contemplates taking the water from the Great Falls of the Potomac, and consequently I gave to it my approval.

For the progress and present condition of this important work and for its demands so far as appropriations are concerned I refer you to the report of the Secretary of War.

The present judicial system of the United States has now been in operation for so long a period of time and has in its general theory and much of its details become so familiar to the country and acquired so entirely the public confidence that if modified in any respect it should only be in those particulars which may adapt it to the increased extent, population, and legal business of the United States. In this relation the organization of the courts is now confessedly inadequate to the duties to be performed by them, in consequence of which the States of Florida, Wisconsin, Iowa, Texas, and California, and districts of other States, are in effect excluded from the full benefits of the general system by the functions of the circuit court being devolved on the district judges in all those States or parts of States.

The spirit of the Constitution and a due regard to justice require that all the States of the Union should be placed on the same footing in regard to the judicial tribunals. I therefore commend to your consideration this important subject, which in my judgment demands the speedy action of Congress. I will present to you, if deemed desirable, a plan which I am prepared to recommend for the enlargement and modification of the present judicial system.

The act of Congress establishing the Smithsonian Institution provided that the President of the United States and other persons therein designated should constitute an "establishment" by that name, and that the members should hold stated and special meetings for the supervision of the affairs of the Institution. The organization not having taken place, it seemed to me proper that it should be effected without delay. This has been done; and an occasion was thereby presented for inspecting the condition of the Institution and appreciating its successful progress thus far and its high promise of great and general usefulness.

I have omitted to ask your favorable consideration for the estimates of works of a local character in twenty-seven of the thirty-one States, amounting to $1,754,500, because, independently of the grounds which have so often been urged against the application of the Federal revenue for works of this character, inequality, with consequent injustice, is inherent in the nature of the proposition, and because the plan has proved entirely inadequate to the accomplishment of the objects sought.

The subject of internal improvements, claiming alike the interest and good will of all, has, nevertheless, been the basis of much political discussion and has stood as a deep-graven line of division between statesmen of eminent ability and patriotism. The rule of strict construction of all powers delegated by the States to the General Government has arrayed itself from time to time against the rapid progress of expenditures from the National Treasury on works of a local character within the States. Memorable as an epoch in the history of this subject is the message of President Jackson of the 27th of May, 1830, which met the system of internal improvements in its comparative infancy; but so rapid had been its growth that the projected appropriations in that year for works of this character had risen to the alarming amount of more than $100,000,000.

In that message the President admitted the difficulty of bringing back the operations of the Government to the construction of the Constitution set up in 1798, and marked it as an admonitory proof of the necessity of guarding that instrument with sleepless vigilance against the authority of precedents which had not the sanction of its most plainly defined powers.

Our Government exists under a written compact between sovereign States, uniting for specific objects and with specific grants to their general agent. If, then, in the progress of its administration there have been departures from the terms and intent of the compact, it is and will ever be proper to refer back to the fixed standard which our fathers left us and to make a stern effort to conform our action to it. It would seem that the fact of a principle having been resisted from the first by many of the wisest and most patriotic men of the Republic, and a policy having provoked constant strife without arriving at a conclusion which can be regarded as satisfactory to its most earnest advocates, should suggest the inquiry whether there may not be a plan likely to be crowned by happier results. Without perceiving any sound distinction or intending to assert any principle as opposed to improvements needed for the protection of internal commerce which does not equally apply to improvements upon the seaboard for the protection of foreign commerce, I submit to you whether it may not be safely anticipated that if the policy were once settled against appropriations by the General Government for local improvements for the benefit of commerce, localities requiring expenditures would not, by modes and means clearly legitimate and proper, raise the fund necessary for such constructions as the safety or other interests of their commerce might require.

If that can be regarded as a system which in the experience of more than thirty years has at no time so commanded the public judgment as to give it the character of a settled policy; which, though it has produced some works of conceded importance, has been attended with an expenditure quite disproportionate to their value and has resulted in squandering large sums upon objects which have answered no valuable purpose, the interests of all the States require it to be abandoned unless hopes may be indulged for the future which find no warrant in the past.

With an anxious desire for the completion of the works which are regarded by all good citizens with sincere interest, I have deemed it my duty to ask at your hands a deliberate reconsideration of the question, with a hope that, animated by a desire to promote the permanent and substantial interests of the country, your wisdom may prove equal to the task of devising and maturing a plan which, applied to this subject, may promise something better than constant strife, the suspension of the powers of local enterprise, the exciting of vain hopes, and the disappointment of cherished expectations.

In expending the appropriations made by the last Congress several cases have arisen in relation to works for the improvement of harbors which involve questions as to the right of soil and jurisdiction, and have threatened conflict between the authority of the State and General Governments. The right to construct a breakwater, jetty, or dam would seem necessarily to carry with it the power to protect and preserve such constructions. This can only be effectually done by having jurisdiction over the soil. But no clause of the Constitution is found on which to rest the claim of the United States to exercise jurisdiction over the soil of a State except that conferred by the eighth section of the first article of the Constitution. It is, then, submitted whether, in all cases where constructions are to be erected by the General Government, the right of soil should not first be obtained and legislative provision be made to cover all such cases.

For the progress made in the construction of roads within the Territories, as provided for in the appropriations of the last Congress, I refer you to the report of the Secretary of War.

There is one subject of a domestic nature which, from its intrinsic importance and the many interesting questions of future policy which it involves, can not fail to receive your early attention. I allude to the means of communication by which different parts of the wide expanse of our country are to be placed in closer connection for purposes both of defense and commercial intercourse, and more especially such as appertain to the communication of those great divisions of the Union which lie on the opposite sides of the Rocky Mountains.

That the Government has not been unmindful of this heretofore is apparent from the aid it has afforded through appropriations for mail facilities and other purposes. But the general subject will now present itself under aspects more imposing and more purely national by reason of the surveys ordered by Congress, and now in the process of completion, for communication by railway across the continent, and wholly within the limits of the United States.

The power to declare war, to raise and support armies, to provide and maintain a navy, and to call forth the militia to execute the laws, suppress insurrections, and repel invasions was conferred upon Congress as means to provide for the common defense and to protect a territory and a population now widespread and vastly multiplied. As incidental to and indispensable for the exercise of this power, it must sometimes be necessary to construct military roads and protect harbors of refuge. To appropriations by Congress for such objects no sound objection can be raised. Happily for our country, its peaceful policy and rapidly increasing population impose upon us no urgent necessity for preparation, and leave but few trackless deserts between assailable points and a patriotic people ever ready and generally able to protect them. These necessary links the enterprise and energy of our people are steadily and boldly struggling to supply. All experience affirms that wherever private enterprise will avail it is most wise for the General Government to leave to that and individual watchfulness the location and execution of all means of communication.

The surveys before alluded to were designed to ascertain the most practicable and economical route for a railroad from the river Mississippi to the Pacific Ocean. Parties are now in the field making explorations, where previous examinations had not supplied sufficient data and where there was the best reason to hope the object sought might be found. The means and time being both limited, it is not to be expected that all the accurate knowledge desired will be obtained, but it is hoped that much and important information will be added to the stock previously possessed, and that partial, if not full, reports of the surveys ordered will be received in time for transmission to the two Houses of Congress on or before the first Monday in February next, as required by the act of appropriation. The magnitude of the enterprise contemplated has aroused and will doubtless continue to excite a very general interest throughout the country. In its political, its commercial, and its military bearings it has varied, great, and increasing claims to consideration. The heavy expense, the great delay, and, at times, fatality attending travel by either of the Isthmus routes have demonstrated the advantage which would result from interterritorial communication by such safe and rapid means as a railroad would supply.

These difficulties, which have been encountered in a period of peace, would be magnified and still further increased in time of war. But whilst the embarrassments already encountered and others under new contingencies to be anticipated may serve strikingly to exhibit the importance of such a work, neither these nor all considerations combined can have an appreciable value when weighed against the obligation strictly to adhere to the Constitution and faithfully to execute the powers it confers.

Within this limit and to the extent of the interest of the Government involved it would seem both expedient and proper if an economical and practicable route shall be found to aid by all constitutional means in the construction of a road which will unite by speedy transit the populations of the Pacific and Atlantic States. To guard against misconception, it should be remarked that although the power to construct or aid in the construction of a road within the limits of a Territory is not embarrassed by that question of jurisdiction which would arise within the limits of a State, it is, nevertheless, held to be of doubtful power and more than doubtful propriety, even within the limits of a Territory, for the General Government to undertake to administer the affairs of a railroad, a canal, or other similar construction, and therefore that its connection with a work of this character should be incidental rather than primary. I will only add at present that, fully appreciating the magnitude of the subject and solicitous that the Atlantic and Pacific shores of the Republic may be bound together by inseparable ties of common interest, as well as of common fealty and attachment to the Union, I shall be disposed, so far as my own action is concerned, to follow the lights of the Constitution as expounded and illustrated by those whose opinions and expositions constitute the standard of my political faith in regard to the powers of the Federal Government. It is, I trust, not necessary to say that no grandeur of enterprise and no present urgent inducement promising popular favor will lead me to disregard those lights or to depart from that path which experience has proved to be safe, and which is now radiant with the glow of prosperity and legitimate constitutional progress. We can afford to wait, but we can not afford to overlook the ark of our security.

It is no part of my purpose to give prominence to any subject which may properly be regarded as set at rest by the deliberate judgment of the people. But while the present is bright with promise and the future full of demand and inducement for the exercise of active intelligence, the past can never be without useful lessons of admonition and instruction. If its dangers serve not as beacons, they will evidently fail to fulfill the object of a wise design. When the grave shall have closed over all who are now endeavoring to meet the obligations of duty, the year 1850 will be recurred to as a period filled with anxious apprehension. A successful war had just terminated. Peace brought with it a vast augmentation of territory. Disturbing questions arose bearing upon the domestic institutions of one portion of the Confederacy and involving the constitutional rights of the States. But notwithstanding differences of opinion and sentiment which then existed in relation to details and specific provisions, the acquiescence of distinguished citizens, whose devotion to the Union can never be doubted, has given renewed vigor to our institutions and restored a sense of repose and security to the public mind throughout the Confederacy. That this repose is to suffer no shock during my official term, if I have power to avert it, those who placed me here may be assured. The wisdom of men who knew what independence cost, who had put all at stake upon the issue of the Revolutionary struggle, disposed of the subject to which I refer in the only way consistent with the Union of these States and with the march of power and prosperity which has made us what we are. It is a significant fact that from the adoption of the Constitution until the officers and soldiers of the Revolution had passed to their graves, or, through the infirmities of age and wounds, had ceased to participate actively in public affairs, there was not merely a quiet acquiescence in, but a prompt vindication of, the constitutional rights of the States. The reserved powers were scrupulously respected. No statesman put forth the narrow views of casuists to justify interference and agitation, but the spirit of the compact was regarded as sacred in the eye of honor and indispensable for the great experiment of civil liberty, which, environed by inherent difficulties, was yet borne forward in apparent weakness by a power superior to all obstacles. There is no condemnation which the voice of freedom will not pronounce upon us should we prove faithless to this great trust. While men inhabiting different parts of this vast continent can no more be expected to hold the same opinions or entertain the same sentiments than every variety of climate or soil can be expected to furnish the same agricultural products, they can unite in a common object and sustain common principles essential to the maintenance of that object. The gallant men of the South and the North could stand together during the struggle of the Revolution; they could stand together in the more trying period which succeeded the clangor of arms. As their united valor was adequate to all the trials of the camp and dangers of the field, so their united wisdom proved equal to the greater task of founding upon a deep and broad basis institutions which it has been our privilege to enjoy and will ever be our most sacred duty to sustain. It is but the feeble expression of a faith strong and universal to say that their sons, whose blood mingled so often upon the same field during the War of 1812 and who have more recently borne in triumph the flag of the country upon a foreign soil, will never permit alienation of feeling to weaken the power of their united efforts nor internal dissensions to paralyze the great arm of freedom, uplifted for the vindication of self-government.

I have thus briefly presented such suggestions as seem to me especially worthy of your consideration. In providing for the present you can hardly fail to avail yourselves of the light which the experience of the past casts upon the future.

The growth of our population has now brought us, in the destined career of our national history, to a point at which it well behooves us to expand our vision over the vast prospective.

The successive decennial returns of the census since the adoption of the Constitution have revealed a law of steady, progressive development, which may be stated in general terms as a duplication every quarter century. Carried forward from the point already reached for only a short period of time, as applicable to the existence of a nation, this law of progress, if unchecked, will bring us to almost incredible results. A large allowance for a diminished proportional effect of emigration would not very materially reduce the estimate, while the increased average duration of human life known to have already resulted from the scientific and hygienic improvements of the past fifty years will tend to keep up through the next fifty, or perhaps hundred, the same ratio of growth which has been thus revealed in our past progress; and to the influence of these causes may be added the influx of laboring masses from eastern Asia to the Pacific side of our possessions, together with the probable accession of the populations already existing in other parts of our hemisphere, which within the period in question will feel with yearly increasing force the natural attraction of so vast, powerful, and prosperous a confederation of self-governing republics and will seek the privilege of being admitted within its safe and happy bosom, transferring with themselves, by a peaceful and healthy process of incorporation, spacious regions of virgin and exuberant soil, which are destined to swarm with the fast-growing and fast-spreading millions of our race.

These considerations seem fully to justify the presumption that the law of population above stated will continue to act with undiminished effect through at least the next half century, and that thousands of persons who have already arrived at maturity and are now exercising the rights of freemen will close their eyes on the spectacle of more than 100,000,000 of population embraced within the majestic proportions of the American Union. It is not merely as an interesting topic of speculation that I present these views for your consideration. They have important practical bearings upon all the political duties we are called upon to perform. Heretofore our system of government has worked on what may be termed a miniature scale in comparison with the development which it must thus assume within a future so near at hand as scarcely to be beyond the present of the existing generation.

It is evident that a confederation so vast and so varied, both in numbers and in territorial extent, in habits and in interests, could only be kept in national cohesion by the strictest fidelity to the principles of the Constitution as understood by those who have adhered to the most restricted construction of the powers granted by the people and the States. Interpreted and applied according to those principles, the great compact adapts itself with healthy ease and freedom to an unlimited extension of that benign system of federative self-government of which it is our glorious and, I trust, immortal charter. Let us, then, with redoubled vigilance, be on our guard against yielding to the temptation of the exercise of doubtful powers, even under the pressure of the motives of conceded temporary advantage and apparent temporary expediency.

The minimum of Federal government compatible with the maintenance of national unity and efficient action in our relations with the rest of the world should afford the rule and measure of construction of our powers under the general clauses of the Constitution. A spirit of strict deference to the sovereign rights and dignity of every State, rather than a disposition to subordinate the States into a provincial relation to the central authority, should characterize all our exercise of the respective powers temporarily vested in us as a sacred trust from the generous confidence of our constituents.

In like manner, as a manifestly indispensable condition of the perpetuation of the Union and of the realization of that magnificent national future adverted to, does the duty become yearly stronger and clearer upon us, as citizens of the several States, to cultivate a fraternal and affectionate spirit, language, and conduct in regard to other States and in relation to the varied interests, institutions, and habits of sentiment and opinion which may respectively characterize them. Mutual forbearance, respect, and noninterference in our personal action as citizens and an enlarged exercise of the most liberal principles of comity in the public dealings of State with State, whether in legislation or in the execution of laws, are the means to perpetuate that confidence and fraternity the decay of which a mere political union, on so vast a scale, could not long survive.

In still another point of view is an important practical duty suggested by this consideration of the magnitude of dimensions to which our political system, with its corresponding machinery of government, is so rapidly expanding. With increased vigilance does it require us to cultivate the cardinal virtues of public frugality and official integrity and purity. Public affairs ought to be so conducted that a settled conviction shall pervade the entire Union that nothing short of the highest tone and standard of public morality marks every part of the administration and legislation of the General Government. Thus will the federal system, whatever expansion time and progress may give it, continue more and more deeply rooted in the love and confidence of the people.

That wise economy which is as far removed from parsimony as from corrupt and corrupting extravagance; that single regard for the public good which will frown upon all attempts to approach the Treasury with insidious projects of private interest cloaked under public pretexts; that sound fiscal administration which, in the legislative department, guards against the dangerous temptations incident to overflowing revenue, and, in the executive, maintains an unsleeping watchfulness against the tendency of all national expenditure to extravagance, while they are admitted elementary political duties, may, I trust, be deemed as properly adverted to and urged in view of the more impressive sense of that necessity which is directly suggested by the considerations now presented.

Since the adjournment of Congress the Vice-President of the United States has passed from the scenes of earth, without having entered upon the duties of the station to which he had been called by the voice of his countrymen. Having occupied almost continuously for more than thirty years a seat in one or the other of the two Houses of Congress, and having by his singular purity and wisdom secured unbounded confidence and universal respect, his failing health was watched by the nation with painful solicitude. His loss to the country, under all the circumstances, has been justly regarded as irreparable.

In compliance with the act of Congress of March 2, 1853, the oath of office was administered to him on the 24th of that month at Ariadne estate, near Matanzas, in the island of Cuba; but his strength gradually declined, and was hardly sufficient to enable him to return to his home in Alabama, where, on the 18th day of April, in the most calm and peaceful way, his long and eminently useful career was terminated.

Entertaining unlimited confidence in your intelligent and patriotic devotion to the public interest, and being conscious of no motives on my part which are not inseparable from the honor and advancement of my country, I hope it may be my privilege to deserve and secure not only your cordial cooperation in great public measures, but also those relations of mutual confidence and regard which it is always so desirable to cultivate between members of coordinate branches of the Government.

FRANKLIN PIERCE.

SPECIAL MESSAGES.

WASHINGTON, *December 12, 1853.*

To the Senate of the United States:

In answer to the resolutions of the Senate of the 17th of August, 1852, and 23d of February last, requesting a copy of correspondence relative to the claim on the Government of Portugal in the case of the brig *General Armstrong*, I transmit a report from the Secretary of State, to whose Department the resolutions were referred.

FRANKLIN PIERCE.

WASHINGTON, *December 12, 1853.*

To the Senate of the United States:

I transmit to the Senate, for its consideration with a view to ratification, a treaty of friendship, commerce, and navigation between the United States and Paraguay, concluded on the 4th of March last.

FRANKLIN PIERCE.

WASHINGTON, *December 12, 1853.*

To the Senate of the United States:

I transmit to the Senate, for its consideration with a view to ratification, a treaty for the free navigation of the rivers Parana and Uruguay between the United States and the Argentine Confederation, concluded on the 10th of July last.

FRANKLIN PIERCE.

WASHINGTON, *December 12, 1853.*

To the Senate of the United States:

I transmit to the Senate, for its consideration with a view to ratification, a treaty of friendship, commerce, and navigation between the United States and the Argentine Confederation, concluded on the 27th of July last.

FRANKLIN PIERCE.

WASHINGTON, *December 12, 1853.*

To the Senate of the United States:

I transmit to the Senate, for its consideration with a view to ratification, a convention for the mutual extradition of fugitives from justice in certain cases, concluded at London on the 12th day of September last between the Government of the United States and the Kingdom of Bavaria.

FRANKLIN PIERCE.

WASHINGTON, *December 19, 1853.*

To the Senate of the United States:

I transmit certain documents in answer to the resolution of the Senate of the 6th of April ultimo, requesting information in regard to transactions between Captain Hollins, of the *Cyane*, and the authorities at San Juan de Nicaragua.

FRANKLIN PIERCE.

WASHINGTON, *December 23, 1853.*

To the Senate of the United States:

In answer to the resolution of the Senate of the 18th January, 1853, in regard to the claims of American citizens against Hayti and to the correspondence of the special agent sent to Hayti and St. Domingo in 1849, I transmit a report from the Secretary of State and the documents by which it is accompanied.

FRANKLIN PIERCE.

WASHINGTON, *December 31, 1853.*

To the Senate of the United States:

I transmit to the Senate a report from the Secretary of State, with accompanying papers,* in answer to their resolution of the 12th instant.

FRANKLIN PIERCE.

WASHINGTON CITY, *January 9, 1854.*

To the Senate of the United States:

I herewith communicate to the Senate a letter from the Secretary of the Interior, accompanied by a report of the result of an investigation of the charge of fraud and misconduct in office alleged against Alexander Ramsey, superintendent of Indian affairs in Minnesota, which I have caused to be made in compliance with the Senate's resolution of the 5th of April last.

FRANKLIN PIERCE.

*Correspondence relative to the treaty of Washington of July 4, 1850, between Great Britain and the United States.

WASHINGTON, *January 9, 1854.*

To the House of Representatives:

In answer to the resolution of the House of Representatives of the 3d of January, 1854, I have the honor to transmit herewith a letter of the Secretary of the Navy and the papers* accompanying it.

FRANKLIN PIERCE.

WASHINGTON, *January 19, 1854.*

To the House of Representatives:

I transmit herewith a report from the Secretary of State, with accompanying documents,† in compliance with the resolution of the House of Representatives of the 3d instant.   FRANKLIN PIERCE.

WASHINGTON, *January 23, 1854.*

To the Senate and House of Representatives:

I transmit to Congress a report of the Secretary of State, together with the set of works illustrative of the exhibition in London of 1851 to which it refers, in order that such disposal may be made of them as may be deemed advisable.   FRANKLIN PIERCE.

WASHINGTON, *January 25, 1854.*

To the Senate of the United States:

I transmit herewith a report from the Secretary of State, with accompanying documents,‡ in compliance with a resolution of the Senate of the 23d instant.   FRANKLIN PIERCE.

WASHINGTON, *February 2, 1854.*

To the House of Representatives:

I transmit herewith a report from the Secretary of State, with accompanying documents,§ in compliance with the resolution of the House of Representatives of the 30th ultimo.   FRANKLIN PIERCE.

---

*Correspondence with and orders to commanders of vessels or squadrons on the Atlantic coast of British North America relative to protecting the rights of fishing and navigation secured to citizens of the United States under treaties with Great Britain.

†Relating to seizure and imprisonment by Spanish authorities at Puerto Rico of officers and crew of schooner *North Carolina.*

‡Relating to a complimentary mission to the United States of Archbishop Gaetano Bedini, apostolic nuncio to the Empire of Brazil, for the purpose of conveying, in the name of Pope Pius IX, sentiments of regard for the President of the United States.

§Correspondence with the American chargé to Austria relative to the claim of Simon Tousig to the protection of the United States.

EXECUTIVE OFFICE, *February 4, 1854.*

To the Senate of the United States:

I submit to the Senate herewith, for their constitutional action thereon, a treaty negotiated on the 27th of July, 1853, by Agent Thomas Fitzpatrick, on behalf of the United States, with the Comanche, Kiowa, and Apache Indians inhabiting the territory on the Arkansas River.

FRANKLIN PIERCE.

EXECUTIVE OFFICE, *February 4, 1854.*

To the Senate of the United States:

I submit to the Senate herewith, for their constitutional action thereon, two treaties, one negotiated on the 10th day of September, 1853, by Superintendent Joel Palmer and Agent Samuel H. Culver, on the part of the United States, and the chiefs and headmen of the bands of the Rogue River tribe of Indians in Oregon; the other negotiated on the 19th of the same month, on behalf of the Government by the said superintendent, with the chiefs of the Crow Creek band of Umpqua Indians in said Territory.

FRANKLIN PIERCE.

WASHINGTON, *February 6, 1854.*

To the House of Representatives:

I transmit a report from the Secretary of State upon the subject of the resolution* of the House of Representatives of the 14th of December last, and recommend that the appropriation therein suggested as being necessary to enable him to comply with the resolution be made.

FRANKLIN PIERCE.

WASHINGTON, *February 10, 1854.*

To the Senate and House of Representatives:

I herewith transmit a communication from the Secretary of the Navy, accompanied by the second part of Lieutenant Herndon's report of the exploration of the valley of the Amazon and its tributaries, made by him in connection with Lieutenant Lardner Gibbon under instructions from the Navy Department.

FRANKLIN PIERCE.

WASHINGTON, *February 10, 1854.*

To the Senate of the United States:

I transmit to the Senate, for its consideration with a view to ratification, a treaty between the United States and the Mexican Republic, signed by the plenipotentiaries of the parties in the City of Mexico on

---

* Requesting a statement of the privileges and restrictions of the commercial intercourse of the United States with foreign nations and a comparative statement between the tariff of the United States and other nations.

the 30th of December last. Certain amendments are proposed to the instrument, as hereinafter specified, viz:

In order to make the duties and obligations stipulated in the second article reciprocal, it is proposed to add to that article the following:

And the Government of Mexico agrees that the stipulations contained in this article to be performed by the United States shall be reciprocal, and Mexico shall be under like obligations to the United States and the citizens thereof as those hereinabove imposed on the latter in favor of the Republic of Mexico and Mexican citizens.

It is also recommended that for the third article of the original treaty the following shall be adopted as a substitute:

In consideration of the grants received by the United States and the obligations relinquished by the Mexican Republic pursuant to this treaty, the former agree to pay to the latter the sum of $15,000,000 in gold or silver coin at the Treasury at Washington, one-fifth of the amount on the exchange of ratifications of the present treaty at Washington and the remaining four-fifths in monthly installments of three millions each, with interest at the rate of 6 per cent per annum until the whole be paid, the Government of the United States reserving the right to pay up the whole sum of fifteen millions at an earlier date, as may be to it convenient.

The United States also agree to assume all the claims of their citizens against the Mexican Republic which may have arisen under treaty or the law of nations since the date of the signature of the treaty of Guadalupe, and the Mexican Republic agrees to exonerate the United States of America from all claims of Mexico or Mexican citizens which may have arisen under treaty or the law of nations since the date of the treaty of Guadalupe, so that each Government, in the most formal and effective manner, shall be exempted and exonerated of all such obligations to each other respectively.

I also recommend that the eighth article be modified by striking out all after the word "attempts" in the twenty-third line of that article. The part to be omitted is as follows:

They mutually and especially obligate themselves, in all cases of such lawless enterprises which may not have been prevented through the civil authorities before formation, to aid with the naval and military forces, on due notice being given by the aggrieved party of the aggressions of the citizens and subjects of the other, so that the lawless adventurers may be pursued and overtaken on the high seas, their elements of war destroyed, and the deluded captives held responsible in their persons and meet with the merited retribution inflicted by the laws of nations against all such disturbers of the peace and happiness of contiguous and friendly powers. It being understood that in all cases of successful pursuit and capture the delinquents so captured shall be judged and punished by the government of that nation to which the vessel capturing them may belong, conformably to the laws of each nation.

At the close of the instrument it will also be advisable to substitute "seventy-eighth" for "seventy-seventh" year of the Independence of the United States.

FRANKLIN PIERCE.

WASHINGTON, *February 13, 1854.*

To the Senate of the United States:

I transmit to the Senate, for its consideration with a view to ratification, an additional article to the convention for the establishment of international copyright, which was concluded at Washington on the 17th of February, 1853, between the United States of America and Her Britannic Majesty, extending the time limited in that convention for the exchange of the ratifications of the same.

FRANKLIN PIERCE.

WASHINGTON, *February 23, 1854.*

To the Senate of the United States:

I communicate herewith a report from the Secretary of State and the documents* therein referred to, in compliance with the resolution of the Senate of the 13th instant.

FRANKLIN PIERCE.

WASHINGTON, *March 1, 1854.*

To the Senate of the United States:

I transmit to the Senate a report from the Secretary of State, with accompanying documents,† in compliance with their resolution of the 2d ultimo.

FRANKLIN PIERCE.

WASHINGTON, *March 1, 1854.*

To the House of Representatives:

In accordance with the resolution of the House of Representatives of the 13th instant, requesting information respecting negotiations with Peru for the removal of restrictions upon the exportation of guano, I transmit herewith a report from the Secretary of State, with the correspondence therein referred to.

FRANKLIN PIERCE.

WASHINGTON, *March 1, 1854.*

To the House of Representatives of the United States:

In compliance with the resolution of the House of Representatives of the 23d January last, "that the President of the United States be respectfully requested to furnish this House with copies of all contracts made by and correspondence subsequently with the Chief of the Bureau of Topographical Engineers for furnishing materials of wood and stone for improving the harbors and rivers on Lake Michigan, under and by virtue of the act making appropriations for the improvement of certain harbors and rivers," approved August 30, 1852, I transmit a letter of the Secretary of War submitting a report of the Colonel of Topographical Engineers inclosing copies of the contracts and correspondence called for.

FRANKLIN PIERCE.

*Relating to the repair of the United States frigate *Susquehanna* at Rio de Janeiro.

†Communications from the American legation at Constantinople respecting the seizure of Martin Koszta by Austrian authorities at Smyrna.

WASHINGTON, *March 1, 1854.*

To the Senate of the United States:

In answer to the resolution of the Senate of the 7th of December last, requesting me to present to the Senate the plan referred to in my annual message to Congress, and recommended therein, for the enlargement and modification of the present judicial system of the United States, I transmit a report from the Attorney-General, to whom the resolution was referred.

FRANKLIN PIERCE.

WASHINGTON, *March 1, 1854.*

To the House of Representatives:

I transmit herewith a report of the Attorney-General, in answer to the resolutions of the House of the 22d of December, requesting me to communicate to the House the plan for the modification and enlargement of the judicial system of the United States, recommended in my annual message to Congress.

FRANKLIN PIERCE.

WASHINGTON, *March 7, 1854.*

To the Senate of the United States:

I transmit herewith a report from the Secretary of State and the documents* therein referred to, in answer to the resolution of the Senate of the 26th March, 1853.

FRANKLIN PIERCE.

WASHINGTON, *March 7, 1854.*

To the Senate of the United States:

I transmit herewith a report from the Secretary of State and the documents† therein referred to, in answer to the resolution of the Senate in executive session of the 3d January, 1854.

FRANKLIN PIERCE.

WASHINGTON, *March 11, 1854.*

To the Senate of the United States:

I transmit herewith to the Senate a report of the Secretary of State, with accompanying documents,‡ in compliance with their resolution of the 9th of March, 1853.

FRANKLIN PIERCE.

*Correspondence with R. C. Schenck, United States minister to Brazil, relative to the African slave trade.

†Correspondence with the Mexican Republic touching the eleventh article of the treaty of Guadalupe Hidalgo, and copies of instructions on that subject to the United States minister to Mexico.

‡ Correspondence relative to the imprisonment, etc., of James H. West in the island of Cuba.

WASHINGTON, *March 14, 1854.*

To the Senate of the United States:

In transmitting to the Senate the report of the Secretary of State, together with the documents therein referred to, being the correspondence called for by the resolution of that body of the 9th of January last, I deem it proper to state briefly the reasons which have deterred me from sending to the Senate for ratification the proposed convention between the United States of America and the United Mexican States, concluded by the respective plenipotentiaries of the two Governments on the 21st day of March, 1853, on the subject of a transit way across the Isthmus of Tehuantepec.

Without adverting to the want of authority on the part of the American minister to conclude any such convention, or to the action of this Government in relation to the rights of certain of its citizens under the grant for a like object originally made to José Garay, the objections to it upon its face are numerous, and should, in my judgment, be regarded as conclusive.

Prominent among these objections is the fact that the convention binds us to a foreign Government, to guarantee the contract of a private company with that Government for the construction of the contemplated transit way, "to protect the persons engaged and property employed in the construction of the said work from the commencement thereof to its completion against all confiscation, spoliation, or violence of whatsoever nature," and to guarantee the entire security of the capital invested therein during the continuance of the contract. Such is the substance of the second and third articles.

Hence it will be perceived that the obligations which this Government is asked to assume are not to terminate in a few years, or even with the present generation.

And again: "If the regulations which may be prescribed concerning the traffic on said transit way shall be clearly contrary to the spirit and intention of this convention," even then this Government is not to be at liberty to withdraw its "protection and guaranty" without first giving one year's notice to the Mexican Government.

When the fact is duly considered that the responsibility of this Government is thus pledged for a long series of years to the interests of a private company established for purposes of internal improvement in a foreign country, and that country peculiarly subject to civil wars and other public vicissitudes, it will be seen how comprehensive and embarrassing would be those engagements to the Government of the United States.

Not less important than this objection is the consideration that the United States can not agree to the terms of this convention without disregarding the provisions of the eighth article of the convention which this Government entered into with Great Britain on April 19, 1850, which expressly includes any interoceanic communication whatever by the Isthmus of Tehuantepec. However inconvenient may be the conditions of that convention, still they exist, and the obligations of good faith rest alike upon the United States and Great Britain.

Without enlarging upon these and other questionable features of the proposed convention which will suggest themselves to your minds, I will only add that after the most careful consideration I have deemed it my duty not to ask for its ratification by the Senate.

FRANKLIN PIERCE.

WASHINGTON, *March 15, 1854.*

To the House of Representatives:

In compliance with the resolution of the House of Representatives of the 10th instant, I herewith transmit a report of the Secretary of State, containing all the information received at the Department in relation to the seizure of the *Black Warrior* at Havana on the 28th ultimo.

There have been in the course of a few years past many other instances of aggression upon our commerce, violations of the rights of American citizens, and insults to the national flag by the Spanish authorities in Cuba, and all attempts to obtain redress have led to protracted, and as yet fruitless, negotiations.

The documents in these cases are voluminous, and when prepared will be sent to Congress.

Those now transmitted relate exclusively to the seizure of the *Black Warrior*, and present so clear a case of wrong that it would be reasonable to expect full indemnity therefor as soon as this unjustifiable and offensive conduct shall be made known to Her Catholic Majesty's Government; but similar expectations in other cases have not been realized.

The offending party is at our doors with large powers for aggression, but none, it is alleged, for reparation. The source of redress is in another hemisphere, and the answers to our just complaints made to the home Government are but the repetition of excuses rendered by inferior officials to their superiors in reply to representations of misconduct. The peculiar situation of the parties has undoubtedly much aggravated the annoyances and injuries which our citizens have suffered from the Cuban authorities, and Spain does not seem to appreciate to its full extent her responsibility for the conduct of these authorities. In giving very extraordinary powers to them she owes it to justice and to her friendly relations with this Government to guard with great vigilance against the exorbitant exercise of these powers, and in case of injuries to provide for prompt redress.

I have already taken measures to present to the Government of Spain the wanton injury of the Cuban authorities in the detention and seizure of the *Black Warrior*, and to demand immediate indemnity for the injury which has thereby resulted to our citizens.

In view of the position of the island of Cuba, its proximity to our coast, the relations which it must ever bear to our commercial and other interests, it is vain to expect that a series of unfriendly acts infringing our commercial rights and the adoption of a policy threatening the honor and security of these States can long consist with peaceful relations.

In case the measures taken for amicable adjustment of our difficulties with Spain should, unfortunately, fail, I shall not hesitate to use the authority and means which Congress may grant to insure the observance of our just rights, to obtain redress for injuries received, and to vindicate the honor of our flag.

In anticipation of that contingency, which I earnestly hope may not arise, I suggest to Congress the propriety of adopting such provisional measures as the exigency may seem to demand.

FRANKLIN PIERCE.

EXECUTIVE OFFICE,
Washington, March 17, 1854.

To the Senate of the United States:

I communicate to the Senate herewith, for its constitutional action, two treaties recently negotiated by the Commissioner of Indian Affairs, as commissioner on the part of the United States, with the delegates now at the seat of Government representing the confederated tribes of Otoes and Missourias and the Omaha Indians, for the extinguishment of their titles to lands west of the Missouri River.

FRANKLIN PIERCE.

EXECUTIVE OFFICE,
Washington, March 18, 1854.

Hon. LINN BOYD,
   Speaker of the House of Representatives.

SIR: I transmit to you herewith a report of the present date from the Secretary of the Interior, accompanied by a tabular statement containing the information* called for by resolution of the House of Representatives adopted the 13th ultimo.

FRANKLIN PIERCE.

WASHINGTON, *March 21, 1854.*

To the Senate of the United States:

In answer to the resolution of the Senate of the 15th instant, adopted in executive session, I transmit confidentially a report from the Secretary of State and the documents† by which it was accompanied. Pursuant

---

*Area of each State and Territory; extent of the public domain remaining in each State and Territory, and the extent alienated by sales, grants, etc.

†Instructions and correspondence relative to the negotiation of the treaty with Mexico of December 30, 1853, etc.

to the suggestion in the report, it is desirable that such of the papers as may be originals should be returned to the Department of State.

FRANKLIN PIERCE.

EXECUTIVE OFFICE, *March 25, 1854.*

Hon. LINN BOYD,
Speaker of the House of Representatives:

I communicate to the House of Representatives herewith a report from the Secretary of the Interior, dated the 24th instant, containing so much of the information called for by the resolution of the 17th instant as it is practicable or compatible with the public interest to furnish at the present time, respecting the proceedings which have been had and negotiations entered into for the extinguishment of the Indian titles to lands west of the States of Missouri and Iowa.

FRANKLIN PIERCE.

WASHINGTON, *March 29, 1854.*

To the Senate of the United States:

In answer to the resolution of the Senate of the 21st instant, adopted in executive session, relative to the claims of the Mexican Government and of citizens of the Mexican Republic on this Government, and of citizens of the United States on the Government of that Republic, I transmit a report from the Secretary of State, to whom the resolution was referred.

FRANKLIN PIERCE.

WASHINGTON, *March 31, 1854.*

To the Senate of the United States:

In answer to the resolution of the Senate of the 13th instant, requesting a confidential communication of information touching the expedition under the authority of this Government for the purpose of opening trade with Japan, I transmit a report from the Secretary of State, to whom the resolution was referred.

FRANKLIN PIERCE.

WASHINGTON, D. C., *April 1, 1854.*

To the Senate of the United States:

I transmit herewith the report of the Secretary of State in reply to the resolution of the Senate of the 27th ultimo.

That part of the document which purports to recite my official instructions is strictly correct; that which is avowedly unofficial and unauthorized, it can hardly be necessary for me to say, in view of the documents already before the Senate, does not convey a correct impression of my "views and wishes."

At no time after an intention was entertained of sending Mr. Ward as special agent to Mexico was either the Garay grant or the convention entered into by Mr. Conkling alluded to otherwise than as subjects which might embarrass the negotiation of the treaty, and were consequently not included in the instructions.

While the departure of Mr. Ward, under any circumstances or in any respect, from the instructions committed to him is a matter of regret, it is just to say that, although he failed to convey in his letter to General Gadsden the correct import of remarks made by me anterior to his appointment as special agent, I impute to him no design of misrepresentation.

FRANKLIN PIERCE.

WASHINGTON, *April 5, 1854.*

To the Senate of the United States:

I transmit to the Senate a report of the Secretary of State, with accompanying documents,* in compliance with their resolution of the 14th ultimo.

FRANKLIN PIERCE.

WASHINGTON, *April 5, 1854.*

To the House of Representatives of the United States:

I transmit herewith to the House of Representatives a report of the Secretary of State, with accompanying documents,† in further compliance with their resolution of the 10th of March, 1854.

FRANKLIN PIERCE.

WASHINGTON, *April 5, 1854.*

To the Senate of the United States:

I transmit herewith a report ‡ from the Secretary of State, in answer to the resolution of the Senate in executive session of the 3d instant.

FRANKLIN PIERCE.

WASHINGTON, *April 8, 1854.*

To the House of Representatives:

I transmit herewith to the House of Representatives a report § of the Secretary of State, in answer to their resolution of the 3d instant.

FRANKLIN PIERCE.

---

*Correspondence relative to the seizure of Martin Koszta by Austrian authorities at Smyrna.

†Relating to violations of the rights of American citizens by Spanish authorities and their refusal to allow United States vessels to enter ports of Cuba, etc.

‡ Relating to expeditions organized in California for the invasion of Sonora, Mexico.

§ Stating that the correspondence relative to the refusal by the authorities of Cuba to permit the United States mail steamer *Crescent City* to land mail and passengers at Havana had been transmitted with the message to the House of April 5, 1854.

WASHINGTON, *April 10, 1854.*

To the Senate of the United States:

I communicate to the Senate herewith a communication from the Secretary of the Interior, accompanied by the articles of a convention recently entered into for an exchange of country for the future residence of the Winnebago Indians, and recommend their ratification with the amendment suggested by the Secretary of the Interior.

FRANKLIN PIERCE.

WASHINGTON, *April 11, 1854.*

To the Senate of the United States:

I transmit herewith a report* from the Secretary of State, in reply to the Senate's resolution of yesterday passed in executive session.

FRANKLIN PIERCE.

WASHINGTON, *April 12, 1854.*

To the House of Representatives:

I transmit herewith a report from the Secretary of State, with accompanying documents,† in compliance with the resolution of the House of Representatives of the 4th instant.

FRANKLIN PIERCE.

WASHINGTON, *April 13, 1854.*

To the Senate of the United States:

I transmit herewith a report ‡ from the Secretary of State, in reply to the resolution of the Senate adopted in executive session yesterday.

FRANKLIN PIERCE.

WASHINGTON, *April 24, 1854.*

To the Senate of the United States:

I have the honor to transmit herewith a report of the Attorney-General, suggesting modifications in the manner of conducting the legal business of the Government, which are respectfully commended to your favorable consideration.

FRANKLIN PIERCE.

[The same message was also addressed to the Speaker of the House of Representatives.]

---

*Relating to claims growing out of the eleventh article of the treaty of Guadalupe Hidalgo.
†Correspondence relative to the seizure of Martin Koszta by Austrian authorities at Smyrna.
‡Relating to the abrogation of the eleventh article of the treaty of Guadalupe Hidalgo, etc.

WASHINGTON, *April 27, 1854.*

To the Senate and House of Representatives:

I transmit to Congress a copy of a correspondence between the Secretary of State and Her Britannic Majesty's minister accredited to this Government, and between the Secretary of State and the Secretary of the Treasury, relative to the expediency of further measures for the safety, health, and comfort of immigrants to the United States by sea. As it is probable that further legislation may be necessary for the purpose of securing those desirable objects, I commend the subject to the consideration of Congress.

FRANKLIN PIERCE.

WASHINGTON, *May 2, 1854.*

To the House of Representatives:

I transmit the report* of the Secretary of State in compliance with a resolution of the House of Representatives of the 5th ultimo.

It is presumed that the omission from the resolution of the usual clause giving the Executive a discretion in its answer was accidental, and as there does not appear to be anything in the accompanying papers which upon public considerations should require them to be withheld, they are communicated accordingly.

FRANKLIN PIERCE.

WASHINGTON, *May 5, 1854.*

To the Senate of the United States:

I transmit herewith a report from the Secretary of State, with accompanying documents,† in compliance with the resolution of the Senate of the 12th ultimo.

FRANKLIN PIERCE.

WASHINGTON, *May 5, 1854.*

To the Senate of the United States:

I transmit herewith a report ‡ from the Secretary of State, together with the documents therein referred to, in compliance with the resolution of the Senate of the 12th January last.

FRANKLIN PIERCE.

---

*Relating to the application of Rev. James Cook Richmond for redress of wrongs alleged to have been committed by Austrian authorities in Pest, and to the refusal to grant an exequatur upon the commission of the United States consul appointed for Trieste.

†Correspondence relative to the arrest and detention at Bremen of Conrad Schmidt, and arrest and maltreatment at Heidelberg of E. T. Dana, W. B. Dingle, and David Ramsay, all citizens of the United States; correspondence with the King of Prussia relative to religious toleration.

‡Relating to the impressment of seamen from the United States whale ship *Addison* at Valparaiso, and imprisonment of William A. Stewart, an American citizen, at Valparaiso on the charge of murder, and on conviction released by Chilean authorities.

WASHINGTON, *May 11, 1854.*

To the House of Representatives:

I transmit a report from the Secretary of State, with accompanying papers,* in answer to the resolution of the House of Representatives of the 1st instant.

FRANKLIN PIERCE.

WASHINGTON, *May 20, 1854.*

To the Senate of the United States:

I transmit herewith a report from the Secretary of State, with accompanying documents,† in compliance with the Senate's resolution of the 30th of January last.

FRANKLIN PIERCE.

WASHINGTON, *May 23, 1854.*

To the Senate of the United States:

I transmit a report from the Secretary of State, on the subject of documents‡ called for by the resolution of the Senate of the 9th instant.

FRANKLIN PIERCE.

WASHINGTON, *May 25, 1854.*

To the Senate of the United States:

I communicate to the Senate herewith, for its constitutional action thereon, four several treaties recently negotiated in this city by George W. Manypenny, as commissioner on the part of the United States, with the delegates of the Delaware, Ioway, Kickapoo, and Sac and Fox tribes of Indians.

FRANKLIN PIERCE.

WASHINGTON, *May 29, 1854.*

To the Senate of the United States:

I communicate to the Senate herewith, for its constitutional action thereon, a treaty negotiated on the 12th instant at the Falls of Wolf River, in Wisconsin, by Francis Huebschmann, superintendent of Indian affairs for the northern superintendency, and the Menomonee Indians, by the chiefs, headmen, and warriors of that tribe.

FRANKLIN PIERCE.

---

*Relating to the rights accorded to neutrals and the rights claimed by belligerents in the war between certain European powers.

†Correspondence relative to the difficulties between Rev. Jonas King and the Government of Greece.

‡Researches of H. S. Sanford, late chargé d'affaires at Paris, on the condition of penal law in continental Europe, etc.; also a "Memoir on the Administrative Changes in France since the Revolution of 1848," by H. S. Sanford.

WASHINGTON, *May 30, 1854.*

To the House of Representatives of the United States:

I transmit herewith a report from the Secretary of State, with accompanying documents,* in compliance with the resolution of the House of Representatives of the 20th December last.

FRANKLIN PIERCE.

To the House of Representatives: WASHINGTON, *June 12, 1854.*

I transmit a report from the Secretary of State, with accompanying papers,† in answer to the resolution of the House of Representatives of the 24th of April last.

FRANKLIN PIERCE.

To the House of Representatives: WASHINGTON, *June 19, 1854.*

I transmit herewith a report from the Secretary of State, with accompanying documents,‡ in compliance with the resolution of the House of Representatives of the 30th ultimo.

FRANKLIN PIERCE.

To the House of Representatives: WASHINGTON, *June 20, 1854.*

I have received information that the Government of Mexico has agreed to the several amendments proposed by the Senate to the treaty between the United States and the Republic of Mexico signed on the 30th of December last, and has authorized its envoy extraordinary to this Government to exchange the ratifications thereof. The time within which the ratifications can be exchanged will expire on the 30th instant.

There is a provision in the treaty for the payment by the United States to Mexico of the sum of $7,000,000 on the exchange of ratifications and the further sum of $3,000,000 when the boundaries of the ceded territory shall be settled.

To be enabled to comply with the stipulation according to the terms of the treaty relative to the payments therein mentioned, it will be necessary that Congress should make an appropriation of $7,000,000 for that purpose before the 30th instant, and also the further sum of $3,000,000, to be paid when the boundaries shall be established.

I therefore respectfully request that these sums may be put at the disposal of the Executive.

I herewith transmit to the House of Representatives a copy of the said treaty.

FRANKLIN PIERCE.

---

* Correspondence relative to the imposition of Sound dues, etc., upon United States commerce to the Baltic.

† Relating to the instructions referred to by President Monroe in his annual message of December 2, 1823, on the subject of the issue of commissions to private armed vessels.

‡ Correspondence of the American minister to Turkey relative to the expulsion of the Greeks from Constantinople.

WASHINGTON, *June 20, 1854.*

To the Senate of the United States:

I transmit to the Senate, for its consideration with a view to ratification, a treaty extending the right of fishing and regulating the commerce and navigation between Her Britannic Majesty's possessions in North America and the United States, concluded in this city on the 5th instant between the United States and Her Britannic Majesty.

FRANKLIN PIERCE.

WASHINGTON, *June 24, 1854.*

To the Senate and House of Representatives:

I transmit to Congress the copy of two communications of the 26th ultimo and 4th instant, respectively, from Her Britannic Majesty's minister accredited to this Government to the Secretary of State, relative to the health on shipboard of immigrants from foreign countries to the United States. This was the subject of my message to Congress of the 27th of April last.

FRANKLIN PIERCE.

WASHINGTON CITY, *June 29, 1854.*

To the Senate of the United States:

I herewith communicate to the Senate, for its constitutional action thereon, three treaties recently negotiated in this city by George W. Manypenny, as commissioner on the part of the United States; one concluded on the 19th ultimo with the delegates of the Shawnee Indians, one on the 5th instant with the Miami Indians, and the other on the 30th ultimo with the united tribes of Kaskaskia and Peoria and Wea and Piankeshaw Indians.

FRANKLIN PIERCE.

WASHINGTON, *July 3, 1854.*

To the Senate of the United States:

I transmit herewith to the Senate, for its constitutional action thereon, an article of agreement made on the 13th day of June, 1854, by William H. Garrett, agent on the part of the United States, and a delegation of Creek Indians, supplementary to the Creek treaty of 1838.

FRANKLIN PIERCE.

WASHINGTON, *July 5, 1854.*

To the Senate of the United States:

In compliance with the resolution of the Senate of the 1st instant, I herewith return the articles of convention made and concluded with the Winnebago Indians on the 6th of August, 1853, together with the Senate resolution of the 9th ultimo, advising and consenting to the ratification of the same with amendments.

FRANKLIN PIERCE.

To the House of Representatives: WASHINGTON, *July 12, 1854.*

I transmit herewith the inclosed communication from the Secretary of the Navy, respecting the observations of Lieutenant James M. Gillis, of the United States Navy, and the accompanying documents.*

FRANKLIN PIERCE.

WASHINGTON, *July 12, 1854.*
To the Senate of the United States:

I transmit to the Senate, for its consideration with a view to ratification, a treaty between the United States and the Empire of Japan, signed at Kanagawa on the 31st day of March last by the plenipotentiaries of the two Governments. The Chinese and Dutch translations of the instrument and the chart and sketch to which it refers are also herewith communicated.

FRANKLIN PIERCE.

WASHINGTON, *July 17, 1854.*
To the Senate of the United States:

I transmit to the Senate, for its consideration with a view to ratification, a convention between the United States and Her Britannic Majesty for the extension of the period limited for the duration of the mixed commission under convention between the United States and Great Britain of the 8th of February, 1853.

FRANKLIN PIERCE.

To the House of Representatives: WASHINGTON, *July 19, 1854.*

I transmit a report from the Secretary of State, with accompanying papers,† in answer to the resolution of the House of Representatives of the 6th of February last.

FRANKLIN PIERCE.

WASHINGTON, *July 22, 1854.*
To the Senate of the United States:

I have this day given my signature to the "Act making further appropriations for the improvement of the Cape Fear River, in North Carolina."

The occasion seems to render it proper for me to deviate from the ordinary course of announcing the approval of bills by an oral statement only, and, for the purpose of preventing any misapprehension which might otherwise arise from the phraseology of this act, to communicate in writing that my approval is given to it on the ground that the obstructions which the proposed appropriation is intended to remove are the result of acts of the General Government.

FRANKLIN PIERCE.

---

*Report of the United States naval astronomical expedition to the Southern Hemisphere.
†Correspondence of Humphrey Marshall, commissioner to China.

WASHINGTON, *July 24, 1854.*

To the Senate of the United States:

I transmit to the Senate, for its consideration with a view to ratification, a convention concerning the rights of neutrals, concluded in this city on the 22d instant between the United States and His Majesty the Emperor of all the Russias. FRANKLIN PIERCE.

WASHINGTON, *July 26, 1854.*

To the Senate of the United States:

I transmit a report from the Secretary of State, in answer to the resolution of the Senate of the 23d of May last, relative to the slave trade in the island of Cuba.

The information contained in the papers accompanying the report will, it is believed, be considered important, and perhaps necessary to enable the Senate to form an opinion upon the subjects to which they relate; but doubts may be entertained in regard to the expediency of publishing some of the documents at this juncture.

This communication is accordingly addressed to the Senate in executive session, in order that a discretion may be exercised in regard to its publication. FRANKLIN PIERCE.

WASHINGTON, *July 27, 1854.*

The PRESIDENT OF THE SENATE:

In compliance with the resolution of the Senate of the 24th instant, requesting me to cause to be transmitted to the Senate the Fourth Meteorological Report of Professor Espy, the accompanying papers and charts are respectfully submitted. FRANKLIN PIERCE.

WASHINGTON, *July 29, 1854.*

To the Senate of the United States:

In compliance with the Senate resolution of the 10th July instant, requesting that I would "cause to be communicated to the Senate copies of all the correspondence and other official documents on file in the Department of the Interior respecting the claims of persons for services performed and supplies and subsistence furnished to Indians in California under contracts with Indian agents in the year 1851, and embracing the names of claimants, the amount, respectively, of their claims, on what account created and by what authority, if any," I transmit herewith a communication from the Secretary of the Interior, accompanied by copies of all the papers called for which have not heretofore been furnished. As it appears that most of the papers called for were communicated to the Senate at its first and special sessions of the Thirty-second Congress, I have not supposed that it was the intention of the Senate to have them again sent, and I have therefore not directed them to be copied.

FRANKLIN PIERCE.

WASHINGTON, *July 31, 1854.*

To the Senate of the United States:

In compliance with a resolution of the Senate of the 28th instant, requesting information in respect to the bombardment of San Juan de Nicaragua, I transmit reports from the Secretaries of State and of the Navy, with the documents which accompanied them.

FRANKLIN PIERCE.

WASHINGTON, *July 31, 1854.*

To the House of Representatives:

In answer to the resolution of the House of Representatives of the 28th instant, requesting information in regard to the destruction of San Juan de Nicaragua, I transmit reports from the Secretaries of State and of the Navy, with the documents accompanying them.

FRANKLIN PIERCE.

WASHINGTON, *August 1, 1854.*

To the Senate of the United States:

I hasten to respond briefly to the resolution of the Senate of this date, "requesting the President to inform the Senate, if in his opinion it be not incompatible with the public interest, whether anything has arisen since the date of his message to the House of Representatives of the 15th of March last concerning our relations with the Government of Spain which in his opinion may dispense with the suggestions therein contained touching the propriety of 'provisional measures' by Congress to meet any exigency that may arise in the recess of Congress affecting those relations."

In the message to the House of Representatives referred to I availed myself of the occasion to present the following reflections and suggestions:

In view of the position of the island of Cuba, its proximity to our coast, the relations which it must ever bear to our commercial and other interests, it is vain to expect that a series of unfriendly acts infringing our commercial rights and the adoption of a policy threatening the honor and security of these States can long consist with peaceful relations.

In case the measures taken for amicable adjustment of our difficulties with Spain should, unfortunately, fail, I shall not hesitate to use the authority and means which Congress may grant to insure the observance of our just rights, to obtain redress for injuries received, and to vindicate the honor of our flag.

In anticipation of that contingency, which I earnestly hope may not arise, I suggest to Congress the propriety of adopting such provisional measures as the exigency may seem to demand.

The two Houses of Congress may have anticipated that the hope then expressed would be realized before the period of its adjournment, and that our relations with Spain would have assumed a satisfactory condition, so as to remove past causes of complaint and afford better security for tranquillity and justice in the future. But I am constrained to say that such is not the fact. The formal demand for immediate reparation in the case of the *Black Warrior*, instead of having been met on the part of Spain by prompt satisfaction, has only served to call forth a justification of the local authorities of Cuba, and thus to transfer the responsibility for their acts to the Spanish Government itself.

Meanwhile information, not only reliable in its nature, but of an official character, was received to the effect that preparation was making within the limits of the United States by private individuals under military organization for a descent upon the island of Cuba with a view to wrest that colony from the dominion of Spain. International comity, the obligations of treaties, and the express provisions of law alike required, in my judgment, that all the constitutional power of the Executive should be exerted to prevent the consummation of such a violation of positive law and of that good faith on which mainly the amicable relations of neighboring nations must depend. In conformity with these convictions of public duty, a proclamation was issued to warn all persons not to participate in the contemplated enterprise and to invoke the interposition in this behalf of the proper officers of the Government. No provocation whatever can justify private expeditions of hostility against a country at peace with the United States. The power to declare war is vested by the Constitution in Congress, and the experience of our past history leaves no room to doubt that the wisdom of this arrangement of constitutional power will continue to be verified whenever the national interest and honor shall demand a resort to ultimate measures of redress. Pending negotiations by the Executive, and before the action of Congress, individuals could not be permitted to embarrass the operations of the one and usurp the powers of the other of these depositaries of the functions of Government.

I have only to add that nothing has arisen since the date of my former message to "dispense with the suggestions therein contained touching the propriety of provisional measures by Congress."

FRANKLIN PIERCE.

WASHINGTON, *August 2, 1854.*

To the Senate of the United States:

I transmit herewith a report of the Secretary of State, with the accompanying documents,* in answer to the resolution of the Senate of the 5th ultimo.

FRANKLIN PIERCE.

*Correspondence relative to the imprisonment of George Marsden and to the seizure of the cargo of the American bark *Griffon* by the authorities of Brazil.

WASHINGTON, *August 2, 1854.*

To the House of Representatives:

I herewith transmit to you a copy of a treaty between the United States and Great Britain, negotiated at Washington on the 5th of June last. It has been concurred in by the Senate, and I have no doubt that the ratifications of it will be soon exchanged. It will be observed that by the provision of the fifth article the treaty does not go into operation until after legislation thereon by the respective parties.

Should Congress at its present session pass the requisite law on the part of the United States to give effect to its stipulations, the fishing grounds on the coasts of the British North American Provinces, from which our fishermen have been heretofore excluded, may be opened to them during the present season, and apprehended collisions between them and British fishermen avoided.

For this reason and for the purpose of securing to the citizens of the United States at the earliest practicable period other advantages which it is believed they will derive from this treaty, I recommend the passage by Congress at the present session of such a law as is necessary on the part of the United States to give effect to its provisions.

FRANKLIN PIERCE.

VETO MESSAGES.

WASHINGTON, *May 3, 1854.*

To the Senate of the United States:

The bill entitled "An act making a grant of public lands to the several States for the benefit of indigent insane persons," which was presented to me on the 27th ultimo, has been maturely considered, and is returned to the Senate, the House in which it originated, with a statement of the objections which have required me to withhold from it my approval.

In the performance of this duty, prescribed by the Constitution, I have been compelled to resist the deep sympathies of my own heart in favor of the humane purpose sought to be accomplished and to overcome the reluctance with which I dissent from the conclusions of the two Houses of Congress, and present my own opinions in opposition to the action of a coordinate branch of the Government which possesses so fully my confidence and respect.

If in presenting my objections to this bill I should say more than strictly belongs to the measure or is required for the discharge of my official obligation, let it be attributed to a sincere desire to justify my act before those whose good opinion I so highly value and to that earnestness which springs from my deliberate conviction that a strict adherence to the terms and purposes of the federal compact offers the best, if not the only, security for the preservation of our blessed inheritance of representative liberty.

The bill provides in substance:

First. That 10,000,000 acres of land be granted to the several States, to be apportioned among them in the compound ratio of the geographical area and representation of said States in the House of Representatives.

Second. That wherever there are public lands in a State subject to sale at the regular price of private entry, the proportion of said 10,000,000 acres falling to such State shall be selected from such lands within it, and that to the States in which there are no such public lands land scrip shall be issued to the amount of their distributive shares, respectively, said scrip not to be entered by said States, but to be sold by them and subject to entry by their assignees: *Provided*, That none of it shall be sold at less than $1 per acre, under penalty of forfeiture of the same to the United States.

Third. That the expenses of the management and superintendence of said lands and of the moneys received therefrom shall be paid by the States to which they may belong out of the treasury of said States.

Fourth. That the gross proceeds of the sales of such lands or land scrip so granted shall be invested by the several States in safe stocks, to constitute a perpetual fund, the principal of which shall remain forever undiminished, and the interest to be appropriated to the maintenance of the indigent insane within the several States.

Fifth. That annual returns of lands or scrip sold shall be made by the States to the Secretary of the Interior, and the whole grant be subject to certain conditions and limitations prescribed in the bill, to be assented to by legislative acts of said States.

This bill therefore proposes that the Federal Government shall make provision to the amount of the value of 10,000,000 acres of land for an eleemosynary object within the several States, to be administered by the political authority of the same; and it presents at the threshold the question whether any such act on the part of the Federal Government is warranted and sanctioned by the Constitution, the provisions and principles of which are to be protected and sustained as a first and paramount duty.

It can not be questioned that if Congress has power to make provision for the indigent insane without the limits of this District it has the same power to provide for the indigent who are not insane, and thus to transfer to the Federal Government the charge of all the poor in all the States. It has the same power to provide hospitals and other local establishments for the care and cure of every species of human infirmity, and thus to assume all that duty of either public philanthropy or public necessity to the dependent, the orphan, the sick, or the needy which is now discharged by the States themselves or by corporate institutions or private endowments existing under the legislation of the States. The whole field of public beneficence is thrown open to the care and culture of the Federal Government. Generous impulses no longer encounter the limitations and control of our imperious fundamental law; for however worthy may be the present object in itself, it is only one of a class. It is not exclusively worthy of benevolent regard. Whatever considerations dictate sympathy for this particular object apply in like manner, if not in the same degree, to idiocy, to physical disease, to extreme destitution. If Congress may and ought to provide for any one of these objects, it may and ought to provide for them all. And if it be done in this case, what answer shall be given when Congress shall be called upon, as it doubtless will be, to pursue a similar course of legislation in the others? It will obviously be vain to reply that the object is worthy, but that the application has taken a wrong direction. The power will have been deliberately assumed, the general obligation will by this act have been acknowledged, and the question of means and expediency will alone be left for consideration. The decision upon the principle in any one case determines it for the whole class. The question presented, therefore, clearly is upon the constitutionality and propriety of the Federal Government assuming to enter into a novel and vast field of legislation, namely, that of providing for the care and support of all those among the people of the United States who by any form of calamity become fit objects of public philanthropy.

I readily and, I trust, feelingly acknowledge the duty incumbent on us all as men and citizens, and as among the highest and holiest of our duties, to provide for those who, in the mysterious order of Providence, are subject to want and to disease of body or mind; but I can not find any authority in the Constitution for making the Federal Government the great almoner of public charity throughout the United States. To do so would, in my judgment, be contrary to the letter and spirit of the Constitution and subversive of the whole theory upon which the Union of these States is founded. And if it were admissible to contemplate the exercise of this power for any object whatever, I can not avoid the belief that it would in the end be prejudicial rather than beneficial in the noble offices of charity to have the charge of them transferred from the States to the Federal Government. Are we not too prone to forget that the Federal Union is the creature of the States, not they of the Federal Union? We were the inhabitants of colonies distinct in local government one from the other before the Revolution. By that Revolution the colonies each became an independent State. They achieved that independence and secured its recognition by the agency of a consulting body, which, from being an assembly of the ministers of distinct sovereignties instructed to agree to no form of government which did not leave the domestic concerns of each State to itself, was appropriately denominated a Congress. When, having tried the experiment of the Confederation, they resolved to change that for the present Federal Union, and thus to confer on the Federal Government more ample authority, they scrupulously measured such of the functions of their cherished sovereignty as they chose to delegate to the General Government. With this aim and to this end the fathers of the Republic framed the Constitution, in and by which the independent and sovereign States united themselves for certain specified objects and purposes, and for those only, leaving all powers not therein set forth as conferred on one or another of the three great departments—the legislative, the executive, and the judicial—indubitably with the States. And when the people of the several States had in their State conventions, and thus alone, given effect and force to the Constitution, not content that any doubt should in future arise as to the scope and character of this act, they ingrafted thereon the explicit declaration that "the powers not delegated to the United States by the Constitution nor prohibited by it to the States are reserved to the States respectively or to the people." Can it be controverted that the great mass of the business of Government—that involved in the social relations, the internal arrangements of the body politic, the mental and moral culture of men, the development of local resources of wealth, the punishment of crimes in general, the preservation of order, the relief of the needy or otherwise unfortunate members of society—did in practice remain with the States; that none of these objects of local concern are by the Constitution expressly or impliedly prohibited to the States, and that none of them are by any express language of the Constitution transferred to the United States? Can it be claimed that any of these functions of local administration and legislation are vested in the Federal Government by any implication? I have never found anything in the Constitution which is susceptible of such a construction. No one of the enumerated powers touches the subject or has even a remote analogy to it. The powers conferred upon the United States have reference to federal relations, or to the means of accomplishing or executing things of federal relation. So also of the same character are the powers taken away from the States by enumeration. In either case the powers granted and the powers restricted were so granted or so restricted only where it was requisite for the maintenance of peace and harmony between the States or for the purpose of protecting their common interests and defending their common sovereignty against aggression from abroad or insurrection at home.

I shall not discuss at length the question of power sometimes claimed for the General Government under the clause of the eighth section of the Constitution, which gives Congress the power "to lay and collect taxes, duties, imposts, and excises, to pay debts and provide for the common defense and general welfare of the United States," because if it has not already been settled upon sound reason and authority it never will be. I take the received and just construction of that article, as if written to lay and collect taxes, duties, imposts, and excises *in order* to pay the debts and *in order* to provide for the common defense and general welfare. It is not a substantive general power to provide for the welfare of the United States, but is a limitation on the grant of power to raise money by taxes, duties, and imposts. If it were otherwise, all the rest of the Constitution, consisting of carefully enumerated and cautiously guarded grants of specific powers, would have been useless, if not delusive. It would be impossible in that view to escape from the conclusion that these were inserted only to mislead for the present, and, instead of enlightening and defining the pathway of the future, to involve its action in the mazes of doubtful construction. Such a conclusion the character of the men who framed that sacred instrument will never permit us to form. Indeed, to suppose it susceptible of any other construction would be to consign all the rights of the States and of the people of the States to the mere discretion of Congress, and thus to clothe the Federal Government with authority to control the sovereign States, by which they would have been dwarfed into provinces or departments and all sovereignty vested in an absolute consolidated central power, against which the spirit of liberty has so often and in so many countries struggled in vain. In my judgment you can not by tributes to humanity make any adequate compensation for the wrong you would inflict by removing the sources of power and political action from those who are to be thereby affected. If the time shall ever arrive when, for an object appealing, however strongly, to our sympathies, the dignity of the States shall bow to the dictation of Congress by conforming their legislation thereto, when the power and majesty and honor of those who created shall become subordinate to the thing of their creation, I but feebly utter my apprehensions when I express my firm conviction that we shall see "the beginning of the end."

Fortunately, we are not left in doubt as to the purpose of the Constitution any more than as to its express language, for although the history of its formation, as recorded in the Madison Papers, shows that the Federal Government in its present form emerged from the conflict of opposing influences which have continued to divide statesmen from that day to this, yet the rule of clearly defined powers and of strict construction presided over the actual conclusion and subsequent adoption of the Constitution. President Madison, in the Federalist, says:

The powers delegated by the proposed Constitution are few and defined. Those which are to remain in the State governments are numerous and indefinite. * * * Its [the General Government's] jurisdiction extends to certain enumerated objects only, and leaves to the several States a residuary and inviolable sovereignty over all other objects.

In the same spirit President Jefferson invokes "the support of the State governments in all their rights as the most competent administrations for our domestic concerns and the surest bulwarks against antirepublican tendencies;" and President Jackson said that our true strength and wisdom are not promoted by invasions of the rights and powers of

the several States, but that, on the contrary, they consist "not in binding the States more closely to the center, but in leaving each more unobstructed in its proper orbit."

The framers of the Constitution, in refusing to confer on the Federal
Government any jurisdiction over these purely local objects, in my judgment manifested a wise forecast and broad comprehension of the true
interests of these objects themselves. It is clear that public charities
within the States can be efficiently administered only by their authority.
The bill before me concedes this, for it does not commit the funds it provides to the administration of any other authority.

I can not but repeat what I have before expressed, that if the several
States, many of which have already laid the foundation of munificent
establishments of local beneficence, and nearly all of which are proceeding to establish them, shall be led to suppose, as, should this bill become
a law, they will be, that Congress is to make provision for such objects,
the fountains of charity will be dried up at home, and the several States,
instead of bestowing their own means on the social wants of their own
people, may themselves, through the strong temptation which appeals
to states as to individuals, become humble suppliants for the bounty of
the Federal Government, reversing their true relations to this Union.

Having stated my views of the limitation of the powers conferred by
the eighth section of the first article of the Constitution, I deem it proper
to call attention to the third section of the fourth article and to the provisions of the sixth article bearing directly upon the question under
consideration, which, instead of aiding the claim to power exercised in
this case, tend, it is believed, strongly to illustrate and explain positions
which, even without such support, I can not regard as questionable. The
third section of the fourth article of the Constitution is in the following
terms:

The Congress shall have power to *dispose* of and make all needful rules and regulations respecting the territory or other property belonging to the United States;
and nothing in this Constitution shall be so construed as to prejudice any claims of
the United States or of any particular State.

The sixth article is as follows, to wit, that—

All debts contracted and engagements entered into before the adoption of this
Constitution shall be as valid against the United States under this Constitution as
under the Confederation.

For a correct understanding of the terms used in the third section of
the fourth article, above quoted, reference should be had to the history
of the times in which the Constitution was formed and adopted. It
was decided upon in convention on the 17th September, 1787, and by it
Congress was empowered "to dispose of," etc., "the territory or other
property belonging to the United States." The only territory then
belonging to the United States was that then recently ceded by the
several States, to wit: By New York in 1781, by Virginia in 1784, by

Massachusetts in 1785, and by South Carolina in August, 1787, only the month before the formation of the Constitution. The cession from Virginia contained the following provision:

That all the lands within the territory so ceded to the United States, and not reserved for or appropriated to any of the before-mentioned purposes or disposed of in bounties to the officers and soldiers of the American Army, shall be considered a common fund for the use and benefit of such of the United States as have become or shall become members of the Confederation or Federal Alliance of the said States, Virginia included, according to their usual respective proportions in the general charge and expenditure, and shall be faithfully and *bona fide disposed of* for that purpose and for no other use or purpose whatsoever.

Here the object for which these lands are to be disposed of is clearly set forth, and the power to dispose of them granted by the third section of the fourth article of the Constitution clearly contemplates such disposition only. If such be the fact, and in my mind there can be no doubt of it, then you have again not only no implication in favor of the contemplated grant, but the strongest authority against it. Furthermore, this bill is in violation of the faith of the Government pledged in the act of January 28, 1847. The nineteenth section of that act declares:

That for the payment of the stock which may be created under the provisions of this act the sales of the public lands are hereby pledged; and it is hereby made the duty of the Secretary of the Treasury to use and apply all moneys which may be received into the Treasury for the sales of the public lands after the 1st day of January, 1848, first, to pay the interest on all stocks issued by virtue of this act, and, secondly, to use the balance of said receipts, after paying the interest aforesaid, in the purchase of said stocks at their market value, etc.

The debts then contracted have not been liquidated, and the language of this section and the obligations of the United States under it are too plain to need comment.

I have been unable to discover any distinction on constitutional grounds or grounds of expediency between an appropriation of $10,000,000 directly from the money in the Treasury for the object contemplated and the appropriation of lands presented for my sanction, and yet I can not doubt that if the bill proposed $10,000,000 from the Treasury of the United States for the support of the indigent insane in the several States that the constitutional question involved in the act would have attracted forcibly the attention of Congress.

I respectfully submit that in a constitutional point of view it is wholly immaterial whether the appropriation be in money or in land.

The public domain is the common property of the Union just as much as the surplus proceeds of that and of duties on imports remaining unexpended in the Treasury. As such it has been pledged, is now pledged, and may need to be so pledged again for public indebtedness.

As property it is distinguished from actual money chiefly in this respect, that its profitable management sometimes requires that portions of it be appropriated to local objects in the States wherein it may happen to lie, as would be done by any prudent proprietor to enhance the sale value of his private domain. All such grants of land are in fact a disposal of it for value received, but they afford no precedent or constitutional reason for giving away the public lands. Still less do they give sanction to appropriations for objects which have not been intrusted to the Federal Government, and therefore belong exclusively to the States.

To assume that the public lands are applicable to ordinary State objects, whether of public structures, police, charity, or expenses of State administration, would be to disregard to the amount of the value of the public lands all the limitations of the Constitution and confound to that extent all distinctions between the rights and powers of the States and those of the United States; for if the public lands may be applied to the support of the poor, whether sane or insane, if the disposal of them and their proceeds be not subject to the ordinary limitations of the Constitution, then Congress possesses unqualified power to provide for expenditures in the States by means of the public lands, even to the degree of defraying the salaries of governors, judges, and all other expenses of the government and internal administration within the several States.

The conclusion from the general survey of the whole subject is to my mind irresistible, and closes the question both of right and of expediency so far as regards the principle of the appropriation proposed in this bill. Would not the admission of such power in Congress to dispose of the public domain work the practical abrogation of some of the most important provisions of the Constitution?

If the systematic reservation of a definite portion of the public lands (the sixteenth sections) in the States for the purposes of education and occasional grants for similar purposes be cited as contradicting these conclusions, the answer as it appears to me is obvious and satisfactory. Such reservations and grants, besides being a part of the conditions on which the proprietary right of the United States is maintained, along with the eminent domain of a particular State, and by which the public land remains free from taxation in the State in which it lies as long as it remains the property of the United States, are the acts of a mere land-owner disposing of a small share of his property in a way to augment the value of the residue and in this mode to encourage the early occupation of it by the industrious and intelligent pioneer.

The great example of apparent donation of lands to the States likely to be relied upon as sustaining the principles of this bill is the relinquishment of swamp lands to the States in which they are situated, but this also, like other grants already referred to, was based expressly upon grounds clearly distinguishable in principle from any which can be assumed for the bill herewith returned, viz, upon the interest and duty of the proprietor. They were charged, and not without reason, to be a nuisance to the inhabitants of the surrounding country. The measure was predicated not only upon the ground of the disease inflicted upon the people of the States, which the United States could not justify as a just and honest proprietor, but also upon an express limitation of the application of the proceeds in the first instance to purposes of levees and drains, thus protecting the health of the inhabitants and at the same time enhancing the value of the remaining lands belonging to the General Government.

It is not to be denied that Congress, while administering the public lands as a proprietor within the principle distinctly announced in my annual message, may sometimes have failed to distinguish accurately between objects which are and which are not within its constitutional powers.

After the most careful examination I find but two examples in the acts of Congress which furnish any precedent for the present bill, and those examples will, in my opinion, serve rather as a warning than as an induce- ment to tread in the same path.

The first is the act of March 3, 1819, granting a township of land to the Connecticut asylum for the education of the deaf and dumb; the second, that of April 5, 1826, making a similar grant of land to the Ken- tucky asylum for teaching the deaf and dumb—the first more than thirty years after the adoption of the Constitution and the second more than a quarter of a century ago. These acts were unimportant as to the amount appropriated, and so far as I can ascertain were passed on two grounds: First, that the object was a charitable one, and, secondly, that it was national. To say that it was a charitable object is only to say that it was an object of expenditure proper for the competent authority; but it no more tended to show that it was a proper object of expenditure by the United States than is any other purely local object appealing to the best sympathies of the human heart in any of the States. And the sugges- tion that a school for the mental culture of the deaf and dumb in Con- necticut or Kentucky is a national object only shows how loosely this expression has been used when the purpose was to procure appropria- tions by Congress. It is not perceived how a school of this character is otherwise national than is any establishment of religious or moral instruc- tion. All the pursuits of industry, everything which promotes the mate- rial or intellectual well-being of the race, every ear of corn or boll of cotton which grows, is national in the same sense, for each one of these things goes to swell the aggregate of national prosperity and happiness of the United States; but it confounds all meaning of language to say that these things are "national," as equivalent to "Federal," so as to come within any of the classes of appropriation for which Congress is authorized by the Constitution to legislate.

It is a marked point of the history of the Constitution that when it was proposed to empower Congress to establish a university the prop- osition was confined to the District intended for the future seat of Gov- ernment of the United States, and that even that proposed clause was omitted in consideration of the exclusive powers conferred on Congress to legislate for that District.   Could a more decisive indication of the true construction and the spirit of the Constitution in regard to all matters of this nature have been given?   It proves that such objects were considered by the Convention as appertaining to local legislation only; that they were not comprehended, either expressly or by implication, in the grant of general power to Congress, and that consequently they remained with the several States.

The general result at which I have arrived is the necessary consequence of those views of the relative rights, powers, and duties of the States and of the Federal Government which I have long entertained and often expressed and in reference to which my convictions do but increase in force with time and experience.

I have thus discharged the unwelcome duty of respectfully stating my objections to this bill, with which I cheerfully submit the whole subject to the wisdom of Congress.

FRANKLIN PIERCE.

WASHINGTON, *August 4, 1854.*

To the House of Representatives:

I have received the bill entitled "An act making appropriations for the repair, preservation, and completion of certain public works heretofore commenced under the authority of law."   It reaches me in the expiring hours of the session, and time does not allow full opportunity for examining and considering its provisions or of stating at length the reasons which forbid me to give it my signature.

It belongs to that class of measures which are commonly known as internal improvements by the General Government, and which from a very early period have been deemed of doubtful constitutionality and expediency, and have thus failed to obtain the approbation of successive Chief Magistrates.

On such an examination of this bill as it has been in my power to make, I recognize in it certain provisions national in their character, and which, if they stood alone, it would be compatible with my convictions of public duty to assent to; but at the same time, it embraces others which are merely local, and not, in my judgment, warranted by any safe or true construction of the Constitution.

To make proper and sound discriminations between these different provisions would require a deliberate discussion of general principles, as well as a careful scrutiny of details for the purpose of rightfully applying those principles to each separate item of appropriation.

Public opinion with regard to the value and importance of internal improvements in the country is undivided.   There is a disposition on all hands to have them prosecuted with energy and to see the benefits sought to be attained by them fully realized.

The prominent point of difference between those who have been regarded as the friends of a system of internal improvements by the General Government and those adverse to such a system has been one of constitutional power, though more or less connected with considerations of expediency.

My own judgment, it is well known, has on both grounds been opposed to "a general system of internal improvements" by the Federal Government. I have entertained the most serious doubts from the inherent difficulties of its application, as well as from past unsatisfactory experience, whether the power could be so exercised by the General Government as to render its use advantageous either to the country at large or effectual for the accomplishment of the object contemplated.

I shall consider it incumbent on me to present to Congress at its next session a matured view of the whole subject, and to endeavor to define, approximately at least, and according to my own convictions, what appropriations of this nature by the General Government the great interests of the United States require and the Constitution will admit and sanction, in case no substitute should be devised capable of reconciling differences both of constitutionality and expediency.

In the absence of the requisite means and time for duly considering the whole subject at present and discussing such possible substitute, it becomes necessary to return this bill to the House of Representatives, in which it originated, and for the reasons thus briefly submitted to the consideration of Congress to withhold from it my approval.

FRANKLIN PIERCE.

[The following message is inserted here because it is an exposition of the reasons of the President for the veto of August 4, 1854, immediately preceding.]

WASHINGTON, *December 30, 1854.*

To the Senate and House of Representatives:

In returning to the House of Representatives, in which it originated, a bill entitled "An act making appropriations for the repair, preservation, and completion of certain public works heretofore commenced under the authority of law," it became necessary for me, owing to the late day at which the bill was passed, to state my objections to it very briefly, announcing at the same time a purpose to resume the subject for more deliberate discussion at the present session of Congress; for, while by no means insensible of the arduousness of the task thus undertaken by me, I conceived that the two Houses were entitled to an exposition of the considerations which had induced dissent on my part from their conclusions in this instance.

The great constitutional question of the power of the General Government in relation to internal improvements has been the subject of earnest difference of opinion at every period of the history of the United States.

Annual and special messages of successive Presidents have been occupied with it, sometimes in remarks on the general topic and frequently in objection to particular bills. The conflicting sentiments of eminent statesmen, expressed in Congress or in conventions called expressly to devise, if possible, some plan calculated to relieve the subject of the embarrassments with which it is environed, while they have directed public attention strongly to the magnitude of the interests involved, have yet left unsettled the limits, not merely of expediency, but of constitutional power, in relation to works of this class by the General Government.

What is intended by the phrase "internal improvements"? What does it embrace and what exclude? No such language is found in the Constitution. Not only is it not an expression of ascertainable constitutional power, but it has no sufficient exactness of meaning to be of any value as the basis of a safe conclusion either of constitutional law or of practical statesmanship.

President John Quincy Adams, in claiming on one occasion, after his retirement from office, the authorship of the idea of introducing into the administration of the affairs of the General Government "a permanent and regular system" of internal improvements, speaks of it as a system by which "the whole Union would have been checkered over with railroads and canals," affording "high wages and constant employment to hundreds of thousands of laborers;" and he places it in express contrast with the construction of such works by the legislation of the States and by private enterprise.

It is quite obvious that if there be any constitutional power which authorizes the construction of "railroads and canals" by Congress, the same power must comprehend turnpikes and ordinary carriage roads; nay, it must extend to the construction of bridges, to the draining of marshes, to the erection of levees, to the construction of canals of irrigation; in a word, to all the possible means of the material improvement of the earth, by developing its natural resources anywhere and everywhere, even within the proper jurisdiction of the several States. But if there be any constitutional power thus comprehensive in its nature, must not the same power embrace within its scope other kinds of improvement of equal utility in themselves and equally important to the welfare of the whole country? President Jefferson, while intimating the expediency of so amending the Constitution as to comprise objects of physical progress and well-being, does not fail to perceive that "other objects of public improvement," including "public education" by name, belong to the same class of powers. In fact, not only public instruction, but hospitals, establishments of science and art, libraries, and, indeed, everything appertaining to the internal welfare of the country, are just as much objects of internal improvement, or, in other words, of internal utility, as canals and railways.

The admission of the power in either of its senses implies its existence in the other; and since if it exists at all it involves dangerous augmentation of the political functions and of the patronage of the Federal Government, we ought to see clearly by what clause or clauses of the Constitution it is conferred.

I have had occasion more than once to express, and deem it proper now to repeat, that it is, in my judgment, to be taken for granted, as a fundamental proposition not requiring elucidation, that the Federal Government is the creature of the individual States and of the people of the States severally; that the sovereign power was in them alone; that all the powers of the Federal Government are derivative ones, the enumeration and limitations of which are contained in the instrument which organized it; and by express terms ''the powers not delegated to the United States by the Constitution nor prohibited by it to the States are reserved to the States respectively or to the people.''

Starting from this foundation of our constitutional faith and proceeaing to inquire in what part of the Constitution the power of making appropriations for internal improvements is found, it is necessary to reject all idea of there being any grant of power in the preamble. When that instrument says, ''We, the people of the United States, in order to form a more perfect union, establish justice, insure domestic tranquillity, provide for the common defense, promote the general welfare, and secure the blessings of liberty to ourselves and our posterity,'' it only declares the inducements and the anticipated results of the things ordained and established by it. To assume that anything more can be designed by the language of the preamble would be to convert all the body of the Constitution, with its carefully weighed enumerations and limitations, into mere surplusage. The same may be said of the phrase in the grant of the power to Congress ''to pay the debts and provide for the common defense and general welfare of the United States;'' or, to construe the words more exactly, they are not significant of grant or concession, but of restriction of the specific grants, having the effect of saying that in laying and collecting taxes for each of the precise objects of power granted to the General Government Congress must exercise any such definite and undoubted power in strict subordination to the purpose of the common defense and general welfare of all the States.

There being no specific grant in the Constitution of a power to sanction appropriations for internal improvements, and no general provision broad enough to cover any such indefinite object, it becomes necessary to look for particular powers to which one or another of the things included in the phrase ''internal improvements'' may be referred.

In the discussions of this question by the advocates of the organization of a '' general system of internal improvements '' under the auspices of the Federal Government, reliance is had for the justification of the measure on several of the powers expressly granted to Congress, such as to establish post-offices and post-roads, to declare war, to provide and maintain a navy, to raise and support armies, to regulate commerce, and to dispose of the territory and other public property of the United States.

As to the last of these sources of power, that of disposing of the territory and other public property of the United States, it may be conceded that it authorizes Congress, in the management of the public property, to make improvements essential to the successful execution of the trust; but this must be the primary object of any such improvement, and it would be an abuse of the trust to sacrifice the interest of the property to incidental purposes.

As to the other assumed sources of a general power over internal improvements, they being specific powers of which this is supposed to be the incident, if the framers of the Constitution, wise and thoughtful men as they were, intended to confer on Congress the power over a subject so wide as the whole field of internal improvements, it is remarkable that they did not use language clearly to express it, or, in other words, that they did not give it as a distinct and substantive power instead of making it the implied incident of some other one; for such is the magnitude of the supposed incidental power and its capacity of expansion that any system established under it would exceed each of the others in the amount of expenditure and number of the persons employed, which would thus be thrown upon the General Government.

This position may be illustrated by taking as a single example one of the many things comprehended clearly in the idea of ''a general system of internal improvements,'' namely, roads. Let it be supposed that the power to construct roads over the whole Union, according to the suggestion of President J. Q. Adams in 1807, whilst a member of the Senate of the United States, had been conceded. Congress would have begun, in pursuance of the state of knowledge at the time, by constructing turnpikes; then, as knowledge advanced, it would have constructed canals, and at the present time it would have been embarked in an almost limitless scheme of railroads.

Now there are in the United States, the results of State or private enterprise, upward of 17,000 miles of railroads and 5,000 miles of canals; in all, 22,000 miles, the total cost of which may be estimated at little short of $600,000,000; and if the same works had been constructed by the Federal Government, supposing the thing to have been practicable, the cost would have probably been not less than $900,000,000. The number of persons employed in superintending, managing, and keeping up these canals and railroads may be stated at 126,000 or thereabouts, to which are to be added 70,000 or 80,000 employed on the railroads in construction, making a total of at least 200,000 persons, representing in families nearly 1,000,000 souls, employed on or maintained by this one class of public works in the United States.

In view of all this, it is not easy to estimate the disastrous consequences which must have resulted from such extended local improvements being undertaken by the General Government. State legislation upon this subject would have been suspended and private enterprise paralyzed, while applications for appropriations would have perverted the legislation of Congress, exhausted the National Treasury, and left the people burdened with a heavy public debt, beyond the capacity of generations to discharge.

Is it conceivable that the framers of the Constitution intended that authority drawing after it such immense consequences should be inferred by implication as the incident of enumerated powers? I can not think this, and the impossibility of supposing it would be still more glaring if similar calculations were carried out in regard to the numerous objects of material, moral, and political usefulness of which the idea of internal improvement admits. It may be safely inferred that if the framers of the Constitution had intended to confer the power to make appropriations for the objects indicated, it would have been enumerated among the grants expressly made to Congress. When, therefore, any one of the powers actually enumerated is adduced or referred to as the ground of an assumption to warrant the incidental or implied power of "internal improvement," that hypothesis must be rejected, or at least can be no further admitted than as the particular act of internal improvement may happen to be necessary to the exercise of the granted power. Thus, when the object of a given road, the clearing of a particular channel, or the construction of a particular harbor of refuge is manifestly required by the exigencies of the naval or military service of the country, then it seems to me undeniable that it may be constitutionally comprehended in the powers to declare war, to provide and maintain a navy, and to raise and support armies. At the same time, it would be a misuse of these powers and a violation of the Constitution to undertake to build upon them a great system of internal improvements. And similar reasoning applies to the assumption of any such power as is involved in that to establish post-roads and to regulate commerce. If the particular improvement, whether by land or sea, be necessary to the execution of the enumerated powers, then, but not otherwise, it falls within the jurisdiction of Congress. To this extent only can the power be claimed as the incident of any express grant to the Federal Government.

But there is one clause of the Constitution in which it has been suggested that express authority to construct works of internal improvement has been conferred on Congress, namely, that which empowers it "to exercise exclusive legislation in all cases whatsoever over such district (not exceeding 10 miles square) as may by cession of particular States and the acceptance of Congress become the seat of the Government of the United States, and to exercise like authority over all places purchased by the consent of the legislature of the State in which the same shall be for the erection of forts, magazines, arsenals, dockyards, and *other needful buildings.*" But any such supposition will be seen to be groundless when this provision is carefully examined and compared with other parts of the Constitution.

It is undoubtedly true that "like authority" refers back to "exclusive legislation in all cases whatsoever" as applied to the District of Columbia, and there is in the District no division of powers as between the General and the State Governments.

In those places which the United States has purchased or retains within any of the States—sites for dockyards or forts, for example—legal process of the given State is still permitted to run for some purposes, and therefore the jurisdiction of the United States is not absolutely perfect. But let us assume for the argument's sake that the jurisdiction of the United States in a tract of land ceded to it for the purpose of a dockyard or fort by Virginia or Maryland is as complete as in that ceded by them for the seat of Government, and then proceed to analyze this clause of the Constitution.

It provides that Congress shall have certain legislative authority over all places purchased by the United States for certain purposes. It implies that Congress has otherwise the power to purchase. But where does Congress get the power to purchase? Manifestly it must be from some other clause of the Constitution, for it is not conferred by this one. Now, as it is a fundamental principle that the Constitution is one of limited powers, the authority to purchase must be conferred in one of the enumerations of legislative power; so that the power to purchase is itself not an unlimited one, but is limited by the objects in regard to which legislative authority is directly conferred.

The other expressions of the clause in question confirm this conclusion, since the jurisdiction is given as to places purchased for certain enumerated objects or purposes. Of these the first great division—forts, magazines, arsenals, and dockyards—is obviously referable to recognized heads of specific constitutional power. There remains only the phrase "and other *needful* buildings." Wherefore needful? Needful for any possible purpose within the whole range of the business of society and of Government? Clearly not; but only such "buildings" as are "needful" to the United States in the exercise of any of the powers conferred on Congress.

Thus the United States need, in the exercise of admitted powers, not only forts, magazines, arsenals, and dockyards, but also court-houses, prisons, custom-houses, and post-offices within the respective States. Places for the erection of such buildings the General Government may constitutionally purchase, and, having purchased them, the jurisdiction over them belongs to the United States. So if the General Government has the power to build a light-house or a beacon, it may purchase a place for that object; and having purchased it, then this clause of the Constitution gives jurisdiction over it. Still, the power to purchase for the purpose of erecting a light-house or beacon must depend on the existence of the power to erect, and if that power exists it must be sought after in some other clause of the Constitution.

From whatever point of view, therefore, the subject is regarded, whether as a question of express or implied power, the conclusion is the same, that Congress has no constitutional authority to carry on a system of internal improvements; and in this conviction the system has been steadily opposed by the soundest expositors of the functions of the Government.

It is not to be supposed that in no conceivable case shall there be doubt as to whether a given object be or not a necessary incident of the military, naval, or any other power. As man is imperfect, so are his methods of uttering his thoughts. Human language, save in expressions for the exact sciences, must always fail to preclude all possibility of controversy. Hence it is that in one branch of the subject—the question of the power of Congress to make appropriations in aid of navigation—there is less of positive conviction than in regard to the general subject; and it therefore seems proper in this respect to revert to the history of the practice of the Government.

Among the very earliest acts of the first session of Congress was that for the establishment and support of light-houses, approved by President Washington on the 7th of August, 1789, which contains the following provisions:

That all expenses which shall accrue from and after the 15th day of August, 1789, in the necessary support, maintenance, and repairs of all light-houses, beacons, buoys, and public piers erected, placed, or sunk before the passing of this act at the entrance of or within any bay, inlet, harbor, or port of the United States, for rendering the navigation thereof easy and safe, shall be defrayed out of the Treasury of the United States: *Provided, nevertheless,* That none of the said expenses shall continue to be so defrayed after the expiration of one year from the day aforesaid unless such light-houses, beacons, buoys, and public piers shall in the meantime be ceded to and vested in the United States by the State or States, respectively, in which the same may be, together with the lands and tenements thereunto belonging and together with the jurisdiction of the same.

Acts containing appropriations for this class of public works were passed in 1791, 1792, 1793, and so on from year to year down to the present time; and the tenor of these acts, when examined with reference to other parts of the subject, is worthy of special consideration.

It is a remarkable fact that for a period of more than thirty years after the adoption of the Constitution all appropriations of this class were confined, with scarcely an apparent exception, to the construction of light-houses, beacons, buoys, and public piers and the stakage of channels; to render navigation "safe and easy," it is true, but only by indicating to the navigator obstacles in his way, not by removing those obstacles nor in any other respect changing, artificially, the preexisting natural condition of the earth and sea. It is obvious, however, that works of art for the removal of natural impediments to navigation, or to prevent their formation, or for supplying harbors where these do not exist, are also means of rendering navigation safe and easy, and may in supposable cases be the most efficient, as well as the most economical, of such means. Nevertheless, it is not until the year 1824 that in an act to improve the navigation of the rivers Ohio and Mississippi and in another act making appropriations for deepening the channel leading into the harbor of Presque Isle, on Lake Erie, and for repairing Plymouth Beach, in Massachusetts Bay, we have any example of an appropriation for the improvement of harbors in the nature of those provided for in the bill returned by me to the House of Representatives.

It appears not probable that the abstinence of Congress in this respect is attributable altogether to considerations of economy or to any failure to perceive that the removal of an obstacle to navigation might be not less useful than the indication of it for avoidance, and it may be well assumed that the course of legislation so long pursued was induced, in whole or in part, by solicitous consideration in regard to the constitutional power over such matters vested in Congress.

One other peculiarity in this course of legislation is not less remarkable. It is that when the General Government first took charge of light-houses and beacons it required the works themselves and the lands on which they were situated to be ceded to the United States. And although for a time this precaution was neglected in the case of new works, in the sequel it was provided by general laws that no light-house should be constructed on any site previous to the jurisdiction over the same being ceded to the United States.

Constitutional authority for the construction and support of many of the public works of this nature, it is certain, may be found in the power of Congress to maintain a navy and provide for the general defense; but their number, and in many instances their location, preclude the idea of their being fully justified as necessary and proper incidents of that power. And they do not seem susceptible of being referred to any other of the specific powers vested in Congress by the Constitution, unless it be that to raise revenue in so far as this relates to navigation. The practice under all my predecessors in office, the express admissions of some of them, and absence of denial by any sufficiently manifest their belief that the power to erect light-houses, beacons, and piers is possessed by the General Government. In the acts of Congress, as we have already seen, the inducement and object of the appropriations are expressly declared, those appropriations being for "light-houses, beacons, buoys, and public piers" erected or placed "within any bay, inlet, harbor, or port of the United States for rendering the navigation thereof easy and safe."

If it be contended that this review of the history of appropriations of this class leads to the inference that, beyond the purposes of national defense and maintenance of a navy, there is authority in the Constitution to construct certain works in aid of navigation, it is at the same time to be remembered that the conclusions thus deduced from cotemporaneous construction and long-continued acquiescence are themselves directly suggestive of limitations of constitutionality, as well as expediency, regarding the nature and the description of those aids to navigation which Congress may provide as incident to the revenue power; for at this point controversy begins, not so much as to the principle as to its application.

In accordance with long-established legislative usage, Congress may construct light-houses and beacons and provide, as it does, other means to prevent shipwrecks on the coasts of the United States. But the General Government can not go beyond this and make improvements of rivers and harbors of the nature and to the degree of all the provisions of the bill of the last session of Congress.

To justify such extended power, it has been urged that if it be constitutional to appropriate money for the purpose of pointing out, by the construction of light-houses or beacons, where an obstacle to navigation exists, it is equally so to remove such obstacle or to avoid it by the creation of an artificial channel; that if the object be lawful, then the means adopted solely with reference to the end must be lawful, and that therefore it is not material, constitutionally speaking, whether a given obstruction to navigation be indicated for avoidance or be actually avoided by excavating a new channel; that if it be a legitimate object of expenditure to preserve a ship from wreck by means of a beacon or of revenue cutters, it must be not less so to provide places of safety by the improvement of harbors, or, where none exist, by their artificial construction; and thence the argument naturally passes to the propriety of improving rivers for the benefit of internal navigation, because all these objects are of more or less importance to the commercial as well as the naval interests of the United States.

The answer to all this is that the question of opening speedy and easy communication to and through all parts of the country is substantially the same, whether done by land or water; that the uses of roads and canals in facilitating commercial intercourse and uniting by community of interests the most remote quarters of the country by land communication are the same in their nature as the uses of navigable waters; and that therefore the question of the facilities and aids to be provided to navigation, by whatsoever means, is but a subdivision of the great question of the constitutionality and expediency of internal improvements by the General Government. In confirmation of this it is to be remarked that one of the most important acts of appropriation of this class, that of the year 1833, under the Administration of President Jackson, by including together and providing for in one bill as well river and harbor works as road works, impliedly recognizes the fact that they are alike branches of the same great subject of internal improvements.

As the population, territory, and wealth of the country increased and settlements extended into remote regions, the necessity for additional means of communication impressed itself upon all minds with a force which had not been experienced at the date of the formation of the Constitution, and more and more embarrassed those who were most anxious to abstain scrupulously from any exercise of doubtful power. Hence the recognition in the messages of Presidents Jefferson, Madison, and Monroe of the eminent desirableness of such works, with admission that some of them could lawfully and should be conducted by the General Government, but with obvious uncertainty of opinion as to the line between such as are constitutional and such as are not, such as ought to receive appropriations from Congress and such as ought to be consigned to private enterprise or the legislation of the several States.

This uncertainty has not been removed by the practical working of our institutions in later times; for although the acquisition of additional territory and the application of steam to the propulsion of vessels have greatly magnified the importance of internal commerce, this fact has at the same time complicated the question of the power of the General Government over the present subject.

In fine, a careful review of the opinions of all my predecessors and of the legislative history of the country does not indicate any fixed rule by which to decide what, of the infinite variety of possible river and harbor improvements, are within the scope of the power delegated by the Constitution; and the question still remains unsettled. President Jackson conceded the constitutionality, under suitable circumstances, of the improvement of rivers and harbors through the agency of Congress, and President Polk admitted the propriety of the establishment and support by appropriations from the Treasury of light-houses, beacons, buoys, and other improvements within the bays, inlets, and harbors of the ocean and lake coasts immediately connected with foreign commerce.

But if the distinction thus made rests upon the differences between foreign and domestic commerce it can not be restricted thereby to the bays, inlets, and harbors of the oceans and lakes, because foreign commerce has already penetrated thousands of miles into the interior of the continent by means of our great rivers, and will continue so to extend itself with the progress of settlement until it reaches the limit of navigability.

At the time of the adoption of the Constitution the vast Valley of the Mississippi, now teeming with population and supplying almost boundless resources, was literally an unexplored wilderness. Our advancement has outstripped even the most sanguine anticipations of the fathers of the Republic, and it illustrates the fact that no rule is admissible which undertakes to discriminate, so far as regards river and harbor improvements, between the Atlantic or Pacific coasts and the great lakes and rivers of the interior regions of North America. Indeed, it is quite erroneous to suppose that any such discrimination has ever existed in the practice of the Government. To the contrary of which is the significant fact, before stated, that when, after abstaining from all such appropriations for more than thirty years, Congress entered upon the policy of improving the navigation of rivers and harbors, it commenced with the rivers Mississippi and Ohio.

The Congress of the Union, adopting in this respect one of the ideas of that of the Confederation, has taken heed to declare from time to time, as occasion required, either in acts for disposing of the public lands in the Territories or in acts for admitting new States, that all navigable rivers within the same "shall be deemed to be and remain public highways."

Out of this condition of things arose a question which at successive periods of our public annals has occupied the attention of the best minds in the Union. This question is, What waters are public navigable waters, so as not to be of State character and jurisdiction, but of Federal jurisdiction and character, in the intent of the Constitution and of Congress? A proximate, but imperfect, answer to this important question is furnished by the acts of Congress and the decisions of the Supreme Court of the United States defining the constitutional limits of the maritime jurisdiction of the General Government. That jurisdiction is entirely independent of the revenue power. It is not derived from that, nor is it measured thereby.

In that act of Congress which, in the first year of the Government, organized our judicial system, and which, whether we look to the subject, the comprehensive wisdom with which it was treated, or the deference with which its provisions have come to be regarded, is only second to the Constitution itself, there is a section in which the statesmen who framed the Constitution have placed on record their construction of it in this matter. It enacts that the district courts of the United States "shall have exclusive cognizance of all civil cases of admiralty and maritime jurisdiction, including all seizures under the law of impost, navigation, or trade of the United States, when the seizures are made on waters which are navigable from the sea by vessels of 10 or more tons burden, within their respective districts, as well as upon the high seas." In this cotemporaneous exposition of the Constitution there is no trace or suggestion that nationality of jurisdiction is limited to the sea, or even to tide waters. The law is marked by a sagacious apprehension of the fact that the Great Lakes and the Mississippi were navigable waters of the United States even then, before the acquisition of Louisiana had made wholly our own the territorial greatness of the West. It repudiates unequivocally the rule of the common law, according to which the question of whether a water is public navigable water or not depends on whether it is salt or not, and therefore, in a river, confines that quality to tide water—a rule resulting from the geographical condition of England and applicable to an island with small and narrow streams, the only navigable portion of which, for ships, is in immediate contact with the ocean, but wholly inapplicable to the great inland fresh-water seas of America and its mighty rivers, with secondary branches exceeding in magnitude the largest rivers of Great Britain.

At a later period it is true that, in disregard of the more comprehensive definition of navigability afforded by that act of Congress, it was for a time held by many that the rule established for England was to be received in the United States, the effect of which was to exclude from the jurisdiction of the General Government not only the waters of the Mississippi, but also those of the Great Lakes. To this construction it was with truth objected that, in so far as concerns the lakes, they are in fact seas, although of fresh water; that they are the natural marine communications between a series of populous States and between them and the possessions of a foreign nation; that they are actually navigated by ships of commerce of the largest capacity; that they had once been and might again be the scene of foreign war; and that therefore it was doing violence to all reason to undertake by means of an arbitrary doctrine of technical foreign law to exclude such waters from the jurisdiction of the General Government. In regard to the river Mississippi, it was objected that to draw a line across that river at the point of ebb and flood of tide, and say that the part below was public navigable water and the part above not, while in the latter the water was at least equally deep and navigable and its commerce as rich as in the former, with numerous ports of foreign entry and delivery, was to sanction a distinction artificial and unjust, because regardless of the real fact of navigability.

We may conceive that some such considerations led to the enactment in the year 1845 of an act in addition to that of 1789, declaring that—

The district courts of the United States shall have, possess, and exercise the same jurisdiction in matters of contract and tort arising in, upon, or concerning steamboats and other vessels of 20 tons burden and upward, enrolled and licensed for the coasting trade and at the time employed in business of commerce and navigation between ports and places in different States and Territories upon the lakes and navigable waters connecting said lakes, as is now possessed and exercised by the said courts in cases of the like steamboats and other vessels employed in navigation and commerce upon the high seas or tide waters within the admiralty and maritime jurisdiction of the United States.

It is observable that the act of 1789 applies the jurisdiction of the United States to all "waters which are navigable from the sea" for vessels of 10 tons burden, and that of 1845 extends the jurisdiction to enrolled vessels of 20 tons burden, on the lakes and navigable waters connecting said lakes, though not waters navigable from the sea, provided such vessels be employed between places in different States and Territories.

Thus it appears that these provisions of law in effect prescribe conditions by which to determine whether any waters are public navigable waters, subject to the authority of the Federal Government. The conditions include all waters, whether salt or fresh, and whether of sea, lake, or river, provided they be capable of navigation by vessels of a certain tonnage, and for commerce either between the United States and foreign countries or between any two or more of the States or Territories of the Union. This excludes water wholly within any particular State, and not used as the means of commercial communication with any other State, and subject to be improved or obstructed at will by the State within which it may happen to be.

The constitutionality of these provisions of statute has been called in question. Their constitutionality has been maintained, however, by repeated decisions of the Supreme Court of the United States, and they are therefore the law of the land by the concurrent act of the legislative, the executive, and the judicial departments of the Government. Regarded as affording a criterion of what is navigable water, and as such subject to the maritime jurisdiction of the Supreme Court and of Congress, these acts are objectionable in this, that the rule of navigability is an arbitrary one, that Congress may repeal the present rule and adopt a new one, and that thus a legislative definition will be able to restrict or enlarge the limits of constitutional power. Yet this variableness of standard seems inherent in the nature of things. At any rate, neither the First Congress, composed of the statesmen of the era when the Constitution was adopted, nor any subsequent Congress has afforded us the means of attaining greater precision of construction as to this part of the Constitution.

This reflection may serve to relieve from undeserved reproach an idea of one of the greatest men of the Republic—President Jackson. He, seeking amid all the difficulties of the subject for some practical rule of action in regard to appropriations for the improvement of rivers and harbors, prescribed for his own official conduct the rule of confining such appropriations to ''places below the ports of entry or delivery established by law.'' He saw clearly, as the authors of the above-mentioned acts of 1789 and 1845 did, that there is no inflexible natural line of discrimination between what is national and what local by means of which to determine absolutely and unerringly at what point on a river the jurisdiction of the United States shall end. He perceived, and of course admitted, that the Constitution, while conferring on the General Government some power of action to render navigation safe and easy, had of necessity left to Congress much of discretion in this matter. He confided in the patriotism of Congress to exercise that discretion wisely, not permitting himself to suppose it possible that a port of entry or delivery would ever be established by law for the express and only purpose of evading the Constitution.

It remains, therefore, to consider the question of the measure of discretion in the exercise by Congress of the power to provide for the improvement of rivers and harbors, and also that of the legitimate responsibility of the Executive in the same relation.

In matters of legislation of the most unquestionable constitutionality it is always material to consider what amount of public money shall be appropriated for any particular object. The same consideration applies with augmented force to a class of appropriations which are in their nature peculiarly prone to run to excess, and which, being made in the exercise of incidental powers, have intrinsic tendency to overstep the bounds of constitutionality.

If an appropriation for improving the navigability of a river or deepening or protecting a harbor have reference to military or naval purposes, then its rightfulness, whether in amount or in the objects to which it is applied, depends, manifestly, on the military or naval exigency; and the subject-matter affords its own measure of legislative discretion. But if the appropriation for such an object have no distinct relation to the military or naval wants of the country, and is wholly, or even mainly, intended to promote the revenue from commerce, then the very vagueness of the proposed purpose of the expenditure constitutes a perpetual admonition of reserve and caution. Through disregard of this it is undeniable that in many cases appropriations of this nature have been made unwisely, without accomplishing beneficial results commensurate with the cost, and sometimes for evil rather than good, independently of their dubious rela·· tion to the Constitution.

Among the radical changes of the course of legislation in these mat· ters which, in my judgment, the public interest demands, one is a return to the primitive idea of Congress, which required in this class of public works, as in all others, a conveyance of the soil and a cession of the jurisdiction to the United States. I think this condition ought never to have been waived in the case of any harbor improvement of a permanent nature, as where piers, jetties, sea walls, and other like works are to be constructed and maintained. It would powerfully tend to counteract endeavors to obtain appropriations of a local character and chiefly calculated to promote individual interests. The want of such a provision is the occasion of abuses in regard to existing works, exposing them to private encroachment without sufficient means of redress by law. Indeed, the absence in such cases of a cession of jurisdiction has constituted one of the constitutional objections to appropriations of this class. It is not easy to perceive any sufficient reason for requiring it in the case of arsenals or forts which does not equally apply to all other public works. If to be constructed and maintained by Congress in the exercise of a constitutional power of appropriation, they should be brought within the jurisdiction of the United States.

There is another measure of precaution in regard to such appropriations which seems to me to be worthy of the consideration of Congress. It is to make appropriation for every work in a separate bill, so that each one shall stand on its own independent merits, and if it pass shall do so under circumstances of legislative scrutiny entitling it to be regarded as of general interest and a proper subject of charge on the Treasury of the Union.

During that period of time in which the country had not come to look to Congress for appropriations of this nature several of the States whose productions or geographical position invited foreign commerce had entered upon plans for the improvement of their harbors by themselves and through means of support drawn directly from that commerce, in virtue of an express constitutional power, needing for its exercise only the permission of Congress.   Harbor improvements thus constructed and maintained, the expenditures upon them being defrayed by the very facilities they afford, are a voluntary charge on those only who see fit to avail themselves of such facilities, and can be justly complained of by none.   On the other hand, so long as these improvements are carried on by appropriations from the Treasury the benefits will continue to inure to those alone who enjoy the facilities afforded, while the expenditure will be a burden upon the whole country and the discrimination a double injury to places equally requiring improvement, but not equally favored by appropriations.

These considerations, added to the embarrassments of the whole question, amply suffice to suggest the policy of confining appropriations by the General Government to works necessary to the execution of its undoubted powers and of leaving all others to individual enterprise or to the separate States, to be provided for out of their own resources or by recurrence to the provision of the Constitution which authorizes the States to lay duties of tonnage with the consent of Congress.

FRANKLIN PIERCE.

PROCLAMATIONS.

By the President of the United States.

A PROCLAMATION.

Whereas information has been received by me that an unlawful expedition has been fitted out in the State of California with a view to invade Mexico, a nation maintaining friendly relations with the United States, and that other expeditions are organizing within the United States for the same unlawful purpose; and

Whereas certain citizens and inhabitants of this country, unmindful of their obligations and duties and of the rights of a friendly power, have participated and are about to participate in these enterprises, so derogatory to our national character and so threatening to our tranquillity, and are thereby incurring the severe penalties imposed by law against such offenders:

Now, therefore, I, Franklin Pierce, President of the United States, have issued this my proclamation, warning all persons who shall connect themselves with any such enterprise or expedition that the penalties of the law denounced against such criminal conduct will be rigidly enforced; and I exhort all good citizens, as they regard our national character, as they respect our laws or the law of nations, as they value the blessings of peace and the welfare of their country, to discountenance and by all lawful means prevent such criminal enterprises; and I call upon all officers of this Government, civil and military, to use any efforts which may be in their power to arrest for trial and punishment every such offender.

Given under my hand and the seal of the United States, at Washington, this 18th day of January, A. D. 1854, and the seventy-eighth of the Independence of the United States.

[SEAL.]

FRANKLIN PIERCE.

By the President:
W. L. MARCY,
Secretary of State.

BY THE PRESIDENT OF THE UNITED STATES.

A PROCLAMATION.

Whereas information has been received that sundry persons, citizens of the United States and others residing therein, are engaged in organizing and fitting out a military expedition for the invasion of the island of Cuba; and

Whereas the said undertaking is contrary to the spirit and express stipulations of treaties between the United States and Spain, derogatory to the character of this nation, and in violation of the obvious duties and obligations of faithful and patriotic citizens; and

Whereas it is the duty of the constituted authorities of the United States to hold and maintain the control of the great question of peace or war, and not suffer the same to be lawlessly complicated under any pretense whatever; and

Whereas to that end all private enterprises of a hostile character within the United States against any foreign power with which the United States are at peace are forbidden and declared to be a high misdemeanor by an express act of Congress:

Now, therefore, in virtue of the authority vested by the Constitution in the President of the United States, I do issue this proclamation to warn all persons that the General Government claims it as a right and duty to interpose itself for the honor of its flag, the rights of its citizens, the national security, and the preservation of the public tranquillity, from whatever quarter menaced, and it will not fail to prosecute with due energy all those who, unmindful of their own and their country's fame, presume thus to disregard the laws of the land and our treaty obligations.

By the President of the United States.

A Proclamation.

Whereas, information has been received, that sundry persons, citizens of the United States, and others residing therein, are engaged in organizing and fitting out, a military expedition for the invasion of the Island of Cuba:

And whereas, the said undertaking is contrary to the spirit, and express stipulations of treaties between the United States and Spain, derogatory to the character of this nation, and in violation of the obvious duties and obligations of faithful and patriotic citizens.

And whereas, it is the duty of the constituted authorities of the United States, to hold and maintain the control of the great question of peace or war, and not suffer the same to be lawlessly complicated, under any pretence whatever;

And whereas, to that end, all private enterprises of a hostile character, within the United States, against any foreign power, with which the United States are at peace, are forbidden, and declared to be a high misdemeanor by an express act of Congress.

FIRST PAGE OF PRESIDENT PIERCE'S PROCLAMATION
AGAINST FILIBUSTERING EXPEDITIONS TO CUBA.

Now, therefore, in virtue of the authority, vested by the Constitution in the President of the United States, I do issue this proclamation to warn all persons that, the general government claims, as a right and duty, to interpose itself for the honor of its flag, the rights of its citizens, the national security, and the preservation of the public tranquillity from whatever quarter menaced; and it will not fail to prosecute with due energy all those, who, unmindful of their own, and their country's fame, presume thus to disregard the laws of the land and our treaty obligations.

I earnestly exhort all good citizens to discountenance and prevent any movement, in conflict with law and national faith; especially charging the several district attorneys, collectors, and other officers of the United States, civil or military, having lawful power in the premises, to exert the same for the purpose of maintaining the authority and preserving the peace of the United States.

Given under my hand and the seal of the United States at Washington the thirty first day of May in the year of our Lord one thousand eight hundred and fifty four, and the seventy eighth of the Independence of the United States.

Franklin Pierce

By the President:
W. L. Marcy   Secretary of State

LAST PAGE OF PROCLAMATION AGAINST FILIBUSTERING
BY PRESIDENT PIERCE.

I earnestly exhort all good citizens to discountenance and prevent any movement in conflict with law and national faith, especially charging the several district attorneys, collectors, and other officers of the United States, civil or military, having lawful power in the premises, to exert the same for the purpose of maintaining the authority and preserving the peace of the United States.

Given under my hand and the seal of the United States, at Washington, the 31st day of May, A. D. 1854, and the seventy-eighth [SEAL.] of the Independence of the United States.

FRANKLIN PIERCE.

By the President:
    W. L. MARCY,
        Secretary of State.

SECOND ANNUAL MESSAGE.

WASHINGTON, *December 4, 1854.*

Fellow-Citizens of the Senate and of the House of Representatives:

The past has been an eventful year, and will be hereafter referred to as a marked epoch in the history of the world. While we have been happily preserved from the calamities of war, our domestic prosperity has not been entirely uninterrupted. The crops in portions of the country have been nearly cut off. Disease has prevailed to a greater extent than usual, and the sacrifice of human life through casualties by sea and land is without parallel. But the pestilence has swept by, and restored salubrity invites the absent to their homes and the return of business to its ordinary channels. If the earth has rewarded the labor of the husbandman less bountifully than in preceding seasons, it has left him with abundance for domestic wants and a large surplus for exportation. In the present, therefore, as in the past, we find ample grounds for reverent thankfulness to the God of grace and providence for His protecting care and merciful dealings with us as a people.

Although our attention has been arrested by painful interest in passing events, yet our country feels no more than the slight vibrations of the convulsions which have shaken Europe. As individuals we can not repress sympathy with human suffering nor regret for the causes which produce it; as a nation we are reminded that whatever interrupts the peace or checks the prosperity of any part of Christendom tends more or less to involve our own. The condition of States is not unlike that of individuals; they are mutually dependent upon each other. Amicable relations between them and reciprocal good will are essential for the promotion of whatever is desirable in their moral, social, and political condition.   Hence it has been my earnest endeavor to maintain peace and friendly intercourse with all nations.

The wise theory of this Government, so early adopted and steadily pursued, of avoiding all entangling alliances has hitherto exempted it from many complications in which it would otherwise have become involved.   Notwithstanding this our clearly defined and well-sustained course of action and our geographical position, so remote from Europe, increasing disposition has been manifested by some of its Governments to supervise and in certain respects to direct our foreign policy.   In plans for adjusting the balance of power among themselves they have assumed to take us into account, and would constrain us to conform our conduct to their views.   One or another of the powers of Europe has from time to time undertaken to enforce arbitrary regulations contrary in many respects to established principles of international law.   That law the United States have in their foreign intercourse uniformly respected and observed, and they can not recognize any such interpolations therein as the temporary interests of others may suggest.   They do not admit that the sovereigns of one continent or of a particular community of states can legislate for all others.

Leaving the transatlantic nations to adjust their political system in the way they may think best for their common welfare, the independent powers of this continent may well assert the right to be exempt from all annoying interference on their part.   Systematic abstinence from intimate political connection with distant foreign nations does not conflict with giving the widest range to our foreign commerce.   This distinction, so clearly marked in history, seems to have been overlooked or disregarded by some leading foreign states.   Our refusal to be brought within and subjected to their peculiar system has, I fear, created a jealous distrust of our conduct and induced on their part occasional acts of disturbing effect upon our foreign relations.   Our present attitude and past course give assurances, which should not be questioned, that our purposes are not aggressive nor threatening to the safety and welfare of other nations.   Our military establishment in time of peace is adapted to maintain exterior defenses and to preserve order among the aboriginal tribes within the limits of the Union.   Our naval force is intended only for the protection of our citizens abroad and of our commerce, diffused, as it is, over all the seas of the globe.   The Government of the United States, being essentially pacific in policy, stands prepared to repel invasion by the voluntary service of a patriotic people, and provides no permanent means of foreign aggression.   These considerations should allay all apprehension that we are disposed to encroach on the rights or endanger the security of other states.

Some European powers have regarded with disquieting concern the territorial expansion of the United States.   This rapid growth has resulted from the legitimate exercise of sovereign rights belonging alike to all nations, and by many liberally exercised. Under such circumstances it could hardly have been expected that those among them which have within a comparatively recent period subdued and absorbed ancient kingdoms, planted their standards on every continent, and now possess or claim the control of the islands of every ocean as their appropriate domain would look with unfriendly sentiments upon the acquisitions of this country, in every instance hororably obtained, or would feel themselves justified in imputing our advancement to a spirit of aggression or to a passion for political predominance.

Our foreign commerce has reached a magnitude and extent nearly equal to that of the first maritime power of the earth, and exceeding that of any other. Over this great interest, in which not only our merchants, but all classes of citizens, at least indirectly, are concerned, it is the duty of the executive and legislative branches of the Government to exercise a careful supervision and adopt proper measures for its protection. The policy which I had in view in regard to this interest embraces its future as well as its present security. Long experience has shown that, in general, when the principal powers of Europe are engaged in war the rights of neutral nations are endangered. This consideration led, in the progress of the War of our Independence, to the formation of the celebrated confederacy of armed neutrality, a primary object of which was to assert the doctrine that free ships make free goods, except in the case of articles contraband of war—a doctrine which from the very commencement of our national being has been a cherished idea of the statesmen of this country. At one period or another every maritime power has by some solemn treaty stipulation recognized that principle, and it might have been hoped that it would come to be universally received and respected as a rule of international law. But the refusal of one power prevented this, and in the next great war which ensued—that of the French Revolution—it failed to be respected among the belligerent States of Europe. Notwithstanding this, the principle is generally admitted to be a sound and salutary one, so much so that at the commencement of the existing war in Europe Great Britain and France announced their purpose to observe it for the present; not, however, as a recognized international right, but as a mere concession for the time being. The cooperation, however, of these two powerful maritime nations in the interest of neutral rights appeared to me to afford an occasion inviting and justifying on the part of the United States a renewed effort to make the doctrine in question a principle of international law, by means of special conventions between the several powers of Europe and America. Accordingly, a proposition embracing not only the rule that free ships make free goods, except contraband articles, but also the less contested one that neutral property other than contraband, though on board enemy's ships, shall be exempt from confiscation, has been submitted by this Government to those of Europe and America.

Russia acted promptly in this matter, and a convention was concluded between that country and the United States providing for the observance of the principles announced, not only as between themselves, but also as between them and all other nations which shall enter into like stipulations. None of the other powers have as yet taken final action on the subject. I am not aware, however, that any objection to the proposed stipulations has been made, but, on the contrary, they are acknowledged to be essential to the security of neutral commerce, and the only apparent obstacle to their general adoption is in the possibility that it may be encumbered by inadmissible conditions.

The King of the Two Sicilies has expressed to our minister at Naples his readiness to concur in our proposition relative to neutral rights and to enter into a convention on that subject.

The King of Prussia entirely approves of the project of a treaty to the same effect submitted to him, but proposes an additional article providing for the renunciation of privateering. Such an article, for most obvious reasons, is much desired by nations having naval establishments large in proportion to their foreign commerce. If it were adopted as an international rule, the commerce of a nation having comparatively a small naval force would be very much at the mercy of its enemy in case of war with a power of decided naval superiority. The bare statement of the condition in which the United States would be placed, after having surrendered the right to resort to privateers, in the event of war with a belligerent of naval supremacy will show that this Government could never listen to such a proposition. The navy of the first maritime power in Europe is at least ten times as large as that of the United States. The foreign commerce of the two countries is nearly equal, and about equally exposed to hostile depredations. In war between that power and the United States, without resort on our part to our mercantile marine the means of our enemy to inflict injury upon our commerce would be tenfold greater than ours to retaliate. We could not extricate our country from this unequal condition, with such an enemy, unless we at once departed from our present peaceful policy and became a great naval power. Nor would this country be better situated in war with one of the secondary naval powers. Though the naval disparity would be less, the greater extent and more exposed condition of our widespread commerce would give any of them a like advantage over us.

The proposition to enter into engagements to forego a resort to privateers in case this country should be forced into war with a great naval power is not entitled to more favorable consideration than would be a proposition to agree not to accept the services of volunteers for operations on land. When the honor or the rights of our country require it to assume a hostile attitude, it confidently relies upon the patriotism of its citizens, not ordinarily devoted to the military profession, to augment the Army and the Navy so as to make them fully adequate to the emergency which calls them into action. The proposal to surrender the right to employ privateers is professedly founded upon the principle that private property of unoffending noncombatants, though enemies, should be exempt from the ravages of war; but the proposed surrender goes but little way in carrying out that principle, which equally requires that such private property should not be seized or molested by national ships of war. Should the leading powers of Europe concur in proposing as a rule of international law to exempt private property upon the ocean from seizure by public armed cruisers as well as by privateers, the United States will readily meet them upon that broad ground.

Since the adjournment of Congress the ratifications of the treaty between the United States and Great Britain relative to coast fisheries and to reciprocal trade with the British North American Provinces have been exchanged, and some of its anticipated advantages are already enjoyed by us, although its full execution was to abide certain acts of legislation not yet fully performed. So soon as it was ratified Great Britain opened to our commerce the free navigation of the river St. Lawrence and to our fishermen unmolested access to the shores and bays, from which they had been previously excluded, on the coasts of her North American Provinces; in return for which she asked for the introduction free of duty into the ports of the United States of the fish caught on the same coast by British fishermen. This being the compensation stipulated in the treaty for privileges of the highest importance and value to the United States, which were thus voluntarily yielded before it became effective, the request seemed to me to be a reasonable one; but it could not be acceded to from want of authority to suspend our laws imposing duties upon all foreign fish. In the meantime the Treasury Department issued a regulation for ascertaining the duties paid or secured by bonds on fish caught on the coasts of the British Provinces and brought to our markets by British subjects after the fishing grounds had been made fully accessible to the citizens of the United States. I recommend to your favorable consideration a proposition, which will be submitted to you, for authority to refund the duties and cancel the bonds thus received. The Provinces of Canada and New Brunswick have also anticipated the full operation of the treaty by legislative arrangements, respectively, to admit free of duty the products of the United States mentioned in the free list of the treaty; and an arrangement similar to that regarding British fish has been made for duties now chargeable on the products of those Provinces enumerated in the same free list and introduced therefrom into the United States, a proposition for refunding which will, in my judgment, be in like manner entitled to your favorable consideration.

There is difference of opinion between the United States and Great Britain as to the boundary line of the Territory of Washington adjoining the British possessions on the Pacific, which has already led to difficulties on the part of the citizens and local authorities of the two Governments.

I recommend that provision be made for a commission, to be joined by one on the part of Her Britannic Majesty, for the purpose of running and establishing the line in controversy.   Certain stipulations of the third and fourth articles of the treaty concluded by the United States and Great Britain in 1846, regarding possessory rights of the Hudsons Bay Company and property of the Pugets Sound Agricultural Company, have given rise to serious disputes, and it is important to all concerned that summary means of settling them amicably should be devised.   I have reason to believe that an arrangement can be made on just terms for the extinguishment of the rights in question, embracing also the right of the Hudsons Bay Company to the navigation of the river Columbia; and I therefore suggest to your consideration the expediency of making a contingent appropriation for that purpose.

France was the early and efficient ally of the United States in their struggle for independence.   From that time to the present, with occasional slight interruptions, cordial relations of friendship have existed between the Governments and people of the two countries.   The kindly sentiments cherished alike by both nations have led to extensive social and commercial intercourse, which I trust will not be interrupted or checked by any casual event of an apparently unsatisfactory character.   The French consul at San Francisco was not long since brought into the United States district court at that place by compulsory process as a witness in favor of another foreign consul, in violation, as the French Government conceives, of his privileges under our consular convention with France.   There being nothing in the transaction which could imply any disrespect to France or its consul, such explanation has been made as, I hope, will be satisfactory.   Subsequently misunderstanding arose on the subject of the French Government having, as it appeared, abruptly excluded the American minister to Spain from passing through France on his way from London to Madrid.   But that Government has unequivocally disavowed any design to deny the right of transit to the minister of the United States, and after explanations to this effect he has resumed his journey and actually returned through France to Spain.   I herewith lay before Congress the correspondence on this subject between our envoy at Paris and the minister of foreign relations of the French Government.

The position of our affairs with Spain remains as at the close of the last session.   Internal agitation, assuming very nearly the character of political revolution, has recently convulsed that country.   The late ministers were violently expelled from power, and men of very different views in relation to its internal affairs have succeeded.   Since this change there has been no propitious opportunity to resume and press on negotiations for the adjustment of serious questions of difficulty between the Spanish Government and the United States.   There is reason to believe that our minister will find the present Government more favorably inclined than the preceding to comply with our just demands and to make suitable arrangements for restoring harmony and preserving peace between the two countries.

Negotiations are pending with Denmark to discontinue the practice of levying tolls on our vessels and their cargoes passing through the Sound. I do not doubt that we can claim exemption therefrom as a matter of right. It is admitted on all hands that this exaction is sanctioned, not by the general principles of the law of nations, but only by special conventions which most of the commercial nations have entered into with Denmark. The fifth article of our treaty of 1826 with Denmark provides that there shall not be paid on the vessels of the United States and their cargoes when passing through the Sound higher duties than those of the most favored nations. This may be regarded as an implied agreement to submit to the tolls during the continuance of the treaty, and consequently may embarrass the assertion of our right to be released therefrom. There are also other provisions in the treaty which ought to be modified. It was to remain in force for ten years and until one year after either party should give notice to the other of intention to terminate it. I deem it expedient that the contemplated notice should be given to the Government of Denmark.

The naval expedition dispatched about two years since for the purpose of establishing relations with the Empire of Japan has been ably and skillfully conducted to a successful termination by the officer to whom it was intrusted. A treaty opening certain of the ports of that populous country has been negotiated, and in order to give full effect thereto it only remains to exchange ratifications and adopt requisite commercial regulations.

The treaty lately concluded between the United States and Mexico settled some of our most embarrassing difficulties with that country, but numerous claims upon it for wrongs and injuries to our citizens remained unadjusted, and many new cases have been recently added to the former list of grievances. Our legation has been earnest in its endeavors to obtain from the Mexican Government a favorable consideration of these claims, but hitherto without success. This failure is probably in some measure to be ascribed to the disturbed condition of that country. It has been my anxious desire to maintain friendly relations with the Mexican Republic and to cause its rights and territories to be respected, not only by our citizens, but by foreigners who have resorted to the United States for the purpose of organizing hostile expeditions against some of the States of that Republic. The defenseless condition in which its frontiers have been left has stimulated lawless adventurers to embark in these enterprises and greatly increased the difficulty of enforcing our obligations of neutrality. Regarding it as my solemn duty to fulfill efficiently these obligations, not only toward Mexico, but other foreign nations, I have exerted all the powers with which I am invested to defeat such proceedings and bring to punishment those who by taking a part therein violated our laws. The energy and activity of our civil and military authorities have frustrated the designs of those who meditated expeditions of this character except in two instances. One of these, composed of foreigners, was at first countenanced and aided by the Mexican Government itself, it having been deceived as to their real object. The other, small in number, eluded the vigilance of the magistrates at San Francisco and succeeded in reaching the Mexican territories; but the effective measures taken by this Government compelled the abandonment of the undertaking.

The commission to establish the new line between the United States and Mexico, according to the provisions of the treaty of the 30th of December last, has been organized, and the work is already commenced.

Our treaties with the Argentine Confederation and with the Republics of Uruguay and Paraguay secure to us the free navigation of the river La Plata and some of its larger tributaries, but the same success has not attended our endeavors to open the Amazon. The reasons in favor of the free use of that river I had occasion to present fully in a former message, and, considering the cordial relations which have long existed between this Government and Brazil, it may be expected that pending negotiations will eventually reach a favorable result.

Convenient means of transit between the several parts of a country are not only desirable for the objects of commercial and personal communication, but essential to its existence under one government. Separated, as are the Atlantic and Pacific coasts of the United States, by the whole breadth of the continent, still the inhabitants of each are closely bound together by community of origin and institutions and by strong attachment to the Union. Hence the constant and increasing intercourse and vast interchange of commercial productions between these remote divisions of the Republic. At the present time the most practicable and only commodious routes for communication between them are by the way of the isthmus of Central America. It is the duty of the Government to secure these avenues against all danger of interruption.

In relation to Central America, perplexing questions existed between the United States and Great Britain at the time of the cession of California. These, as well as questions which subsequently arose concerning interoceanic communication across the Isthmus, were, as it was supposed, adjusted by the treaty of April 19, 1850, but, unfortunately, they have been reopened by serious misunderstanding as to the import of some of its provisions, a readjustment of which is now under consideration. Our minister at London has made strenuous efforts to accomplish this desirable object, but has not yet found it possible to bring the negotiations to a termination.

As incidental to these questions, I deem it proper to notice an occurrence which happened in Central America near the close of the last session of Congress. So soon as the necessity was perceived of establishing interoceanic communications across the Isthmus a company was organized, under the authority of the State of Nicaragua, but composed for the most part of citizens of the United States, for the purpose of opening such a transit way by the river San Juan and Lake Nicaragua, which soon became an eligible and much used route in the transportation of our citizens and their property between the Atlantic and Pacific. Meanwhile, and in anticipation of the completion and importance of this transit way, a number of adventurers had taken possession of the old Spanish port at the mouth of the river San Juan in open defiance of the State or States of Central America, which upon their becoming independent had rightfully succeeded to the local sovereignty and jurisdiction of Spain. These adventurers undertook to change the name of the place from San Juan del Norte to Greytown, and though at first pretending to act as the subjects of the fictitious sovereign of the Mosquito Indians, they subsequently repudiated the control of any power whatever, assumed to adopt a distinct political organization, and declared themselves an independent sovereign state. If at some time a faint hope was entertained that they might become a stable and respectable community, that hope soon vanished. They proceeded to assert unfounded claims to civil jurisdiction over Punta Arenas, a position on the opposite side of the river San Juan, which was in possession, under a title wholly independent of them, of citizens of the United States interested in the Nicaragua Transit Company, and which was indispensably necessary to the prosperous operation of that route across the Isthmus. The company resisted their groundless claims, whereupon they proceeded to destroy some of its buildings and attempted violently to dispossess it.

At a later period they organized a strong force for the purpose of demolishing the establishment at Punta Arenas, but this mischievous design was defeated by the interposition of one of our ships of war at that time in the harbor of San Juan. Subsequently to this, in May last, a body of men from Greytown crossed over to Punta Arenas, arrogating authority to arrest on the charge of murder a captain of one of the steamboats of the Transit Company. Being well aware that the claim to exercise jurisdiction there would be resisted then, as it had been on previous occasions, they went prepared to assert it by force of arms. Our minister to Central America happened to be present on that occasion. Believing that the captain of the steamboat was innocent (for he witnessed the transaction on which the charge was founded), and believing also that the intruding party, having no jurisdiction over the place where they proposed to make the arrest, would encounter desperate resistance if they persisted in their purpose, he interposed, effectually, to prevent violence and bloodshed. The American minister afterwards visited Greytown, and whilst he was there a mob, including certain of the so-called public functionaries of the place, surrounded the house in which he was, avowing that they had come to arrest him by order of some person exercising the chief authority.   While parleying with them he was wounded by a missile from the crowd.   A boat dispatched from the American steamer *Northern Light* to release him from the perilous situation in which he was understood to be was fired into by the town guard and compelled to return.   These incidents, together with the known character of the population of Greytown and their excited state, induced just apprehensions that the lives and property of our citizens at Punta Arenas would be in imminent danger after the departure of the steamer, with her passengers, for New York, unless a guard was left for their protection.   For this purpose, and in order to insure the safety of passengers and property passing over the route, a temporary force was organized, at considerable expense to the United States, for which provision was made at the last session of Congress.

This pretended community, a heterogeneous assemblage gathered from various countries, and composed for the most part of blacks and persons of mixed blood, had previously given other indications of mischievous and dangerous propensities.   Early in the same month property was clandestinely abstracted from the depot of the Transit Company and taken to Greytown.   The plunderers obtained shelter there and their pursuers were driven back by its people, who not only protected the wrongdoers and shared the plunder, but treated with rudeness and violence those who sought to recover their property.

Such, in substance, are the facts submitted to my consideration, and proved by trustworthy evidence.   I could not doubt that the case demanded the interposition of this Government.   Justice required that reparation should be made for so many and such gross wrongs, and that a course of insolence and plunder, tending directly to the insecurity of the lives of numerous travelers and of the rich treasure belonging to our citizens passing over this transit way, should be peremptorily arrested. Whatever it might be in other respects, the community in question, in power to do mischief, was not despicable.   It was well provided with ordnance, small arms, and ammunition, and might easily seize on the unarmed boats, freighted with millions of property, which passed almost daily within its reach.   It did not profess to belong to any regular government, and had, in fact, no recognized dependence on or connection with anyone to which the United States or their injured citizens might apply for redress or which could be held responsible in any way for the outrages committed.   Not standing before the world in the attitude of an organized political society, being neither competent to exercise the rights nor to discharge the obligations of a government, it was, in fact, a marauding establishment too dangerous to be disregarded and too guilty to pass unpunished, and yet incapable of being treated in any other way than as a piratical resort of outlaws or a camp of savages depredating on emigrant trains or caravans and the frontier settlements of civilized states.

Seasonable notice was given to the people of Greytown that this Government required them to repair the injuries they had done to our citizens and to make suitable apology for their insult of our minister, and that a ship of war would be dispatched thither to enforce compliance with these demands. But the notice passed unheeded. Thereupon a commander of the Navy, in charge of the sloop of war *Cyane*, was ordered to repeat the demands and to insist upon a compliance therewith. Finding that neither the populace nor those assuming to have authority over them manifested any disposition to make the required reparation, or even to offer excuse for their conduct, he warned them by a public proclamation that if they did not give satisfaction within a time specified he would bombard the town. By this procedure he afforded them opportunity to provide for their personal safety. To those also who desired to avoid loss of property in the punishment about to be inflicted on the offending town he furnished the means of removing their effects by the boats of his own ship and of a steamer which he procured and tendered to them for that purpose. At length, perceiving no disposition on the part of the town to comply with his requisitions, he appealed to the commander of Her Britannic Majesty's schooner *Bermuda*, who was seen to have intercourse and apparently much influence with the leaders among them, to interpose and persuade them to take some course calculated to save the necessity of resorting to the extreme measure indicated in his proclamation; but that officer, instead of acceding to the request, did nothing more than to protest against the contemplated bombardment. No steps of any sort were taken by the people to give the satisfaction required. No individuals, if any there were, who regarded themselves as not responsible for the misconduct of the community adopted any means to separate themselves from the fate of the guilty. The several charges on which the demands for redress were founded had been publicly known to all for some time, and were again announced to them. They did not deny any of these charges; they offered no explanation, nothing in extenuation of their conduct, but contumaciously refused to hold any intercourse with the commander of the *Cyane*. By their obstinate silence they seemed rather desirous to provoke chastisement than to escape it. There is ample reason to believe that this conduct of wanton defiance on their part is imputable chiefly to the delusive idea that the American Government would be deterred from punishing them through fear of displeasing a formidable foreign power, which they presumed to think looked with complacency upon their aggressive and insulting deportment toward the United States. The *Cyane* at length fired upon the town. Before much injury had been done the fire was twice suspended in order to afford opportunity for an arrangement, but this was declined. Most of the buildings of the place, of little value generally, were in the sequel destroyed, but, owing to the considerate precautions taken by our naval commander, there was no destruction of life.

When the *Cyane* was ordered to Central America, it was confidently hoped and expected that no occasion would arise for "a resort to violence and destruction of property and loss of life." Instructions to that effect were given to her commander; and no extreme act would have been requisite had not the people themselves, by their extraordinary conduct in the affair, frustrated all the possible mild measures for obtaining satisfaction. A withdrawal from the place, the object of his visit entirely defeated, would under the circumstances in which the commander of the *Cyane* found himself have been absolute abandonment of all claim of our citizens for indemnification and submissive acquiescence in national indignity. It would have encouraged in these lawless men a spirit of insolence and rapine most dangerous to the lives and property of our citizens at Punta Arenas, and probably emboldened them to grasp at the treasures and valuable merchandise continually passing over the Nicaragua route. It certainly would have been most satisfactory to me if the objects of the *Cyane's* mission could have been consummated without any act of public force, but the arrogant contumacy of the offenders rendered it impossible to avoid the alternative either to break up their establishment or to leave them impressed with the idea that they might persevere with impunity in a career of insolence and plunder.

This transaction has been the subject of complaint on the part of some foreign powers, and has been characterized with more of harshness than of justice. If comparisons were to be instituted, it would not be difficult to present repeated instances in the history of states standing in the very front of modern civilization where communities far less offending and more defenseless than Greytown have been chastised with much greater severity, and where not cities only have been laid in ruins, but human life has been recklessly sacrificed and the blood of the innocent made profusely to mingle with that of the guilty.

Passing from foreign to domestic affairs, your attention is naturally directed to the financial condition of the country, always a subject of general interest. For complete and exact information regarding the finances and the various branches of the public service connected therewith I refer you to the report of the Secretary of the Treasury, from which it will appear that the amount of revenue during the last fiscal year from all sources was $73,549,705, and that the public expenditures for the same period, exclusive of payments on account of the public debt, amounted to $51,018,249. During the same period the payments made in redemption of the public debt, including interest and premium, amounted to $24,336,-380. To the sum total of the receipts of that year is to be added a balance remaining in the Treasury at the commencement thereof, amounting to $21,942,892; and at the close of the same year a corresponding balance, amounting to $20,137,967, of receipts above expenditures also remained in the Treasury. Although, in the opinion of the Secretary of the Treasury, the receipts of the current fiscal year are not likely to equal in amount those of the last, yet they will undoubtedly exceed the amount of expenditures by at least $15,000,000. I shall therefore continue to direct that the surplus revenue be applied, so far as it can be judiciously and economically done, to the reduction of the public debt, the amount of which at the commencement of the last fiscal year was $67,340,628; of which there had been paid on the 20th day of November, 1854, the sum of $22,365,172, leaving a balance of outstanding public debt of only $44,975,456, redeemable at different periods within fourteen years. There are also remnants of other Government stocks, most of which are already due, and on which the interest has ceased, but which have not yet been presented for payment, amounting to $233,179. This statement exhibits the fact that the annual income of the Government greatly exceeds the amount of its public debt, which latter remains unpaid only because the time of payment has not yet matured, and it can not be discharged at once except at the option of public creditors, who prefer to retain the securities of the United States; and the other fact, not less striking, that the annual revenue from all sources exceeds by many millions of dollars the amount needed for a prudent and economical administration of the Government.

The estimates presented to Congress from the different Executive Departments at the last session amounted to $38,406,581 and the appropriations made to the sum of $58,116,958. Of this excess of appropriations over estimates, however, more than twenty millions was applicable to extraordinary objects, having no reference to the usual annual expenditures. Among these objects was embraced ten millions to meet the third article of the treaty between the United States and Mexico; so that, in fact, for objects of ordinary expenditure the appropriations were limited to considerably less than $40,000,000. I therefore renew my recommendation for a reduction of the duties on imports. The report of the Secretary of the Treasury presents a series of tables showing the operation of the revenue system for several successive years; and as the general principle of reduction of duties with a view to revenue, and not protection, may now be regarded as the settled policy of the country, I trust that little difficulty will be encountered in settling the details of a measure to that effect.

In connection with this subject I recommend a change in the laws, which recent experience has shown to be essential to the protection of the Government. There is no express provision of law requiring the records and papers of a public character of the several officers of the Government to be left in their offices for the use of their successors, nor any provision declaring it felony on their part to make false entries in the books or return false accounts. In the absence of such express provision by law, the outgoing officers in many instances have claimed and exercised the right to take into their own possession important books and papers, on the ground that these were their private property, and have placed them beyond the reach of the Government.   Conduct of this character, brought in several instances to the notice of the present Secretary of the Treasury, naturally awakened his suspicion, and resulted in the disclosure that at four ports—namely, Oswego, Toledo, Sandusky, and Milwaukee—the Treasury had, by false entries, been defrauded within the four years next preceding March, 1853, of the sum of $198,000.   The great difficulty with which the detection of these frauds has been attended, in consequence of the abstraction of books and papers by the retiring officers, and the facility with which similar frauds in the public service may be perpetrated render the necessity of new legal enactments in the respects above referred to quite obvious.   For other material modifications of the revenue laws which seem to me desirable, I refer you to the report of the Secretary of the Treasury.   That report and the tables which accompany it furnish ample proofs of the solid foundation on which the financial security of the country rests and of the salutary influence of the independent-treasury system upon commerce and all monetary operations.

The experience of the last year furnishes additional reasons, I regret to say, of a painful character, for the recommendation heretofore made to provide for increasing the military force employed in the Territory inhabited by the Indians.   The settlers on the frontier have suffered much from the incursions of predatory bands, and large parties of emigrants to our Pacific possessions have been massacred with impunity.   The recurrence of such scenes can only be prevented by teaching these wild tribes the power of and their responsibility to the United States.   From the garrisons of our frontier posts it is only possible to detach troops in small bodies; and though these have on all occasions displayed a gallantry and a stern devotion to duty which on a larger field would have commanded universal admiration, they have usually suffered severely in these conflicts with superior numbers, and have sometimes been entirely sacrificed.   All the disposable force of the Army is already employed on this service, and is known to be wholly inadequate to the protection which should be afforded.   The public mind of the country has been recently shocked by savage atrocities committed upon defenseless emigrants and border settlements, and hardly less by the unnecessary destruction of valuable lives where inadequate detachments of troops have undertaken to furnish the needed aid.   Without increase of the military force these scenes will be repeated, it is to be feared, on a larger scale and with more disastrous consequences.   Congress, I am sure, will perceive that the plainest duties and responsibilities of Government are involved in this question, and I doubt not that prompt action may be confidently anticipated when delay must be attended by such fearful hazards.

The bill of the last session providing for an increase of the pay of the rank and file of the Army has had beneficial results, not only in facilitating enlistments, but in obvious improvement in the class of men who enter the service. I regret that corresponding consideration was not bestowed on the officers, who, in view of their character and services and the expenses to which they are necessarily subject, receive at present what is, in my judgment, inadequate compensation.

The valuable services constantly rendered by the Army and its inestimable importance as the nucleus around which the volunteer forces of the nation can promptly gather in the hour of danger, sufficiently attest the wisdom of maintaining a military peace establishment; but the theory of our system and the wise practice under it require that any proposed augmentation in time of peace be only commensurate with our extended limits and frontier relations. While scrupulously adhering to this principle, I find in existing circumstances a necessity for increase of our military force, and it is believed that four new regiments, two of infantry and two of mounted men, will be sufficient to meet the present exigency. If it were necessary carefully to weigh the cost in a case of such urgency, it would be shown that the additional expense would be comparatively light.

With the increase of the numerical force of the Army should, I think, be combined certain measures of reform in its organic arrangement and administration. The present organization is the result of partial legislation often directed to special objects and interests; and the laws regulating rank and command, having been adopted many years ago from the British code, are not always applicable to our service. It is not surprising, therefore, that the system should be deficient in the symmetry and simplicity essential to the harmonious working of its several parts, and require a careful revision.

The present organization, by maintaining large staff corps or departments, separates many officers from that close connection with troops and those active duties in the field which are deemed requisite to qualify them for the varied responsibilities of high command. Were the duties of the Army staff mainly discharged by officers detached from their regiments, it is believed that the special service would be equally well performed and the discipline and instruction of the Army be improved. While due regard to the security of the rights of officers and to the nice sense of honor which should be cultivated among them would seem to exact compliance with the established rule of promotion in ordinary cases, still it can hardly be doubted that the range of promotion by selection, which is now practically confined to the grade of general officers, might be somewhat extended with benefit to the public service. Observance of the rule of seniority sometimes leads, especially in time of peace, to the promotion of officers who, after meritorious and even distinguished service, may have been rendered by age or infirmity incapable of performing active duty, and whose advancement, therefore, would tend to impair the efficiency of the Army. Suitable provision for this class of officers, by the creation of a retired list, would remedy the evil without wounding the just pride of men who by past services have established a claim to high consideration. In again commending this measure to the favorable consideration of Congress I would suggest that the power of placing officers on the retired list be limited to one year. The practical operation of the measure would thus be tested, and if after the lapse of years there should be occasion to renew the provision it can be reproduced with any improvements which experience may indicate. The present organization of the artillery into regiments is liable to obvious objections. The service of artillery is that of batteries, and an organization of batteries into a corps of artillery would be more consistent with the nature of their duties. A large part of the troops now called artillery are, and have been, on duty as infantry, the distinction between the two arms being merely nominal. This nominal artillery in our service is disproportionate to the whole force and greater than the wants of the country demand. I therefore commend the discontinuance of a distinction which has no foundation in either the arms used or the character of the service expected to be performed.

In connection with the proposition for the increase of the Army, I have presented these suggestions with regard to certain measures of reform as the complement of a system which would produce the happiest results from a given expenditure, and which, I hope, may attract the early attention and be deemed worthy of the approval of Congress.

The recommendation of the Secretary of the Navy having reference to more ample provisions for the discipline and general improvement in the character of seamen and for the reorganization and gradual increase of the Navy I deem eminently worthy of your favorable consideration. The principles which have controlled our policy in relation to the permanent military force by sea and land are sound, consistent with the theory of our system, and should by no means be disregarded. But, limiting the force to the objects particularly set forth in the preceding part of this message, we should not overlook the present magnitude and prospective extension of our commercial marine, nor fail to give due weight to the fact that besides the 2,000 miles of Atlantic seaboard we have now a Pacific coast stretching from Mexico to the British possessions in the north, teeming with wealth and enterprise and demanding the constant presence of ships of war. The augmentation of the Navy has not kept pace with the duties properly and profitably assigned to it in time of peace, and it is inadequate for the large field of its operations, not merely in the present, but still more in the progressively increasing exigencies of the commerce of the United States. I cordially approve of the proposed apprentice system for our national vessels recommended by the Secretary of the Navy.

The occurrence during the last few months of marine disasters of the most tragic nature, involving great loss of human life, has produced intense emotions of sympathy and sorrow throughout the country. It may well be doubted whether all these calamitous events are wholly attributable to the necessary and inevitable dangers of the sea. The merchants, mariners, and shipbuilders of the United States are, it is true, unsurpassed in far-reaching enterprise, skill, intelligence, and courage by any others in the world. But with the increasing amount of our commercial tonnage in the aggregate and the larger size and improved equipment of the ships now constructed a deficiency in the supply of reliable seamen begins to be very seriously felt. The inconvenience may perhaps be met in part by due regulation for the introduction into our merchant ships of indented apprentices, which, while it would afford useful and eligible occupation to numerous young men, would have a tendency to raise the character of seamen as a class. And it is deserving of serious reflection whether it may not be desirable to revise the existing laws for the maintenance of discipline at sea, upon which the security of life and property on the ocean must to so great an extent depend. Although much attention has already been given by Congress to the proper construction and arrangement of steam vessels and all passenger ships, still it is believed that the resources of science and mechanical skill in this direction have not been exhausted. No good reason exists for the marked distinction which appears upon our statutes between the laws for protecting life and property at sea and those for protecting them on land. In most of the States severe penalties are provided to punish conductors of trains, engineers, and others employed in the transportation of persons by railway or by steamboats on rivers. Why should not the same principle be applied to acts of insubordination, cowardice, or other misconduct on the part of masters and mariners producing injury or death to passengers on the high seas, beyond the jurisdiction of any of the States, and where such delinquencies can be reached only by the power of Congress? The whole subject is earnestly commended to your consideration.

The report of the Postmaster-General, to which you are referred for many interesting details in relation to this important and rapidly extending branch of the public service, shows that the expenditure of the year ending June 30, 1854, including $133,483 of balance due to foreign offices, amounted to $8,710,907. The gross receipts during the same period amounted to $6,955,586, exhibiting an expenditure over income of $1,755,321 and a diminution of deficiency as compared with the last year of $361,756. The increase of the revenue of the Department for the year ending June 30, 1854, over the preceding year was $970,399. No proportionate increase, however, can be anticipated for the current year, in consequence of the act of Congress of June 23, 1854, providing for increased compensation to all postmasters. From these statements it is apparent that the Post-Office Department, instead of defraying its expenses according to the design at the time of its creation, is now, and under existing laws must continue to be, to no small extent a charge upon the general Treasury. The cost of mail transportation during the year ending June 30, 1854, exceeds the cost of the preceding year by $495,074. I again call your attention to the subject of mail transportation by ocean steamers, and commend the suggestions of the Postmaster-General to your early attention.

During the last fiscal year 11,070,935 acres of the public lands have been surveyed and 8,190,017 acres brought into market. The number of acres sold is 7,035,735 and the amount received therefor $9,285,533. The aggregate amount of lands sold, located under military scrip and land warrants, selected as swamp lands by States, and by locating under grants for roads is upward of 23,000,000 acres. The increase of lands sold over the previous year is about 6,000,000 acres, and the sales during the first two quarters of the current year present the extraordinary result of five and a half millions sold, exceeding by nearly 4,000,000 acres the sales of the corresponding quarters of the last year.

The commendable policy of the Government in relation to setting apart public domain for those who have served their country in time of war is illustrated by the fact that since 1790 no less than 30,000,000 acres have been applied to this object.

The suggestions which I submitted in my annual message of last year in reference to grants of land in aid of the construction of railways were less full and explicit than the magnitude of the subject and subsequent developments would seem to render proper and desirable. Of the soundness of the principle then asserted with regard to the limitation of the power of Congress I entertain no doubt, but in its application it is not enough that the value of lands in a particular locality may be enhanced; that, in fact, a larger amount of money may probably be received in a given time for alternate sections than could have been realized for all the sections without the impulse and influence of the proposed improvements. A prudent proprietor looks beyond limited sections of his domain, beyond present results to the ultimate effect which a particular line of policy is likely to produce upon all his possessions and interests. The Government, which is trustee in this matter for the people of the States, is bound to take the same wise and comprehensive view. Prior to and during the last session of Congress upward of 30,000,000 acres of land were withdrawn from public sale with a view to applications for grants of this character pending before Congress. A careful review of the whole subject led me to direct that all such orders be abrogated and the lands restored to market, and instructions were immediately given to that effect. The applications at the last session contemplated the construction of more than 5,000 miles of road and grants to the amount of nearly 20,000,000 acres of the public domain. Even admitting the right on the part of Congress to be unquestionable, is it quite clear that the proposed grants would be productive of good, and not evil? The different projects are confined for the present to eleven States of this Union and one Territory. The reasons assigned for the grants show that it is proposed to put the works speedily in process of construction. When we reflect that since the commencement of the construction of railways in the United States, stimulated, as they have been, by the large dividends realized from the earlier works over the great thoroughfares and between the most important points of commerce and population, encouraged by State legislation, and pressed forward by the amazing energy of private enterprise, only 17,000 miles have been completed in all the States in a quarter of a century; when we see the crippled condition of many works commenced and prosecuted upon what were deemed to be sound principles and safe calculations; when we contemplate the enormous absorption of capital withdrawn from the ordinary channels of business, the extravagant rates of interest at this moment paid to continue operations, the bankruptcies, not merely in money but in character, and the inevitable effect upon finances generally, can it be doubted that the tendency is to run to excess in this matter? Is it wise to augment this excess by encouraging hopes of sudden wealth expected to flow from magnificent schemes dependent upon the action of Congress? Does the spirit which has produced such results need to be stimulated or checked? Is it not the better rule to leave all these works to private enterprise, regulated and, when expedient, aided by the cooperation of States? If constructed by private capital the stimulant and the check go together and furnish a salutary restraint against speculative schemes and extravagance. But it is manifest that with the most effective guards there is danger of going too fast and too far.

We may well pause before a proposition contemplating a simultaneous movement for the construction of railroads which in extent will equal, exclusive of the great Pacific road and all its branches, nearly one-third of the entire length of such works now completed in the United States, and which can not cost with equipments less than $150,000,000. The dangers likely to result from combinations of interests of this character can hardly be overestimated. But independently of these considerations, where is the accurate knowledge, the comprehensive intelligence, which shall discriminate between the relative claims of these twenty-eight proposed roads in eleven States and one Territory? Where will you begin and where end? If to enable these companies to execute their proposed works it is necessary that the aid of the General Government be primarily given, the policy will present a problem so comprehensive in its bearings and so important to our political and social well-being as to claim in anticipation the severest analysis. Entertaining these views, I recur with satisfaction to the experience and action of the last session of Congress as furnishing assurance that the subject will not fail to elicit a careful reexamination and rigid scrutiny.

It was my intention to present on this occasion some suggestions regarding internal improvements by the General Government, which want of time at the close of the last session prevented my submitting on the return to the House of Representatives with objections of the bill entitled "An act making appropriations for the repair, preservation, and completion of certain public works heretofore commenced under the authority of law;" but the space in this communication already occupied with other matter of immediate public exigency constrains me to reserve that subject for a special message, which will be transmitted to the two Houses of Congress at an early day.

The judicial establishment of the United States requires modification, and certain reforms in the manner of conducting the legal business of the Government are also much needed; but as I have addressed you upon both of these subjects at length before, I have only to call your attention to the suggestions then made.

My former recommendations in relation to suitable provision for various objects of deep interest to the inhabitants of the District of Columbia are renewed. Many of these objects partake largely of a national character, and are important independently of their relation to the prosperity of the only considerable organized community in the Union entirely unrepresented in Congress.

I have thus presented suggestions on such subjects as appear to me to be of particular interest or importance, and therefore most worthy of consideration during the short remaining period allotted to the labors of the present Congress.

Our forefathers of the thirteen united colonies, in acquiring their independence and in founding this Republic of the United States of America, have devolved upon us, their descendants, the greatest and the most noble trust ever committed to the hands of man, imposing upon all, and especially such as the public will may have invested for the time being with political functions, the most sacred obligations. We have to maintain inviolate the great doctrine of the inherent right of popular self-government; to reconcile the largest liberty of the individual citizen with complete security of the public order; to render cheerful obedience to the laws of the land, to unite in enforcing their execution, and to frown indignantly on all combinations to resist them; to harmonize a sincere and ardent devotion to the institutions of religious faith with the most universal religious toleration; to preserve the rights of all by causing each to respect those of the other; to carry forward every social improvement to the uttermost limit of human perfectibility, by the free action of mind upon mind, not by the obtrusive intervention of misapplied force; to uphold the integrity and guard the limitations of our organic law; to preserve sacred from all touch of usurpation, as the very palladium of our political salvation, the reserved rights and powers of the several States and of the people; to cherish with loyal fealty and devoted affection this Union, as the only sure foundation on which the hopes of civil liberty rest; to administer government with vigilant integrity and rigid economy; to cultivate peace and friendship with foreign nations, and to demand and exact equal justice from all, but to do wrong to none; to eschew intermeddling with the national policy and the domestic repose of other governments, and to repel it from our own; never to shrink from war when the rights and the honor of the country call us to arms, but to cultivate in preference the arts of peace, seek enlargement of the rights of neutrality, and elevate and liberalize the intercourse of nations; and by such just and honorable means, and such only, whilst exalting the condition of the Republic, to assure to it the legitimate influence and the benign authority of a great example amongst all the powers of Christendom.

Under the solemnity of these convictions the blessing of Almighty God is earnestly invoked to attend upon your deliberations and upon all the counsels and acts of the Government, to the end that, with common zeal and common efforts, we may, in humble submission to the divine will, cooperate for the promotion of the supreme good of these United States.

FRANKLIN PIERCE.

SPECIAL MESSAGES.

WASHINGTON, *December 5, 1854.*

To the Senate of the United States:

I transmit to the Senate, for its consideration with a view to approval, a compact between the United States and the royal Government of Lew Chew, entered into at Napa on the 11th day of July last, for securing certain privileges to vessels of the United States resorting to the Lew Chew Islands.

A copy of the instructions of the Secretary of State upon the subject is also herewith transmitted. FRANKLIN PIERCE.

WASHINGTON, *December 5, 1854.*

To the Senate of the United States:

I transmit to the Senate, for its consideration with a view to ratification, a convention for regulating the right of inheriting and acquiring property, concluded in this city on the 21st day of August last between the United States and His Highness the Duke of Brunswick and Luneburg. FRANKLIN PIERCE.

WASHINGTON, *December 11, 1854.*

To the Senate and House of Representatives:

An act for the relief of the legal representatives of Samuel Prioleau, deceased, which provided for the payment of the sum of $6,928.60 to the legal representatives of said Prioleau by the proper accounting officer of the Treasury, was approved by me July 27, 1854. It having been ascertained that the identical claim provided for in this act was liquidated and paid under the provisions of the general act of August 4, 1790, and of the special act of January 24, 1795, the First Comptroller of the Treasury declined to give effect to the law first above referred to without communicating the facts for my consideration. This refusal I regard as fully justified by the facts upon which it was predicated.

In view of the destruction of valuable papers by fire in the building occupied by the Treasury Department in 1814 and again in 1833, it is not surprising that cases like this should, more than seventy years after the transaction with which they were connected, be involved in much doubt. The report of the Comptroller, however, shows conclusively by record evidence still preserved in the Department and elsewhere that the sum of $6,122.44, with $3,918.36 interest thereon from the date of the destruction of the property, making the sum of $10,040.80, was allowed to Samuel Prioleau under the act for his relief passed in 1795.

That amount was reported by the Auditor to the Comptroller on the 4th day of February, 1795, to be funded as follows, to wit:

Two-thirds of $6,122.44, called 6 per cent stock	$4,081.63
One-third, called deferred stock	2,040.81
Interest on the principal, called 3 per cent stock	3,918.36
Total	10,040.80
On the books of the loan office of South Carolina, under date of April 27, 1795, is an entry showing that there was issued of the funded 6 per cent stock to Samuel Prioleau	4,081.63
Of the deferred stock	2,040.81
Of the 3 per cent stock	3,918.36
Total	10,040.80

On the ledger of said loan office an account was opened with Samuel Prioleau, in which he was credited with the three items of stock and deputed by the transfer of each certificate to certain persons named, under dates of May 20, 1795, August 24, 1795, and April 19, 1796.

These records show that the account of Samuel Prioleau, required to be settled by the act of January 28, 1795, was settled; that the value of the property destroyed was allowed; that the amount so found due was funded by said Prioleau and entered by his order on the loan-office books of South Carolina, and soon thereafter by him sold and transferred. That the entire funded debt of the United States was long since paid is matter of history.

It is apparent that the claim has been prosecuted under a misapprehension on the part of the present claimants.

I present the evidence in the case collected by the First Comptroller and embodied in his report for your consideration, together with a copy of a letter just received by that officer from the executor of P. G. Prioleau, and respectfully recommend the repeal of the act of July 27, 1854.

FRANKLIN PIERCE.

CARTOON ON TEMPERANCE CRAZE OF 1854, DURING
FRANKLIN PIERCE'S ADMINISTRATION.

TEMPERANCE AGITATION OF FRANKLIN PIERCE'S TERM.

WASHINGTON, *December 11, 1854.*

To the House of Representatives:

I transmit herewith a report from the Secretary of State, with accompanying documents,* in compliance with the resolution of the House of Representatives of the 27th of July last.

FRANKLIN PIERCE.

WASHINGTON, *December 11, 1854.*

To the Senate:

I herewith transmit a communication from the Secretary of the Treasury, requesting authority to invest the sum of $6,561.80, received from the sales of lands in the Chickasaw cession, in stocks for the benefit of the Chickasaw national fund, as required by the eleventh article of the treaty with the Chickasaws of the 20th October, 1832, and the act of Congress of 11th September, 1841.

FRANKLIN PIERCE.

WASHINGTON, *December 12, 1854.*

To the Senate of the United States:

Herewith I transmit a report of the Secretary of State, with accompanying papers,† in answer to the resolution of the Senate of the 3d of August last.

FRANKLIN PIERCE.

WASHINGTON, *December 16, 1854.*

To the House of Representatives:

I transmit a report from the Secretary of State, with accompanying papers,‡ in answer to the resolution of the House of Representatives of the 27th of July last.

FRANKLIN PIERCE.

WASHINGTON, *December 18, 1854.*

To the House of Representatives:

I transmit a report from the Secretary of War, with accompanying papers, in answer to the resolution of the House of Representatives of the 2d of August last, requesting such information as may be in the possession of the War Department touching the cause of any difficulties which may have arisen between the Creek and Seminole Indians since their removal west of the Mississippi and other matters concerning the tribes.

FRANKLIN PIERCE.

*Correspondence of the American consul-general at Cairo relative to the expulsion of the Greeks from Egypt.

†Correspondence relative to difficulties between Rev. Jonas King and the Government of Greece.

‡Relating to the case of Walter M. Gibson, held in duress by the Dutch authorities at Batavia, island of Java, on a charge of having attempted to excite the native chiefs of Sumatra to throw off their allegiance to the Dutch Government.

WASHINGTON, *December 20, 1854.*

To the Senate of the United States:

I herewith transmit to the Senate, for its constitutional action thereon, a treaty made at the Neosho Agency on the 12th August, 1854, by Andrew J. Dorn, commissioner on the part of the United States, and the chiefs and warriors of the Quapaw tribe of Indians.

FRANKLIN PIERCE.

WASHINGTON, *December 20, 1854.*

To the Senate of the United States:

I herewith transmit to the Senate, for its constitutional action thereon, a treaty made by Andrew J. Dorn, commissioner on the part of the United States, on the 23d of August, 1854, and the chiefs and warriors of the Senecas of Sandusky and the Senecas and Shawnees of Lewistown, designated by the treaty of 1832 as the United Nation of Seneca and Shawnee Indians.

FRANKLIN PIERCE.

WASHINGTON, *December 20, 1854.*

To the Senate of the United States:

I herewith transmit to the Senate, for its constitutional action thereon, a treaty made at La Pointe, Wis., on the 30th of September, 1854, by Henry C. Gilbert and David B. Harriman, commissioners on the part of the United States, and the chiefs and headmen of the Chippewas of Lake Superior and the Mississippi.

FRANKLIN PIERCE.

WASHINGTON, *December 26, 1854.*

To the Senate of the United States:

In compliance with the resolution of the Senate of the 5th instant, requesting me, if not incompatible with the public interests, to communicate to that body ''copies of all instructions and correspondence between the different Departments of the Government and Major-General Wool, commanding the Pacific division of the Army, in regard to his operations on that coast,'' I transmit the accompanying documents.

FRANKLIN PIERCE.

[For message of December 30, 1854, giving an exposition of the reasons of the President for vetoing ''An act making appropriations for the repair, preservation, and completion of certain public works heretofore commenced under the authority of law,'' see pp. 257–271.]

WASHINGTON, D. C., *January 1, 1855.*

To the House of Representatives:

In response to the resolution of the House of Representatives of the 11th ultimo, requesting the President ''to communicate to this House any proposition which may have been made to the Government by the city authorities of Memphis relative to the navy-yard property recently ceded to that city, together with his views and those of the Navy Department as to the propriety of accepting the proposed re-cession and of reestablishing a naval depot and yard of construction at Memphis,'' I transmit herewith a report of the Secretary of the Navy, and have only to add my concurrence in the views by him presented.

FRANKLIN PIERCE.

WASHINGTON, *January 9, 1855.*

To the Senate of the United States:

I transmit herewith to the Senate, for its constitutional action thereon, an article of agreement and convention made and concluded on the 9th day of December, 1854, between the United States, by George Hepner, United States Indian agent, and the chiefs and headmen of the confederate tribes of Otoe and Missouria Indians, being a supplement to the treaty made between the United States and said confederate tribes on the 15th day of March, 1854. FRANKLIN PIERCE.

WASHINGTON, *January 10, 1855.*

To the House of Representatives of the United States:

I transmit herewith a report of the Attorney-General, with the accompanying documents, communicating the information required by the following resolution of the House of Representatives, of the 28th ultimo:

Resolved, That the President of the United States be requested to communicate to this House any information possessed by him regarding a suit instituted in the Territory of Minnesota by or in the name of the United States against the Minnesota and Northwestern Railroad Company.

FRANKLIN PIERCE.

WASHINGTON, *January 11, 1855.*

To the Senate of the United States:

In compliance with the resolution of the Senate of the 3d instant, requesting ''a statement of the names of the ministers, chargés d'affaires, and the secretaries of legation of the United States appointed since the 4th of March, 1849, together with the dates of their commissions, the time of the commencement of their compensation, of their departure for their posts, and of their entering upon their official duties thereat,'' I transmit the accompanying report from the Secretary of State.

FRANKLIN PIERCE.

WASHINGTON, *January 16, 1855.*

To the Senate and House of Representatives:

I transmit herewith a letter of the Secretary of War upon the subject of Indian hostilities. The employment of volunteer troops, as suggested by the Secretary, seems to afford the only practicable means of providing for the present emergency.

There is much reason to believe that other cases similar in character to those particularly referred to in the accompanying papers will at an early day require vigorous measures and the exhibition of a strong military force. The proposed temporary provision to meet a special demand, so far from obviating, in my judgment only serves to illustrate the urgent necessity of an increase of the Regular Army, at least to the extent recommended in my late annual message. Unless by the plan proposed, or some other equally effective, a force can be early brought into the field adequate to the suppression of existing hostilities, the combination of predatory bands will be extended and the difficulty of restoring order and security greatly magnified. On the other hand, without a permanent military force of suffcient strength to control the unfriendly Indians, it may be expected that hostilities will soon be renewed and that years of border warfare will afflict the country, retarding the progress of settlement, exposing emigrant trains to savage barbarities and consuming millions of the public money.

The state of things made known in various letters recently received at the War Department, extracts from a portion of which are herewith inclosed, is calculated to augment the deep solicitude which this matter has for some time past awakened, and which has been earnestly expressed in previous messages and in the annual reports of the Secretary of War.

I respectfully submit that the facts now communicated urgently call for immediate action on the part of Congress.

FRANKLIN PIERCE.

WASHINGTON, *January 17, 1855.*

To the Senate of the United States:

In further compliance with the resolution of the Senate of the 5th of December last, requesting copies of correspondence* between Major-General Wool and the different Departments of the Government, I transmit a report from the Secretary of State and the documents by which it was accompanied.

FRANKLIN PIERCE.

WASHINGTON, *January 19, 1855.*

To the House of Representatives:

In further compliance with the resolution of the House of Representatives of the 27th of July last, upon the subject of the case of Walter M. Gibson, I transmit a report from the Secretary of State.

FRANKLIN PIERCE.

---

*Relating to affairs on the Pacific Coast.

WASHINGTON, *January 19, 1855.*

To the Senate of the United States:

I communicate to the Senate herewith a letter from the Secretary of the Interior, dated the 18th instant, covering a communication from the Commissioner of Indian Affairs, with accompanying papers, and asking that certain appropriations be made for the service of the Indian Department.

FRANKLIN PIERCE.

WASHINGTON, *January 22, 1855.*

To the Senate and House of Representatives of the United States:

I communicate to Congress herewith a communication of this date from the Secretary of the Interior, with accompanying papers, and recommend that the appropriation* therein asked for be made.

FRANKLIN PIERCE.

WASHINGTON, *January 24, 1855.*

To the Senate and House of Representatives:

I transmit herewith a report of the Secretary of the Interior and the Postmaster-General, together with accompanying documents, communicating what has been done in execution of the act of Congress of August 2, 1854, entitled "An act to provide for the accommodation of the courts of the United States in the cities of New York and Philadelphia."

I have deemed it best under the circumstances not to enter into contracts for the purchase of sites, but to submit all proposals made, in response to public advertisement for several weeks in the principal newspapers in each of the cities designated, to Congress, for such action as it may deem proper to take in fulfillment of the original design of the before-mentioned act.

FRANKLIN PIERCE.

WASHINGTON, *January 29, 1855.*

To the Senate and House of Representatives of the United States:

I transmit to Congress herewith a communication of this date from the Secretary of the Interior, with accompanying papers, and recommend that the appropriations therein asked for be made.

I avail myself of the occasion to suggest a modification of existing laws, with a view to enable me more effectually to carry into execution the treaties with the different Indian tribes in Kansas Territory.

With an earnest desire to promote the early settlement of the ceded lands, as well as those held in trust and to be sold for the benefit of the Indians, I shall exercise all the power intrusted to me to maintain strictly and in good faith our treaty obligations.

* For payment of interest due the Cherokee Indians.

I respectfully recommend that provisions be made by law requiring the lands which are to be sold on account of the Indians by the Government to be appraised and classified; a minimum price to be fixed, for a less sum than which no sales shall be made without further provision of law; and authorizing the sale of the lands in such quantities and at such times and places as the obligations of the Government, the rights of the Indian tribes, and the public interest, with reference to speedy settlement, may render expedient.

FRANKLIN PIERCE.

WASHINGTON, *January 30, 1855.*

To the Senate of the United States:

In compliance with the resolution of the Senate of the 6th of December last, requesting the President "to communicate to the Senate, if in his opinion not incompatible with the public interest, the instructions, correspondence, and other documents relating to the naval expedition to Japan, and the proceedings and negotiations resulting in a treaty with the Government thereof," I transmit the inclosed report from the Secretary of the Navy, with the accompanying documents.

FRANKLIN PIERCE.

WASHINGTON, *February 1, 1855.*

To the Senate of the United States:

I transmit to the Senate, with a view to ratification, a convention which was concluded between the United States and Mexico at the City of Mexico on the 8th day of January last.

FRANKLIN PIERCE.

WASHINGTON, *February 4, 1855.*

To the Senate and House of Representatives of the United States:

I communicate to Congress herewith, for its consideration, the accompanying papers from the Secretary of the Interior, on the subject of the proviso of the act of July 31, 1854, in relation to the removal of the California Indians.

FRANKLIN PIERCE.

WASHINGTON, *February 4, 1855.*

To the Senate and House of Representatives of the United States:

I communicate to Congress the accompanying papers* from the Secretary of the Interior, and recommend that the appropriations therein asked for may be made.

FRANKLIN PIERCE.

*Relating to the expenses necessary to be incurred in colonizing the Texas Indians.

WASHINGTON, *February 5, 1855.*

To the Senate of the United States:

I communicate to the Senate herewith, for its constitutional action thereon, articles of agreement and convention made and concluded at the city of Washington on the 31st day of January, 1855, by George W. Manypenny, as commissioner on the part of the United States, and the chiefs and delegates of the Wyandott tribe of Indians.

FRANKLIN PIERCE.

WASHINGTON, *February 6, 1855.*

To the Senate of the United States:

In compliance with the resolution of the Senate of the 11th ultimo, in relation to the case of Francis W. Rice,* late United States consul at Acapulco, I transmit a report from the Secretary of State, with the accompanying documents.

FRANKLIN PIERCE

WASHINGTON, *February 6, 1855.*

To the House of Representatives:

I transmit herewith a report † from the Secretary of State, in answer to the resolution of the House of Representatives of the 27th ultimo.

FRANKLIN PIERCE.

WASHINGTON, *February 7, 1855.*

To the Senate of the United States:

I transmit to the Senate, for its advice with regard to ratification, a convention for the mutual extradition of fugitives from justice in certain cases between the United States and His Majesty the King of Hanover, signed by the plenipotentiaries of the two Governments at London on the 18th of January last. An extract from a dispatch of Mr. Buchanan to the Secretary of State relative to the convention is also herewith communicated.

FRANKLIN PIERCE.

WASHINGTON, *February 7, 1855.*

To the Senate and House of Representatives of the United States:

I communicate to Congress herewith a letter and accompanying papers from the Secretary of the Interior, of the 5th instant, on the subject of the colonization of the Indians in the State of California, and recommend that the appropriation therein asked for may be made.

FRANKLIN PIERCE.

---

*Arrested and imprisoned at Acapulco, Mexico.

†Stating that the information relative to the applicability to the Spanish colonies of the treaty of 1795 with Spain, and whether American citizens residing in said colonies are entitled to the benefits of its provisions, had been already transmitted.

WASHINGTON, *February 7, 1855.*

To the Senate and House of Representatives of the United States:

I communicate to Congress the accompanying letter from the Secretary of the Interior, with its inclosure, on the subject of a treaty between the United States and the Chippewa Indians of Lake Superior, and recommend that the appropriation therein asked for may be made.

FRANKLIN PIERCE.

WASHINGTON, *February 9, 1855.*

To the Senate of the United States:

I communicate to the Senate herewith a report from the Secretary of the Treasury, and also one from the Secretary of the Interior, with accompanying papers, containing information called for by the resolution adopted by the Senate on the 30th ultimo, respecting the advance of public moneys to the marshal of the United States for the western district of Arkansas.

FRANKLIN PIERCE.

WASHINGTON, *February 9, 1855.*

To the Senate of the United States:

I herewith communicate to the Senate, for its constitutional action thereon, the articles of convention and agreement between the Choctaw and Chickasaw tribes of Indians made on the 4th day of November, 1854, at Doaksville, near Fort Towson, Choctaw Nation.

FRANKLIN PIERCE.

WASHINGTON, *February 12, 1855.*

To the Senate of the United States:

The resolution of the Senate of the 11th of December last, requesting a copy of the official correspondence relative to the late difficulties between the consul of France at San Francisco and the authorities of the United States in California, has been under consideration, and it was hoped that the negotiations on the subject might have been brought to a close, so as to have obviated any objection to a compliance with the resolution at this session of Congress. Those negotiations, however, are still pending, but I entertain a confident expectation that the affair will be definitely and satisfactorily adjusted prior to the next session.

FRANKLIN PIERCE.

WASHINGTON, *February 14, 1855.*

To the Senate of the United States:

I transmit to the Senate, for its consideration with a view to ratification, a convention between the United States and His Majesty the King of the Netherlands, upon the subject of the admission of the United States consuls into the ports of the Dutch colonies.

FRANKLIN PIERCE.

WASHINGTON, *February 14, 1855.*

To the Senate of the United States:

I transmit to the Senate, for its consideration with a view to ratification, a convention between the United States and His Majesty the King of the Kingdom of the Two Sicilies, relative to the rights of neutrals during war.

FRANKLIN PIERCE.

WASHINGTON, *February 17, 1855.*

To the Senate and House of Representatives of the United States:

I communicate herewith a letter* of the Secretary of the Interior and accompanying paper, for the consideration of Congress.

FRANKLIN PIERCE.

WASHINGTON, *February 19, 1855.*

To the Senate of the United States:

I transmit herewith, for the constitutional action of the Senate, a treaty made on the 15th day of November, 1854, by Joel Palmer, superintendent of Indian affairs, on the part of the United States, and the chiefs and headmen of the Rogue River Indians in Oregon Territory.

FRANKLIN PIERCE.

WASHINGTON, *February 19, 1855.*

To the Senate of the United States:

I transmit herewith, for the constitutional action of the Senate, a treaty made by Isaac I. Stevens, governor and superintendent of Indian affairs in Washington Territory, on the part of the United States, and the chiefs, headmen, and delegates of the Nesqually, Puyallup, Steilacoom, Squawksin, S'Homamish, Ste'h-chass, F'peeksin, Squi-aitl, and Sa-heh-wamish tribes and bands of Indians occupying the lands lying around the head of Pugets Sound and the adjacent inlets in Washington Territory.

FRANKLIN PIERCE.

WASHINGTON, *February 19, 1855.*

To the Senate of the United States:

I transmit herewith, for the constitutional action of the Senate, two treaties, one made on the 18th day of November, 1854, by Joel Palmer,

---

*Recommending an appropriation to supply a deficit in the amount held on Indian account, caused by the failure of Selden, Withers & Co., with whom it was deposited.

superintendent of Indian affairs, on the part of the United States, and the chiefs and headmen of the Quil-si-eton and Na-hel-ta bands of the Chasta tribe of Indians, the Cow-non-ti-co, Sa-cher-i-ton, and Na-al-ye bands of Scotans, and the Grave Creek band of Umpqua Indians in Oregon Territory; the other, made on the 29th of November, 1854, by Joel Palmer, superintendent of Indian affairs, on the part of the United States, and the chiefs and headmen of the confederated bands of the Umpqua tribe of Indians and the Calaponas, residing in Umpqua Valley, Oregon Territory.

FRANKLIN PIERCE.

WASHINGTON, *February 21, 1855.*

To the Senate and House of Representatives of the United States:

I communicate to Congress a communication of this date from the Secretary of the Interior, with the accompanying paper, and recommend that the appropriation * therein asked for be made.

FRANKLIN PIERCE.

WASHINGTON, *February 22, 1855.*

To the Senate of the United States:

In compliance with the resolution of the Senate of the 21st instant, I transmit a report from the Secretary of State, inclosing a copy of the letter † addressed to the Department of State on the 17th November, 1852, by Mr. Joaquin J. de Osma, envoy extraordinary and minister plenipotentiary of the Republic of Peru.

FRANKLIN PIERCE.

WASHINGTON, *February 23, 1855.*

To the Senate and House of Representatives of the United States:

I communicate to Congress herewith a communication of this date from the Secretary of the Interior, with accompanying estimates, and recommend that the appropriation ‡ therein asked for be made.

FRANKLIN PIERCE.

WASHINGTON, *February 24, 1855.*

To the Senate of the United States:

In compliance with the resolution of the Senate of the 22d instant, I transmit a report from the Secretary of State, together with the copy of a communication from Francis W. Rice,§ therein referred to.

FRANKLIN PIERCE.

* For extending and improving the culvert running from the United States Capitol Grounds down the center of South Capitol street toward the canal.

† Proposing a settlement of the Lobos Islands controversy.

‡ To fulfill treaty stipulations with the Wyandotte Indians.

§ Late United States consul at Acapulco, relative to outrages committed upon him by authorities of Mexico.

WASHINGTON, *February 26, 1855.*

To the Senate of the United States:

I transmit herewith a report of the Secretary of the Navy, in compliance with a resolution of the Senate of the 20th instant, requesting the President "to communicate to the Senate a copy of the order issued by the Navy Department to the officer in command of the Home Squadron in pursuance of which the United States sloop of war *Albany* was ordered on her last cruise to Carthagena and Aspinwall, etc.; also of the orders given by such officer to Commander Gerry to proceed upon such cruise, and also of any reports or letters from the captain of the *Albany* on the necessity of repairs to said vessel."

FRANKLIN PIERCE.

WASHINGTON, *February 27, 1855.*

To the Senate and House of Representatives of the United States:

I transmit to Congress herewith a communication of this date from the Secretary of the Interior, and recommend that the appropriation* therein asked for be made.

FRANKLIN PIERCE.

WASHINGTON, *February 27, 1855.*

To the Senate and House of Representatives of the United States:

I communicate herewith, for the consideration of Congress, a letter of this date from the Secretary of the Interior, and accompanying paper, recommending certain appropriations† on account of the Indian service.

FRANKLIN PIERCE.

WASHINGTON, *February 27, 1855.*

To the Senate of the United States:

I communicate to the Senate herewith, for its constitutional action thereon, a treaty made in this city on the 22d instant between the United States and the Mississippi, the Pillager, and the Lake Winnibigoshish bands of Chippewa Indians.

FRANKLIN PIERCE.

WASHINGTON, *February 28, 1855.*

To the Senate of the United States:

For eminent services in the late war with Mexico, I nominate Major-General Winfield Scott, of the Army of the United States, to be lieutenant-general by brevet in the same, to take rank as such from March

---

*For surveying public lands in the northern part of Minnesota Territory acquired from the Chippewa Indians.

†For running the boundary line between the Chickasaw and Choctaw nations of Indians and for negotiations with the Menominee Indians.

29, 1847, the day on which the United States forces under his command captured Vera Cruz and the castle of San Juan de Ulua.

FRANKLIN PIERCE.

WASHINGTON, *February 28, 1855.*

To the Senate of the United States:

I communicate to the Senate herewith, for its constitutional action thereon, a treaty made and concluded in this city on the 27th day of February, 1855, between George W. Manypenny, commissioner on the part of the United States, and the chiefs and delegates of the Winnebago tribe of Indians.

FRANKLIN PIERCE.

WASHINGTON, *March 1, 1855.*

To the Senate and House of Representatives of the United States:

I communicate to Congress herewith a copy of an act of the legislature of the State of Texas, approved the 11th of February, 1854, making partial provision for running and marking the boundary line between the said State and the territories of the United States from the point where the said line leaves the Red River to its intersection with the Rio Grande, and appropriating $10,000 toward carrying the same into effect, when the United States shall have made provision by the enactment of a law for the appointment of the necessary officers to join in the execution of said survey.

It will be perceived from the accompanying papers that the early demarcation of said boundary line is urgently desired on the part of Texas, and, acquiescing in the importance thereof, I recommend that provision be made by law for the appointment of officers to act in conjunction with those to be appointed by the State of Texas, and that the sum of $10,000 at least be appropriated for the payment of their salaries and necessary incidental expenses.

FRANKLIN PIERCE.

WASHINGTON, *March 2, 1855.*

To the Senate of the United States:

I communicate to the Senate herewith, for its constitutional action thereon, the articles of a treaty negotiated on the 4th of January, 1855, between Joel Palmer, superintendent of Indian affairs in Oregon, and the chiefs of certain confederated tribes of Indians residing in the Willamette Valley of Oregon.

FRANKLIN PIERCE.

EXECUTIVE MANSION, *March 2, 1855.*

To the Senate of the United States:

I herewith submit a report of the Secretary of War, containing all the information that can now be furnished in reply to the resolution of the Senate of the 28th ultimo, requesting "a statement of the number of muskets, rifles, and other arms and equipments delivered to the State arsenals, respectively, the number remaining on hand, and the number sold and accounted for; also, the date and amount of such sales."

FRANKLIN PIERCE.

WASHINGTON, *March 2, 1855.*

To the Senate and House of Representatives of the United States:

I transmit to Congress herewith a communication of this date from the Secretary of the Interior, with accompanying papers,* and recommend that the appropriations therein asked for be made.

FRANKLIN PIERCE.

WASHINGTON, *March 2, 1855.*

To the Senate and House of Representatives of the United States:

I transmit to Congress herewith a communication of this date from the Secretary of the Interior, with its inclosure,† and recommend that the appropriations therein asked for be made.

FRANKLIN PIERCE.

WASHINGTON, *March 3, 1855.*

To the House of Representatives:

I transmit herewith to the House of Representatives a report from the Secretary of State, with accompanying documents,‡ in answer to their resolutions of the 30th of January and 23d February last.

FRANKLIN PIERCE.

VETO MESSAGES.

WASHINGTON, *February 17, 1855.*

To the House of Representatives:

I have received and carefully considered the bill entitled "An act to provide for the ascertainment of claims of American citizens for spoliations committed by the French prior to the 31st of July, 1801," and in the discharge of a duty imperatively enjoined on me by the Constitution I return the same with my objections to the House of Representatives, in which it originated.

In the organization of the Government of the United States the legislative and executive functions were separated and placed in distinct

---

* Estimates of appropriations necessary for carrying out the bounty-land law.
† Additional estimate of appropriations necessary for pay of Indian agents.
‡ Correspondence relative to the causes disturbing the friendly relations between Spain and the United States and instructions to United States diplomatic agents relative to ˙ne same; correspondence relative to Cuba, etc.

hands. Although the President is required from time to time to recommend to the consideration of Congress such measures as he shall judge necessary and expedient, his participation in the formal business of legislation is limited to the single duty, in a certain contingency, of demanding for a bill a particular form of vote prescribed by the Constitution before it can become a law. He is not invested with power to defeat legislation by an absolute veto, but only to restrain it, and is charged with the duty, in case he disapproves a measure, of invoking a second and a more deliberate and solemn consideration of it on the part of Congress. It is not incumbent on the President to sign a bill as a matter of course, and thus merely to authenticate the action of Congress, for he must exercise intelligent judgment or be faithless to the trust reposed in him. If he approve a bill, he shall sign it, but if not he shall return it with his objections to that House in which it shall have originated for such further action as the Constitution demands, which is its enactment, if at all, not by a bare numerical majority, as in the first instance, but by a constitutional majority of two-thirds of both Houses.

While the Constitution thus confers on the legislative bodies the complete power of legislation in all cases, it proceeds, in the spirit of justice, to provide for the protection of the responsibility of the President. It does not compel him to affix the signature of approval to any bill unless it actually have his approbation; for while it requires him to sign if he approve, it, in my judgment, imposes upon him the duty of withholding his signature if he do not approve. In the execution of his official duty in this respect he is not to perform a mere mechanical part, but is to decide and act according to conscientious convictions of the rightfulness or wrongfulness of the proposed law. In a matter as to which he is doubtful in his own mind he may well defer to the majority of the two Houses. Individual members of the respective Houses, owing to the nature, variety, and amount of business pending, must necessarily rely for their guidance in many, perhaps most, cases, when the matters involved are not of popular interest, upon the investigation of appropriate committees, or, it may be, that of a single member, whose attention has been particularly directed to the subject. For similar reasons, but even to a greater extent, from the number and variety of subjects daily urged upon his attention, the President naturally relies much upon the investigation had and the results arrived at by the two Houses, and hence those results, in large classes of cases, constitute the basis upon which his approval rests. The President's responsibility is to the whole people of the United States, as that of a Senator is to the people of a particular State, that of a Representative to the people of a State or district; and it may be safely assumed that he will not resort to the clearly defined and limited power of arresting legislation and calling for reconsideration of any measure except in obedience to requirements of duty: When, however, he entertains a decisive and fixed conclusion, not merely of the unconstitutionality, but of the impropriety, or injustice in other respects, of any measure, if he declare that he approves it he is false to his oath, and he deliberately disregards his constitutional obligations.

I cheerfully recognize the weight of authority which attaches to the action of a majority of the two Houses. But in this case, as in some others, the framers of our Constitution, for wise considerations of public good, provided that nothing less than a two-thirds vote of one or both of the Houses of Congress shall become effective to bind the coordinate departments of the Government, the people, and the several States. If there be anything of seeming invidiousness in the official right thus conferred on the President, it is in appearance only, for the same right of approving or disapproving a bill, according to each one's own judgment, is conferred on every member of the Senate and of the House of Representatives.

It is apparent, therefore, that the circumstances must be extraordinary which would induce the President to withhold approval from a bill involving no violation of the Constitution. The amount of the claims proposed to be discharged by the bill before me, the nature of the transactions in which those claims are alleged to have originated, the length of time during which they have occupied the attention of Congress and the country, present such an exigency. Their history renders it impossible that a President who has participated to any considerable degree in public affairs could have failed to form respecting them a decided opinion upon what he would deem satisfactory grounds. Nevertheless, instead of resting on former opinions, it has seemed to me proper to review and more carefully examine the whole subject, so as satisfactorily to determine the nature and extent of my obligations in the premises.

I feel called upon at the threshold to notice an assertion, often repeated, that the refusal of the United States to satisfy these claims in the manner provided by the present bill rests as a stain on the justice of our country. If it be so, the imputation on the public honor is aggravated by the consideration that the claims are coeval with the present century, and it has been a persistent wrong during that whole period of time. The allegation is that private property has been taken for public use without just compensation, in violation of express provision of the Constitution, and that reparation has been withheld and justice denied until the injured parties have for the most part descended to the grave. But it is not to be forgotten or overlooked that those who represented the people in different capacities at the time when the alleged obligations were incurred, and to whom the charge of injustice attaches in the first instance, have also passed away and borne with them the special information which controlled their decision and, it may be well presumed, constituted the justification of their acts.

If, however, the charge in question be well founded, although its admission would inscribe on our history a page which we might desire most of all to obliterate, and although, if true, it must painfully disturb our confidence in the justice and the high sense of moral and political responsibility of those whose memories we have been taught to cherish with so much reverence and respect, still we have only one course of action left to us, and that is to make the most prompt and ample reparation in our power and consign the wrong as far as may be to forgetfulness.

But no such heavy sentence of condemnation should be lightly passed upon the sagacious and patriotic men who participated in the transactions out of which these claims are supposed to have arisen, and who, from their ample means of knowledge of the general subject in its minute details and from their official position, are peculiarly responsible for whatever there is of wrong or injustice in the decisions of the Government.

Their justification consists in that which constitutes the objection to the present bill, namely, the absence of any indebtedness on the part of the United States. The charge of denial of justice in this case, and consequent stain upon our national character, has not yet been indorsed by the American people. But if it were otherwise, this bill, so far from relieving the past, would only stamp on the present a more deep and indelible stigma. It admits the justice of the claims, concedes that payment has been wrongfully withheld for fifty years, and then proposes not to pay them, but to compound with the public creditors by providing that, whether the claims shall be presented or not, whether the sum appropriated shall pay much or little of what shall be found due, the law itself shall constitute a perpetual bar to all future demands. This is not, in my judgment, the way to atone for wrongs if they exist, nor to meet subsisting obligations.

If new facts, not known or not accessible during the Administration of Mr. Jefferson, Mr. Madison, or Mr. Monroe, had since been brought to light, or new sources of information discovered, this would greatly relieve the subject of embarrassment. But nothing of this nature has occurred.

That those eminent statesmen had the best means of arriving at a correct conclusion no one will deny. That they never recognized the alleged obligation on the part of the Government is shown by the history of their respective Administrations. Indeed, it stands not as a matter of controlling authority, but as a fact of history, that these claims have never since our existence as a nation been deemed by any President worthy of recommendation to Congress.

Claims to payment can rest only on the plea of indebtedness on the part of the Government. This requires that it should be shown that the United States have incurred liability to the claimants, either by such acts as deprived them of their property or by having actually taken it for public use without making just compensation for it.

The first branch of the proposition—that on which an equitable claim to be indemnified by the United States for losses sustained might rest—requires at least a cursory examination of the history of the transactions on which the claims depend. The first link which in the chain of events arrests attention is the treaties of alliance and of amity and commerce between the United States and France negotiated in 1778. By those treaties peculiar privileges were secured to the armed vessels of each of the contracting parties in the ports of the other, the freedom of trade was greatly enlarged, and mutual obligations were incurred by each to guarantee to the other their territorial possessions in America.

In 1792–93, when war broke out between France and Great Britain, the former claimed privileges in American ports which our Government did not admit as deducible from the treaties of 1778, and which it was held were in conflict with obligations to the other belligerent powers. The liberal principle of one of the treaties referred to—that free ships make free goods, and that subsistence and supplies were not contraband of war unless destined to a blockaded port—was found, in a commercial view, to operate disadvantageously to France as compared with her enemy, Great Britain, the latter asserting, under the law of nations, the right to capture as contraband supplies when bound for an enemy's port.

Induced mainly, it is believed, by these considerations, the Government of France decreed on the 9th of May, 1793, the first year of the war, that "the French people are no longer permitted to fulfill toward the neutral powers in general the vows they have so often manifested, and which they constantly make for the full and entire liberty of commerce and navigation," and, as a counter measure to the course of Great Britain, authorized the seizure of neutral vessels bound to an enemy's port in like manner as that was done by her great maritime rival. This decree was made to act retrospectively, and to continue until the enemies of France should desist from depredations on the neutral vessels bound to the ports of France. Then followed the embargo, by which our vessels were detained in Bordeaux; the seizure of British goods on board of our ships, and of the property of American citizens under the pretense that it belonged to English subjects, and the imprisonment of American citizens captured on the high seas.

Against these infractions of existing treaties and violations of our rights as a neutral power we complained and remonstrated. For the property of our injured citizens we demanded that due compensation should be made, and from 1793 to 1797 used every means, ordinary and extraordinary, to obtain redress by negotiation. In the last-mentioned year these efforts were met by a refusal to receive a minister sent by our Government with special instructions to represent the amicable disposition of the Government and people of the United States and their desire to remove jealousies and to restore confidence by showing that the complaints against them

were groundless. Failing in this, another attempt to adjust all differences between the two Republics was made in the form of an extraordinary mission, composed of three distinguished citizens, but the refusal
to receive was offensively repeated, and thus terminated this last effort to
preserve peace and restore kind relations with our early friend and ally,
to whom a debt of gratitude was due which the American people have
never been willing to depreciate or to forget. Years of negotiation had
not only failed to secure indemnity for our citizens and exemption from
further depredation, but these long-continued efforts had brought upon
the Government the suspension of diplomatic intercourse with France
and such indignities as to induce President Adams, in his message of
May 16, 1797, to Congress, convened in special session, to present it as
the particular matter for their consideration and to speak of it in terms
of the highest indignation. Thenceforward the action of our Government
assumed a character which clearly indicates that hope was no longer
entertained from the amicable feeling or justice of the Government of
France, and hence the subsequent measures were those of force.

On the 28th of May, 1798, an act was passed for the employment of
the Navy of the United States against "armed vessels of the Republic
of France," and authorized their capture if "found hovering on the
coast of the United States for the purpose of committing depredations
on the vessels belonging to the citizens thereof;" on the 18th of June,
1798, an act was passed prohibiting commercial intercourse with France
under the penalty of the forfeiture of the vessels so employed; on the
25th of June, the same year, an act to arm the merchant marine to oppose
searches, capture aggressors, and recapture American vessels taken by
the French; on the 28th of June, same year, an act for the condemnation
and sale of French vessels captured by authority of the act of 28th of May
preceding; on the 27th of July, same year, an act abrogating the treaties and the convention which had been concluded between the United
States and France, and declaring "that the same shall not henceforth
be regarded as legally obligatory on the Government or citizens of the
United States;" on the 9th of the same month an act was passed which
enlarged the limits of the hostilities then existing by authorizing our
public vessels to capture armed vessels of France wherever found upon
the high seas, and conferred power on the President to issue commissions to private armed vessels to engage in like service.

These acts, though short of a declaration of war, which would put all
the citizens of each country in hostility with those of the other, were,
nevertheless, actual war, partial in its application, maritime in its character, but which required the expenditure of much of our public treasure
and much of the blood of our patriotic citizens, who, in vessels but little
suited to the purposes of war, went forth to battle on the high seas for
the rights and security of their fellow-citizens and to repel indignities
offered to the national honor.

It is not, then, because of any failure to use all available means, diplomatic and military, to obtain reparation that liability for private claims can have been incurred by the United States, and if there is any pretense for such liability it must flow from the action, not from the neglect, of the United States. The first complaint on the part of France was against the proclamation of President Washington of April 22, 1793. At that early period in the war which involved Austria, Prussia, Sardinia, the United Netherlands, and Great Britain on the one part and France on the other, the great and wise man who was the Chief Executive, as he was and had been the guardian of our then infant Republic, proclaimed that "the duty and interest of the United States require that they should with sincerity and good faith adopt and pursue a conduct friendly and impartial toward the belligerent powers." This attitude of neutrality, it was pretended, was in disregard of the obligations of alliance between the United States and France. And this, together with the often-renewed complaint that the stipulations of the treaties of 1778 had not been observed and executed by the United States, formed the pretext for the series of outrages upon our Government and its citizens which finally drove us to seek redress and safety by an appeal to force. The treaties of 1778, so long the subject of French complaints, are now understood to be the foundation upon which are laid these claims of indemnity from the United States for spoliations committed by the French prior to 1800. The act of our Government which abrogated not only the treaties of 1778, but also the subsequent consular convention of 1788, has already been referred to, and it may be well here to inquire what the course of France was in relation thereto. By the decrees of 9th of May, 1793, 7th of July, 1796, and 2d of March, 1797, the stipulations which were then and subsequently most important to the United States were rendered wholly inoperative. The highly injurious effects which these decrees are known to have produced show how vital were the provisions of treaty which they violated, and make manifest the incontrovertible right of the United States to declare, as the consequence of these acts of the other contracting party, the treaties at an end.

The next step in this inquiry is whether the act declaring the treaties null and void was ever repealed, or whether by any other means the treaties were ever revived so as to be either the subject or the source of national obligation. The war which has been described was terminated by the treaty of Paris of 1800, and to that instrument it is necessary to turn to find how much of preexisting obligations between the two Governments outlived the hostilities in which they had been engaged. By the second article of the treaty of 1800 it was declared that the ministers plenipotentiary of the two parties not being able to agree respecting the treaties of alliance, amity, and commerce of 1778 and the convention of 1788, nor upon the indemnities mutually due or claimed, the parties will negotiate further on these subjects at a convenient time; and until they shall have agreed upon these points the said treaties and convention shall have no operation.

When the treaty was submitted to the Senate of the United States, the second article was disagreed to and the treaty amended by striking it out and inserting a provision that the convention then made should continue in force eight years from the date of ratification, which convention, thus amended, was accepted by the First Consul of France, with the addition of a note explanatory of his construction of the convention, to the effect that by the retrenchment of the second article the two States renounce the respective pretensions which were the object of the said article.

It will be perceived by the language of the second article, as originally framed by the negotiators, that they had found themselves unable to adjust the controversies on which years of diplomacy and of hostilities had been expended, and that they were at last compelled to postpone the discussion of those questions to that most indefinite period, a "convenient time." All, then, of these subjects which was revived by the convention was the right to renew, when it should be convenient to the parties, a discussion which had already exhausted negotiation, involved the two countries in a maritime war, and on which the parties had approached no nearer to concurrence than they were when the controversy began.

The obligations of the treaties of 1778 and the convention of 1788 were mutual, and estimated to be equal. But however onerous they may have been to the United States, they had been abrogated, and were not revived by the convention of 1800, but expressly spoken of as suspended until an event which could only occur by the pleasure of the United States. It seems clear, then, that the United States were relieved of no obligation to France by the retrenchment of the second article of the convention, and if thereby France was relieved of any valid claims against her the United States received no consideration in return, and that if private property was taken by the United States from their own citizens it was not for public use. But it is here proper to inquire whether the United States did relieve France from valid claims against her on the part of citizens of the United States, and did thus deprive them of their property.

The complaints and counter complaints of the two Governments had been that treaties were violated and that both public and individual rights and interests had been sacrificed. The correspondence of our ministers engaged in negotiations, both before and after the convention of 1800, sufficiently proves how hopeless was the effort to obtain full indemnity from France for injuries inflicted on our commerce from 1793 to 1800, unless it should be by an account in which the rival pretensions of the two Governments should each be acknowledged and the balance struck between them.

It is supposable, and may be inferred from the contemporaneous history as probable, that had the United States agreed in 1800 to revive the treaties of 1778 and 1788 with the construction which France had placed upon them, that the latter Government would, on the other hand, have agreed to make indemnity for those spoliations which were committed under the pretext that the United States were faithless to the obligations of the alliance between the two countries.

Hence the conclusion that the United States did not sacrifice private rights or property to get rid of public obligations, but only refused to reassume public obligations for the purpose of obtaining the recognition of the claims of American citizens on the part of France.

All those claims which the French Government was willing to admit were carefully provided for elsewhere in the convention, and the declaration of the First Consul, which was appended in his additional note, had no other application than to the claims which had been mutually made by the Governments, but on which they had never approximated to an adjustment. In confirmation of the fact that our Government did not intend to cease from the prosecution of the just claims of our citizens against France, reference is here made to the annual message of President Jefferson of December 8, 1801, which opens with expressions of his gratification at the restoration of peace among sister nations; and, after speaking of the assurances received from all nations with whom we had principal relations and of the confidence thus inspired that our peace with them would not have been disturbed if they had continued at war with each other, he proceeds to say:

But a cessation of irregularities which had affected the commerce of neutral nations, and of the irritations and injuries produced by them, can not but add to this confidence, and strengthens at the same time the hope that wrongs committed on unoffending friends under a pressure of circumstances will now be reviewed with candor, and will be considered as founding just claims of retribution for the past and new assurance for the future.

The zeal and diligence with which the claims of our citizens against France were prosecuted appear in the diplomatic correspondence of the three years next succeeding the convention of 1800, and the effect of these efforts is made manifest in the convention of 1803, in which provision was made for payment of a class of cases the consideration of which France had at all previous periods refused to entertain, and which are of that very class which it has been often assumed were released by striking out the second article of the convention of 1800. This is shown by reference to the preamble and to the fourth and fifth articles of the convention of 1803, by which were admitted among the debts due by France to citizens of the United States the amounts chargeable for "prizes made at sea in which the appeal has been properly lodged within the time mentioned in the said convention of the 30th of September, 1800;" and this class was further defined to be only "captures of which the council of prizes shall have ordered restitution, it being well understood that the claimant can not have recourse to the United States otherwise than he might have had to the French Republic, and only in case of the insufficiency of the captors.''

If, as was affirmed on all hands, the convention of 1803 was intended to close all questions between the Governments of France and the United States, and 20,000,000 francs were set apart as a sum which might exceed, but could not fall short of, the debts due by France to the citizens of the United States, how are we to reconcile the claim now presented with the estimates made by those who were of the time and immediately connected with the events, and whose intelligence and integrity have in no small degree contributed to the character and prosperity of the country in which we live? Is it rational to assume that the claimants who now present themselves for indemnity by the United States represent debts which would have been admitted and paid by France but for the intervention of the United States? And is it possible to escape from the effect of the voluminous evidence tending to establish the fact that France resisted all these claims; that it was only after long and skillful negotiation that the agents of the United States obtained the recognition of such of the claims as were provided for in the conventions of 1800 and 1803? And is it not conclusive against any pretensions of possible success on the part of the claimants, if left unaided to make their applications to France, that the only debts due to American citizens which have been paid by France are those which were assumed by the United States as part of the consideration in the purchase of Louisiana?

There is little which is creditable either to the judgment or patriotism of those of our fellow-citizens who at this day arraign the justice, the fidelity, or love of country of the men who founded the Republic in representing them as having bartered away the property of individuals to escape from public obligations, and then to have withheld from them just compensation. It has been gratifying to me in tracing the history of these claims to find that ample evidence exists to refute an accusation which would impeach the purity, the justice, and the magnanimity of the illustrious men who guided and controlled the early destinies of the Republic.

I pass from this review of the history of the subject, and, omitting many substantial objections to these claims, proceed to examine somewhat more closely the only grounds upon which they can by possibility be maintained.

Before entering on this it may be proper to state distinctly certain propositions which it is admitted on all hands are essential to prove the obligations of the Government.

First. That at the date of the treaty of September 30, 1800, these claims were valid and subsisting as against France.

Second. That they were released or extinguished by the United States in that treaty and by the manner of its ratification.

Third. That they were so released or extinguished for a consideration valuable to the Government, but in which the claimants had no more interest than any other citizens.

The convention between the French Republic and the United States of America signed at Paris on the 30th day of September, 1800, purports in the preamble to be founded on the equal desire of the First Consul (Napoleon Bonaparte) and the President of the United States to terminate the differences which have arisen between the two States. It declares, in the first place, that there shall be firm, inviolable, and universal peace and a true and sincere friendship between the French Republic and the United States. Next it proceeds, in the second, third, fourth, and fifth articles, to make provision in sundry respects, having reference to past differences and the transition from the state of war between the two countries to that of general and permanent peace. Finally, in the residue of the twenty-seventh article, it stipulates anew the conditions of amity and intercourse, commercial and political, thereafter to exist, and, of course, to be substituted in place of the previous conditions of the treaties of alliance and of commerce and the consular convention, which are thus tacitly but unequivocally recognized as no longer in force, but in effect abrogated, either by the state of war or by the political action of the two Republics.

Except in so far as the whole convention goes to establish the fact that the previous treaties were admitted on both sides to be at an end, none of the articles are directly material to the present question save the following:

ART. II. The ministers plenipotentiary of the two parties not being able to agree at present respecting the treaty of alliance of 6th February, 1778, the treaty of amity and commerce of the same date, and the convention of 14th of November, 1788, nor upon the indemnities mutually due or claimed, the parties will negotiate further on these subjects at a convenient time; and until they may have agreed upon these points the said treaties and convention shall have no operation, and the relations of the two countries shall be regulated as follows:

*   *   *   *   *   *   *

ART. V. The debts contracted by one of the two nations with individuals of the other, or by the individuals of one with the individuals of the other, shall be paid, or the payment may be prosecuted, in the same manner as if there had been no misunderstanding between the two States. But this clause shall not extend to indemnities claimed on account of captures or confiscations.

On this convention being submitted to the Senate of the United States, they consented and advised to its ratification with the following proviso:

Provided, That the second article be expunged, and that the following article be added or inserted: It is agreed that the present convention shall be in force for the term of eight years from the time of the exchange of ratifications.

The spirit and purpose of this change are apparent and unmistakable. The convention as signed by the respective plenipotentiaries did not adjust all the points of controversy. Both nations, however, desired the restoration of peace.   Accordingly, as to those matters in the relations of the two countries concerning which they could agree, they did agree for the time being; and as to the rest, concerning which they could not agree, they suspended and postponed further negotiation.

They abandoned no pretensions, they relinquished no right on either side, but simply adjourned the question until "a convenient time." Meanwhile, and until the arrival of such convenient time, the relations of the two countries were to be regulated by the stipulations of the convention.

Of course the convention was on its face a temporary and provisional one, but in the worst possible form of prospective termination.   It was to cease at a convenient time.   But how should that convenient time be ascertained?   It is plain that such a stipulation, while professedly not disposing of the present controversy, had within itself the germ of a fresh one, for the two Governments might at any moment fall into dispute on the question whether that convenient time had or had not arrived.   The Senate of the United States anticipated and prevented this question by the only possible expedient; that is, the designation of a precise date.   This being done, the remaining parts of the second article became superfluous and useless, for as all the provisions of the convention would expire in eight years, it would necessarily follow that negotiations must be renewed within that period, more especially as the operation of the amendment which covered the whole convention was that even the stipulation of peace in the first article became temporary and expired in eight years, whereas that article, and that article alone, was permanent according to the original tenor of the convention.

The convention thus amended, being submitted to the First Consul, was ratified by him, his act of acceptance being accompanied with the following declaratory note:

The Government of the United States having added in its ratification that the convention should be in force for the space of eight years, and having omitted the second article, the Government of the French Republic consents to accept, ratify, and confirm the above convention with the addition importing that the convention shall be in force for the space of eight years and with the retrenchment of the second article: *Provided*, That by this retrenchment the two States renounce the respective pretensions which are the object of the said article.

The convention, as thus ratified by the First Consul, having been again submitted to the Senate of the United States, that body resolved that "they considered the convention as fully ratified," and returned the same to the President for promulgation, and it was accordingly promulgated in the usual form by President Jefferson.

Now it is clear that in simply resolving that "they considered the convention as fully ratified" the Senate did in fact abstain from any express declaration of dissent or assent to the construction put by the First Consul on the retrenchment of the second article.   If any inference beyond this can be drawn from their resolution, it is that they regarded the proviso annexed by the First Consul to his declaration of acceptance as foreign to the subject, as nugatory, or as without consequence or effect. Notwithstanding this proviso, they considered the ratification as full. If the new proviso made any change in the previous import of the convention, then it was not full; and in considering it a full ratification they in substance deny that the proviso did in any respect change the tenor of the convention.

By the second article, as it originally stood, neither Republic had relinquished its existing rights or pretensions, either as to other previous treaties or the indemnities mutually due or claimed, but only deferred the consideration of them to a convenient time. By the amendment of the Senate of the United States that convenient time, instead of being left indefinite, was fixed at eight years; but no right or pretension of either party was surrendered or abandoned.

If the Senate erred in assuming that the proviso added by the First Consul did not affect the question, then the transaction would amount to nothing more than to have raised a new question, to be disposed of on resuming the negotiations, namely, the question whether the proviso of the First Consul did or not modify or impair the effect of the convention as it had been ratified by the Senate.

That such, and such only, was the true meaning and effect of the transaction; that it was not, and was not intended to be, a relinquishment by the United States of any existing claim on France, and especially that it was not an abandonment of any claims of individual citizens, nor the set off of these against any conceded national obligations to France, is shown by the fact that President Jefferson did at once resume and prosecute to successful conclusion negotiations to obtain from France indemnification for the claims of citizens of the United States existing at the date of that convention; for on the 30th of April, 1803, three treaties were concluded at Paris between the United States of America and the French Republic, one of which embraced the cession of Louisiana; another stipulated for the payment of 60,000,000 francs by the United States to France; and a third provided that, for the satisfaction of sums due by France to citizens of the United States at the conclusion of the convention of September 30, 1800, and in express compliance with the second and fifth articles thereof, a further sum of 20,000,000 francs should be appropriated and paid by the United States. In the preamble to the first of these treaties, which ceded Louisiana, it is set forth that—

The President of the United States of America and the First Consul of the French Republic, in the name of the French people, desiring to remove all source of misunderstanding relative to objects of discussion mentioned in the second and fifth articles of the convention of the 8th Vendémiaire, an 9 (30th September, 1800), relative to the rights claimed by the United States in virtue of the treaty concluded at Madrid the 27th of October, 1795, between His Catholic Majesty and the said United States, and willing to strengthen the union and friendship which at the time of the said convention was happily reestablished between the two nations, have respectively named their plenipotentiaries, * * * who * * * have agreed to the following articles.

Here is the most distinct and categorical declaration of the two Governments that the matters of claim in the second article of the convention of 1800 had not been ceded away, relinquished, or set off, but they were still subsisting subjects of demand against France. The same declaration appears in equally emphatic language in the third of these treaties, bearing the same date, the preamble of which recites that—

The President of the United States of America and the First Consul of the French Republic, in the name of the French people, having by a treaty of this date terminated all difficulties relative to Louisiana and established on a solid foundation the friendship which unites the two nations, and being desirous, in compliance with the second and fifth articles of the convention of the 8th Vendémiaire, ninth year of the French Republic (30th September, 1800), to secure the payment of the sums due by France to the citizens of the United States, have appointed plenipotentiaries—

who agreed to the following among other articles:

ART. I. The debts due by France to citizens of the United States, contracted before the 8th of Vendémiaire, ninth year of the French Republic (30th September, 1800), shall be paid according to the following regulations, with interest at 6 per cent, to commence from the periods when the accounts and vouchers were presented to the French Government.

ART. II. The debts provided for by the preceding article are those whose result is comprised in the conjectural note annexed to the present convention, and which, with the interest, can not exceed the sum of 20,000,000 francs. The claims comprised in the said note which fall within the exceptions of the following articles shall not be admitted to the benefit of this provision.

*   *   *   *   *   *

ART. IV. It is expressly agreed that the preceding articles shall comprehend no debts but such as are due to citizens of the United States who have been and are yet creditors of France for supplies, for embargoes, and prizes made at sea in which the appeal has been properly lodged within the time mentioned in the said convention, 8th Vendémiaire, ninth year (30th September, 1800).

ART. V. The preceding articles shall apply only, first, to captures of which the council of prizes shall have ordered restitution, it being well understood that the claimant can not have recourse to the United States otherwise than he might have had to the Government of the French Republic, and only in case of insufficiency of the captors; second, the debts mentioned in the said fifth article of the convention, contracted before the 8th Vendémiaire, an 9 (30th September, 1800), the payment of which has been heretofore claimed of the actual Government of France and for which the creditors have a right to the protection of the United States; the said fifth article does not comprehend prizes whose condemnation has been or shall be confirmed. It is the express intention of the contracting parties not to extend the benefit of the present convention to reclamations of American citizens who shall have established houses of commerce in France, England, or other countries than the United States, in partnership with foreigners, and who by that reason and the nature of their commerce ought to be regarded as domiciliated in the places where such houses exist. All agreements and bargains concerning merchandise which shall not be the property of American citizens are equally excepted from the benefit of the said convention, saving, however, to such persons their claims in like manner as if this treaty had not been made.

*   *   *   *   *   *   *

ART. XII. In case of claims for debts contracted by the Government of France with citizens of the United States since the 8th Vendémiaire, ninth year (30th September, 1800), not being comprised in this convention, may be pursued, and the payment demanded in the same manner as if it had not been made.

Other articles of the treaty provide for the appointment of agents to liquidate the claims intended to be secured, and for the payment of them as allowed at the Treasury of the United States. The following is the concluding clause of the tenth article:

The rejection of any claim shall have no other effect than to exempt the United States from the payment of it, the French Government reserving to itself the right to decide definitively on such claim so far as it concerns itself.

Now, from the provisions of the treaties thus collated the following deductions undeniably follow, namely:

First. Neither the second article of the convention of 1800, as it originally stood, nor the retrenchment of that article, nor the proviso in the ratification by the First Consul, nor the action of the Senate of the United States thereon, was regarded by either France or the United States as the renouncement of any claims of American citizens against France.

Second. On the contrary, in the treaties of 1803 the two Governments took up the question precisely where it was left on the day of the signature of that of 1800, without suggestion on the part of France that the claims of our citizens were excluded by the retrenchment of the second article or the note of the First Consul, and proceeded to make ample provision for such as France could be induced to admit were justly due, and they were accordingly discharged in full, with interest, by the United States in the stead and behalf of France.

Third. The United States, not having admitted in the convention of 1800 that they were under any obligations to France by reason of the abrogation of the treaties of 1778 and 1788, persevered in this view of the question by the tenor of the treaties of 1803, and therefore had no such national obligation to discharge, and did not, either in purpose or in fact, at any time undertake to discharge themselves from any such obligation at the expense and with the property of individual citizens of the United States.

Fourth. By the treaties of 1803 the United States obtained from France the acknowledgment and payment, as part of the indemnity for the cession of Louisiana, of claims of citizens of the United States for spoliations, so far as France would admit her liability in the premises; but even then the United States did not relinquish any claim of American citizens not provided for by those treaties; so far from it, to the honor of France be it remembered, she expressly reserved to herself the right to reconsider any rejected claims of citizens of the United States.

Fifth. As to claims of citizens of the United States against France, which had been the subject of controversy between the two countries prior to the signature of the convention of 1800, and the further consideration of which was reserved for a more convenient time by the second article of that convention, for these claims, and these only, provision was made in the treaties of 1803, all other claims being expressly excluded by them from their scope and purview.

It is not to be overlooked, though not necessary to the conclusion, that by the convention between France and the United States of the 4th of July, 1831, complete provision was made for the liquidation, discharge, and payment on both sides of all claims of citizens of either against the other for unlawful seizures, captures, sequestrations, or destructions of the vessels, cargoes, or other property, without any limitation of time, so as in terms to run back to the date of the last preceding settlement, at least to that of 1803, if not to the commencement of our national relations with France.

This review of the successive treaties between France and the United States has brought my mind to the undoubting conviction that while the United States have in the most ample and the completest manner discharged their duty toward such of their citizens as may have been at any time aggrieved by acts of the French Government, so also France has honorably discharged herself of all obligations in the premises toward the United States. To concede what this bill assumes would be to impute undeserved reproach both to France and to the United States.

I am, of course, aware that the bill proposes only to provide indemnification for such valid claims of citizens of the United States against France as shall not have been stipulated for and embraced in any of the treaties enumerated. But in excluding all such claims it excludes all, in fact, for which, during the negotiations, France could be persuaded to agree that she was in any wise liable to the United States or our citizens. What remains? And for what is five millions appropriated? In view of what has been said there would seem to be no ground on which to raise a liability of the United States, unless it be the assumption that the United States are to be considered the insurer and the guarantor of all claims, of whatever nature, which any individual citizen may have against a foreign nation.

FRANKLIN PIERCE.

WASHINGTON, *March 3*, [*1855.*]

To the House of Representatives:

I return herewith to the House of Representatives, in which it originated, the bill entitled "An act making appropriations for the transportation of the United States mail, by ocean steamers and otherwise, during the fiscal years ending the 30th of June, 1855, and the 30th of June, 1856," with a brief statement of the reasons which prevent its receiving my approval. The bill provides, among other things, that—

The following sums be, and the same are hereby, appropriated, to be paid out of any money in the Treasury not otherwise appropriated, for the year ending the 30th of June, 1856:

For transportation of the mails from New York to Liverpool and back, $858,000;

and that the proviso contained in the first section of the act entitled "An act to supply deficiencies in the appropriations for the service of the fiscal year ending the 30th of June, 1852," approved the 21st of July, 1852, be, and the same is hereby, repealed: *Provided*, That Edward K. Collins and his associates shall proceed with all due diligence to build another steamship, in accordance with the terms of their contract, and have the same ready for the mail service in two years from and after the passage of this act; and if the said steamship is not ready within the time above mentioned, by reason of any neglect or want of diligence on their part, then the said Edward K. Collins and his associates shall carry the United States mails between New York and Liverpool from the expiration of the said two years, every fortnight, free of any charge to the Government, until the new steamship shall have commenced the said mail service.

The original contract was predicated upon the proposition of E. K. Collins of March 6, 1846, made with abundant means of knowledge as to the advantages and disadvantages of the terms which he then submitted for the acceptance of the Government. The proposition was in the following terms:

WASHINGTON, *March 6, 1846.*

E. K. Collins and his associates propose to carry the United States mail between New York and Liverpool twice each month during eight months of the year and once a month during the other four months for the sum of $385,000 per annum, payable quarterly. For this purpose they will agree to build five steamships of not less than 2,000 tons measurement and of 1,000 horsepower each, which vessels shall be built for great speed and sufficiently strong for war purposes.

Four of said vessels to be ready for service in eighteen months from the signing of the contract. The fifth vessel to be built as early as possibly practicable, and when not employed in the mail service to be subject to the orders of the Government for carrying dispatches, for which service a fair compensation is to be paid. Contract to be for the term of ten years. It is also proposed to secure to the United States the privilege of purchasing said steamships whenever they may be required for public purposes, at a fair valuation, to be ascertained by appraisers appointed by the United States and by the owners. EDWARD K. COLLINS.

The act of March 3, 1847, provides—

That from and immediately after the passage of this act it shall be the duty of the Secretary of the Navy to accept, on the part of the Government of the United States, the proposals of E. K. Collins and his associates, of the city of New York, submitted to the Postmaster-General, and dated at Washington, March 6, 1846, for the transportation of the United States mail between New York and Liverpool, and to contract with the said E. K. Collins and his associates for the faithful fulfillment of the stipulations therein contained, and in accordance with the provisions of this act.

And under this proposition and enactment the original contract was made.

According to the terms of that contract the parties were to receive from the United States for twenty round trips each year the sum of $19,250 the trip, or $385,000 per annum; and they were to construct and provide five ships of a stipulated size and quality for the performance of this or other service for the Government.

Of the ships contracted for, only four have been furnished—the *Atlantic, Pacific, Arctic,* and *Baltic*—and the present bill proposes to dispense entirely with the original condition of a fifth ship, by only requiring the construction of one, which would but supply the place of the *Arctic*, recently lost by peril of the sea. Certain minor conditions involving expense to the contractors, among which was one for the accommodation and subsistence of a certain number of passed midshipmen on each vessel, had previously been dispensed with on the part of the United States.

By act of Congress of July 21, 1852, the amount of compensation to the contractors was increased from $19,250 to $33,000 a trip and the number of trips from twenty to twenty-six each year, making the whole compensation $858,000 per annum. During the period of time from the commencement of the service of these contractors, on the 27th of April, 1850, to the end of the last fiscal year, June 30, 1854, the sum paid to them by the United States amounted to $2,620,906, without reckoning public money advanced on loan to aid them in the construction of the ships; while the whole amount of postages derived to the Department has been only $734,056, showing an excess of expenditure above receipts of $1,886,440 to the charge of the Government. In the meantime, in addition to the payments from the Treasury, the parties have been in the enjoyment of large receipts from the transportation of passengers and merchandise, the profits of which are in addition to the amount allowed by the United States.

It does not appear that the liberal conditions heretofore enjoyed by the parties were less than a proper compensation for the service to be performed, including whatever there may have been of hazard in a new undertaking, nor that any hardship can be justly alleged calling for relief on the part of the Government.

On the other hand, the construction of five ships of great speed, and sufficiently strong for war purposes, and the services of passed midshipmen on board of them, so as thus to augment the contingent force and the actual efficiency of the Navy, were among the inducements of the Government to enter into the contract.

The act of July 21, 1852, provides "that it shall be in the power of Congress at any time after the 31st day of December, 1854, to terminate the arrangement for the additional allowance herein provided for upon giving six months' notice;" and it will be seen that, with the exception of the six additional trips required by the act of July 21, 1852, there has been no departure from the original engagement but to relieve the contractors from obligation, and yet by the act last named the compensation was increased from $385,000 to $858,000, with no other protection to the public interests provided than the right which Congress reserved to itself to terminate the contract, so far as this increased compensation was concerned, after six months' notice. This last provision, certainly a primary consideration for the more generous action of the Government, the present bill proposes to repeal, so as to leave Congress no power to terminate the new arrangement.

To this repeal the objections are, in my mind, insuperable, because in terms it deprives the United States of all future discretion as to the increased service and compensation, whatever changes may occur in the art of navigation, its expenses, or the policy and political condition of the country. The gravity of this objection is enhanced by other considerations. While the contractors are to be paid a compensation nearly double the rate of the original contract, they are exempted from several of its conditions, which has the effect of adding still more to that rate; while the further advantage is conceded to them of placing their new privileges beyond the control even of Congress.

It will be regarded as a less serious objection than that already stated, but one which should not be overlooked, that the privileges bestowed upon the contractors are without corresponding advantages to the Government, which receives no sufficient pecuniary or other return for the immense outlay involved, which could obtain the same service of other parties at less cost, and which, if the bill becomes a law, will pay them a large amount of public money without adequate consideration; that is, will in effect confer a gratuity whilst nominally making provision for the transportation of the mails of the United States.

To provide for making a donation of such magnitude and to give to the arrangement the character of permanence which this bill proposes would be to deprive commercial enterprise of the benefits of free competition and to establish a monopoly in violation of the soundest principles of public policy and of doubtful compatibility with the Constitution.

I am, of course, not unmindful of the fact that the bill comprises various other appropriations which are more or less important to the public interests, for which reason my objections to it are communicated at the first meeting of the House following its presentation to me, in the hope that by amendment to bills now pending or otherwise suitable provision for all the objects in question may be made before the adjournment of Congress.

FRANKLIN PIERCE.

PROCLAMATIONS.

BY THE PRESIDENT OF THE UNITED STATES OF AMERICA.

A PROCLAMATION.

Whereas by an act of the Congress of the United States approved the 5th day of August, 1854, entitled "An act to carry into effect a treaty between the United States and Great Britain signed on the 5th day of June, 1854," it is provided that whenever the President of the United States shall receive satisfactory evidence that the Imperial Parliament of Great Britain and the Provincial Parliaments of Canada, New Brunswick,

Nova Scotia, and Prince Edwards Island have passed laws on their part to give full effect to the provisions of the said treaty, he is authorized to issue his proclamation declaring that he has such evidence; and

Whereas satisfactory information has been received by me that the Imperial Parliament of Great Britain and the Provincial Parliaments of Canada, New Brunswick, Nova Scotia, and Prince Edwards Island have passed laws on their part to give full effect to the provisions of the treaty aforesaid:

Now, therefore, I, Franklin Pierce, President of the United States of America, do hereby declare and proclaim that from this date the following articles, being the growth and produce of the said Provinces of Canada, New Brunswick, Nova Scotia, and Prince Edwards Island, to wit: Grain, flour, and breadstuffs of all kinds; animals of all kinds; fresh, smoked, and salted meats; cotton wool, seeds and vegetables, undried fruits, dried fruits, fish of all kinds, products of fish and all other creatures living in the water, poultry, eggs; hides, furs, skins, or tails, undressed; stone or marble in its crude or unwrought state, slate, butter, cheese, tallow, lard, horns, manures, ores of metals of all kinds, coal, pitch, tar, turpentine, ashes; timber and lumber of all kinds, round, hewed, and sawed, unmanufactured in whole or in part; firewood; plants, shrubs, and trees; pelts, wool, fish oil, rice, broom corn, and bark; gypsum, ground or unground; hewn or wrought or unwrought burr or grind stones; dyestuffs; flax, hemp, and tow, unmanufactured; unmanufactured tobacco, rags—shall be introduced into the United States free of duty so long as the said treaty shall remain in force, subject, however, to be suspended in relation to the trade with Canada on the condition mentioned in the fourth article of the said treaty, and that all the other provisions of the said treaty shall go into effect and be observed on the part of the United States.

Given under my hand, at the city of Washington, the 16th day of March, A. D. 1855, and of the Independence of the United
[SEAL.] States the seventy-ninth.

FRANKLIN PIERCE.

By the President:

W. L. MARCY,
Secretary of State.

BY THE PRESIDENT OF THE UNITED STATES OF AMERICA.

A PROCLAMATION.

Whereas the act of Congress of the 28th of September, 1850, entitled "An act to create additional collection districts in the State of California and to change the existing district therein, and to modify the existing collection districts in the United States," extends to merchandise warehoused under bond the privilege of being exported to the British North

American Provinces adjoining the United States in the manner prescribed in the act of Congress of the 3d of March, 1845, which designates certain frontier ports through which merchandise may be exported, and further provides "that such other ports situated on the frontiers of the United States adjoining the British North American Provinces as may hereafter be found expedient may have extended to them the like privileges on the recommendation of the Secretary of the Treasury and proclamation duly made by the President of the United States specially designating the ports to which the aforesaid privileges are to be extended:"

Now, therefore, I, Franklin Pierce, President of the United States of America, in accordance with the recommendation of the Secretary of the Treasury, do hereby declare and proclaim that the ports of Rouses Point, Cape Vincent, Suspension Bridge, and Dunkirk, in the State of New York; Swanton, Alburg, and Island Pond, in the State of Vermont; Toledo, in the State of Ohio; Chicago, in the State of Illinois; Milwaukee, in the State of Wisconsin; Michilimackinac, in the State of Michigan; Eastport, in the State of Maine; and Pembina, in the Territory of Minnesota, are and shall be entitled to all the privileges in regard to the exportation of merchandise in bond to the British North American Provinces adjoining the United States which are extended to the ports enumerated in the seventh section of the act of Congress of the 3d of March, 1845, aforesaid, from and after the date of this proclamation.

In witness whereof I have hereunto set my hand and caused the seal of the United States to be affixed.

Done at the city of Washington, this 2d day of July, A. D. [SEAL.] 1855, and of the Independence of the United States of America the seventy-ninth.   FRANKLIN PIERCE.

By the President:
  W. L. MARCY,
      Secretary of State.

THIRD ANNUAL MESSAGE.

WASHINGTON, *December 31, 1855.*

Fellow-Citizens of the Senate and of the House of Representatives:

The Constitution of the United States provides that Congress shall assemble annually on the first Monday of December, and it has been usual for the President to make no communication of a public character to the Senate and House of Representatives until advised of their readiness to receive it. I have deferred to this usage until the close of the first month of the session, but my convictions of duty will not permit me longer to postpone the discharge of the obligation enjoined by the

Constitution upon the President "to give to the Congress information of the state of the Union and recommend to their consideration such measures as he shall judge necessary and expedient."

It is matter of congratulation that the Republic is tranquilly advancing in a career of prosperity and peace.

Whilst relations of amity continue to exist between the United States and all foreign powers, with some of them grave questions are depending which may require the consideration of Congress.

Of such questions, the most important is that which has arisen out of the negotiations with Great Britain in reference to Central America.

By the convention concluded between the two Governments on the 19th of April, 1850, both parties covenanted that "neither will ever" "occupy, or fortify, or colonize, or assume or exercise any dominion over Nicaragua. Costa Rica, the Mosquito Coast, or any part of Central America."

It was the undoubted understanding of the United States in making this treaty that all the present States of the former Republic of Central America and the entire territory of each would thenceforth enjoy complete independence, and that both contracting parties engaged equally and to the same extent, for the present and for the future, that if either then had any claim of right in Central America such claim and all occupation or authority under it were unreservedly relinquished by the stipulations of the convention, and that no dominion was thereafter to be exercised or assumed in any part of Central America by Great Britain or the United States.

This Government consented to restrictions in regard to a region of country wherein we had specific and peculiar interests only upon the conviction that the like restrictions were in the same sense obligatory on Great Britain. But for this understanding of the force and effect of the convention it would never have been concluded by us.

So clear was this understanding on the part of the United States that in correspondence contemporaneous with the ratification of the convention it was distinctly expressed that the mutual covenants of nonoccupation were not intended to apply to the British establishment at the Balize. This qualification is to be ascribed to the fact that, in virtue of successive treaties with previous sovereigns of the country, Great Britain had obtained a concession of the right to cut mahogany or dyewoods at the Balize, but with positive exclusion of all domain or sovereignty; and thus it confirms the natural construction and understood import of the treaty as to all the rest of the region to which the stipulations applied.

It, however, became apparent at an early day after entering upon the discharge of my present functions that Great Britain still continued in the exercise or assertion of large authority in all that part of Central America commonly called the Mosquito Coast, and covering the entire length of the State of Nicaragua and a part of Costa Rica; that she regarded the Balize as her absolute domain and was gradually extending its limits at the expense of the State of Honduras, and that she had formally colonized a considerable insular group known as the Bay Islands, and belonging of right to that State.

All these acts or pretensions of Great Britain, being contrary to the rights of the States of Central America and to the manifest tenor of her stipulations with the United States as understood by this Government, have been made the subject of negotiation through the American minister in London. I transmit herewith the instructions to him on the subject and the correspondence between him and the British secretary for foreign affairs, by which you will perceive that the two Governments differ widely and irreconcilably as to the construction of the convention and its effect on their respective relations to Central America.

Great Britain so construes the convention as to maintain unchanged all her previous pretensions over the Mosquito Coast and in different parts of Central America. These pretensions as to the Mosquito Coast are founded on the assumption of political relation between Great Britain and the remnant of a tribe of Indians on that coast, entered into at a time when the whole country was a colonial possession of Spain. It can not be successfully controverted that by the public law of Europe and America no possible act of such Indians or their predecessors could confer on Great Britain any political rights.

Great Britain does not allege the assent of Spain as the origin of her claims on the Mosquito Coast. She has, on the contrary, by repeated and successive treaties renounced and relinquished all pretensions of her own and recognized the full and sovereign rights of Spain in the most unequivocal terms. Yet these pretensions, so without solid foundation in the beginning and thus repeatedly abjured, were at a recent period revived by Great Britain against the Central American States, the legitimate successors to all the ancient jurisdiction of Spain in that region. They were first applied only to a defined part of the coast of Nicaragua, afterwards to the whole of its Atlantic coast, and lastly to a part of the coast of Costa Rica, and they are now reasserted to this extent notwithstanding engagements to the United States.

On the eastern coast of Nicaragua and Costa Rica the interference of Great Britain, though exerted at one time in the form of military occupation of the port of San Juan del Norte, then in the peaceful possession of the appropriate authorities of the Central American States, is now presented by her as the rightful exercise of a protectorship over the Mosquito tribe of Indians.

But the establishment at the Balize, now reaching far beyond its treaty limits into the State of Honduras, and that of the Bay Islands, appertaining of right to the same State, are as distinctly colonial governments as those of Jamaica or Canada, and therefore contrary to the very letter, as well as the spirit, of the convention with the United States as it was at the time of ratification and now is understood by this Government.

The interpretation which the British Government thus, in assertion and act, persists in ascribing to the convention entirely changes its character. While it holds us to all our obligations, it in a great measure releases Great Britain from those which constituted the consideration of this Government for entering into the convention. It is impossible, in my judgment, for the United States to acquiesce in such a construction of the respective relations of the two Governments to Central America.

To a renewed call by this Government upon Great Britain to abide by and carry into effect the stipulations of the convention according to its obvious import by withdrawing from the possession or colonization of portions of the Central American States of Honduras, Nicaragua, and Costa Rica, the British Government has at length replied, affirming that the operation of the treaty is prospective only and did not require Great Britain to abandon or contract any possessions held by her in Central America at the date of its conclusion.

This reply substitutes a partial issue in the place of the general one presented by the United States. The British Government passes over the question of the rights of Great Britain, real or supposed, in Central America, and assumes that she had such rights at the date of the treaty and that those rights comprehended the protectorship of the Mosquito Indians, the extended jurisdiction and limits of the Balize, and the colony of the Bay Islands, and thereupon proceeds by implication to infer that if the stipulations of the treaty be merely future in effect Great Britain may still continue to hold the contested portions of Central America. The United States can not admit either the inference or the premises. We steadily deny that at the date of the treaty Great Britain had any possessions there other than the limited and peculiar establishment at the Balize, and maintain that if she had any they were surrendered by the convention.

This Government, recognizing the obligations of the treaty, has, of course, desired to see it executed in good faith by both parties, and in the discussion, therefore, has not looked to rights which we might assert independently of the treaty in consideration of our geographical position and of other circumstances which create for us relations to the Central American States different from those of any government of Europe.

The British Government, in its last communication, although well knowing the views of the United States, still declares that it sees no reason why a conciliatory spirit may not enable the two Governments to overcome all obstacles to a satisfactory adjustment of the subject.

Assured of the correctness of the construction of the treaty constantly adhered to by this Government and resolved to insist on the rights of the United States, yet actuated also by the same desire which is avowed by the British Government, to remove all causes of serious misunderstanding between two nations associated by so many ties of interest and kindred, it has appeared to me proper not to consider an amicable solution of the controversy hopeless.

There is, however, reason to apprehend that with Great Britain in the actual occupation of the disputed territories, and the treaty therefore practically null so far as regards our rights, this international difficulty can not long remain undetermined without involving in serious danger the friendly relations which it is the interest as well as the duty of both countries to cherish and preserve. It will afford me sincere gratification if future efforts shall result in the success anticipated heretofore with more confidence than the aspect of the case permits me now to entertain.

One other subject of discussion between the United States and Great Britain has grown out of the attempt, which the exigencies of the war in which she is engaged with Russia induced her to make, to draw recruits from the United States.

It is the traditional and settled policy of the United States to maintain impartial neutrality during the wars which from time to time occur among the great powers of the world. Performing all the duties of neutrality toward the respective belligerent states, we may reasonably expect them not to interfere with our lawful enjoyment of its benefits. Notwithstanding the existence of such hostilities, our citizens retained the individual right to continue all their accustomed pursuits, by land or by sea, at home or abroad, subject only to such restrictions in this relation as the laws of war, the usage of nations, or special treaties may impose; and it is our sovereign right that our territory and jurisdiction shall not be invaded by either of the belligerent parties for the transit of their armies, the operations of their fleets, the levy of troops for their service, the fitting out of cruisers by or against either, or any other act or incident of war. And these undeniable rights of neutrality, individual and national, the United States will under no circumstances surrender.

In pursuance of this policy, the laws of the United States do not forbid their citizens to sell to either of the belligerent powers articles contraband of war or take munitions of war or soldiers on board their private ships for transportation; and although in so doing the individual citizen exposes his property or person to some of the hazards of war, his acts do not involve any breach of national neutrality nor of themselves implicate the Government. Thus, during the progress of the present war in Europe, our citizens have, without national responsibility therefor, sold gunpowder and arms to all buyers, regardless of the destination of those articles. Our merchantmen have been, and still continue to be, largely employed by Great Britain and by France in transporting troops, provisions, and munitions of war to the principal seat of military operations and in bringing home their sick and wounded soldiers; but such use of our mercantile marine is not interdicted either by the international or by our municipal law, and therefore does not compromit our neutral relations with Russia

But our municipal law, in accordance with the law of nations, peremptorily forbids not only foreigners, but our own citizens, to fit out within the United States a vessel to commit hostilities against any state with which the United States are at peace, or to increase the force of any foreign armed vessel intended for such hostilities against a friendly state.

Whatever concern may have been felt by either of the belligerent powers lest private armed cruisers or other vessels in the service of one might be fitted out in the ports of this country to depredate on the property of the other, all such fears have proved to be utterly groundless. Our citizens have been withheld from any such act or purpose by good faith and by respect for the law.

While the laws of the Union are thus peremptory in their prohibition of the equipment or armament of belligerent cruisers in our ports, they provide not less absolutely that no person shall, within the territory or jurisdiction of the United States, enlist or enter himself, or hire or retain another person to enlist or enter himself, or to go beyond the limits or jurisdiction of the United States with intent to be enlisted or entered, in the service of any foreign state, either as a soldier or as a marine or seaman on board of any vessel of war, letter of marque, or privateer. And these enactments are also in strict conformity with the law of nations, which declares that no state has the right to raise troops for land or sea service in another state without its consent, and that, whether forbidden by the municipal law or not, the very attempt to do it without such consent is an attack on the national sovereignty.

Such being the public rights and the municipal law of the United States, no solicitude on the subject was entertained by this Government when, a year since, the British Parliament passed an act to provide for the enlistment of foreigners in the military service of Great Britain. Nothing on the face of the act or in its public history indicated that the British Government proposed to attempt recruitment in the United States, nor did it ever give intimation of such intention to this Government. It was matter of surprise, therefore, to find subsequently that the engagement of persons within the United States to proceed to Halifax, in the British Province of Nova Scotia, and there enlist in the service of Great Britain, was going on extensively, with little or no disguise. Ordinary legal steps were immediately taken to arrest and punish parties concerned, and so put an end to acts infringing the municipal law and derogatory to our sovereignty. Meanwhile suitable representations on the subject were addressed to the British Government.

Thereupon it became known, by the admission of the British Government itself, that the attempt to draw recruits from this country originated with it, or at least had its approval and sanction; but it also appeared that the public agents engaged in it had "stringent instructions" not to violate the municipal law of the United States.

It is difficult to understand how it should have been supposed that troops could be raised here by Great Britain without violation of the municipal law. The unmistakable object of the law was to prevent every such act which if performed must be either in violation of the law or in studied evasion of it, and in either alternative the act done would be alike injurious to the sovereignty of the United States.

In the meantime the matter acquired additional importance by the recruitments in the United States not being discontinued, and the disclosure of the fact that they were prosecuted upon a systematic plan devised by official authority; that recruiting rendezvous had been opened in our principal cities and depots for the reception of recruits established on our frontier, and the whole business conducted under the supervision and by the regular cooperation of British officers, civil and military, some in the North American Provinces and some in the United States. The complicity of those officers in an undertaking which could only be accomplished by defying our laws, throwing suspicion over our attitude of neutrality, and disregarding our territorial rights is conclusively proved by the evidence elicited on the trial of such of their agents as have been apprehended and convicted. Some of the officers thus implicated are of high official position, and many of them beyond our jurisdiction, so that legal proceedings could not reach the source of the mischief.

These considerations, and the fact that the cause of complaint was not a mere casual occurrence, but a deliberate design, entered upon with full knowledge of our laws and national policy and conducted by responsible public functionaries, impelled me to present the case to the British Government, in order to secure not only a cessation of the wrong, but its reparation. The subject is still under discussion, the result of which will be communicated to you in due time.

I repeat the recommendation submitted to the last Congress, that provision be made for the appointment of a commissioner, in connection with Great Britain, to survey and establish the boundary line which divides the Territory of Washington from the contiguous British possessions. By reason of the extent and importance of the country in dispute, there has been imminent danger of collision between the subjects of Great Britain and the citizens of the United States, including their respective authorities, in that quarter. The prospect of a speedy arrangement has contributed hitherto to induce on both sides forbearance to assert by force what each claims as a right. Continuance of delay on the part of the two Governments to act in the matter will increase the dangers and difficulties of the controversy.

Misunderstanding exists as to the extent, character, and value of the possessory rights of the Hudsons Bay Company and the property of the Pugets Sound Agricultural Company reserved in our treaty with Great Britain relative to the Territory of Oregon. I have reason to believe that a cession of the rights of both companies to the United States, which would be the readiest means of terminating all questions, can be obtained on reasonable terms, and with a view to this end I present the subject to the attention of Congress.

The colony of Newfoundland, having enacted the laws required by the treaty of the 5th of June, 1854, is now placed on the same footing in respect to commercial intercourse with the United States as the other British North American Provinces.

The commission which that treaty contemplated, for determining the rights of fishery in rivers and mouths of rivers on the coasts of the United States and the British North American Provinces, has been organized, and has commenced its labors, to complete which there are needed further appropriations for the service of another season.

In pursuance of the authority conferred by a resolution of the Senate of the United States passed on the 3d of March last, notice was given to Denmark on the 14th day of April of the intention of this Government to avail itself of the stipulation of the subsisting convention of friendship, commerce, and navigation between that Kingdom and the United States whereby either party might after ten years terminate the same at the expiration of one year from the date of notice for that purpose.

The considerations which led me to call the attention of Congress to that convention and induced the Senate to adopt the resolution referred to still continue in full force. The convention contains an article which, although it does not directly engage the United States to submit to the imposition of tolls on the vessels and cargoes of Americans passing into or from the Baltic Sea during the continuance of the treaty, yet may by possibility be construed as implying such submission. The exaction of those tolls not being justified by any principle of international law, it became the right and duty of the United States to relieve themselves from the implication of engagement on the subject, so as to be perfectly free to act in the premises in such way as their public interests and honor shall demand.

I remain of the opinion that the United States ought not to submit to the payment of the Sound dues, not so much because of their amount, which is a secondary matter, but because it is in effect the recognition of the right of Denmark to treat one of the great maritime highways of nations as a close sea, and prevent the navigation of it as a privilege, for which tribute may be imposed upon those who have occasion to use it.

This Government on a former occasion, not unlike the present, signalized its determination to maintain the freedom of the seas and of the great natural channels of navigation. The Barbary States had for a long time coerced the payment of tribute from all nations whose ships frequented the Mediterranean. To the last demand of such payment made by them the United States, although suffering less by their depredations than many other nations, returned the explicit answer that we preferred war to tribute, and thus opened the way to the relief of the commerce of the world from an ignominious tax, so long submitted to by the more powerful nations of Europe.

If the manner of payment of the Sound dues differ from that of the tribute formerly conceded to the Barbary States, still their exaction by Denmark has no better foundation in right. Each was in its origin nothing but a tax on a common natural right, extorted by those who were at that time able to obstruct the free and secure enjoyment of it, but who no longer possess that power.

Denmark, while resisting our assertion of the freedom of the Baltic Sound and Belts, has indicated a readiness to make some new arrangement on the subject, and has invited the governments interested, including the United States, to be represented in a convention to assemble for the purpose of receiving and considering a proposition which she intends to submit for the capitalization of the Sound dues and the distribution of the sum to be paid as commutation among the governments according to the respective proportions of their maritime commerce to and from the Baltic. I have declined, in behalf of the United States, to accept this invitation, for the most cogent reasons. One is that Denmark does not offer to submit to the convention the question of her right to levy the Sound dues. The second is that if the convention were allowed to take cognizance of that particular question, still it would not be competent to deal with the great international principle involved, which affects the right in other cases of navigation and commercial freedom, as well as that of access to the Baltic. Above all, by the express terms of the proposition it is contemplated that the consideration of the Sound dues shall be commingled with and made subordinate to a matter wholly extraneous—the balance of power among the Governments of Europe.

While, however, rejecting this proposition and insisting on the right of free transit into and from the Baltic, I have expressed to Denmark a willingness on the part of the United States to share liberally with other powers in compensating her for any advantages which commerce shall hereafter derive from expenditures made by her for the improvement and safety of the navigation of the Sound or Belts.

I lay before you herewith sundry documents on the subject, in which my views are more fully disclosed. Should no satisfactory arrangement be soon concluded, I shall again call your attention to the subject, with recommendation of such measures as may appear to be required in order to assert and secure the rights of the United States, so far as they are affected by the pretensions of Denmark.

I announce with much gratification that since the adjournment of the last Congress the question then existing between this Government and that of France respecting the French consul at San Francisco has been satisfactorily determined, and that the relations of the two Governments continue to be of the most friendly nature.

A question, also, which has been pending for several years between the

United States and the Kingdom of Greece, growing out of the sequestration by public authorities of that country of property belonging to the present American consul at Athens, and which had been the subject of very earnest discussion heretofore, has recently been settled to the satisfaction of the party interested and of both Governments.

With Spain peaceful relations are still maintained, and some progress has been made in securing the redress of wrongs complained of by this Government. Spain has not only disavowed and disapproved the conduct of the officers who illegally seized and detained the steamer *Black Warrior* at Havana, but has also paid the sum claimed as indemnity for the loss thereby inflicted on citizens of the United States.

In consequence of a destructive hurricane which visited Cuba in 1844, the supreme authority of that island issued a decree permitting the importation for the period of six months of certain building materials and provisions free of duty, but revoked it when about half the period only had elapsed, to the injury of citizens of the United States who had proceeded to act on the faith of that decree. The Spanish Government refused indemnification to the parties aggrieved until recently, when it was assented to, payment being promised to be made so soon as the amount due can be ascertained.

Satisfaction claimed for the arrest and search of the steamer *El Dorado* has not yet been accorded, but there is reason to believe that it will be; and that case, with others, continues to be urged on the attention of the Spanish Government. I do not abandon the hope of concluding with Spain some general arrangement which, if it do not wholly prevent the recurrence of difficulties in Cuba, will render them less frequent, and, whenever they shall occur, facilitate their more speedy settlement.

The interposition of this Government has been invoked by many of its citizens on account of injuries done to their persons and property for which the Mexican Republic is responsible. The unhappy situation of that country for some time past has not allowed its Government to give due consideration to claims of private reparation, and has appeared to call for and justify some forbearance in such matters on the part of this Government. But if the revolutionary movements which have lately occurred in that Republic end in the organization of a stable government, urgent appeals to its justice will then be made, and, it may be hoped, with success, for the redress of all complaints of our citizens.

In regard to the American Republics, which from their proximity and other considerations have peculiar relations to this Government, while it has been my constant aim strictly to observe all the obligations of political friendship and of good neighborhood, obstacles to this have arisen in some of them from their own insufficient power to check lawless irruptions, which in effect throws most of the task on the United States. Thus it is that the distracted internal condition of the State of Nicaragua has made it incumbent on me to appeal to the good faith of our citizens to abstain from unlawful intervention in its affairs and to adopt preventive measures to the same end, which on a similar occasion had the best results in reassuring the peace of the Mexican States of Sonora and Lower California.

Since the last session of Congress a treaty of amity, commerce, and navigation and for the surrender of fugitive criminals with the Kingdom of the Two Sicilies; a treaty of friendship, commerce, and navigation with Nicaragua, and a convention of commercial reciprocity with the Hawaiian Kingdom have been negotiated. The latter Kingdom and the State of Nicaragua have also acceded to a declaration recognizing as international rights the principles contained in the convention between the United States and Russia of July 22, 1854. These treaties and conventions will be laid before the Senate for ratification.

The statements made in my last annual message respecting the anticipated receipts and expenditures of the Treasury have been substantially verified.

It appears from the report of the Secretary of the Treasury that the receipts during the last fiscal year, ending June 30, 1855, from all sources were $65,003,930, and that the public expenditures for the same period, exclusive of payments on account of the public debt, amounted to $56,-365,393. During the same period the payments made in redemption of the public debt, including interest and premium, amounted to $9,844,528.

The balance in the Treasury at the beginning of the present fiscal year, July 1, 1855, was $18,931,976; the receipts for the first quarter and the estimated receipts for the remaining three quarters amount together to $67,918,734; thus affording in all, as the available resources of the current fiscal year, the sum of $86,856,710.

If to the actual expenditures of the first quarter of the current fiscal year be added the probable expenditures for the remaining three quarters, as estimated by the Secretary of the Treasury, the sum total will be $71,226,846, thereby leaving an estimated balance in the Treasury on July 1, 1856, of $15,623,863.41.

In the above-estimated expenditures of the present fiscal year are included $3,000,000 to meet the last installment of the ten millions provided for in the late treaty with Mexico and $7,750,000 appropriated on account of the debt due to Texas, which two sums make an aggregate amount of $10,750,000 and reduce the expenditures, actual or estimated, for ordinary objects of the year to the sum of $60,476,000.

The amount of the public debt at the commencement of the present fiscal year was $40,583,631, and, deduction being made of subsequent payments, the whole public debt of the Federal Government remaining at this time is less than $40,000,000. The remnant of certain other Government stocks, amounting to $243,000, referred to in my last message as outstanding, has since been paid.

I am fully persuaded that it would be difficult to devise a system superior to that by which the fiscal business of the Government is now conducted. Notwithstanding the great number of public agents of collection and disbursement, it is believed that the checks and guards provided, including the requirement of monthly returns, render it scarcely possible for any considerable fraud on the part of those agents or neglect involving hazard of serious public loss to escape detection. I renew, however, the recommendation heretofore made by me of the enactment of a law declaring it felony on the part of public officers to insert false entries in their books of record or account or to make false returns, and also requiring them on the termination of their service to deliver to their successors all books, records, and other objects of a public nature in their custody.

Derived, as our public revenue is, in chief part from duties on imports, its magnitude affords gratifying evidence of the prosperity, not only of our commerce, but of the other great interests upon which that depends.

The principle that all moneys not required for the current expenses of the Government should remain for active employment in the hands of the people and the conspicuous fact that the annual revenue from all sources exceeds by many millions of dollars the amount needed for a prudent and economical administration of public affairs can not fail to suggest the propriety of an early revision and reduction of the tariff of duties on imports. It is now so generally conceded that the purpose of revenue alone can justify the imposition of duties on imports that in readjusting the impost tables and schedules, which unquestionably require essential modifications, a departure from the principles of the present tariff is not anticipated.

The Army during the past year has been actively engaged in defending the Indian frontier, the state of the service permitting but few and small garrisons in our permanent fortifications. The additional regiments authorized at the last session of Congress have been recruited and organized, and a large portion of the troops have already been sent to the field. All the duties which devolve on the military establishment have been satisfactorily performed, and the dangers and privations incident to the character of the service required of our troops have furnished additional evidence of their courage, zeal, and capacity to meet any requisition which their country may make upon them. For the details of the military operations, the distribution of the troops, and additional provisions required for the military service, I refer to the report of the Secretary of War and the accompanying documents.

Experience gathered from events which have transpired since my last annual message has but served to confirm the opinion then expressed of the propriety of making provision by a retired list for disabled officers and for increased compensation to the officers retained on the list for active duty. All the reasons which existed when these measures were recommended on former occasions continue without modification, except so far as circumstances have given to some of them additional force.

The recommendations heretofore made for a partial reorganization of the Army are also renewed. The thorough elementary education given to those officers who commence their service with the grade of cadet qualifies them to a considerable extent to perform the duties of every arm of the service; but to give the highest efficiency to artillery requires the practice and special study of many years, and it is not, therefore, believed to be advisable to maintain in time of peace a larger force of that arm than can be usually employed in the duties appertaining to the service of field and siege artillery. The duties of the staff in all its various branches belong to the movements of troops, and the efficiency of an army in the field would materially depend upon the ability with which those duties are discharged. It is not, as in the case of the artillery, a specialty, but requires also an intimate knowledge of the duties of an officer of the line, and it is not doubted that to complete the education of an officer for either the line or the general staff it is desirable that he shall have served in both. With this view, it was recommended on a former occasion that the duties of the staff should be mainly performed by details from the line, and, with conviction of the advantages which would result from such a change, it is again presented for the consideration of Congress.

The report of the Secretary of the Navy, herewith submitted, exhibits in full the naval operations of the past year, together with the present condition of the service, and it makes suggestions of further legislation, to which your attention is invited.

The construction of the six steam frigates for which appropriations were made by the last Congress has proceeded in the most satisfactory manner and with such expedition as to warrant the belief that they will be ready for service early in the coming spring. Important as this addition to our naval force is, it still remains inadequate to the contingent exigencies of the protection of the extensive seacoast and vast commercial interests of the United States. In view of this fact and of the acknowledged wisdom of the policy of a gradual and systematic increase of the Navy an appropriation is recommended for the construction of six steam sloops of war.

In regard to the steps taken in execution of the act of Congress to promote the efficiency of the Navy, it is unnecessary for me to say more than to express entire concurrence in the observations on that subject presented by the Secretary in his report.

It will be perceived by the report of the Postmaster-General that the gross expenditure of the Department for the last fiscal year was $9,968,-342 and the gross receipts $7,342,136, making an excess of expenditure over receipts of $2,626,206; and that the cost of mail transportation during that year was $674,952 greater than the previous year. Much of the heavy expenditures to which the Treasury is thus subjected is to be ascribed to the large quantity of printed matter conveyed by the mails, either franked or liable to no postage by law or to very low rates of postage compared with that charged on letters, and to the great cost of mail service on railroads and by ocean steamers. The suggestions of the Postmaster-General on the subject deserve the consideration of Congress.

The report of the Secretary of the Interior will engage your attention as well for useful suggestions it contains as for the interest and importance of the subjects to which they refer.

The aggregate amount of public land sold during the last fiscal year, located with military scrip or land warrants, taken up under grants for roads, and selected as swamp lands by States is 24,557,409 acres, of which the portion sold was 15,729,524 acres, yielding in receipts the sum of $11,485,380. In the same period of time 8,723,854 acres have been surveyed, but, in consideration of the quantity already subject to entry, no additional tracts have been brought into market.

The peculiar relation of the General Government to the District of Columbia renders it proper to commend to your care not only its material but also its moral interests, including education, more especially in those parts of the District outside of the cities of Washington and Georgetown.

The commissioners appointed to revise and codify the laws of the District have made such progress in the performance of their task as to insure its completion in the time prescribed by the act of Congress.

Information has recently been received that the peace of the settlements in the Territories of Oregon and Washington is disturbed by hostilities on the part of the Indians, with indications of extensive combinations of a hostile character among the tribes in that quarter, the more serious in their possible effect by reason of the undetermined foreign interests existing in those Territories, to which your attention has already been especially invited. Efficient measures have been taken, which, it is believed, will restore quiet and afford protection to our citizens.

In the Territory of Kansas there have been acts prejudicial to good order, but as yet none have occurred under circumstances to justify the interposition of the Federal Executive. That could only be in case of obstruction to Federal law or of organized resistance to Territorial law, assuming the character of insurrection, which, if it should occur, it would be my duty promptly to overcome and suppress. I cherish the hope, however, that the occurrence of any such untoward event will be prevented by the sound sense of the people of the Territory, who by its organic law, possessing the right to determine their own domestic institutions, are entitled while deporting themselves peacefully to the free exercise of that right, and must be protected in the enjoyment of it without interference on the part of the citizens of any of the States.

The southern boundary line of this Territory has never been surveyed and established. The rapidly extending settlements in that region and the fact that the main route between Independence, in the State of Missouri, and New Mexico is contiguous in this line suggest the probability that embarrassing questions of jurisdiction may consequently arise.

For these and other considerations I commend the subject to your early attention.

I have thus passed in review the general state of the Union, including such particular concerns of the Federal Government, whether of domestic or foreign relation, as it appeared to me desirable and useful to bring to the special notice of Congress. Unlike the great States of Europe and Asia and many of those of America, these United States are wasting their strength neither in foreign war nor domestic strife. Whatever of discontent or public dissatisfaction exists is attributable to the imperfections of human nature or is incident to all governments, however perfect, which human wisdom can devise. Such subjects of political agitation as occupy the public mind consist to a great extent of exaggeration of inevitable evils, or overzeal in social improvement, or mere imagination of grievance, having but remote connection with any of the constitutional functions or duties of the Federal Government. To whatever extent these questions exhibit a tendency menacing to the stability of the Constitution or the integrity of the Union, and no further, they demand the consideration of the Executive and require to be presented by him to Congress.

Before the thirteen colonies became a confederation of independent States they were associated only by community of transatlantic origin, by geographical position, and by the mutual tie of common dependence on Great Britain. When that tie was sundered they severally assumed the powers and rights of absolute self-government. The municipal and social institutions of each, its laws of property and of personal relation, even its political organization, were such only as each one chose to establish, wholly without interference from any other. In the language of the Declaration of Independence, each State had "full power to levy war, conclude peace, contract alliances, establish commerce, and to do all other acts and things which independent states may of right do." The several colonies differed in climate, in soil, in natural productions, in religion, in systems of education, in legislation, and in the forms of political administration, and they continued to differ in these respects when they voluntarily allied themselves as States to carry on the War of the Revolution. The object of that war was to disenthrall the united colonies from foreign rule, which had proved to be oppressive, and to separate them permanently from the mother country. The political result was the foundation of a Federal Republic of the free white men of the colonies, constituted, as they were, in distinct and reciprocally independent State governments. As for the subject races, whether Indian or African, the wise and brave statesmen of that day, being engaged in no extravagant scheme of social change, left them as they were, and thus preserved themselves and their posterity from the anarchy and the ever-recurring civil wars which have prevailed in other revolutionized European colonies of America.

When the confederated States found it convenient to modify the conditions of their association by giving to the General Government direct access in some respects to the people of the States, instead of confining it to action on the States as such, they proceeded to frame the existing Constitution, adhering steadily to one guiding thought, which was to delegate only such power as was necessary and proper to the execution of specific purposes, or, in other words, to retain as much as possible consistently with those purposes of the independent powers of the individual States. For objects of common defense and security, they intrusted to the General Government certain carefully defined functions, leaving all others as the undelegated rights of the separate independent sovereignties.

Such is the constitutional theory of our Government, the practical observance of which has carried us, and us alone among modern republics, through nearly three generations of time without the cost of one drop of blood shed in civil war. With freedom and concert of action, it has enabled us to contend successfully on the battlefield against foreign foes, has elevated the feeble colonies into powerful States, and has raised our industrial productions and our commerce which transports them to the level of the richest and the greatest nations of Europe. And the admirable adaptation of our political institutions to their objects, combining local self-government with aggregate strength, has established the practicability of a government like ours to cover a continent with confederate states.

The Congress of the United States is in effect that congress of sovereignties which good men in the Old World have sought for, but could never attain, and which imparts to America an exemption from the mutable leagues for common action, from the wars, the mutual invasions, and vague aspirations after the balance of power which convulse from time to time the Governments of Europe. Our cooperative action rests in the conditions of permanent confederation prescribed by the Constitution. Our balance of power is in the separate reserved rights of the States and their equal representation in the Senate. That independent sovereignty in every one of the States, with its reserved rights of local self-government assured to each by their coequal power in the Senate, was the fundamental condition of the Constitution. Without it the Union would never have existed. However desirous the larger States might be to reorganize the Government so as to give to their population its proportionate weight in the common counsels, they knew it was impossible unless they conceded to the smaller ones authority to exercise at least a negative influence on all the measures of the Government, whether legislative or executive, through their equal representation in the Senate. Indeed, the larger States themselves could not have failed to perceive that the same power was equally necessary to them for the security of their own domestic interests against the aggregate force of the General Government. In a word, the original States went into this permanent league on the agreed premises of exerting their common strength for the defense of the whole and of all its parts, but of utterly excluding all capability of reciprocal aggression. Each solemnly bound itself to all the others neither to undertake nor permit any encroachment upon or intermeddling with another's reserved rights.

Where it was deemed expedient particular rights of the States were expressly guaranteed by the Constitution, but in all things besides these rights were guarded by the limitation of the powers granted and by express reservation of all powers not granted in the compact of union. Thus the great power of taxation was limited to purposes of common defense and general welfare, excluding objects appertaining to the local legislation of the several States; and those purposes of general welfare and common defense were afterwards defined by specific enumeration as being matters only of co-relation between the States themselves or between them and foreign governments, which, because of their common and general nature, could not be left to the separate control of each State.

Of the circumstances of local condition, interest, and rights in which a portion of the States, constituting one great section of the Union, differed from the rest and from another section, the most important was the peculiarity of a larger relative colored population in the Southern than in the Northern States.

A population of this class, held in subjection, existed in nearly all the States, but was more numerous and of more serious concernment in the South than in the North on account of natural differences of climate and production; and it was foreseen that, for the same reasons, while this population would diminish and sooner or later cease to exist in some States, it might increase in others. The peculiar character and magnitude of this question of local rights, not in material relations only, but still more in social ones, caused it to enter into the special stipulations of the Constitution.

Hence, while the General Government, as well by the enumerated powers granted to it as by those not enumerated, and therefore refused to it, was forbidden to touch this matter in the sense of attack or offense, it was placed under the general safeguard of the Union in the sense of defense against either invasion or domestic violence, like all other local interests of the several States. Each State expressly stipulated, as well for itself as for each and all of its citizens, and every citizen of each State became solemnly bound by his allegiance to the Constitution that any person held to service or labor in one State, escaping into another, should not, in consequence of any law or regulation thereof, be discharged from such service or labor, but should be delivered up on claim of the party to whom such service or labor might be due by the laws of his State.

Thus and thus only, by the reciprocal guaranty of all the rights of every State against interference on the part of another, was the present form of government established by our fathers and transmitted to us, and by no other means is it possible for it to exist. If one State ceases to respect the rights of another and obtrusively intermeddles with its local interests; if a portion of the States assume to impose their institutions on the others or refuse to fulfill their obligations to them, we are no longer united, friendly States, but distracted, hostile ones, with little capacity left of common advantage, but abundant means of reciprocal injury and mischief. Practically it is immaterial whether aggressive interference between the States or deliberate refusal on the part of any one of them to comply with constitutional obligations arise from erroneous conviction or blind prejudice, whether it be perpetrated by direction or indirection. In either case it is full of threat and of danger to the durability of the Union.

Placed in the office of Chief Magistrate as the executive agent of the whole country, bound to take care that the laws be faithfully executed, and specially enjoined by the Constitution to give information to Congress on the state of the Union, it would be palpable neglect of duty on my part to pass over a subject like this, which beyond all things at the present time vitally concerns individual and public security.

It has been matter of painful regret to see States conspicuous for their services in founding this Republic and equally sharing its advantages disregard their constitutional obligations to it. Although conscious of their inability to heal admitted and palpable social evils of their own, and which are completely within their jurisdiction, they engage in the offensive and hopeless undertaking of reforming the domestic institutions of other States, wholly beyond their control and authority. In the vain pursuit of ends by them entirely unattainable, and which they may not legally attempt to compass, they peril the very existence of the Constitution and all the countless benefits which it has conferred. While the people of the Southern States confine their attention to their own affairs, not presuming officiously to intermeddle with the social institutions of the Northern States, too many of the inhabitants of the latter are permanently organized in associations to inflict injury on the former by wrongful acts, which would be cause of war as between foreign powers and only fail to be such in our system because perpetrated under cover of the Union.

Is it possible to present this subject as truth and the occasion require without noticing the reiterated but groundless allegation that the South has persistently asserted claims and obtained advantages in the practical administration of the General Government to the prejudice of the North, and in which the latter has acquiesced? That is, the States which either promote or tolerate attacks on the rights of persons and of property in other States, to disguise their own injustice, pretend or imagine, and constantly aver, that they, whose constitutional rights are thus systematically assailed, are themselves the aggressors. At the present time this imputed aggression, resting, as it does, only in the vague declamatory charges of political agitators, resolves itself into misapprehension, or misinterpretation, of the principles and facts of the political organization of the new Territories of the United States.

What is the voice of history? When the ordinance which provided for the government of the territory northwest of the river Ohio and for its eventual subdivision into new States was adopted in the Congress of the Confederation, it is not to be supposed that the question of future relative power as between the States which retained and those which did not retain a numerous colored population escaped notice or failed to be considered. And yet the concession of that vast territory to the interests and opinions of the Northern States, a territory now the seat of five among the largest members of the Union, was in great measure the act of the State of Virginia and of the South.

When Louisiana was acquired by the United States, it was an acquisition not less to the North than to the South; for while it was important to the country at the mouth of the river Mississippi to become the emporium of the country above it, so also it was even more important to the whole Union to have that emporium; and although the new province, by reason of its imperfect settlement, was mainly regarded as on the Gulf of Mexico, yet in fact it extended to the opposite boundaries of the United States, with far greater breadth above than below, and was in territory, as in everything else, equally at least an accession to the Northern States. It is mere delusion and prejudice, therefore, to speak of Louisiana as acquisition in the special interest of the South.

The patriotic and just men who participated in that act were influenced by motives far above all sectional jealousies. It was in truth the great event which, by completing for us the possession of the Valley of the Mississippi, with commercial access to the Gulf of Mexico, imparted unity and strength to the whole Confederation and attached together by indissoluble ties the East and the West, as well as the North and the South.

As to Florida, that was but the transfer by Spain to the United States of territory on the east side of the river Mississippi in exchange for large territory which the United States transferred to Spain on the west side of that river, as the entire diplomatic history of the transaction serves to demonstrate. Moreover, it was an acquisition demanded by the commercial interests and the security of the whole Union.

In the meantime the people of the United States had grown up to a proper consciousness of their strength, and in a brief contest with France and in a second serious war with Great Britain they had shaken off all which remained of undue reverence for Europe, and emerged from the atmosphere of those transatlantic influences which surrounded the infant Republic, and had begun to turn their attention to the full and systematic development of the internal resources of the Union.

Among the evanescent controversies of that period the most conspicuous was the question of regulation by Congress of the social condition of the future States to be founded in the territory of Louisiana.

The ordinance for the government of the territory northwest of the river Ohio had contained a provision which prohibited the use of servile labor therein, subject to the condition of the extraditions of fugitives from service due in any other part of the United States. Subsequently to the adoption of the Constitution this provision ceased to remain as a law, for its operation as such was absolutely superseded by the Constitution. But the recollection of the fact excited the zeal of social propagandism in some sections of the Confederation, and when a second State, that of Missouri, came to be formed in the territory of Louisiana proposition was made to extend to the latter territory the restriction originally applied to the country situated between the rivers Ohio and Mississippi.

Most questionable as was this proposition in all its constitutional relations, nevertheless it received the sanction of Congress, with some slight modifications of line, to save the existing rights of the intended new State. It was reluctantly acquiesced in by Southern States as a sacrifice to the cause of peace and of the Union, not only of the rights stipulated by the treaty of Louisiana, but of the principle of equality among the States guaranteed by the Constitution. It was received by the Northern States with angry and resentful condemnation and complaint, because it did not concede all which they had exactingly demanded. Having passed through the forms of legislation, it took its place in the statute book, standing open to repeal, like any other act of doubtful constitutionality, subject to be pronounced null and void by the courts of law, and possessing no possible efficacy to control the rights of the States which might thereafter be organized out of any part of the original territory of Louisiana.

In all this, if any aggression there were, any innovation upon preexisting rights, to which portion of the Union are they justly chargeable?

This controversy passed away with the occasion, nothing surviving it save the dormant letter of the statute.

But long afterwards, when by the proposed accession of the Republic of Texas the United States were to take their next step in territorial greatness, a similar contingency occurred and became the occasion for systematized attempts to intervene in the domestic affairs of one section of the Union, in defiance of their rights as States and of the stipulations of the Constitution. These attempts assumed a practical direction in the shape of persevering endeavors by some of the Representatives in both Houses of Congress to deprive the Southern States of the supposed benefit of the provisions of the act authorizing the organization of the State of Missouri.

But the good sense of the people and the vital force of the Constitution triumphed over sectional prejudice and the political errors of the day, and the State of Texas returned to the Union as she was, with social institutions which her people had chosen for themselves and with express agreement by the reannexing act that she should be susceptible of subdivision into a plurality of States.

Whatever advantage the interests of the Southern States, as such, gained by this were far inferior in results, as they unfolded in the progress of time, to those which sprang from previous concessions made by the South.

To every thoughtful friend of the Union, to the true lovers of their country, to all who longed and labored for the full success of this great experiment of republican institutions, it was cause of gratulation that such an opportunity had occurred to illustrate our advancing power on this continent and to furnish to the world additional assurance of the strength and stability of the Constitution. Who would wish to see Florida still a European colony? Who would rejoice to hail Texas as a lone star instead of one in the galaxy of States? Who does not appreciate the incalculable benefits of the acquisition of Louisiana? And yet narrow views and sectional purposes would inevitably have excluded them all from the Union.

But another struggle on the same point ensued when our victorious armies returned from Mexico and it devolved on Congress to provide for the territories acquired by the treaty of Guadalupe Hidalgo. The great relations of the subject had now become distinct and clear to the perception of the public mind, which appreciated the evils of sectional controversy upon the question of the admission of new States. In that crisis intense solicitude pervaded the nation. But the patriotic impulses of the popular heart, guided by the admonitory advice of the Father of his Country, rose superior to all the difficulties of the incorporation of a new empire into the Union. In the counsels of Congress there was manifested extreme antagonism of opinion and action between some Representatives, who sought by the abusive and unconstitutional employment of the legislative powers of the Government to interfere in the condition of the inchoate States and to impose their own social theories upon the latter, and other Representatives, who repelled the interposition of the General Government in this respect and maintained the self-constituting rights of the States. In truth, the thing attempted was in form alone action of the General Government, while in reality it was the endeavor, by abuse of legislative power, to force the ideas of internal policy entertained in particular States upon allied independent States. Once more the Constitution and the Union triumphed signally. The new territories were organized without restrictions on the disputed point, and were thus left to judge in that particular for themselves; and the sense of constitutional faith proved vigorous enough in Congress not only to accomplish this primary object, but also the incidental and hardly less important one of so amending the provisions of the statute for the extradition of fugitives. from service as to place that public duty under the safeguard of the General Government, and thus relieve it from obstacles raised up by the legislation of some of the States.

Vain declamation regarding the provisions of law for the extradition of fugitives from service, with occasional episodes of frantic effort to obstruct their execution by riot and murder, continued for a brief time to agitate certain localities. But the true principle of leaving each State and Territory to regulate its own laws of labor according to its own sense of right and expediency had acquired fast hold of the public judgment, to such a degree that by common consent it was observed in the organization of the Territory of Washington.

When, more recently, it became requisite to organize the Territories of Nebraska and Kansas, it was the natural and legitimate, if not the inevitable, consequence of previous events and legislation that the same great and sound principle which had already been applied to Utah and New Mexico should be applied to them—that they should stand exempt from the restrictions proposed in the act relative to the State of Missouri.

These restrictions were, in the estimation of many thoughtful men, null from the beginning, unauthorized by the Constitution, contrary to the treaty stipulations for the cession of Louisiana, and inconsistent with the equality of these States.

They had been stripped of all moral authority by persistent efforts to procure their indirect repeal through contradictory enactments. They had been practically abrogated by the legislation attending the organization of Utah, New Mexico, and Washington. If any vitality remained in them it would have been taken away, in effect, by the new Territorial acts in the form originally proposed to the Senate at the first session of the last Congress. It was manly and ingenuous, as well as patriotic and just, to do this directly and plainly, and thus relieve the statute book of an act which might be of possible future injury, but of no possible future benefit; and the measure of its repeal was the final consummation and complete recognition of the principle that no portion of the United States shall undertake through assumption of the powers of the General Government to dictate the social institutions of any other portion.

The scope and effect of the language of repeal were not left in doubt. It was declared in terms to be "the true intent and meaning of this act not to legislate slavery into any Territory or State, nor to exclude it therefrom, but to leave the people thereof perfectly free to form and regulate their domestic institutions in their own way, subject only to the Constitution of the United States."

The measure could not be withstood upon its merits alone. It was attacked with violence on the false or delusive pretext that it constituted a breach of faith. Never was objection more utterly destitute of substantial justification. When before was it imagined by sensible men that a regulative or declarative statute, whether enacted ten or forty years ago, is irrepealable; that an act of Congress is above the Constitution? If, indeed, there were in the facts any cause to impute bad faith, it would attach to those only who have never ceased, from the time of the enactment of the restrictive provision to the present day, to denounce and condemn it; who have constantly refused to complete it by needful supplementary legislation; who have spared no exertion to deprive it of moral force; who have themselves again and again attempted its repeal by the enactment of incompatible provisions, and who, by the inevitable reactionary effect of their own violence on the subject, awakened the country to perception of the true constitutional principle of leaving the matter involved to the discretion of the people of the respective existing or incipient States.

It is not pretended that this principle or any other precludes the possibility of evils in practice, disturbed, as political action is liable to be, by human passions. No form of government is exempt from inconveniences; but in this case they are the result of the abuse, and not of the legitimate exercise, of the powers reserved or conferred in the organization of a Territory. They are not to be charged to the great principle of popular sovereignty. On the contrary, they disappear before the intelligence and patriotism of the people, exerting through the ballot box their peaceful and silent but irresistible power.

If the friends of the Constitution are to have another struggle, its enemies could not present a more acceptable issue than that of a State whose constitution clearly embraces "a republican form of government" being excluded from the Union because its domestic institutions may not in all respects comport with the ideas of what is wise and expedient entertained in some other State. Fresh from groundless imputations of breach of faith against others, men will commence the agitation of this new question with indubitable violation of an express compact between the independent sovereign powers of the United States and of the Republic of Texas, as well as of the older and equally solemn compacts which assure the equality of all the States.

But deplorable as would be such a violation of compact in itself and in all its direct consequences, that is the very least of the evils involved. When sectional agitators shall have succeeded in forcing on this issue, can their pretensions fail to be met by counter pretensions? Will not different States be compelled, respectively, to meet extremes with extremes? And if either extreme carry its point, what is that so far forth but dissolution of the Union? If a new State, formed from the territory of the United States, be absolutely excluded from admission therein, that fact of itself constitutes the disruption of union between it and the other States. But the process of dissolution could not stop there. Would not a sectional decision producing such result by a majority of votes, either Northern or Southern, of necessity drive out the oppressed and aggrieved minority and place in presence of each other two irreconcilably hostile confederations?

It is necessary to speak thus plainly of projects the offspring of that sectional agitation now prevailing in some of the States, which are as impracticable as they are unconstitutional, and which if persevered in must and will end calamitously. It is either disunion and civil war or it is mere angry, idle, aimless disturbance of public peace and tranquillity. Disunion for what? If the passionate rage of fanaticism and partisan spirit did not force the fact upon our attention, it would be difficult to believe that any considerable portion of the people of this enlightened country could have so surrendered themselves to a fanatical devotion to the supposed interests of the relatively few Africans in the United States as totally to abandon and disregard the interests of the 25,000,000 Americans; to trample under foot the injunctions of moral and constitutional obligation, and to engage in plans of vindictive hostility against those who are associated with them in the enjoyment of the common heritage of our national institutions.

Nor is it hostility against their fellow-citizens of one section of the Union alone. The interests, the honor, the duty, the peace, and the prosperity of the people of all sections are equally involved and imperiled in this question. And are patriotic men in any part of the Union prepared on such issue thus madly to invite all the consequences of the forfeiture of their constitutional engagements? It is impossible. The storm of frenzy and faction must inevitably dash itself in vain against the unshaken rock of the Constitution. I shall never doubt it. I know that the Union is stronger a thousand times than all the wild and chimerical schemes of social change which are generated one after another in the unstable minds of visionary sophists and interested agitators. I rely confidently on the patriotism of the people, on the dignity and self-respect of the States, on the wisdom of Congress, and, above all, on the continued gracious favor of Almighty God to maintain against all enemies, whether at home or abroad, the sanctity of the Constitution and the integrity of the Union.

FRANKLIN PIERCE.

SPECIAL MESSAGES.

WASHINGTON, *December 26, 1855.*

To the Senate of the United States:

In compliance with a resolution of the Senate of the 17th instant, I send herewith the "memorial of citizens of New Orleans, complaining of the irregularity of the mail service between Washington and New Orleans." I deem it proper also to transmit with the memorial my note of the 18th instant to the memorialists and a copy of the letter of the Postmaster-General therein referred to.

FRANKLIN PIERCE.

WASHINGTON, *December 27, 1855.*

To the Senate of the United States:

I transmit to the Senate, for consideration with a view to ratification, a treaty between the United States and Nicaragua, signed at Granada on the 20th day of June, A. D. 1855.

FRANKLIN PIERCE.

WASHINGTON, *December 27, 1855.*

To the Senate of the United States:

I transmit to the Senate, for consideration with a view to ratification, a treaty between the United States and the Kingdom of the Two Sicilies and a declaration as to the construction thereof, both signed at Naples on the 1st day of October last.

FRANKLIN PIERCE.

WASHINGTON, *December 27, 1855.*

To the Senate of the United States:

I transmit to the Senate, for consideration with a view to ratification, a treaty between the United States and His Majesty the King of the Hawaiian Islands, signed in Washington the 20th day of July, A. D. 1855.

FRANKLIN PIERCE.

WASHINGTON CITY, *January 3, 1856.*

To the Senate of the United States:

I herewith lay before the Senate, for its constitutional action thereon, the following-described Indian treaties, negotiated by George W. Manypenny and Henry C. Gilbert, as commissioners on the part of the United States:

A. Treaty with the Chippewas of Saginaw, Swan Creek, and Black River, dated 2d August, 1855.

B. Treaty with the Chippewas of Sault Ste. Marie, dated August 2, 1855.

C. Treaty with the Ottawas and Chippewas, dated July 31, 1855.

FRANKLIN PIERCE.

WASHINGTON, *January 11, 1856.*

To the Senate of the United States:

I transmit to the Senate a report from the Secretary of State, with the accompanying document,* in answer to their resolution of yesterday.

FRANKLIN PIERCE.

WASHINGTON CITY, *January 21, 1856.*

To the Senate of the United States:

I communicate to the Senate herewith a letter from the Secretary of the Interior, accompanying six several treaties negotiated by Governor Meriwether, of New Mexico, with the Indians in that Territory, for its constitutional action thereon.

FRANKLIN PIERCE.

*Letter of Lord John Russell declaring that the British Government intends to adhere to the treaty of Washington of April 19, 1850, and not to assume any sovereignty in Central America.

WASHINGTON, *January 23, 1856.*

To the Senate of the United States:

I communicate herewith to the Senate, for its constitutional action thereon, a treaty between the United States and the Choctaw and Chickasaw tribes of Indians, made and concluded in this city on the 22d day of June, 1855.

FRANKLIN PIERCE.

WASHINGTON, *January 24, 1856.*

To the Senate and House of Representatives:

Circumstances have occurred to disturb the course of governmental organization in the Territory of Kansas and produce there a condition of things which renders it incumbent on me to call your attention to the subject and urgently to recommend the adoption by you of such measures of legislation as the grave exigencies of the case appear to require.

A brief exposition of the circumstances referred to and of their causes will be necessary to the full understanding of the recommendations which it is proposed to submit.

The act to organize the Territories of Nebraska and Kansas was a manifestation of the legislative opinion of Congress on two great points of constitutional construction: One, that the designation of the boundaries of a new Territory and provision for its political organization and administration as a Territory are measures which of right fall within the powers of the General Government; and the other, that the inhabitants of any such Territory, considered as an inchoate State, are entitled, in the exercise of self-government, to determine for themselves what shall be their own domestic institutions, subject only to the Constitution and the laws duly enacted by Congress under it and to the power of the existing States to decide, according to the provisions and principles of the Constitution, at what time the Territory shall be received as a State into the Union. Such are the great political rights which are solemnly declared and affirmed by that act.

Based upon this theory, the act of Congress defined for each Territory the outlines of republican government, distributing public authority among lawfully created agents—executive, judicial, and legislative—to be appointed either by the General Government or by the Territory. The legislative functions were intrusted to a council and a house of representatives, duly elected, and empowered to enact all the local laws which they might deem essential to their prosperity, happiness, and good government. Acting in the same spirit, Congress also defined the persons who were in the first instance to be considered as the people of each Territory, enacting that every free white male inhabitant of the same above the age of 21 years, being an actual resident thereof and possessing the qualifications hereafter described, should be entitled to vote at the first election and be eligible to any office within the Territory, but that the qualification of voters and holding office at all subsequent elections should be such as might be prescribed by the legislative assembly; provided, however, that the right of suffrage and of holding office should be exercised only by citizens of the United States and those who should have declared on oath their intention to become such and have taken an oath to support the Constitution of the United States and the provisions of the act; and provided further, that no officer, soldier, seaman, or marine or other person in the Army or Navy of the United States or attached to troops in their service should be allowed to vote or hold office in either Territory by reason of being on service therein.

Such of the public officers of the Territories as by the provisions of the act were to be appointed by the General Government, including the governors, were appointed and commissioned in due season, the law having been enacted on the 30th of May, 1854, and the commission of the governor of the Territory of Nebraska being dated on the 2d day of August, 1854, and of the Territory of Kansas on the 29th day of June, 1854. Among the duties imposed by the act on the governors was that of directing and superintending the political organization of the respective Territories.

The governor of Kansas was required to cause a census or enumeration of the inhabitants and qualified voters of the several counties and districts of the Territory to be taken by such persons and in such mode as he might designate and appoint; to appoint and direct the time and places of holding the first elections, and the manner of conducting them, both as to the persons to superintend such elections and the returns thereof; to declare the number of the members of the council and the house of representatives for each county or district; to declare what persons might appear to be duly elected, and to appoint the time and place of the first meeting of the legislative assembly. In substance, the same duties were devolved on the governor of Nebraska.

While by this act the principle of constitution for each of the Territories was one and the same and the details of organic legislation regarding both were as nearly as could be identical, and while the Territory of Nebraska was tranquilly and successfully organized in the due course of law, and its first legislative assembly met on the 16th of January, 1855, the organization of Kansas was long delayed, and has been attended with serious difficulties and embarrassments, partly the consequence of local maladministration and partly of the unjustifiable interference of the inhabitants of some of the States, foreign by residence, interests, and rights to the Territory.

The governor of the Territory of Kansas, commissioned as before stated, on the 29th of June, 1854, did not reach the designated seat of his government until the 7th of the ensuing October, and even then failed to make the first step in its legal organization, that of ordering the census or enumeration of its inhabitants, until so late a day that the election of the members of the legislative assembly did not take place until the 30th of March, 1855, nor its meeting until the 2d of July, 1855. So that for a year after the Territory was constituted by the act of Congress and the officers to be appointed by the Federal Executive had been commissioned it was without a complete government, without any legislative authority, without local law, and, of course, without the ordinary guaranties of peace and public order.

In other respects the governor, instead of exercising constant vigilance and putting forth all his energies to prevent or counteract the tendencies to illegality which are prone to exist in all imperfectly organized and newly associated communities, allowed his attention to be diverted from official obligations by other objects, and himself set an example of the violation of law in the performance of acts which rendered it my duty in the sequel to remove him from the office of chief executive magistrate of the Territory.

Before the requisite preparation was accomplished for election of a Territorial legislature, an election of Delegate to Congress had been held in the Territory on the 29th day of November, 1854, and the Delegate took his seat in the House of Representatives without challenge. If arrangements had been perfected by the governor so that the election for members of the legislative assembly might be held in the several precincts at the same time as for Delegate to Congress, any question appertaining to the qualification of the persons voting as people of the Territory would have passed necessarily and at once under the supervision of Congress, as the judge of the validity of the return of the Delegate, and would have been determined before conflicting passions had become inflamed by time, and before opportunity could have been afforded for systematic interference of the people of individual States.

This interference, in so far as concerns its primary causes and its immediate commencement, was one of the incidents of that pernicious agitation on the subject of the condition of the colored persons held to service in some of the States which has so long disturbed the repose of our country and excited individuals, otherwise patriotic and law abiding, to toil with misdirected zeal in the attempt to propagate their social theories by the perversion and abuse of the powers of Congress.

The persons and the parties whom the tenor of the act to organize the Territories of Nebraska and Kansas thwarted in the endeavor to impose, through the agency of Congress, their particular views of social organization on the people of the future new States now perceiving that the policy of leaving the inhabitants of each State to judge for themselves in this respect was ineradicably rooted in the convictions of the people of the Union, then had recourse, in the pursuit of their general object, to the extraordinary measure of propagandist colonization of the Territory of Kansas to prevent the free and natural action of its inhabitants in its internal organization, and thus to anticipate or to force the determination of that question in this inchoate State.

With such views associations were organized in some of the States, and their purposes were proclaimed through the press in language extremely irritating and offensive to those of whom the colonists were to become the neighbors. Those designs and acts had the necessary consequence to awaken emotions of intense indignation in States near to the Territory of Kansas, and especially in the adjoining State of Missouri, whose domestic peace was thus the most directly endangered; but they are far from justifying the illegal and reprehensible countermovements which ensued.

Under these inauspicious circumstances the primary elections for members of the legislative assembly were held in most, if not all, of the precincts at the time and the places and by the persons designated and appointed by the governor according to law.

Angry accusations that illegal votes had been polled abounded on all sides, and imputations were made both of fraud and violence. But the governor, in the exercise of the power and the discharge of the duty conferred and imposed by law on him alone, officially received and considered the returns, declared a large majority of the members of the council and the house of representatives "duly elected," withheld certificates from others because of alleged illegality of votes, appointed a new election to supply the places of the persons not certified, and thus at length, in all the forms of statute, and with his own official authentication, complete legality was given to the first legislative assembly of the Territory.

Those decisions of the returning officers and of the governor are final, except that by the parliamentary usage of the country applied to the organic law it may be conceded that each house of the assembly must have been competent to determine in the last resort the qualifications and the election of its members. The subject was by its nature one appertaining exclusively to the jurisdiction of the local authorities of the Territory. Whatever irregularities may have occurred in the elections, it seems too late now to raise that question. At all events, it is a question as to which, neither now nor at any previous time, has the least possible legal authority been possessed by the President of the United States. For all present purposes the legislative body thus constituted and elected was the legitimate legislative assembly of the Territory.

Accordingly the governor by proclamation convened the assembly thus elected to meet at a place called Pawnee City; the two houses met and were duly organized in the ordinary parliamentary form; each sent to and received from the governor the official communications usual on such occasions; an elaborate message opening the session was communicated by the governor, and the general business of legislation was entered upon by the legislative assembly.

But after a few days the assembly resolved to adjourn to another place in the Territory. A law was accordingly passed, against the consent of the governor, but in due form otherwise, to remove the seat of government temporarily to the "Shawnee Manual Labor School" (or mission), and thither the assembly proceeded. After this, receiving a bill for the establishment of a ferry at the town of Kickapoo, the governor refused to sign it, and by special message assigned for reason of refusal not anything objectionable in the bill itself nor any pretense of the illegality or incompetency of the assembly as such, but only the fact that the assembly had by its act transferred the seat of government temporarily from Pawnee City to the Shawnee Mission. For the same reason he continued to refuse to sign other bills until in the course of a few days he by official message communicated to the assembly the fact that he had received notification of the termination of his functions as governor, and that the duties of the office were legally devolved on the secretary of the Territory; thus to the last recognizing the body as a duly elected and constituted legislative assembly.

It will be perceived that if any constitutional defect attached to the legislative acts of the assembly it is not pretended to consist in irregularity of election or want of qualification of the members, but only in the change of its place of session. However trivial this objection may seem to be, it requires to be considered, because upon it is founded all that superstructure of acts, plainly against law, which now threaten the peace, not only of the Territory of Kansas, but of the Union.

Such an objection to the proceedings of the legislative assembly was of exceptionable origin, for the reason that by the express terms of the organic law the seat of government of the Territory was "located temporarily at Fort Leavenworth;" and yet the governor himself remained there less than two months, and of his own discretion transferred the seat of government to the Shawnee Mission, where it in fact was at the time the assembly were called to meet at Pawnee City. If the governor had any such right to change temporarily the seat of government, still more had the legislative assembly. The objections are of exceptionable origin for the further reason that the place indicated by the governor, without having any exclusive claim of preference in itself, was a proposed town site only, which he and others were attempting to locate unlawfully upon land within a military reservation, and for participation in which illegal act the commandant of the post, a superior officer in the Army, has been dismissed by sentence of court-martial. Nor is it easy to see why the legislative assembly might not with propriety pass the Territorial act transferring its sittings to the Shawnee Mission. If it could not, that must be on account of some prohibitory or incompatible provision of act of Congress; but no such provision exists. The organic act, as already quoted, says "the seat of government is hereby located temporarily at Fort Leavenworth;" and it then provides that certain of the public buildings there "may be occupied and used under the direction of the governor and legislative assembly." These expressions might possibly be construed to imply that when, in a previous section of the act, it was enacted that "the first legislative assembly shall meet at such place and on such day as the governor shall appoint," the word "place" means place at Fort Leavenworth, not place anywhere in the Territory. If so, the governor would have been the first to err in this matter, not only in himself having removed the seat of government to the Shawnee Mission, but in again removing it to Pawnee City. If there was any departure from the letter of the law, therefore, it was his in both instances. But however this may be, it is most unreasonable to suppose that by the terms of the organic act Congress intended to do impliedly what it has not done expressly—that is, to forbid to the legislative assembly the power to choose any place it might see fit as the temporary seat of its deliberations. That is proved by the significant language of one of the subsequent acts of Congress on the subject—that of March 3, 1855—which, in making appropriation for public buildings of the Territory, enacts that the same shall not be expended "until the legislature of said Territory shall have fixed by law the permanent seat of government." Congress in these expressions does not profess to be granting the power to fix the permanent seat of government, but recognizes the power as one already granted. But how? Undoubtedly by the comprehensive provision of the organic act itself, which declares that "the legislative power of the Territory shall extend to all rightful subjects of legislation consistent with the Constitution of the United States and the provisions of this act." If in view of this act the legislative assembly had the large power to fix the permanent seat of government at any place in its discretion, of course by the same enactment it had the less and the included power to fix it temporarily.

Nevertheless, the allegation that the acts of the legislative assembly were illegal by reason of this removal of its place of session was brought forward to justify the first great movement in disregard of law within the Territory. One of the acts of the legislative assembly provided for the election of a Delegate to the present Congress, and a Delegate was elected under that law. But subsequently to this a portion of the people of the Territory proceeded without authority of law to elect another Delegate.

Following upon this movement was another and more important one of the same general character. Persons confessedly not constituting the body politic or all the inhabitants, but merely a party of the inhabitants, and without law, have undertaken to summon a convention for the purpose of transforming the Territory into a State, and have framed a constitution, adopted it, and under it elected a governor and other officers and a Representative to Congress. In extenuation of these illegal acts it is alleged that the States of California, Michigan, and others were self-organized, and as such were admitted into the Union without a previous enabling act of Congress. It is true that while in a majority of cases a previous act of Congress has been passed to authorize the Territory to present itself as a State, and that this is deemed the most regular course, yet such an act has not been held to be indispensable, and in some cases the Territory has proceeded without it, and has nevertheless been admitted into the Union as a State. It lies with Congress to authorize beforehand or to confirm afterwards, in its discretion. But in no instance has a State been admitted upon the application of persons acting against authorities duly constituted by act of Congress. In every case it is the people of the Territory, not a party among them, who have the power to form a constitution and ask for admission as a State. No principle of public law, no practice or precedent under the Constitution of the United States, no rule of reason, right, or common sense, confers any such power as that now claimed by a mere party in the Territory. In fact what has been done is of revolutionary character. It is avowedly so in motive and in aim as respects the local law of the Territory. It will become treasonable insurrection if it reach the length of organized resistance by force to the fundamental or any other Federal law and to the authority of the General Government. In such an event the path of duty for the Executive is plain. The Constitution requiring him to take care that the laws of the United States be faithfully executed, if they be opposed in the Territory of Kansas he may, and should, place at the disposal of the marshal any public force of the United States which happens to be within the jurisdiction, to be used as a portion of the *posse comitatus;* and if that do not suffice to maintain order, then he may call forth the militia of one or more States for that object, or employ for the same object any part of the land or naval force of the United States. So, also, if the obstruction be to the laws of the Territory, and it be duly presented to him as a case of insurrection, he may employ for its suppression the militia of any State or the land or naval force of the United States. And if the Territory be invaded by the citizens of other States, whether for the purpose of deciding elections or for any other, and the local authorities find themselves unable to repel or withstand it, they will be entitled to, and upon the fact being fully ascertained they shall most certainly receive, the aid of the General Government.

But it is not the duty of the President of the United States to volunteer interposition by force to preserve the purity of elections either in a State or Territory. To do so would be subversive of public freedom. And whether a law be wise or unwise, just or unjust, is not a question for him to judge. If it be constitutional—that is, if it be the law of the land—it is his duty to cause it to be executed, or to sustain the authorities of any State or Territory in executing it in opposition to all insurrectionary movements.

Our system affords no justification of revolutionary acts, for the constitutional means of relieving the people of unjust administration and laws, by a change of public agents and by repeal, are ample, and more prompt and effective than illegal violence. These means must be scrupulously guarded, this great prerogative of popular sovereignty sacredly respected.

It is the undoubted right of the peaceable and orderly people of the Territory of Kansas to elect their own legislative body, make their own laws, and regulate their own social institutions, without foreign or domestic molestation. Interference on the one hand to procure the abolition or prohibition of slave labor in the Territory has produced mischievous interference on the other for its maintenance or introduction. One wrong begets another. Statements entirely unfounded, or grossly exaggerated, concerning events within the Territory are sedulously diffused through remote States to feed the flame of sectional animosity there, and the agitators there exert themselves indefatigably in return to encourage and stimulate strife within the Territory.

The inflammatory agitation, of which the present is but a part, has for twenty years produced nothing save unmitigated evil, North and South. But for it the character of the domestic institutions of the future new State would have been a matter of too little interest to the inhabitants of the contiguous States, personally or collectively, to produce among them any political emotion. Climate, soil, production, hopes of rapid advancement and the pursuit of happiness on the part of the settlers themselves, with good wishes, but with no interference from without, would have quietly determined the question which is at this time of such disturbing character.

But we are constrained to turn our attention to the circumstances of embarrassment as they now exist. It is the duty of the people of Kansas to discountenance every act or purpose of resistance to its laws. Above all, the emergency appeals to the citizens of the States, and especially of those contiguous to the Territory, neither by intervention of nonresidents in elections nor by unauthorized military force to attempt to encroach upon or usurp the authority of the inhabitants of the Territory.

No citizen of our country should permit himself to forget that he is a part of its Government and entitled to be heard in the determination of its policy and its measures, and that therefore the highest considerations of personal honor and patriotism require him to maintain by whatever of power or influence he may possess the integrity of the laws of the Republic.

Entertaining these views, it will be my imperative duty to exert the whole power of the Federal Executive to support public order in the Territory; to vindicate its laws, whether Federal or local, against all attempts of organized resistance, and so to protect its people in the establishment of their own institutions, undisturbed by encroachment from without, and in the full enjoyment of the rights of self-government assured to them by the Constitution and the organic act of Congress.

Although serious and threatening disturbances in the Territory of Kansas, announced to me by the governor in December last, were speedily quieted without the effusion of blood and in a satisfactory manner, there is, I regret to say, reason to apprehend that disorders will continue to occur there, with increasing tendency to violence, until some decisive measure be taken to dispose of the question itself which constitutes the inducement or occasion of internal agitation and of external interference.

This, it seems to me, can best be accomplished by providing that when the inhabitants of Kansas may desire it and shall be of sufficient number to constitute a State, a convention of delegates, duly elected by the qualified voters, shall assemble to frame a constitution, and thus to prepare through regular and lawful means for its admission into the Union as a State.

I respectfully recommend the enactment of a law to that effect.

I recommend also that a special appropriation be made to defray any expense which may become requisite in the execution of the laws or the maintenance of public order in the Territory of Kansas.

FRANKLIN PIERCE.

WASHINGTON, *January 25, 1856.*

To the Senate of the United States:

By the inclosed letter of the Secretary of the Treasury it appears that $24,233 belonging to the Chickasaw Indians should be invested in stocks of the United States, by and with the advice and consent of the Senate. I therefore recommend that the necessary authority be given for that purpose.

FRANKLIN PIERCE.

WASHINGTON, *January 28, 1856.*

To the Senate of the United States:

I transmit herewith a report from the Secretary of State, in answer to the resolution of the Senate of the 10th of January, calling for the correspondence between the Secretary of State and Edward Worrell while the latter was acting as consul at Matanzas in relation to the estates of deceased American citizens on the island of Cuba.

FRANKLIN PIERCE.

To the Senate: WASHINGTON, *January, 1856.*

I transmit herewith a copy of the "proceedings of the court-martial in the case of Colonel Montgomery, of the United States Army," as requested by the resolution of the Senate of the 7th instant.

FRANKLIN PIERCE.

WASHINGTON, *February 5, 1856.*

To the Senate of the United States:

In further compliance with the Senate's resolution adopted in executive session on the 15th January last, in respect to the correspondence relating to the estates of deceased American citizens on the island of Cuba, I transmit a report from the Secretary of State, with the papers which accompanied it.

FRANKLIN PIERCE.

WASHINGTON, *February 14, 1856.*

To the Senate of the United States:

I transmit a report from the Secretary of State, in answer to the resolution of the Senate of the 17th ultimo, requesting transcripts of certain correspondence and other papers touching the Republics of Nicaragua and Costa Rica, the Mosquito Indians, and the convention between the United States and Great Britain of April 19, 1850.

FRANKLIN PIERCE.

WASHINGTON, *February 18, 1856.*

To the Senate of the United States:

In compliance with the resolution of the Senate of the 4th instant, requesting transcripts of certain papers relative to the affairs of the Territory of Kansas, I transmit a report from the Secretary of State and the documents which accompanied it.

FRANKLIN PIERCE.

WASHINGTON, *February 21, 1856.*

To the Senate of the United States:

I communicate herewith a report of the Secretary of War and accompanying documents, also of the Secretary of the Navy and accompanying documents, in answer to a resolution of the Senate passed the 11th February, "that the President of the United States be requested to communicate to the Senate copies of all the correspondence between the different Departments of the Government and the officers of the Army and Navy (not heretofore communicated) on the Pacific Coast touching the Indian disturbances in California, Oregon, and Washington."

FRANKLIN PIERCE.

WASHINGTON, *February 25, 1856.*

To the Senate and House of Representatives:

I transmit a copy of a letter of the 7th of March last from the acting commissioner of the United States in China, and of the regulations and notification which accompanied it, for such revision thereof as Congress may deem expedient, pursuant to the sixth section of the act approved 11th August, 1848.

FRANKLIN PIERCE.

WASHINGTON, *February 25, 1856.*

To the Senate of the United States:

I communicate to the Senate herewith, for its constitutional action thereon, a treaty made and concluded on the 17th October, 1855, by and between A. Cumming and Isaac I. Stevens, commissioners on the part of the United States, and the Blackfeet and other tribes of Indians on the Upper Missouri and Yellowstone rivers.

FRANKLIN PIERCE.

WASHINGTON, *February 26, 1856.*

To the Senate and House of Representatives of the United States:

I herewith transmit and recommend to the favorable consideration of Congress a communication from the Secretary of War, asking a special appropriation of $3,000,000 to prepare armaments and ammunition for the fortifications, to increase the supply of improved small arms, and to apply recent improvements to arms of old patterns belonging to the United States and the several States.

FRANKLIN PIERCE.

WASHINGTON, *February 27, 1856.*

To the Senate of the United States:

In answer to the resolution of the Senate of the 25th instant, I transmit reports* from the Secretary of State and the Attorney-General, to whom the resolution was referred.

FRANKLIN PIERCE.

WASHINGTON, *February 29, 1856.*

To the Senate of the United States:

I transmit a report from the Secretary of State, with accompanying papers,† in answer to the resolution of the Senate of yesterday.

FRANKLIN PIERCE.

WASHINGTON, *March 4, 1856.*

To the House of Representatives:

I transmit a report on the commercial relations of the United States with all foreign nations, in answer to the resolution of the House of Representatives of December 14, 1853.

FRANKLIN PIERCE.

---

*Relating to the enlistment of soldiers within the United States by agents of the British Government.

†Relating to an offer of the British Government to refer to the arbitrament of some friendly power the questions of difference between the United States and Great Britain upon the construction of the convention of April 19, 1850.

WASHINGTON, *March 4, 1856.*

To the Senate of the United States:

I herewith communicate to the Senate, for its constitutional action thereon, two treaties recently negotiated by Francis Huebochmann, the superintendent of Indian affairs for the northern superintendency, one with the Menominee Indians and the other with the Stockbridge and Munsee Indians, and more particularly referred to in the accompanying communications of the Secretary of the Interior of this date.

FRANKLIN PIERCE.

WASHINGTON, *March 5, 1856.*

To the Senate of the United States:

In compliance with the resolution of the Senate of the 21st ultimo, I transmit herewith a report from the Secretary of the Interior, with accompanying papers.*

FRANKLIN PIERCE.

EXECUTIVE OFFICE, *March 5, 1856.*

To the Senate and House of Representatives of the United States:

I present herewith a communication from the Secretary of the Interior, in relation to Indian disturbances in the Territories of Oregon and Washington, and recommending an immediate appropriation of $300,000.

I commend this subject to your early consideration.

FRANKLIN PIERCE.

WASHINGTON, *March 5, 1856.*

To the Senate of the United States:

In answer to the resolution of the Senate of the 26th ultimo, requesting information in regard to the site selected for the building to be used for the preservation of the ordnance, arms, etc., of the United States, under the act approved March 3, 1855, I transmit a letter from the Secretary of War, with an accompanying report of the Chief of Ordnance, containing the information.

FRANKLIN PIERCE.

WASHINGTON, *March 10, 1856.*

To the Senate of the United States:

In compliance with a resolution of the Senate of the 21st ultimo, requesting the President of the United States to "communicate to the Senate any correspondence which may have taken place between the Illinois Central Railroad Company and any of the Departments of the Government," etc., I transmit herewith communications from the Secretary of the Treasury and from the Postmaster-General, together with the accompanying papers.*

FRANKLIN PIERCE.

*Correspondence relative to transportation of the mails, etc., over the Illinois Central Railroad.

WASHINGTON, *March 14, 1856.*

To the House of Representatives:

I herewith communicate to the House of Representatives, in compliance with their resolution of the 28th ultimo, a report from the Secretary of the Interior, containing such information as is in possession of his Department touching the cause of the difficulties existing between the Creek and Seminole Indians since their emigration west of the Mississippi River.

FRANKLIN PIERCE.

To the House of Representatives:

I herewith transmit to the House of Representatives a report of the Secretary of War, with copies prepared in compliance with a resolution of the House of the 28th ultimo, requesting ''copies of all correspondence, documents, and papers in relation to the compensation and emoluments of Brevet Lieutenant-General Scott under the joint resolution of Congress approved February 15, 1855.''

MARCH 17, 1856.

FRANKLIN PIERCE.

WASHINGTON, *March 17, 1856.*

To the House of Representatives:

In answer to the resolution of the House of Representatives of the 27th ultimo, on the subject of correspondence between this Government and that of Great Britain touching the Clayton and Bulwer convention, I transmit a report from the Secretary of State, to whom the resolution was referred.

FRANKLIN PIERCE.

WASHINGTON, *March 17, 1856.*

To the Senate and House of Representatives:

I transmit to Congress the copy of a correspondence which has recently taken place between Her Britannic Majesty's minister accredited to this Government and the Secretary of State, in order that the expediency of sanctioning the acceptance by the officers of the United States who were in the American expedition in search of Sir John Franklin of such token of thankfulness as may be offered to them on the part of Her Majesty's Government for their services on the occasion referred to may be taken into consideration.

FRANKLIN PIERCE.

WASHINGTON, *March 20, 1856.*

To the Senate of the United States:

In compliance with a resolution of the Senate of the 26th ultimo, I herewith communicate ''a copy of the report, with the maps, of an exploration of the Big Witchitaw and the head waters of the Brazos rivers, made by Captain R. B. Marcy, of the United States Army, while engaged in locating lands for the Indians of Texas in the year 1854."

FRANKLIN PIERCE.

WASHINGTON, *March 24, 1856.*

To the House of Representatives:

In answer to the resolution of the House of Representatives of the 18th of last month, requesting the transmission of documents touching the affairs of the Territory of Kansas, I transmit a report from the Secretary of State, to whom the resolution was referred.

FRANKLIN PIERCE.

EXECUTIVE OFFICE,
Washington, March 24, 1856.

Hon. NATHANIEL P. BANKS,
Speaker of the House of Representatives:

I herewith transmit to the House of Representatives, in obedience to their resolution of the 17th instant, a communication from the Secretary of the Interior, accompanied by a copy of the report of Superintendent Cumming in regard to his late expedition among the tribes of Indians on the Upper Missouri. FRANKLIN PIERCE.

WASHINGTON, *April 1, 1856.*

To the Senate of the United States:

I transmit to the Senate, for its consideration with a view to ratification, a convention between the United States and the Grand Duchy of Baden for the mutual surrender of fugitive criminals, concluded at Berlin on the 10th ultimo. FRANKLIN PIERCE.

WASHINGTON, *April 3, 1856.*

To the Senate of the United States:

In answer to the resolution of the Senate of the 27th ultimo, requesting additional documents relating to the condition of affairs in Kansas Territory, I transmit a report from the Secretary of State, to whom the resolution was referred. FRANKLIN PIERCE.

WASHINGTON, *April 9, 1856.*

To the Senate and House of Representatives:

In execution of an act of Congress entitled "An act to provide for the accommodation of the courts of the United States for the district of Maryland and for a post-office at Baltimore city, Md.," approved February 17,

1855, I communicate herewith, for the consideration of Congress, copies of conditional contracts which I have caused to be executed for two sites, with buildings thereon, together with plans and estimates for fitting up and furnishing the same.   FRANKLIN PIERCE.

WASHINGTON, *April 9, 1856.*

To the House of Representatives:

I transmit herewith a report from the Secretary of State, with accompanying document,* in compliance with the resolution of the House of Representatives of the 4th instant.   FRANKLIN PIERCE.

WASHINGTON, *April 10, 1856.*

To the Senate of the United States:

I transmit herewith a report of the Secretary of the Interior, with accompanying documents, in compliance with a resolution of the Senate of the 6th ultimo.   The documents, it is believed, contain all the information in the Executive Departments upon the subject† to which the resolution refers.   FRANKLIN PIERCE.

WASHINGTON, *April, 1856.*

To the Senate and House of Representatives of the United States:

I communicate to Congress herewith a letter from the Secretary of the Interior and a copy of a conditional contract entered into, under instructions from that Department, for the purchase of a lot and the building thereon, for the use of the United States courts at Philadelphia, in the State of Pennsylvania, and recommend that an appropriation of $78,000 be made to complete the same.   FRANKLIN PIERCE.

WASHINGTON, *April 14, 1856.*

To the Senate of the United States:

I transmit herewith the report of the Secretary of War, with the accompanying documents, in answer to the resolution of the Senate of the 7th instant, respecting ''the steps pursued in execution of the clause of the act making appropriations for the civil and diplomatic expenses of the Government, approved March 3, 1855, which provides for the construction of an armory for the District of Columbia.''

The selection of the site was made after a full hearing of the parties interested and a personal examination by myself of all the sites suggested as suitable for the purpose.

*Dispatch from the United States minister at Naples relative to the saving from shipwreck of certain American vessels and their crews by officers of the Neapolitan navy and marine service.
†Claim of Richard W. Thompson for alleged services to the Menominee Indians.

It will be perceived upon an examination of the accompanying documents that although two additional purposes were added by Congress after the estimate of the War Department was made, and the expense of the structure consequently increased, still by the terms of my indorsement on the report of the colonel of ordnance fixing the site, the size and arrangement of the building were to be such that it could be *completed* without exceeding the appropriation of $30,000, and that this requirement has been strictly adhered to in every stage of the proceedings.

FRANKLIN PIERCE.

WASHINGTON, *April 14, 1856.*

To the Senate of the United States:

I transmit herewith the report of the Secretary of State, with the accompanying documents, in answer to the resolution of the Senate of the 20th ultimo, respecting the adjustment of the boundary line and the payment of the three millions under the treaty with Mexico of the 30th June [December], 1853.

FRANKLIN PIERCE.

WASHINGTON, *April 17, 1856.*

The SPEAKER OF THE HOUSE OF REPRESENTATIVES:

I transmit herewith reports of the Secretaries of the War and Interior Departments, in response to the resolution of the House of Representatives of the 31st ultimo, calling for information in relation to the origin, progress, and present condition of Indian hostilities in the Territories of Oregon and Washington, and also of the means which have been adopted to preserve peace and protect the inhabitants of said Territories.

FRANKLIN PIERCE.

WASHINGTON, *April 29, 1856.*

To the Senate of the United States:

I transmit herewith the report of the Secretary of State, with the accompanying documents, in answer to the resolution of the Senate of the 24th February, 1855, in relation to the settlement of the controversy respecting the Lobos Islands.

FRANKLIN PIERCE.

WASHINGTON, *April 30, 1856.*

To the House of Representatives:

I transmit herewith to the House of Representatives a report* from the Secretary of State, in answer to their resolution of the 7th instant.

FRANKLIN PIERCE.

* Relating to indemnification by the Spanish Government of the captains, owners, and crews of the bark *Georgiana* and the brig *Susan Loud* for their capture and confiscation by the Spanish authorities.

WASHINGTON, *May 1, 1856.*

To the Senate and House of Representatives:

I communicate herewith a letter of the Postmaster-General, with accompanying correspondence, in relation to mail transportation between our Atlantic and Pacific possessions, and earnestly commend the subject to the early consideration of Congress.

FRANKLIN PIERCE.

WASHINGTON, *May 3, 1856.*

To the Senate of the United States:

I communicate herewith a letter from the Secretary of War, with accompanying papers, in response to a resolution of the Senate of the 21st ultimo, upon the subject of damages which will be "incurred by the United States in case of the repeal of so much of the act of March 3, 1855, as provides for the construction of an armory in the District of Columbia," and also a further answer from the Secretary of War to the resolution of the Senate of the 7th ultimo, requesting a full report of the steps pursued in execution of the clause of the act making appropriations for the civil and diplomatic expenses of the Government, approved March 2, 1855, which provides for the construction of the armory in this District before referred to.

FRANKLIN PIERCE.

WASHINGTON, *May 15, 1856.*

To the Senate and House of Representatives:

I transmit herewith reports of the Secretary of State, the Secretary of the Navy, and the Attorney-General, in reply to a resolution of the Senate of the 24th of March last, and also to a resolution of the House of Representatives of the 8th of May instant, both having reference to the routes of transit between the Atlantic and Pacific oceans through the Republics of New Granada and Nicaragua and to the condition of affairs in Central America.

These documents relate to questions of the highest importance and interest to the people of the United States.

The narrow isthmus which connects the continents of North and South America, by the facilities it affords for easy transit between the Atlantic and Pacific oceans, rendered the countries of Central America an object of special consideration to all maritime nations, which has been greatly augmented in modern times by the operation of changes in commercial relations, especially those produced by the general use of steam as a motive power by land and sea. To us, on account of its geographical position and of our political interest as an American State of primary magnitude, that isthmus is of peculiar importance, just as the Isthmus of Suez is, for corresponding reasons, to the maritime powers of Europe.

But above all, the importance to the United States of securing free transit across the American isthmus has rendered it of paramount interest to us since the settlement of the Territories of Oregon and Washington and the accession of California to the Union.

Impelled by these considerations, the United States took steps at an early day to assure suitable means of commercial transit by canal railway, or otherwise across this isthmus.

We concluded, in the first place, a treaty of peace, amity, navigation, and commerce with the Republic of New Granada, among the conditions of which was a stipulation on the part of New Granada guaranteeing to the United States the right of way or transit across that part of the Isthmus which lies in the territory of New Granada, in consideration of which the United States guaranteed in respect of the same territory the rights of sovereignty and property of New Granada.

The effect of this treaty was to afford to the people of the United States facilities for at once opening a common road from Chagres to Panama and for at length constructing a railway in the same direction, to connect regularly with steamships, for the transportation of mails, specie, and passengers to and fro between the Atlantic and Pacific States and Territories of the United States.

The United States also endeavored, but unsuccessfully, to obtain from the Mexican Republic the cession of the right of way at the northern extremity of the Isthmus by Tehuantepec, and that line of communication continues to be an object of solicitude to the people of this Republic.

In the meantime, intervening between the Republic of New Granada and the Mexican Republic lie the States of Guatemala, Salvador, Honduras, Nicaragua, and Costa Rica, the several members of the former Republic of Central America. Here, in the territory of the Central American States, is the narrowest part of the Isthmus, and hither, of course, public attention has been directed as the most inviting field for enterprises of interoceanic communication between the opposite shores of America, and more especially to the territory of the States of Nicaragua and Honduras.

Paramount to that of any European State, as was the interest of the United States in the security and freedom of projected lines of travel across the Isthmus by the way of Nicaragua and Honduras, still we did not yield in this respect to any suggestions of territorial aggrandizement, or even of exclusive advantage, either of communication or of commerce. Opportunities had not been wanting to the United States to procure such advantage by peaceful means and with full and free assent of those who alone had any legitimate authority in the matter. We disregarded those opportunities from considerations alike of domestic and foreign policy, just as, even to the present day, we have persevered in a system of justice and respect for the rights and interests of others as well as our own in regard to each and all of the States of Central America.

It was with surprise and regret, therefore, that the United States learned a few days after the conclusion of the treaty of Guadalupe Hidalgo, by which the United States became, with the consent of the Mexican Republic, the rightful owners of California, and thus invested with augmented special interest in the political condition of Central America, that a military expedition, under the authority of the British Government, had landed at San Juan del Norte, in the State of Nicaragua, and taken forcible possession of that port, the necessary terminus of any canal or railway across the Isthmus within the territories of Nicaragua.

It did not diminish the unwelcomeness to us of this act on the part of Great Britain to find that she assumed to justify it on the ground of an alleged protectorship of a small and obscure band of uncivilized Indians, whose proper name had even become lost to history, who did not constitute a state capable of territorial sovereignty either in fact or of right, and all political interest in whom and in the territory they occupied Great Britain had previously renounced by successive treaties with Spain when Spain was sovereign to the country and subsequently with independent Spanish America.

Nevertheless, and injuriously affected as the United States conceived themselves to have been by this act of the British Government and by its occupation about the same time of insular and of continental portions of the territory of the State of Honduras, we remembered the many and powerful ties and mutual interests by which Great Britain and the United States are associated, and we proceeded in earnest good faith and with a sincere desire to do whatever might strengthen the bonds of peace between us to negotiate with Great Britain a convention to assure the perfect neutrality of all interoceanic communications across the Isthmus and, as the indispensable condition of such neutrality, the absolute independence of the States of Central America and their complete sovereignty within the limits of their own territory as well against Great Britain as against the United States. We supposed we had accomplished that object by the convention of April 19, 1850, which would never have been signed nor ratified on the part of the United States but for the conviction that in virtue of its provisions neither Great Britain nor the United States was thereafter to exercise any territorial sovereignty in fact or in name in any part of Central America, however or whensoever acquired, either before or afterwards. The essential object of the convention—the neutralization of the Isthmus—would, of course, become a nullity if either Great Britain or the United States were to continue to hold exclusively islands or mainland of the Isthmus, and more especially if, under any claim of protectorship of Indians, either Government were to remain forever sovereign in fact of the Atlantic shores of the three States of Costa Rica, Nicaragua, and Honduras.

I have already communicated to the two Houses of Congress full information of the protracted and hitherto fruitless efforts which the United

States have made to arrange this international question with Great Britain. It is referred to on the present occasion only because of its intimate connection with the special object now to be brought to the attention of Congress.

The unsettled political condition of some of the Spanish American Republics has never ceased to be regarded by this Government with solicitude and regret on their own account, while it has been the source of continual embarrassment in our public and private relations with them. In the midst of the violent revolutions and the wars by which they are continually agitated, their public authorities are unable to afford due protection to foreigners and to foreign interests within their territory, or even to defend their own soil against individual aggressors, foreign or domestic, the burden of the inconveniences and losses of which therefore devolves in no inconsiderable degree upon the foreign states associated with them in close relations of geographical vicinity or of commercial intercourse.

Such is more emphatically the situation of the United States with respect to the Republics of Mexico and of Central America. Notwithstanding, however, the relative remoteness of the European States from America, facts of the same order have not failed to appear conspicuously in their intercourse with Spanish American Republics. Great Britain has repeatedly been constrained to recur to measures of force for the protection of British interests in those countries. France found it necessary to attack the castle of San Juan de Uloa and even to debark troops at Vera Cruz in order to obtain redress of wrongs done to Frenchmen in Mexico.

What is memorable in this respect in the conduct and policy of the United States is that while it would be as easy for us to annex and absorb new territories in America as it is for European States to do this in Asia or Africa, and while if done by us it might be justified as well on the alleged ground of the advantage which would accrue therefrom to the territories annexed and absorbed, yet we have abstained from doing it, in obedience to considerations of right not less than of policy; and that while the courageous and self-reliant spirit of our people prompts them to hardy enterprises, and they occasionally yield to the temptation of taking part in the troubles of countries near at hand, where they know how potential their influence, moral and material, must be, the American Government has uniformly and steadily resisted all attempts of individuals in the United States to undertake armed aggression against friendly Spanish American Republics.

While the present incumbent of the executive office has been in discharge of its duties he has never failed to exert all the authority in him vested to repress such enterprises, because they are in violation of the law of the land, which the Constitution requires him to execute faithfully; because they are contrary to the policy of the Government, and because to permit them would be a departure from good faith toward those American Republics in amity with us, which are entitled to, and will never cease to enjoy, in their calamities the cordial sympathy, and in their prosperity the efficient good will, of the Government and of the people of the United States.

To say that our laws in this respect are sometimes violated or successfully evaded is only to say what is true of all laws in all countries, but not more so in the United States than in any one whatever of the countries of Europe. Suffice it to repeat that the laws of the United States prohibiting all foreign military enlistments or expeditions within our territory have been executed with impartial good faith, and, so far as the nature of things permits, as well in repression of private persons as of the official agents of other Governments, both of Europe and America.

Among the Central American Republics to which modern events have imparted most prominence is that of Nicaragua, by reason of its particular position on the Isthmus. Citizens of the United States have established in its territory a regular interoceanic transit route, second only in utility and value to the one previously established in the territory of New Granada. The condition of Nicaragua would, it is believed, have been much more prosperous than it has been but for the occupation of its only Atlantic port by a foreign power, and of the disturbing authority set up and sustained by the same power in a portion of its territory, by means of which its domestic sovereignty was impaired, its public lands were withheld from settlement, and it was deprived of all the maritime revenue which it would otherwise collect on imported merchandise at San Juan del Norte.

In these circumstances of the political debility of the Republic of Nicaragua, and when its inhabitants were exhausted by long-continued civil war between parties neither of them strong enough to overcome the other or permanently maintain internal tranquillity, one of the contending factions of the Republic invited the assistance and cooperation of a small body of citizens of the United States from the State of California, whose presence, as it appears, put an end at once to civil war and restored apparent order throughout the territory of Nicaragua, with a new administration, having at its head a distinguished individual, by birth a citizen of the Republic, D. Patricio Rivas, as its provisional President.

It is the established policy of the United States to recognize all governments without question of their source or their organization, or of the means by which the governing persons attain their power, provided there be a government *de facto* accepted by the people of the country, and with reserve only of the time as to the recognition of revolutionary governments arising out of the subdivision of parent states with which we are in relations of amity. We do not go behind the fact of a foreign government exercising actual power to investigate questions of legitimacy; we do not inquire into the causes which may have led to a change of government. To us it is indifferent whether a successful revolution has been aided by foreign intervention or not; whether insurrection has overthrown existing government, and another has been established in its place according to preexisting forms or in a manner adopted for the occasion by those whom we may find in the actual possession of power. All these matters we leave to the people and public authorities of the particular country to determine; and their determination, whether it be by positive action or by ascertained acquiescence, is to us a sufficient warranty of the legitimacy of the new government.

During the sixty-seven years which have elapsed since the establishment of the existing Government of the United States, in all which time this Union has maintained undisturbed domestic tranquillity, we have had occasion to recognize governments *de facto*, founded either by domestic revolution or by military invasion from abroad, in many of the Governments of Europe.

It is the more imperatively necessary to apply this rule to the Spanish American Republics, in consideration of the frequent and not seldom anomalous changes of organization or administration which they undergo and the revolutionary nature of most of these changes, of which the recent series of revolutions in the Mexican Republic is an example, where five successive revolutionary governments have made their appearance in the course of a few months and been recognized successively, each as the political power of that country, by the United States.

When, therefore, some time since, a new minister from the Republic of Nicaragua presented himself, bearing the commission of President Rivas, he must and would have been received as such, unless he was found on inquiry subject to personal exception, but for the absence of satisfactory information upon the question whether President Rivas was *in fact* the head of an established Government of the Republic of Nicaragua, doubt as to which arose not only from the circumstances of his avowed association with armed emigrants recently from the United States, but that the proposed minister himself was of that class of persons, and not otherwise or previously a citizen of Nicaragua.

Another minister from the Republic of Nicaragua has now presented himself, and has been received as such, satisfactory evidence appearing that he represents the Government *de facto* and, so far as such exists, the Government *de jure* of that Republic.

That reception, while in accordance with the established policy of the United States, was likewise called for by the most imperative special exigencies, which require that this Government shall enter at once into diplomatic relations with that of Nicaragua. In the first place, a difference has occurred between the Government of President Rivas and the Nicaragua Transit Company, which involves the necessity of inquiry into rights of citizens of the United States, who allege that they have been aggrieved by the acts of the former and claim protection and redress at the hands of their Government. In the second place, the interoceanic communication by the way of Nicaragua is effectually interrupted, and the persons and property of unoffending private citizens of the United States in that country require the attention of their Government. Neither of these objects can receive due consideration without resumption of diplomatic intercourse with the Government of Nicaragua.

Further than this, the documents communicated show that while the interoceanic transit by the way of Nicaragua is cut off, disturbances at Panama have occurred to obstruct, temporarily at least, that by the way of New Granada, involving the sacrifice of the lives and property of citizens of the United States. A special commissioner has been dispatched to Panama to investigate the facts of this occurrence with a view particularly to the redress of parties aggrieved. But measures of another class will be demanded for the future security of interoceanic communication by this as by the other routes of the Isthmus.

It would be difficult to suggest a single object of interest, external or internal, more important to the United States than the maintenance of the communication, by land and sea, between the Atlantic and Pacific States and Territories of the Union It is a material element of the national integrity and sovereignty.

I have adopted such precautionary measures and have taken such action for the purpose of affording security to the several transit routes of Central America and to the persons and property of citizens of the United States connected with or using the same as are within my constitutional power and as existing circumstances have seemed to demand. Should these measures prove inadequate to the object, that fact will be communicated to Congress with such recommendations as the exigency of the case may indicate.

FRANKLIN PIERCE.

EXECUTIVE OFFICE,
Washington, May 16, 1856.

To the Senate and House of Representatives:

I communicate to Congress a report from the Secretary of the Interior, containing estimates of appropriations required in the fulfillment of treaty stipulations with certain Indian tribes, and recommend that the appropriations asked for be made in the manner therein suggested.

FRANKLIN PIERCE.

WASHINGTON, *May 19, 1856.*

To the House of Representatives:

In compliance with a resolution of the House of Representatives of the 7th ultimo, requesting the President "to communicate what information he may possess in regard to citizens of the United States being engaged in the slave trade, or in the transportation in American ships of coolies from China to Cuba and other countries with the intention of placing or continuing them in a state of slavery or servitude, and whether such traffic is not, in his opinion, a violation of the spirit of existing treaties, rendering those engaged in it liable to indictment for piracy; and especially that he be requested to communicate to this House the facts and circumstances attending the shipment from China of some 500 coolies in the ship *Sea Witch*, of the city of New York, lately wrecked on the coast of Cuba," I transmit the accompanying report of the Secretary of State.

FRANKLIN PIERCE.

WASHINGTON, *May 20, 1856.*

To the Senate of the United States:

I transmit a copy of and extracts from dispatches of the late minister of the United States at London, and of his correspondence with Lord Clarendon which accompanied them, relative to the enlistment of soldiers for the British army within the United States by agents of the Government of Great Britain. These dispatches have been received since my message to the Senate upon the subject of the 27th of February last.

FRANKLIN PIERCE.

WASHINGTON, *May 22, 1856.*

To the House of Representatives:

I communicate herewith a report from the Secretary of War, in response to a resolution of the House of Representatives of the 12th instant, requesting me to inform the House "whether United States soldiers have been employed in the Territory of Kansas to arrest persons charged with a violation of certain supposed laws enacted by a supposed legislature assembled at Shawnee Mission."

FRANKLIN PIERCE.

WASHINGTON, *May 29, 1856.*

To the Senate and House of Representatives:

I have ceased to hold intercourse with the envoy extraordinary and minister plenipotentiary of Her Majesty the Queen of the United Kingdom of Great Britain and Ireland near this Government.

In making communication of this fact it has been deemed by me proper also to lay before Congress the considerations of indispensable public duty which have led to the adoption of a measure of so much importance. They appear in the documents herewith transmitted to both Houses.

FRANKLIN PIERCE.

WASHINGTON, *May 29, 1856.*

To the Senate of the United States:

In further answer to the resolution of the Senate of the 17th of January last, requesting a copy of any official correspondence not previously communicated touching the construction and purport of the convention between the United States and Great Britain of the 19th of April, 1850, I transmit a copy of an instruction of the 24th instant from the Secretary of State to the minister of the United States at London.

FRANKLIN PIERCE.

WASHINGTON, *June 3, 1856.*

To the Senate and House of Representatives of the United States:

I herewith communicate a letter of the 26th instant from the Secretary of the Interior, and accompanying papers, relative to the conflict of jurisdiction between the Federal and Cherokee courts and the inadequacy of protection against the intrusion of improper persons into the Cherokee country, and recommend the subject to the consideration of Congress.

FRANKLIN PIERCE.

WASHINGTON, *June 3, 1856.*

To the House of Representatives:

I transmit a report* from the Secretary of State, in answer to a resolution of the House of Representatives of the 29th ultimo.

FRANKLIN PIERCE.

WASHINGTON, *June 4, 1856.*

To the House of Representatives:

In answer to the resolution of the House of Representatives of the 8th of last month, requesting information in regard to a contemplated imposition of additional duties on American leaf tobacco by the Zollverein or Commercial Union of the German States, I transmit a report from the Secretary of State, to whom the resolution was referred.

FRANKLIN PIERCE.

WASHINGTON, *June 13, 1856.*

To the House of Representatives:

In compliance with a resolution of the House of Representatives of the 18th of February last, requesting me to communicate to the House "the report of Captain E. B. Boutwell, and all the documents accompanying it, relative to the operations of the United States sloop of war *John Adams,* under his command, at the Fejee Islands in the year 1855," I transmit herewith a report of the Secretary of the Navy.

FRANKLIN PIERCE.

---

*Stating that no information relative to the action of the leading powers of Europe on the subject of privateering has been officially communicated by any foreign government.

WASHINGTON, *June 18, 1856.*

To the Senate of the United States:

I transmit a report from the Secretary of State, with accompanying documents,* in answer to the resolution of the Senate of the 16th instant.

FRANKLIN PIERCE.

WASHINGTON, *June 20, 1856.*

To the Senate and House of Representatives of the United States:

I communicate herewith a letter from the Secretary of the Interior and accompanying papers, respecting the sum of $16,024.80 now in the hands of the agent of the Choctaw Indians, being a balance remaining from the sales of Choctaw orphan reservations under the nineteenth article of the treaty of 1830, and commend the subject to the favorable consideration of Congress.

FRANKLIN PIERCE.

WASHINGTON, *June 23, 1856.*

To the Senate of the United States:

I transmit to the Senate, for its consideration with a view to ratification, a convention for the mutual delivery of criminals fugitives from justice in certain cases, and for other purposes, concluded at The Hague on the 29th ultimo between the United States and His Majesty the King of the Netherlands.

FRANKLIN PIERCE.

WASHINGTON, *July 3, 1856.*

To the House of Representatives of the United States:

In response to a resolution of the House of Representatives of the 18th ultimo, requesting me to inform the House "what measures, if any, have been taken to carry out the provisions of a late act of Congress authorizing the President to contract with Hiram Powers, the great American sculptor, now in Italy, for some work of art for the new Capitol, and appropriating $25,000 for that purpose," I transmit herewith copies of three letters—one from Mr. Powers to Hon. Edward Everett and two from myself to the same gentleman.

Since the date of my letter of July 24, 1855, I have communicated with Mr. Everett upon the subject verbally and in writing, and the final proposition on my part, resulting therefrom, will be found in the accompanying extract of a letter dated June 5, 1856.

FRANKLIN PIERCE.

*Instructions to Mr. Buchanan, late minister to England, on the subject of free ships making free goods, and letter from Mr. Buchanan to Lord Clarendon on the same subject.

WASHINGTON, *July 7, 1856.*

To the Senate of the United States:

In compliance with a resolution of the Senate of the 6th ultimo, respecting the location of the District armory upon the Mall in this city, I transmit the accompanying report from the Secretary of War.

FRANKLIN PIERCE.

WASHINGTON, *July 7, 1856.*

To the Senate of the United States:

I transmit to the Senate, for its consideration with a view to ratification, a convention for the mutual delivery of criminals fugitives from justice between the United States and Austria, signed in this city on the 3d instant.

FRANKLIN PIERCE.

WASHINGTON, *July 8, 1856.*

To the House of Representatives:

I communicate herewith a report of the Secretary of War, in reply to a resolution of the House of the 25th ultimo, "on the subject of Indian hostilities in Oregon and Washington Territories."

FRANKLIN PIERCE.

WASHINGTON, *July 11, 1856.*

To the Senate of the United States:

In reply to a resolution of the Senate of May 23, requesting a "detailed statement of the sums which have been paid to newspapers published in Washington for advertisements or other printing published or executed under the orders or by authority of the several Departments since the 4th day of March, 1853," I communicate herewith reports from the several Departments.

FRANKLIN PIERCE.

WASHINGTON, *July 15, 1856.*

To the Senate and House of Representatives:

I transmit a copy of a letter of November 27, 1854, from the commissioner of the United States in China, and of the regulations, orders, and decrees which accompanied it, for such revision thereof as Congress may deem expedient, pursuant to the sixth section of the act approved August 11, 1848.

FRANKLIN PIERCE.

EXECUTIVE OFFICE, *Washington, July 21, 1856.*

To the Senate and House of Representatives of the United States:

I communicate to Congress herewith a letter from the Postmaster-General and a copy of a conditional contract entered into under instructions from me for the purchase of a lot and building thereon for a post-office in the city of Philadelphia, together with a copy of a report of Edward Clark, architect of the Patent Office building, in relation to the site and building selected, and recommend that an appropriation of $250,000 be made to complete the purchase, and also an appropriation of $50,000 to make the required alterations and furnish the necessary cases, boxes, etc., to fit it up for a city post-office.

FRANKLIN PIERCE.

WASHINGTON, *July 22, 1856.*

To the Senate of the United States:

I transmit to the Senate, for its consideration with a view to ratification, a treaty of friendship, commerce, navigation, and extradition between the United States and the Republic of Chili, signed at Santiago, in that Republic, on the 27th of May last.

FRANKLIN PIERCE.

WASHINGTON, *July 24, 1856.*

To the Senate and House of Representatives:

I herewith present to Congress a copy of "minutes of a council held at Fort Pierre, Nebraska Territory, on the 1st day of March, 1856, by Brevet Brigadier-General William S. Harney, United States Army, commanding the Sioux expedition, with the delegations from nine of the bands of the Sioux;" also copies of sundry papers upon the same subject.

Regarding the stipulations between General Harney and the nine bands of the Sioux as just and desirable, both for the United States and for the Indians, I respectfully recommend an appropriation by Congress of the sum of $100,000 to enable the Government to execute the stipulations entered into by General Harney.

FRANKLIN PIERCE.

WASHINGTON, *July 29, 1856.*

To the Senate of the United States:

I herewith lay before the Senate, for its constitutional action thereon, a treaty made and concluded at Múckl-te-oh, or Point Elliott, by Isaac I. Stevens, governor and superintendent of Indian affairs of Washington Territory, on the part of the United States, and chiefs, headmen, and delegates of the Dwámish, Suquámish, Sk-táhl-mish, Sam-áhmish, Smalh-kamish, Skope-áhmish, St-káh-mish, Snoquálmoo, Skai-wha-mish, N'Quentl-má-mish, Sk-táh-le-jum, Stoluck-whá-mish, Sno-ho-mish, Ská-git, Kik-i-állus, Swin-á-mish, Squin-áh-mish, Sah-ku-méhu, Noo-whá-há, Nook-wa-cháh-mish, Mee-sée-qua-guilch, Cho-bah-áh-bish, and other allied and subordinate tribes and bands of Indians in said Territory.

Also a treaty made and concluded at Hahd Skus, or Point no Point, on the 26th day of January, 1855, by and between the same commissioner on the part of the United States and the chiefs, headmen, and delegates of the different villages of the S'Klallams Indians in said Territory.

Also a treaty made and concluded at Neah Bay on the 31st day of January, 1855, by and between the same commissioner on the part of the United States and the chiefs, headmen, and delegates of the same villages of the Makah tribe of Indians in the said Territory.

FRANKLIN PIERCE.

WASHINGTON, *July 29, 1856.*

To the Senate of the United States:

I herewith lay before the Senate, for its constitutional action thereon, a treaty made and concluded by and between Isaac I. Stevens, governor and superintendent of Indian affairs of the Territory of Washington, on the part of the United States, and the chiefs, headmen, and delegates of the different tribes and bands of the Qui-nai-elt and Quil-leh-ute Indians in Washington Territory.

Said treaty was made on the 1st of July, 1855, and 25th January, 1856.

FRANKLIN PIERCE.

WASHINGTON, *July 29, 1856.*

To the Senate of the United States:

I herewith lay before the Senate, for its constitutional action thereon, a treaty made and concluded at the treaty ground at Hell Gate, in the Bitter Root Valley, on the 16th day of July, 1855, by and between Isaac I. Stevens, governor and superintendent of Indian affairs for the Territory of Washington, on the part of the United States, and the chiefs, headmen, and delegates of the confederate tribes of the Flathead, Kootenay, and Upper Pend d'Oreilles Indians, who by the treaty are constituted a nation, under the name of the Flat Head Nation.

FRANKLIN PIERCE.

WASHINGTON, *July 29, 1856.*

To the Senate of the United States:

I herewith lay before the Senate, for its constitutional action thereon, a treaty made and concluded at Wasco, near the Dalles of the Columbia River, in Oregon Territory, by and between Joel Palmer, superintendent of Indian affairs, on the part of the United States, and the chiefs and headmen of the confederated tribes and bands of Walla-Wallas and Wascoes Indians residing in middle Oregon. Said treaty was made on the 25th day of June, 1855.

FRANKLIN PIERCE.

WASHINGTON, *July 29, 1856.*

To the Senate of the United States:

I herewith lay before the Senate, for its constitutional action thereon, a treaty made and concluded on the 21st day of December, 1855, by and between Joel Palmer, superintendent of Indian affairs, on the part of the United States, and the chiefs and headmen of the Mo-lal-la-las, or Molel, tribe of Indians in Oregon Territory.

FRANKLIN PIERCE.

WASHINGTON, *July 29, 1856.*

To the Senate of the United States:

I herewith lay before the Senate, for its constitutional action thereon, a treaty made on the 9th of June, 1855, by and between Isaac I. Stevens, governor and superintendent of Indian affairs of the Territory of Washington, and Joel Palmer, superintendent of Indian affairs of the Territory of Oregon, on the part of the United States, and the chiefs, headmen, and delegates of the Walla-Wallas, Cayuses, and Umatilla tribes and bands of Indians, who for the purposes of the treaty are to be regarded as one nation. Also a treaty made on the 11th of June, 1855, by and between the same commissioners on the part of the United States and the chiefs, headmen, and delegates of the Nez Percé tribe of Indians.

The lands ceded by the treaties herewith lie partly in Washington and partly in Oregon Territories.

FRANKLIN PIERCE.

WASHINGTON, *July 29, 1856.*

To the Senate of the United States:

I herewith lay before the Senate, for its constitutional action thereon, a treaty made and concluded at Camp Stevens, Walla Walla Valley, on the 9th day of June, 1855, by and between Isaac I. Stevens, governor of and superintendent of Indian affairs for Washington Territory, on the part of the United States, and the head chiefs, chiefs, headmen, and delegates of the Yakama, Palouse, Pisquouse, Wenatshapam, Klikatat, Klin-quit, Kow-was-say-ee, Li-ay-was, Skin-pah, Wish-ham, Shyiks, Oche-chotes, Kah-milt-pah, and Se-ap-cat tribes and bands of Indians, who for the purposes of the treaty are to be known as the "Yakama" Nation of Indians.

FRANKLIN PIERCE.

WASHINGTON, *July 30, 1856.*

To the Senate of the United States:

By the sixteenth article of the treaty of 4th March, 1853, between the United States and the Republic of Paraguay, as amended by a resolution of the Senate of the 1st May, 1854, it was provided that the exchange of the ratifications of that instrument should be effected within twenty-four months of its date; that is, on or before the 4th March, 1855.

From circumstances, however, over which the Government of the United States had no control, but which are not supposed to indicate any indisposition on the part of the Paraguayan Government to consummate the final formalities necessary to give full force and validity to the treaty, the exchange of ratifications has not yet been effected.

A similar condition exists in regard to the treaty between the United States and the Oriental Republic of Uruguay of the 28th August, 1852. The Senate, by a resolution of 13th June, 1854, extended the time within which the ratifications of that treaty might be exchanged to thirty months from its date. That limit, however, has expired, and the exchange has not been effected.

I deem it expedient to direct a renewal of negotiations with the Governments referred to, with a view to secure the exchange of the ratifications of these important conventions. But as the limit prescribed by the Senate in both cases has passed by, it is necessary that authority be conferred on the Executive for that purpose.

I consequently recommend that the Senate sanction an exchange of the ratifications of the treaties above mentioned at any time which may be deemed expedient by the President within three years from the date of the resolution to that effect.

FRANKLIN PIERCE.

WASHINGTON, *August 1, 1856.*

To the Senate and House of Representatives of the United States:

I communicate to Congress herewith the report of Major W. H. Emory, United States commissioner, on the survey of the boundary between the United States and the Republic of Mexico, referred to in the accompanying letter of this date from the Secretary of the Interior.

FRANKLIN PIERCE.

EXECUTIVE OFFICE,
Washington, August 4, 1856.

To the House of Representatives of the United States:

I herewith lay before the House of Representatives a report of the Secretary of War, in reply to a resolution of the House requesting "information in regard to the construction of the Capitol and Post-Office extensions."

FRANKLIN PIERCE.

EXECUTIVE OFFICE, *August 4, 1856.*

To the Senate of the United States:

I communicate herewith a report of the Secretary of War, in response to a resolution of the Senate calling for information in relation to instructions "issued to any military officer in command in Kansas to disperse any unarmed meeting of the people of that Territory, or to prevent by military power any assemblage of the people of that Territory."

FRANKLIN PIERCE.

WASHINGTON, *August 4, 1856.*

To the Senate of the United States:

In answer to the resolution of the Senate of the 1st instant, requesting a copy of papers touching recent events in the Territory of Washington, I transmit a report from the Secretary of State and the documents by which it was accompanied.

FRANKLIN PIERCE.

EXECUTIVE OFFICE,
Washington, August 6, 1856.

To the Senate of the United States:

In compliance with a resolution of the Senate of the 28th ultimo, requesting the President to inform the Senate in relation to any application "by the governor of the State of California to maintain the laws and peace of the said State against the usurped authority of an organization calling itself the committee of vigilance in the city and county of San Francisco," and also "to lay before the Senate whatever information he may have in respect to the proceedings of the said committee of vigilance," I transmit the accompanying reports from the Secretary of State and the Secretary of the Navy.

FRANKLIN PIERCE.

WASHINGTON, *August 8, 1856.*

To the Senate of the United States:

I herewith submit to the Senate, for its constitutional action thereon, a treaty negotiated with the Creek and Seminole Indians, together with the accompanying papers.

FRANKLIN PIERCE.

WASHINGTON, *August 9, 1856.*

To the Senate of the United States:

With a message of the 23d of June last I transmitted, for the consideration of the Senate, a convention for the mutual delivery of criminals fugitives from justice in certain cases, and for other purposes, concluded at The Hague on the 29th of May last between the United States and His Majesty the King of the Netherlands. Deeming it advisable to withdraw that instrument from the consideration of the Senate, I request that it may be returned to me.

FRANKLIN PIERCE.

To the Senate of the United States:

I transmit to the Senate, for its consideration with a view to ratification, a treaty of amity, commerce, and navigation, and for the surrender of fugitive criminals, between the United States and the Republic of Venezuela, signed at Caracas on the 10th of July last.

AUGUST 9, 1856.   FRANKLIN PIERCE.

WASHINGTON, *August 11, 1856.*

To the Senate of the United States:

In compliance with the resolution of the Senate of the 3d March, 1855, requesting information relative to the proceedings of the commissioners for the adjustment of claims under the convention with Great Britain of the 8th of February, 1853, I transmit a report from the Secretary of State, to whom the resolution was referred.

FRANKLIN PIERCE.

WASHINGTON, *August 11, 1856.*

To the House of Representatives of the United States:

I transmit herewith a report of the Secretary of War, in reply to a resolution of the House of Representatives of May 26, 1856, in relation to the Capitol and Post-Office extensions.

FRANKLIN PIERCE.

WASHINGTON, *August 12, 1856.*

To the Senate of the United States:

I transmit a report from the Secretary of State, with accompanying papers,* in answer to the resolution of the Senate of yesterday.

FRANKLIN PIERCE.

WASHINGTON, *August 12, 1856.*

To the Senate of the United States:

In compliance with the resolution of the Senate of the 7th instant, in relation to the refusal of the Government of Honduras to receive a commercial agent from this country, I transmit a report from the Secretary of State and the documents which accompanied it.

FRANKLIN PIERCE.

WASHINGTON, *August 13, 1856.*

To the Senate and House of Representatives:

I transmit herewith a communication from the Secretary of War, inclosing a report of Captain M. C. Meigs, stating that the sum of $750,000

---

*Relating to "The declaration concerning maritime law," adopted by the plenipotentiaries of Great Britain, Austria, France, Prussia, Russia, Sardinia, and Turkey at Paris April 16, 1856.

will be necessary for the prosecution of the Capitol extension until the close of the next session of Congress, and recommend that that amount may be appropriated.

FRANKLIN PIERCE.

WASHINGTON, *August 15, 1856.*

To the House of Representatives:

In answer to the resolution of the House of Representatives of the 4th instant, requesting a copy of letters and papers touching the pardons or remission of the imprisonment of Daniel Drayton and Edward Sayres in August, 1852, I transmit a report from the Secretary of State, to whom the resolution was referred.

FRANKLIN PIERCE.

WASHINGTON, *August 15, 1856.*

To the Senate and House of Representatives:

I transmit herewith a report from the Secretary of War, in relation to an error in a communication* of Captain Meigs.

FRANKLIN PIERCE.

WASHINGTON, *August 16, 1856.*

To the Senate of the United States:

In compliance with a resolution of the Senate of the 11th instant, in relation to the public accounts of John C. Frémont, I transmit the accompanying report from the Secretary of the Treasury, to whom the resolution was referred.

FRANKLIN PIERCE.

WASHINGTON, *August 16, 1856.*

To the House of Representatives:

In compliance with a resolution of the House of Representatives of the 17th April, 1856, requesting me to have prepared and presented to the House of Representatives "a statement showing the appropriations made by the Thirty-first, Thirty-second, and Thirty-third Congresses, distinguishing the appropriations made at each session of each Congress, distinguishing also the appropriations made on the recommendations of the President, heads of Departments, or heads of bureaus from those that were made without such recommendation, and showing what expenditures have been made by the Government in each fiscal year, commencing with the 1st day of July, 1850, and ending on the 30th day of June, 1855; and also what, if any, defalcations have occurred from the 30th day of June, 1850, to the 1st day of July, 1855, and the amount of such defalcations severally, and such other information as may be in his power bearing upon the matters above mentioned," I submit the following reports from the Secretaries of the Treasury, War, Navy, and Interior Departments and the Postmaster-General.

FRANKLIN PIERCE.

---

*Relating to the Capitol extension.

VETO MESSAGES.

WASHINGTON, *May 19, 1856.*

To the Senate of the United States:

I return herewith to the Senate, in which it originated, the bill entitled "An act to remove obstructions to navigation in the mouth of the Mississippi River at the Southwest Pass and Pass à l'Outre," which proposes to appropriate a sum of money, to be expended under the superintendence of the Secretary of War, "for the opening and keeping open ship channels of sufficient capacity to accommodate the wants of commerce through the Southwest Pass and Pass à l'Outre, leading from the Mississippi River to the Gulf of Mexico."

In a communication addressed by me to the two Houses of Congress on the 30th of December, 1854, my views were exhibited in full on the subject of the relation of the General Government to internal improvements. I set forth on that occasion the constitutional impediments, which in my mind are insuperable, to the prosecution of a system of internal improvements by means of appropriations from the Treasury of the United States, more especially the consideration that the Constitution does not confer on the General Government any express power to make such appropriations, that they are not a necessary and proper incident of any of the express powers, and that the assumption of authority on the part of the Federal Government to commence and carry on a general system of internal improvements, while exceptionable for the want of constitutional power, is in other respects prejudicial to the several interests and inconsistent with the true relation to one another of the Union and of the individual States.

These objections apply to the whole system of internal improvements, whether such improvements consist of works on land or in navigable waters, either of the seacoast or of the interior lakes or rivers.

I have not been able, after the most careful reflection, to regard the bill before me in any other light than as part of a general system of internal improvements, and therefore feel constrained to submit it, with these objections, to the reconsideration of Congress.

FRANKLIN PIERCE.

WASHINGTON, *May 19, 1856.*

To the Senate of the United States:

I return herewith to the Senate, in which it originated, a bill entitled "An act making an appropriation for deepening the channel over the St. Clair flats, in the State of Michigan," and submit it for reconsideration, because it is, in my judgment, liable to the objections to the prosecution of internal improvements by the General Government which have already been presented by me in previous communications to Congress.

In considering this bill under the restriction that the power of Congress to construct a work of internal improvement is limited to cases in which the work is manifestly needful and proper for the execution of some one or more of the powers expressly delegated to the General Government, I have not been able to find for the proposed expenditure any such relation, unless it be to the power to provide for the common defense and to maintain an army and navy. But a careful examination of the subject, with the aid of information officially received since my last annual message was communicated to Congress, has convinced me that the expenditure of the sum proposed would serve no valuable purpose as contributing to the common defense, because all which could be effected by it would be to afford a channel of 12 feet depth and of so temporary a character that unless the work was done immediately before the necessity for its use should arise it could not be relied on for the vessels of even the small draft the passage of which it would permit.

Under existing circumstances, therefore, it can not be considered as a necessary means for the common defense, and is subject to those objections which apply to other works designed to facilitate commerce and contribute to the convenience and local prosperity of those more immediately concerned—an object not to be constitutionally and justly attained by the taxation of the people of the whole country.

FRANKLIN PIERCE.

WASHINGTON, *May 22, 1856.*

To the Senate of the United States:

Having considered the bill, which originated in the Senate, entitled "An act making an appropriation for deepening the channel over the flats of the St. Marys River, in the State of Michigan," it is herewith returned without my approval.

The appropriation proposed by this bill is not, in my judgment, a necessary means for the execution of any of the expressly granted powers of the Federal Government. The work contemplated belongs to a general class of improvements, embracing roads, rivers, and canals, designed to afford additional facilities for intercourse and for the transit of commerce, and no reason has been suggested to my mind for excepting it from the objections which apply to appropriations by the General Government for deepening the channels of rivers wherever shoals or other obstacles impede their navigation, and thus obstruct communication and impose restraints upon commerce within the States or between the States or Territories of the Union. I therefore submit it to the reconsideration of Congress, on account of the same objections which have been presented in my previous communications on the subject of internal improvements.

FRANKLIN PIERCE.

WASHINGTON, *August 11, 1856.*

To the House of Representatives:

I return herewith to the House of Representatives, in which it originated, a bill entitled "An act for continuing the improvement of the Des Moines Rapids, in the Mississippi River," and submit it for reconsideration, because it is, in my judgment, liable to the objections to the prosecution of internal improvements by the General Government set forth at length in a communication addressed by me to the two Houses of Congress on the 30th day of December, 1854, and in other subsequent messages upon the same subject, to which on this occasion I respectfully refer.

FRANKLIN PIERCE.

WASHINGTON, *August 14, 1856.*

To the Senate of the United States:

I return herewith to the Senate, in which it originated, a bill entitled "An act for the improvement of the navigation of the Patapsco River and to render the port of Baltimore accessible to the war steamers of the United States," and submit it for reconsideration, because it is, in my judgment, liable to the objections to the prosecution of internal improvements by the General Government set forth at length in a communication addressed by me to the two Houses of Congress on the 30th day of December, 1854, and other subsequent messages upon the same subject, to which on this occasion I respectfully refer.

FRANKLIN PIERCE.

PROCLAMATIONS.

BY THE PRESIDENT OF THE UNITED STATES OF AMERICA.

A PROCLAMATION.

Whereas information has been received by me that sundry persons, citizens of the United States and others resident therein, are preparing, within the jurisdiction of the same, to enlist, or enter themselves, or to hire or retain others to participate in military operations within the State of Nicaragua:

Now, therefore, I, Franklin Pierce, President of the United States, do warn all persons against connecting themselves with any such enterprise or undertaking, as being contrary to their duty as good citizens and to the laws of their country and threatening to the peace of the United States.

I do further admonish all persons who may depart from the United States, either singly or in numbers, organized or unorganized, for any such purpose, that they will thereby cease to be entitled to the protection of this Government.

I exhort all good citizens to discountenance and prevent any such disreputable and criminal undertaking as aforesaid, charging all officers, civil and military, having lawful power in the premises, to exercise the same for the purpose of maintaining the authority and enforcing the laws of the United States.

In testimony whereof I have hereunto set my hand and caused the seal of the United States to be affixed to these presents.

[SEAL.] Done at the city of Washington, the 8th day of December, 1855, and of the Independence of the United States the eightieth.

FRANKLIN PIERCE.

By the President:

W. L. MARCY,
Secretary of State.

BY THE PRESIDENT OF THE UNITED STATES OF AMERICA.

A PROCLAMATION.

Whereas by the second section of an act of the Congress of the United States approved the 5th day of August, 1854, entitled "An act to carry into effect a treaty between the United States and Great Britain signed on the 5th day of June, 1854," it is provided that whenever the island of Newfoundland shall give its consent to the application of the stipulations and provisions of the said treaty to that Province and the legislature thereof and the Imperial Parliament shall pass the necessary laws for that purpose, grain, flour, and breadstuffs of all kinds; animals of all kinds; fresh, smoked, and salted meats; cotton wool, seeds and vegetables, undried fruits, dried fruits, fish of all kinds, products of fish and all other creatures living in the water, poultry, eggs; hides, furs, skins, or tails, undressed; stone or marble in its crude or unwrought state, slate, butter, cheese, tallow, lard, horns, manures, ores of metals of all kinds, coal, pitch, tar, turpentine, ashes; timber and lumber of all kinds, round, hewed, and sawed, unmanufactured in whole or in part; firewood; plants, shrubs, and trees; pelts, wool, fish oil, rice, broom corn, and bark; gypsum, ground or unground; hewn or wrought or unwrought burr or grind stones, dyestuffs; flax, hemp, and tow, unmanufactured; unmanufactured tobacco, and rags—shall be admitted free of duty from that Province into the United States from and after the date of a proclamation by the President of the United States declaring that he has satisfactory evidence that the said Province has consented in a due and proper manner to have the provisions of the treaty extended to it and to allow the United States the full benefits of all the stipulations therein contained; and

Whereas I have satisfactory evidence that the Province of Newfoundland has consented in a due and proper manner to have the provisions of the aforesaid treaty extended to it and to allow the United States the full benefits of all the stipulations therein contained, so far as they are applicable to that Province:

Now, therefore, I, Franklin Pierce, President of the United States of America, do hereby declare and proclaim that from this date the articles enumerated in the preamble of this proclamation, being the growth and produce of the British North American colonies, shall be admitted from the aforesaid Province of Newfoundland into the United States free of duty so long as the aforesaid treaty shall remain in force.

In testimony whereof I have hereunto set my hand and caused the seal of the United States to be affixed to these presents.

[SEAL.]   Done at the city of Washington, the 12th day of December, A. D. 1855, and of the Independence of the United States the eightieth.

FRANKLIN PIERCE.

By the President:

    W. L. MARCY,
      Secretary of State.

BY THE PRESIDENT OF THE UNITED STATES OF AMERICA.

A PROCLAMATION.

Whereas indications exist that public tranquillity and the supremacy of law in the Territory of Kansas are endangered by the reprehensible acts or purposes of persons, both within and without the same, who propose to direct and control its political organization by force. It appearing that combinations have been formed therein to resist the execution of the Territorial laws, and thus in effect subvert by violence all present constitutional and legal authority; it also appearing that persons residing without the Territory, but near its borders, contemplate armed intervention in the affairs thereof; it also appearing that other persons, inhabitants of remote States, are collecting money, engaging men, and providing arms for the same purpose; and it further appearing that combinations within the Territory are endeavoring, by the agency of emissaries and otherwise, to induce individual States of the Union to intervene in the affairs thereof, in violation of the Constitution of the United States; and

Whereas all such plans for the determination of the future institutions of the Territory, if carried into action from within the same, will constitute the fact of insurrection, and if from without that of invasive aggression, and will in either case justify and require the forcible interposition of the whole power of the General Government, as well to maintain the laws of the Territory as those of the Union:

Now, therefore, I, Franklin Pierce, President of the United States, do issue this my proclamation to command all persons engaged in unlawful combinations against the constituted authority of the Territory of Kansas or of the United States to disperse and retire peaceably to their respective abodes, and to warn all such persons that any attempted insurrection in said Territory or aggressive intrusion into the same will be resisted not only by the employment of the local militia, but also by that of any available forces of the United States, to the end of assuring immunity from violence and full protection to the persons, property, and civil rights of all peaceable and law-abiding inhabitants of the Territory.

If, in any part of the Union, the fury of faction or fanaticism, inflamed into disregard of the great principles of popular sovereignty which, under the Constitution, are fundamental in the whole structure of our institutions is to bring on the country the dire calamity of an arbitrament of arms in that Territory, it shall be between lawless violence on the one side and conservative force on the other, wielded by legal authority of the General Government.

I call on the citizens, both of adjoining and of distant States, to abstain from unauthorized intermeddling in the local concerns of the Territory, admonishing them that its organic law is to be executed with impartial justice, that all individual acts of illegal interference will incur condign punishment, and that any endeavor to intervene by organized force will be firmly withstood.

I invoke all good citizens to promote order by rendering obedience to the law, to seek remedy for temporary evils by peaceful means, to discountenance and repulse the counsels and the instigations of agitators and of disorganizers, and to testify their attachment to their country, their pride in its greatness, their appreciation of the blessings they enjoy, and their determination that republican institutions shall not fail in their hands by cooperating to uphold the majesty of the laws and to vindicate the sanctity of the Constitution.

In testimony whereof I have hereunto set my hand and caused the seal of the United States to be affixed to these presents.

[SEAL.] Done at the city of Washington, the 11th day of February, A. D. 1856, and of the Independence of the United States the eightieth.

FRANKLIN PIERCE.

By the President:
  W. L. MARCY,
    Secretary of State.

FRANKLIN PIERCE, PRESIDENT OF THE UNITED STATES OF AMERICA.

To all whom it may concern:

Whereas by letters patent under the seal of the United States bearing date the 2d day of March, A. D. 1843, the President recognized Anthony Barclay as consul of Her Britannic Majesty at New York and declared him free to exercise and enjoy such functions, powers, and privileges as are allowed to the consuls of the most favored nations, but, for good and sufficient reasons, it is deemed proper that he should no longer exercise the said functions within the United States:

Now, therefore, be it known that I, Franklin Pierce, President of the United States of America, do hereby declare that the powers and privileges conferred as aforesaid on the said Anthony Barclay are revoked and annulled.

In testimony whereof I have caused these letters to be made patent and the seal of the United States to be hereunto affixed.

[SEAL.]   Given under my hand, at the city of Washington, the 28th day of May, A. D. 1856, and of the Independence of the United States of America the eightieth.

FRANKLIN PIERCE.

By the President:
    W. L. MARCY, *Secretary of State.*

FRANKLIN PIERCE, PRESIDENT OF THE UNITED STATES OF AMERICA.

To all whom it may concern:

Whereas by letters patent under the seal of the United States bearing date the 2d day of August, A. D. 1853, the President recognized George Benvenuto Mathew as consul of Her Britannic Majesty at Philadelphia and declared him free to exercise and enjoy such functions, powers, and privileges as are allowed to the consuls of the most favored nations, but, for good and sufficient reasons, it is deemed proper that he should no longer exercise the said functions within the United States:

Now, therefore, be it known that I, Franklin Pierce, President of the United States of America, do hereby declare that the powers and privileges conferred as aforesaid on the said George Benvenuto Mathew are revoked and annulled.

In testimony whereof I have caused these letters to be made patent and the seal of the United States to be hereunto affixed.

[SEAL.]   Given under my hand, at the city of Washington, the 28th day of May, A. D. 1856, and of the Independence of the United States of America the eightieth.

FRANKLIN PIERCE.

By the President:
    W. L. MARCY, *Secretary of State.*

FRANKLIN PIERCE, PRESIDENT OF THE UNITED STATES OF AMERICA.

To all whom it may concern:

Whereas by letters patent under the seal of the United States bearing date the 17th day of August, A. D. 1852, the President recognized Charles Rowcroft as consul of Her Britannic Majesty at Cincinnati and declared him free to exercise and enjoy such functions, powers, and privileges as are allowed to the consuls of the most favored nations, but, for good and sufficient reasons, it is deemed proper that he should no longer exercise the said functions within the United States:

Now, therefore, be it known that I, Franklin Pierce, President of the United States of America, do hereby declare that the powers and privileges conferred as aforesaid on the said Charles Rowcroft are revoked and annulled.

In testimony whereof I have caused these letters to be made patent and the seal of the United States to be hereunto affixed.

[SEAL.] Given under my hand, at the city of Washington, the 28th day of May, A. D. 1856, and of the Independence of the United States of America the eightieth.

FRANKLIN PIERCE.

By the President:

W. L. MARCY,
Secretary of State.

BY THE PRESIDENT OF THE UNITED STATES OF AMERICA.

A PROCLAMATION.

Whereas, pursuant to the first article of the treaty between the United States and the Mexican Republic of the 30th day of December, 1853, the true limits between the territories of the contracting parties were declared to be as follows:

Retaining the same dividing line between the two Californias as already defined and established according to the fifth article of the treaty of Guadalupe Hidalgo, the limits between the two Republics shall be as follows:

Beginning in the Gulf of Mexico 3 leagues from land, opposite the mouth of the Rio Grande, as provided in the fifth article of the treaty of Guadalupe Hidalgo; thence, as defined in the said article, up the middle of that river to the point where the parallel of 31° 47′ north latitude crosses the same; thence due west 100 miles; thence south to the parallel of 31° 20′ north latitude; thence along the said parallel of 31° 20′ to the one hundred and eleventh meridian of longitude west of Greenwich; thence in a straight line to a point on the Colorado River 20 English miles below the junction of the Gila and Colorado rivers; thence up the middle of the said river Colorado until it intersects the present line between the United States and Mexico.

And whereas the said dividing line has been surveyed, marked out, and established by the respective commissioners of the contracting parties, pursuant to the same article of the said treaty:

Now, therefore, be it known that I, Franklin Pierce, President of the United States of America, do hereby declare to all whom it may concern that the line aforesaid shall be held and considered as the boundary between the United States and the Mexican Republic and shall be respected as such by the United States and the citizens thereof.

In testimony whereof I have caused the seal of the United States to be hereunto affixed.

[SEAL.]   Given under my hand, at the city of Washington, this 2d day of June, A. D. 1856, and of the Independence of the United States the eightieth.

FRANKLIN PIERCE.

By the President:

W. L. MARCY,
Secretary of State.

BY THE PRESIDENT OF THE UNITED STATES OF AMERICA.

A PROCLAMATION.

Whereas whilst hostilities exist with various Indian tribes on the remote frontiers of the United States, and whilst in other respects the public peace is seriously threatened, Congress has adjourned without granting necessary supplies for the Army, depriving the Executive of the power to perform his duty in relation to the common defense and security, and an extraordinary occasion has thus arisen for assembling the two Houses of Congress, I do therefore by this my proclamation convene the said Houses to meet in the Capitol, at the city of Washington, on Thursday, the 21st day of August instant, hereby requiring the respective Senators and Representatives then and there to assemble to consult and determine on such measures as the state of the Union may seem to require.

In testimony whereof I have caused the seal of the United States to be hereunto affixed and signed the same with my hand.

[SEAL.]   Done at the city of Washington, the 18th day of August, A. D. 1856, and of the Independence of the United States the eighty-first.

FRANKLIN PIERCE.

By order:

W. L. MARCY,
Secretary of State.

SPECIAL SESSION MESSAGE.

WASHINGTON, *August 21, 1856.*

Fellow-Citizens of the Senate and House of Representatives:

In consequence of the failure of Congress at its recent session to make provision for the support of the Army, it became imperatively incumbent on me to exercise the power which the Constitution confers on the Executive for extraordinary occasions, and promptly to convene the two

Houses in order to afford them an opportunity of reconsidering a subject of such vital interest to the peace and welfare of the Union.

With the exception of a partial authority vested by law in the Secretary of War to contract for the supply of clothing and subsistence, the Army is wholly dependent on the appropriations annually made by Congress. The omission of Congress to act in this respect before the termination of the fiscal year had already caused embarrassments to the service, which were overcome only in expectation of appropriations before the close of the present month. If the requisite funds be not speedily provided, the Executive will no longer be able to furnish the transportation, equipments, and munitions which are essential to the effectiveness of a military force in the field. With no provision for the pay of troops the contracts of enlistment would be broken and the Army must in effect be disbanded, the consequences of which would be so disastrous as to demand all possible efforts to avert the calamity.

It is not merely that the officers and enlisted men of the Army are to be thus deprived of the pay and emoluments to which they are entitled by standing laws; that the construction of arms at the public armories, the repair and construction of ordnance at the arsenals, and the manufacture of military clothing and camp equipage must be discontinued, and the persons connected with this branch of the public service thus be deprived suddenly of the employment essential to their subsistence; nor is it merely the waste consequent on the forced abandonment of the seaboard fortifications and of the interior military posts and other establishments, and the enormous expense of recruiting and reorganizing the Army and again distributing it over the vast regions which it now occupies. These are evils which may, it is true, be repaired hereafter by taxes imposed on the country; but other evils are involved, which no expenditures, however lavish, could remedy, in comparison with which local and personal injuries or interests sink into insignificance.

A great part of the Army is situated on the remote frontier or in the deserts and mountains of the interior. To discharge large bodies of men in such places without the means of regaining their homes, and where few, if any, could obtain subsistence by honest industry, would be to subject them to suffering and temptation, with disregard of justice and right most derogatory to the Government.

In the Territories of Washington and Oregon numerous bands of Indians are in arms and are waging a war of extermination against the white inhabitants; and although our troops are actively carrying on the campaign, we have no intelligence as yet of a successful result. On the Western plains, notwithstanding the imposing display of military force recently made there and the chastisement inflicted on the rebellious tribes, others, far from being dismayed, have manifested hostile intentions and been guilty of outrages which, if not designed to provoke a conflict, serve to show that the apprehension of it is insufficient wholly to restrain their vicious propensities. A strong force in the State of Texas has produced a temporary suspension of hostilities there, but in New Mexico incessant activity on the part of the troops is required to keep in check the marauding tribes which infest that Territory. The hostile Indians have not been removed from the State of Florida, and the withdrawal of the troops therefrom, leaving that object unaccomplished, would be most injurious to the inhabitants and a breach of the positive engagement of the General Government.

To refuse supplies to the Army, therefore, is to compel the complete cessation of all its operations and its practical disbandment, and thus to invite hordes of predatory savages from the Western plains and the Rocky Mountains to spread devastation along a frontier of more than 4,000 miles in extent and to deliver up the sparse population of a vast tract of country to rapine and murder.

Such, in substance, would be the direct and immediate effects of the refusal of Congress, for the first time in the history of the Government, to grant supplies for the maintenance of the Army—the inevitable waste of millions of public treasure; the infliction of extreme wrong upon all persons connected with the military establishment by service, employment, or contracts; the recall of our forces from the field; the fearful sacrifice of life and incalculable destruction of property on the remote frontiers; the striking of our national flag on the battlements of the fortresses which defend our maritime cities against foreign invasion; the violation of the public honor and good faith, and the discredit of the United States in the eyes of the civilized world.

I confidently trust that these considerations, and others appertaining to the domestic peace of the country which can not fail to suggest themselves to every patriotic mind, will on reflection be duly appreciated by both Houses of Congress and induce the enactment of the requisite provisions of law for the support of the Army of the United States.

FRANKLIN PIERCE.

SPECIAL MESSAGE.

EXECUTIVE OFFICE,
Washington, August 21, 1856.

To the Senate and House of Representatives:

I transmit herewith a letter from the Secretary of War, in relation to the balances remaining in the Treasury from the last appropriation for the support of the Army.

FRANKLIN PIERCE.

FOURTH ANNUAL MESSAGE.

WASHINGTON, *December 2, 1856.*

Fellow-Citizens of the Senate and of the House of Representatives:

The Constitution requires that the President shall from time to time not only recommend to the consideration of Congress such measures as he may judge necessary and expedient, but also that he shall give information to them of the state of the Union. To do this fully involves exposition of all matters in the actual condition of the country, domestic or foreign, which essentially concern the general welfare. While performing his constitutional duty in this respect, the President does not speak merely to express personal convictions, but as the executive minister of the Government, enabled by his position and called upon by his official obligations to scan with an impartial eye the interests of the whole and of every part of the United States.

Of the condition of the domestic interests of the Union—its agriculture, mines, manufactures, navigation, and commerce—it is necessary only to say that the internal prosperity of the country, its continuous and steady advancement in wealth and population and in private as well as public well-being, attest the wisdom of our institutions and the predominant spirit of intelligence and patriotism which, notwithstanding occasional irregularities of opinion or action resulting from popular freedom, has distinguished and characterized the people of America.

In the brief interval between the termination of the last and the commencement of the present session of Congress the public mind has been occupied with the care of selecting for another constitutional term the President and Vice-President of the United States.

The determination of the persons who are of right, or contingently, to preside over the administration of the Government is under our system committed to the States and the people. We appeal to them, by their voice pronounced in the forms of law, to call whomsoever they will to the high post of Chief Magistrate.

And thus it is that as the Senators represent the respective States of the Union and the members of the House of Representatives the several constituencies of each State, so the President represents the aggregate population of the United States. Their election of him is the explicit and solemn act of the sole sovereign authority of the Union.

It is impossible to misapprehend the great principles which by their recent political action the people of the United States have sanctioned and announced.

They have asserted the constitutional equality of each and all of the States of the Union as States; they have affirmed the constitutional equality of each and all of the citizens of the United States as citizens, whatever their religion, wherever their birth or their residence; they have maintained the inviolability of the constitutional rights of the different sections of the Union, and they have proclaimed their devoted and unalterable attachment to the Union and to the Constitution, as objects of interest superior to all subjects of local or sectional controversy, as the safeguard of the rights of all, as the spirit and the essence of the liberty, peace, and greatness of the Republic.

In doing this they have at the same time emphatically condemned the idea of organizing in these United States mere geographical parties, of marshaling in hostile array toward each other the different parts of the country, North or South, East or West.

Schemes of this nature, fraught with incalculable mischief, and which the considerate sense of the people has rejected, could have had countenance in no part of the country had they not been disguised by suggestions plausible in appearance, acting upon an excited state of the public mind, induced by causes temporary in their character and, it is to be hoped, transient in their influence.

Perfect liberty of association for political objects and the widest scope of discussion are the received and ordinary conditions of government in our country. Our institutions, framed in the spirit of confidence in the intelligence and integrity of the people, do not forbid citizens, either individually or associated together, to attack by writing, speech, or any other methods short of physical force the Constitution and the very existence of the Union. Under the shelter of this great liberty, and protected by the laws and usages of the Government they assail, associations have been formed in some of the States of individuals who, pretending to seek only to prevent the spread of the institution of slavery into the present or future inchoate States of the Union, are really inflamed with desire to change the domestic institutions of existing States. To accomplish their objects they dedicate themselves to the odious task of depreciating the government organization which stands in their way and of calumniating with indiscriminate invective not only the citizens of particular States with whose laws they find fault, but all others of their fellow-citizens throughout the country who do not participate with them in their assaults upon the Constitution, framed and adopted by our fathers, and claiming for the privileges it has secured and the blessings it has conferred the steady support and grateful reverence of their children. They seek an object which they well know to be a revolutionary one. They are perfectly aware that the change in the relative condition of the white and black races in the slaveholding States which they would promote is beyond their lawful authority; that to them it is a foreign object; that it can not be effected by any peaceful instrumentality of theirs; that for them and the States of which they are citizens the only path to its accomplishment is through burning cities, and ravaged fields, and slaughtered populations, and all there is most terrible in foreign complicated with civil and servile war; and that the first step in the attempt is the forcible disruption of a country embracing in its broad bosom a degree of liberty and an amount of individual and public prosperity to which there is no parallel in history, and substituting in its place hostile governments, driven at once and inevitably into mutual devastation and fratricidal carnage, transforming the now peaceful and felicitous brotherhood into a vast permanent camp of armed men like the rival monarchies of Europe and Asia. Well knowing that such, and such only, are the means and the consequences of their plans and purposes, they endeavor to prepare the people of the United States for civil war by doing everything in their power to deprive the Constitution and the laws of moral authority and to undermine the fabric of the Union by appeals to passion and sectional prejudice, by indoctrinating its people with reciprocal hatred, and by educating them to stand face to face as enemies, rather than shoulder to shoulder as friends.

It is by the agency of such unwarrantable interference, foreign and domestic, that the minds of many otherwise good citizens have been so inflamed into the passionate condemnation of the domestic institutions of the Southern States as at length to pass insensibly to almost equally passionate hostility toward their fellow-citizens of those States, and thus finally to fall into temporary fellowship with the avowed and active enemies of the Constitution. Ardently attached to liberty in the abstract, they do not stop to consider practically how the objects they would attain can be accomplished, nor to reflect that, even if the evil were as great as they deem it, they have no remedy to apply, and that it can be only aggravated by their violence and unconstitutional action. A question which is one of the most difficult of all the problems of social institution, political economy, and statesmanship they treat with unreasoning intemperance of thought and language. Extremes beget extremes. Violent attack from the North finds its inevitable consequence in the growth of a spirit of angry defiance at the South. Thus in the progress of events we had reached that consummation, which the voice of the people has now so pointedly rebuked, of the attempt of a portion of the States, by a sectional organization and movement, to usurp the control of the Government of the United States.

I confidently believe that the great body of those who inconsiderately took this fatal step are sincerely attached to the Constitution and the Union. They would upon deliberation shrink with unaffected horror from any conscious act of disunion or civil war. But they have entered into a path which leads nowhere unless it be to civil war and disunion, and which has no other possible outlet. They have proceeded thus far in that direction in consequence of the successive stages of their progress having consisted of a series of secondary issues, each of which professed to be confined within constitutional and peaceful limits, but which attempted indirectly what few men were willing to do directly; that is, to act aggressively against the constitutional rights of nearly one-half of the thirty-one States.

In the long series of acts of indirect aggression, the first was the strenuous agitation by citizens of the Northern States, in Congress and out of it, of the question of negro emancipation in the Southern States.

The second step in this path of evil consisted of acts of the people of the Northern States, and in several instances of their governments, aimed to facilitate the escape of persons held to service in the Southern States and to prevent their extradition when reclaimed according to law and in virtue of express provisions of the Constitution. To promote this object, legislative enactments and other means were adopted to take away or defeat rights which the Constitution solemnly guaranteed. In order to nullify the then existing act of Congress concerning the extradition of fugitives from service, laws were enacted in many States forbidding their officers, under the severest penalties, to participate in the execution of any act of Congress whatever. In this way that system of harmonious cooperation between the authorities of the United States and of the several States, for the maintenance of their common institutions, which existed in the early years of the Republic was destroyed; conflicts of jurisdiction came to be frequent, and Congress found itself compelled, for the support of the Constitution and the vindication of its power, to authorize the appointment of new officers charged with the execution of its acts, as if they and the officers of the States were the ministers, respectively, of foreign governments in a state of mutual hostility rather than fellow-magistrates of a common country peacefully subsisting under the protection of one well-constituted Union. Thus here also aggression was followed by reaction, and the attacks upon the Constitution at this point did but serve to raise up new barriers for its defense and security.

The third stage of this unhappy sectional controversy was in connection with the organization of Territorial governments and the admission of new States into the Union. When it was proposed to admit the State of Maine, by separation of territory from that of Massachusetts, and the State of Missouri, formed of a portion of the territory ceded by France to the United States, representatives in Congress objected to the admission of the latter unless with conditions suited to particular views of public policy. The imposition of such a condition was successfully resisted; but at the same period the question was presented of imposing restrictions upon the residue of the territory ceded by France. That question was for the time disposed of by the adoption of a geographical line of limitation.

In this connection it should not be forgotten that when France, of her own accord, resolved, for considerations of the most far-sighted sagacity, to cede Louisiana to the United States, and that accession was accepted by the United States, the latter expressly engaged that "the inhabitants of the ceded territory shall be incorporated in the Union of the United

States and admitted as soon as possible, according to the principles of the Federal Constitution, to the enjoyment of all the rights, advantages, and immunities of citizens of the United States; and in the meantime they shall be maintained and protected in the free enjoyment of their *liberty, property,* and the religion which they profess;" that is to say, while it remains in a Territorial condition its inhabitants are maintained and protected in the free enjoyment of their liberty and property, with a right then to pass into the condition of States on a footing of perfect equality with the original States.

The enactment which established the restrictive geographical line was acquiesced in rather than approved by the States of the Union. It stood on the statute book, however, for a number of years; and the people of the respective States acquiesced in the reenactment of the principle as applied to the State of Texas, and it was proposed to acquiesce in its further application to the territory acquired by the United States from Mexico. But this proposition was successfully resisted by the representatives from the Northern States, who, regardless of the statute line, insisted upon applying restriction to the new territory generally, whether lying north or south of it, thereby repealing it as a legislative compromise, and, on the part of the North, persistently violating the compact, if compact there was.

Thereupon this enactment ceased to have binding virtue in any sense, whether as respects the North or the South, and so in effect it was treated on the occasion of the admission of the State of California and the organization of the Territories of New Mexico, Utah, and Washington.

Such was the state of this question when the time arrived for the organization of the Territories of Kansas and Nebraska. In the progress of constitutional inquiry and reflection it had now at length come to be seen clearly that Congress does not possess constitutional power to impose restrictions of this character upon any present or future State of the Union. In a long series of decisions, on the fullest argument and after the most deliberate consideration, the Supreme Court of the United States had finally determined this point in every form under which the question could arise, whether as affecting public or private rights—in questions of the public domain, of religion, of navigation, and of servitude.

The several States of the Union are by force of the Constitution coequal in domestic legislative power. Congress can not change a law of domestic relation in the State of Maine; no more can it in the State of Missouri. Any statute which proposes to do this is a mere nullity; it takes away no right, it confers none. If it remains on the statute book unrepealed, it remains there only as a monument of error and a beacon of warning to the legislator and the statesman. To repeal it will be only to remove imperfection from the statutes, without affecting, either in the sense of permission or of prohibition, the action of the States or of their citizens.

Still, when the nominal restriction of this nature, already a dead letter in law, was in terms repealed by the last Congress, in a clause of the act organizing the Territories of Kansas and Nebraska, that repeal was made the occasion of a widespread and dangerous agitation.

It was alleged that the original enactment being a compact of perpetual moral obligation, its repeal constituted an odious breach of faith.

An act of Congress, while it remains unrepealed, more especially if it be constitutionally valid in the judgment of those public functionaries whose duty it is to pronounce on that point, is undoubtedly binding on the conscience of each good citizen of the Republic. But in what sense can it be asserted that the enactment in question was invested with perpetuity and entitled to the respect of a solemn compact? Between whom was the compact? No distinct contending powers of the Government, no separate sections of the Union treating as such, entered into treaty stipulations on the subject. It was a mere clause of an act of Congress, and, like any other controverted matter of legislation, received its final shape and was passed by compromise of the conflicting opinions or sentiments of the members of Congress. But if it had moral authority over men's consciences, to whom did this authority attach? Not to those of the North, who had repeatedly refused to confirm it by extension and who had zealously striven to establish other and incompatible regulations upon the subject. And if, as it thus appears, the supposed compact had no obligatory force as to the North, of course it could not have had any as to the South, for all such compacts must be mutual and of reciprocal obligation.

It has not unfrequently happened that lawgivers, with undue estima- tion of the value of the law they give or in the view of imparting to it peculiar strength, make it perpetual in terms; but they can not thus bind the conscience, the judgment, and the will of those who may suc- ceed them, invested with similar responsibilities and clothed with equal authority. More careful investigation may prove the law to be unsound in principle. Experience may show it to be imperfect in detail and im- practicable in execution. And then both reason and right combine not merely to justify but to require its repeal.

The Constitution, supreme, as it is, over all the departments of the Government—legislative, executive, and judicial—is open to amendment by its very terms; and Congress or the States may, in their discretion, propose amendment to it, solemn compact though it in truth is between the sovereign States of the Union. In the present instance a political enactment which had ceased to have legal power or authority of any kind was repealed. The position assumed that Congress had no moral right to enact such repeal was strange enough, and singularly so in view of the fact that the argument came from those who openly refused obedi- ence to existing laws of the land, having the same popular designation and quality as compromise acts; nay, more, who unequivocally disregarded and condemned the most positive and obligatory injunctions of the Constitution itself, and sought by every means within their reach to deprive a portion of their fellow-citizens of the equal enjoyment of those rights and privileges guaranteed alike to all by the fundamental compact of our Union.

This argument against the repeal of the statute line in question was accompanied by another of congenial character and equally with the former destitute of foundation in reason and truth. It was imputed that the measure originated in the conception of extending the limits of slave labor beyond those previously assigned to it, and that such was its natural as well as intended effect; and these baseless assumptions were made, in the Northern States, the ground of unceasing assault upon constitutional right.

The repeal in terms of a statute, which was already obsolete and also null for unconstitutionality, could have no influence to obstruct or to promote the propagation of conflicting views of political or social institution. When the act organizing the Territories of Kansas and Nebraska was passed, the inherent effect upon that portion of the public domain thus opened to legal settlement was to admit settlers from all the States of the Union alike, each with his convictions of public policy and private interest, there to found, in their discretion, subject to such limitations as the Constitution and acts of Congress might prescribe, new States, hereafter to be admitted into the Union. It was a free field, open alike to all, whether the statute line of assumed restriction were repealed or not. That repeal did not open to free competition of the diverse opinions and domestic institutions a field which without such repeal would have been closed against them; it found that field of competition already opened, in fact and in law. All the repeal did was to relieve the statute book of an objectionable enactment, unconstitutional in effect and injurious in terms to a large portion of the States.

Is it the fact that in all the unsettled regions of the United States, if emigration be left free to act in this respect for itself, without legal prohibitions on either side, slave labor will spontaneously go everywhere in preference to free labor? Is it the fact that the peculiar domestic institutions of the Southern States possess relatively so much of vigor that wheresoever an avenue is freely opened to all the world they will penetrate to the exclusion of those of the Northern States? Is it the fact that the former enjoy, compared with the latter, such irresistibly superior vitality, independent of climate, soil, and all other accidental circumstances, as to be able to produce the supposed result in spite of the assumed moral and natural obstacles to its accomplishment and of the more numerous population of the Northern States?

The argument of those who advocate the enactment of new laws of restriction and condemn the repeal of old ones in effect avers that their particular views of government have no self-extending or self-sustaining power of their own, and will go nowhere unless forced by act of Congress. And if Congress do but pause for a moment in the policy of stern coercion; if it venture to try the experiment of leaving men to judge for themselves what institutions will best suit them; if it be not strained up to perpetual legislative exertion on this point—if Congress proceed thus to act in the very spirit of liberty, it is at once charged with aiming to extend slave labor into all the new Territories of the United States.

Of course these imputations on the intentions of Congress in this respect, conceived, as they were, in prejudice and disseminated in passion, are utterly destitute of any justification in the nature of things and contrary to all the fundamental doctrines and principles of civil liberty and self-government.

While, therefore, in general, the people of the Northern States have never at any time arrogated for the Federal Government the power to interfere directly with the domestic condition of persons in the Southern States, but, on the contrary, have disavowed all such intentions and have shrunk from conspicuous affiliation with those few who pursue their fanatical objects avowedly through the contemplated means of revolutionary change of the Government and with acceptance of the necessary consequences—a civil and servile war—yet many citizens have suffered themselves to be drawn into one evanescent political issue of agitation after another, appertaining to the same set of opinions, and which subsided as rapidly as they arose when it came to be seen, as it uniformly did, that they were incompatible with the compacts of the Constitution and the existence of the Union. Thus when the acts of some of the States to nullify the existing extradition law imposed upon Congress the duty of passing a new one, the country was invited by agitators to enter into party organization for its repeal; but that agitation speedily ceased by reason of the impracticability of its object. So when the statute restriction upon the institutions of new States by a geographical line had been repealed, the country was urged to demand its restoration, and that project also died almost with its birth. Then followed the cry of alarm from the North against imputed Southern encroachments, which cry sprang in reality from the spirit of revolutionary attack on the domestic institutions of the South, and, after a troubled existence of a few months, has been rebuked by the voice of a patriotic people.

Of this last agitation, one lamentable feature was that it was carried on at the immediate expense of the peace and happiness of the people of the Territory of Kansas. That was made the battlefield, not so much of opposing factions or interests within itself as of the conflicting passions of the whole people of the United States. Revolutionary disorder in Kansas had its origin in projects of intervention deliberately arranged by certain members of that Congress which enacted the law for the organization of the Territory; and when propagandist colonization of Kansas had thus been undertaken in one section of the Union for the systematic promotion of its peculiar views of policy there ensued as a matter of course a counteraction with opposite views in other sections of the Union.

In consequence of these and other incidents, many acts of disorder, it is undeniable, have been perpetrated in Kansas, to the occasional interruption rather than the permanent suspension of regular government. Aggressive and most reprehensible incursions into the Territory were undertaken both in the North and the South, and entered it on its northern border by the way of Iowa, as well as on the eastern by way of Missouri; and there has existed within it a state of insurrection against the constituted authorities, not without countenance from inconsiderate persons in each of the great sections of the Union. But the difficulties in that Territory have been extravagantly exaggerated for purposes of political agitation elsewhere. The number and gravity of the acts of violence have been magnified partly by statements entirely untrue and partly by reiterated accounts of the same rumors or facts. Thus the Territory has been seemingly filled with extreme violence, when the whole amount of such acts has not been greater than what occasionally passes before us in single cities to the regret of all good citizens, but without being regarded as of general or permanent political consequence.

Imputed irregularities in the elections had in Kansas, like occasional irregularities of the same description in the States, were beyond the sphere of action of the Executive. But incidents of actual violence or of organized obstruction of law, pertinaciously renewed from time to time, have been met as they occurred by such means as were available and as the circumstances required, and nothing of this character now remains to affect the general peace of the Union. The attempt of a part of the inhabitants of the Territory to erect a revolutionary government, though sedulously encouraged and supplied with pecuniary aid from active agents of disorder in some of the States, has completely failed. Bodies of armed men, foreign to the Territory, have been prevented from entering or compelled to leave it; predatory bands, engaged in acts of rapine under cover of the existing political disturbances, have been arrested or dispersed, and every well-disposed person is now enabled once more to devote himself in peace to the pursuits of prosperous industry, for the prosecution of which he undertook to participate in the settlement of the Territory.

It affords me unmingled satisfaction thus to announce the peaceful condition of things in Kansas, especially considering the means to which it was necessary to have recourse for the attainment of the end, namely, the employment of a part of the military force of the United States. The withdrawal of that force from its proper duty of defending the country against foreign foes or the savages of the frontier to employ it for the suppression of domestic insurrection is, when the exigency occurs, a matter of the most earnest solicitude. On this occasion of imperative necessity it has been done with the best results, and my satisfaction in the attainment of such results by such means is greatly enhanced by the consideration that, through the wisdom and energy of the present executive of Kansas and the prudence, firmness, and vigilance of the military officers on duty there tranquillity has been restored without one drop of blood having been shed in its accomplishment by the forces of the United States.

The restoration of comparative tranquillity in that Territory furnishes the means of observing calmly and appreciating at their just value the events which have occurred there and the discussions of which the government of the Territory has been the subject.

We perceive that controversy concerning its future domestic institutions was inevitable; that no human prudence, no form of legislation, no wisdom on the part of Congress, could have prevented it.

It is idle to suppose that the particular provisions of their organic law were the cause of agitation. Those provisions were but the occasion, or the pretext, of an agitation which was inherent in the nature of things. Congress legislated upon the subject in such terms as were most consonant with the principle of popular sovereignty which underlies our Government. It could not have legislated otherwise without doing violence to another great principle of our institutions—the imprescriptible right of equality of the several States.

We perceive also that sectional interests and party passions have been the great impediment to the salutary operation of the organic principles adopted and the chief cause of the successive disturbances in Kansas. The assumption that because in the organization of the Territories of Nebraska and Kansas Congress abstained from imposing restraints upon them to which certain other Territories had been subject, therefore disorders occurred in the latter Territory, is emphatically contradicted by the fact that none have occurred in the former. Those disorders were not the consequence, in Kansas, of the freedom of self-government conceded to that Territory by Congress, but of unjust interference on the part of persons not inhabitants of the Territory. Such interference, wherever it has exhibited itself by acts of insurrectionary character or of obstruction to process of law, has been repelled or suppressed by all the means which the Constitution and the laws place in the hands of the Executive.

In those parts of the United States where, by reason of the inflamed state of the public mind, false rumors and misrepresentations have the greatest currency it has been assumed that it was the duty of the Executive not only to suppress insurrectionary movements in Kansas, but also to see to the regularity of local elections. It needs little argument to show that the President has no such power. All government in the United States rests substantially upon popular election. The freedom of elections is liable to be impaired by the intrusion of unlawful votes or the exclusion of lawful ones, by improper influences, by violence, or by fraud. But the people of the United States are themselves the all-sufficient guardians of their own rights, and to suppose that they will not remedy in due season any such incidents of civil freedom is to suppose them to have ceased to be capable of self-government. The President of the United States has not power to interpose in elections, to see to their freedom, to canvass their votes, or to pass upon their legality in the Territories any more than in the States. If he had such power the Government might be republican in form, but it would be a monarchy in fact; and if he had undertaken to exercise it in the case of Kansas he would have been justly subject to the charge of usurpation and of violation of the dearest rights of the people of the United States.

Unwise laws, equally with irregularities at elections, are in periods of great excitement the occasional incidents of even the freest and best political institutions; but all experience demonstrates that in a country like ours, where the right of self-constitution exists in the completest form, the attempt to remedy unwise legislation by resort to revolution is totally out of place, inasmuch as existing legal institutions afford more prompt and efficacious means for the redress of wrong.

I confidently trust that now, when the peaceful condition of Kansas affords opportunity for calm reflection and wise legislation, either the legislative assembly of the Territory or Congress will see that no act shall remain on its statute book violative of the provisions of the Constitution or subversive of the great objects for which that was ordained and established, and will take all other necessary steps to assure to its inhabitants the enjoyment, without obstruction or abridgment, of all the constitutional rights, privileges, and immunities of citizens of the United States, as contemplated by the organic law of the Territory.

Full information in relation to recent events in this Territory will be found in the documents communicated herewith from the Departments of State and War.

I refer you to the report of the Secretary of the Treasury for particular information concerning the financial condition of the Government and the various branches of the public service connected with the Treasury Department.

During the last fiscal year the receipts from customs were for the first time more than $64,000,000, and from all sources $73,918,141, which, with the balance on hand up to the 1st of July, 1855, made the total resources of the year amount to $92,850,117. The expenditures, including $3,000,000 in execution of the treaty with Mexico and excluding sums paid on account of the public debt, amounted to $60,172,401, and including the latter to $72,948,792, the payment on this account having amounted to $12,776,390.

On the 4th of March, 1853, the amount of the public debt was $69,-129,937. There was a subsequent increase of $2,750,000 for the debt of

Texas, making a total of $71,879,937. Of this the sum of $45,525,319, including premium, has been discharged, reducing the debt to $30,963,-909, all which might be paid within a year without embarrassing the public service, but being not yet due and only redeemable at the option of the holder, can not be pressed to payment by the Government.

On examining the expenditures of the last five years it will be seen that the average, deducting payments on account of the public debt and $10,000,000 paid by treaty to Mexico, has been but about $48,000,000. It is believed that under an economical administration of the Government the average expenditure for the ensuing five years will not exceed that sum, unless extraordinary occasion for its increase should occur. The acts granting bounty lands will soon have been executed, while the extension of our frontier settlements will cause a continued demand for lands and augmented receipts, probably, from that source. These considerations will justify a reduction of the revenue from customs so as not to exceed forty-eight or fifty million dollars. I think the exigency for such reduction is imperative, and again urge it upon the consideration of Congress.

The amount of reduction, as well as the manner of effecting it, are questions of great and general interest, it being essential to industrial enterprise and the public prosperity, as well as the dictate of obvious justice, that the burden of taxation be made to rest as equally as possible upon all classes and all sections and interests of the country.

I have heretofore recommended to your consideration the revision of the revenue laws, prepared under the direction of the Secretary of the Treasury, and also legislation upon some special questions affecting the business of that Department, more especially the enactment of a law to punish the abstraction of official books or papers from the files of the Government and requiring all such books and papers and all other public property to be turned over by the outgoing officer to his successor; of a law requiring disbursing officers to deposit all public money in the vaults of the Treasury or in other legal depositories, where the same are conveniently accessible, and a law to extend existing penal provisions to all persons who may become possessed of public money by deposit or otherwise and who shall refuse or neglect on due demand to pay the same into the Treasury. I invite your attention anew to each of these objects.

The Army during the past year has been so constantly employed against hostile Indians in various quarters that it can scarcely be said, with propriety of language, to have been a peace establishment. Its duties have been satisfactorily performed, and we have reason to expect as a result of the year's operations greater security to the frontier inhabitants than has been hitherto enjoyed. Extensive combinations among the hostile Indians of the Territories of Washington and Oregon at one time threatened the devastation of the newly formed settlements of that remote portion of the country. From recent information we are permitted to hope that the energetic and successful operations conducted there will prevent such combinations in future and secure to those Territories an opportunity to make steady progress in the development of their agricultural and mineral resources.

Legislation has been recommended by me on previous occasions to cure defects in the existing organization and to increase the efficiency of the Army, and further observation has but served to confirm me in the views then expressed and to enforce on my mind the conviction that such measures are not only proper, but necessary.

I have, in addition, to invite the attention of Congress to a change of policy in the distribution of troops and to the necessity of providing a more rapid increase of the military armament. For details of these and other subjects relating to the Army I refer to the report of the Secretary of War.

The condition of the Navy is not merely satisfactory, but exhibits the most gratifying evidences of increased vigor. As it is comparatively small, it is more important that it should be as complete as possible in all the elements of strength; that it should be efficient in the character of its officers, in the zeal and discipline of its men, in the reliability of its ordnance, and in the capacity of its ships. In all these various qualities the Navy has made great progress within the last few years. The execution of the law of Congress of February 28, 1855, "to promote the efficiency of the Navy," has been attended by the most advantageous results. The law for promoting discipline among the men is found convenient and salutary. The system of granting an honorable discharge to faithful seamen on the expiration of the period of their enlistment and permitting them to reenlist after a leave of absence of a few months without cessation of pay is highly beneficial in its influence. The apprentice system recently adopted is evidently destined to incorporate into the service a large number of our countrymen, hitherto so difficult to procure. Several hundred American boys are now on a three years' cruise in our national vessels and will return well-trained seamen. In the Ordnance Department there is a decided and gratifying indication of progress, creditable to it and to the country. The suggestions of the Secretary of the Navy in regard to further improvement in that branch of the service I commend to your favorable action.

The new frigates ordered by Congress are now afloat and two of them in active service. They are superior models of naval architecture, and with their formidable battery add largely to public strength and security. I concur in the views expressed by the Secretary of the Department in favor of a still further increase of our naval force.

The report of the Secretary of the Interior presents facts and views in relation to internal affairs over which the supervision of his Department extends of much interest and importance.

The aggregate sales of the public lands during the last fiscal year amount to 9,227,878 acres, for which has been received the sum of $8,821,414. During the same period there have been located with military scrip and land warrants and for other purposes 30,100,230 acres, thus making a total aggregate of 39,328,108 acres. On the 30th of September last surveys had been made of 16,873,699 acres, a large proportion of which is ready for market.

The suggestions in this report in regard to the complication and progressive expansion of the business of the different bureaus of the Department, to the pension system, to the colonization of Indian tribes, and the recommendations in relation to various improvements in the District of Columbia are especially commended to your consideration.

The report of the Postmaster-General presents fully the condition of that Department of the Government. Its expenditures for the last fiscal year were $10,407,868 and its gross receipts $7,620,801, making an excess of expenditure over receipts of $2,787,046. The deficiency of this Department is thus $744,000 greater than for the year ending June 30, 1853. Of this deficiency $330,000 is to be attributed to the additional compensation allowed to postmasters by the act of Congress of June 22, 1854. The mail facilities in every part of the country have been very much increased in that period, and the large addition of railroad service, amounting to 7,908 miles, has added largely to the cost of transportation.

The inconsiderable augmentation of the income of the Post-Office Department under the reduced rates of postage and its increasing expenditures must for the present make it dependent to some extent upon the Treasury for support. The recommendations of the Postmaster-General in relation to the abolition of the franking privilege and his views on the establishment of mail steamship lines deserve the consideration of Congress. I also call the special attention of Congress to the statement of the Postmaster-General respecting the sums now paid for the transportation of mails to the Panama Railroad Company, and commend to their early and favorable consideration the suggestions of that officer in relation to new contracts for mail transportation upon that route, and also upon the Tehuantepec and Nicaragua routes.

The United States continue in the enjoyment of amicable relations with all foreign powers.

When my last annual message was transmitted to Congress two subjects of controversy, one relating to the enlistment of soldiers in this country for foreign service and the other to Central America, threatened to disturb the good understanding between the United States and Great Britain. Of the progress and termination of the former question you were informed at the time, and the other is now in the way of satisfactory adjustment.

The object of the convention between the United States and Great Britain of the 19th of April, 1850, was to secure for the benefit of all

nations the neutrality and the common use of any transit way or interoceanic communication across the Isthmus of Panama which might be
opened within the limits of Central America. The pretensions subsequently asserted by Great Britain to dominion or control over territories
in .or near two of the routes, those of Nicaragua and Honduras, were
deemed by the United States not merely incompatible with the main
object of the treaty, but opposed even to its express stipulations. Occasion of controversy on this point has been removed by an additional treaty,
which our minister at London has concluded, and which will be immediately submitted to the Senate for its consideration. Should the proposed
supplemental arrangement be concurred in by all the parties to be affected
by it, the objects contemplated by the original convention will have been
fully attained.

The treaty between the United States and Great Britain of the 5th of
June, 1854, which went into effective operation in 1855, put an end to
causes of irritation between the two countries, by securing to the United
States the right of fishery on the coast of the British North American
Provinces, with advantages equal to those enjoyed by British subjects.
Besides the signal benefits of this treaty to a large class of our citizens
engaged in a pursuit connected to no inconsiderable degree with our national prosperity and strength, it has had a favorable effect upon other
interests in the provision it made for reciprocal freedom of trade between
the United States and the British Provinces in America.

The exports of domestic articles to those Provinces during the last year
amounted to more than $22,000,000, exceeding those of the preceding
year by nearly $7,000,000; and the imports therefrom during the same
period amounted to more than twenty-one million, an increase of six
million upon those of the previous year.

The improved condition of this branch of our commerce is mainly
attributable to the above-mentioned treaty.

Provision was made in the first article of that treaty for a commission
to designate the mouths of rivers to which the common right of fishery
on the coast of the United States and the British Provinces was not to
extend. This commission has been employed a part of two seasons, but
without much progress in accomplishing the object for which it was instituted, in consequence of a serious difference of opinion between the commissioners, not only as to the precise point where the rivers terminate,
but in many instances as to what constitutes a river. These difficulties,
however, may be overcome by resort to the umpirage provided for by the
treaty.

The efforts perseveringly prosecuted since the commencement of my
Administration to relieve our trade to the Baltic from the exaction of
Sound dues by Denmark have not yet been attended with success. Other
governments have also sought to obtain a like relief to their commerce,
and Denmark was thus induced to propose an arrangement to all the

European powers interested in the subject, and the manner in which her proposition was received warranting her to believe that a satisfactory arrangement with them could soon be concluded, she made a strong appeal to this Government for temporary suspension of definite action on its part, in consideration of the embarrassment which might result to her European negotiations by an immediate adjustment of the question with the United States. This request has been acceded to upon the condition that the sums collected after the 16th of June last and until the 16th of June next from vessels and cargoes belonging to our merchants are to be considered as paid under protest and subject to future adjustment. There is reason to believe that an arrangement between Denmark and the maritime powers of Europe on the subject will be soon concluded, and that the pending negotiation with the United States may then be resumed and terminated in a satisfactory manner.

With Spain no new difficulties have arisen, nor has much progress been made in the adjustment of pending ones.

Negotiations entered into for the purpose of relieving our commercial intercourse with the island of Cuba of some of its burdens and providing for the more speedy settlement of local disputes growing out of that intercourse have not yet been attended with any results.

Soon after the commencement of the late war in Europe this Government submitted to the consideration of all maritime nations two principles for the security of neutral commerce—one that the neutral flag should cover enemies' goods, except articles contraband of war, and the other that neutral property on board merchant vessels of belligerents should be exempt from condemnation, with the exception of contraband articles. These were not presented as new rules of international law, having been generally claimed by neutrals, though not always admitted by belligerents. One of the parties to the war (Russia), as well as several neutral powers, promptly acceded to these propositions, and the two other principal belligerents (Great Britain and France) having consented to observe them for the present occasion, a favorable opportunity seemed to be presented for obtaining a general recognition of them, both in Europe and America.

But Great Britain and France, in common with most of the States of Europe, while forbearing to reject, did not affirmatively act upon the overtures of the United States.

While the question was in this position the representatives of Russia, France, Great Britain, Austria, Prussia, Sardinia, and Turkey, assembled at Paris, took into consideration the subject of maritime rights, and put forth a declaration containing the two principles which this Government had submitted nearly two years before to the consideration of maritime powers, and adding thereto the following propositions: "Privateering is and remains abolished," and "Blockades in order to be binding must be effective; that is to say, maintained by a force sufficient really to prevent access to the coast of the enemy;'' and to the declaration thus composed of four points, two of which had already been proposed by the United States, this Government has been invited to accede by all the powers represented at Paris except Great Britain and Turkey. To the last of the two additional propositions—that in relation to blockades—there can certainly be no objection. It is merely the definition of what shall constitute the effectual investment of a blockaded place, a definition for which this Government has always contended, claiming indemnity for losses where a practical violation of the rule thus defined has been injurious to our commerce. As to the remaining article of the declaration of the conference of Paris, that ''privateering is and remains abolished,'' I certainly can not ascribe to the powers represented in the conference of Paris any but liberal and philanthropic views in the attempt to change the unquestionable rule of maritime law in regard to privateering. Their proposition was doubtless intended to imply approval of the principle that private property upon the ocean, although it might belong to the citizens of a belligerent state, should be exempted from capture; and had that proposition been so framed as to give full effect to the principle, it would have received my ready assent on behalf of the United States. But the measure proposed is inadequate to that purpose. It is true that if adopted private property upon the ocean would be withdrawn from one mode of plunder, but left exposed meanwhile to another mode, which could be used with increased effectiveness. The aggressive capacity of great naval powers would be thereby augmented, while the defensive ability of others would be reduced. Though the surrender of the means of prosecuting hostilities by employing privateers, as proposed by the conference of Paris, is mutual in terms, yet in practical effect it would be the relinquishment of a right of little value to one class of states, but of essential importance to another and a far larger class. It ought not to have been anticipated that a measure so inadequate to the accomplishment of the proposed object and so unequal in its operation would receive the assent of all maritime powers. Private property would be still left to the depredations of the public armed cruisers.

I have expressed a readiness on the part of this Government to accede to all the principles contained in the declaration of the conference of Paris provided that the one relating to the abandonment of privateering can be so amended as to effect the object for which, as is presumed, it was intended—the immunity of private property on the ocean from hostile capture. To effect this object, it is proposed to add to the declaration that ''privateering is and remains abolished'' the following amendment:

And that the private property of subjects and citizens of a belligerent on the high seas shall be exempt from seizure by the public armed vessels of the other belligerent, except it be contraband.

This amendment has been presented not only to the powers which have asked our assent to the declaration to abolish privateering, but to all other maritime states. Thus far it has not been rejected by any, and is favorably entertained by all which have made any communication in reply.

Several of the governments regarding with favor the proposition of the United States have delayed definitive action upon it only for the purpose of consulting with others, parties to the conference of Paris. I have the satisfaction of stating, however, that the Emperor of Russia has entirely and explicitly approved of that modification and will cooperate in endeavoring to obtain the assent of other powers, and that assurances of a similar purport have been received in relation to the disposition of the Emperor of the French.

The present aspect of this important subject allows us to cherish the hope that a principle so humane in its character, so just and equal in its operation, so essential to the prosperity of commercial nations, and so consonant to the sentiments of this enlightened period of the world will command the approbation of all maritime powers, and thus be incorporated into the code of international law.

My views on the subject are more fully set forth in the reply of the Secretary of State, a copy of which is herewith transmitted, to the communications on the subject made to this Government, especially to the communication of France.

The Government of the United States has at all times regarded with friendly interest the other States of America, formerly, like this country, European colonies, and now independent members of the great family of nations. But the unsettled condition of some of them, distracted by frequent revolutions, and thus incapable of regular and firm internal administration, has tended to embarrass occasionally our public intercourse by reason of wrongs which our citizens suffer at their hands, and which they are slow to redress.

Unfortunately, it is against the Republic of Mexico, with which it is our special desire to maintain a good understanding, that such complaints are most numerous; and although earnestly urged upon its attention, they have not as yet received the consideration which this Government had a right to expect. While reparation for past injuries has been withheld, others have been added. The political condition of that country, however, has been such as to demand forbearance on the part of the United States. I shall continue my efforts to procure for the wrongs of our citizens that redress which is indispensable to the continued friendly association of the two Republics.

The peculiar condition of affairs in Nicaragua in the early part of the present year rendered it important that this Government should have diplomatic relations with that State. Through its territory had been opened one of the principal thoroughfares across the isthmus connecting North and South America, on which a vast amount of property was transported and to which our citizens resorted in great numbers in passing between the Atlantic and Pacific coasts of the United States. The protection of both required that the existing power in that State should be regarded as a responsible Government, and its minister was accordingly received. But he remained here only a short time. Soon thereafter the political affairs of Nicaragua underwent unfavorable change and became involved in much uncertainty and confusion. Diplomatic representatives from two contending parties have been recently sent to this Government, but with the imperfect information possessed it was not possible to decide which was the Government *de facto*, and, awaiting further developments, I have refused to receive either.

Questions of the most serious nature are pending between the United States and the Republic of New Granada. The Government of that Republic undertook a year since to impose tonnage duties on foreign vessels in her ports, but the purpose was resisted by this Government as being contrary to existing treaty stipulations with the United States and to rights conferred by charter upon the Panama Railroad Company, and was accordingly relinquished at that time, it being admitted that our vessels were entitled to be exempt from tonnage duty in the free ports of Panama and Aspinwall. But the purpose has been recently revived on the part of New Granada by the enactment of a law to subject vessels visiting her ports to the tonnage duty of 40 cents per ton, and although the law has not been put in force, yet the right to enforce it is still asserted and may at any time be acted on by the Government of that Republic.

The Congress of New Granada has also enacted a law during the last year which levies a tax of more than $3 on every pound of mail matter transported across the Isthmus. The sum thus required to be paid on the mails of the United States would be nearly $2,000,000 annually in addition to the large sum payable by contract to the Panama Railroad Company. If the only objection to this exaction were the exorbitancy of its amount, it could not be submitted to by the United States.

The imposition of it, however, would obviously contravene our treaty with New Granada and infringe the contract of that Republic with the Panama Railroad Company. The law providing for this tax was by its terms to take effect on the 1st of September last, but the local authorities on the Isthmus have been induced to suspend its execution and to await further instructions on the subject from the Government of the Republic. I am not yet advised of the determination of that Government. If a measure so extraordinary in its character and so clearly contrary to treaty stipulations and the contract rights of the Panama Railroad Company, composed mostly of American citizens, should be persisted in, it will be the duty of the United States to resist its execution.

I regret exceedingly that occasion exists to invite your attention to a subject of still graver import in our relations with the Republic of New

Granada. On the 15th day of April last a riotous assemblage of the inhabitants of Panama committed a violent and outrageous attack on the premises of the railroad company and the passengers and other persons in or near the same, involving the death of several citizens of the United States, the pillage of many others, and the destruction of a large amount of property belonging to the railroad company. I caused full investigation of that event to be made, and the result shows satisfactorily that complete responsibility for what occurred attaches to the Government of New Granada. I have therefore demanded of that Government that the perpetrators of the wrongs in question should be punished; that provision should be made for the families of citizens of the United States who were killed, with full indemnity for the property pillaged or destroyed.

The present condition of the Isthmus of Panama, in so far as regards the security of persons and property passing over it, requires serious consideration. Recent incidents tend to show that the local authorities can not be relied on to maintain the public peace of Panama, and there is just ground for apprehension that a portion of the inhabitants are meditating further outrages, without adequate measures for the security and protection of persons or property having been taken, either by the State of Panama or by the General Government of New Granada.

Under the guaranties of treaty, citizens of the United States have, by the outlay of several million dollars, constructed a railroad across the Isthmus, and it has become the main route between our Atlantic and Pacific possessions, over which multitudes of our citizens and a vast amount of property are constantly passing; to the security and protection of all which and the continuance of the public advantages involved it is impossible for the Government of the United States to be indifferent.

I have deemed the danger of the recurrence of scenes of lawless violence in this quarter so imminent as to make it my duty to station a part of our naval force in the harbors of Panama and Aspinwall, in order to protect the persons and property of the citizens of the United States in those ports and to insure to them safe passage across the Isthmus. And it would, in my judgment, be unwise to withdraw the naval force now in those ports until, by the spontaneous action of the Republic of New Granada or otherwise, some adequate arrangement shall have been made for the protection and security of a line of interoceanic communication, so important at this time not to the United States only, but to all other maritime states, both of Europe and America.

Meanwhile negotiations have been instituted, by means of a special commission, to obtain from New Granada full indemnity for injuries sustained by our citizens on the Isthmus and satisfactory security for the general interests of the United States.

In addressing to you my last annual message the occasion seems to me an appropriate one to express my congratulations, in view of the peace, greatness, and felicity which the United States now possess and enjoy. To point you to the state of the various Departments of the Government and of all the great branches of the public service, civil and military, in order to speak of the intelligence and the integrity which pervades the whole, would be to indicate but imperfectly the administrative condition of the country and the beneficial effects of that on the general welfare. Nor would it suffice to say that the nation is actually at peace at home and abroad; that its industrial interests are prosperous; that the canvas of its mariners whitens every sea, and the plow of its husbandmen is marching steadily onward to the bloodless conquest of the continent; that cities and populous States are springing up, as if by enchantment, from the bosom of our Western wilds, and that the courageous energy of our people is making of these United States the great Republic of the world. These results have not been attained without passing through trials and perils, by experience of which, and thus only, nations can harden into manhood. Our forefathers were trained to the wisdom which conceived and the courage which achieved independence by the circumstances which surrounded them, and they were thus made capable of the creation of the Republic. It devolved on the next generation to consolidate the work of the Revolution, to deliver the country entirely from the influences of conflicting transatlantic partialities or antipathies which attached to our colonial and Revolutionary history, and to organize the practical operation of the constitutional and legal institutions of the Union. To us of this generation remains the not less noble task of maintaining and extending the national power. We have at length reached that stage of our country's career in which the dangers to be encountered and the exertions to be made are the incidents, not of weakness, but of strength. In foreign relations we have to attemper our power to the less happy condition of other Republics in America and to place ourselves in the calmness and conscious dignity of right by the side of the greatest and wealthiest of the Empires of Europe. In domestic relations we have to guard against the shock of the discontents, the ambitions, the interests, and the exuberant, and therefore sometimes irregular, impulses of opinion or of action which are the natural product of the present political elevation, the self-reliance, and the restless spirit of enterprise of the people of the United States.

I shall prepare to surrender the Executive trust to my successor and retire to private life with sentiments of profound gratitude to the good Providence which during the period of my Administration has vouchsafed to carry the country through many difficulties, domestic and foreign, and which enables me to contemplate the spectacle of amicable and respectful relations between ours and all other governments and the establishment of constitutional order and tranquillity throughout the Union.

FRANKLIN PIERCE.

SPECIAL MESSAGES.

WASHINGTON, *December 2, 1856.*

To the House of Representatives:

I transmit herewith a report* from the Secretary of State, in compliance with the resolution of the House of Representatives of the 7th of August last. FRANKLIN PIERCE

WASHINGTON, *December 8, 1856.*

To the Senate of the United States:

I transmit to the Senate, for its consideration with a view to ratification, a treaty between the United States and Siam, concluded at Bangkok on the 29th day of May last. FRANKLIN PIERCE.

WASHINGTON, *December 10, 1856.*

To the Senate of the United States:

I transmit to the Senate, for its consideration with a view to ratification, a treaty for the settlement of the questions which have come into discussion between the United States and Great Britain relative to Central America, concluded and signed at London on the 17th day of October last between the United States and Great Britain.

FRANKLIN PIERCE.

WASHINGTON, *December 12, 1856.*

To the Senate and House of Representatives:

I transmit a copy of a letter of the 20th of May last from the commissioner of the United States in China, and of the decree and regulations† which accompanied it, for such revision thereof as Congress may deem expedient, pursuant to the sixth section of the act approved 11th August, 1848. FRANKLIN PIERCE.

WASHINGTON, *December 15, 1856.*

To the Senate and House of Representatives:

I transmit to Congress an extract from a letter of the 22d ultimo from the governor of the Territory of Kansas to the Secretary of State, with a copy of the executive minutes ‡ to which it refers. These documents have been received since the date of my message at the opening of the present session. FRANKLIN PIERCE.

---

*Stating that the correspondence in the Departments of State and of the Navy relative to Hamet Caramally had been transmitted to Congress.

†For judicial jurisdiction by acting consuls or vice-consuls of the United States in China.

‡Containing a history of Kansas affairs.

WASHINGTON, *December 29, 1856.*

To the Senate of the United States:

In compliance with a resolution of the Senate of the 23d instant, requesting the President "to communicate to the Senate, if not incompatible with the public interest, such information as he may have concerning the present condition and prospects of a proposed plan for connecting by submarine wires the magnetic telegraph lines on this continent and Europe," I transmit the accompanying report from the Secretary of State.

FRANKLIN PIERCE.

WASHINGTON, *January 6, 1857.*

To the Senate of the United States:

I transmit a report from the Secretary of State, with accompanying papers,* in answer to the resolution of the Senate of the 2d instant.

FRANKLIN PIERCE.

WASHINGTON, *January 12, 1857.*

To the Senate of the United States:

In compliance with the resolution of the Senate of the 4th August, 1856, and 9th January instant, I transmit herewith a report from the Secretary of State, together with the documents† therein referred to.

FRANKLIN PIERCE.

WASHINGTON, *January 12, 1857.*

To the Senate of the United States:

I again transmit to the Senate, for its advice and consent with a view to ratification, the convention between the United States and His Majesty the King of the Netherlands, for the mutual delivery of criminals fugitives from justice in certain cases, and for other purposes, which was concluded at The Hague on the 29th day of May, 1856.

FRANKLIN PIERCE.

WASHINGTON, *January 12, 1857.*

To the Senate of the United States:

I transmit a report from the Secretary of State, with accompanying papers,‡ in answer to the resolution of the Senate of the 7th instant.

FRANKLIN PIERCE.

*Relating to the refusal of the minister to the United States from the Netherlands to testify before the criminal court of the District of Columbia.

†Relating to the claims of certain American citizens for losses consequent upon their expulsion by Venezuelan authorities from one of the Aves Islands, while collecting guano.

‡Correspondence and documents connected with the treaty concluded at London between the United States and Great Britain October 17, 1856, relative to Central America.

WASHINGTON, *January 12, 1857.*

The SPEAKER OF THE HOUSE OF REPRESENTATIVES:

In compliance with the resolution of the House of Representatives of the 22d ultimo, in relation to information with regard to expenditures and liabilities for persons called into the service of the United States in the Territory of Kansas, I transmit the accompanying report of the Secretary of War.

FRANKLIN PIERCE.

WASHINGTON, *January 13, 1857.*

To the Senate of the United States:

I transmit to the Senate, for its consideration with a view to ratification, a convention between the United States and the Republic of Peru relative to the rights of neutrals at sea, signed at Lima by the plenipotentiaries of the parties on the 22d of July last.

FRANKLIN PIERCE.

WASHINGTON, *January 16, 1857.*

To the Senate of the United States:

I communicate to the Senate herewith, for its constitutional action thereon, a treaty made and concluded at Fort Leavenworth, Kansas Territory, on the 16th day of December, 1856, between Indian Agent Benjamin F. Robinson, commissioner on the part of the United States, the principal men of the Christian Indians, and Gottleib F. Oehler, on behalf of the board of elders of the northern diocese of the Church of the United Brethren in the United States of America.

Among the papers which accompany the treaty is a communication from the Commissioner of Indian Affairs, containing a recommendation, concurred in by the Secretary of the Interior, that the treaty be ratified with an amendment which is therein explained.

FRANKLIN PIERCE.

WASHINGTON, *January 19, 1857.*

To the Senate and House of Representatives:

Soon after the close of the last session of Congress I directed steps to be taken to carry into effect the joint resolution of August 28, 1856, relative to the restoration of the ship *Resolute* to Her Britannic Majesty's service. The ship was purchased of the salvors at the sum appropriated for the purchase, and "after being fully repaired and equipped" was sent to England under control of the Secretary of the Navy. The letter from Her Majesty's minister for foreign affairs, now communicated to Congress in conformity with his request, and copies of correspondence from the files of the Departments of State and of the Navy, also transmitted herewith, will apprise you of the manner in which the joint resolution has been fully executed and show how agreeable the proceeding has been to Her Majesty's Government.

FRANKLIN PIERCE.

WASHINGTON, *January, 1857.*

To the Senate and House of Representatives:

I transmit to Congress copies of a communication from His Excellency Andrew Johnson, governor of the State of Tennessee, tendering to the Government of the United States "500 acres of the late residence of Andrew Jackson, deceased, including the mansion, tomb, and other improvements, known as the Hermitage," upon the terms and conditions of an act of the legislature of said State, a copy of which is also herewith communicated.

FRANKLIN PIERCE.

WASHINGTON, *January 20, 1857.*

To the House of Representatives:

In response to a resolution of January 5, 1857, requesting the President to inform the House of Representatives "by what authority a Government architect is employed and paid for designing and erecting all public buildings, and also for placing said buildings under the supervision of military engineers," I submit the accompanying reports from the Secretary of the Treasury and the Secretary of War.

FRANKLIN PIERCE.

WASHINGTON, *January 21, 1857.*

To the House of Representatives:

In further compliance with resolution of the House of Representatives of the 22d ultimo, calling upon me for "statements of the amounts of money paid and liabilities incurred for the pay, support, and other expenses of persons called into the service of the United States in the Territory of Kansas, either under the designation of the militia of Kansas or of posses summoned by the civil officers in that Territory, since the date of its establishment; also statements of the amounts paid to marshals, sheriffs, and other deputies, and to witnesses and for other expenses in the arrest, detention, and trial of persons charged in said Territory with treason against the United States or with violations of the alleged laws of said Territory," I transmit a report from the Secretary of the Treasury, with accompanying documents.

FRANKLIN PIERCE.

WASHINGTON, *January 28, 1857.*

To the Senate of the United States:

I communicate to the Senate herewith, for its constitutional action thereon, a treaty made and concluded at Grand Portage, in the Territory of Minnesota, on the 16th day of September, 1856, between Henry C. Gilbert, Indian agent, acting as commissioner on the part of the United States, and the Bois Porte bands of Chippewa Indians, by their chiefs and headmen.

The treaty is accompanied by communications from the Secretary of the Interior, transmitting a letter to him from the Commissioner of Indian Affairs and a report from Agent Gilbert of the 24th December, 1856.

FRANKLIN PIERCE.

WASHINGTON, *January 30, 1857.*

To the Senate of the United States:

In compliance with a resolution of the Senate passed December 23, 1856, requesting "any information upon the files of the Department in relation to pay and emoluments of Lieutenant-General Scott or his staff under the resolution of February 15, 1855, which may not have been communicated in Executive Document No. 56, first session Thirty-fourth Congress," and a resolution passed December 30, requesting "a statement of all payments and allowances which have been made, and of all claims which have been disallowed, to Brevet Lieutenant-General Scott from the date when he joined the army serving in Mexico up to December 1, 1856," and "also copies of all correspondence on file in the Executive Departments relating to said claims, payments, or allowances," I herewith transmit a report of the Secretary of War, to whom the resolutions were referred in order that the information, statements, and copies of correspondence therein required might be prepared and furnished.

FRANKLIN PIERCE.

WASHINGTON, *February 4, 1857.*

To the Senate of the United States:

In answer to the resolutions of the Senate of yesterday, adopted in executive session, I transmit reports* from the Secretary of State, to whom they were referred.

FRANKLIN PIERCE.

WASHINGTON, *February 4, 1857.*

To the House of Representatives:

I transmit a report from the Secretary of State, with accompanying documents,† in answer to the resolution of the House of December 26, 1854.

FRANKLIN PIERCE.

---

*Relating to the convention between Great Britain and Honduras respecting the island of Ruatan.

†Consular returns on shipping, shipbuilding, etc., in foreign countries.

WASHINGTON, *February 9, 1857.*

To the Senate of the United States:

I transmit a report from the Secretary of State, with accompanying papers,* in answer to the resolution of the Senate of the 30th ultimo.

FRANKLIN PIERCE.

WASHINGTON, *February 11, 1857.*

To the Senate of the United States:

In further compliance with a resolution of the Senate of the 5th instant, requesting me to communicate transcripts of papers relative to the proclamation of martial law by Governor Stevens, of Washington Territory, I transmit the accompanying report from the Secretary of War.

FRANKLIN PIERCE.

WASHINGTON, *February 11, 1857.*

To the Senate of the United States:

I transmit to the Senate, for its consideration with a view to ratification, a treaty of friendship and commerce between the United States and the Shah of Persia, signed by the plenipotentiaries of the parties at Constantinople on the 13th of December last.

FRANKLIN PIERCE.

WASHINGTON, *February 11, 1857.*

To the Senate of the United States:

I communicate to the Senate herewith, for its constitutional action thereon, articles of agreement and convention made and concluded at the places and dates therein named by Joel Palmer, superintendent of Indian affairs, on the part of the United States, and the chiefs and headmen of the confederate tribes and bands of Indians residing along the coast west of the summit of the Coast Range of mountains and between the Columbia River on the north and the southern boundary of Oregon on the south. A letter from the Secretary of the Interior, including one from the Commissioner of Indian Affairs, accompanies the treaty.

FRANKLIN PIERCE.

WASHINGTON, *February 14, 1857.*

To the House of Representatives:

In compliance with a resolution of the House of Representatives of the 19th ultimo, requesting me "to furnish to the House all correspondence and documents, not incompatible with the public interest, relating

---

* Relating to the proclamation of martial law in Washington Territory, etc.

to Indian affairs in the Department of the Pacific, those of the Interior as well as those of the War Department,'' I transmit the accompanying report and documents from the Secretary of War.

FRANKLIN PIERCE.

WASHINGTON, *February, 1857.*

To the House of Representatives of the United States:

I communicate herewith a letter of the Secretary of War, recommending an appropriation of $10,000 for the purpose of instituting a series of researches for the discovery of a more efficient mode of manufacturing niter.

FRANKLIN PIERCE.

WASHINGTON, *February 16, 1857.*

To the Senate of the United States:

In compliance with the resolution of the Senate of the 4th of August last, calling for information in relation to certain internal improvements, I transmit reports* from the Secretary of the Treasury and the Secretary of War.

FRANKLIN PIERCE.

WASHINGTON, *February 19, 1857.*

To the Senate of the United States:

I transmit for the consideration of the Senate with a view to ratification a consular convention between the United States and the Republic of Chili, signed by the plenipotentiaries of the parties at the city of Santiago on the 1st day of December last.

FRANKLIN PIERCE.

WASHINGTON, *February 23, 1857.*

To the House of Representatives:

I transmit a report from the Secretary of State, with accompanying papers,† in answer to the resolution of the House of Representatives of the 6th instant.

FRANKLIN PIERCE.

---

* Appropriations made by Congress within eleven years for light-houses, beacons, buoys, etc., on Lakes Superior, Michigan, Huron, St. Clair, Erie, Ontario, and Champlain; duties collected and expenses of collection at each of the lake ports annually for eleven fiscal years, ending June 30, 1856; tonnage of the lake ports, etc.

† Relating to the claim of F. Dainese for salary, expenses, etc., while acting consul at Constantinople.

To the Senate of the United States:

I transmit herewith a report from the Attorney-General, in reply to the resolution* of the Senate in executive session of the 19th instant.

FEBRUARY 23, 1857. FRANKLIN PIERCE.

To the Senate of the United States:

I communicate herewith a report from the Attorney-General, in reply to the resolution of the Senate of the 20th instant, asking for correspondence of Samuel D. Lecompte, chief justice of the Territory of Kansas.†

FEBRUARY 23, 1857. FRANKLIN PIERCE.

WASHINGTON, *March 2, 1857.*

To the Senate of the United States:

I communicate herewith a letter ‡ from the Secretary of the Navy, in response to a resolution of the Senate of August 15, 1856.

Concurring in the views presented in the documents to which the Secretary of the Navy refers, I am not prepared at this time to recommend any legislation on the subject. FRANKLIN PIERCE.

WASHINGTON, *March 3, 1857.*

To the Senate of the United States:

In compliance with a resolution of the Senate of the 20th ultimo, in relation to correspondence between the Treasury and Interior Departments and Edward F. Beale, late superintendent of Indian affairs in California, and accounts of remittances, etc., I transmit the accompanying report from the Secretary of the Treasury.

FRANKLIN PIERCE.

WASHINGTON, *March 3, 1857.*

To the House of Representatives:

As a further answer to resolutions of the House of Representatives adopted on the 6th and 10th of February, I transmit a second report from the Secretary of State, relating to the "accounts," "claims," and "difficulties" at Constantinople, referred to in said resolutions.

FRANKLIN PIERCE.

---

*Asking whether Samuel D. Lecompte has been allowed to perform the functions of chief justice of the Territory of Kansas since the nomination of J. O. Harrison to that office.

†Explanatory of his judicial conduct in the Territory of Kansas.

‡Relating to the discontinuance or change of location of any navy-yard or naval station on the Atlantic Seaboard.

PROCLAMATION.

By the President of the United States of America.

A PROCLAMATION.

Whereas objects of interest to the United States require that the Senate should be convened at 12 o'clock on the 4th of March next to receive and act upon such communications as may be made to it on the part of the Executive:

Now, therefore, I, Franklin Pierce, President of the United States, have considered it to be my duty to issue this my proclamation, declaring that an extraordinary occasion requires the Senate of the United States to convene for the transaction of business at the Capitol, in the city of Washington, on the 4th day of March next, at 12 o'clock at noon of that day, of which all who shall at that time be entitled to act as members of that body are hereby required to take notice.

Given under my hand and the seal of the United States, at Washing-[SEAL.] ton, this 16th day of February, A. D. 1857, and of the Independence of the United States the eighty-first.

FRANKLIN PIERCE.

By the President:

W. L. MARCY,
Secretary of State.

James Buchanan

March 4, 1857, to March 4, 1861

427

HOME AT WHEATLAND, PENNSYLVANIA, OF

JAMES BUCHANAN

With official portrait engraved from copy of original in steel

JAMES BUCHANAN

James Buchanan

JAMES BUCHANAN was born near Mercersburg, Pa., April 23, 1791.
His father, James Buchanan, a Scotch-Irish farmer, came from the county
of Donegal, Ireland, in 1783. His mother was Elizabeth Speer. The
future President was educated at a school in Mercersburg and at Dickin-
son College, Pennsylvania, where he was graduated in 1809. Began to
practice law in Lancaster in 1812. His first public address was made at
the age of 23 on the occasion of a popular meeting in Lancaster after the
capture of Washington by the British in 1814. Although a Federalist
and with his party opposed to the war, he urged the enlistment of volunteers for the defense of Baltimore, and was among the first to enroll his
name. In October, 1814, was elected to the legislature of Pennsylvania
for Lancaster County, and again elected in 1815. At the close of his term
in the legislature retired to the practice of the law, gaining early distinction. In 1820 was elected to Congress to represent a district composed
of Lancaster, York, and Dauphin counties, and took his seat in December, 1821. He was called a Federalist, but the party distinctions of that
time were not clearly defined, and Mr. Buchanan's political principles as a
national statesman were yet to be formed. His first speech in Congress
was made in January, 1822, sustaining the Administration of President
Monroe, and of John C. Calhoun, Secretary of War, in particular, with
reference to a military establishment. President Monroe's veto, in May,
1822, of a bill imposing tolls for the support of the Cumberland road, for
which Mr. Buchanan had voted, produced a strong effect upon his constitutional views, and he began to perceive the dividing line between the
Federal and the State powers. He remained in the House of Representatives ten years—during Mr. Monroe's second term, through the Administration of John Quincy Adams, and during the first two years of Jackson's
Administration. In December, 1829, became chairman of the Judiciary
Committee of the House. During Mr. Adams's term the friends of the
Administration began to take the name of National Republicans, while
the opposing party assumed the name of Democrats. Mr. Buchanan was
one of the leaders of the opposition in the House of Representatives.
Was always a strong supporter and warm personal friend of General Jackson. In March, 1831, at the close of the Twenty-first Congress, it was

Mr. Buchanan's wish to retire from public life, but at the request of President Jackson he accepted the mission to Russia; negotiated a commercial treaty with that country. August 8, 1833, left St. Petersburg, spent a short time in Paris and London, and reached home in November. In 1834 was appointed one of the commissioners on the part of Pennsylvania to arrange with commissioners from New Jersey concerning the use of the waters of the Delaware River. December 6, 1834, was elected to the United States Senate to fill a vacancy, and was reelected in January, 1837. Was conspicuous in the Senate as a supporter of Jackson's financial policy throughout his Administration and that of his successor, Mr. Van Buren, of the same party. In 1839 declined the office of Attorney-General, tendered by President Van Buren. In 1843 was elected to the Senate for a third term, and in 1844 his name was brought forward as the Democratic candidate of Pennsylvania for the Presidential nomination, but before the national convention met he withdrew his name. At the beginning of the Administration of James K. Polk became Secretary of State, and as such had a number of important questions to deal with, including the settlement of the boundary between Oregon Territory and the British possessions and the annexation of Texas, which resulted in the Mexican War. On the accession of Mr. Taylor to the Presidency Mr. Buchanan retired for a time from official life. Was an unsuccessful candidate for the Presidential nomination before the Democratic national convention June 1, 1852. In April, 1853, was appointed minister to England by President Pierce; was recalled at his own request in 1855. June 3, 1856, was nominated for President of the United States by the Democratic national convention at Cincinnati, Ohio, and on November 4, 1856, was elected, receiving 174 electoral votes to 114 for John C. Frémont and 8 for Millard Fillmore. Was inaugurated March 4, 1857. In 1860 refused the use of his name for renomination. At the conclusion of his term returned to his home at Wheatland, near Lancaster, Pa. Died June 1, 1868, and was buried at Wheatland.

INAUGURAL ADDRESS.

Fellow-Citizens: I appear before you this day to take the solemn oath "that I will faithfully execute the office of President of the United States and will to the best of my ability preserve, protect, and defend the Constitution of the United States."

In entering upon this great office I must humbly invoke the God of our fathers for wisdom and firmness to execute its high and responsible duties in such a manner as to restore harmony and ancient friendship among the people of the several States and to preserve our free institutions throughout many generations. Convinced that I owe my election to the inherent love for the Constitution and the Union which still animates the hearts of the American people, let me earnestly ask their powerful support in sustaining all just measures calculated to perpetuate these, the richest political blessings which Heaven has ever bestowed upon any nation. Having determined not to become a candidate for reelection, I shall have no motive to influence my conduct in administering the Government except the desire ably and faithfully to serve my country and to live in the grateful memory of my countrymen.

We have recently passed through a Presidential contest in which the passions of our fellow-citizens were excited to the highest degree by questions of deep and vital importance; but when the people proclaimed their will the tempest at once subsided and all was calm.

The voice of the majority, speaking in the manner prescribed by the Constitution, was heard, and instant submission followed. Our own country could alone have exhibited so grand and striking a spectacle of the capacity of man for self-government.

What a happy conception, then, was it for Congress to apply this simple rule, that the will of the majority shall govern, to the settlement of the question of domestic slavery in the Territories! Congress is neither "to legislate slavery into any Territory or State nor to exclude it therefrom, but to leave the people thereof perfectly free to form and regulate their domestic institutions in their own way, subject only to the Constitution of the United States."

As a natural consequence, Congress has also prescribed that when the Territory of Kansas shall be admitted as a State it "shall be received into the Union with or without slavery, as their constitution may prescribe at the time of their admission."

A difference of opinion has arisen in regard to the point of time when the people of a Territory shall decide this question for themselves.

This is, happily, a matter of but little practical importance. Besides, it is a judicial question, which legitimately belongs to the Supreme Court of the United States, before whom it is now pending, and will, it is understood, be speedily and finally settled. To their decision, in common with all good citizens, I shall cheerfully submit, whatever this may be, though it has ever been my individual opinion that under the Nebraska-Kansas act the appropriate period will be when the number of actual residents in the Territory shall justify the formation of a constitution with a view to its admission as a State into the Union. But be this as it may, it is the imperative and indispensable duty of the Government of the United States to secure to every resident inhabitant the free and independent expression of his opinion by his vote. This sacred right of each individual must be preserved. That being accomplished, nothing can be fairer than to leave the people of a Territory free from all foreign interference to decide their own destiny for themselves, subject only to the Constitution of the United States.

The whole Territorial question being thus settled upon the principle of popular sovereignty—a principle as ancient as free government itself—everything of a practical nature has been decided. No other question remains for adjustment, because all agree that under the Constitution slavery in the States is beyond the reach of any human power except that of the respective States themselves wherein it exists. May we not, then, hope that the long agitation on this subject is approaching its end, and that the geographical parties to which it has given birth, so much dreaded by the Father of his Country, will speedily become extinct? Most happy will it be for the country when the public mind shall be diverted from this question to others of more pressing and practical importance. Throughout the whole progress of this agitation, which has scarcely known any intermission for more than twenty years, whilst it has been productive of no positive good to any human being it has been the prolific source of great evils to the master, to the slave, and to the whole country. It has alienated and estranged the people of the sister States from each other, and has even seriously endangered the very existence of the Union. Nor has the danger yet entirely ceased. Under our system there is a remedy for all mere political evils in the sound sense and sober judgment of the people. Time is a great corrective. Political subjects which but a few years ago excited and exasperated the public mind have passed away and are now nearly forgotten. But this question of domestic slavery is of far graver importance than any mere political question, because should the agitation continue it may eventually endanger the personal safety of a large portion of our countrymen where the institution exists. In that event no form of government, however admirable in itself and however productive of material benefits, can compensate for the loss of peace and domestic security around the family altar. Let every Union-loving man, therefore, exert his best influence to suppress this agitation, which since the recent legislation of Congress is without any legitimate object.

It is an evil omen of the times that men have undertaken to calculate the mere material value of the Union. Reasoned estimates have been presented of the pecuniary profits and local advantages which would result to different States and sections from its dissolution and of the comparative injuries which such an event would inflict on other States and sections. Even descending to this low and narrow view of the mighty question, all such calculations are at fault. The bare reference to a single consideration will be conclusive on this point. We at present enjoy a free trade throughout our extensive and expanding country such as the world has never witnessed. This trade is conducted on railroads and canals, on noble rivers and arms of the sea, which bind together the North and the South, the East and the West, of our Confederacy. Annihilate this trade, arrest its free progress by the geographical lines of jealous and hostile States, and you destroy the prosperity and onward march of the whole and every part and involve all in one common ruin. But such considerations, important as they are in themselves, sink into insignificance when we reflect on the terrific evils which would result from disunion to every portion of the Confederacy—to the North not more than to the South, to the East not more than to the West. These I shall not attempt to portray, because I feel an humble confidence that the kind Providence which inspired our fathers with wisdom to frame the most perfect form of government and union ever devised by man will not suffer it to perish until it shall have been peacefully instrumental by its example in the extension of civil and religious liberty throughout the world.

Next in importance to the maintenance of the Constitution and the Union is the duty of preserving the Government free from the taint or even the suspicion of corruption. Public virtue is the vital spirit of republics, and history proves that when this has decayed and the love of money has usurped its place, although the forms of free government may remain for a season, the substance has departed forever.

Our present financial condition is without a parallel in history. No nation has ever before been embarrassed from too large a surplus in its treasury. This almost necessarily gives birth to extravagant legislation. It produces wild schemes of expenditure and begets a race of speculators and jobbers, whose ingenuity is exerted in contriving and promoting expedients to obtain public money. The purity of official agents, whether rightfully or wrongfully, is suspected, and the character of the government suffers in the estimation of the people. This is in itself a very great evil.

The natural mode of relief from this embarrassment is to appropriate the surplus in the Treasury to great national objects for which a clear warrant can be found in the Constitution. Among these I might mention the extinguishment of the public debt, a reasonable increase of the Navy, which is at present inadequate to the protection of our vast tonnage afloat, now greater than that of any other nation, as well as to the defense of our extended seacoast.

It is beyond all question the true principle that no more revenue ought to be collected from the people than the amount necessary to defray the expenses of a wise, economical, and efficient administration of the Government. To reach this point it was necessary to resort to a modification of the tariff, and this has, I trust, been accomplished in such a manner as to do as little injury as may have been practicable to our domestic manufactures, especially those necessary for the defense of the country. Any discrimination against a particular branch for the purpose of benefiting favored corporations, individuals, or interests would have been unjust to the rest of the community and inconsistent with that spirit of fairness and equality which ought to govern in the adjustment of a revenue tariff.

But the squandering of the public money sinks into comparative insignificance as a temptation to corruption when compared with the squandering of the public lands.

No nation in the tide of time has ever been blessed with so rich and noble an inheritance as we enjoy in the public lands. In administering this important trust, whilst it may be wise to grant portions of them for the improvement of the remainder, yet we should never forget that it is our cardinal policy to reserve these lands, as much as may be, for actual settlers, and this at moderate prices. We shall thus not only best promote the prosperity of the new States and Territories, by furnishing them a hardy and independent race of honest and industrious citizens, but shall secure homes for our children and our children's children, as well as for those exiles from foreign shores who may seek in this country to improve their condition and to enjoy the blessings of civil and religious liberty. Such emigrants have done much to promote the growth and prosperity of the country. They have proved faithful both in peace and in war. After becoming citizens they are entitled, under the Constitution and laws, to be placed on a perfect equality with native-born citizens, and in this character they should ever be kindly recognized.

The Federal Constitution is a grant from the States to Congress of certain specific powers, and the question whether this grant should be liberally or strictly construed has more or less divided political parties from the beginning. Without entering into the argument, I desire to state at the commencement of my Administration that long experience and observation have convinced me that a strict construction of the powers of the Government is the only true, as well as the only safe, theory of the Constitution. Whenever in our past history doubtful powers have been exercised by Congress, these have never failed to produce injurious and unhappy consequences. Many such instances might be adduced if this were the proper occasion. Neither is it necessary for the public service to strain the language of the Constitution, because all the great and useful powers required for a successful administration of the Government, both in peace and in war, have been granted, either in express terms or by the plainest implication.

Whilst deeply convinced of these truths, I yet consider it clear that under the war-making power Congress may appropriate money toward the construction of a military road when this is absolutely necessary for the defense of any State or Territory of the Union against foreign invasion. Under the Constitution Congress has power "to declare war," "to raise and support armies," "to provide and maintain a navy," and to call forth the militia to "repel invasions." Thus endowed, in an ample manner, with the war-making power, the corresponding duty is required that "the United States shall protect each of them [the States] against invasion." Now, how is it possible to afford this protection to California and our Pacific possessions except by means of a military road

through the Territories of the United States, over which men and munitions of war may be speedily transported from the Atlantic States to
meet and to repel the invader? In the event of a war with a naval power
much stronger than our own we should then have no other available
access to the Pacific Coast, because such a power would instantly close
the route across the isthmus of Central America. It is impossible to
conceive that whilst the Constitution has expressly required Congress
to defend all the States it should yet deny to them, by any fair construction, the only possible means by which one of these States can be
defended. Besides, the Government, ever since its origin, has been in
the constant practice of constructing military roads. It might also be
wise to consider whether the love for the Union which now animates
our fellow-citizens on the Pacific Coast may not be impaired by our
neglect or refusal to provide for them, in their remote and isolated condition, the only means by which the power of the States on this side of
the Rocky Mountains can reach them in sufficient time to ''protect''
them ''against invasion.'' I forbear for the present from expressing an
opinion as to the wisest and most economical mode in which the Government can lend its aid in accomplishing this great and necessary work.
I believe that many of the difficulties in the way, which now appear
formidable, will in a great degree vanish as soon as the nearest and best
route shall have been satisfactorily ascertained.

It may be proper that on this occasion I should make some brief
remarks in regard to our rights and duties as a member of the great
family of nations. In our intercourse with them there are some plain
principles, approved by our own experience, from which we should never
depart. We ought to cultivate peace, commerce, and friendship with
all nations, and this not merely as the best means of promoting our own
material interests, but in a spirit of Christian benevolence toward our
fellow-men, wherever their lot may be cast. Our diplomacy should be
direct and frank, neither seeking to obtain more nor accepting less than
is our due. We ought to cherish a sacred regard for the independence
of all nations, and never attempt to interfere in the domestic concerns of
any unless this shall be imperatively required by the great law of self-
preservation. To avoid entangling alliances has been a maxim of our
policy ever since the days of Washington, and its wisdom no one will
attempt to dispute. In short, we ought to do justice in a kindly spirit to
all nations and require justice from them in return.

It is our glory that whilst other nations have extended their dominions by the sword we have never acquired any territory except by fair
purchase or, as in the case of Texas, by the voluntary determination
of a brave, kindred, and independent people to blend their destinies
with our own. Even our acquisitions from Mexico form no exception.
Unwilling to take advantage of the fortune of war against a sister republic, we purchased these possessions under the treaty of peace for a sum

which was considered at the time a fair equivalent. Our past history forbids that we shall in the future acquire territory unless this be sanctioned by the laws of justice and honor. Acting on this principle, no nation will have a right to interfere or to complain if in the progress of events we shall still further extend our possessions. Hitherto in all our acquisitions the people, under the protection of the American flag, have enjoyed civil and religious liberty, as well as equal and just laws, and have been contented, prosperous, and happy. Their trade with the rest of the world has rapidly increased, and thus every commercial nation has shared largely in their successful progress.

I shall now proceed to take the oath prescribed by the Constitution, whilst humbly invoking the blessing of Divine Providence on this great people.

MARCH 4, 1857.

FIRST ANNUAL MESSAGE.

WASHINGTON, *December 8, 1857.*

Fellow-Citizens of the Senate and House of Representatives:

In obedience to the command of the Constitution, it has now become my duty "to give to Congress information of the state of the Union and recommend to their consideration such measures" as I judge to be "necessary and expedient."

But first and above all, our thanks are due to Almighty God for the numerous benefits which He has bestowed upon this people, and our united prayers ought to ascend to Him that He would continue to bless our great Republic in time to come as He has blessed it in time past. Since the adjournment of the last Congress our constituents have enjoyed an unusual degree of health. The earth has yielded her fruits abundantly and has bountifully rewarded the toil of the husbandman. Our great staples have commanded high prices, and up till within a brief period our manufacturing, mineral, and mechanical occupations have largely partaken of the general prosperity. We have possessed all the elements of material wealth in rich abundance, and yet, notwithstanding all these advantages, our country in its monetary interests is at the present moment in a deplorable condition. In the midst of unsurpassed plenty in all the productions of agriculture and in all the elements of national wealth, we find our manufactures suspended, our public works retarded, our private enterprises of different kinds abandoned, and thousands of useful laborers thrown out of employment and reduced to want. The revenue of the Government, which is chiefly derived from duties on imports from abroad, has been greatly reduced, whilst the appropriations made by Congress at its last session for the current fiscal year are very large in amount.

Under these circumstances a loan may be required before the close of your present session; but this, although deeply to be regretted, would prove to be only a slight misfortune when compared with the suffering and distress prevailing among the people. With this the Government can not fail deeply to sympathize, though it may be without the power to extend relief.

It is our duty to inquire what has produced such unfortunate results and whether their recurrence can be prevented. In all former revulsions the blame might have been fairly attributed to a variety of cooperating causes, but not so upon the present occasion. It is apparent that our existing misfortunes have proceeded solely from our extravagant and vicious system of paper currency and bank credits, exciting the people to wild speculations and gambling in stocks. These revulsions must continue to recur at successive intervals so long as the amount of the paper currency and bank loans and discounts of the country shall be left to the discretion of 1,400 irresponsible banking institutions, which from the very law of their nature will consult the interest of their stockholders rather than the public welfare.

The framers of the Constitution, when they gave to Congress the power "to coin money and to regulate the value thereof" and prohibited the States from coining money, emitting bills of credit, or making anything but gold and silver coin a tender in payment of debts, supposed they had protected the people against the evils of an excessive and irredeemable paper currency. They are not responsible for the existing anomaly that a Government endowed with the sovereign attribute of coining money and regulating the value thereof should have no power to prevent others from driving this coin out of the country and filling up the channels of circulation with paper which does not represent gold and silver.

It is one of the highest and most responsible duties of Government to insure to the people a sound circulating medium, the amount of which ought to be adapted with the utmost possible wisdom and skill to the wants of internal trade and foreign exchanges. If this be either greatly above or greatly below the proper standard, the marketable value of every man's property is increased or diminished in the same proportion, and injustice to individuals as well as incalculable evils to the community are the consequence.

Unfortunately, under the construction of the Federal Constitution which has now prevailed too long to be changed this important and delicate duty has been dissevered from the coining power and virtually transferred to more than 1,400 State banks acting independently of each other and regulating their paper issues almost exclusively by a regard to the present interest of their stockholders. Exercising the sovereign power of providing a paper currency instead of coin for the country, the first duty which these banks owe to the public is to keep in their vaults a sufficient amount of gold and silver to insure the convertibility of their notes into coin at all times and under all circumstances. No bank ought ever to be chartered without such restrictions on its business as to secure this result. All other restrictions are comparatively vain. This is the only true touchstone, the only efficient regulator of a paper currency—the only one which can guard the public against overissues and bank suspensions. As a collateral and eventual security, it is doubtless wise, and in all cases ought to be required, that banks shall hold an amount of United States or State securities equal to their notes in circulation and pledged for their redemption. This, however, furnishes no adequate security against overissues. On the contrary, it may be perverted to inflate the currency. Indeed, it is possible by this means to convert all the debts of the United States and State Governments into bank notes, without reference to the specie required to redeem them. However valuable these securities may be in themselves, they can not be converted into gold and silver at the moment of pressure, as our experience teaches, in sufficient time to prevent bank suspensions and the depreciation of bank notes. In England, which is to a considerable extent a paper-money country, though vastly behind our own in this respect, it was deemed advisable, anterior to the act of Parliament of 1844, which wisely separated the issue of notes from the banking department, for the Bank of England always to keep on hand gold and silver equal to one-third of its combined circulation and deposits. If this proportion was no more than sufficient to secure the convertibility of its notes with the whole of Great Britain and to some extent the continent of Europe as a field for its circulation, rendering it almost impossible that a sudden and immediate run to a dangerous amount should be made upon it, the same proportion would certainly be insufficient under our banking system. Each of our 1,400 banks has but a limited circumference for its circulation, and in the course of a very few days the depositors and note holders might demand from such a bank a sufficient amount in specie to compel it to suspend, even although it had coin in its vaults equal to one-third of its immediate liabilities. And yet I am not aware, with the exception of the banks of Louisiana, that any State bank throughout the Union has been required by its charter to keep this or any other proportion of gold and silver compared with the amount of its combined circulation and deposits. What has been the consequence? In a recent report made by the Treasury Department on the condition of the banks throughout the different States, according to returns dated nearest to January, 1857, the aggregate amount of actual specie in their vaults is $58,349,838, of their circulation $214,778,822, and of their deposits $230,351,352. Thus it appears that these banks in the aggregate have considerably less than one dollar in seven of gold and silver compared with their circulation and deposits. It was palpable,

CARTOON ON BUCHANAN'S CURRENCY POLICY

therefore, that the very first pressure must drive them to suspension and deprive the people of a convertible currency, with all its disastrous consequences. It is truly wonderful that they should have so long continued to preserve their credit when a demand for the payment of one-seventh of their immediate liabilities would have driven them into insolvency. And this is the condition of the banks, notwithstanding that four hundred millions of gold from California have flowed in upon us within the last eight years, and the tide still continues to flow. Indeed, such has been the extravagance of bank credits that the banks now hold a considerably less amount of specie, either in proportion to their capital or to their circulation and deposits combined, than they did before the discovery of gold in California. Whilst in the year 1848 their specie in proportion to their capital was more than equal to one dollar for four and a half, in 1857 it does not amount to one dollar for every six dollars and thirty-three cents of their capital. In the year 1848 the specie was equal within a very small fraction to one dollar in five of their circulation and deposits; in 1857 it is not equal to one dollar in seven and a half of their circulation and deposits.

From this statement it is easy to account for our financial history for the last forty years. It has been a history of extravagant expansions in the business of the country, followed by ruinous contractions. At successive intervals the best and most enterprising men have been tempted to their ruin by excessive bank loans of mere paper credit, exciting them to extravagant importations of foreign goods, wild speculations, and ruinous and demoralizing stock gambling. When the crisis arrives, as arrive it must, the banks can extend no relief to the people. In a vain struggle to redeem their liabilities in specie they are compelled to contract their loans and their issues, and at last, in the hour of distress, when their assistance is most needed, they and their debtors together sink into insolvency.

It is this paper system of extravagant expansion, raising the nominal price of every article far beyond its real value when compared with the cost of similar articles in countries whose circulation is wisely regulated, which has prevented us from competing in our own markets with foreign manufacturers, has produced extravagant importations, and has counteracted the effect of the large incidental protection afforded to our domestic manufactures by the present revenue tariff. But for this the branches of our manufactures composed of raw materials, the production of our own country—such as cotton, iron, and woolen fabrics—would not only have acquired almost exclusive possession of the home market, but would have created for themselves a foreign market throughout the world.

Deplorable, however, as may be our present financial condition, we may yet indulge in bright hopes for the future. No other nation has ever existed which could have endured such violent expansions and contractions of paper credits without lasting injury; yet the buoyancy of youth, the energies of our population, and the spirit which never quails before difficulties will enable us soon to recover from our present financial embarrassments, and may even occasion us speedily to forget the lesson which they have taught.

In the meantime it is the duty of the Government, by all proper means within its power, to aid in alleviating the sufferings of the people occasioned by the suspension of the banks and to provide against a recurrence of the same calamity. Unfortunately, in either aspect of the case it can do but little. Thanks to the independent treasury, the Government has not suspended payment, as it was compelled to do by the failure of the banks in 1837. It will continue to discharge its liabilities to the people in gold and silver. Its disbursements in coin will pass into circulation and materially assist in restoring a sound currency. From its high credit, should we be compelled to make a temporary loan, it can be effected on advantageous terms. This, however, shall if possible be avoided, but if not, then the amount shall be limited to the lowest practicable sum.

I have therefore determined that whilst no useful Government works already in progress shall be suspended, new works not already commenced will be postponed if this can be done without injury to the country. Those necessary for its defense shall proceed as though there had been no crisis in our monetary affairs.

But the Federal Government can not do much to provide against a recurrence of existing evils. Even if insurmountable constitutional objections did not exist against the creation of a national bank, this would furnish no adequate preventive security. The history of the last Bank of the United States abundantly proves the truth of this assertion. Such a bank could not, if it would, regulate the issues and credits of 1,400 State banks in such a manner as to prevent the ruinous expansions and contractions in our currency which afflicted the country throughout the existence of the late bank, or secure us against future suspensions. In 1825 an effort was made by the Bank of England to curtail the issues of the country banks under the most favorable circumstances. The paper currency had been expanded to a ruinous extent, and the bank put forth all its power to contract it in order to reduce prices and restore the equilibrium of the foreign exchanges. It accordingly commenced a system of curtailment of its loans and issues, in the vain hope that the joint stock and private banks of the Kingdom would be compelled to follow its example. It found, however, that as it contracted they expanded, and at the end of the process, to employ the language of a very high official authority, "whatever reduction of the paper circulation was effected by the Bank of England (in 1825) was more than made up by the issues of the country banks."

But a bank of the United States would not, if it could, restrain the issues and loans of the State banks, because its duty as a regulator of the currency must often be in direct conflict with the immediate interest of its stockholders. If we expect one agent to restrain or control another, their interests must, at least in some degree, be antagonistic. But the directors of a bank of the United States would feel the same interest and the same inclination with the directors of the State banks to expand the currency, to accommodate their favorites and friends with loans, and to declare large dividends. Such has been our experience in regard to the last bank.

After all, we must mainly rely upon the patriotism and wisdom of the States for the prevention and redress of the evil. If they will afford us a real specie basis for our paper circulation by increasing the denomination of bank notes, first to twenty and afterwards to fifty dollars; if they will require that the banks shall at all times keep on hand at least one dollar of gold and silver for every three dollars of their circulation and deposits, and if they will provide by a self-executing enactment, which nothing can arrest, that the moment they suspend they shall go into liquidation, I believe that such provisions, with a weekly publication by each bank of a statement of its condition, would go far to secure us against future suspensions of specie payments.

Congress, in my opinion, possess the power to pass a uniform bankrupt law applicable to all banking institutions throughout the United States, and I strongly recommend its exercise. This would make it the irreversible organic law of each bank's existence that a suspension of specie payments shall produce its civil death. The instinct of self-preservation would then compel it to perform its duties in such a manner as to escape the penalty and preserve its life.

The existence of banks and the circulation of bank paper are so identified with the habits of our people that they can not at this day be suddenly abolished without much immediate injury to the country. If we could confine them to their appropriate sphere and prevent them from administering to the spirit of wild and reckless speculation by extravagant loans and issues, they might be continued with advantage to the public.

But this I say, after long and much reflection: If experience shall prove it to be impossible to enjoy the facilities which well-regulated banks might afford without at the same time suffering the calamities which the excesses of the banks have hitherto inflicted upon the country, it would then be far the lesser evil to deprive them altogether of the power to issue a paper currency and confine them to the functions of banks of deposit and discount.

Our relations with foreign governments are upon the whole in a satisfactory condition.

The diplomatic difficulties which existed between the Government of the United States and that of Great Britain at the adjournment of the last Congress have been happily terminated by the appointment of a British minister to this country, who has been cordially received.

Whilst it is greatly to the interest, as I am convinced it is the sincere desire, of the Governments and people of the two countries to be on terms of intimate friendship with each other, it has been our misfortune almost always to have had some irritating, if not dangerous, outstanding question with Great Britain.

Since the origin of the Government we have been employed in negotiating treaties with that power, and afterwards in discussing their true intent and meaning. In this respect the convention of April 19, 1850, commonly called the Clayton and Bulwer treaty, has been the most unfortunate of all, because the two Governments place directly opposite and contradictory constructions upon its first and most important article. Whilst in the United States we believed that this treaty would place both powers upon an exact equality by the stipulation that neither will ever "occupy, or fortify, or colonize, or assume, or exercise any dominion" over any part of Central America, it is contended by the British Government that the true construction of this language has left them in the rightful possession of all that portion of Central America which was in their occupancy at the date of the treaty; in fact, that the treaty is a virtual recognition on the part of the United States of the right of Great Britain, either as owner or protector, to the whole extensive coast of Central America, sweeping round from the Rio Hondo to the port and harbor of San Juan de Nicaragua, together with the adjacent Bay Islands, except the comparatively small portion of this between the Sarstoon and Cape Honduras. According to their construction, the treaty does no more than simply prohibit them from extending their possessions in Central America beyond the present limits. It is not too much to assert that if in the United States the treaty had been considered susceptible of such a construction it never would have been negotiated under the authority of the President, nor would it have received the approbation of the Senate. The universal conviction in the United States was that when our Government consented to violate its traditional and time-honored policy and to stipulate with a foreign government never to occupy or acquire territory in the Central American portion of our own continent, the consideration for this sacrifice was that Great Britain should, in this respect at least, be placed in the same position with ourselves. Whilst we have no right to doubt the sincerity of the British Government in their construction of the treaty, it is at the same time my deliberate conviction that this construction is in opposition both to its letter and its spirit.

Under the late Administration negotiations were instituted between the two Governments for the purpose, if possible, of removing these difficulties, and a treaty having this laudable object in view was signed at London on the 17th October, 1856, and was submitted by the President to the Senate on the following 10th of December. Whether this treaty, either in its original or amended form, would have accomplished the object intended without giving birth to new and embarrassing complications between the two Governments, may perhaps be well questioned. Certain it is, however, it was rendered much less objectionable by the different amendments made to it by the Senate. The treaty as amended was ratified by me on the 12th March, 1857, and was transmitted to London for ratification by the British Government. That Government expressed its willingness to concur in all the amendments made by the Senate with the single exception of the clause relating to Ruatan and the other islands in the Bay of Honduras. The article in the original treaty as submitted to the Senate, after reciting that these islands and their inhabitants "having been, by a convention bearing date the 27th day of August, 1856, between Her Britannic Majesty and the Republic of Honduras, constituted and declared a free territory under the sovereignty of the said Republic of Honduras," stipulated that "the two contracting parties do hereby mutually engage to recognize and respect in all future time the independence and rights of the said free territory as a part of the Republic of Honduras."

Upon an examination of this convention between Great Britain and Honduras of the 27th August, 1856, it was found that whilst declaring the Bay Islands to be "a free territory under the sovereignty of the Republic of Honduras" it deprived that Republic of rights without which its sovereignty over them could scarcely be said to exist. It divided them from the remainder of Honduras and gave to their inhabitants a separate government of their own, with legislative, executive, and judicial officers elected by themselves. It deprived the Government of Honduras of the taxing power in every form and exempted the people of the islands from the performance of military duty except for their own exclusive defense. It also prohibited that Republic from erecting fortifications upon them for their protection, thus leaving them open to invasion from any quarter; and, finally, it provided "that slavery shall not at any time hereafter be permitted to exist therein."

Had Honduras ratified this convention, she would have ratified the establishment of a state substantially independent within her own limits, and a state at all times subject to British influence and control. Moreover, had the United States ratified the treaty with Great Britain in its original form, we should have been bound "to recognize and respect in all future time" these stipulations to the prejudice of Honduras. Being in direct opposition to the spirit and meaning of the Clayton and Bulwer treaty as understood in the United States, the Senate rejected the entire clause, and substituted in its stead a simple recognition of the sovereign right of Honduras to these islands in the following language:

The two contracting parties do hereby mutually engage to recognize and respect the islands of Ruatan, Bonaco, Utila, Barbaretta, Helena, and Morat, situate in the Bay of Honduras and off the coast of the Republic of Honduras, as under the sovereignty and as part of the said Republic of Honduras.

Great Britain rejected this amendment, assigning as the only reason that the ratifications of the convention of the 27th August, 1856, between her and Honduras had not been "exchanged, owing to the hesitation of that Government." Had this been done, it is stated that "Her Majesty's Government would have had little difficulty in agreeing to the modification proposed by the Senate, which then would have had in effect the same signification as the original wording." Whether this would have been the effect, whether the mere circumstance of the exchange of the ratifications of the British convention with Honduras prior in point of time to the ratification of our treaty with Great Britain would "in effect" have had "the same signification as the original wording," and thus have nullified the amendment of the Senate, may well be doubted. It is, perhaps, fortunate that the question has never arisen.

The British Government, immediately after rejecting the treaty as amended, proposed to enter into a new treaty with the United States, similar in all respects to the treaty which they had just refused to ratify, if the United States would consent to add to the Senate's clear and unqualified recognition of the sovereignty of Honduras over the Bay Islands the following conditional stipulation:

Whenever and so soon as the Republic of Honduras shall have concluded and ratified a treaty with Great Britain by which Great Britain shall have ceded and the Republic of Honduras shall have accepted the said islands, subject to the provisions and conditions contained in such treaty.

This proposition was, of course, rejected. After the Senate had refused to recognize the British convention with Honduras of the 27th August, 1856, with full knowledge of its contents, it was impossible for me, necessarily ignorant of "the provisions and conditions" which might be contained in a future convention between the same parties, to sanction them in advance.

The fact is that when two nations like Great Britain and the United States, mutually desirous, as they are, and I trust ever may be, of maintaining the most friendly relations with each other, have unfortunately concluded a treaty which they understand in senses directly opposite, the wisest course is to abrogate such a treaty by mutual consent and to commence anew. Had this been done promptly, all difficulties in Central America would most probably ere this have been adjusted to the satisfaction of both parties. The time spent in discussing the meaning of the Clayton and Bulwer treaty would have been devoted to this praiseworthy purpose, and the task would have been the more easily accomplished because the interest of the two countries in Central America is identical, being confined to securing safe transits over all the routes across the Isthmus.

Whilst entertaining these sentiments, I shall, nevertheless, not refuse to contribute to any reasonable adjustment of the Central American questions which is not practically inconsistent with the American interpretation of the treaty. Overtures for this purpose have been recently made by the British Government in a friendly spirit, which I cordially reciprocate, but whether this renewed effort will result in success I am not yet prepared to express an opinion. A brief period will determine.

With France our ancient relations of friendship still continue to exist. The French Government have in several recent instances, which need not be enumerated, evinced a spirit of good will and kindness toward our country, which I heartily reciprocate. It is, notwithstanding, much to be regretted that two nations whose productions are of such a character as to invite the most extensive exchanges and freest commercial intercourse should continue to enforce ancient and obsolete restrictions of trade against each other. Our commercial treaty with France is in this respect an exception from our treaties with all other commercial nations. It jealously levies discriminating duties both on tonnage and on articles the growth, produce, or manufacture of the one country when arriving in vessels belonging to the other.

More than forty years ago, on the 3d March, 1815, Congress passed an act offering to all nations to admit their vessels laden with their national productions into the ports of the United States upon the same terms with our own vessels provided they would reciprocate to us similar advantages. This act confined the reciprocity to the productions of the respective foreign nations who might enter into the proposed arrangement with the United States. The act of May 24, 1828, removed this restriction and offered a similar reciprocity to all such vessels without reference to the origin of their cargoes. Upon these principles our commercial treaties and arrangements have been founded, except with France, and let us hope that this exception may not long exist.

Our relations with Russia remain, as they have ever been, on the most friendly footing. The present Emperor, as well as his predecessors, have never failed when the occasion offered to manifest their good will to our country, and their friendship has always been highly appreciated by the Government and people of the United States.

With all other European Governments, except that of Spain, our relations are as peaceful as we could desire. I regret to say that no progress whatever has been made since the adjournment of Congress toward the settlement of any of the numerous claims of our citizens against the Spanish Government. Besides, the outrage committed on our flag by the Spanish war frigate *Ferrolana* on the high seas off the coast of Cuba in March, 1855, by firing into the American mail steamer *El Dorado* and detaining and searching her, remains unacknowledged and unredressed. The general tone and temper of the Spanish Government toward that of the United States are much to be regretted. Our present envoy extraordinary and minister plenipotentiary to Madrid has asked to be recalled, and it is my purpose to send out a new minister to Spain with special instructions on all questions pending between the two Governments, and with a determination to have them speedily and amicably adjusted if this be possible. In the meantime, whenever our minister urges the just claims of our citizens on the notice of the Spanish Government he is met with the objection that Congress has never made the appropriation recommended by President Polk in his annual message of December, 1847, "to be paid to the Spanish Government for the purpose of distribution among the claimants in the *Amistad* case." A similar recommendation was made by my immediate predecessor in his message of December, 1853, and entirely concurring with both in the opinion that this indemnity is justly due under the treaty with Spain of the 27th of October, 1795, I earnestly recommend such an appropriation to the favorable consideration of Congress.

A treaty of friendship and commerce was concluded at Constantinople on the 13th December, 1856, between the United States and Persia, the ratifications of which were exchanged at Constantinople on the 13th June, 1857, and the treaty was proclaimed by the President on the 18th August, 1857. This treaty, it is believed, will prove beneficial to American commerce. The Shah has manifested an earnest disposition to cultivate friendly relations with our country, and has expressed a strong wish that we should be represented at Teheran by a minister plenipotentiary; and I recommend that an appropriation be made for this purpose.

Recent occurrences in China have been unfavorable to a revision of the treaty with that Empire of the 3d July, 1844, with a view to the security and extension of our commerce. The twenty-fourth article of this treaty stipulated for a revision of it in case experience should prove this to be requisite, "in which case the two Governments will, at the expiration of twelve years from the date of said convention, treat amicably concerning the same by means of suitable persons appointed to conduct such negotiations." These twelve years expired on the 3d July, 1856, but long before that period it was ascertained that important changes in the treaty were necessary, and several fruitless attempts were made by the commissioner of the United States to effect these changes. Another effort was about to be made for the same purpose by our commissioner in conjunction with the ministers of England and France, but this was suspended by the occurrence of hostilities in the Canton River between Great Britain and the Chinese Empire. These hostilities have necessarily interrupted the trade of all nations with Canton, which is now in a state of blockade, and have occasioned a serious loss of life and property. Meanwhile the insurrection within the Empire against the existing imperial dynasty still continues, and it is difficult to anticipate what will be the result.

Under these circumstances I have deemed it advisable to appoint a distinguished citizen of Pennsylvania envoy extraordinary and minister plenipotentiary to proceed to China and to avail himself of any opportunities which may offer to effect changes in the existing treaty favorable to American commerce. He left the United States for the place of his destination in July last in the war steamer *Minnesota*. Special ministers to China have also been appointed by the Governments of Great Britain and France.

Whilst our minister has been instructed to occupy a neutral position in reference to the existing hostilities at Canton, he will cordially cooperate with the British and French ministers in all peaceful measures to secure by treaty stipulations those just concessions to commerce which the nations of the world have a right to expect and which China can not long be permitted to withhold. From assurances received I entertain no doubt that the three ministers will act in harmonious concert to obtain similar commercial treaties for each of the powers they represent.

We can not fail to feel a deep interest in all that concerns the welfare of the independent Republics on our own continent, as well as of the Empire of Brazil.

Our difficulties with New Granada, which a short time since bore so threatening an aspect, are, it is to be hoped, in a fair train of settlement in a manner just and honorable to both parties.

The isthmus of Central America, including that of Panama, is the great highway between the Atlantic and Pacific over which a large portion of the commerce of the world is destined to pass. The United States are more deeply interested than any other nation in preserving the freedom and security of all the communications across this isthmus. It is our duty, therefore, to take care that they shall not be interrupted either by invasions from our own country or by wars between the independent States of Central America. Under our treaty with New Granada of the 12th December, 1846, we are bound to guarantee the neutrality of the Isthmus of Panama, through which the Panama Railroad passes, "as well as the rights of sovereignty and property which New Granada has and possesses over the said territory." This obligation is founded upon equivalents granted by the treaty to the Government and people of the United States.

Under these circumstances I recommend to Congress the passage of an act authorizing the President, in case of necessity, to employ the land and naval forces of the United States to carry into effect this guaranty of neutrality and protection. I also recommend similar legislation for the security of any other route across the Isthmus in which we may acquire an interest by treaty.

With the independent Republics on this continent it is both our duty and our interest to cultivate the most friendly relations. We can never feel indifferent to their fate, and must always rejoice in their prosperity. Unfortunately both for them and for us, our example and advice have lost much of their influence in consequence of the lawless expeditions which have been fitted out against some of them within the limits of our country. Nothing is better calculated to retard our steady material progress or impair our character as a nation than the toleration of such enterprises in violation of the law of nations.

It is one of the first and highest duties of any independent state in its relations with the members of the great family of nations to restrain its people from acts of hostile aggression against their citizens or subjects. The most eminent writers on public law do not hesitate to denounce such hostile acts as robbery and murder.

Weak and feeble states like those of Central America may not feel themselves able to assert and vindicate their rights. The case would be far different if expeditions were set on foot within our own territories to make private war against a powerful nation. If such expeditions were fitted out from abroad against any portion of our own country, to burn down our cities, murder and plunder our people, and usurp our Government, we should call any power on earth to the strictest account for not preventing such enormities.

Ever since the Administration of General Washington acts of Congress have been enforced to punish severely the crime of setting on foot a military expedition within the limits of the United States to proceed from thence against a nation or state with whom we are at peace. The present neutrality act of April 20, 1818, is but little more than a collection of preexisting laws. Under this act the President is empowered to employ the land and naval forces and the militia "for the purpose of preventing the carrying on of any such expedition or enterprise from the territories and jurisdiction of the United States," and the collectors of customs are authorized and required to detain any vessel in port when there is reason to believe she is about to take part in such lawless enterprises.

When it was first rendered probable that an attempt would be made to get up another unlawful expedition against Nicaragua, the Secretary of State issued instructions to the marshals and district attorneys, which were directed by the Secretaries of War and the Navy to the appropriate army and navy officers, requiring them to be vigilant and to use their best exertions in carrying into effect the provisions of the act of 1818. Notwithstanding these precautions, the expedition has escaped from our shores. Such enterprises can do no possible good to the country, but have already inflicted much injury both on its interests and its character. They have prevented peaceful emigration from the United States to the States of Central America, which could not fail to prove highly beneficial to all the parties concerned. In a pecuniary point of view alone our citizens have sustained heavy losses from the seizure and closing of the transit route by the San Juan between the two oceans.

The leader of the recent expedition was arrested at New Orleans, but was discharged on giving bail for his appearance in the insufficient sum of $2,000.

I commend the whole subject to the serious attention of Congress, believing that our duty and our interest, as well as our national character, require that we should adopt such measures as will be effectual in restraining our citizens from committing such outrages.

I regret to inform you that the President of Paraguay has refused to ratify the treaty between the United States and that State as amended by the Senate, the signature of which was mentioned in the message of my predecessor to Congress at the opening of its session in December, 1853. The reasons assigned for this refusal will appear in the correspondence herewith submitted.

It being desirable to ascertain the fitness of the river La Plata and its tributaries for navigation by steam, the United States steamer *Water Witch* was sent thither for that purpose in 1853. This enterprise was successfully carried on until February, 1855, when, whilst in the peaceful prosecution of her voyage up the Parana River, the steamer was fired upon by a Paraguayan fort. The fire was returned, but as the *Water Witch* was of small force and not designed for offensive operations, she retired from the conflict. The pretext upon which the attack was made was a decree of the President of Paraguay of October, 1854, prohibiting foreign vessels of war from navigating the rivers of that State. As Paraguay, however, was the owner of but one bank of the river of that name, the other belonging to Corientes, a State of the Argentine Confederation, the right of its Government to expect that such a decree would be obeyed can not be acknowledged. But the *Water Witch* was not, properly speaking, a vessel of war. She was a small steamer engaged in a scientific enterprise intended for the advantage of commercial states generally. Under these circumstances I am constrained to consider the attack upon her as unjustifiable and as calling for satisfaction from the Paraguayan Government.

Citizens of the United States also who were established in business in Paraguay have had their property seized and taken from them, and have otherwise been treated by the authorities in an insulting and arbitrary manner, which requires redress.

A demand for these purposes will be made in a firm but conciliatory spirit. This will the more probably be granted if the Executive shall have authority to use other means in the event of a refusal. This is accordingly recommended.

It is unnecessary to state in detail the alarming condition of the Territory of Kansas at the time of my inauguration. The opposing parties then stood in hostile array against each other, and any accident might have relighted the flames of civil war. Besides, at this critical moment Kansas was left without a governor by the resignation of Governor Geary.

On the 19th of February previous the Territorial legislature had passed a law providing for the election of delegates on the third Monday of June to a convention to meet on the first Monday of September for the purpose of framing a constitution preparatory to admission into the Union. This law was in the main fair and just, and it is to be regretted that all the qualified electors had not registered themselves and voted under its provisions.

At the time of the election for delegates an extensive organization existed in the Territory whose avowed object it was, if need be, to put down the lawful government by force and to establish a government of their own under the so-called Topeka constitution. The persons attached to this revolutionary organization abstained from taking any part in the election.

The act of the Territorial legislature had omitted to provide for submitting to the people the constitution which might be framed by the convention, and in the excited state of public feeling throughout Kansas an apprehension extensively prevailed that a design existed to force upon them a constitution in relation to slavery against their will. In this emergency it became my duty, as it was my unquestionable right, having in view the union of all good citizens in support of the Territorial laws, to express an opinion on the true construction of the provisions concerning slavery contained in the organic act of Congress of the 30th May, 1854. Congress declared it to be "the true intent and meaning of this act not to legislate slavery into any Territory or State, nor to exclude it therefrom, but to leave the people thereof perfectly free to form and regulate their domestic institutions in their own way." Under it Kansas, "when admitted as a State," was to "be received into the Union with or without slavery, as their constitution may prescribe at the time of their admission."

Did Congress mean by this language that the delegates elected to frame a constitution should have authority finally to decide the question of slavery, or did they intend by leaving it to the people that the people of Kansas themselves should decide this question by a direct vote? On this subject I confess I had never entertained a serious doubt, and therefore in my instructions to Governor Walker of the 28th March last I merely said that when "a constitution shall be submitted to the people of the Territory they must be protected in the exercise of their right of voting for or against that instrument, and the fair expression of the popular will must not be interrupted by fraud or violence."

In expressing this opinion it was far from my intention to interfere with the decision of the people of Kansas, either for or against slavery. From this I have always carefully abstained. Intrusted with the duty of taking "care that the laws be faithfully executed," my only desire was that the people of Kansas should furnish to Congress the evidence required by the organic act, whether for or against slavery, and in this manner smooth their passage into the Union. In emerging from the condition of Territorial dependence into that of a sovereign State it was their duty, in my opinion, to make known their will by the votes of the majority on the direct question whether this important domestic institution should or should not continue to exist. Indeed, this was the only possible mode in which their will could be authentically ascertained.

The election of delegates to a convention must necessarily take place in separate districts. From this cause it may readily happen, as has often been the case, that a majority of the people of a State or Territory are on one side of a question, whilst a majority of the representatives from the several districts into which it is divided may be upon the other side. This arises from the fact that in some districts delegates may be elected by small majorities, whilst in others those of different sentiments may receive majorities sufficiently great not only to overcome the votes given for the former, but to leave a large majority of the whole people in direct opposition to a majority of the delegates. Besides, our history proves that influences may be brought to bear on the representative sufficiently powerful to induce him to disregard the will of his constituents. The truth is that no other authentic and satisfactory mode exists of ascertaining the will of a majority of the people of any State or Territory on an important and exciting question like that of slavery in Kansas except by leaving it to a direct vote. How wise, then, was it for Congress to pass over all subordinate and intermediate agencies and proceed directly to the source of all legitimate power under our institutions!

How vain would any other principle prove in practice! This may be illustrated by the case of Kansas. Should she be admitted into the Union with a constitution either maintaining or abolishing slavery against the sentiment of the people, this could have no other effect than to continue and to exasperate the existing agitation during the brief period required to make the constitution conform to the irresistible will of the majority.

The friends and supporters of the Nebraska and Kansas act, when struggling on a recent occasion to sustain its wise provisions before the great tribunal of the American people, never differed about its true meaning on this subject. Everywhere throughout the Union they publicly pledged their faith and their honor that they would cheerfully submit the question of slavery to the decision of the *bona fide* people of Kansas, without any restriction or qualification whatever. All were cordially united upon the great doctrine of popular sovereignty, which is the vital principle of our free institutions. Had it then been insinuated from any quarter that it would be a sufficient compliance with the requisitions of the organic law for the members of a convention thereafter to be elected to withhold the question of slavery from the people and to substitute their own will for that of a legally ascertained majority of all their constituents, this would have been instantly rejected. Everywhere they remained true to the resolution adopted on a celebrated occasion recognizing "the right of the people of all the Territories, including Kansas and Nebraska, acting through the legally and fairly expressed will of a majority of actual residents, and whenever the number of their inhabitants justifies it, to form a constitution with or without slavery and be admitted into the Union upon terms of perfect equality with the other States."

The convention to frame a constitution for Kansas met on the first Monday of September last. They were called together by virtue of an act of the Territorial legislature, whose lawful existence had been recognized by Congress in different forms and by different enactments. A large proportion of the citizens of Kansas did not think proper to register their names and to vote at the election for delegates; but an opportunity to do this having been fairly afforded, their refusal to avail themselves of their right could in no manner affect the legality of the convention.

This convention proceeded to frame a constitution for Kansas, and finally adjourned on the 7th day of November. But little difficulty occurred in the convention except on the subject of slavery. The truth is that the general provisions of our recent State constitutions are so similar and, I may add, so excellent that the difference between them is not essential. Under the earlier practice of the Government no constitution framed by the convention of a Territory preparatory to its admission into the Union as a State had been submitted to the people. I trust, however, the example set by the last Congress, requiring that the constitution of Minnesota "should be subject to the approval and ratification of the people of the proposed State," may be followed on future occasions. I took it for granted that the convention of Kansas would act in accordance with this example, founded, as it is, on correct principles, and hence my instructions to Governor Walker in favor of submitting the constitution to the people were expressed in general and unqualified terms.

In the Kansas-Nebraska act, however, this requirement, as applicable to the whole constitution, had not been inserted, and the convention were not bound by its terms to submit any other portion of the instrument to an election except that which relates to the "domestic institution" of slavery. This will be rendered clear by a simple reference to its language. It was "not to legislate slavery into any Territory or State, nor to exclude it therefrom, but to leave the people thereof perfectly free to form and regulate their domestic institutions in their own way." According to the plain construction of the sentence, the words "domestic institutions" have a direct, as they have an appropriate, reference to slavery. "Domestic institutions" are limited to the family The relation between master and slave and a few others are "domestic institutions," and are entirely distinct from institutions of a political character. Besides, there was no question then before Congress, nor, indeed, has there since been any serious question before the people of Kansas or the country, except that which relates to the "domestic institution" of slavery.

The convention, after an angry and excited debate, finally determined, by a majority of only two, to submit the question of slavery to the people, though at the last forty-three of the fifty delegates present affixed their signatures to the constitution.

A large majority of the convention were in favor of establishing slavery in Kansas. They accordingly inserted an article in the constitution for this purpose similar in form to those which had been adopted by other Territorial conventions. In the schedule, however, providing for the transition from a Territorial to a State government the question has been fairly and explicitly referred to the people whether they will have a constitution "with or without slavery." It declares that before the constitution adopted by the convention "shall be sent to Congress for admission into the Union as a State" an election shall be held to decide this question, at which all the white male inhabitants of the Territory above the age of 21 are entitled to vote. They are to vote by ballot, and "the ballots cast at said election shall be indorsed 'constitution with slavery' and 'constitution with no slavery.'" If there be a majority in favor of the "constitution with slavery," then it is to be transmitted to Congress by the president of the convention in its original form; if, on the contrary, there shall be a majority in favor of the "constitution with no slavery," "then the article providing for slavery shall be stricken from the constitution by the president of this convention;" and it is expressly declared that "no slavery shall exist in the State of Kansas, except that the right of property in slaves now in the Territory shall in no manner be interfered with;" and in that event it is made his duty to have the constitution thus ratified transmitted to the Congress of the United States for the admission of the State into the Union.

At this election every citizen will have an opportunity of expressing his opinion by his vote "whether Kansas shall be received into the Union with or without slavery," and thus this exciting question may be peacefully settled in the very mode required by the organic law. The election will be held under legitimate authority, and if any portion of the inhabitants shall refuse to vote, a fair opportunity to do so having been presented, this will be their own voluntary act and they alone will be responsible for the consequences.

Whether Kansas shall be a free or a slave State must eventually, under some authority, be decided by an election; and the question can never be more clearly or distinctly presented to the people than it is at the present moment. Should this opportunity be rejected she may be involved for years in domestic discord, and possibly in civil war, before she can again make up the issue now so fortunately tendered and again reach the point she has already attained.

Kansas has for some years occupied too much of the public attention. It is high time this should be directed to far more important objects. When once admitted into the Union, whether with or without slavery, the excitement beyond her own limits will speedily pass away, and she will then for the first time be left, as she ought to have been long since, to manage her own affairs in her own way. If her constitution on the subject of slavery or on any other subject be displeasing to a majority of the people, no human power can prevent them from changing it within a brief period. Under these circumstances it may well be questioned whether the peace and quiet of the whole country are not of greater importance than the mere temporary triumph of either of the political parties in Kansas.

Should the constitution without slavery be adopted by the votes of the majority, the rights of property in slaves now in the Territory are reserved. The number of these is very small, but if it were greater the provision would be equally just and reasonable. The slaves were brought into the Territory under the Constitution of the United States and are now the property of their masters. This point has at length been finally decided by the highest judicial tribunal of the country, and this upon the plain principle that when a confederacy of sovereign States acquire a new territory at their joint expense both equality and justice demand that the citizens of one and all of them shall have the right to take into it whatsoever is recognized as property by the common Constitution. To have summarily confiscated the property in slaves already in the Territory would have been an act of gross injustice and contrary to the practice of the older States of the Union which have abolished slavery.

A Territorial government was established for Utah by act of Congress approved the 9th September, 1850, and the Constitution and laws of the United States were thereby extended over it "so far as the same or any provisions thereof may be applicable." This act provided for the appointment by the President, by and with the advice and consent of the Senate, of a governor (who was to be *ex officio* superintendent of Indian affairs), a secretary, three judges of the supreme court, a marshal, and a district attorney. Subsequent acts provided for the appointment of the officers necessary to extend our land and our Indian system over the Territory. Brigham Young was appointed the first governor on the 20th September, 1850, and has held the office ever since. Whilst Governor Young has been both governor and superintendent of Indian affairs throughout this period, he has been at the same time the head of the church called the Latter-day Saints, and professes to govern its members and dispose of their property by direct inspiration and authority from the Almighty. His power has been, therefore, absolute over both church and state.

The people of Utah almost exclusively belong to this church, and believing with a fanatical spirit that he is governor of the Territory by divine appointment, they obey his commands as if these were direct revelations from Heaven. If, therefore, he chooses that his government shall come into collision with the Government of the United States, the members of the Mormon Church will yield implicit obedience to his will. Unfortunately, existing facts leave but little doubt that such is his determination. Without entering upon a minute history of occurrences, it is sufficient to say that all the officers of the United States, judicial and executive, with the single exception of two Indian agents, have found it necessary for their own personal safety to withdraw from the Territory, and there no longer remains any government in Utah but the despotism of Brigham Young. This being the condition of affairs in the Territory, I could not mistake the path of duty. As Chief Executive Magistrate I was bound to restore the supremacy of the Constitution and laws within its limits. In order to effect this purpose, I appointed a new governor and other Federal officers for Utah and sent with them a military force for their protection and to aid as a *posse comitatus* in case of need in the execution of the laws.

With the religious opinions of the Mormons, as long as they remained mere opinions, however deplorable in themselves and revolting to the moral and religious sentiments of all Christendom, I had no right to in terfere. Actions alone, when in violation of the Constitution and laws of the United States, become the legitimate subjects for the jurisdiction of the civil magistrate. My instructions to Governor Cumming have therefore been framed in strict accordance with these principles. At their date a hope was indulged that no necessity might exist for employ ing the military in restoring and maintaining the authority of the law, but this hope has now vanished. Governor Young has by proclama tion declared his determination to maintain his power by force, and has already committed acts of hostility against the United States. Unless he should retrace his steps the Territory of Utah will be in a state of open rebellion. He has committed these acts of hostility notwithstanding Major Van Vliet, an officer of the Army, sent to Utah by the Command ing General to purchase provisions for the troops, had given him the strongest assurances of the peaceful intentions of the Government, and that the troops would only be employed as a *posse comitatus* when called on by the civil authority to aid in the execution of the laws.

There is reason to believe that Governor Young has long contemplated this result. He knows that the continuance of his despotic power depends upon the exclusion of all settlers from the Territory except those who will acknowledge his divine mission and implicitly obey his will, and that an enlightened public opinion there would soon prostrate institutions at war with the laws both of God and man. He has there fore for several years, in order to maintain his independence, been indus triously employed in collecting and fabricating arms and munitions of war and in disciplining the Mormons for military service. As superin tendent of Indian affairs he has had an opportunity of tampering with the Indian tribes and exciting their hostile feelings against the United States. This, according to our information, he has accomplished in regard to some of these tribes, while others have remained true to their allegiance and have communicated his intrigues to our Indian agents. He has laid in a store of provisions for three years, which in case of ne cessity, as he informed Major Van Vliet, he will conceal, "and then take to the mountains and bid defiance to all the powers of the Government."

A great part of all this may be idle boasting, but yet no wise government will lightly estimate the efforts which may be inspired by such frenzied fanaticism as exists among the Mormons in Utah. This is the first rebellion which has existed in our Territories, and humanity itself requires that we should put it down in such a manner that it shall be the last. To trifle with it would be to encourage it and to render it formidable. We ought to go there with such an imposing force as to convince these deluded people that resistance would be vain, and thus spare the effusion of blood. We can in this manner best convince them that we are their friends, not their enemies. In order to accomplish this object it will be necessary, according to the estimate of the War Department, to raise four additional regiments; and this I earnestly recommend to Congress. At the present moment of depression in the revenues of the country I am sorry to be obliged to recommend such a measure; but I feel confident of the support of Congress, cost what it may, in suppressing the insurrection and in restoring and maintaining the sovereignty of the Constitution and laws over the Territory of Utah.

I recommend to Congress the establishment of a Territorial government over Arizona, incorporating with it such portions of New Mexico as they may deem expedient. I need scarcely adduce arguments in support of this recommendation. We are bound to protect the lives and the property of our citizens inhabiting Arizona, and these are now without any efficient protection. Their present number is already considerable, and is rapidly increasing, notwithstanding the disadvantages under which they labor. Besides, the proposed Territory is believed to be rich in mineral and agricultural resources, especially in silver and copper. The mails of the United States to California are now carried over it throughout its whole extent, and this route is known to be the nearest and believed to be the best to the Pacific.

Long experience has deeply convinced me that a strict construction of the powers granted to Congress is the only true, as well as the only safe, theory of the Constitution. Whilst this principle shall guide my public conduct, I consider it clear that under the war-making power Congress may appropriate money for the construction of a military road through the Territories of the United States when this is absolutely necessary for the defense of any of the States against foreign invasion. The Constitution has conferred upon Congress power "to declare war," "to raise and support armies," "to provide and maintain a navy," and to call forth the militia to "repel invasions." These high sovereign powers necessarily involve important and responsible public duties, and among them there is none so sacred and so imperative as that of preserving our soil from the invasion of a foreign enemy. The Constitution has therefore left nothing on this point to construction, but expressly requires that "the United States shall protect each of them [the States] against invasion." Now if a military road over our own Territories be indispensably necessary to enable us to meet and repel the invader, it follows as a necessary consequence not only that we possess the power, but it is our imperative duty to construct such a road. It would be an absurdity to invest a government with the unlimited power to make and conduct war and at the same time deny to it the only means of reaching and defeating the enemy at the frontier. Without such a road it is quite evident we can not "protect" California and our Pacific possessions "against invasion." We can not by any other means transport men and munitions of war from the Atlantic States in sufficient time successfully to defend these remote and distant portions of the Republic.

Experience has proved that the routes across the isthmus of Central America are at best but a very uncertain and unreliable mode of communication. But even if this were not the case, they would at once be closed against us in the event of war with a naval power so much stronger than our own as to enable it to blockade the ports at either end of these routes. After all, therefore, we can only rely upon a military road through our own Territories; and ever since the origin of the Government Congress has been in the practice of appropriating money from the public Treasury for the construction of such roads.

The difficulties and the expense of constructing a military railroad to connect our Atlantic and Pacific States have been greatly exaggerated. The distance on the Arizona route, near the thirty-second parallel of north latitude, between the western boundary of Texas, on the Rio Grande, and the eastern boundary of California, on the Colorado, from the best explorations now within our knowledge, does not exceed 470 miles, and the face of the country is in the main favorable. For obvious reasons the Government ought not to undertake the work itself by means of its own agents. This ought to be committed to other agencies, which Congress might assist, either by grants of land or money, or by both, upon such terms and conditions as they may deem most beneficial for the country. Provision might thus be made not only for the safe, rapid, and economical transportation of troops and munitions of war, but also of the public mails. The commercial interests of the whole country, both East and West, would be greatly promoted by such a road, and, above all, it would be a powerful additional bond of union. And although advantages of this kind, whether postal, commercial, or political, can not confer constitutional power, yet they may furnish auxiliary arguments in favor of expediting a work which, in my judgment, is clearly embraced within the war-making power.

For these reasons I commend to the friendly consideration of Congress the subject of the Pacific Railroad, without finally committing myself to any particular route.

The report of the Secretary of the Treasury will furnish a detailed statement of the condition of the public finances and of the respective branches of the public service devolved upon that Department of the

Government. By this report it appears that the amount of revenue received from all sources into the Treasury during the fiscal year ending the 30th June, 1857, was $68,631,513.67, which amount, with the balance of $19,901,325.45 remaining in the Treasury at the commencement of the year, made an aggregate for the service of the year of $88,532,839.12.

The public expenditures for the fiscal year ending 30th June, 1857, amounted to $70,822,724.85, of which $5,943,896.91 were applied to the redemption of the public debt, including interest and premium, leaving in the Treasury at the commencement of the present fiscal year, on the 1st July, 1857, $17,710,114.27.

The receipts into the Treasury for the first quarter of the present fiscal year, commencing 1st July, 1857, were $20,929,819.81, and the estimated receipts of the remaining three quarters to the 30th June, 1858, are $36,750,000, making, with the balance before stated, an aggregate of $75,389,934.08 for the service of the present fiscal year.

The actual expenditures during the first quarter of the present fiscal year were $23,714,528.37, of which $3,895,232.39 were applied to the redemption of the public debt, including interest and premium. The probable expenditures of the remaining three quarters to 30th June, 1858, are $51,248,530.04, including interest on the public debt, making an aggregate of $74,963,058.41, leaving an estimated balance in the Treasury at the close of the present fiscal year of $426,875.67.

The amount of the public debt at the commencement of the present fiscal year was $29,060,386.90.

The amount redeemed since the 1st of July was $3,895,232.39, leaving a balance unredeemed at this time of $25,165,154.51.

The amount of estimated expenditures for the remaining three quarters of the present fiscal year will in all probability be increased from the causes set forth in the report of the Secretary. His suggestion, therefore, that authority should be given to supply any temporary deficiency by the issue of a limited amount of Treasury notes is approved, and I accordingly recommend the passage of such a law.

As stated in the report of the Secretary, the tariff of March 3, 1857, has been in operation for so short a period of time and under circumstances so unfavorable to a just development of its results as a revenue measure that I should regard it as inexpedient, at least for the present, to undertake its revision.

I transmit herewith the reports made to me by the Secretaries of War and of the Navy, of the Interior, and of the Postmaster-General. They all contain valuable and important information and suggestions, which I commend to the favorable consideration of Congress.

I have already recommended the raising of four additional regiments, and the report of the Secretary of War presents strong reasons proving this increase of the Army under existing circumstances to be indispensable.

I would call the special attention of Congress to the recommendation of the Secretary of the Navy in favor of the construction of ten small war steamers of light draft. For some years the Government has been obliged on many occasions to hire such steamers from individuals to supply its pressing wants. At the present moment we have no armed vessel in the Navy which can penetrate the rivers of China. We have but few which can enter any of the harbors south of Norfolk, although many millions of foreign and domestic commerce annually pass in and out of these harbors. Some of our most valuable interests and most vulnerable points are thus left exposed. This class of vessels of light draft, great speed, and heavy guns would be formidable in coast defense. The cost of their construction will not be great and they will require but a comparatively small expenditure to keep them in commission. In time of peace they will prove as effective as much larger vessels and more useful. One of them should be at every station where we maintain a squadron, and three or four should be constantly employed on our Atlantic and Pacific coasts. Economy, utility, and efficiency combine to recommend them as almost indispensable. Ten of these small vessels would be of incalculable advantage to the naval service, and the whole cost of their construction would not exceed $2,300,000, or $230,000 each.

The report of the Secretary of the Interior is worthy of grave consideration. It treats of the numerous important and diversified branches of domestic administration intrusted to him by law. Among these the most prominent are the public lands and our relations with the Indians.

Our system for the disposal of the public lands, originating with the fathers of the Republic, has been improved as experience pointed the way, and gradually adapted to the growth and settlement of our Western States and Territories. It has worked well in practice. Already thirteen States and seven Territories have been carved out of these lands, and still more than a thousand millions of acres remain unsold. What a boundless prospect this presents to our country of future prosperity and power!

We have heretofore disposed of 363,862,464 acres of the public land.

Whilst the public lands, as a source of revenue, are of great importance, their importance is far greater as furnishing homes for a hardy and independent race of honest and industrious citizens who desire to subdue and cultivate the soil. They ought to be administered mainly with a view of promoting this wise and benevolent policy. In appropriating them for any other purpose we ought to use even greater economy than if they had been converted into money and the proceeds were already in the public Treasury. To squander away this richest and noblest inheritance which any people have ever enjoyed upon objects of doubtful constitutionality or expediency would be to violate one of the most important trusts ever committed to any people. Whilst I do not deny to Congress the power, when acting *bona fide* as a proprietor, to give away portions of them for the purpose of increasing the value of the remainder, yet, considering the great temptation to abuse this power, we can not be too cautious in its exercise.

Actual settlers under existing laws are protected against other purchasers at the public sales in their right of preemption to the extent of a quarter section, or 160 acres, of land. The remainder may then be disposed of at public or entered at private sale in unlimited quantities.

Speculation has of late years prevailed to a great extent in the public lands. The consequence has been that large portions of them have become the property of individuals and companies, and thus the price is greatly enhanced to those who desire to purchase for actual settlement. In order to limit the area of speculation as much as possible, the extinction of the Indian title and the extension of the public surveys ought only to keep pace with the tide of emigration.

If Congress should hereafter grant alternate sections to States or companies, as they have done heretofore, I recommend that the intermediate sections retained by the Government should be subject to preemption by actual settlers.

It ought ever to be our cardinal policy to reserve the public lands as much as may be for actual settlers, and this at moderate prices. We shall thus not only best promote the prosperity of the new States and Territories and the power of the Union, but shall secure homes for our posterity for many generations.

The extension of our limits has brought within our jurisdiction many additional and populous tribes of Indians, a large proportion of which are wild, untractable, and difficult to control. Predatory and warlike in their disposition and habits, it is impossible altogether to restrain them from committing aggressions on each other, as well as upon our frontier citizens and those emigrating to our distant States and Territories. Hence expensive military expeditions are frequently necessary to overawe and chastise the more lawless and hostile.

The present system of making them valuable presents to influence them to remain at peace has proved ineffectual. It is believed to be the better policy to colonize them in suitable localities where they can receive the rudiments of education and be gradually induced to adopt habits of industry. So far as the experiment has been tried it has worked well in practice, and it will doubtless prove to be less expensive than the present system.

The whole number of Indians within our territorial limits is believed to be, from the best data in the Interior Department, about 325,000.

The tribes of Cherokees, Choctaws, Chickasaws, and Creeks settled in the Territory set apart for them west of Arkansas are rapidly advancing in education and in all the arts of civilization and self-government, and we may indulge the agreeable anticipation that at no very distant day they will be incorporated into the Union as one of the sovereign States.

It will be seen from the report of the Postmaster-General that the Post-Office Department still continues to depend on the Treasury, as it has been compelled to do for several years past, for an important portion of the means of sustaining and extending its operations. Their rapid growth and expansion are shown by a decennial statement of the number of post-offices and the length of post-roads, commencing with the year 1827. In that year there were 7,000 post-offices; in 1837, 11,177; in 1847, 15,146, and in 1857 they number 26,586. In this year 1,725 post-offices have been established and 704 discontinued, leaving a net increase of 1,021. The postmasters of 368 offices are appointed by the President.

The length of post-roads in 1827 was 105,336 miles; in 1837, 141,242 miles; in 1847, 153,818 miles, and in the year 1857 there are 242,601 miles of post-road, including 22,530 miles of railroad on which the mails are transported.

The expenditures of the Department for the fiscal year ending on the 30th June, 1857, as adjusted by the Auditor, amounted to $11,507,670. To defray these expenditures there was to the credit of the Department on the 1st July, 1856, the sum of $789,599; the gross revenue of the year, including the annual allowances for the transportation of free mail matter, produced $8,053,951, and the remainder was supplied by the appropriation from the Treasury of $2,250,000 granted by the act of Congress approved August 18, 1856, and by the appropriation of $666,883 made by the act of March 3, 1857, leaving $252,763 to be carried to the credit of the Department in the accounts of the current year. I commend to your consideration the report of the Department in relation to the establishment of the overland mail route from the Mississippi River to San Francisco, Cal. The route was selected with my full concurrence, as the one, in my judgment, best calculated to attain the important objects contemplated by Congress.

The late disastrous monetary revulsion may have one good effect should it cause both the Government and the people to return to the practice of a wise and judicious economy both in public and private expenditures.

An overflowing Treasury has led to habits of prodigality and extravagance in our legislation. It has induced Congress to make large appropriations to objects for which they never would have provided had it been necessary to raise the amount of revenue required to meet them by increased taxation or by loans. We are now compelled to pause in our career and to scrutinize our expenditures with the utmost vigilance; and in performing this duty I pledge my cooperation to the extent of my constitutional competency.

It ought to be observed at the same time that true public economy does not consist in withholding the means necessary to accomplish important national objects intrusted to us by the Constitution, and especially such as may be necessary for the common defense. In the present crisis of the country it is our duty to confine our appropriations to objects of this character, unless in cases where justice to individuals may demand a different course. In all cases care ought to be taken that the money granted by Congress shall be faithfully and economically applied.

Under the Federal Constitution "every bill which shall have passed the House of Representatives and the Senate shall, before it become a law," be approved and signed by the President; and if not approved, "he shall return it with his objections to that House in which it shall have originated." In order to perform this high and responsible duty, sufficient time must be allowed the President to read and examine every bill presented to him for approval. Unless this be afforded, the Constitution becomes a dead letter in this particular, and, even worse, it becomes a means of deception. Our constituents, seeing the President's approval and signature attached to each act of Congress, are induced to believe that he has actually performed his duty, when in truth nothing is in many cases more unfounded.

From the practice of Congress such an examination of each bill as the Constitution requires has been rendered impossible. The most important business of each session is generally crowded into its last hours, and the alternative presented to the President is either to violate the constitutional duty which he owes to the people and approve bills which for want of time it is impossible he should have examined, or by his refusal to do this subject the country and individuals to great loss and inconvenience.

Besides, a practice has grown up of late years to legislate in appropriation bills at the last hours of the session on new and important subjects. This practice constrains the President either to suffer measures to become laws which he does not approve or to incur the risk of stopping the wheels of the Government by vetoing an appropriation bill. Formerly such bills were confined to specific appropriations for carrying into effect existing laws and the well-established policy of the country, and little time was then required by the President for their examination.

For my own part, I have deliberately determined that I shall approve no bills which I have not examined, and it will be a case of extreme and most urgent necessity which shall ever induce me to depart from this rule. I therefore respectfully but earnestly recommend that the two Houses would allow the President at least two days previous to the adjournment of each session within which no new bill shall be presented to him for approval. Under the existing joint rule one day is allowed, but this rule has been hitherto so constantly suspended in practice that important bills continue to be presented to him up till the very last moments of the session. In a large majority of cases no great public inconvenience can arise from the want of time to examine their provisions, because the Constitution has declared that if a bill be presented to the President within the last ten days of the session he is not required to return it, either with an approval or with a veto, "in which case it shall not be a law." It may then lie over and be taken up and passed at the next session. Great inconvenience would only be experienced in regard to appropriation bills, but, fortunately, under the late excellent law allowing a salary instead of a per diem to members of Congress the expense and inconvenience of a called session will be greatly reduced.

I can not conclude without commending to your favorable consideration the interest of the people of this District. Without a representative on the floor of Congress, they have for this very reason peculiar claims upon our just regard. To this I know, from my long acquaintance with them, they are eminently entitled.

JAMES BUCHANAN.

SPECIAL MESSAGES.

WASHINGTON, December 8, 1857.

To the Senate of the United States:

Herewith I transmit to the Senate, for its consideration with a view to ratification, a convention between the United States and His Majesty the King of Denmark for the discontinuance of the Sound dues, signed in this city on the 11th day of April last.

JAMES BUCHANAN.

WASHINGTON, December 10, 1857.

To the Senate and House of Representatives:

I transmit a copy of a letter of the 30th of May last from the commissioner of the United States in China, and of the decree and regulation which accompanied it, for such revision thereof as Congress may deem expedient, pursuant to the sixth section of the act approved the 11th of August, 1848.

JAMES BUCHANAN.

WASHINGTON, December 17, 1857.

To the Senate of the United States:

I transmit to the Senate, for its consideration with a view to ratification, a convention for the mutual delivery of criminals fugitives from justice in certain cases, and for other purposes, concluded at The Hague on the 21st day of August last, between the United States and His Majesty the King of the Netherlands. The instrument in this form embodies the Senate's amendments of the 16th of February last to the convention between the same parties of the 29th of May, 1856, and is in fact a mere copy of that instrument as amended by the Senate. Pursuant to the usual course in such cases, the Senate's amendments were not included in the text of the United States exchange copy of the convention, but appeared in the act of ratification only. As the Dutch Government objected to this, it is now proposed to substitute the new convention herewith submitted.

JAMES BUCHANAN.

WASHINGTON, *December 22, 1857.*

To the Senate of the United States:

In answer to resolutions of the Senate of the 16th and 18th instant, requesting correspondence and documents relative to the Territory of Kansas, I transmit a report from the Secretary of State and the papers by which it was accompanied.

JAMES BUCHANAN.

WASHINGTON, *December 23, 1857.*

To the Senate of the United States:

I herewith transmit to the Senate a communication, dated on the 22d instant, with the accompanying papers, received from the Department of State, in compliance with a resolution adopted by the Senate on the 17th instant, requesting the President, if compatible with the public interest, to communicate to that body copies of any correspondence which may have taken place between the Department of State and the British and French ministers on the subject of claims for losses alleged to have been sustained by subjects of Great Britain and France at the bombardment of Greytown.

JAMES BUCHANAN.

WASHINGTON, *December 29, 1857.*

To the Senate of the United States:

Herewith I transmit a report of the Secretary of State, with accompanying documents,* in compliance with the resolution of the Senate of the 18th instant.

JAMES BUCHANAN.

To the Senate: WASHINGTON, *January 5, 1858.*

I transmit herewith, for the constitutional action of the Senate, a treaty recently concluded with the Pawnee Indians, with accompanying papers.

JAMES BUCHANAN.

WASHINGTON, *January 6, 1858.*

To the Senate of the United States:

In compliance with the resolution of the Senate of the 28th of February last, requesting a communication of all the correspondence of John W.

---

*Correspondence with the minister of Bremen relative to claims for losses alleged to have been sustained by subjects of the Hanse towns at the bombardment of Greytown.

Geary, late governor of the Territory of Kansas, not heretofore communicated to Congress, I transmit a report from the Secretary of State and the documents by which it was accompanied.

JAMES BUCHANAN.

WASHINGTON, *January 6, 1858.*

To the Senate of the United States:

In answer to the resolution of the Senate of the 18th of last month, requesting certain information relative to the Territory of Kansas, I transmit a report of the Secretary of State and the documents by which it was accompanied.

JAMES BUCHANAN.

WASHINGTON, *January 6, 1858.*

To the Senate of the United States:

I nominate Alexander W. Reynolds, late of the Quartermaster's Department of the Army, to be assistant quartermaster with the rank of captain, to date from August 5, 1847, and to take place on the Army Register next below Captain S. Van Vliet, agreeably to the recommendation of the Secretary of War.

JAMES BUCHANAN.

WAR DEPARTMENT, *January 6, 1858.*

The PRESIDENT OF THE UNITED STATES.

SIR: Under date of October 9, 1855, Captain A. W. Reynolds, assistant quartermaster, was dismissed from the public service in virtue of the third section of the act approved January 31, 1823.

Shortly afterwards suit was brought in the United States district court for the eastern district of Pennsylvania for the purpose of recovering the amounts alleged to be due the United States from Captain Reynolds, and which were stated at $126,307.20. At the suggestion of the United States district attorney, and with the consent of the Secretary of the Treasury, the matter was referred for a full and careful reexamination to three gentlemen, of whom one is understood to have been an experienced clerk of the Treasury Department of the United States. The verdict of the referees, fully concurred in by the United States district attorney, subsequently confirmed by a jury, and according to which judgment was rendered by the court, is that the United States are, on the contrary, indebted to Captain Reynolds in the sum of $430.63.

In addition to this high judicial award in Captain Reynolds's favor, numerous petitions have been received—from the district attorney, from the referees who examined the case, from his brother officers of the Army—all testifying to their assured belief in his perfect integrity, no less than in his high character as a gentleman and a soldier, and earnestly requesting of the President of the United States that he would be pleased to reinstate him in the position which he formerly held in the Quartermaster's Department of the Army.

Among the last description of petitions are many of the highest officers, in rank as well as reputation, who served with Captain Reynolds in New Mexico, the theater of his difficulties, and they respectfully urge their conviction that were the President "cognizant," as many of them declare themselves to be, of the circumstances "under which Captain Reynolds was made responsible for public property over which ne had no control," that he could feel no hesitation about restoring him to the service.

In view of all which facts I have the honor to submit his case for your consideration, and respectfully recommend that he be nominated for restoration to his original rank and place in the Army.

I am, sir, with great respect, your obedient servant,

JOHN B. FLOYD,
Secretary of War.

WASHINGTON, *January 7, 1858.*

To the House of Representatives:

I transmit a report from the Secretary of State, in answer to the resolution of the House of Representatives of the 4th instant, requesting to be informed if any complaint had been made against our Government by the Government of Nicaragua on account of the recent arrest of William Walker and his followers by Captain Paulding within the territory of that Republic.
JAMES BUCHANAN.

WASHINGTON CITY, *January 7, 1858.*

To the Senate of the United States:

I herewith transmit to the Senate a report from the Secretary of the Navy, with the accompanying documents, containing the information called for by the resolution of the Senate of the 4th instant, requesting me "to communicate to the Senate the correspondence, instructions, and orders to the United States naval forces on the coast of Central America connected with the arrest of William Walker and his associates," etc.

In submitting to the Senate the papers for which they have called I deem it proper to make a few observations.

In capturing General Walker and his command after they had landed on the soil of Nicaragua Commodore Paulding has, in my opinion, committed a grave error. It is quite evident, however, from the communications herewith transmitted that this was done from pure and patriotic motives and in the sincere conviction that he was promoting the interest and vindicating the honor of his country. In regard to Nicaragua, she has sustained no injury by the act of Commodore Paulding. This has inured to her benefit and relieved her from a dreaded invasion. She alone would have any right to complain of the violation of her territory, and it is quite certain she will never exercise this right. It unquestionably does not lie in the mouth of her invaders to complain in her name that she has been rescued by Commodore Paulding from their assaults. The error of this gallant officer consists in exceeding his instructions and landing his sailors and marines in Nicaragua, whether with or without her consent, for the purpose of making war upon any military force whatever which he might find in the country, no matter from whence they came. This power certainly did not belong to him. Obedience to law and conformity to instructions are the best and safest guides for all officers, civil and military, and when they transcend these limits and act upon their own personal responsibility evil consequences almost inevitably follow.

Under these circumstances, when Marshal Rynders presented himself at the State Department on the 29th ultimo with General Walker in custody, the Secretary informed him "that the executive department of the Government did not recognize General Walker as a prisoner, that it had no directions to give concerning him, and that it is only through the action of the judiciary that he could be lawfully held in custody to answer any charges that might be brought against him."

In thus far disapproving the conduct of Commodore Paulding no inference must be drawn that I am less determined than I have ever been to execute the neutrality laws of the United States. This is my imperative duty, and I shall continue to perform it by all the means which the Constitution and the laws have placed in my power. My opinion of the value and importance of these laws corresponds entirely with that expressed by Mr. Monroe in his message to Congress of December 7, 1819. That wise, prudent, and patriotic statesman says:

It is of the highest importance to our national character and indispensable to the morality of our citizens that all violations of our neutrality should be prevented. No door should be left open for the evasion of our laws, no opportunity afforded to any who may be disposed to take advantage of it to compromit the interest or the honor of the nation.

The crime of setting on foot or providing the means for a military expedition within the United States to make war against a foreign state with which we are at peace is one of an aggravated and dangerous character, and early engaged the attention of Congress. Whether the executive government possesses any, or what, power under the Constitution, independently of Congress, to prevent or punish this and similar offenses against the law of nations was a subject which engaged the attention of our most eminent statesmen in the time of the Administration of General Washington and on the occasion of the French Revolution. The act of Congress of the 5th of June, 1794, fortunately removed all the difficulties on this question which had theretofore existed. The fifth and seventh sections of this act, which relate to the present question, are the same in substance with the sixth and eighth sections of the act of April 20, 1818, and have now been in force for a period more than sixty years.

The military expedition rendered criminal by the act must have its origin, must "begin" or be "set on foot," in the United States; but the great object of the law was to save foreign states with whom we were at peace from the ravages of these lawless expeditions proceeding from our shores. The seventh section alone, therefore, which simply defines the crime and its punishment, would have been inadequate to accomplish this purpose and enforce our international duties. In order to render the law effectual it was necessary to prevent "the carrying on" of such expeditions to their consummation after they had succeeded in leaving our shores.   This has been done effectually and in clear and explicit language by the authority given to the President under the eighth section of the act to employ the land and naval forces of the United States "for the purpose of preventing the carrying on of any such expedition or enterprise from the territories or jurisdiction of the United States against the territories or dominions of any foreign prince or state or of any colony, district, or people with whom the United States are at peace."

For these reasons, had Commodore Paulding intercepted the steamer *Fashion*, with General Walker and his command on board, at any period before they entered the port of San Juan de Nicaragua and conducted them back to Mobile, this would have prevented them from "carrying on" the expedition and have been not only a justifiable but a praiseworthy act.

The crime well deserves the punishment inflicted upon it by our laws. It violates the principles of Christianity, morality, and humanity, held sacred by all civilized nations and by none more than by the people of the United States.   Disguise it as we may, such a military expedition is an invitation to reckless and lawless men to enlist under the banner of any adventurer to rob, plunder, and murder the unoffending citizens of neighboring states, who have never done them harm.   It is a usurpation of the war-making power, which belongs alone to Congress; and the Government itself, at least in the estimation of the world, becomes an accomplice in the commission of this crime unless it adopts all the means necessary to prevent and to punish it.

It would be far better and more in accordance with the bold and manly character of our countrymen for the Government itself to get up such expeditions than to allow them to proceed under the command of irresponsible adventurers.   We could then at least exercise some control over our own agents and prevent them from burning down cities and committing other acts of enormity of which we have read.

The avowed principle which lies at the foundation of the law of nations is contained in the divine command that "all things whatsoever ye would that men should do to you do ye even so to them."   Tried by this unerring rule, we should be severely condemned if we shall not use our best exertions to arrest such expeditions against our feeble sister Republic of Nicaragua.   One thing is very certain, that a people never existed who would call any other nation to a stricter account than we should ourselves for tolerating lawless expeditions from their shores to make war upon any portion of our territories.   By tolerating such expeditions we shall soon lose the high character which we have enjoyed ever since the days of Washington for the faithful performance of our international obligations and duties, and inspire distrust against us among the members of the great family of civilized nations.

But if motives of duty were not sufficient to restrain us from engaging in such lawless enterprises, our evident interest ought to dictate this policy. These expeditions are the most effectual mode of retarding American progress, although to promote this is the avowed object of the leaders and contributors in such undertakings.

It is beyond question the destiny of our race to spread themselves over the continent of North America, and this at no distant day should events be permitted to take their natural course. The tide of emigrants will flow to the south, and nothing can eventually arrest its progress. If permitted to go there peacefully, Central America will soon contain an American population which will confer blessings and benefits as well upon the natives as their respective Governments. Liberty under the restraint of law will preserve domestic peace, whilst the different transit routes across the Isthmus, in which we are so deeply interested, will have assured protection.

Nothing has retarded this happy condition of affairs so much as the unlawful expeditions which have been fitted out in the United States to make war upon the Central American States. Had one-half the number of American citizens who have miserably perished in the first disastrous expedition of General Walker settled in Nicaragua as peaceful emigrants, the object which we all desire would ere this have been in a great degree accomplished. These expeditions have caused the people of the Central American States to regard us with dread and suspicion. It is our true policy to remove this apprehension and to convince them that we intend to do them good, and not evil. We desire, as the leading power on this continent, to open and, if need be, to protect every transit route across the Isthmus, not only for our own benefit, but that of the world, and thus open a free access to Central America, and through it to our Pacific possessions. This policy was commenced under favorable auspices when the expedition under the command of General Walker escaped from our territories and proceeded to Punta Arenas. Should another expedition of a similar character again evade the vigilance of our officers and proceed to Nicaragua, this would be fatal, at least for a season, to the peaceful settlement of these countries and to the policy of American progress. The truth is that no Administration can successfully conduct the foreign affairs of the country in Central America or anywhere else if it is to be interfered with at every step by lawless military expeditions "set on foot" in the United States.

JAMES BUCHANAN.

WASHINGTON, *January 11, 1858.*

To the Senate and House of Representatives of the United States:

I have received from Samuel Medary, governor of the Territory of Minnesota, a copy of the constitution of Minnesota, "together with an abstract of the votes polled for and against said constitution" at the election held in that Territory on the second Tuesday of October last, certified by the governor in due form, which I now lay before Congress in the manner prescribed by that instrument.

Having received but a single copy of the constitution, I transmit this to the Senate.   JAMES BUCHANAN.

WASHINGTON, *January 11, 1858.*

To the House of Representatives:

I herewith transmit to the House of Representatives the reports of the Secretaries of State, of the Treasury, of the Navy, and of the Attorney-General, with the accompanying documents, containing the information called for by the resolution of the House of the 4th instant, concerning "the late seizure of General William Walker and his followers in Nicaragua," etc.   JAMES BUCHANAN.

To the Senate of the United States:

I transmit to the Senate, for its consideration with a view to ratification, a convention between the United States and the Republic of Peru, signed on the 4th July last at Lima by the plenipotentiaries of the contracting parties, with regard to the interpretation to be given to article 12 of the treaty of the 26th July, 1851.

JANUARY 12, 1858.   JAMES BUCHANAN.

WASHINGTON, *January 14, 1858.*

To the Senate and House of Representatives:

I transmit to Congress a copy of a convention between the United States and His Majesty the King of Denmark, for the discontinuance of the Sound dues, the ratifications of which were exchanged in this city on the 12th instant, and recommend that an appropriation be made to enable the Executive seasonably to carry into effect the stipulations in regard to the sums payable to His Danish Majesty's Government.

JAMES BUCHANAN.

WASHINGTON, *January 27, 1858.*

To the Senate of the United States:

In answer to the resolution of the Senate of the 7th instant, requesting information on the subject of contracts made in Europe for inland-passage tickets for intending emigrants to the United States, I transmit a report from the Secretary of State and the documents by which it was accompanied.   JAMES BUCHANAN.

WASHINGTON, *January 28, 1858.*

To the House of Representatives:

I herewith transmit to the House of Representatives a report from the Secretary of the Interior, under date of the 27th instant, with the accompanying papers, in compliance with a resolution adopted by the House on the 18th instant, requesting the President to communicate to that body "whether the census of the Territory of Minnesota has been taken in accordance with the provisions of the fourth section of the act of Congress providing for the admission of Minnesota as a State, approved February 26, 1857, and if said census has been taken and returned to him or any Department of the Government to communicate the same to this House, and if the said census has not been so taken and returned to state the reasons, if any exist to his knowledge, why it has not been done."

JAMES BUCHANAN.

WASHINGTON, *February 2, 1858.*

To the Senate and House of Representatives of the United States:

I have received from J. Calhoun, esq., president of the late constitutional convention of Kansas, a copy, duly certified by himself, of the constitution framed by that body, with the expression of a hope that I would submit the same to the consideration of Congress "with the view of the admission of Kansas into the Union as an independent State." In compliance with this request, I herewith transmit to Congress, for their action, the constitution of Kansas, with the ordinance respecting the public lands, as well as the letter of Mr. Calhoun, dated at Lecompton on the 14th ultimo, by which they were accompanied. Having received but a single copy of the constitution and ordinance, I send this to the Senate.

A great delusion seems to pervade the public mind in relation to the condition of parties in Kansas. This arises from the difficulty of inducing the American people to realize the fact that any portion of them should be in a state of rebellion against the government under which they live. When we speak of the affairs of Kansas, we are apt to refer merely to the existence of two violent political parties in that Territory, divided on the question of slavery, just as we speak of such parties in the States. This presents no adequate idea of the true state of the case. The dividing line there is not between two political parties, both acknowledging the lawful existence of the government, but between those who are loyal to this government and those who have endeavored to destroy its existence by force and by usurpation—between those who sustain and those who have done all in their power to overthrow the Territorial government established by Congress. This government they would long since have subverted had it not been protected from their assaults by the troops of the United States. Such has been the condition of affairs since my inauguration. Ever since that period a large portion of the people of Kansas have been in a state of rebellion against the government, with a military leader at their head of a most turbulent and dangerous character. They have never acknowledged, but have constantly renounced and defied, the government to which they owe allegiance, and have been all the time in a state of resistance against its authority. They have all the time been endeavoring to subvert it and to establish a revolutionary government, under the so-called Topeka constitution, in its stead. Even at this very moment the Topeka legislature are in session. Whoever has read the correspondence of Governor Walker with the State Department, recently communicated to the Senate, will be convinced that this picture is not overdrawn. He always protested against the withdrawal of any portion of the military force of the United States from the Territory, deeming its presence absolutely necessary for the preservation of the regular government and the execution of the laws. In his very first dispatch to the Secretary of State, dated June 2, 1857, he says:

The most alarming movement, however, proceeds from the assembling on the 9th June of the so-called Topeka legislature, with a view to the enactment of an entire code of laws. Of course it will be my endeavor to prevent such a result, as it would lead to inevitable and disastrous collision, and, in fact, renew the civil war in Kansas.

This was with difficulty prevented by the efforts of Governor Walker; but soon thereafter, on the 14th of July, we find him requesting General Harney to furnish him a regiment of dragoons to proceed to the city of Lawrence; and this for the reason that he had received authentic intelligence, verified by his own actual observation, that a dangerous rebellion had occurred, "involving an open defiance of the laws and the establishment of an insurgent government in that city."

In the governor's dispatch of July 15 he informs the Secretary of State that—

This movement at Lawrence was the beginning of a plan, originating in that city, to organize insurrection throughout the Territory, and especially in all towns, cities, or counties where the Republican party have a majority. Lawrence is the hotbed of all the abolition movements in this Territory. It is the town established by the abolition societies of the East, and whilst there are respectable people there, it is filled by a considerable number of mercenaries who are paid by abolition societies to perpetuate and diffuse agitation throughout Kansas and prevent a peaceful settlement of this question. Having failed in inducing their own so-called Topeka State legislature to organize this insurrection, Lawrence has commenced it herself, and if not arrested the rebellion will extend throughout the Territory.

And again:

In order to send this communication immediately by mail, I must close by assuring you that the spirit of rebellion pervades the great mass of the Republican party of this Territory, instigated, as I entertain no doubt they are, by Eastern societies, having in view results most disastrous to the government and to the Union; and that the continued presence of General Harney here is indispensable, as originally stipulated by me, with a large body of dragoons and several batteries.

On the 20th July, 1857, General Lane, under the authority of the Topeka convention, undertook, as Governor Walker informs us—

to organize the whole so-called Free-State party into volunteers and to take the names of all who refuse enrollment. The professed object is to protect the polls, at the election in August, of the new insurgent Topeka State legislature.

* * * * * * *

The object of taking the names of all who refuse enrollment is to terrify the Free-State conservatives into submission. This is proved by recent atrocities committed on such men by Topekaites. The speedy location of large bodies of regular troops here, with two batteries, is necessary. The Lawrence insurgents await the development of this new revolutionary military organization. * * *

In the governor's dispatch of July 27 he says that "General Lane and his staff everywhere deny the authority of the Territorial laws and counsel a total disregard of these enactments."

Without making further quotations of a similar character from other dispatches of Governor Walker, it appears by a reference to Mr. Stanton's communication to General Cass of the 9th of December last that the "important step of calling the legislature together was taken after I [he] had become satisfied that the election ordered by the convention on the 21st instant could not be conducted without collision and bloodshed." So intense was the disloyal feeling among the enemies of the government established by Congress that an election which afforded them an opportunity, if in the majority, of making Kansas a free State, according to their own professed desire, could not be conducted without collision and bloodshed.

The truth is that up till the present moment the enemies of the existing government still adhere to their Topeka revolutionary constitution and government. The very first paragraph of the message of Governor Robinson, dated on the 7th of December, to the Topeka legislature now assembled at Lawrence contains an open defiance of the Constitution and laws of the United States. The governor says:

The convention which framed the constitution at Topeka originated with the people of Kansas Territory. They have adopted and ratified the same twice by a direct vote, and also indirectly through two elections of State officers and members of the State legislature. Yet it has pleased the Administration to regard the whole proceeding revolutionary.

This Topeka government, adhered to with such treasonable pertinacity, is a government in direct opposition to the existing government prescribed and recognized by Congress. It is a usurpation of the same character as it would be for a portion of the people of any State of the Union to undertake to establish a separate government within its limits for the purpose of redressing any grievance, real or imaginary, of which they might complain against the legitimate State government. Such a principle, if carried into execution, would destroy all lawful authority and produce universal anarchy.

From this statement of facts the reason becomes palpable why the enemies of the government authorized by Congress have refused to vote for delegates to the Kansas constitutional convention, and also afterwards on the question of slavery, submitted by it to the people. It is because they have ever refused to sanction or recognize any other constitution than that framed at Topeka.

Had the whole Lecompton constitution been submitted to the people the adherents of this organization would doubtless have voted against it, because if successful they would thus have removed an obstacle out of the way of their own revolutionary constitution. They would have done this, not upon a consideration of the merits of the whole or any part of the Lecompton constitution, but simply because they have ever resisted the authority of the government authorized by Congress, from which it emanated.

Such being the unfortunate condition of affairs in the Territory, what was the right as well as the duty of the law-abiding people? Were they silently and patiently to submit to the Topeka usurpation, or adopt the necessary measures to establish a constitution under the authority of the organic law of Congress?

That this law recognized the right of the people of the Territory, without any enabling act from Congress, to form a State constitution is too clear for argument. For Congress "to leave the people of the Territory perfectly free," in framing their constitution, "to form and regulate their domestic institutions in their own way, subject only to the Constitution of the United States," and then to say that they shall not be permitted to proceed and frame a constitution in their own way without an express authority from Congress, appears to be almost a contradiction in terms. It would be much more plausible to contend that Congress had no power to pass such an enabling act than to argue that the people of a Territory might be kept out of the Union for an indefinite period, and until it might please Congress to permit them to exercise the right of self-government. This would be to adopt not "their own way," but the way which Congress might prescribe.

It is impossible that any people could have proceeded with more regularity in the formation of a constitution than the people of Kansas have done. It was necessary, first, to ascertain whether it was the desire of the people to be relieved from their Territorial dependence and establish a State government. For this purpose the Territorial legislature in 1855 passed a law "for taking the sense of the people of this Territory upon the expediency of calling a convention to form a State constitution," at the general election to be held in October, 1856. The "sense of the people" was accordingly taken and they decided in favor of a convention. It is true that at this election the enemies of the Territorial government did not vote, because they were then engaged at Topeka, without the slightest pretext of lawful authority, in framing a constitution of their own for the purpose of subverting the Territorial government.

In pursuance of this decision of the people in favor of a convention, the Territorial legislature, on the 27th day of February, 1857, passed an act for the election of delegates on the third Monday of June, 1857, to frame a State constitution. This law is as fair in its provisions as any that ever passed a legislative body for a similar purpose. The right of suffrage at this election is clearly and justly defined. "Every *bona fide* inhabitant of the Territory of Kansas," on the third Monday of June, the day of the election, who was a citizen of the United States above the age of 21, and had resided therein for three months previous to that date, was entitled to vote. In order to avoid all interference from neighboring States or Territories with the freedom and fairness of the election, provision was made for the registry of the qualified voters, and in pursuance thereof 9,251 voters were registered. Governor Walker did his whole duty in urging all the qualified citizens of Kansas to vote at this election. In his inaugural address, on the 27th May last, he informed them that—

Under our practice the preliminary act of framing a State constitution is uniformly performed through the instrumentality of a convention of delegates chosen by the people themselves. That convention is now about to be elected by you under the call of the Territorial legislature, created and still recognized by the authority of Congress and clothed by it, in the comprehensive language of the organic law, with full power to make such an enactment. The Territorial legislature, then, in assembling this convention, were fully sustained by the act of Congress, and the authority of the convention is distinctly recognized in my instructions from the President of the United States.

The governor also clearly and distinctly warns them what would be the consequences if they should not participate in the election.

The people of Kansas, then [he says], are invited by the highest authority known to the Constitution to participate freely and fairly in the election of delegates to frame a constitution and State government. The law has performed its entire appropriate function when it extends to the people the right of suffrage, but it can not compel the performance of that duty. Throughout our whole Union, however, and wherever free government prevails those who abstain from the exercise of the right of suffrage authorize those who do vote to act for them in that contingency; and the absentees are as much bound under the law and Constitution, where there is no fraud or violence, by the act of the majority of those who do vote as if all had participated in the election. Otherwise, as voting must be voluntary, self-government would be impracticable and monarchy or despotism would remain as the only alternative.

It may also be observed that at this period any hope, if such had existed, that the Topeka constitution would ever be recognized by Congress must have been abandoned. Congress had adjourned on the 3d March previous, having recognized the legal existence of the Territorial legislature in a variety of forms, which I need not enumerate. Indeed, the Delegate elected to the House of Representatives under a Territorial law had been admitted to his seat and had just completed his term of service on the day previous to my inauguration.

This was the propitious moment for settling all difficulties in Kansas.

This was the time for abandoning the revolutionary Topeka organization and for the enemies of the existing government to conform to the laws and to unite with its friends in framing a State constitution; but this they refused to do, and the consequences of their refusal to submit to lawful authority and vote at the election of delegates may yet prove to be of a most deplorable character. Would that the respect for the laws of the land which so eminently distinguished the men of the past generation could be revived. It is a disregard and violation of law which have for years kept the Territory of Kansas in a state of almost open rebellion against its government. It is the same spirit which has produced actual rebellion in Utah. Our only safety consists in obedience and conformity to law. Should a general spirit against its enforcement prevail, this will prove fatal to us as a nation. We acknowledge no master but the law, and should we cut loose from its restraints and everyone do what seemeth good in his own eyes our case will indeed be hopeless.

The enemies of the Territorial government determined still to resist the authority of Congress. They refused to vote for delegates to the convention, not because, from circumstances which I need not detail, there was an omission to register the comparatively few voters who were inhabitants of certain counties of Kansas in the early spring of 1857, but because they had predetermined at all hazards to adhere to their revolutionary organization and defeat the establishment of any other constitution than that which they had framed at Topeka. The election was therefore suffered to pass by default. But of this result the qualified electors who refused to vote can never justly complain.

From this review it is manifest that the Lecompton convention, according to every principle of constitutional law, was legally constituted and was invested with power to frame a constitution.

The sacred principle of popular sovereignty has been invoked in favor of the enemies of law and order in Kansas. But in what manner is popular sovereignty to be exercised in this country if not through the instrumentality of established law? In certain small republics of ancient times the people did assemble in primary meetings, passed laws, and directed public affairs. In our country this is manifestly impossible. Popular sovereignty can be exercised here only through the ballot box; and if the people will refuse to exercise it in this manner, as they have done in Kansas at the election of delegates, it is not for them to complain that their rights have been violated.

The Kansas convention, thus lawfully constituted, proceeded to frame a constitution, and, having completed their work, finally adjourned on the 7th day of November last. They did not think proper to submit the whole of this constitution to a popular vote, but they did submit the question whether Kansas should be a free or a slave State to the people. This was the question which had convulsed the Union and shaken it to its very center. This was the question which had lighted up the flames of civil war in Kansas and had produced dangerous sectional parties throughout the Confederacy. It was of a character so paramount in respect to the condition of Kansas as to rivet the anxious attention of the people of the whole country upon it, and it alone. No person thought of any other question. For my own part, when I instructed Governor Walker in general terms in favor of submitting the constitution to the people, I had no object in view except the all-absorbing question of slavery. In what manner the people of Kansas might regulate their other concerns was not a subject which attracted any attention. In fact, the general provisions of our recent State constitutions, after an experience of eight years, are so similar and so excellent that it would be difficult to go far wrong at the present day in framing a new constitution.

I then believed and still believe that under the organic act the Kansas convention were bound to submit this all-important question of slavery to the people. It was never, however, my opinion that, independently of this act, they would have been bound to submit any portion of the constitution to a popular vote in order to give it validity. Had I entertained such an opinion, this would have been in opposition to many precedents in our history, commencing in the very best age of the Republic. It would have been in opposition to the principle which pervades our institutions, and which is every day carried out into practice, that the people have the right to delegate to representatives chosen by themselves their sovereign power to frame constitutions, enact laws, and perform many other important acts without requiring that these should be subjected to their subsequent approbation. It would be a most inconvenient limitation of their own power, imposed by the people upon themselves, to exclude them from exercising their sovereignty in any lawful manner they think proper. It is true that the people of Kansas might, if they had pleased, have required the convention to submit the constitution to a popular vote; but this they have not done. The only remedy, therefore, in this case is that which exists in all other similar cases. If the delegates who framed the Kansas constitution have in any manner violated the will of their constituents, the people always possess the power to change their constitution or their laws according to their own pleasure.

The question of slavery was submitted to an election of the people of Kansas on the 21st December last, in obedience to the mandate of the constitution. Here again a fair opportunity was presented to the adherents of the Topeka constitution, if they were the majority, to decide this exciting question "in their own way" and thus restore peace to the distracted Territory; but they again refused to exercise their right of popular sovereignty, and again suffered the election to pass by default.

I heartily rejoice that a wiser and better spirit prevailed among a large majority of these people on the first Monday of January, and that they did on that day vote under the Lecompton constitution for a governor and other State officers, a Member of Congress, and for members of the legislature. This election was warmly contested by the parties, and a larger vote was polled than at any previous election in the Territory. We may now reasonably hope that the revolutionary Topeka organization will be speedily and finally abandoned, and this will go far toward the final settlement of the unhappy differences in Kansas. If frauds have been committed at this election, either by one or both parties, the legislature and the people of Kansas, under their constitution, will know how to redress themselves and punish these detestable but too common crimes without any outside interference.

The people of Kansas have, then, "in their own way" and in strict accordance with the organic act, framed a constitution and State government, have submitted the all-important question of slavery to the people, and have elected a governor, a Member to represent them in Congress, members of the State legislature, and other State officers. They now ask admission into the Union under this constitution, which is republican in its form. It is for Congress to decide whether they will admit or reject the State which has thus been created. For my own part, I am decidedly in favor of its admission, and thus terminating the Kansas question. This will carry out the great principle of nonintervention recognized and sanctioned by the organic act, which declares in express language in favor of "nonintervention by Congress with slavery in the States or Territories," leaving "the people thereof perfectly free to form and regulate their domestic institutions in their own way, subject only to the Constitution of the United States." In this manner, by localizing the question of slavery and confining it to the people whom it immediately concerned, every patriot anxiously expected that this question would be banished from the halls of Congress, where it has always exerted a baneful influence throughout the whole country.

It is proper that I should briefly refer to the election held under an act of the Territorial legislature on the first Monday of January last on the Lecompton constitution. This election was held after the Territory had been prepared for admission into the Union as a sovereign State, and when no authority existed in the Territorial legislature which could possibly destroy its existence or change its character. The election, which was peaceably conducted under my instructions, involved a strange inconsistency. A large majority of the persons who voted against the Lecompton constitution were at the very same time and place recognizing its valid existence in the most solemn and authentic manner by voting under its provisions. I have yet received no official information of the result of this election.

As a question of expediency, after the right has been maintained, it may be wise to reflect upon the benefits to Kansas and to the whole country which would result from its immediate admission into the Union, as well as the disasters which may follow its rejection. Domestic peace will be the happy consequence of its admission, and that fine Territory, which has hitherto been torn by dissensions, will rapidly increase in population and wealth and speedily realize the blessings and the comforts which follow in the train of agricultural and mechanical industry. The people will then be sovereign and can regulate their own affairs in their own way. If a majority of them desire to abolish domestic slavery within the State, there is no other possible mode by which this can be effected so speedily as by prompt admission. The will of the majority is supreme and irresistible when expressed in an orderly and lawful manner. They can make and unmake constitutions at pleasure. It would be absurd to say that they can impose fetters upon their own power which they can not afterwards remove. If they could do this, they might tie their own hands for a hundred as well as for ten years. These are fundamental principles of American freedom, and are recognized, I believe, in some form or other by every State constitution; and if Congress, in the act of admission, should think proper to recognize them I can perceive no objection to such a course. This has been done emphatically in the constitution of Kansas. It declares in the bill of rights that "all political power is inherent in the people and all free governments are founded on their authority and instituted for their benefit, and therefore they have at all times an inalienable and indefeasible right to alter, reform, or abolish their form of government in such manner as they may think proper." The great State of New York is at this moment governed under a constitution framed and established in direct opposition to the mode prescribed by the previous constitution. If, therefore, the provision changing the Kansas constitution after the year 1864 could by possibility be construed into a prohibition to make such a change previous to that period, this prohibition would be wholly unavailing. The legislature already elected may at its very first session submit the question to a vote of the people whether they will or will not have a convention to amend their constitution and adopt all necessary means for giving effect to the popular will.

It has been solemnly adjudged by the highest judicial tribunal known to our laws that slavery exists in Kansas by virtue of the Constitution of the United States. Kansas is therefore at this moment as much a slave State as Georgia or South Carolina. Without this the equality of the sovereign States composing the Union would be violated and the use and enjoyment of a territory acquired by the common treasure of all the States would be closed against the people and the property of nearly half the members of the Confederacy. Slavery can therefore never be prohibited in Kansas except by means of a constitutional provision, and in no other manner can this be obtained so promptly, if a majority of the people desire it, as by admitting it into the Union under its present constitution.

On the other hand, should Congress reject the constitution under the idea of affording the disaffected in Kansas a third opportunity of prohibiting slavery in the State, which they might have done twice before if in the majority, no man can foretell the consequences.

If Congress, for the sake of those men who refused to vote for delegates to the convention when they might have excluded slavery from the constitution, and who afterwards refused to vote on the 21st December last, when they might, as they claim, have stricken slavery from the constitution, should now reject the State because slavery remains in the constitution, it is manifest that the agitation upon this dangerous subject will be renewed in a more alarming form than it has ever yet assumed.

Every patriot in the country had indulged the hope that the Kansas and Nebraska act would put a final end to the slavery agitation, at least in Congress, which had for more than twenty years convulsed the country and endangered the Union. This act involved great and fundamental principles, and if fairly carried into effect will settle the question. Should the agitation be again revived, should the people of the sister States be again estranged from each other with more than their former bitterness, this will arise from a cause, so far as the interests of Kansas are concerned, more trifling and insignificant than has ever stirred the elements of a great people into commotion. To the people of Kansas the only practical difference between admission or rejection depends simply upon the fact whether they can themselves more speedily change the present constitution if it does not accord with the will of the majority, or frame a second constitution to be submitted to Congress hereafter. Even if this were a question of mere expediency, and not of right, the small difference of time one way or the other is of not the least importance when contrasted with the evils which must necessarily result to the whole country from a revival of the slavery agitation.

In considering this question it should never be forgotten that in proportion to its insignificance, let the decision be what it may so far as it may affect the few thousand inhabitants of Kansas who have from the beginning resisted the constitution and the laws, for this very reason the rejection of the constitution will be so much the more keenly felt by the people of fourteen of the States of this Union, where slavery is recognized under the Constitution of the United States.

Again, the speedy admission of Kansas into the Union would restore peace and quiet to the whole country. Already the affairs of this Territory have engrossed an undue proportion of public attention. They have sadly affected the friendly relations of the people of the States with each other and alarmed the fears of patriots for the safety of the Union. Kansas once admitted into the Union, the excitement becomes localized and will soon die away for want of outside aliment. Then every difficulty will be settled at the ballot box.

Besides—and this is no trifling consideration—I shall then be enabled to withdraw the troops of the United States from Kansas and employ them on branches of service where they are much needed. They have been kept there, on the earnest importunity of Governor Walker, to maintain the existence of the Territorial government and secure the execution of the laws. He considered that at least 2,000 regular troops, under the command of General Harney, were necessary for this purpose. Acting upon his reliable information, I have been obliged in some degree to interfere with the expedition to Utah in order to keep down rebellion in Kansas. This has involved a very heavy expense to the Government. Kansas once admitted, it is believed there will no longer be any occasion there for troops of the United States.

I have thus performed my duty on this important question, under a deep sense of responsibility to God and my country. My public life will terminate within a brief period, and I have no other object of earthly ambition than to leave my country in a peaceful and prosperous condition and to live in the affections and respect of my countrymen. The dark and ominous clouds which now appear to be impending over the Union I conscientiously believe may be dissipated with honor to every portion of it by the admission of Kansas during the present session of Congress, whereas if she should be rejected I greatly fear these clouds will become darker and more ominous than any which have ever yet threatened the Consitution and the Union.

JAMES BUCHANAN.

To the Senate of the United States:

I transmit to the Senate for its consideration with a view to ratification, a convention for the purpose of further regulating the intercourse of American citizens within the Empire of Japan, signed at Simoda on the 17th day of June last by Townsend Harris, consul-general of the United States, and by the governors of Simoda, empowered for that purpose by their respective Governments.

FEBRUARY 10, 1858.

JAMES BUCHANAN.

WASHINGTON, *February 11, 1858.*

To the Senate of the United States:

I transmit to the Senate, for its consideration with a view to ratification, an additional article to the extradition convention between the United States and France of the 9th of November, 1843, and the additional article thereto of the 24th February, 1845, signed in this city yesterday by the Secretary of State and the minister of His Imperial Majesty the Emperor of the French.

JAMES BUCHANAN.

WASHINGTON, *February 12, 1858.*

To the House of Representatives:

I herewith transmit a report from the Secretary of State, with the accompanying documents, in reply to the resolution of the House of

Representatives of the 18th ultimo, requesting to be furnished with official information and correspondence in relation to the execution of Colonel Crabb and his associates within or near the limits of the Republic of Mexico.

JAMES BUCHANAN.

WASHINGTON CITY, *February 26, 1858.*

To the House of Representatives:

I herewith transmit to the House of Representatives the reports of the Secretaries of State, of War, of the Interior, and of the Attorney-General, containing the information called for by a resolution of the House of the 27th ultimo, requesting "the President, if not incompatible with the public interest, to communicate to the House of Representatives the information which gave rise to the military expeditions ordered to Utah Territory, the instructions to the army officers in connection with the same, and all correspondence which has taken place with said army officers, with Brigham Young and his followers, or with others throwing light upon the question as to how far said Brigham Young and his followers are in a state of rebellion or resistance to the Government of the United States."

JAMES BUCHANAN.

WASHINGTON, *March 2, 1858.*

To the Senate of the United States:

I herewith transmit to the Senate a report from the Secretary of the Navy, dated on the 24th instant [ultimo], furnishing the information called for by a resolution of the Senate adopted on the 16th instant [ultimo], requesting me "to inform the Senate in executive session on what evidence the nominees for the Marine Corps are stated to be taken from the States as designated in his message communicating the nominations of January 13."

JAMES BUCHANAN.

WASHINGTON CITY, *March 4, 1858.*

To the House of Representatives:

I herewith transmit to the House of Representatives communications from the Secretary of War and Secretary of the Interior, in answer to the resolution adopted by the House on the 5th ultimo, requesting the President to furnish certain information in relation to the number of troops, whether regulars, volunteers, drafted men, or militia, who were engaged in the service of the United States in the last war with Great Britain, etc.

JAMES BUCHANAN.

WASHINGTON, *March 9, 1858.*

To the Senate and House of Representatives:

I transmit herewith a report of the Attorney-General, with accompanying papers, dated March 1, 1858, detailing proceedings under the act approved March 3, 1855, entitled ''An act to improve the laws of the District of Columbia and to codify the same.''

JAMES BUCHANAN.

WASHINGTON, *March 23, 1858.*

To the House of Representatives:

In compliance with a resolution of the House of Representatives of the 26th of January, requesting the President to communicate to the House ''so much of the correspondence between the late Secretary of War and Major-General John E. Wool, late commander of the Pacific Department, relative to the affairs of such department, as has not heretofore been published under a call of this House,'' I herewith transmit all the correspondence called for so far as is afforded by the files of the War Department.

JAMES BUCHANAN.

WASHINGTON, *April 7, 1858.*

To the Senate of the United States:

I submit to the Senate, for its consideration and constitutional action, a treaty made with the Tonawanda Indians, of New York, on the 5th of November, 1857, with the accompanying papers from the Department of the Interior.

JAMES BUCHANAN.

WASHINGTON, *April 9, 1858.*

To the House of Representatives:

I transmit to the House of Representatives a memorial addressed to myself by a committee appointed by the citizens of that portion of the Territory of Utah which is situated west of the Goose Creek range of mountains, commonly known as '' Carsons Valley,'' in favor of the establishment of a Territorial government over them, and containing the request that I should communicate it to Congress. I have received but one copy of this memorial, which I transmit to the House upon the suggestion of James M. Crane, esq., the Delegate elect of the people of the proposed new Territory, for the reason, as he alleges, that the subject is now under consideration before the Committee on the Territories of that body.

JAMES BUCHANAN.

WASHINGTON, *April 20, 1858.*

To the Senate of the United States:

I transmit a report from the Secretary of State, with accompanying papers,* in answer to the resolution of the Senate of the 5th instant.

JAMES BUCHANAN.

WASHINGTON, *April 21, 1858.*

To the Senate of the United States:

I herewith transmit the reports of the Secretary of State and the Secretary of the Navy, with accompanying papers,† in answer to the resolution of the Senate of the 19th of January last.

JAMES BUCHANAN.

WASHINGTON, *April 28, 1858.*

To the Senate of the United States:

I transmit a report from the Secretary of State, in answer to the resolution of the Senate of the 24th ultimo, requesting information relative to the seizure in the Valley of Sitana, in Peru, by authorities of Chile of a sum of money belonging to citizens of the United States.

JAMES BUCHANAN.

WASHINGTON, *May 1, 1858.*

To the Senate of the United States:

In compliance with the resolution of the Senate of the 24th ultimo, I herewith transmit a report of the Secretary of State, with accompanying documents.‡

JAMES BUCHANAN.

WASHINGTON, *May, 1858.*

To the Senate of the United States:

I transmit herewith, for the constitutional action of the Senate, a treaty negotiated with the Ponca tribe of Indians on the 12th of March, 1858, with the accompanying documents from the Department of the Interior.

JAMES BUCHANAN.

WASHINGTON, *May 3, 1858.*

To the House of Representatives:

In compliance with the resolutions of the House of Representatives of the 19th January, 1857, and 3d February, 1858, I herewith transmit the report of the Secretary of the Interior, with accompanying documents.§

JAMES BUCHANAN.

---

*Instructions to William B. Reed, United States commissioner to China.

†Relating to the African slave trade and to movements of the French Government to establish a colony in the possessions of that Government from the coast of Africa.

‡Relating to outrages committed against the family of Walter Dickson, an American citizen residing at Jaffa, Palestine.

§ Relating to Indian affairs in Oregon and Washington Territories and to the official conduct of Anson Dart, superintendent of Indian affairs in Oregon Territory.

WASHINGTON, *May 6, 1858.*

To the House of Representatives:

In compliance with the resolution of the House of Representatives of the 3d of February, 1858, I transmit herewith a report from the Secretary of War, with all papers and correspondence* so far as the same is afforded by the files of the Department.

JAMES BUCHANAN.

WASHINGTON CITY, *May 13, 1858.*

Hon. JAMES L. ORR,
   Speaker of the House of Representatives.

SIR: I herewith transmit, to be laid before the House of Representatives, the letter of the Secretary of the Interior, dated the 12th instant, covering the report, maps, etc., of the geological survey of Oregon and Washington Territories, which has been made by John Evans, esq., United States geologist, under appropriations made by Congress for that purpose.

   Respectfully,   JAMES BUCHANAN.

WASHINGTON, *May 13, 1858.*

To the Senate of the United States:

I transmit herewith, for the constitutional action of the Senate, a treaty negotiated on the 19th of April, 1858, with the Yancton tribe of Sioux or Dacotah Indians, with accompanying papers from the Department of the Interior.

JAMES BUCHANAN.

WASHINGTON, *May, 1858.*

To the Senate of the United States:

I transmit to the Senate a report, dated 13th instant, with the accompanying papers, received from the Secretary of State in answer to the resolution of the Senate of the 5th instant, requesting information in regard to measures which may have been adopted for the protection of American commerce in the ports of Mexico.

JAMES BUCHANAN.

WASHINGTON CITY, *May 18, 1858.*

Hon. J. C. BRECKINRIDGE,
   Vice-President of the United States.

SIR: In reply to the resolutions of the Senate of the United States of the 20th February and 14th March, 1857, I herewith transmit, to be laid before that body, copies of all correspondence, vouchers, and other papers having reference to the accounts of Edward F. Beale, esq., late superintendent of Indian affairs in California, which are of file or record in the Departments of the Treasury and Interior.

JAMES BUCHANAN.

---

*Relating to Indian affairs in Oregon and Washington Territories and to the official conduct of Anson Dart, superintendent of Indian affairs in Oregon Territory.

WASHINGTON, *May 19, 1858.*

To the Senate of the United States:

In answer to the resolution of the Senate of the 14th instant, requesting information concerning the recent search or seizure of American vessels by foreign armed cruisers in the Gulf of Mexico, I transmit reports from the Secretaries of State and of the Navy.

JAMES BUCHANAN.

WASHINGTON, *May 27, 1858.*

To the Senate of the United States:

I transmit herewith, in compliance with the resolution of the Senate of the 19th of May, a communication from the Secretary of the Navy with copies of the correspondence, etc.,* as afforded by the files of the Department.

JAMES BUCHANAN.

WASHINGTON, *May 29, 1858.*

To the Senate of the United States:

I transmit a report from the Secretary of State, with accompanying papers, in answer to the resolution of the Senate of the 22d instant, requesting information in regard to the seizure of the American vessel *Panchita* on the coast of Africa.

JAMES BUCHANAN.

WASHINGTON, *May 31, 1858.*

To the House of Representatives:

In answer to the resolution of the House of Representatives of the 17th instant, requesting information relative to attacks upon United States vessels in the Gulf of Mexico and on the coast of Cuba, I transmit a report from the Secretary of State, with the papers by which it was accompanied.

JAMES BUCHANAN.

WASHINGTON, *June 1, 1858.*

To the Senate of the United States:

I transmit herewith a report from the Secretaries of State and Navy, with the accompanying papers, in compliance with the resolution of the Senate of the 11th of March, 1858, requesting the President "to communicate to the Senate any information in possession of any of the Executive Departments in relation to alleged discoveries of guano in the year 1855 and the measures taken to ascertain the correctness of the same, and also any report made to the Navy Department in relation to the discovery of guano in Jarvis and Bakers islands, with the charts, soundings, and sailing directions for those islands.

JAMES BUCHANAN.

*Relating to the arrest of William Walker and associates within the territory of Nicaragua by the naval forces under Commodore Paulding.

WASHINGTON, *June 4, 1858.*

To the Senate of the United States:

I transmit herewith a report from the Secretary of State, together with the documents by which it is accompanied, as embracing all the information which it is practicable or expedient to communicate in reply to the resolution of the Senate of the 31st ultimo, on the subject of guano.

JAMES BUCHANAN.

WASHINGTON, *June 10, 1858.*

To the Senate and House of Representatives:

I transmit a copy of a dispatch from Governor Cumming to the Secretary of State, dated at Great Salt Lake City on the 2d of May and received at the Department of State on yesterday. From this there is reason to believe that our difficulties with the Territory of Utah have terminated and the reign of the Constitution and the laws has been restored. I congratulate you on this auspicious event.

I lose no time in communicating this information and in expressing the opinion that there will now be no occasion to make any appropriation for the purpose of calling into service the two regiments of volunteers authorized by the act of Congress approved on the 7th of April last for the purpose of quelling disturbances in the Territory of Utah, for the protection of supply and emigrant trains, and the suppression of Indian hostilities on the frontier.

I am the more gratified at this satisfactory intelligence from Utah because it will afford some relief to the Treasury at a time demanding from us the strictest economy, and when the question which now arises upon every new appropriation is whether it be of a character so important and urgent as to brook no delay and to justify and require a loan and most probably a tax upon the people to raise the money necessary for its payment.

In regard to the regiment of volunteers authorized by the same act of Congress to be called into service for the defense of the frontiers of Texas against Indian hostilities, I desire to leave this question to Congress, observing at the same time that in my opinion the State can be defended for the present by the regular troops which have not yet been withdrawn from its limits.

JAMES BUCHANAN.

WASHINGTON, *June 11, 1858.*

To the Senate of the United States:

In answer to the resolution of the Senate of the 19th ultimo, respecting the Isthmus of Tehuantepec, I transmit herewith a report from the Secretary of State, with the documents by which it is accompanied, together with the copy of a letter from the Postmaster-General of the 21st ultimo to the Department of State.

JAMES BUCHANAN.

WASHINGTON CITY, *June 11, 1858.*

To the House of Representatives:

I transmit herewith a report from the Secretary of War, with the accompanying papers,* in obedience to the resolution of the House of Representatives of the 2d of June, 1858.

JAMES BUCHANAN.

WASHINGTON CITY, *June 12, 1858.*

To the Senate and House of Representatives:

I feel it to be an indispensable duty to call your attention to the condition of the Treasury. On the 19th day of May last the Secretary of the Treasury submitted a report to Congress "on the present condition of the finances of the Government." In this report he states that after a call upon the heads of Departments he had received official information that the sum of $37,000,000 would probably be required during the first two quarters of the next fiscal year, from the 1st of July until the 1st of January. "This sum," the Secretary says, "does not include such amounts as may be appropriated by Congress over and above the estimates submitted to them by the Departments, and I have no data on which to estimate for such expenditures. Upon this point Congress is better able to form a correct opinion than I am."

The Secretary then estimates that the receipts into the Treasury from all sources between the 1st of July and the 1st of January would amount to $25,000,000, leaving a deficit of $15,000,000, inclusive of the sum of about $3,000,000, the least amount required to be in the Treasury at all times to secure its successful operation. For this amount he recommends a loan. This loan, it will be observed, was required, after a close calculation, to meet the estimates from the different Departments, and not such appropriations as might be made by Congress over and above these estimates.

There was embraced in this sum of $15,000,000 estimates to the amount of about $1,750,000 for the three volunteer regiments authorized by the act of Congress approved April 7, 1858, for two of which, if not for the third, no appropriation will now be required. To this extent a portion of the loan of $15,000,000 may be applied to pay the appropriations made by Congress beyond the estimates from the different Departments, referred to in the report of the Secretary of the Treasury.

To what extent a probable deficiency may exist in the Treasury between the 1st July and the 1st January next can not be ascertained until the appropriation bills, as well as the private bills containing appropriations, shall have finally passed.

Adversity teaches useful lessons to nations as well as individuals. The habit of extravagant expenditures, fostered by a large surplus in

---

* Copies of contracts for deepening the channels of the Southwest Pass and Pass à l'Outre, at the mouth of the Mississippi River, etc.

the Treasury, must now be corrected or the country will be involved in serious financial difficulties.

Under any form of government extravagance in expenditure must be the natural consequence when those who authorize the expenditure feel no responsibility in providing the means of payment. Such had been for a number of years our condition previously to the late monetary revulsion in the country. Fortunately, at least for the cause of public economy, the case is now reversed, and to the extent of the appropriations, whatever these may be, ingrafted on the different appropriation bills, as well as those made by private bills, over and above the estimates of the different Departments, it will be necessary for Congress to provide the means of payment before their adjournment. Without this the Treasury will be exhausted before the 1st of January and the public credit will be seriously impaired. This disgrace must not fall upon the country.

It is impossible for me, however, now to ascertain this amount, nor does there at present seem to be the least probability that this can be done and the necessary means provided by Congress to meet any deficiency which may exist in the Treasury before Monday next at 12 o'clock, the hour fixed for adjournment, it being now Saturday morning at half-past 11 o'clock. To accomplish this object the appropriation bills, as they shall have finally passed Congress, must be before me, and time must be allowed to ascertain the amount of the moneys appropriated and to enable Congress to provide the necessary means. At this writing it is understood that several of these bills are yet before the committee of conference and the amendments to some of them have not even been printed.

Foreseeing that such a state of things might exist at the close of the session, I stated in the annual message to Congress of December last that—

From the practice of Congress such an examination of each bill as the Constitution requires has been rendered impossible. The most important business of each session is generally crowded into its last hours, and the alternative presented to the President is either to violate the constitutional duty which he owes to the people and approve bills which for want of time it is impossible he should have examined, or by his refusal to do this subject the country and individuals to great loss and inconvenience.

*   *   *   *   *   *   *

For my own part, I have deliberately determined that I shall approve no bills which I have not examined, and it will be a case of extreme and most urgent necessity which shall ever induce me to depart from this rule.

The present condition of the Treasury absolutely requires that I should adhere to this resolution on the present occasion, for the reasons which I have heretofore presented.

In former times it was believed to be the true character of an appropriation bill simply to carry into effect existing laws and the established policy of the country. A practice has, however, grown up of late years to ingraft on such bills at the last hours of the session large appropriations for new and important objects not provided for by preexisting laws and when no time is left to the Executive for their examination and investigation. No alternative is thus left to the President but either to approve measures without examination or by vetoing an appropriation bill seriously to embarrass the operations of the Government. This practice could never have prevailed without a surplus in the Treasury sufficiently large to cover an indefinite amount of appropriations. Necessity now compels us to arrest it, at least so far as to afford time to ascertain the amount appropriated and to provide the means of its payment.

For all these reasons I recommend to Congress to postpone the day of adjournment for a brief period. I promise that not an hour shall be lost in ascertaining the amount of appropriations made by them for which it will be necessary to provide. I know it will be inconvenient for the members to attend a called session, and this above all things I desire to avoid.

JAMES BUCHANAN.

PROCLAMATIONS.

[From Statutes at Large (Little, Brown & Co.), Vol. XI, p. 794.]

By the President of the United States of America.

A PROCLAMATION.

Whereas by an act of Congress approved March 3, 1855, entitled "An act to improve the laws of the District of Columbia and to codify the same," the President of the United States was directed to appoint a time and place for taking the sense of the citizens of the District of Columbia for or against the adoption of the code prepared in pursuance of said act, and, further, to provide and proclaim the mode and rules of conducting such election:

Now, therefore, be it known that I do hereby appoint Monday, the 15th day of February, 1858, as the day for taking the sense of the citizens of the District of Columbia as aforesaid.

The polls will be opened at 9 o'clock a. m. and closed at 5 o'clock p. m. Every free white male citizen of the United States above the age of 21 years who shall have resided in the District of Columbia for one year next preceding the said 15th day of February, 1858, shall be allowed to vote at said election.

The voting shall be by ballot. Those in favor of the adoption of the revised code will vote a ballot with the words "for the revised code" written or printed upon the same, and those opposed to the adoption of the said code will vote a ballot with the words "against the revised code" written or printed upon the same.

The places where the said election shall be held and the judges who shall conduct and preside over the same will be as follows:

For the First Ward, in the city of Washington, at Samuel Drury's office, on Pennsylvania avenue. Judges: Southey S. Parker, Terence Drury, and Alexander H. Mechlin.

For the Second Ward, on Twelfth street, one door above Pennsylvania avenue. Judges: Charles L. Coltman, Charles J. Canfield, and Edward C. Dyer.

For the Third Ward, near the corner of Ninth street, between F and G, west of the Patent Office. Judges: Valentine Harbaugh, Joseph Bryan, and Harvey Cruttenden.

For the Fourth Ward, at the west end of City Hall. Judges: William A. Kennedy, John T. Clements, and Francis Mohun.

For the Fifth Ward, at the Columbia engine house. Judges: Henry C. Purdy, Thomas Hutchinson, and James A. Brown.

For the Sixth Ward, at the Anacostia engine house. Judges: John D. Brandt, George A. Bohrer, and George R. Ruff.

For the Seventh Ward, at Island Hall. Judges: Samuel Pumphrey, James Espey, and John L. Smith.

For Georgetown, at the mayor's office. Judges: Edward Chapman, John L. Kidwell, and William H. Edes.

For that portion of the county of Washington which lies west of Rock Creek, at Conrad's Tavern, in Tenallytown. Judges: Joshua Peirce, Charles R. Belt, and William D. C. Murdock.

For that portion of said county which lies between Rock Creek and the Eastern Branch of the Potomac, at Seventh street tollgate. Judges: Thomas Blagden, Dr. Henry Haw, and Abner Shoemaker.

And for that portion of said county which lies east of the Eastern Branch of the Potomac, at Goodhope Tavern. Judges: Selby B. Scaggs, Fenwick Young, and Dr. Wellford Manning.

The judges presiding at the respective places of holding the elections shall be sworn to perform their duties faithfully; and immediately after the close of the polls they shall count up the votes and certify what number were given "for the revised code" and what number "against the revised code," which certificates shall be transmitted within twenty-four hours to the Attorney-General of the United States, who will report the same to me.

Given under my hand this 24th day of December, A. D. 1857, and of Independence the eighty-second.

[SEAL.]   JAMES BUCHANAN.

BY THE PRESIDENT OF THE UNITED STATES OF AMERICA.

A PROCLAMATION.

Whereas by an act of Congress of the United States of the 24th of May, 1828, entitled "An act in addition to an act entitled 'An act concerning discriminating duties of tonnage and impost,' and to equalize the duties on Prussian vessels and their cargoes," it is provided that upon satisfactory evidence being given to the President of the United States by the government of any foreign nation that no discriminating duties of tonnage or impost are imposed or levied in the ports of the said nation upon vessels wholly belonging to citizens of the United States, or upon the produce, manufactures, or merchandise imported in the same from the United States or from any foreign country, the President is thereby authorized to issue his proclamation declaring that the foreign discriminating duties of tonnage and impost within the United States are and shall be suspended and discontinued so far as respects the vessels of the said foreign nation and the produce, manufactures, or merchandise imported into the United States in the same from the said foreign nation or from any other foreign country, the said suspension to take effect from the time of such notification being given to the President of the United States and to continue so long as the reciprocal exemption of vessels belonging to citizens of the United States and their cargoes, as aforesaid, shall be continued, and no longer; and

Whereas satisfactory evidence has lately been received from the Government of His Holiness the Pope, through an official communication addressed by Cardinal Antonelli, his secretary of state, to the minister resident of the United States at Rome, under date of the 7th day of December, 1857, that no discriminating duties of tonnage or impost are imposed or levied in the ports of the Pontifical States upon vessels wholly belonging to citizens of the United States, or upon the produce, manufactures, or merchandise imported in the same from the United States or from any foreign country:

Now, therefore, I, James Buchanan, President of the United States of America, do hereby declare and proclaim that the foreign discriminating duties of tonnage and impost within the United States are and shall be suspended and discontinued so far as respects the vessels of the subjects of His Holiness the Pope and the produce, manufactures, or merchandise imported into the United States in the same from the Pontifical States or from any other foreign country, the said suspension to take effect from the 7th day of December, 1857, above mentioned, and to continue so long as the reciprocal exemption of vessels belonging to citizens of the United States and their cargoes, as aforesaid, shall be continued, and no longer.

Given under my hand, at the city of Washington, the 25th day of February, A. D. 1858, and of the Independence of the United States the eighty-second.

[SEAL.]

JAMES BUCHANAN.

By the President:

LEWIS CASS,
   Secretary of State.

By James Buchanan, President of the United States of
America.

A PROCLAMATION.

Whereas the Territory of Utah was settled by certain emigrants from
the States and from foreign countries who have for several years past
manifested a spirit of insubordination to the Constitution and laws of the
United States. The great mass of those settlers, acting under the influence of leaders to whom they seem to have surrendered their judgment,
refuse to be controlled by any other authority. They have been often
advised to obedience, and these friendly counsels have been answered
with defiance. The officers of the Federal Government have been driven
from the Territory for no offense but an effort to do their sworn duty;
others have been prevented from going there by threats of assassination;
judges have been violently interrupted in the performance of their functions, and the records of the courts have been seized and destroyed or
concealed. Many other acts of unlawful violence have been perpetrated, and the right to repeat them has been openly claimed by the
leading inhabitants, with at least the silent acquiescence of nearly all
the others. Their hostility to the lawful government of the country has
at length become so violent that no officer bearing a commission from
the Chief Magistrate of the Union can enter the Territory or remain
there with safety, and all those officers recently appointed have been
unable to go to Salt Lake or anywhere else in Utah beyond the immediate power of the Army. Indeed, such is believed to be the condition to
which a strange system of terrorism has brought the inhabitants of that
region that no one among them could express an opinion favorable to
this Government, or even propose to obey its laws, without exposing his
life and property to peril.

After carefully considering this state of affairs and maturely weighing
the obligation I was under to see the laws faithfully executed, it seemed
to me right and proper that I should make such use of the military force
at my disposal as might be necessary to protect the Federal officers in
going into the Territory of Utah and in performing their duties after
arriving there. I accordingly ordered a detachment of the Army to
march for the city of Salt Lake, or within reach of that place, and to act
in case of need as a posse for the enforcement of the laws. But in the
meantime the hatred of that misguided people for the just and legal
authority of the Government had become so intense that they resolved
to measure their military strength with that of the Union. They have
organized an armed force far from contemptible in point of numbers and
trained it, if not with skill, at least with great assiduity and perseverance.
While the troops of the United States were on their march a train of
baggage wagons, which happened to be unprotected, was attacked and
destroyed by a portion of the Mormon forces and the provisions and

stores with which the train was laden were wantonly burnt. In short, their present attitude is one of decided and unreserved enmity to the United States and to all their loyal citizens. Their determination to oppose the authority of the Government by military force has not only been expressed in words, but manifested in overt acts of the most unequivocal character.

Fellow-citizens of Utah, this is rebellion against the Government to which you owe allegiance; it is levying war against the United States, and involves you in the guilt of treason. Persistence in it will bring you to condign punishment, to ruin, and to shame; for it is mere madness to suppose that with your limited resources you can successfully resist the force of this great and powerful nation.

If you have calculated upon the forbearance of the United States, if you have permitted yourselves to suppose that this Government will fail to put forth its strength and bring you to submission, you have fallen into a grave mistake. You have settled upon territory which lies, geographically, in the heart of the Union. The land you live upon was purchased by the United States and paid for out of their Treasury; the proprietary right and title to it is in them, and not in you. Utah is bounded on every side by States and Territories whose people are true to the Union. It is absurd to believe that they will or can permit you to erect in their very midst a government of your own, not only independent of the authority which they all acknowledge, but hostile to them and their interests.

Do not deceive yourselves nor try to mislead others by propagating the idea that this is a crusade against your religion. The Constitution and laws of this country can take no notice of your creed, whether it be true or false. That is a question between your God and yourselves, in which I disclaim all right to interfere. If you obey the laws, keep the peace, and respect the just rights of others, you will be perfectly secure, and may live on in your present faith or change it for another at your pleasure. Every intelligent man among you knows very well that this Government has never, directly or indirectly, sought to molest you in your worship, to control you in your ecclesiastical affairs, or even to influence you in your religious opinions.

This rebellion is not merely a violation of your legal duty; it is without just cause, without reason, without excuse. You never made a complaint that was not listened to with patience; you never exhibited a real grievance that was not redressed as promptly as it could be. The laws and regulations enacted for your government by Congress have been equal and just, and their enforcement was manifestly necessary for your own welfare and happiness. You have never asked their repeal. They are similar in every material respect to the laws which have been passed for the other Territories of the Union, and which everywhere else (with one partial exception) have been cheerfully obeyed. No people ever lived who were freer from unnecessary legal restraints than you. Human wisdom never devised a political system which bestowed more blessings or imposed lighter burdens than the Government of the United States in its operation upon the Territories.

But being anxious to save the effusion of blood and to avoid the indiscriminate punishment of a whole people for crimes of which it is not probable that all are equally guilty, I offer now a free and full pardon to all who will submit themselves to the just authority of the Federal Government. If you refuse to accept it, let the consequences fall upon your own heads. But I conjure you to pause deliberately and reflect well before you reject this tender of peace and good will.

Now, therefore, I, James Buchanan, President of the United States, have thought proper to issue this my proclamation, enjoining upon all public officers in the Territory of Utah to be diligent and faithful, to the full extent of their power, in the execution of the laws; commanding all citizens of the United States in said Territory to aid and assist the officers in the performance of their duties; offering to the inhabitants of Utah who shall submit to the laws a free pardon for the seditions and treasons heretofore by them committed; warning those who shall persist, after notice of this proclamation, in the present rebellion against the United States that they must expect no further lenity, but look to be rigorously dealt with according to their deserts; and declaring that the military forces now in Utah and hereafter to be sent there will not be withdrawn until the inhabitants of that Territory shall manifest a proper sense of the duty which they owe to this Government.

In testimony whereof I have hereunto set my hand and caused the seal of the United States to be affixed to these presents.

[SEAL.]   Done at the city of Washington the 6th day of April, 1858, and of the Independence of the United States the eighty-second.

JAMES BUCHANAN.

By the President:

LEWIS CASS, *Secretary of State.*

BY THE PRESIDENT OF THE UNITED STATES OF AMERICA.

A PROCLAMATION.

Whereas an extraordinary occasion has occurred rendering it necessary and proper that the Senate of the United States shall be convened to receive and act upon such communications as have been or may be made to it on the part of the Executive:

Now, therefore, I, James Buchanan, President of the United States, do issue this my proclamation, declaring that an extraordinary occasion requires the Senate of the United States to convene for the transaction of business at the Capitol, in the city of Washington, on the 15th day of this month, at 12 o'clock at noon of that day, of which all who shall at that time be entitled to act as members of that body are hereby required to take notice.

Given under my hand and the seal of the United States, at Washington, this 14th day of June, A. D. 1858, and of the Independence of the United States the eighty-second.

[SEAL.]

JAMES BUCHANAN.

By the President:

LEWIS CASS,

Secretary of State.

BY JAMES BUCHANAN, PRESIDENT OF THE UNITED STATES OF AMERICA.

A PROCLAMATION.

Whereas information has reached me from sources which I can not disregard that certain persons, in violation of the neutrality laws of the United States, are making a third attempt to set on foot a military expedition within their territory against Nicaragua, a foreign State with which they are at peace. In order to raise money for equipping and maintaining this expedition, persons connected therewith, as I have reason to believe, have issued and sold bonds and other contracts pledging the public lands of Nicaragua and the transit route through its territory as a security for their redemption and fulfillment.

The hostile design of this expedition is rendered manifest by the fact that these bonds and contracts can be of no possible value to their holders unless the present Government of Nicaragua shall be overthrown by force. Besides, the envoy extraordinary and minister plenipotentiary of that Government in the United States has issued a notice, in pursuance of his instructions, dated on the 27th instant, forbidding the citizens or subjects of any nation, except passengers intending to proceed through Nicaragua over the transit route from ocean to ocean, to enter its territory without a regular passport, signed by the proper minister or consul-general of the Republic resident in the country from whence they shall have departed. Such persons, with this exception, ''will be stopped and compelled to return by the same conveyance that took them to the country.'' From these circumstances the inference is irresistible that persons engaged in this expedition will leave the United States with hostile purposes against Nicaragua. They can not, under the guise which they have assumed that they are peaceful emigrants, conceal their real intentions, and especially when they know in advance that their landing will be resisted and can only be accomplished by an overpowering force. This expedient was successfully resorted to previous to the last expedition, and the vessel in which those composing it were conveyed to Nicaragua obtained a clearance from the collector of the port of Mobile Although, after a careful examination, no arms or munitions of war were discovered on board, yet when they arrived in Nicaragua they were found to be armed and equipped and immediately commenced hostilities.

The leaders of former illegal expeditions of the same character have openly expressed their intention to renew hostilities against Nicaragua. One of them, who has already been twice expelled from Nicaragua, has invited through the public newspapers American citizens to emigrate to that Republic, and has designated Mobile as the place of rendezvous and departure and San Juan del Norte as the port to which they are bound. This person, who has renounced his allegiance to the United States and claims to be President of Nicaragua, has given notice to the collector of the port of Mobile that two or three hundred of these emigrants will be prepared to embark from that port about the middle of November.

For these and other good reasons, and for the purpose of saving American citizens who may have been honestly deluded into the belief that they are about to proceed to Nicaragua as peaceful emigrants, if any such there be, from the disastrous consequences to which they will be exposed, I, James Buchanan, President of the United States, have thought it fit to issue this my proclamation, enjoining upon all officers of the Government, civil and military, in their respective spheres, to be vigilant, active, and faithful in suppressing these illegal enterprises and in carrying out their standing instructions to that effect; exhorting all good citizens, by their respect for the laws and their regard for the peace and welfare of the country, to aid the efforts of the public authorities in the discharge of their duties.

In testimony whereof I have hereunto set my hand and caused the seal of the United States to be affixed to these presents.

[SEAL.] Done at the city of Washington the 30th day of October, 1858, and of the Independence of the United States the eighty-third.

JAMES BUCHANAN.

By the President:

LEWIS CASS, *Secretary of State.*

SECOND ANNUAL MESSAGE.

WASHINGTON CITY, *December 6, 1858.*

Fellow-Citizens of the Senate and House of Representatives:

When we compare the condition of the country at the present day with what it was one year ago at the meeting of Congress, we have much reason for gratitude to that Almighty Providence which has never failed to interpose for our relief at the most critical periods of our history. One year ago the sectional strife between the North and the

South on the dangerous subject of slavery had again become so intense as to threaten the peace and perpetuity of the Confederacy. The application for the admission of Kansas as a State into the Union fostered this unhappy agitation and brought the whole subject once more before Congress. It was the desire of every patriot that such measures of legislation might be adopted as would remove the excitement from the States and confine it to the Territory where it legitimately belonged. Much has been done, I am happy to say, toward the accomplishment of this object during the last session of Congress.

The Supreme Court of the United States had previously decided that all American citizens have an equal right to take into the Territories whatever is held as property under the laws of any of the States, and to hold such property there under the guardianship of the Federal Constitution so long as the Territorial condition shall remain.

This is now a well-established position, and the proceedings of the last session were alone wanting to give it practical effect. The principle has been recognized in some form or other by an almost unanimous vote of both Houses of Congress that a Territory has a right to come into the Union either as a free or a slave State, according to the will of a majority of its people. The just equality of all the States has thus been vindicated and a fruitful source of dangerous dissension among them has been removed.

Whilst such has been the beneficial tendency of your legislative proceedings outside of Kansas, their influence has nowhere been so happy as within that Territory itself. Left to manage and control its own affairs in its own way, without the pressure of external influence, the revolutionary Topeka organization and all resistance to the Territorial government established by Congress have been finally abandoned. As a natural consequence that fine Territory now appears to be tranquil and prosperous and is attracting increasing thousands of immigrants to make it their happy home.

The past unfortunate experience of Kansas has enforced the lesson, so often already taught, that resistance to lawful authority under our form of government can not fail in the end to prove disastrous to its authors. Had the people of the Territory yielded obedience to the laws enacted by their legislature, it would at the present moment have contained a large additional population of industrious and enterprising citizens, who have been deterred from entering its borders by the existence of civil strife and organized rebellion.

It was the resistance to rightful authority and the persevering attempts to establish a revolutionary government under the Topeka constitution which caused the people of Kansas to commit the grave error of refusing to vote for delegates to the convention to frame a constitution under a law not denied to be fair and just in its provisions. This refusal to vote has been the prolific source of all the evils which have followed. In their hostility to the Territorial government they disregarded the principle, absolutely essential to the working of our form of government, that a majority of those who vote, not the majority who may remain at home, from whatever cause, must decide the result of an election. For this reason, seeking to take advantage of their own error, they denied the authority of the convention thus elected to frame a constitution.

The convention, notwithstanding, proceeded to adopt a constitution unexceptionable in its general features, and providing for the submission of the slavery question to a vote of the people, which, in my opinion, they were bound to do under the Kansas and Nebraska act. This was the all-important question which had alone convulsed the Territory; and yet the opponents of the lawful government, persisting in their first error, refrained from exercising their right to vote, and preferred that slavery should continue rather than surrender their revolutionary Topeka organization.

A wiser and better spirit seemed to prevail before the first Monday of January last, when an election was held under the constitution. A majority of the people then voted for a governor and other State officers, for a Member of Congress and members of the State legislature. This election was warmly contested by the two political parties in Kansas, and a greater vote was polled than at any previous election. A large majority of the members of the legislature elect belonged to that party which had previously refused to vote. The antislavery party were thus placed in the ascendant, and the political power of the State was in their own hands. Had Congress admitted Kansas into the Union under the Lecompton constitution, the legislature might at its very first session have submitted the question to a vote of the people whether they would or would not have a convention to amend their constitution, either on the slavery or any other question, and have adopted all necessary means for giving speedy effect to the will of the majority. Thus the Kansas question would have been immediately and finally settled.

Under these circumstances I submitted to Congress the constitution thus framed, with all the officers already elected necessary to put the State government into operation, accompanied by a strong recommendation in favor of the admission of Kansas as a State. In the course of my long public life I have never performed any official act which in the retrospect has afforded me more heartfelt satisfaction. Its admission could have inflicted no possible injury on any human being, whilst it would within a brief period have restored peace to Kansas and harmony to the Union. In that event the slavery question would ere this have been finally settled according to the legally expressed will of a majority of the voters, and popular sovereignty would thus have been vindicated in a constitutional manner.

With my deep convictions of duty I could have pursued no other course. It is true that as an individual I had expressed an opinion, both before and during the session of the convention, in favor of submitting the remaining clauses of the constitution, as well as that concerning slavery, to the people. But, acting in an official character, neither myself nor any human authority had the power to rejudge the proceedings of the convention and declare the constitution which it had framed to be a nullity. To have done this would have been a violation of the Kansas and Nebraska act, which left the people of the Territory "perfectly free to form and regulate their domestic institutions in their own way, subject only to the Constitution of the United States." It would equally have violated the great principle of popular sovereignty, at the foundation of our institutions, to deprive the people of the power, if they thought proper to exercise it, of confiding to delegates elected by themselves the trust of framing a constitution without requiring them to subject their constituents to the trouble, expense, and delay of a second election. It would have been in opposition to many precedents in our history, commencing in the very best age of the Republic, of the admission of Territories as States into the Union without a previous vote of the people approving their constitution.

It is to be lamented that a question so insignificant when viewed in its practical effects on the people of Kansas, whether decided one way or the other, should have kindled such a flame of excitement throughout the country. This reflection may prove to be a lesson of wisdom and of warning for our future guidance. Practically considered, the question is simply whether the people of that Territory should first come into the Union and then change any provision in their constitution not agreeable to themselves, or accomplish the very same object by remaining out of the Union and framing another constitution in accordance with their will. In either case the result would be precisely the same. The only difference, in point of fact, is that the object would have been much sooner attained and the pacification of Kansas more speedily effected had it been admitted as a State during the last session of Congress.

My recommendation, however, for the immediate admission of Kansas failed to meet the approbation of Congress. They deemed it wiser to adopt a different measure for the settlement of the question. For my own part, I should have been willing to yield my assent to almost any constitutional measure to accomplish this object. I therefore cordially acquiesced in what has been called the English compromise and approved the "act for the admission of the State of Kansas into the Union" upon the terms therein prescribed.

Under the ordinance which accompanied the Lecompton constitution the people of Kansas had claimed double the quantity of public lands for the support of common schools which had ever been previously granted to any State upon entering the Union, and also the alternate sections of land for 12 miles on each side of two railroads proposed to be constructed from the northern to the southern boundary and from the eastern to the western boundary of the State. Congress, deeming these claims unreasonable, provided by the act of May 4, 1858, to which I have just referred, for the admission of the State on an equal footing with the original States, but "upon the fundamental condition precedent" that a majority of the people thereof, at an election to be held for that purpose, should, in place of the very large grants of public lands which they had demanded under the ordinance, accept such grants as had been made to Minnesota and other new States. Under this act, should a majority reject the proposition offered them, "it shall be deemed and held that the people of Kansas do not desire admission into the Union with said constitution under the conditions set forth in said proposition." In that event the act authorizes the people of the Territory to elect delegates to form a constitution and State government for themselves "whenever, and not before, it is ascertained by a census, duly and legally taken, that the population of said Territory equals or exceeds the ratio of representation required for a member of the House of Representatives of the Congress of the United States." The delegates thus assembled "shall first determine by a vote whether it is the wish of the people of the proposed State to be admitted into the Union at that time, and, if so, shall proceed to form a constitution and take all necessary steps for the establishment of a State government in conformity with the Federal Constitution." After this constitution shall have been formed, Congress, carrying out the principles of popular sovereignty and nonintervention, have left "the mode and manner of its approval or ratification by the people of the proposed State" to be "prescribed by law," and they "shall then be admitted into the Union as a State under such constitution, thus fairly and legally made, with or without slavery, as said constitution may prescribe."

An election was held throughout Kansas, in pursuance of the provisions of this act, on the 2d day of August last, and it resulted in the rejection by a large majority of the proposition submitted to the people by Congress. This being the case, they are now authorized to form another constitution, preparatory to admission into the Union, but not until their number, as ascertained by a census, shall equal or exceed the ratio required to elect a member to the House of Representatives.

It is not probable, in the present state of the case, that a third constitution can be lawfully framed and presented to Congress by Kansas before its population shall have reached the designated number. Nor is it to be presumed that after their sad experience in resisting the Territorial laws they will attempt to adopt a constitution in express violation of the provisions of an act of Congress. During the session of 1856 much of the time of Congress was occupied on the question of admitting Kansas under the Topeka constitution. Again, nearly the whole of the last session was devoted to the question of its admission under the Lecompton constitution. Surely it is not unreasonable to require the people of Kansas to wait before making a third attempt until the number of their inhabitants shall amount to 93,420. During this brief period the harmony of the States as well as the great business interests of the country demand that the people of the Union shall not for a third time be convulsed by another agitation on the Kansas question. By waiting for a short time and acting in obedience to law Kansas will glide into the Union without the slightest impediment.

This excellent provision, which Congress have applied to Kansas. ought to be extended and rendered applicable to all Territories which may hereafter seek admission into the Union.

Whilst Congress possess the undoubted power of admitting a new State into the Union, however small may be the number of its inhabitants, yet this power ought not, in my opinion, to be exercised before the population shall amount to the ratio required by the act for the admission of Kansas. Had this been previously the rule, the country would have escaped all the evils and misfortunes to which it has been exposed by the Kansas question.

Of course it would be unjust to give this rule a retrospective application, and exclude a State which, acting upon the past practice of the Government, has already formed its constitution, elected its legislature and other officers, and is now prepared to enter the Union.

The rule ought to be adopted, whether we consider its bearing on the people of the Territories or upon the people of the existing States. Many of the serious dissensions which have prevailed in Congress and throughout the country would have been avoided had this rule been established at an earlier period of the Government.

Immediately upon the formation of a new Territory people from different States and from foreign countries rush into it for the laudable purpose of improving their condition. Their first duty to themselves is to open and cultivate farms, to construct roads, to establish schools, to erect places of religious worship, and to devote their energies generally to reclaim the wilderness and to lay the foundations of a flourishing and prosperous commonwealth. If in this incipient condition, with a population of a few thousand, they should prematurely enter the Union, they are oppressed by the burden of State taxation, and the means necessary for the improvement of the Territory and the advancement of their own interests are thus diverted to very different purposes.

The Federal Government has ever been a liberal parent to the Territories and a generous contributor to the useful enterprises of the early settlers. It has paid the expenses of their governments and legislative assemblies out of the common Treasury, and thus relieved them from a heavy charge. Under these circumstances nothing can be better calculated to retard their material progress than to divert them from their useful employments by prematurely exciting angry political contests among themselves for the benefit of aspiring leaders. It is surely no hardship for embryo governors, Senators, and Members of Congress to wait until the number of inhabitants shall equal those of a single Congressional district. They surely ought not to be permitted to rush into the Union with a population less than one-half of several of the large counties in the interior of some of the States. This was the condition of Kansas when it made application to be admitted under the Topeka constitution. Besides, it requires some time to render the mass of a population collected in a new Territory at all homogeneous and to unite them on anything like a fixed policy. Establish the rule, and all will look forward to it and govern themselves accordingly.

But justice to the people of the several States requires that this rule should be established by Congress. Each State is entitled to two Senators and at least one Representative in Congress. Should the people of the States fail to elect a Vice-President, the power devolves upon the Senate to select this officer from the two highest candidates on the list. In case of the death of the President, the Vice-President thus elected by the Senate becomes President of the United States. On all questions of legislation the Senators from the smallest States of the Union have an equal vote with those from the largest. The same may be said in regard to the ratification of treaties and of Executive appointments. All this has worked admirably in practice, whilst it conforms in principle with the character of a Government instituted by sovereign States. I presume no American citizen would desire the slightest change in the arrangement. Still, is it not unjust and unequal to the existing States to invest some 40,000 or 50,000 people collected in a Territory with the attributes of sovereignty and place them on an equal footing with Virginia and New York in the Senate of the United States?

For these reasons I earnestly recommend the passage of a general act which shall provide that, upon the application of a Territorial legislature declaring their belief that the Territory contains a number of inhabitants which, if in a State, would entitle them to elect a Member of Congress, it shall be the duty of the President to cause a census of the inhabitants to be taken, and if found sufficient then by the terms of this act to authorize them to proceed "in their own way" to frame a State constitution preparatory to admission into the Union. I also recommend that an appropriation may be made to enable the President to take a census of the people of Kansas.

The present condition of the Territory of Utah, when contrasted with what it was one year ago, is a subject for congratulation. It was then in a state of open rebellion, and, cost what it might, the character of the Government required that this rebellion should be suppressed and the Mormons compelled to yield obedience to the Constitution and the laws. In order to accomplish this object, as I informed you in my last annual message, I appointed a new governor instead of Brigham Young, and other Federal officers to take the place of those who, consulting their personal safety, had found it necessary to withdraw from the Territory.

.To protect these civil officers, and to aid them, as a *posse comitatus*, in the execution of the laws in case of need, I ordered a detachment of the Army to accompany them to Utah. The necessity for adopting these measures is now demonstrated.

On the 15th of September, 1857, Governor Young issued his proclamation, in the style of an independent sovereign, announcing his purpose to resist by force of arms the entry of the United States troops into our own Territory of Utah. By this he required all the forces in the Territory to "hold themselves in readiness to march at a moment's notice to repel any and all such invasion," and established martial law from its date throughout the Territory. These proved to be no idle threats. Forts Bridger and Supply were vacated and burnt down by the Mormons to deprive our troops of a shelter after their long and fatiguing march. Orders were issued by Daniel H. Wells, styling himself "Lieutenant-General, Nauvoo Legion," to stampede the animals of the United States troops on their march, to set fire to their trains, to burn the grass and the whole country before them and on their flanks, to keep them from sleeping by night surprises, and to blockade the road by felling trees and destroying the fords of rivers, etc.

These orders were promptly and effectually obeyed. On the 4th of October, 1857, the Mormons captured and burned, on Green River, three of our supply trains, consisting of seventy-five wagons loaded with provisions and tents for the army, and carried away several hundred animals. This diminished the supply of provisions so materially that General Johnston was obliged to reduce the ration, and even with this precaution there was only sufficient left to subsist the troops until the 1st of June.

Our little army behaved admirably in their encampment at Fort Bridger under these trying privations. In the midst of the mountains, in a dreary, unsettled, and inhospitable region, more than a thousand miles from home, they passed the severe and inclement winter without a murmur. They looked forward with confidence for relief from their country in due season, and in this they were not disappointed.

The Secretary of War employed all his energies to forward them the necessary supplies and to muster and send such a military force to Utah as would render resistance on the part of the Mormons hopeless, and thus terminate the war without the effusion of blood. In his efforts he was efficiently sustained by Congress. They granted appropriations sufficient to cover the deficiency thus necessarily created, and also provided for raising two regiments of volunteers "for the purpose of quelling disturbances in the Territory of Utah, for the protection of supply and emigrant trains, and the suppression of Indian hostilities on the frontiers." Happily, there was no occasion to call these regiments into service. If there had been, I should have felt serious embarrassment in selecting them, so great was the number of our brave and patriotic citizens anxious to serve their country in this distant and apparently dangerous expedition. Thus it has ever been, and thus may it ever be.

The wisdom and economy of sending sufficient reenforcements to Utah are established, not only by the event, but in the opinion of those who from their position and opportunities are the most capable of forming a correct judgment. General Johnston, the commander of the forces, in addressing the Secretary of War from Fort Bridger under date of October 18, 1857, expresses the opinion that "unless a large force is sent here, from the nature of the country a protracted war on their [the Mormons's] part is inevitable." This he considered necessary to terminate the war "speedily and more economically than if attempted by insufficient means."

In the meantime it was my anxious desire that the Mormons should yield obedience to the Constitution and the laws without rendering it necessary to resort to military force. To aid in accomplishing this object, I deemed it advisable in April last to dispatch two distinguished citizens of the United States, Messrs. Powell and McCulloch, to Utah. They bore with them a proclamation addressed by myself to the inhabitants of Utah, dated on the 6th day of that month, warning them of their true condition and how hopeless it was on their part to persist in rebellion against the United States, and offering all those who should submit to the laws a full pardon for their past seditions and treasons. At the same time I assured those who should persist in rebellion against the United States that they must expect no further lenity, but look to be rigorously dealt with according to their deserts. The instructions to these agents, as well as a copy of the proclamation and their reports, are herewith submitted. It will be seen by their report of the 3d of July last that they have fully confirmed the opinion expressed by General Johnston in the previous October as to the necessity of sending reenforcements to Utah. In this they state that they "are firmly impressed with the belief that the presence of the Army here and the large additional force that had been ordered to this Territory were the chief inducements that caused the Mormons to abandon the idea of resisting the authority of the United States. A less decisive policy would probably have resulted in a long, bloody, and expensive war."

These gentlemen conducted themselves to my entire satisfaction and rendered useful services in executing the humane intentions of the Government.

It also affords me great satisfaction to state that Governor Cumming has performed his duty in an able and conciliatory manner and with the happiest effect. I can not in this connection refrain from mentioning the valuable services of Colonel Thomas L. Kane, who, from motives of pure benevolence and without any official character or pecuniary compensation, visited Utah during the last inclement winter for the purpose of contributing to the pacification of the Territory.

I am happy to inform you that the governor and other civil officers of

Utah are now performing their appropriate functions without resistance. The authority of the Constitution and the laws has been fully restored and peace prevails throughout the Territory.

A portion of the troops sent to Utah are now encamped in Cedar Valley, 44 miles southwest of Salt Lake City, and the remainder have been ordered to Oregon to suppress Indian hostilities.

The march of the army to Salt Lake City through the Indian Territory has had a powerful effect in restraining the hostile feelings against the United States which existed among the Indians in that region and in securing emigrants to the far West against their depredations. This will also be the means of establishing military posts and promoting settlements along the route.

I recommend that the benefits of our land laws and preemption system be extended to the people of Utah by the establishment of a land office in that Territory.

I have occasion also to congratulate you on the result of our negotiations with China.

You were informed by my last annual message that our minister had been instructed to occupy a neutral position in the hostilities conducted by Great Britain and France against Canton. He was, however, at the same time directed to cooperate cordially with the British and French ministers in all peaceful measures to secure by treaty those just concessions to foreign commerce which the nations of the world had a right to demand. It was impossible for me to proceed further than this on my own authority without usurping the war-making power, which under the Constitution belongs exclusively to Congress.

Besides, after a careful examination of the nature and extent of our grievances, I did not believe they were of such a pressing and aggravated character as would have justified Congress in declaring war against the Chinese Empire without first making another earnest attempt to adjust them by peaceful negotiation. I was the more inclined to this opinion because of the severe chastisement which had then but recently been inflicted upon the Chinese by our squadron in the capture and destruction of the Barrier forts to avenge an alleged insult to our flag.

The event has proved the wisdom of our neutrality. Our minister has executed his instructions with eminent skill and ability. In conjunction with the Russian plenipotentiary, he has peacefully, but effectually, cooperated with the English and French plenipotentiaries, and each of the four powers has concluded a separate treaty with China of a highly satisfactory character. The treaty concluded by our own plenipotentiary will immediately be submitted to the Senate.

I am happy to announce that through the energetic yet conciliatory efforts of our consul-general in Japan a new treaty has been concluded with that Empire, which may be expected materially to augment our trade and intercourse in that quarter and remove from our countrymen the disabilities which have heretofore been imposed upon the exercise of their religion. The treaty shall be submitted to the Senate for approval without delay.

It is my earnest desire that every misunderstanding with the Government of Great Britain should be amicably and speedily adjusted. It has been the misfortune of both countries, almost ever since the period of the Revolution, to have been annoyed by a succession of irritating and dangerous questions, threatening their friendly relations. This has partially prevented the full development of those feelings of mutual friendship between the people of the two countries so natural in themselves and so conducive to their common interest. Any serious interruption of the commerce between the United States and Great Britain would be equally injurious to both. In fact, no two nations have ever existed on the face of the earth which could do each other so much good or so much harm.

Entertaining these sentiments, I am gratified to inform you that the long-pending controversy between the two Governments in relation to the question of visitation and search has been amicably adjusted. The claim on the part of Great Britain forcibly to visit American vessels on the high seas in time of peace could not be sustained under the law of nations, and it had been overruled by her own most eminent jurists. This question was recently brought to an issue by the repeated acts of British cruisers in boarding and searching our merchant vessels in the Gulf of Mexico and the adjacent seas. These acts were the more injurious and annoying, as these waters are traversed by a large portion of the commerce and navigation of the United States and their free and unrestricted use is essential to the security of the coastwise trade between the different States of the Union. Such vexatious interruptions could not fail to excite the feelings of the country and to require the interposition of the Government. Remonstrances were addressed to the British Government against these violations of our rights of sovereignty, and a naval force was at the same time ordered to the Cuban waters with directions "to protect all vessels of the United States on the high seas from search or detention by the vessels of war of any other nation." These measures received the unqualified and even enthusiastic approbation of the American people. Most fortunately, however, no collision took place, and the British Government promptly avowed its recognition of the principles of international law upon this subject as laid down by the Government of the United States in the note of the Secretary of State to the British minister at Washington of April 10, 1858, which secure the vessels of the United States upon the high seas from visitation or search in time of peace under any circumstances whatever. The claim has been abandoned in a manner reflecting honor on the British Government and evincing a just regard for the law of nations, and can not fail to strengthen the amicable relations between the two countries.

The British Government at the same time proposed to the United States that some mode should be adopted, by mutual arrangement between the two countries, of a character which may be found effective without being offensive, for verifying the nationality of vessels suspected on good grounds of carrying false colors.   They have also invited the United States to take the initiative and propose measures for this purpose. Whilst declining to assume so grave a responsibility, the Secretary of State has informed the British Government that we are ready to receive any proposals which they may feel disposed to offer having this object in view, and to consider them in an amicable spirit.   A strong opinion is, however, expressed that the occasional abuse of the flag of any nation is an evil far less to be deprecated than would be the establishment of any regulations which might be incompatible with the freedom of the seas. This Government has yet received no communication specifying the manner in which the British Government would propose to carry out their suggestion, and I am inclined to believe that no plan which can be devised will be free from grave embarrassments.   Still, I shall form no decided opinion on the subject until I shall have carefully and in the best spirit examined any proposals which they may think proper to make.

I am truly sorry I can not also inform you that the complications between Great Britain and the United States arising out of the Clayton and Bulwer treaty of April, 1850, have been finally adjusted.

At the commencement of your last session I had reason to hope that, emancipating themselves from further unavailing discussions, the two Governments would proceed to settle the Central American questions in a practical manner, alike honorable and satisfactory to both; and this hope I have not yet abandoned.   In my last annual message I stated that overtures had been made by the British Government for this purpose in a friendly spirit, which I cordially reciprocated.   Their proposal was to withdraw these questions from direct negotiation between the two Governments, but to accomplish the same object by a negotiation between the British Government and each of the Central American Republics whose territorial interests are immediately involved.   The settlement was to be made in accordance with the general tenor of the interpretation placed upon the Clayton and Bulwer treaty by the United States, with certain modifications.   As negotiations are still pending upon this basis, it would not be proper for me now to communicate their present condition.   A final settlement of these questions is greatly to be desired, as this would wipe out the last remaining subject of dispute between the two countries.

Our relations with the great Empires of France and Russia, as well as with all other Governments on the continent of Europe, except that of Spain, continue to be of the most friendly character.

With Spain our relations remain in an unsatisfactory condition.   In my message of December last I informed you that our envoy extraordinary and minister plenipotentiary to Madrid had asked for his recall, and it was my purpose to send out a new minister to that Court with special instructions on all questions pending between the two Governments, and with a determination to have them speedily and amicably adjusted if that were possible. This purpose has been hitherto defeated by causes which I need not enumerate.

The mission to Spain has been intrusted to a distinguished citizen of Kentucky, who will proceed to Madrid without delay and make another and a final attempt to obtain justice from that Government.

Spanish officials under the direct control of the Captain-General of Cuba have insulted our national flag and in repeated instances have from time to time inflicted injuries on the persons and property of our citizens. These have given birth to numerous claims against the Spanish Government, the merits of which have been ably discussed for a series of years by our successive diplomatic representatives. Notwithstanding this, we have not arrived at a practical result in any single instance, unless we may except the case of the *Black Warrior*, under the late Administration, and that presented an outrage of such a character as would have justified an immediate resort to war. All our attempts to obtain redress have been baffled and defeated. The frequent and oft-recurring changes in the Spanish ministry have been employed as reasons for delay. We have been compelled to wait again and again until the new minister shall have had time to investigate the justice of our demands.

Even what have been denominated "the Cuban claims," in which more than 100 of our citizens are directly interested, have furnished no exception. These claims were for the refunding of duties unjustly exacted from American vessels at different custom-houses in Cuba so long ago as the year 1844. The principles upon which they rest are so manifestly equitable and just that, after a period of nearly ten years, in 1854 they were recognized by the Spanish Government. Proceedings were afterwards instituted to ascertain their amount, and this was finally fixed, according to their own statement (with which we were satisfied), at the sum of $128,635.54. Just at the moment, after a delay of fourteen years, when we had reason to expect that this sum would be repaid with interest, we have received a proposal offering to refund one-third of that amount ($42,878.41), but without interest, if we would accept this in full satisfaction. The offer is also accompanied by a declaration that this indemnification is not founded on any reason of strict justice, but is made as a special favor.

One alleged cause for procrastination in the examination and adjustment of our claims arises from an obstacle which it is the duty of the Spanish Government to remove. Whilst the Captain-General of Cuba is invested with general despotic authority in the government of that island, the power is withheld from him to examine and redress wrongs committed by officials under his control on citizens of the United States.

Instead of making our complaints directly to him at Havana, we are obliged to present them through our minister at Madrid. These are then referred back to the Captain-General for information, and much time is thus consumed in preliminary investigations and correspondence between Madrid and Cuba before the Spanish Government will consent to proceed to negotiation. Many of the difficulties between the two Governments would be obviated and a long train of negotiation avoided if the Captain-General were invested with authority to settle questions of easy solution on the spot, where all the facts are fresh and could be promptly and satisfactorily ascertained. We have hitherto in vain urged upon the Spanish Government to confer this power upon the Captain-General, and our minister to Spain will again be instructed to urge this subject on their notice. In this respect we occupy a different position from the powers of Europe. Cuba is almost within sight of our shores; our commerce with it is far greater than that of any other nation, including Spain itself, and our citizens are in habits of daily and extended personal intercourse with every part of the island. It is therefore a great grievance that when any difficulty occurs, no matter how unimportant, which might be readily settled at the moment, we should be obliged to resort to Madrid, especially when the very first step to be taken there is to refer it back to Cuba.

The truth is that Cuba, in its existing colonial condition, is a constant source of injury and annoyance to the American people. It is the only spot in the civilized world where the African slave trade is tolerated, and we are bound by treaty with Great Britain to maintain a naval force on the coast of Africa, at much expense both of life and treasure, solely for the purpose of arresting slavers bound to that island. The late serious difficulties between the United States and Great Britain respecting the right of search, now so happily terminated, could never have arisen if Cuba had not afforded a market for slaves. As long as this market shall remain open there can be no hope for the civilization of benighted Africa. Whilst the demand for slaves continues in Cuba wars will be waged among the petty and barbarous chiefs in Africa for the purpose of seizing subjects to supply this trade. In such a condition of affairs it is impossible that the light of civilization and religion can ever penetrate these dark abodes.

It has been made known to the world by my predecessors that the United States have on several occasions endeavored to acquire Cuba from Spain by honorable negotiation. If this were accomplished, the last relic of the African slave trade would instantly disappear. We would not, if we could, acquire Cuba in any other manner. This is due to our national character. All the territory which we have acquired since the origin of the Government has been by fair purchase from France, Spain, and Mexico or by the free and voluntary act of the independent State of Texas in blending her destinies with our own. This course we shall ever pursue, unless circumstances should occur which we do not now anticipate, rendering a departure from it clearly justifiable under the imperative and overruling law of self-preservation.

The island of Cuba, from its geographical position, commands the mouth of the Mississippi and the immense and annually increasing trade, foreign and coastwise, from the valley of that noble river, now embracing half the sovereign States of the Union. With that island under the dominion of a distant foreign power this trade, of vital importance to these States, is exposed to the danger of being destroyed in time of war, and it has hitherto been subjected to perpetual injury and annoyance in time of peace. Our relations with Spain, which ought to be of the most friendly character, must always be placed in jeopardy whilst the existing colonial government over the island shall remain in its present condition.

Whilst the possession of the island would be of vast importance to the United States, its value to Spain is comparatively unimportant. Such was the relative situation of the parties when the great Napoleon transferred Louisiana to the United States. Jealous as he ever was of the national honor and interests of France, no person throughout the world has imputed blame to him for accepting a pecuniary equivalent for this cession.

The publicity which has been given to our former negotiations upon this subject and the large appropriation which may be required to effect the purpose render it expedient before making another attempt to renew the negotiation that I should lay the whole subject before Congress. This is especially necessary, as it may become indispensable to success that I should be intrusted with the means of making an advance to the Spanish Government immediately after the signing of the treaty, without awaiting the ratification of it by the Senate. I am encouraged to make this suggestion by the example of Mr. Jefferson previous to the purchase of Louisiana from France and by that of Mr. Polk in view of the acquisition of territory from Mexico. I refer the whole subject to Congress and commend it to their careful consideration.

I repeat the recommendation made in my message of December last in favor of an appropriation "to be paid to the Spanish Government for the purpose of distribution among the claimants in the *Amistad* case." President Polk first made a similar recommendation in December, 1847, and it was repeated by my immediate predecessor in December, 1853. I entertain no doubt that indemnity is fairly due to these claimants under our treaty with Spain of October 27, 1795; and whilst demanding justice we ought to do justice. An appropriation promptly made for this purpose could not fail to exert a favorable influence on our negotiations with Spain.

Our position in relation to the independent States south of us on this continent, and especially those within the limits of North America, is of a peculiar character. The northern boundary of Mexico is coincident with our own southern boundary from ocean to ocean, and we must necessarily feel a deep interest in all that concerns the well-being and the fate of so near a neighbor.   We have always cherished the kindest wishes for the success of that Republic, and have indulged the hope that it might at last, after all its trials, enjoy peace and prosperity under a free and stable government.   We have never hitherto interfered, directly or indirectly, with its internal affairs, and it is a duty which we owe to ourselves to protect the integrity of its territory against the hostile interference of any other power.   Our geographical position, our direct interest in all that concerns Mexico, and our well-settled policy in regard to the North American continent render this an indispensable duty.

Mexico has been in a state of constant revolution almost ever since it achieved its independence.   One military leader after another has usurped the Government in rapid succession, and the various constitutions from time to time adopted have been set at naught almost as soon as they were proclaimed.   The successive Governments have afforded no adequate protection, either to Mexican citizens or foreign residents, against lawless violence.   Heretofore a seizure of the capital by a military chieftain has been generally followed by at least the nominal submission of the country to his rule for a brief period, but not so at the present crisis of Mexican affairs.   A civil war has been raging for some time throughout the Republic between the central Government at the City of Mexico, which has endeavored to subvert the constitution last framed by military power, and those who maintain the authority of that constitution.   The antagonist parties each hold possession of different States of the Republic, and the fortunes of the war are constantly changing.   Meanwhile the most reprehensible means have been employed by both parties to extort money from foreigners, as well as natives, to carry on this ruinous contest.   The truth is that this fine country, blessed with a productive soil and a benign climate, has been reduced by civil dissension to a condition of almost hopeless anarchy and imbecility.   It would be vain for this Government to attempt to enforce payment in money of the claims of American citizens, now amounting to more than $10,000,000, against Mexico, because she is destitute of all pecuniary means to satisfy these demands.

Our late minister was furnished with ample powers and instructions for the adjustment of all pending questions with the central Government of Mexico, and he performed his duty with zeal and ability.   The claims of our citizens, some of them arising out of the violation of an express provision of the treaty of Guadalupe Hidalgo, and others from gross injuries to persons as well as property, have remained unredressed and even unnoticed.   Remonstrances against these grievances have been addressed without effect to that Government.   Meantime in various parts of the Republic instances have been numerous of the murder, imprisonment, and plunder of our citizens by different parties claiming and exercising a local jurisdiction; but the central Government, although repeatedly urged thereto, have made no effort either to punish the authors of these outrages or to prevent their recurrence. No American citizen can now visit Mexico on lawful business without imminent danger to his person and property. There is no adequate protection to either, and in this respect our treaty with that Republic is almost a dead letter.

This state of affairs was brought to a crisis in May last by the promulgation of a decree levying a contribution *pro rata* upon all the capital in the Republic between certain specified amounts, whether held by Mexicans or foreigners. Mr. Forsyth, regarding this decree in the light of a "forced loan," formally protested against its application to his countrymen and advised them not to pay the contribution, but to suffer it to be forcibly exacted. Acting upon this advice, an American citizen refused to pay the contribution, and his property was seized by armed men to satisfy the amount. Not content with this, the Government proceeded still further and issued a decree banishing him from the country. Our minister immediately notified them that if this decree should be carried into execution he would feel it to be his duty to adopt "the most decided measures that belong to the powers and obligations of the representative office." Notwithstanding this warning, the banishment was enforced, and Mr. Forsyth promptly announced to the Government the suspension of the political relations of his legation with them until the pleasure of his own Government should be ascertained.

This Government did not regard the contribution imposed by the decree of the 15th May last to be in strictness a "forced loan," and as such prohibited by the tenth article of the treaty of 1826 between Great Britain and Mexico, to the benefits of which American citizens are entitled by treaty; yet the imposition of the contribution upon foreigners was considered an unjust and oppressive measure. Besides, internal factions in other parts of the Republic were at the same time levying similar exactions upon the property of our citizens and interrupting their commerce. There had been an entire failure on the part of our minister to secure redress for the wrongs which our citizens had endured, notwithstanding his persevering efforts. And from the temper manifested by the Mexican Government he had repeatedly assured us that no favorable change could be expected until the United States should "give striking evidence of their will and power to protect their citizens," and that "severe chastening is the only earthly remedy for our grievances." From this statement of facts it would have been worse than idle to direct Mr. Forsyth to retrace his steps and resume diplomatic relations with that Government, and it was therefore deemed proper to sanction his withdrawal of the legation from the City of Mexico.

Abundant cause now undoubtedly exists for a resort to hostilities against the Government still holding possession of the capital. Should they succeed in subduing the constitutional forces, all reasonable hope will then have expired of a peaceful settlement of our difficulties.

On the other hand, should the constitutional party prevail and their authority be established over the Republic, there is reason to hope that they will be animated by a less unfriendly spirit and may grant that redress to American citizens which justice requires so far as they may possess the means.   But for this expectation I should at once have recommended to Congress to grant the necessary power to the President to take possession of a sufficient portion of the remote and unsettled territory of Mexico, to be held in pledge until our injuries shall be redressed and our just demands be satisfied.   We have already exhausted every milder means of obtaining justice.   In such a case this remedy of reprisals is recognized by the law of nations, not only as just in itself, but as a means of preventing actual war.

But there is another view of our relations with Mexico, arising from the unhappy condition of affairs along our southwestern frontier, which demands immediate action.   In that remote region, where there are but few white inhabitants, large bands of hostile and predatory Indians roam promiscuously over the Mexican States of Chihuahua and Sonora and our adjoining Territories.   The local governments of these States are perfectly helpless and are kept in a state of constant alarm by the Indians.   They have not the power, if they possessed the will, even to restrain lawless Mexicans from passing the border and committing depredations on our remote settlers.   A state of anarchy and violence prevails throughout that distant frontier.   The laws are a dead letter and life and property wholly insecure.   For this reason the settlement of Arizona is arrested, whilst it is of great importance that a chain of inhabitants should extend all along its southern border sufficient for their own protection and that of the United States mail passing to and from California. Well-founded apprehensions are now entertained that the Indians and wandering Mexicans, equally lawless, may break up the important stage and postal communication recently established between our Atlantic and Pacific possessions.   This passes very near to the Mexican boundary throughout the whole length of Arizona.   I can imagine no possible remedy for these evils and no mode of restoring law and order on that remote and unsettled frontier but for the Government of the United States to assume a temporary protectorate over the northern portions of Chihuahua and Sonora and to establish military posts within the same; and this I earnestly recommend to Congress.   This protection may be withdrawn as soon as local governments shall be established in these Mexican States capable of performing their duties to the United States, restraining the lawless, and preserving peace along the border.

I do not doubt that this measure will be viewed in a friendly spirit by the governments and people of Chihuahua and Sonora, as it will prove equally effectual for the protection of their citizens on that remote and lawless frontier as for citizens of the United States.

And in this connection permit me to recall your attention to the condition of Arizona.   The population of that Territory, numbering, as is alleged, more than 10,000 souls, are practically without a government, without laws, and without any regular administration of justice. Murder and other crimes are committed with impunity. This state of things calls loudly for redress, and I therefore repeat my recommendation for the establishment of a Territorial government over Arizona.

The political condition of the narrow isthmus of Central America, through which transit routes pass between the Atlantic and Pacific oceans, presents a subject of deep interest to all commercial nations. It is over these transits that a large proportion of the trade and travel between the European and Asiatic continents is destined to pass. To the United States these routes are of incalculable importance as a means of communication between their Atlantic and Pacific possessions. The latter now extend throughout seventeen degrees of latitude on the Pacific coast, embracing the important State of California and the flourishing Territories of Oregon and Washington. All commercial nations therefore have a deep and direct interest that these communications shall be rendered secure from interruption. If an arm of the sea connecting the two oceans penetrated through Nicaragua and Costa Rica, it could not be pretended that these States would have the right to arrest or retard its navigation to the injury of other nations. The transit by land over this narrow isthmus occupies nearly the same position. It is a highway in which they themselves have little interest when compared with the vast interests of the rest of the world. Whilst their rights of sovereignty ought to be respected, it is the duty of other nations to require that this important passage shall not be interrupted by the civil wars and revolutionary outbreaks which have so frequently occurred in that region. The stake is too important to be left at the mercy of rival companies claiming to hold conflicting contracts with Nicaragua. The commerce of other nations is not to stand still and await the adjustment of such petty controversies. The Government of the United States expect no more than this, and they will not be satisfied with less. They would not, if they could, derive any advantage from the Nicaragua transit not common to the rest of the world. Its neutrality and protection for the common use of all nations is their only object. They have no objection that Nicaragua shall demand and receive a fair compensation from the companies and individuals who may traverse the route, but they insist that it shall never hereafter be closed by an arbitrary decree of that Government. If disputes arise between it and those with whom they may have entered into contracts, these must be adjusted by some fair tribunal provided for the purpose, and the route must not be closed pending the controversy. This is our whole policy, and it can not fail to be acceptable to other nations.

All these difficulties might be avoided if, consistently with the good faith of Nicaragua, the use of this transit could be thrown open to general competition, providing at the same time for the payment of a reasonable rate to the Nicaraguan Government on passengers and freight.

In August, 1852, the Accessory Transit Company made its first interoceanic trip over the Nicaraguan route, and continued in successful operation, with great advantage to the public, until the 18th February, 1856, when it was closed and the grant to this company as well as its charter were summarily and arbitrarily revoked by the Government of President Rivas. Previous to this date, however, in 1854, serious disputes concerning the settlement of their accounts had arisen between the company and the Government, threatening the interruption of the route at any moment. These the United States in vain endeavored to compose. It would be useless to narrate the various proceedings which took place between the parties up till the time when the transit was discontinued. Suffice it to say that since February, 1856, it has remained closed, greatly to the prejudice of citizens of the United States. Since that time the competition has ceased between the rival routes of Panama and Nicaragua, and in consequence thereof an unjust and unreasonable amount has been exacted from our citizens for their passage to and from California.

A treaty was signed on the 16th day of November, 1857, by the Secretary of State and minister of Nicaragua, under the stipulations of which the use and protection of the transit route would have been secured, not only to the United States, but equally to all other nations. How and on what pretext this treaty has failed to receive the ratification of the Nicaraguan Government will appear by the papers herewith communicated from the State Department. The principal objection seems to have been to the provision authorizing the United States to employ force to keep the route open in case Nicaragua should fail to perform her duty in this respect. From the feebleness of that Republic, its frequent changes of government, and its constant internal dissensions, this had become a most important stipulation, and one essentially necessary, not only for the security of the route, but for the safety of American citizens passing and repassing to and from our Pacific possessions. Were such a stipulation embraced in a treaty between the United States and Nicaragua, the knowledge of this fact would of itself most probably prevent hostile parties from committing aggressions on the route, and render our actual interference for its protection unnecessary.

The executive government of this country in its intercourse with foreign nations is limited to the employment of diplomacy alone. When this fails it can proceed no further. It can not legitimately resort to force without the direct authority of Congress, except in resisting and repelling hostile attacks. It would have no authority to enter the territories of Nicaragua even to prevent the destruction of the transit and protect the lives and property of our own citizens on their passage. It is true that on a sudden emergency of this character the President would direct any armed force in the vicinity to march to their relief, but in doing this he would act upon his own responsibility.

Under these circumstances I earnestly recommend to Congress the passage of an act authorizing the President, under such restrictions as they may deem proper, to employ the land and naval forces of the United States in preventing the transit from being obstructed or closed by lawless violence, and in protecting the lives and property of American citizens traveling thereupon, requiring at the same time that these forces shall be withdrawn the moment the danger shall have passed away. Without such a provision our citizens will be constantly exposed to interruption in their progress and to lawless violence.

A similar necessity exists for the passage of such an act for the protection of the Panama and Tehuantepec routes.

In reference to the Panama route, the United States, by their existing treaty with New Granada, expressly guarantee the neutrality of the Isthmus, "with the view that the free transit from the one to the other sea may not be interrupted or embarrassed in any future time while this treaty exists."

In regard to the Tehuantepec route, which has been recently opened under the most favorable auspices, our treaty with Mexico of the 30th December, 1853, secures to the citizens of the United States a right of transit over it for their persons and merchandise and stipulates that neither Government shall "interpose any obstacle" thereto. It also concedes to the United States the "right to transport across the Isthmus, in closed bags, the mails of the United States not intended for distribution along the line of the communication; also the effects of the United States Government and its citizens which may be intended for transit and not for distribution on the Isthmus, free of custom-house or other charges by the Mexican Government."

These treaty stipulations with New Granada and Mexico, in addition to the considerations applicable to the Nicaragua route, seem to require legislation for the purpose of carrying them into effect.

The injuries which have been inflicted upon our citizens in Costa Rica and Nicaragua during the last two or three years have received the prompt attention of this Government. Some of these injuries were of the most aggravated character. The transaction at Virgin Bay in April, 1856, when a company of unarmed Americans, who were in no way connected with any belligerent conduct or party, were fired upon by the troops of Costa Rica and numbers of them killed and wounded, was brought to the knowledge of Congress by my predecessor soon after its occurrence, and was also presented to the Government of Costa Rica for that immediate investigation and redress which the nature of the case demanded. A similar course was pursued with reference to other outrages in these countries, some of which were hardly less aggravated in their character than the transaction at Virgin Bay. At the time, however, when our present minister to Nicaragua was appointed, in December, 1857, no redress had been obtained for any of these wrongs and no reply even had been received to the demands which had been made by this

Government upon that of Costa Rica more than a year before. Our minister was instructed, therefore, to lose no time in expressing to those Governments the deep regret with which the President had witnessed this inattention to the just claims of the United States and in demanding their prompt and satisfactory adjustment. Unless this demand shall be complied with at an early day it will only remain for this Government to adopt such other measures as may be necessary in order to obtain for itself that justice which it has in vain attempted to secure by peaceful means from the Governments of Nicaragua and Costa Rica. While it has shown, and will continue to show, the most sincere regard for the rights and honor of these Republics, it can not permit this regard to be met by an utter neglect on their part of what is due to the Government and citizens of the United States.

Against New Granada we have long-standing causes of complaint, arising out of the unsatisfied claims of our citizens upon that Republic, and to these have been more recently added the outrages committed upon our citizens at Panama in April, 1856. A treaty for the adjustment of these difficulties was concluded by the Secretary of State and the minister of New Granada in September, 1857, which contained just and acceptable provisions for that purpose. This treaty was transmitted to Bogota and was ratified by the Government of New Granada, but with certain amendments. It was not, however, returned to this city until after the close of the last session of the Senate. It will be immediately transmitted to that body for their advice and consent, and should this be obtained it will remove all our existing causes of complaint against New Granada on the subject of claims.

Questions have arisen between the two Governments as to the right of New Granada to levy a tonnage duty upon the vessels of the United States in its ports of the Isthmus and to levy a passenger tax upon our citizens arriving in that country, whether with a design to remain there or to pass from ocean to ocean by the transit route; and also a tax upon the mail of the United States transported over the Panama Railroad. The Government of New Granada has been informed that the United States would consider the collection of either of these taxes as an act in violation of the treaty between the two countries, and as such would be resisted by the United States. At the same time, we are prepared to discuss these questions in a spirit of amity and justice and with a sincere desire to adjust them in a satisfactory manner. A negotiation for that purpose has already been commenced. No effort has recently been made to collect these taxes nor is any anticipated under present circumstances.

With the Empire of Brazil our relations are of the most friendly character. The productions of the two countries, and especially those of an agricultural nature, are such as to invite extensive mutual exchanges. A large quantity of American flour is consumed in Brazil, whilst more than treble the amount in value of Brazilian coffee is consumed in the United States. Whilst this is the case, a heavy duty has been levied until very recently upon the importation of American flour into Brazil. I am gratified, however, to be able to inform you that in September last this has been reduced from $1.32 to about 49 cents per barrel, and the duties on other articles of our production have been diminished in nearly the same proportion.

I regret to state that the Government of Brazil still continues to levy an export duty of about 11 per cent on coffee, notwithstanding this article is admitted free from duty in the United States. This is a heavy charge upon the consumers of coffee in our country, as we purchase half of the entire surplus crop of that article raised in Brazil. Our minister, under instructions, will reiterate his efforts to have this export duty removed, and it is hoped that the enlightened Government of the Emperor will adopt this wise, just, and equal policy. In that event, there is good reason to believe that the commerce between the two countries will greatly increase, much to the advantage of both.

The claims of our citizens against the Government of Brazil are not in the aggregate of very large amount; but some of these rest upon plain principles of justice and their settlement ought not to be longer delayed. A renewed and earnest, and I trust a successful, effort will be made by our minister to procure their final adjustment.

On the 2d of June last Congress passed a joint resolution authorizing the President "to adopt such measures and use such force as in his judgment may be necessary and advisable" "for the purpose of adjusting the differences between the United States and the Republic of Paraguay in connection with the attack on the United States steamer *Water Witch* and with other measures referred to" in his annual message, and on the 12th of July following they made an appropriation to defray the expenses and compensation of a commissioner to that Republic should the President deem it proper to make such an appointment.

In compliance with these enactments, I have appointed a commissioner, who has proceeded to Paraguay with full powers and instructions to settle these differences in an amicable and peaceful manner if this be practicable. His experience and discretion justify the hope that he may prove successful in convincing the Paraguayan Government that it is due both to honor and justice that they should voluntarily and promptly make atonement for the wrongs which they have committed against the United States and indemnify our injured citizens whom they have forcibly despoiled of their property.

Should our commissioner prove unsuccessful after a sincere and earnest effort to accomplish the object of his mission, then no alternative will remain but the employment of force to obtain "just satisfaction" from Paraguay. In view of this contingency, the Secretary of the Navy, under my direction, has fitted out and dispatched a naval force to rendezvous near Buenos Ayres, which, it is believed, will prove sufficient for the occasion.   It is my earnest desire, however, that it may not be found necessary to resort to this last alternative.

When Congress met in December last the business of the country had just been crushed by one of those periodical revulsions which are the inevitable consequence of our unsound and extravagant system of bank credits and inflated currency.   With all the elements of national wealth in abundance, our manufactures were suspended, our useful public and private enterprises were arrested, and thousands of laborers were deprived of employment and reduced to want.   Universal distress prevailed among the commercial, manufacturing, and mechanical classes.   This revulsion was felt the more severely in the United States because similar causes had produced the like deplorable effects throughout the commercial nations of Europe.   All were experiencing sad reverses at the same moment. Our manufacturers everywhere suffered severely, not because of the recent reduction in the tariff of duties on imports, but because there was no demand at any price for their productions.   The people were obliged to restrict themselves in their purchases to articles of prime necessity.   In the general prostration of business the iron manufacturers in different States probably suffered more than any other class, and much destitution was the inevitable consequence among the great number of workmen who had been employed in this useful branch of industry. There could be no supply where there was no demand.   To present an example, there could be no demand for railroad iron after our magnificent system of railroads, extending its benefits to every portion of the Union, had been brought to a dead pause.   The same consequences have resulted from similar causes to many other branches of useful manufactures.   It is self-evident that where there is no ability to purchase manufactured articles these can not be sold, and consequently must cease to be produced.

No government, and especially a government of such limited powers as that of the United States, could have prevented the late revulsion. The whole commercial world seemed for years to have been rushing to this catastrophe.   The same ruinous consequences would have followed in the United States whether the duties upon foreign imports had remained as they were under the tariff of 1846 or had been raised to a much higher standard.   The tariff of 1857 had no agency in the result.   The general causes existing throughout the world could not have been controlled by the legislation of any particular country.

The periodical revulsions which have existed in our past history must continue to return at intervals so long as our present unbounded system of bank credits shall prevail.   They will, however, probably be the less severe in future, because it is not to be expected, at least for many years to come, that the commercial nations of Europe, with whose interests our own are so materially involved, will expose themselves to similar calamities.   But this subject was treated so much at large in my last

annual message that I shall not now pursue it further. Still, I respectfully renew the recommendation in favor of the passage of a uniform
bankrupt law applicable to banking institutions. This is all the direct
power over the subject which I believe the Federal Government possesses. Such a law would mitigate, though it might not prevent, the
evil. The instinct of self-preservation might produce a wholesome restraint upon their banking business if they knew in advance that a suspension of specie payments would inevitably produce their civil death.

But the effects of the revulsion are now slowly but surely passing
away. The energy and enterprise of our citizens, with our unbounded
resources, will within the period of another year restore a state of wholesome industry and trade. Capital has again accumulated in our large
cities. The rate of interest is there very low. Confidence is gradually
reviving, and so soon as it is discovered that this capital can be profitably employed in commercial and manufacturing enterprises and in the
construction of railroads and other works of public and private improvement prosperity will again smile throughout the land. It is vain, however, to disguise the fact from ourselves that a speculative inflation of
our currency without a corresponding inflation in other countries whose
manufactures come into competition with our own must ever produce
disastrous results to our domestic manufactures. No tariff short of
absolute prohibition can prevent these evil consequences.

In connection with this subject it is proper to refer to our financial
condition. The same causes which have produced pecuniary distress
throughout the country have so reduced the amount of imports from
foreign countries that the revenue has proved inadequate to meet the
necessary expenses of the Government. To supply the deficiency, Congress, by the act of December 23, 1857, authorized the issue of $20,000,000
of Treasury notes; and this proving inadequate, they authorized, by the
act of June 14, 1858, a loan of $20,000,000, "to be applied to the payment
of appropriations made by law."

No statesman would advise that we should go on increasing the national
debt to meet the ordinary expenses of the Government. This would be
a most ruinous policy. In case of war our credit must be our chief
resource, at least for the first year, and this would be greatly impaired
by having contracted a large debt in time of peace. It is our true policy
to increase our revenue so as to equal our expenditures. It would be
ruinous to continue to borrow. Besides, it may be proper to observe
that the incidental protection thus afforded by a revenue tariff would at
the present moment to some extent increase the confidence of the manufacturing interests and give a fresh impulse to our reviving business.
To this surely no person will object.

In regard to the mode of assessing and collecting duties under a strictly
revenue tariff, I have long entertained and often expressed the opinion
that sound policy requires this should be done by specific duties in cases

to which these can be properly applied. They are well adapted to commodities which are usually sold by weight or by measure, and which from their nature are of equal or of nearly equal value. Such, for example, are the articles of iron of different classes, raw sugar, and foreign wines and spirits.

In my deliberate judgment specific duties are the best, if not the only, means of securing the revenue against false and fraudulent invoices, and such has been the practice adopted for this purpose by other commercial nations. Besides, specific duties would afford to the American manufacturer the incidental advantages to which he is fairly entitled under a revenue tariff. The present system is a sliding scale to his disadvantage. Under it, when prices are high and business prosperous, the duties rise in amount when he least requires their aid. On the contrary, when prices fall and he is struggling against adversity, the duties are diminished in the same proportion, greatly to his injury.

Neither would there be danger that a higher rate of duty than that intended by Congress could be levied in the form of specific duties. It would be easy to ascertain the average value of any imported article for a series of years, and, instead of subjecting it to an *ad valorem* duty at a certain rate *per centum*, to substitute in its place an equivalent specific duty.

By such an arrangement the consumer would not be injured. It is true he might have to pay a little more duty on a given article in one year, but, if so, he would pay a little less in another, and in a series of years these would counterbalance each other and amount to the same thing so far as his interest is concerned. This inconvenience would be trifling when contrasted with the additional security thus afforded against frauds upon the revenue, in which every consumer is directly interested.

I have thrown out these suggestions as the fruit of my own observation, to which Congress, in their better judgment, will give such weight as they may justly deserve.

The report of the Secretary of the Treasury will explain in detail the operations of that Department of the Government. The receipts into the Treasury from all sources during the fiscal year ending June 30, 1858, including the Treasury notes authorized by the act of December 23, 1857, were $70,273,869.59, which amount, with the balance of $17,710,114.27 remaining in the Treasury at the commencement of the year, made an aggregate for the service of the year of $87,983,983.86.

The public expenditures during the fiscal year ending June 30, 1858, amounted to $81,585,667.76, of which $9,684,537.99 were applied to the payment of the public debt and the redemption of Treasury notes with the interest thereon, leaving in the Treasury on July 1, 1858, being the commencement of the present fiscal year, $6,398,316.10.

The receipts into the Treasury during the first quarter of the present fiscal year, commencing the 1st of July, 1858, including one-half of the loan of $20,000,000, with the premium upon it, authorized by the act of June 14, 1858, were $25,230,879.46, and the estimated receipts for the remaining three quarters to the 30th of June, 1859, from ordinary sources are $38,500,000, making, with the balance before stated, an aggregate of $70,129,195.56.

The expenditures during the first quarter of the present fiscal year were $21,708,198.51, of which $1,010,142.37 were applied to the payment of the public debt and the redemption of Treasury notes and the interest thereon. The estimated expenditures during the remaining three quarters to June 30, 1859, are $52,357,698.48, making an aggregate of $74,065,896.99, being an excess of expenditure beyond the estimated receipts into the Treasury from ordinary sources during the fiscal year to the 30th of June, 1859, of $3,936,701.43. Extraordinary means are placed by law within the command of the Secretary of the Treasury, by the reissue of Treasury notes redeemed and by negotiating the balance of the loan authorized by the act of June 14, 1858, to the extent of $11,000,000, which, if realized during the present fiscal year, will leave a balance in the Treasury on the 1st day of July, 1859, of $7,063,298.57.

The estimated receipts during the next fiscal year, ending June 30, 1860, are $62,000,000, which, with the above-estimated balance of $7,063,298.57 make an aggregate for the service of the next fiscal year of $69,063,298.57. The estimated expenditures during the next fiscal year, ending June 30, 1860, are $73,139,147.46, which leaves a deficit of estimated means, compared with the estimated expenditures, for that year, commencing on July 1, 1859, of $4,075,848.89.

In addition to this sum the Postmaster-General will require from the Treasury for the service of the Post-Office Department $3,838,728, as explained in the report of the Secretary of the Treasury, which will increase the estimated deficit on June 30, 1860, to $7,914,576.89. To provide for the payment of this estimated deficiency, which will be increased by such appropriations as may be made by Congress not estimated for in the report of the Treasury Department, as well as to provide for the gradual redemption from year to year of the outstanding Treasury notes, the Secretary of the Treasury recommends such a revision of the present tariff as will raise the required amount. After what I have already said I need scarcely add that I concur in the opinion expressed in his report—that the public debt should not be increased by an additional loan—and would therefore strongly urge upon Congress the duty of making at their present session the necessary provision for meeting these liabilities.

The public debt on July 1, 1858, the commencement of the present fiscal year, was $25,155,977.66.

During the first quarter of the present year the sum of $10,000,000 has been negotiated of the loan authorized by the act of June 14, 1858, making the present outstanding public debt, exclusive of Treasury notes,

$35,155,977.66. There was on the 1st of July, 1858, of Treasury notes issued by authority of the act of December 23, 1857, unredeemed, the sum of $19,754,800, making the amount of actual indebtedness at that date $54,910,777.66. To this will be added $10,000,000 during the present fiscal year, this being the remaining half of the loan of $20,000,000 not yet negotiated.

The rapid increase of the public debt and the necessity which exists for a modification of the tariff to meet even the ordinary expenses of the Government ought to admonish us all, in our respective spheres of duty, to the practice of rigid economy. The objects of expenditure should be limited in number, as far as this may be practicable, and the appropriations necessary to carry them into effect ought to be disbursed under the strictest accountability. Enlightened economy does not consist in the refusal to appropriate money for constitutional purposes essential to the defense, progress, and prosperity of the Republic, but in taking care that none of this money shall be wasted by mismanagement in its application to the objects designated by law.

Comparisons between the annual expenditure at the present time and what it was ten or twenty years ago are altogether fallacious. The rapid increase of our country in extent and population renders a corresponding increase of expenditure to some extent unavoidable. This is constantly creating new objects of expenditure and augmenting the amount required for the old. The true questions, then, are, Have these objects been unnecessarily multiplied, or has the amount expended upon any or all of them been larger than comports with due economy? In accordance with these principles, the heads of the different Executive Departments of the Government have been instructed to reduce their estimates for the next fiscal year to the lowest standard consistent with the efficiency of the service, and this duty they have performed in a spirit of just economy. The estimates of the Treasury, War, Navy, and Interior Departments have each been in some degree reduced, and unless a sudden and unforeseen emergency should arise it is not anticipated that a deficiency will exist in either within the present or the next fiscal year. The Post-Office Department is placed in a peculiar position, different from the other Departments, and to this I shall hereafter refer.

I invite Congress to institute a rigid scrutiny to ascertain whether the expenses in all the Departments can not be still further reduced, and I promise them all the aid in my power in pursuing the investigation.

I transmit herewith the reports made to me by the Secretaries of War, of the Navy, of the Interior, and of the Postmaster-General. They each contain valuable information and important recommendations, to which I invite the attention of Congress.

In my last annual message I took occasion to recommend the immediate construction of ten small steamers of light draft, for the purpose of increasing the efficiency of the Navy. Congress responded to the recommendation by authorizing the construction of eight of them. The progress which has been made in executing this authority is stated in the report of the Secretary of the Navy. I concur with him in the opinion that a greater number of this class of vessels is necessary for the purpose of protecting in a more efficient manner the persons and property of American citizens on the high seas and in foreign countries, as well as in guarding more effectually our own coasts. I accordingly recommend the passage of an act for this purpose.

The suggestions contained in the report of the Secretary of the Interior, especially those in regard to the disposition of the public domain, the pension and bounty-land system, the policy toward the Indians, and the amendment of our patent laws, are worthy of the serious consideration of Congress.

The Post-Office Department occupies a position very different from that of the other Departments. For many years it was the policy of the Government to render this a self-sustaining Department; and if this can not now be accomplished, in the present condition of the country, we ought to make as near an approach to it as may be practicable.

The Postmaster-General is placed in a most embarrassing position by the existing laws. He is obliged to carry these into effect. He has no other alternative. He finds, however, that this can not be done without heavy demands upon the Treasury over and above what is received for postage, and these have been progressively increasing from year to year until they amounted for the last fiscal year, ending on the 30th of June, 1858, to more than $4,500,000, whilst it is estimated that for the present fiscal year they will amount to $6,290,000. These sums are exclusive of the annual appropriation of $700,000 for "compensation for the mail service performed for the two Houses of Congress and the other Departments and officers of the Government in the transmission of free matter."

The cause of these large deficits is mainly attributable to the increased expense of transporting the mails. In 1852 the sum paid for this service was but a fraction above four millions and a quarter. Since that year it has annually increased, until in 1858 it has reached more than eight millions and a quarter, and for the service of 1859 it is estimated that it will amount to more than $10,000,000.

The receipts of the Post-Office Department can be made to approach or to equal its expenditure only by means of the legislation of Congress. In applying any remedy care should be taken that the people shall not be deprived of the advantages which they are fairly entitled to enjoy from the Post-Office Department. The principal remedies recommended to the consideration of Congress by the Postmaster-General are to restore the former rate of postage upon single letters to 5 cents; to substitute for the franking privilege the delivery to those now entitled to enjoy it of post-office stamps for their correspondence, and to direct the Department in making contracts for the transportation of the mail to confine itself to the payment of the sum necessary for this single purpose, without requiring it to be transported in post coaches or carriages of any particular description. Under the present system the expense to the Government is greatly increased by requiring that the mail shall be carried in such vehicles as will accommodate passengers. This will be done, without pay from the Department, over all roads where the travel will remunerate the contractors.

These recommendations deserve the grave consideration of Congress.

I would again call your attention to the construction of a Pacific railroad. Time and reflection have but served to confirm me in the truth and justice of the observations which I made on this subject in my last annual message, to which I beg leave respectfully to refer.

It is freely admitted that it would be inexpedient for this Government to exercise the power of constructing the Pacific railroad by its own immediate agents. Such a policy would increase the patronage of the Executive to a dangerous extent, and introduce a system of jobbing and corruption which no vigilance on the part of Federal officials could either prevent or detect. This can only be done by the keen eye and active and careful supervision of individual and private interest. The construction of this road ought therefore to be committed to companies incorporated by the States or other agencies whose pecuniary interests would be directly involved. Congress might then assist them in the work by grants of land or of money, or both, under such conditions and restrictions as would secure the transportation of troops and munitions of war free from any charge and that of the United States mail at a fair and reasonable price.

The progress of events since the commencement of your last session has shown how soon difficulties disappear before a firm and determined resolution. At that time such a road was deemed by wise and patriotic men to be a visionary project. The great distance to be overcome and the intervening mountains and deserts in the way were obstacles which, in the opinion of many, could not be surmounted. Now, after the lapse of but a single year, these obstacles, it has been discovered, are far less formidable than they were supposed to be, and mail stages with passengers now pass and repass regularly twice in each week, by a common wagon road, between San Francisco and St. Louis and Memphis in less than twenty-five days. The service has been as regularly performed as it was in former years between New York and this city.

Whilst disclaiming all authority to appropriate money for the construction of this road, except that derived from the war-making power of the Constitution, there are important collateral considerations urging us to undertake the work as speedily as possible.

The first and most momentous of these is that such a road would be a powerful bond of union between the States east and west of the Rocky Mountains. This is so self-evident as to require no illustration.

But again, in a commercial point of view, I consider this the great question of the day. With the eastern front of our Republic stretching along the Atlantic and its western front along the Pacific, if all the parts should be united by a safe, easy, and rapid intercommunication we must necessarily command a very large proportion of the trade both of Europe and Asia. Our recent treaties with China and Japan will open these rich and populous Empires to our commerce; and the history of the world proves that the nation which has gained possession of the trade with eastern Asia has always become wealthy and powerful. The peculiar geographical position of California and our Pacific possessions invites American capital and enterprise into this fruitful field. To reap the rich harvest, however, it is an indispensable prerequisite that we shall first have a railroad to convey and circulate its products throughout every portion of the Union. Besides, such a railroad through our temperate latitude, which would not be impeded by the frosts and snows of winter nor by the tropical heats of summer, would attract to itself much of the travel and the trade of all nations passing between Europe and Asia.

On the 21st of August last Lieutenant J. N. Maffit, of the United States brig *Dolphin*, captured the slaver *Echo* (formerly the *Putnam*, of New Orleans) near Kay Verde, on the coast of Cuba, with more than 300 African negroes on board. The prize, under the command of Lieutenant Bradford, of the United States Navy, arrived at Charleston on the 27th August, when the negroes, 306 in number, were delivered into the custody of the United States marshal for the district of South Carolina. They were first placed in Castle Pinckney, and afterwards in Fort Sumter, for safe-keeping, and were detained there until the 19th September, when the survivors, 271 in number, were delivered on board the United States steamer *Niagara* to be transported to the coast of Africa under the charge of the agent of the United States, pursuant to the provisions of the act of the 3d March, 1819, "in addition to the acts prohibiting the slave trade." Under the second section of this act the President is "authorized to make such regulations and arrangements as he may deem expedient for the safe-keeping, support, and removal beyond the limits of the United States of all such negroes, mulattoes, or persons of color" captured by vessels of the United States as may be delivered to the marshal of the district into which they are brought, "and to appoint a proper person or persons residing upon the coast of Africa as agent or agents for receiving the negroes, mulattoes, or persons of color delivered from on board vessels seized in the prosecution of the slave trade by commanders of United States armed vessels."

A doubt immediately arose as to the true construction of this act. It is quite clear from its terms that the President was authorized to provide "for the safe-keeping, support, and removal" of these negroes up till the time of their delivery to the agent on the coast of Africa, but no express provision was made for their protection and support after they had reached the place of their destination. Still, an agent was to be appointed to receive them in Africa, and it could not have been supposed that Congress intended he should desert them at the moment they were received and turn them loose on that inhospitable coast to perish for want of food or to become again the victims of the slave trade. Had this been the intention of Congress, the employment of an agent to receive them, who is required to reside on the coast, was unnecessary, and they might have been landed by our vessels anywhere in Africa and left exposed to the sufferings and the fate which would certainly await them.

Mr. Monroe, in his special message of December 17, 1819, at the first session after the act was passed, announced to Congress what in his opinion was its true construction. He believed it to be his duty under it to follow these unfortunates into Africa and make provision for them there until they should be able to provide for themselves. In communicating this interpretation of the act to Congress he stated that some doubt had been entertained as to its true intent and meaning, and he submitted the question to them so that they might, "should it be deemed advisable, amend the same before further proceedings are had under it." Nothing was done by Congress to explain the act, and Mr. Monroe proceeded to carry it into execution according to his own interpretation. This, then, became the practical construction. When the Africans from on board the *Echo* were delivered to the marshal at Charleston, it became my duty to consider what disposition ought to be made of them under the law. For many reasons it was expedient to remove them from that locality as speedily as possible. Although the conduct of the authorities and citizens of Charleston in giving countenance to the execution of the law was just what might have been expected from their high character, yet a prolonged continuance of 300 Africans in the immediate vicinity of that city could not have failed to become a source of inconvenience and anxiety to its inhabitants. Where to send them was the question. There was no portion of the coast of Africa to which they could be removed with any regard to humanity except to Liberia. Under these circumstances an agreement was entered into with the Colonization Society on the 7th of September last, a copy of which is herewith transmitted, under which the society engaged, for the consideration of $45,000, to receive these Africans in Liberia from the agent of the United States and furnish them during the period of one year thereafter with comfortable shelter, clothing, provisions, and medical attendance, causing the children to receive schooling, and all, whether children or adults, to be instructed in the arts of civilized life suitable to their condition. This aggregate of $45,000 was based upon an allowance of $150 for each individual; and as there has been considerable mortality among them and may be more before they reach Africa, the society have agreed, in an equitable spirit, to make such a deduction from the amount as under the circumstances may appear just and reasonable. This can not be fixed until we shall ascertain the actual number which may become a charge to the society.

It was also distinctly agreed that under no circumstances shall this Government be called upon for any additional expenses.

The agents of the society manifested a laudable desire to conform to the wishes of the Government throughout the transaction. They assured me that after a careful calculation they would be required to expend the sum of $150 on each individual in complying with the agreement, and they would have nothing left to remunerate them for their care, trouble, and responsibility. At all events, I could make no better arrangement, and there was no other alternative. During the period when the Government itself, through its own agents, undertook the task of providing for captured negroes in Africa the cost per head was very much greater.

There having been no outstanding appropriation applicable to this purpose, I could not advance any money on the agreement. I therefore recommend that an appropriation may be made of the amount necessary to carry it into effect.

Other captures of a similar character may, and probably will, be made by our naval forces, and I earnestly recommend that Congress may amend the second section of the act of March 3, 1819, so as to free its construction from the ambiguity which has so long existed and render the duty of the President plain in executing its provisions.

I recommend to your favorable regard the local interests of the District of Columbia. As the residence of Congress and the Executive Departments of the Government, we can not fail to feel a deep concern in its welfare. This is heightened by the high character and the peaceful and orderly conduct of its resident inhabitants.

I can not conclude without performing the agreeable duty of expressing my gratification that Congress so kindly responded to the recommendation of my last annual message by affording me sufficient time before the close of their late session for the examination of all the bills presented to me for approval. This change in the practice of Congress has proved to be a wholesome reform. It exerted a beneficial influence on the transaction of legislative business and elicited the general approbation of the country. It enabled Congress to adjourn with that dignity and deliberation so becoming to the representatives of this great Republic, without having crowded into general appropriation bills provisions foreign to their nature and of doubtful constitutionality and expediency. Let me warmly and strongly commend this precedent established by themselves as a guide to their proceedings during the present session.

JAMES BUCHANAN.

SPECIAL MESSAGES.

WASHINGTON, *December 7, 1858.*

To the Senate of the United States:

I transmit to the Senate, for its consideration with a view to ratification, a treaty of amity and commerce between the United States and Japan, concluded at the city of Yeddo on the 29th of July last.

JAMES BUCHANAN.

WASHINGTON, *December 7, 1858.*

To the Senate of the United States:

I transmit to the Senate, for its consideration with a view to ratification, a treaty between the United States and China, signed at Tien-tsin by the plenipotentiaries of the parties on the 18th day of June last.

JAMES BUCHANAN.

EXECUTIVE MANSION, *December 10, 1858.*

The PRESIDENT OF THE SENATE.

SIR: In compliance with the resolution of the Senate of June 12, 1858, I herewith communicate a report from the Secretary of the Interior, showing "the amount of money paid for pensions in each of the States and Territories since the commencement of the present Government."

JAMES BUCHANAN.

WASHINGTON, *December 10, 1858.*

To the Senate and House of Representatives:

I transmit to Congress a copy of the treaty between the United States and the Kingdom of Siam, concluded on the 29th of May, 1856, and proclaimed on the 16th of August last, and call the attention of that body to the necessity of an act for carrying into effect the provisions of Article II of the said treaty, conferring certain judicial powers upon the consul of the United States who may be appointed to reside at Bangkok. I would also suggest that the extension to the Kingdom of Siam of the provisions of the act approved August 11, 1848, entitled "An act to carry into effect certain provisions in the treaties between the United States and China and the Ottoman Porte, giving certain judicial powers to ministers and consuls of the United States in those countries," might obviate the necessity of any other legislation upon the subject.

JAMES BUCHANAN.

EXECUTIVE OFFICE,
Washington, December 15, 1858.

Hon. JAMES L. ORR,
    Speaker of the House of Representatives.

SIR: In compliance with a resolution of the House of Representatives of the 13th instant, requesting the President of the United States, if not inconsistent with the public interest, "to communicate all information in his possession, or which may shortly come into his possession, respecting the reported recent acts of visitation by officers of the British navy of American vessels in the waters of the Gulf of Mexico," I transmit the accompanying reports from the Secretaries of State and the Navy. The report from the Secretary of State is not in strictness embraced by the terms of the resolution, but I deem it advisable to communicate to the House the information therein contained.

JAMES BUCHANAN.

WASHINGTON, *December 20, 1858.*
To the Senate of the United States:

I transmit a report from the Secretary of State, with accompanying documents, in answer to the resolution of the Senate of the 7th of January last, calling for all the official dispatches and correspondence of the Hon. Robert M. McLane and of the Hon. Peter Parker, late commissioners of the United States in China, with the Department of State.

JAMES BUCHANAN.

WASHINGTON, *December 20, 1858.*
To the Senate of the United States:

The Senate will learn from the thirty-five naval nominations herewith submitted the result of my investigations under the resolutions of Congress of March 10 and May 11, 1858. In compliance with these resolutions, I have carefully examined the records of the courts of inquiry in fifty-eight cases, and have arrived at the conclusion that twenty-three of the officers ought to remain in the positions where they have been fixed by the courts of inquiry.

The records are very voluminous and the labor of examination, in which I have been materially assisted by the Secretary of the Navy, the Attorney-General, and the Commissioner of Patents, has consumed much time.

Under the act of January 17, 1857, the courts of inquiry were directed to investigate "the physical, mental, professional, and moral fitness" of each officer who applied to them for relief. These investigations it was my duty to review. They have been very extensive and searching, as the Senate will perceive from an examination of the records, embracing in many instances almost the entire professional life of the individual from his first entrance into the service.

In the performance of my duty I found the greatest difficulty in deciding what should be considered as "moral fitness" for the Navy. Physical, mental, and professional fitness may be decided with a considerable degree of accuracy by a naval court of inquiry, but the question of moral fitness is of a very different character. There has been but one perfect standard of morality on earth, and how far a departure from His precepts and example must proceed in order to disqualify an officer for the naval service is a question on which a great difference of honest opinion must always exist. On this question I have differed in several instances from the courts of inquiry.•

There is one nomination which I regret that I have not the power to present to the Senate, and this is in the case of Commodore Stewart. His name stood on the Register at the head of the list of captains in the Navy until it was removed from this well-earned position by the retiring board and placed on the list of retired officers. The deeply wounded feelings of this veteran officer, who had contributed so much to the efficiency and glory of the Navy from its infancy, prevented him from applying for restoration to his rank and submitting to a court of inquiry composed of his junior officers the question of his "physical, mental, professional, and moral fitness" for the naval service. I would ere this have recommended to Congress the passage of a joint resolution to restore him to his former rank had I not believed this would more appropriately emanate from the legislative branch of Government.

I transmit herewith to the Senate the original records in the fifty-eight cases to which I have referred. After they shall have been examined by the Senate I would respectfully request that they might be returned to the Navy Department.

JAMES BUCHANAN.

WASHINGTON, *December 22, 1858.*

To the Senate of the United States:

I transmit to the Senate, for its consideration with a view to ratification, a convention between the United States and Belgium for regulating the commerce and navigation between the two countries, signed in this city on the 17th of July last.

JAMES BUCHANAN.

WASHINGTON, *December 23, 1858.*

To the Senate of the United States:

I transmit for the consideration of the Senate a convention with New Granada, signed on the 10th day of September, 1857, and a translation of the decree of the President of that Republic ratifying and confirming the same with certain modifications and explanations.

JAMES BUCHANAN.

WASHINGTON, *December 27, 1858.*

To the Senate and House of Representatives:

I transmit a copy of a letter of the 8th of April last from the minister of the United States in China, and of the decree and regulation which accompanied it, for such revision thereof as Congress may deem expedient, pursuant to the sixth section of the act approved 11th August, 1848.

JAMES BUCHANAN.

WASHINGTON, *January 4, 1859.*

To the House of Representatives:

I herewith transmit to the House of Representatives the report of the Secretary of the Treasury, with the accompanying documents, containing the information called for by the resolution of the House of the 23d December, 1858, concerning the correspondence in reference to the clearance of vessels at the port of Mobile.

JAMES BUCHANAN.

WASHINGTON, *January 5, 1859.*

To the Senate of the United States:

I transmit herewith, for the constitutional action of the Senate, the articles of agreement and convention made and concluded on the 19th day of June last with the Mendawakanton and Wahpakoota bands of the Dakota or Sioux Indians.

JAMES BUCHANAN.

WASHINGTON, *January 5, 1859.*

To the Senate of the United States:

I transmit herewith, for the constitutional action of the Senate, the articles of agreement and convention made and concluded on the 19th day of June last (1858) with the Sisseeton and Wahpaton bands of the Dakota or Sioux Indians, with accompanying papers from the Department of the Interior.

JAMES BUCHANAN.

WASHINGTON, *January 5, 1859.*

To the Senate of the United States:

I transmit herewith to the Senate, for its consideration with a view to ratification, a convention between the United States and the Republic of Chili, signed by the plenipotentiaries of the parties on the 10th day of November last, providing for the reference to an arbiter of the questions which have long been in controversy between the two Governments relative to a sum of money, the proceeds of the cargo of the brig *Macedonia*, alleged to have belonged to citizens of the United States, which was seized in the Valley of Sitana, in Peru, by orders of an officer in the service of the Republic of Chili.

JAMES BUCHANAN.

WASHINGTON CITY, *January 6, 1859.*

To the House of Representatives:

I herewith transmit to the House of Representatives a report from the Secretary of the Navy, with accompanying papers, in compliance with a resolution adopted December 23, 1858, requesting the President of the United States "to communicate to the House, if not deemed by him incompatible with the public interest, the instructions which have been given to our naval commanders in the Gulf of Mexico."

JAMES BUCHANAN.

WASHINGTON, *January 7, 1859.*

To the House of Representatives:

I herewith transmit reports from the Secretary of the Treasury and Postmaster-General, with the accompanying papers, in compliance with the resolution of the House adopted December 23, 1858, requesting the President of the United States to report "what action, if any, has been taken under the sixth section of the Post-Office appropriation act approved August 18, 1856, for the adjustment of the damages due Carmick & Ramsey, and if the said section of said law yet remains unexecuted that the President report the reasons therefor."

JAMES BUCHANAN.

WASHINGTON, *January 11, 1859.*

To the Senate of the United States:

In reply to the resolution of the Senate passed on the 16th ultimo, requesting me to communicate, if in my opinion not incompatible with the public interest, any information in my possession in relation to the landing of the bark *Wanderer* on the coast of Georgia with a cargo of slaves, I herewith communicate the report made to me by the Attorney-General, to whom the resolution was referred. From that report it will appear that the offense referred to in the resolution has been committed and that effective measures have been taken to see the laws faithfully executed. I concur with the Attorney-General in the opinion that it would be incompatible with the public interest at this time to communicate the correspondence with the officers of the Government at Savannah or the instructions which they have received. In the meantime every practicable effort has been made, and will be continued, to discover all the guilty parties and to bring them to justice.

JAMES BUCHANAN.

WASHINGTON CITY, *January 13, 1859.*

To the House of Representatives:

I herewith transmit a report from the Comptroller, with a copy of the letter of Messrs. Johnson and Williams, in relation to the decision upon the Carmick & Ramsey claim.

This should have accompanied the papers which have already been transmitted to the House, but was omitted by mistake.

JAMES BUCHANAN.

WASHINGTON, *January 15, 1859.*
To the House of Representatives:

I transmit a report from the Secretary of State, in answer to the resolution of the House of Representatives of the 10th instant, requesting a communication of the correspondence between this Government and France and England respecting the acquisition of Cuba by the United States.

JAMES BUCHANAN.

WASHINGTON, *January 19, 1859.*
To the Senate of the United States:

In compliance with the resolution of the Senate of the 14th of June last, requesting a list of claims of citizens of the United States on foreign governments, I transmit a report from the Secretary of State, with the documents which accompanied it.

JAMES BUCHANAN.

WASHINGTON CITY, *January 21, 1859.*
To the House of Representatives:

I have this day transmitted to the Senate a digest of the statistics of manufactures, according to the returns of the Seventh Census, prepared under the direction of the Secretary of the Interior in accordance with a provision contained in the first section of an act of Congress approved June 12, 1858, entitled "An act making appropriations for sundry civil expenses of the Government for the year ending the 30th of June, 1859." The magnitude of the work has prevented the preparation of another copy.

JAMES BUCHANAN.

WASHINGTON CITY, *January 21, 1859.*
To the Senate of the United States:

I transmit herewith a report from the Secretary of State, in answer to the resolution of the Senate of the 18th instant, requesting the President, if not incompatible with the public interest, "to communicate to the Senate any and all correspondence between the Government of the United States and the Government of Her Catholic Majesty relating to any proposition for the purchase of the island of Cuba, which correspondence has not been furnished to either House of Congress." From this it appears that no such correspondence has taken place which has not already been communicated to Congress. In my late annual message I stated in reference to the purchase of Cuba that "the publicity which has been given to our former negotiations on this subject and the large appropriation which may be required to effect the purpose render it expedient befo e making another attempt to renew the negotiation that I should lay the whole subject before Congress." I still entertain the same opinion, deeming it highly important, if not indispensable to the success of any negotiation which I might institute for this purpose, that the measure should receive the previous sanction of Congress.

JAMES BUCHANAN.

WASHINGTON, *January 21, 1859.*

To the Senate of the United States:

I herewith transmit to the Senate a digest of the statistics of manufactures according to the returns of the Seventh Census, prepared under the direction of the Secretary of the Interior in accordance with a provision in the first section of an act of Congress approved June 12, 1858, entitled "An act making appropriations for sundry civil expenses of the Government for the year ending the 30th of June, 1859."

JAMES BUCHANAN.

WASHINGTON, *January 26, 1859.*

To the Senate of the United States:

I transmit another report from the Secretary of State, in answer to the resolution of the Senate of the 14th of June last, requesting information on the subject of claims of citizens of the United States against foreign governments.

JAMES BUCHANAN.

WASHINGTON, *January 26, 1859.*

To the Senate and House of Representatives:

I transmit to Congress a report, dated the 25th instant, with the accompanying papers, received from the Secretary of State, in compliance with the requirement of the eighteenth section of the act entitled "An act to regulate the diplomatic and consular systems of the United States," approved August 18, 1856.

JAMES BUCHANAN.

WASHINGTON, *January 29, 1859.*

To the Senate and House of Representatives:

I transmit a report from the Secretary of War, with the accompanying documents, recommending the repayment to Governor Douglas, of Vancouvers Island, of the sum of $7,000, advanced by him to Governor Stevens, of Washington Territory, which was applied to the purchase of ammunition and subsistence stores for the forces of the United States in time of need and at a critical period of the late Indian war in that Territory.

As this advance was made by Governor Douglas out of his own private means and from friendly motives toward the United States, I recommend that an appropriation may be made for its immediate payment, with interest.

JAMES BUCHANAN.

WASHINGTON, *January 29, 1859.*

To the Senate of the United States:

In compliance with the resolution of the Senate of the 25th instant, I transmit a copy of the report of the special agent of the United States recently sent to Vancouvers Island and British Columbia.

JAMES BUCHANAN.

WASHINGTON, *February 5, 1859.*

To the Senate of the United States:

In reply to the resolution of the Senate of the 4th ultimo, I transmit a report from the Secretary of State, together with the papers* therein referred to.

JAMES BUCHANAN.

WASHINGTON CITY, *February 8, 1859.*

To the House of Representatives:

I transmit herewith a report from the Secretary of the Navy, in compliance with the resolution of the House of Representatives adopted on the 24th of January, requesting the President of the United States to communicate to the House "the aggregate expenditure, of whatsoever nature, including all salaries, whether special or by virtue of official position in the Army or Navy or otherwise, on account of the preparation and publication of the work known as Wilkes's Exploring Expedition;" also, what number of copies of the said work have been ordered, how they have been distributed, what number of persons are now employed thereon, how long they have been employed, respectively, and the amount of the appropriation now remaining undrawn.

JAMES BUCHANAN.

WASHINGTON, *February 12, 1859.*

To the House of Representatives:

I transmit herewith a report from the Secretary of State, with accompanying papers, in answer to the resolution of the House of Representatives

*Correspondence with the United States minister to Peru and others relative to the guano trade.

of the 14th of June last, requesting the communication of all information and correspondence which may have been received in regard to any consular officer engaged in business in violation of law.

JAMES BUCHANAN.

WASHINGTON CITY, *February 15, 1859.*

To the House of Representatives:

I transmit herewith a report from the Attorney-General, in reply to the resolution of the House of Representatives adopted on the 22d ultimo, requesting the President of the United States to "report what information has been received by him, if any, in regard to the recent importation of Africans into the State of Georgia or any other State of this Union, and what steps have been taken to bring to trial and punishment the persons engaged in this inhuman violation of the laws of the United States and to prevent similar violations hereafter."

JAMES BUCHANAN.

WASHINGTON, *February 18, 1859.*

To the Senate and House of Representatives:

The brief period which remains of your present session and the great urgency and importance of legislative action before its termination for the protection of American citizens and their property whilst in transit across the Isthmus routes between our Atlantic and Pacific possessions render it my duty again to recall this subject to your notice. I have heretofore presented it in my annual messages, both in December, 1857 and 1858, to which I beg leave to refer. In the latter I state that—

The executive government of this country in its intercourse with foreign nations is limited to the employment of diplomacy alone. When this fails it can proceed no further. It can not legitimately resort to force without the direct authority of Congress, except in resisting and repelling hostile attacks. It would have no authority to enter the territories of Nicaragua even to prevent the destruction of the transit and protect the lives and property of our own citizens on their passage. It is true that on a sudden emergency of this character the President would direct any armed force in the vicinity to march to their relief, but in doing this he would act upon his own responsibility.

Under these circumstances I earnestly recommend to Congress the passage of an act authorizing the President, under such restrictions as they may deem proper, to employ the land and naval forces of the United States in preventing the transit from being obstructed or closed by lawless violence and in protecting the lives and property of American citizens traveling thereupon, requiring at the same time that these forces shall be withdrawn the moment the danger shall have passed away. Without such a provision our citizens will be constantly exposed to interruption in their progress and to lawless violence.

A similar necessity exists for the passage of such an act for the protection of the Panama and Tehuantepec routes.

Another subject, equally important, commanded the attention of the Senate at the last session of Congress.

The Republics south of the United States on this continent have, unfortunately, been frequently in a state of revolution and civil war ever since they achieved their independence. As one or the other party has prevailed and obtained possession of the ports open to foreign commerce, they have seized and confiscated American vessels and their cargoes in an arbitrary and lawless manner and exacted money from American citizens by forced loans and other violent proceedings to enable them to carry on hostilities. The executive governments of Great Britain, France, and other countries, possessing the war-making power, can promptly employ the necessary means to enforce immediate redress for similar outrages upon their subjects. Not so the executive government of the United States.

If the President orders a vessel of war to any of these ports to demand prompt redress for outrages committed, the offending parties are well aware that in case of refusal the commander can do no more than remonstrate. He can resort to no hostile act. The question must then be referred to diplomacy, and in many cases adequate redress can never be obtained. Thus American citizens are deprived of the same protection under the flag of their country which the subjects of other nations enjoy. The remedy for this state of things can only be supplied by Congress, since the Constitution has confided to that body alone the power to make war. Without the authority of Congress the Executive can not lawfully direct any force, however near it may be to the scene of difficulty, to enter the territory of Mexico, Nicaragua, or New Granada for the purpose of defending the persons and property of American citizens, even though they may be violently assailed whilst passing in peaceful transit over the Tehuantepec, Nicaragua, or Panama routes. He can not, without transcending his constitutional power, direct a gun to be fired into a port or land a seaman or marine to protect the lives of our countrymen on shore or to obtain redress for a recent outrage on their property. The banditti which infest our neighboring Republic of Mexico, always claiming to belong to one or other of the hostile parties, might make a sudden descent on Vera Cruz or on the Tehuantepec route, and he would have no power to employ the force on shipboard in the vicinity for their relief, either to prevent the plunder of our merchants or the destruction of the transit.

In reference to countries where the local authorities are strong enough to enforce the laws, the difficulty here indicated can seldom happen; but where this is not the case and the local authorities do not possess the physical power, even if they possess the will, to protect our citizens within their limits recent experience has shown that the American Executive should itself be authorized to render this protection. Such a grant of authority, thus limited in its extent, could in no just sense be regarded as a transfer of the war-making power to the Executive, but only as an appropriate exercise of that power by the body to whom it exclusively belongs. The riot at Panama in 1856, in which a great number of our citizens lost their lives, furnishes a pointed illustration of the necessity which may arise for the exertion of this authority.

I therefore earnestly recommend to Congress, on whom the responsibility exclusively rests, to pass a law before their adjournment conferring on the President the power to protect the lives and property of American citizens in the cases which I have indicated, under such restrictions and conditions as they may deem advisable. The knowledge that such a law exists would of itself go far to prevent the outrages which it is intended to redress and to render the employment of force unnecessary.

Without this the President may be placed in a painful position before the meeting of the next Congress. In the present disturbed condition of Mexico and one or more of the other Republics south of us, no person can foresee what occurrences may take place before that period. In case of emergency, our citizens, seeing that they do not enjoy the same protection with subjects of European Governments, will have just cause to complain. On the other hand, should the Executive interpose, and especially should the result prove disastrous and valuable lives be lost, he might subject himself to severe censure for having assumed a power not confided to him by the Constitution. It is to guard against this contingency that I now appeal to Congress.

Having thus recommended to Congress a measure which I deem necessary and expedient for the interest and honor of the country, I leave the whole subject to their wisdom and discretion.

JAMES BUCHANAN.

WASHINGTON, *February 18, 1859.*

To the Senate of the United States:

I transmit to the Senate, for its consideration with a view to ratification, two conventions between the United States and China, one providing for the adjustment of claims of citizens of the United States on the Government of that Empire, the other for the regulation of trade, both signed at Shanghai on the 8th of November last. A copy of the dispatches of Mr. Reed to the Department of State on the subject is also herewith transmitted.

JAMES BUCHANAN.

WASHINGTON CITY, *February 25, 1859.*

To the House of Representatives:

I transmit herewith a report from the Secretary of the Navy, with the accompanying documents, in obedience to the resolution of the House of Representatives adopted on the 28th of January, requesting the President of the United States "to communicate to this House a copy of all instructions given to the commanders of our African squadron since the ratification of the treaty of 1842, called the Washington treaty, with a copy or statement of whatever regulations were entered into by the commanders of the two squadrons for more fully accomplishing the object of the eighth article of said treaty," etc.

JAMES BUCHANAN.

WASHINGTON, *February 26, 1859.*

To the Senate of the United States:

In answer to the resolution of the Senate of the 23d instant, requesting a copy of certain letters of Horatio J. Perry, late secretary to the legation of the United States at Madrid, I transmit a report from the Secretary of State, with the documents which accompanied it.

JAMES BUCHANAN.

WASHINGTON CITY, *March 1, 1859.*

To the Senate of the United States:

I transmit herewith a report from the Secretary of War, with accompanying paper, in obedience to the resolution of the Senate adopted 23d February, requesting the President of the United States "to communicate to the Senate a copy of the opinion of Judge Brewer in the Great Falls land condemnation case, involving a claim for damages to be paid by the United States."

JAMES BUCHANAN.

WASHINGTON, *March 2, 1859.*

To the Senate of the United States:

I transmit to the Senate, in executive session, the report of the Secretary of State, with the accompanying documents, in reply to the resolution of the Senate adopted in open session on the 11th January last, relating to outrages committed on citizens of the United States on the Isthmus of Panama.

JAMES BUCHANAN.

To the House of Representatives:

In compliance with the resolution of the House of Representatives of the 25th ultimo, I transmit a copy of the report of the special agent of the United States recently sent to Vancouvers Island and British Columbia.

JAMES BUCHANAN.

MARCH 3, 1859.

WASHINGTON, *March 3, 1859.*

To the Senate and House of Representatives:

An imperative sense of duty compels me to make an appeal to Congress to preserve the credit of the country. This is the last day of the present Congress, and no provision has yet been made for the payment of appropriations and to meet the outstanding Treasury notes issued under the authority of law. From the information which has already been communicated to Congress by the Secretary of the Treasury it is manifest that the ordinary receipts into the Treasury, even under the most favorable circumstances, will scarcely meet the ordinary expenses of the Government during the remainder of the present fiscal year, ending on the 30th of June. At that time nearly eighteen millions of Treasury notes will have become due, and many of those not yet due are daily paid for duties at the different ports, and there will be no means in the Treasury to meet them. Thus the country, which is full of resources, will be dishonored before the world, and the American people, who are a debt-paying people, will be disgraced by the omission on our part to do our duty. It is impossible to avoid this catastrophe unless we make provision this very day to meet the lawful demands on the public Treasury. If this were the first instead of the last session of a Congress, the case would be different. You might then be convened by proclamation for to-morrow morning. But there are now thirteen States of the Union, entitled to seventy-eight Representatives, in which none have been elected. It will therefore be impracticable for a large majority of these States to elect their Members before the Treasury shall be compelled to stop payment.

Under these circumstances I earnestly recommend to Congress to make provision within the few remaining hours of the session for the preservation of the public credit. The urgency of the case not only justifies but demands that, if necessary, this shall be done by a separate bill. We ought to incur no risk when the good faith of the country is at stake.

JAMES BUCHANAN.

VETO MESSAGES.*

WASHINGTON, *January 7, 1859.*

To the House of Representatives:

On the last day of the last session of Congress, as appears by the Journal of the House of Representatives, "a joint resolution in regard to the carrying the United States mails from Saint Josephs, Missouri, to Placerville, California," was presented to me for my approval. This resolution

---

*The first is a pocket veto.

authorized and directed the Postmaster-General "to order an increase of speed upon said route, requiring the mails to be carried through in thirty days, instead of thirty-eight days, according to the existing contract: *Provided*, The same can be done upon a *pro rata* increase of compensation to the contractors."

I did not approve this joint resolution: First, because it was presented to me at so late a period that I had not the time necessary **on** the day of the adjournment of the last session for an investigation of the subject. Besides, no injury could result to the public, as the Postmaster-General already possessed the discretionary power under existing laws to increase the speed upon this as well as all other mail routes.

Second. Because the Postmaster-General, at the moment in the Capitol, informed me that the contractors themselves had offered to increase the speed on this route to thirty instead of thirty-eight days at a less cost than that authorized by the joint resolution. Upon subsequent examination it has been ascertained at the Post-Office Department that their bid, which is still depending, proposes to perform this service for a sum less by $49,000 than that authorized by the resolution.

JAMES BUCHANAN.

WASHINGTON CITY, February 24, 1859.

To the House of Representatives of the United States:

I return with my objections to the House of Representatives, in which it originated, the bill entitled "An act donating public lands to the several States and Territories which may provide colleges for the benefit of agriculture and the mechanic arts," presented to me on the 18th instant.

This bill makes a donation to the several States of 20,000 acres of the public lands for each Senator and Representative in the present Congress, and also an additional donation of 20,000 acres for each additional Representative to which any State may be entitled under the census of 1860.

According to a report from the Interior Department, based upon the present number of Senators and Representatives, the lands given to the States amount to 6,060,000 acres, and their value, at the minimum Government price of $1.25 per acre, to $7,575,000.

The object of this gift, as stated by the bill, is "the endowment, support, and maintenance of at least one college [in each State] where the leading object shall be, without excluding other scientific or classical studies, to teach such branches of learning as are related to agriculture and the mechanic arts, as the legislatures of the States may respectively prescribe, in order to promote the liberal and practical education of the industrial classes in the several pursuits and professions in life."

As there does not appear from the bill to be any beneficiaries in **ex**istence to which this endowment can be applied, each State is required "to provide, within five years at least, not less than one college, or the grant to said State shall cease." In that event the "said State shall be bound to pay the United States the amount received of any lands previously sold, and that the title to purchasers under the State shall be valid."

The grant in land itself is confined to such States as have public lands within their limits worth $1.25 per acre in the opinion of the governor. For the remaining States the Secretary of the Interior is directed to issue "land scrip to the amount of their distributive shares in acres under the provisions of this act, said scrip to be sold by said States, and the proceeds thereof applied to the uses and purposes prescribed in this act, and for no other use or purpose whatsoever." The lands are granted and the scrip is to be issued "in sections or subdivisions of sections of not less than one-quarter of a section."

According to an estimate from the Interior Department, the number of acres which will probably be accepted by States having public lands within their own limits will not exceed 580,000 acres (and it may be much less), leaving a balance of 5,480,000 acres to be provided for by scrip. These grants of land and land scrip to each of the thirty-three States are made upon certain conditions, the principal of which is that if the fund shall be lost or diminished on account of unfortunate investments or otherwise the deficiency shall be replaced and made good by the respective States.

I shall now proceed to state my objections to this bill. I deem it to be both inexpedient and unconstitutional.

1. This bill has been passed at a period when we can with great difficulty raise sufficient revenue to sustain the expenses of the Government. Should it become a law the Treasury will be deprived of the whole, or nearly the whole, of our income from the sale of public lands, which for the next fiscal year has been estimated at $5,000,000.

A bare statement of the case will make this evident. The minimum price at which we dispose of our lands is $1.25 per acre. At the present moment, however, the price has been reduced to those who purchase the bounty-land warrants of the old soldiers to 85 cents per acre, and of these warrants there are still outstanding and unlocated, as appears by a report (February 12, 1859) from the General Land Office, the amount of 11,990,391 acres. This has already greatly reduced the current sales by the Government and diminished the revenue from this source. If in addition thirty-three States shall enter the market with their land scrip, the price must be greatly reduced below even 85 cents per acre, as much to the prejudice of the old soldiers who have not already parted with their land warrants as to Government. It is easy to perceive that with this glut of the market Government can sell little or no lands at $1.25 per acre, when the price of bounty-land warrants and scrip shall be reduced to half this sum. This source of revenue will be almost entirely dried up. Under the bill the States may sell their land scrip at any price it may bring. There is no limitation whatever in this respect. Indeed, they must sell for what the scrip will bring, for without this fund they can not proceed to establish their colleges within the five years to which they are limited. It is manifest, therefore, that to the extent to which this bill will prevent the sale of public lands at $1.25 per acre, to that amount it will have precisely the same effect upon the Treasury as if we should impose a tax to create a loan to endow these State colleges.

Surely the present is the most unpropitious moment which could have been selected for the passage of this bill.

2. Waiving for the present the question of constitutional power, what effect will this bill have on the relations established between the Federal and State Governments? The Constitution is a grant to Congress of a few enumerated but most important powers, relating chiefly to war, peace, foreign and domestic commerce, negotiation, and other subjects which can be best or alone exercised beneficially by the common Government. All other powers are reserved to the States and to the people. For the efficient and harmonious working of both, it is necessary that their several spheres of action should be kept distinct from each other. This alone can prevent conflict and mutual injury. Should the time ever arrive when the State governments shall look to the Federal Treasury for the means of supporting themselves and maintaining their systems of education and internal policy, the character of both Governments will be greatly deteriorated. The representatives of the States and of the people, feeling a more immediate interest in obtaining money to lighten the burdens of their constituents than for the promotion of the more distant objects intrusted to the Federal Government, will naturally incline to obtain means from the Federal Government for State purposes. If a question shall arise between an appropriation of land or money to carry into effect the objects of the Federal Government and those of the States, their feelings will be enlisted in favor of the latter. This is human nature; and hence the necessity of keeping the two Governments entirely distinct. The preponderance of this home feeling has been manifested by the passage of the present bill. The establishment of these colleges has prevailed over the pressing wants of the common Treasury. No nation ever had such an inheritance as we possess in the public lands. These ought to be managed with the utmost care, but at the same time with a liberal spirit toward actual settlers.

In the first year of a war with a powerful naval nation the revenue from customs must in a great degree cease. A resort to loans will then become necessary, and these can always be obtained, as our fathers obtained them, on advantageous terms by pledging the public lands as security. In this view of the subject it would be wiser to grant money to the States for domestic purposes than to squander away the public lands and transfer them in large bodies into the hands of speculators.

A successful struggle on the part of the State governments with the

General Government for the public lands would deprive the latter of the means of performing its high duties, especially at critical and dangerous periods. Besides, it would operate with equal detriment to the best interests of the States. It would remove the most wholesome of all restraints on legislative bodies—that of being obliged to raise money by taxation from their constituents—and would lead to extravagance, if not to corruption. What is obtained easily and without responsibility will be lavishly expended.

3. This bill, should it become a law, will operate greatly to the injury of the new States. The progress of settlements and the increase of an industrious population owning an interest in the soil they cultivate are the causes which will build them up into great and flourishing commonwealths. Nothing could be more prejudicial to their interests than for wealthy individuals to acquire large tracts of the public land and hold them for speculative purposes. The low price to which this land scrip will probably be reduced will tempt speculators to buy it in large amounts and locate it on the best lands belonging to the Government. The eventual consequence must be that the men who desire to cultivate the soil will be compelled to purchase these very lands at rates much higher than the price at which they could be obtained from the Government.

4. It is extremely doubtful, to say the least, whether this bill would contribute to the advancement of agriculture and the mechanic arts— objects the dignity and value of which can not be too highly appreciated.

The Federal Government, which makes the donation, has confessedly no constitutional power to follow it into the States and enforce the application of the fund to the intended objects. As donors we shall possess no control over our own gift after it shall have passed from our hands. It is true that the State legislatures are required to stipulate that they will faithfully execute the trust in the manner prescribed by the bill. But should they fail to do this, what would be the consequence? The Federal Government has no power, and ought to have no power, to compel the execution of the trust. It would be in as helpless a condition as if, even in this, the time of great need, we were to demand any portion of the many millions of surplus revenue deposited with the States for safekeeping under the act of 1836.

5. This bill will injuriously interfere with existing colleges in the different States, in many of which agriculture is taught as a science and in all of which it ought to be so taught. These institutions of learning have grown up with the growth of the country, under the fostering care of the States and the munificence of individuals, to meet the advancing demands for education. They have proved great blessings to the people. Many, indeed most, of them are poor and sustain themselves with difficulty. What the effect will be on these institutions of creating an indefinite number of rival colleges sustained by the endowment of the Federal Government it is not difficult to determine.

Under this bill it is provided that scientific and classical studies shall not be excluded from them. Indeed, it would be almost impossible to sustain them without such a provision, for no father would incur the expense of sending a son to one of these institutions for the sole purpose of making him a scientific farmer or mechanic. The bill itself negatives this idea, and declares that their object is ''to promote the liberal and practical education of the industrial classes in the several pursuits and professions of life.'' This certainly ought to be the case. In this view of the subject it would be far better, if such an appropriation of land must be made to institutions of learning in the several States, to apply it directly to the establishment of professorships of agriculture and the mechanic arts in existing colleges, without the intervention of the State legislatures. It would be difficult to foresee how these legislatures will manage this fund. Each Representative in Congress for whose district the proportion of 20,000 acres has been granted will probably insist that the proceeds shall be expended within its limits. There will undoubtedly be a struggle between different localities in each State concerning the division of the gift, which may end in disappointing the hopes of the true friends of agriculture. For this state of things we are without remedy. Not so in regard to State colleges. We might grant land to these corporations to establish agricultural and mechanical professorships, and should they fail to comply with the conditions on which they accepted the grant we might enforce specific performance of these before the ordinary courts of justice.

6. But does Congress possess the power under the Constitution to make a donation of public lands to the different States of the Union to provide colleges for the purpose of educating their own people?

I presume the general proposition is undeniable that Congress does not possess the power to appropriate money in the Treasury, raised by taxes on the people of the United States, for the purpose of educating the people of the respective States. It will not be pretended that any such power is to be found among the specific powers granted to Congress nor that ''it is necessary and proper for carrying into execution'' any one of these powers. Should Congress exercise such a power, this would be to break down the barriers which have been so carefully constructed in the Constitution to separate Federal from State authority. We should then not only ''lay and collect taxes, duties, imposts, and excises'' for Federal purposes, but for every State purpose which Congress might deem expedient or useful. This would be an actual consolidation of the Federal and State Governments so far as the great taxing and money power is concerned, and constitute a sort of partnership between the two in the Treasury of the United States, equally ruinous to both.

But it is contended that the public lands are placed upon a different footing from money raised by taxation and that the proceeds arising from their sale are not subject to the limitations of the Constitution, but may be appropriated or given away by Congress, at its own discretion, to States, corporations, or individuals for any purpose they may deem expedient.

The advocates of this bill attempt to sustain their position upon the language of the second clause of the third section of the fourth article of the Constitution, which declares that "the Congress shall have power to dispose of and make all needful rules and regulations respecting the territory or other property belonging to the United States." They contend that by a fair interpretation of the words "dispose of" in this clause Congress possesses the power to make this gift of public lands to the States for purposes of education.

It would require clear and strong evidence to induce the belief that the framers of the Constitution, after having limited the powers of Congress to certain precise and specific objects, intended by employing the words "dispose of" to give that body unlimited power over the vast public domain. It would be a strange anomaly, indeed, to have created two funds—the one by taxation, confined to the execution of the enumerated powers delegated to Congress, and the other from the public lands, applicable to all subjects, foreign and domestic, which Congress might designate; that this fund should be "disposed of," not to pay the debts of the United States, nor "to raise and support armies," nor "to provide and maintain a navy," nor to accomplish any one of the other great objects enumerated in the Constitution, but be diverted from them to pay the debts of the States, to educate their people, and to carry into effect any other measure of their domestic policy. This would be to confer upon Congress a vast and irresponsible authority, utterly at war with the well-known jealousy of Federal power which prevailed at the formation of the Constitution. The natural intendment would be that as the Constitution confined Congress to well-defined specific powers, the funds placed at their command, whether in land or money, should be appropriated to the performance of the duties corresponding with these powers. If not, a Government has been created with all its other powers carefully limited, but without any limitation in respect to the public lands.

But I can not so read the words "dispose of" as to make them embrace the idea of "giving away." The true meaning of words is always to be ascertained by the subject to which they are applied and the known general intent of the lawgiver. Congress is a trustee under the Constitution for the people of the United States to "dispose of" their public lands, and I think I may venture to assert with confidence that no case can be found in which a trustee in the position of Congress has been authorized to "*dispose of*" property by its owner where it has been held that these words authorized such trustee to give away the fund intrusted to his care. No trustee, when called upon to account for the disposition of the property placed under his management before any judicial tribunal, would venture to present such a plea in his defense. The true meaning of these words is clearly stated by Chief Justice Taney in delivering the opinion of the court (19 Howard, p. 436). He says in refer-- ence to this clause of the Constitution:

> It begins its enumeration of powers by that of disposing; in other words, making sale of the lands or raising money from them, which, as we have already said, was the main object of the cession (from the States), and which is the first thing provided for in the article.

It is unnecessary to refer to the history of the times to establish the known fact that this statement of the Chief Justice is perfectly well founded. That it never was intended by the framers of the Constitution that these lands should be given away by Congress is manifest from the concluding portion of the same clause. By it Congress has power not only "to dispose of" the territory, but of the "other property of the United States." In the language of the Chief Justice (p. 437):

> And the same power of making needful rules respecting the territory is in precisely the same language applied to the other property of the United States, associating the power over the territory in this respect with the power over movable or personal property; that is, the ships, arms, or munitions of war which then belonged in common to the State sovereignties.

The question is still clearer in regard to the public lands in the States and Territories within the Louisiana and Florida purchases. These lands were paid for out of the public Treasury from money raised by taxation. Now if Congress had no power to appropriate the money with which these lands were purchased, is it not clear that the power over the lands is equally limited? The mere conversion of this money into land could not confer upon Congress new power over the disposition of land which they had not possessed over money. If it could, then a trustee, by changing the character of the fund intrusted to his care for special objects from money into land, might give the land away or devote it to any purpose he thought proper, however foreign from the trust. The inference is irresistible that this land partakes of the very same character with the money paid for it, and can be devoted to no objects different from those to which the money could have been devoted. If this were not the case, then by the purchase of a new territory from a foreign government out of the public Treasury Congress could enlarge their own powers and appropriate the proceeds of the sales of the land thus purchased, at their own discretion, to other and far different objects from what they could have applied the purchase money which had been raised by taxation.

It has been asserted truly that Congress in numerous instances have granted lands for the purposes of education. These grants have been chiefly, if not exclusively, made to the new States as they successively entered the Union, and consisted at the first of one section and afterwards of two sections of the public land in each township for the use of schools, as well as of additional sections for a State university. Such grants are not, in my opinion, a violation of the Constitution. The United States is a great landed proprietor, and from the very nature of this relation it is both the right and the duty of Congress as their trustee to manage these lands as any other prudent proprietor would manage them for his own best advantage. Now no consideration could be presented of a stronger character to induce the American people to brave the difficulties and hardships of frontier life and to settle upon these lands and to purchase them at a fair price than to give to them and to their children an assurance of the means of education. If any prudent individual had held these lands, he could not have adopted a wiser course to bring them into market and enhance their value than to give a portion of them for purposes of education. As a mere speculation he would pursue this course. No person will contend that donations of land to all the States of the Union for the erection of colleges within the limits of each can be embraced by this principle. It can not be pretended that an agricultural college in New York or Virginia would aid the settlement or facilitate the sale of public lands in Minnesota or California. This can not possibly be embraced within the authority which a prudent proprietor of land would exercise over his own possessions. I purposely avoid any attempt to define what portions of land may be granted, and for what purposes, to improve the value and promote the settlement and sale of the remainder without violating the Constitution. In this case I adopt the rule that "sufficient unto the day is the evil thereof."

JAMES BUCHANAN.

PROCLAMATION.

BY THE PRESIDENT OF THE UNITED STATES OF AMERICA.

A PROCLAMATION.

Whereas an extraordinary occasion has occurred rendering it necessary and proper that the Senate of the United States shall be convened to receive and act upon such communications as have been or may be made to it on the part of the Executive:

Now, therefore, I, James Buchanan, President of the United States, do issue this my proclamation, declaring that an extraordinary occasion requires the Senate of the United States to convene for the transaction of business at the Capitol, in the city of Washington, on the 4th day of next month, at 12 o'clock at noon of that day, of which all who shall then be entitled to act as members of that body are hereby required to take notice.

Given under my hand and the seal of the United States, at Washing-
[SEAL.] ton, this 26th day of February, A. D. 1859, and of the Independence of the United States the eighty-third.

JAMES BUCHANAN.

By the President:
LEWIS CASS, *Secretary of State.*

SPECIAL MESSAGE.

WASHINGTON, *March 9, 1859.*

To the Senate of the United States:

It has become my sad duty to announce to the Senate the death of
Aaron V. Brown, late Postmaster-General, at his residence in this city on
yesterday morning at twenty minutes past 9 o'clock.

The death of this distinguished public officer, especially at the present
moment, when his eminent services are so much needed, is a great loss to
his country. He was able, honest, and indefatigable in the discharge
of his high and responsible duties, whilst his benevolent heart and his
kind deportment endeared him to all who approached him.

Submitting, as I do, with humble resignation to the will of Divine
Providence in this calamitous dispensation, I shall ever cherish his memory with affectionate regard.

JAMES BUCHANAN.

EXECUTIVE ORDERS.

[From the Evening Star, March 10, 1859.]

GENERAL ORDER.

WAR DEPARTMENT,
Washington, March 8, 1859.

Under instructions from the President of the United States, the Secretary of War with unfeigned sorrow announces to the Army the decease
of the Hon. A. V. Brown, Postmaster-General, which occurred in this city
at an early hour this morning.

An enlightened statesman and a distinguished and able member of
the General Government has thus been stricken down at his post. The
nation will mourn the afflicting dispensation which has left so great a
void in its councils. A worthy and estimable citizen has been removed
from the circle of his numerous friends. Society will mingle its grief
with the patriotic regrets which the loss of a statesman will not fail to
call forth.

While the President, with the surviving members of the Cabinet, the legislative and judicial departments of the Government, will unite in every testimonial the sad occasion demands, it is fitting a similar respect should be shown to the memory of the distinguished deceased by the national arms of defense. Accordingly, half-hour guns will be fired from sunrise to sunset at every garrisoned military post the day succeeding the receipt of this order, the national flag will be displayed at half-staff during the same time, and officers of the Army will wear for three months the proper badge of military mourning.

The War Department and its bureaus will be closed until the day succeeding the funeral obsequies.

JOHN B. FLOYD,
Secretary of War.

[From the Daily National Intelligencer, March 10, 1859.]

GENERAL ORDER.

NAVY DEPARTMENT, *March 9, 1859.*

The Secretary of the Navy, by the direction of the President, announces to the Navy and to the Marine Corps the lamented death of the Hon. Aaron V. Brown, Postmaster-General of the United States. He died at his residence in the city of Washington on the 8th of the present month.

As a mark of respect to his high character, his eminent position, and great public services, it is directed that on the day after the receipt of this order by the different navy-yards and stations and vessels of war of the United States in commission the flags be hoisted at half-mast from sunrise to sunset and that seventeen minute guns be fired at noon.

Officers of the Navy and Marine Corps will wear crape on the left arm for thirty days.

The Navy Department will be draped in mourning and will be closed until after the funeral.

ISAAC TOUCEY,
Secretary of the Navy.

THIRD ANNUAL MESSAGE.

WASHINGTON CITY, *December 19, 1859.*

Fellow-Citizens of the Senate and House of Representatives:

Our deep and heartfelt gratitude is due to that Almighty Power which has bestowed upon us such varied and numerous blessings throughout the past year. The general health of the country has been excellent, our harvests have been unusually plentiful, and prosperity smiles throughout the land. Indeed, notwithstanding our demerits, we have much reason to believe from the past events in our history that we have enjoyed the special protection of Divine Providence ever since our origin as a nation. We have been exposed to many threatening and alarming difficulties in our progress, but on each successive occasion the impending cloud has been dissipated at the moment it appeared ready to burst upon our head, and the danger to our institutions has passed away. May we ever be under the divine guidance and protection.

Whilst it is the duty of the President "from time to time to give to Congress information of the state of the Union," I shall not refer in detail to the recent sad and bloody occurrences at Harpers Ferry. Still, it is proper to observe that these events, however bad and cruel in themselves, derive their chief importance from the apprehension that they are but symptoms of an incurable disease in the public mind, which may break out in still more dangerous outrages and terminate at last in an open war by the North to abolish slavery in the South.

Whilst for myself I entertain no such apprehension, they ought to afford a solemn warning to us all to beware of the approach of danger. Our Union is a stake of such inestimable value as to demand our constant and watchful vigilance for its preservation. In this view, let me implore my countrymen, North and South, to cultivate the ancient feelings of mutual forbearance and good will toward each other and strive to allay the demon spirit of sectional hatred and strife now alive in the land. This advice proceeds from the heart of an old public functionary whose service commenced in the last generation, among the wise and conservative statesmen of that day, now nearly all passed away, and whose first and dearest earthly wish is to leave his country tranquil, prosperous, united, and powerful.

We ought to reflect that in this age, and especially in this country, there is an incessant flux and reflux of public opinion. Questions which in their day assumed a most threatening aspect have now nearly gone from the memory of men. They are "volcanoes burnt out, and on the lava and ashes and squalid scoria of old eruptions grow the peaceful olive, the cheering vine, and the sustaining corn." Such, in my opinion, will prove to be the fate of the present sectional excitement should those who wisely seek to apply the remedy continue always to confine their efforts within the pale of the Constitution. If this course be pursued, the existing agitation on the subject of domestic slavery, like everything human, will have its day and give place to other and less threatening controversies. Public opinion in this country is all-powerful, and when it reaches a dangerous excess upon any question the good sense of the people will furnish the corrective and bring it back within safe limits. Still, to hasten this auspicious result at the present crisis we ought to remember that every rational creature must be presumed to intend the natural consequences of his own teachings. Those who announce abstract doctrines subversive of the Constitution and the Union must not be surprised should their heated partisans advance one step further and attempt by violence to carry these doctrines into practical effect. In this view of the subject, it ought never to be forgotten that however great may have been the political advantages resulting from the Union to every portion of our common country, these would all prove to be as nothing should the time ever arrive when they can not be enjoyed without serious danger to the personal safety of the people of fifteen members of the Confederacy. If the peace of the domestic fireside throughout these States should ever be invaded, if the mothers of families within this extensive region should not be able to retire to rest at night without suffering dreadful apprehensions of what may be their own fate and that of their children before the morning, it would be vain to recount to such a people the political benefits which result to them from the Union. Self-preservation is the first instinct of nature, and therefore any state of society in which the sword is all the time suspended over the heads of the people must at last become intolerable. But I indulge in no such gloomy forebodings. On the contrary, I firmly believe that the events at Harpers Ferry, by causing the people to pause and reflect upon the possible peril to their cherished institutions, will be the means under Providence of allaying the existing excitement and preventing further outbreaks of a similar character. They will resolve that the Constitution and the Union shall not be endangered by rash counsels, knowing that should "the silver cord be loosed or the golden bowl be broken * * * at the fountain" human power could never reunite the scattered and hostile fragments.

I cordially congratulate you upon the final settlement by the Supreme Court of the United States of the question of slavery in the Territories, which had presented an aspect so truly formidable at the commencement of my Administration. The right has been established of every citizen to take his property of any kind, including slaves, into the common Territories belonging equally to all the States of the Confederacy, and to have it protected there under the Federal Constitution. Neither Congress nor a Territorial legislature nor any human power has any authority to annul or impair this vested right. The supreme judicial tribunal of the country, which is a coordinate branch of the Government, has sanctioned and affirmed these principles of constitutional law, so manifestly just in themselves and so well calculated to promote peace and harmony among the States. It is a striking proof of the sense of justice which is inherent in our people that the property in slaves has never been disturbed, to my knowledge, in any of the Territories. Even throughout the late troubles in Kansas there has not been any attempt, as I am credibly informed, to interfere in a single instance with the right of the master. Had any such attempt been made, the judiciary would doubtless have afforded an adequate remedy. Should they fail to do this hereafter, it will then be time enough to strengthen their hands by further legislation. Had it been decided that either Congress or the Territorial legislature possess the power to annul or impair the right to property in slaves, the evil would be intolerable. In the latter event there would be a struggle for a majority of the members of the legislature at each successive election, and the sacred rights of property held under the Federal Constitution would depend for the time being on the result. The agitation would thus be rendered incessant whilst the Territorial condition remained, and its baneful influence would keep alive a dangerous excitement among the people of the several States.

Thus has the status of a Territory during the intermediate period from its first settlement until it shall become a State been irrevocably fixed by the final decision of the Supreme Court. Fortunate has this been for the prosperity of the Territories, as well as the tranquillity of the States. Now emigrants from the North and the South, the East and the West, will meet in the Territories on a common platform, having brought with them that species of property best adapted, in their own opinion, to promote their welfare. From natural causes the slavery question will in each case soon virtually settle itself, and before the Territory is prepared for admission as a State into the Union this decision, one way or the other, will have been a foregone conclusion. Meanwhile the settlement of the new Territory will proceed without serious interruption, and its progress and prosperity will not be endangered or retarded by violent political struggles.

When in the progress of events the inhabitants of any Territory shall have reached the number required to form a State, they will then proceed in a regular manner and in the exercise of the rights of popular sovereignty to form a constitution preparatory to admission into the Union. After this has been done, to employ the language of the Kansas and Nebraska act, they "shall be received into the Union with or without slavery, as their constitution may prescribe at the time of their admission." This sound principle has happily been recognized in some form or other by an almost unanimous vote of both Houses of the last Congress.

All lawful means at my command have been employed, and shall continue to be employed, to execute the laws against the African slave trade. After a most careful and rigorous examination of our coasts and a thorough investigation of the subject, we have not been able to discover that any slaves have been imported into the United States except the cargo by the *Wanderer*, numbering between three and four hundred. Those engaged in this unlawful enterprise have been rigorously prosecuted, but not with as much success as their crimes have deserved. A number of them are still under prosecution.

Our history proves that the fathers of the Republic, in advance of all other nations, condemned the African slave trade. It was, notwithstanding, deemed expedient by the framers of the Constitution to deprive Congress of the power to prohibit "the migration or importation of such persons as any of the States now existing shall think proper to admit'' ''prior to the year 1808.'' It will be seen that this restriction on the power of Congress was confined to such States only as might think proper to admit the importation of slaves. It did not extend to other States or to the trade carried on abroad. Accordingly, we find that so early as the 22d March, 1794, Congress passed an act imposing severe penalties and punishments upon citizens and residents of the United States who should engage in this trade between foreign nations. The provisions of this act were extended and enforced by the act of 10th May, 1800.

Again, the States themselves had a clear right to waive the constitutional privilege intended for their benefit, and to prohibit by their own laws this trade at any time they thought proper previous to 1808. Several of them exercised this right before that period, and among them some containing the greatest number of slaves. This gave to Congress the immediate power to act in regard to all such States, because they themselves had removed the constitutional barrier. Congress accordingly passed an act on 28th February, 1803, ''to prevent the importation of certain persons into certain States where by the laws thereof their admission is prohibited.'' In this manner the importation of African slaves into the United States was to a great extent prohibited some years in advance of 1808.

As the year 1808 approached Congress determined not to suffer this trade to exist even for a single day after they had the power to abolish it. On the 2d of March, 1807, they passed an act, to take effect ''from and after the 1st day of January, 1808,'' prohibiting the importation of African slaves into the United States. This was followed by subsequent acts of a similar character, to which I need not specially refer. Such were the principles and such the practice of our ancestors more than fifty years ago in regard to the African slave trade. It did not occur to the revered patriots who had been delegates to the Convention, and afterwards became members of Congress, that in passing these laws they had violated the Constitution which they had framed with so much care and deliberation. They supposed that to prohibit Congress in express terms from exercising a specified power before an appointed day necessarily involved the right to exercise this power after that day had arrived.

If this were not the case, the framers of the Constitution had expended much labor in vain. Had they imagined that Congress would possess no power to prohibit the trade either before or after 1808, they would not have taken so much care to protect the States against the exercise of this power before that period. Nay, more, they would not have attached such vast importance to this provision as to have excluded it from the possibility of future repeal or amendment, to which other portions of the Constitution were exposed. It would, then, have been wholly unnecessary to ingraft on the fifth article of the Constitution, prescribing the mode of its own future amendment, the proviso "that no amendment which may be made prior to the year 1808 shall in any manner affect" the provision in the Constitution securing to the States the right to admit the importation of African slaves previous to that period. According to the adverse construction, the clause itself, on which so much care and discussion had been employed by the members of the Convention, was an absolute nullity from the beginning, and all that has since been done under it a mere usurpation.

It was well and wise to confer this power on Congress, because had it been left to the States its efficient exercise would have been impossible. In that event any one State could have effectually continued the trade, not only for itself, but for all the other slave States, though never so much against their will. And why? Because African slaves, when once brought within the limits of any one State in accordance with its laws, can not practically be excluded from any State where slavery exists. And even if all the States had separately passed laws prohibiting the importation of slaves, these laws would have failed of effect for want of a naval force to capture the slavers and to guard the coast. Such a force no State can employ in time of peace without the consent of Congress.

These acts of Congress, it is believed, have, with very rare and insignificant exceptions, accomplished their purpose. For a period of more than half a century there has been no perceptible addition to the number of our domestic slaves. During this period their advancement in civilization has far surpassed that of any other portion of the African race. The light and the blessings of Christianity have been extended to them, and both their moral and physical condition has been greatly improved.

Reopen the trade and it would be difficult to determine whether the effect would be more deleterious on the interests of the master or on those of the native-born slave. Of the evils to the master, the one most to be dreaded would be the introduction of wild, heathen, and ignorant barbarians among the sober, orderly, and quiet slaves whose ancestors have been on the soil for several generations. This might tend to barbarize, demoralize, and exasperate the whole mass and produce most deplorable consequences.

The effect upon the existing slave would, if possible, be still more deplorable. At present he is treated with kindness and humanity. He is well fed, well clothed, and not overworked. His condition is incomparably better than that of the coolies which modern nations of high civilization have employed as a substitute for African slaves. Both the philanthropy and the self-interest of the master have combined to produce this humane result. But let this trade be reopened and what will be the effect? The same to a considerable extent as on a neighboring island, the only spot now on earth where the African slave trade is openly tolerated, and this in defiance of solemn treaties with a power abundantly able at any moment to enforce their execution. There the master, intent upon present gain, extorts from the slave as much labor as his physical powers are capable of enduring, knowing that when death comes to his relief his place can be supplied at a price reduced to the lowest point by the competition of rival African slave traders. Should this ever be the case in our country, which I do not deem possible, the present useful character of the domestic institution, wherein those too old and too young to work are provided for with care and humanity and those capable of labor are not overtasked, would undergo an unfortunate change. The feeling of reciprocal dependence and attachment which now exists between master and slave would be converted into mutual distrust and hostility.

But we are obliged as a Christian and moral nation to consider what would be the effect upon unhappy Africa itself if we should reopen the slave trade. This would give the trade an impulse and extension which it has never had, even in its palmiest days. The numerous victims required to supply it would convert the whole slave coast into a perfect pandemonium, for which this country would be held responsible in the eyes both of God and man. Its petty tribes would then be constantly engaged in predatory wars against each other for the purpose of seizing slaves to supply the American market. All hopes of African civilization would thus be ended.

On the other hand, when a market for African slaves shall no longer be furnished in Cuba, and thus all the world be closed against this trade, we may then indulge a reasonable hope for the gradual improvement of Africa. The chief motive of war among the tribes will cease whenever there is no longer any demand for slaves. The resources of that fertile but miserable country might then be developed by the hand of industry and afford subjects for legitimate foreign and domestic commerce. In this manner Christianity and civilization may gradually penetrate the existing gloom.

The wisdom of the course pursued by this Government toward China has been vindicated by the event. Whilst we sustained a neutral position in the war waged by Great Britain and France against the Chinese Empire, our late minister, in obedience to his instructions, judiciously coöperated with the ministers of these powers in all peaceful measures to secure by treaty the just concessions demanded by the interests of foreign commerce. The result is that satisfactory treaties have been concluded with China by the respective ministers of the United States, Great Britain, France, and Russia. Our "treaty, or general convention, of peace, amity, and commerce" with that Empire was concluded at Tien-tsin on the 18th June, 1858, and was ratified by the President, by and with the advice and consent of the Senate, on the 21st December following. On the 15th December, 1858, John E. Ward, a distinguished citizen of Georgia, was duly commissioned as envoy extraordinary and minister plenipotentiary to China.

He left the United States for the place of his destination on the 5th of February, 1859, bearing with him the ratified copy of this treaty, and arrived at Shanghai on the 28th May. From thence he proceeded to Peking on the 16th June, but did not arrive in that city until the 27th July. According to the terms of the treaty, the ratifications were to be exchanged on or before the 18th June, 1859. This was rendered impossible by reasons and events beyond his control, not necessary to detail; but still it is due to the Chinese authorities at Shanghai to state that they always assured him no advantage should be taken of the delay, and this pledge has been faithfully redeemed.

On the arrival of Mr. Ward at Peking he requested an audience of the Emperor to present his letter of credence. This he did not obtain, in consequence of his very proper refusal to submit to the humiliating ceremonies required by the etiquette of this strange people in approaching their sovereign. Nevertheless, the interviews on this question were conducted in the most friendly spirit and with all due regard to his personal feelings and the honor of his country. When a presentation to His Majesty was found to be impossible, the letter of credence from the President was received with peculiar honors by Kweiliang, "the Emperor's prime minister and the second man in the Empire to the Emperor himself." The ratifications of the treaty were afterwards, on the 16th of August, exchanged in proper form at Pei-tsang. As the exchange did not take place until after the day prescribed by the treaty, it is deemed proper before its publication again to submit it to the Senate. It is but simple justice to the Chinese authorities to observe that throughout the whole transaction they appear to have acted in good faith and in a friendly spirit toward the United States. It is true this has been done after their own peculiar fashion; but we ought to regard with a lenient eye the ancient customs of an empire dating back for thousands of years, so far as this may be consistent with our own national honor. The conduct of our minister on the occasion has received my entire approbation.

In order to carry out the spirit of this treaty and to give it full effect it became necessary to conclude two supplemental conventions, the one for the adjustment and satisfaction of the claims of our citizens and the other to fix the tariff on imports and exports and to regulate the transit duties and trade of our merchants with China. This duty was satisfactorily performed by our late minister. These conventions bear date at Shanghai on the 8th November, 1858. Having been considered in the light of binding agreements subsidiary to the principal treaty, and to be carried into execution without delay, they do not provide for any formal ratification or exchange of ratifications by the contracting parties. This was not deemed necessary by the Chinese, who are already proceeding in good faith to satisfy the claims of our citizens and, it is hoped, to carry out the other provisions of the conventions. Still, I thought it was proper to submit them to the Senate, by which they were ratified on the

3d of March, 1859. The ratified copies, however, did not reach Shanghai until after the departure of our minister to Peking, and these conventions could not, therefore, be exchanged at the same time with the principal treaty. No doubt is entertained that they will be ratified and exchanged by the Chinese Government should this be thought advisable; but under the circumstances presented I shall consider them binding engagements from their date on both parties, and cause them to be published as such for the information and guidance of our merchants trading with the Chinese Empire.

It affords me much satisfaction to inform you that all our difficulties with the Republic of Paraguay have been satisfactorily adjusted. It happily did not become necessary to employ the force for this purpose which Congress had placed at my command under the joint resolution of 2d June, 1858. On the contrary, the President of that Republic, in a friendly spirit, acceded promptly to the just and reasonable demands of the Government of the United States. Our commissioner arrived at Assumption, the capital of the Republic, on the 25th of January, 1859, and left it on the 17th of February, having in three weeks ably and successfully accomplished all the objects of his mission. The treaties which he has concluded will be immediately submitted to the Senate.

In the view that the employment of other than peaceful means might become necessary to obtain ''just satisfaction'' from Paraguay, a strong naval force was concentrated in the waters of the La Plata to await contingencies whilst our commissioner ascended the rivers to Assumption. The Navy Department is entitled to great credit for the promptness, efficiency, and economy with which this expedition was fitted out and conducted. It consisted of 19 armed vessels, great and small, carrying 200 guns and 2,500 men, all under the command of the veteran and gallant Shubrick. The entire expenses of the expedition have been defrayed out of the ordinary appropriations for the naval service, except the sum of $289,000, applied to the purchase of seven of the steamers constituting a part of it, under the authority of the naval appropriation act of the 3d March last. It is believed that these steamers are worth more than their cost, and they are all now usefully and actively employed in the naval service.

The appearance of so large a force, fitted out in such a prompt manner, in the far-distant waters of the La Plata, and the admirable conduct of the officers and men employed in it, have had a happy effect in favor of our country throughout all that remote portion of the world.

Our relations with the great Empires of France and Russia, as well as with all other governments on the continent of Europe, unless we may except that of Spain, happily continue to be of the most friendly character.

In my last annual message I presented a statement of the unsatisfactory condition of our relations with Spain, and I regret to say that this has not materially improved.

Without special reference to other claims, even the "Cuban claims," the payment of which has been ably urged by our ministers, and in which more than a hundred of our citizens are directly interested, remain unsatisfied, notwithstanding both their justice and their amount ($128,635.54) had been recognized and ascertained by the Spanish Government itself.

I again recommend that an appropriation be made "to be paid to the Spanish Government for the purpose of distribution among the claimants in the *Amistad* case." In common with two of my predecessors, I entertain no doubt that this is required by our treaty with Spain of the 27th October, 1795. The failure to discharge this obligation has been employed by the cabinet of Madrid as a reason against the settlement of our claims.

I need not repeat the arguments which I urged in my last annual message in favor of the acquisition of Cuba by fair purchase. My opinions on that measure remain unchanged. I therefore again invite the serious attention of Congress to this important subject. Without a recognition of this policy on their part it will be almost impossible to institute negotiations with any reasonable prospect of success.

Until a recent period there was good reason to believe that I should be able to announce to you on the present occasion that our difficulties with Great Britain arising out of the Clayton and Bulwer treaty had been finally adjusted in a manner alike honorable and satisfactory to both parties. From causes, however, which the British Government had not anticipated, they have not yet completed treaty arrangements with the Republics of Honduras and Nicaragua, in pursuance of the understanding between the two Governments. It is, nevertheless, confidently expected that this good work will ere long be accomplished.

Whilst indulging the hope that no other subject remained which could disturb the good understanding between the two countries, the question arising out of the adverse claims of the parties to the island of San Juan, under the Oregon treaty of the 15th June, 1846, suddenly assumed a threatening prominence. In order to prevent unfortunate collisions on that remote frontier, the late Secretary of State, on the 17th July, 1855, addressed a note to Mr. Crampton, then British minister at Washington, communicating to him a copy of the instructions which he (Mr. Marcy) had given on the 14th July to Governor Stevens, of Washington Territory, having a special reference to an "apprehended conflict between our citizens and the British subjects on the island of San Juan." To prevent this the governor was instructed "that the officers of the Territory should abstain from all acts on the disputed grounds which are calculated to provoke any conflicts, so far as it can be done without implying the concession to the authorities of Great Britain of an exclusive right over the premises. The title ought to be settled before either party should attempt to exclude the other by force or exercise complete and exclusive sovereign rights within the fairly disputed limits."

In acknowledging the receipt on the next day of Mr. Marcy's note the British minister expressed his entire concurrence "in the propriety of the course recommended to the governor of Washington Territory by your [Mr. Marcy's] instructions to that officer," and stating that he had "lost no time in transmitting a copy of that document to the Governor-General of British North America" and had "earnestly recommended to His Excellency to take such measures as to him may appear best calculated to secure on the part of the British local authorities and the inhabitants of the neighborhood of the line in question the exercise of the same spirit of forbearance which is inculcated by you [Mr. Marcy] on the authorities and citizens of the United States."

Thus matters remained upon the faith of this arrangement until the 9th July last, when General Harney paid a visit to the island. He found upon it twenty-five American residents with their families, and also an establishment of the Hudsons Bay Company for the purpose of raising sheep. A short time before his arrival one of these residents had shot an animal belonging to the company whilst trespassing upon his premises, for which, however, he offered to pay twice its value, but that was refused. Soon after "the chief factor of the company at Victoria, Mr. Dalles, son-in-law of Governor Douglas, came to the island in the British sloop of war *Satellite* and threatened to take this American [Mr. Cutler] by force to Victoria to answer for the trespass he had committed. The American seized his rifle and told Mr. Dalles if any such attempt was made he would kill him upon the spot. The affair then ended."

Under these circumstances the American settlers presented a petition to the General "through the United States inspector of customs, Mr. Hubbs, to place a force upon the island to protect them from the Indians, as well as the oppressive interference of the authorities of the Hudsons Bay Company at Victoria with their rights as American citizens." The General immediately responded to this petition, and ordered Captain George E. Pickett, Ninth Infantry, "to establish his company on Bellevue, or San Juan Island, on some suitable position near the harbor at the southeastern extremity." This order was promptly obeyed and a military post was established at the place designated. The force was afterwards increased, so that by the last return the whole number of troops then on the island amounted in the aggregate to 691 men.

Whilst I do not deem it proper on the present occasion to go further into the subject and discuss the weight which ought to be attached to the statements of the British colonial authorities contesting the accuracy of the information on which the gallant General acted, it was due to him that I should thus present his own reasons for issuing the order to Captain Pickett. From these it is quite clear his object was to prevent the British authorities on Vancouvers Island from exercising jurisdiction over American residents on the island of San Juan, as well as to protect them against the incursions of the Indians. Much excitement prevailed for some time throughout that region, and serious danger of collision between the parties was apprehended. The British had a large naval force in the vicinity, and it is but an act of simple justice to the admiral on that station to state that he wisely and discreetly forbore to commit any hostile act, but determined to refer the whole affair to his Government and await their instructions.

This aspect of the matter, in my opinion, demanded serious attention. It would have been a great calamity for both nations had they been precipitated into acts of hostility, not on the question of title to the island, but merely concerning what should be its condition during the intervening period whilst the two Governments might be employed in settling the question to which of them it belongs. For this reason Lieutenant-General Scott was dispatched, on the 17th of September last, to Washington Territory to take immediate command of the United States forces on the Pacific Coast, should he deem this necessary. The main object of his mission was to carry out the spirit of the precautionary arrangement between the late Secretary of State and the British minister, and thus to preserve the peace and prevent collision between the British and American authorities pending the negotiations between the two Governments. Entertaining no doubt of the validity of our title, I need scarcely add that in any event American citizens were to be placed on a footing at least as favorable as that of British subjects, it being understood that Captain Pickett's company should remain on the island. It is proper to observe that, considering the distance from the scene of action and in ignorance of what might have transpired on the spot before the General's arrival, it was necessary to leave much to his discretion; and I am happy to state the event has proven that this discretion could not have been intrusted to more competent hands. General Scott has recently returned from his mission, having successfully accomplished its objects, and there is no longer any good reason to apprehend a collision between the forces of the two countries during the pendency of the existing negotiations.

I regret to inform you that there has been no improvement in the affairs of Mexico since my last annual message, and I am again obliged to ask the earnest attention of Congress to the unhappy condition of that Republic.

The constituent Congress of Mexico, which adjourned on the 17th February, 1857, adopted a constitution and provided for a popular election. This took place in the following July (1857), and General Comonfort was chosen President almost without opposition. At the same election a new Congress was chosen, whose first session commenced on the 16th of September (1857). By the constitution of 1857 the Presidential term was to begin on the 1st of December (1857) and continue for four years. On that day General Comonfort appeared before the assembled Congress in the City of Mexico, took the oath to support the new constitution, and was duly inaugurated as President. Within a month afterwards he had been driven from the capital and a military rebellion had assigned the supreme power of the Republic to General Zuloaga. The constitution provided that in the absence of the President his office should devolve upon the chief justice of the supreme court; and General Comonfort having left the country, this functionary, General Juarez, proceeded to form at Guanajuato a constitutional Government. Before this was officially known, however, at the capital the Government of Zuloaga had been recognized by the entire diplomatic corps, including the minister of the United States, as the *de facto* Government of Mexico. The constitutional President, nevertheless, maintained his position with firmness, and was soon established, with his cabinet, at Vera Cruz. Meanwhile the Government of Zuloaga was earnestly resisted in many parts of the Republic, and even in the capital, a portion of the army having pronounced against it, its functions were declared terminated, and an assembly of citizens was invited for the choice of a new President. This assembly elected General Miramon, but that officer repudiated the plan under which he was chosen, and Zuloaga was thus restored to his previous position. He assumed it, however, only to withdraw from it; and Miramon, having become by his appointment ''President substitute,'' continues with that title at the head of the insurgent party.

In my last annual message I communicated to Congress the circumstances under which the late minister of the United States suspended his official relations with the central Government and withdrew from the country. It was impossible to maintain friendly intercourse with a government like that at the capital, under whose usurped authority wrongs were constantly committed, but never redressed. Had this been an established government, with its power extending by the consent of the people over the whole of Mexico, a resort to hostilities against it would have been quite justifiable, and, indeed, necessary. But the country was a prey to civil war, and it was hoped that the success of the constitutional President might lead to a condition of things less injurious to the United States. This success became so probable that in January last I employed a reliable agent to visit Mexico and report to me the actual condition and prospects of the contending parties. In consequence of his report and from information which reached me from other sources favorable to the prospects of the constitutional cause, I felt justified in appointing a new minister to Mexico, who might embrace the earliest suitable opportunity of restoring our diplomatic relations with that Republic. For this purpose a distinguished citizen of Maryland was selected, who proceeded on his mission on the 8th of March last, with discretionary authority to recognize the Government of President Juarez if on his arrival in Mexico he should find it entitled to such recognition according to the established practice of the United States.

On the 7th of April following Mr. McLane presented his credentials to President Juarez, having no hesitation ''in pronouncing the Government of Juarez to be the only existing government of the Republic." He was cordially received by the authorities at Vera Cruz, and they have ever since manifested the most friendly disposition toward the United States.

Unhappily, however, the constitutional Government has not been able to establish its power over the whole Republic.

It is supported by a large majority of the people and the States, but there are important parts of the country where it can enforce no obedience.

General Miramon maintains himself at the capital, and in some of the distant Provinces there are military governors who pay little respect to the decrees of either Government. In the meantime the excesses which always attend upon civil war, especially in Mexico, are constantly recurring. Outrages of the worst description are committed both upon persons and property. There is scarcely any form of injury which has not been suffered by our citizens in Mexico during the last few years. We have been nominally at peace with that Republic, but "so far as the interests of our commerce, or of our citizens who have visited the country as merchants, shipmasters, or in other capacities, are concerned, we might as well have been at war." Life has been insecure, property unprotected, and trade impossible except at a risk of loss which prudent men can not be expected to incur. Important contracts, involving large expenditures, entered into by the central Government, have been set at defiance by the local governments. Peaceful American residents, occupying their rightful possessions, have been suddenly expelled the country, in defiance of treaties and by the mere force of arbitrary power. Even the course of justice has not been safe from control, and a recent decree of Miramon permits the intervention of Government in all suits where either party is a foreigner. Vessels of the United States have been seized without law, and a consular officer who protested against such seizure has been fined and imprisoned for disrespect to the authorities. Military contributions have been levied in violation of every principle of right, and the American who resisted the lawless demand has had his property forcibly taken away and has been himself banished. From a conflict of authority in different parts of the country tariff duties which have been paid in one place have been exacted over again in another place. Large numbers of our citizens have been arrested and imprisoned without any form of examination or any opportunity for a hearing, and even when released have only obtained their liberty after much suffering and injury, and without any hope of redress. The wholesale massacre of Crabbe and his associates without trial in Sonora, as well as the seizure and murder of four sick Americans who had taken shelter in the house of an American upon the soil of the United States, was communicated to Congress at its last session. Murders of a still more atrocious character have been committed in the very heart of Mexico, under the authority of Miramon's Government, during the present year. Some of these were only worthy of a barbarous age, and if they had not been clearly proven would have seemed impossible in a country which claims to be civilized. Of this description was the brutal massacre in April last, by order of General Marquez, of three American physicians who were seized in the hospital at Tacubaya while attending upon the sick and the dying of both parties, and without trial, as without crime, were hurried away to speedy execution. Little less shocking was the recent fate of Ormond Chase, who was shot in Tepic on the 7th of August by order of the same Mexican general, not only without a trial, but without any conjecture by his friends of the cause of his arrest. He is represented as a young man of good character and intelligence, who had made numerous friends in Tepic by the courage and humanity which he had displayed on several trying occasions; and his death was as unexpected as it was shocking to the whole community. Other outrages might be enumerated, but these are sufficient to illustrate the wretched state of the country and the unprotected condition of the persons and property of our citizens in Mexico.

In all these cases our ministers have been constant and faithful in their demands for redress, but both they and this Government, which they have successively represented, have been wholly powerless to make their demands effective. Their testimony in this respect and in reference to the only remedy which in their judgments would meet the exigency has been both uniform and emphatic. "Nothing but a manifestation of the power of the Government of the United States," wrote our late minister in 1856, "and of its purpose to punish these wrongs will avail. I assure you that the universal belief here is that there is nothing to be apprehended from the Government of the United States, and that local Mexican officials can commit these outrages upon American citizens with absolute impunity." "I hope the President," wrote our present minister in August last, "will feel authorized to ask from Congress the power to enter Mexico with the military forces of the United States at the call of the constitutional authorities, in order to protect the citizens and the treaty rights of the United States. Unless such a power is conferred upon him, neither the one nor the other will be respected in the existing state of anarchy and disorder, and the outrages already perpetrated will never be chastised; and, as I assured you in my No. 23, all these evils must increase until every vestige of order and government disappears from the country." I have been reluctantly led to the same opinion, and in justice to my countrymen who have suffered wrongs from Mexico and who may still suffer them I feel bound to announce this conclusion to Congress.

The case presented, however, is not merely a case of individual claims, although our just claims against Mexico have reached a very large amount; nor is it merely the case of protection to the lives and property of the few Americans who may still remain in Mexico, although the life and property of every American citizen ought to be sacredly protected in every quarter of the world; but it is a question which relates to the future as well as to the present and the past, and which involves, indirectly at least, the whole subject of our duty to Mexico as a neighboring State. The exercise of the power of the United States in that country to redress the wrongs and protect the rights of our own citizens is none the less to be desired because efficient and necessary aid may thus be rendered at the same time to restore peace and order to Mexico itself. In the accomplishment of this result the people of the United States must necessarily feel a deep and earnest interest. Mexico ought to be a rich and prosperous and powerful Republic. She possesses an extensive territory, a fertile soil, and an incalculable store of mineral wealth. She occupies an important position between the Gulf and the ocean for transit routes and for commerce. Is it possible that such a country as this can be given up to anarchy and ruin without an effort from any quarter for its rescue and its safety? Will the commercial nations of the world, which have so many interests connected with it, remain wholly indifferent to such a result? Can the United States especially, which ought to share most largely in its commercial intercourse, allow their immediate neighbor thus to destroy itself and injure them? Yet without support from some quarter it is impossible to perceive how Mexico can resume her position among nations and enter upon a career which promises any good results. The aid which she requires, and which the interests of all commercial countries require that she should have, it belongs to this Government to render, not only by virtue of our neighborhood to Mexico, along whose territory we have a continuous frontier of nearly a thousand miles, but by virtue also of our established policy, which is inconsistent with the intervention of any European power in the domestic concerns of that Republic.

The wrongs which we have suffered from Mexico are before the world and must deeply impress every American citizen. A government which is either unable or unwilling to redress such wrongs is derelict to its highest duties. The difficulty consists in selecting and enforcing the remedy. We may in vain apply to the constitutional Government at Vera Cruz, although it is well disposed to do us justice, for adequate redress. Whilst its authority is acknowledged in all the important ports and throughout the seacoasts of the Republic, its power does not extend to the City of Mexico and the States in its vicinity, where nearly all the recent outrages have been committed on American citizens. We must penetrate into the interior before we can reach the offenders, and this can only be done by passing through the territory in the occupation of the constitutional Government. The most acceptable and least difficult mode of accomplishing the object will be to act in concert with that Government. Their consent and their aid might, I believe, be obtained; but if not, our obligation to protect our own citizens in their just rights secured by treaty would not be the less imperative. For these reasons I recommend to Congress to pass a law authorizing the President, under such conditions as they may deem expedient, to employ a sufficient military force to enter Mexico for the purpose of obtaining indemnity for the past and security for the future. I purposely refrain from any suggestion as to whether this force shall consist of regular troops or volunteers, or both. This question may be most appropriately left to the decision of Congress. I would merely observe that should volunteers be selected such a force could be easily raised in this country among those who sympathize with the sufferings of our unfortunate fellow-citizens in Mexico and with the unhappy condition of that Republic. Such an accession to the forces of the constitutional Government would enable it soon to reach the City of Mexico and extend its power over the whole Republic. In that event there is no reason to doubt that the just claims of our citizens would be satisfied and adequate redress obtained for the injuries inflicted upon them. The constitutional Government have ever evinced a strong desire to do justice, and this might be secured in advance by a preliminary treaty.

It may be said that these measures will, at least indirectly, be inconsistent with our wise and settled policy not to interfere in the domestic concerns of foreign nations. But does not the present case fairly constitute an exception? An adjoining Republic is in a state of anarchy and confusion from which she has proved wholly unable to extricate herself. She is entirely destitute of the power to maintain peace upon her borders or to prevent the incursions of banditti into our territory. In her fate and in her fortune, in her power to establish and maintain a settled government, we have a far deeper interest, socially, commercially, and politically, than any other nation. She is now a wreck upon the ocean, drifting about as she is impelled by different factions. As a good neighbor, shall we not extend to her a helping hand to save her? If we do not, it would not be surprising should some other nation undertake the task, and thus force us to interfere at last, under circumstances of increased difficulty, for the maintenance of our established policy.

I repeat the recommendation contained in my last annual message that authority may be given to the President to establish one or more temporary military posts across the Mexican line in Sonora and Chihuahua, where these may be necessary to protect the lives and property of American and Mexican citizens against the incursions and depredations of the Indians, as well as of lawless rovers, on that remote region. The establishment of one such post at a point called Arispe, in Sonora, in a country now almost depopulated by the hostile inroads of the Indians from our side of the line, would, it is believed, have prevented much injury and many cruelties during the past season. A state of lawlessness and violence prevails on that distant frontier. Life and property are there wholly insecure. The population of Arizona, now numbering more than 10,000 souls, are practically destitute of government, of laws, or of any regular administration of justice. Murder, rapine, and other crimes are committed with impunity. I therefore again call the attention of Congress to the necessity for establishing a Territorial government over Arizona.

The treaty with Nicaragua of the 16th of February, 1857, to which I referred in my last annual message, failed to receive the ratification of the Government of that Republic, for reasons which I need not enumerate. A similar treaty has been since concluded between the parties, bearing date on the 16th March, 1859, which has already been ratified by the Nicaraguan Congress. This will be immediately submitted to the Senate for their ratification. Its provisions can not, I think, fail to be acceptable to the people of both countries.

Our claims against the Governments of Costa Rica and Nicaragua remain unredressed, though they are pressed in an earnest manner and not without hope of success.

I deem it to be my duty once more earnestly to recommend to Congress the passage of a law authorizing the President to employ the naval force at his command for the purpose of protecting the lives and property of American citizens passing in transit across the Panama, Nicaragua, and Tehuantepec routes against sudden and lawless outbreaks and depredations. I shall not repeat the arguments employed in former messages in support of this measure. Suffice it to say that the lives of many of our people and the security of vast amounts of treasure passing and repassing over one or more of these routes between the Atlantic and Pacific may be deeply involved in the action of Congress on this subject.

I would also again recommend to Congress that authority be given to the President to employ the naval force to protect American merchant vessels, their crews and cargoes, against violent and lawless seizure and confiscation in the ports of Mexico and the Spanish American States when these countries may be in a disturbed and revolutionary condition. The mere knowledge that such an authority had been conferred, as I have already stated, would of itself in a great degree prevent the evil. Neither would this require any additional appropriation for the naval service.

The chief objection urged against the grant of this authority is that Congress by conferring it would violate the Constitution; that it would be a transfer of the war-making, or, strictly speaking, the war-declaring, power to the Executive. If this were well founded, it would, of course, be conclusive. A very brief examination, however, will place this objection at rest.

Congress possess the sole and exclusive power under the Constitution "to declare war." They alone can "raise and support armies" and "provide and maintain a navy." But after Congress shall have declared war and provided the force necessary to carry it on the President, as Commander in Chief of the Army and Navy, can alone employ this force in making war against the enemy. This is the plain language, and history proves that it was the well-known intention of the framers, of the Constitution.

It will not be denied that the general "power to declare war" is without limitation and embraces within itself not only what writers on the law of nations term a public or perfect war, but also an imperfect war, and, in short, every species of hostility, however confined or limited. Without the authority of Congress the President can not fire a hostile gun in any case except to repel the attacks of an enemy. It will not be doubted that under this power Congress could, if they thought proper, authorize the President to employ the force at his command to seize a vessel belonging to an American citizen which had been illegally and unjustly captured in a foreign port and restore it to its owner. But can Congress only act after the fact, after the mischief has been done? Have they no power to confer upon the President the authority in advance to furnish instant redress should such a case afterwards occur? Must they wait until the mischief has been done, and can they apply the remedy only when it is too late? To confer this authority to meet future cases under circumstances strictly specified is as clearly within the war-declaring power as such an authority conferred upon the President by act of Congress after the deed had been done. In the progress of a great nation many exigencies must arise imperatively requiring that Congress should authorize the President to act promptly on certain conditions which may or may not afterwards arise. Our history has already presented a number of such cases. I shall refer only to the latest.

Under the resolution of June 2, 1858, "for the adjustment of difficulties with the Republic of Paraguay," the President is "authorized to adopt such measures and use such force as in his judgment may be necessary and advisable in the event of a refusal of just satisfaction by the Government of Paraguay." "Just satisfaction" for what? For "the attack on the United States steamer *Water Witch*" and "other matters referred to in the annual message of the President." Here the power is expressly granted upon the condition that the Government of Paraguay shall refuse to render this "just satisfaction." In this and other similar cases Congress have conferred upon the President power in advance to employ the Army and Navy upon the happening of contingent future events; and this most certainly is embraced within the power to declare war.

Now, if this conditional and contingent power could be constitutionally conferred upon the President in the case of Paraguay, why may it not be conferred for the purpose of protecting the lives and property of American citizens in the event that they may be violently and unlawfully attacked in passing over the transit routes to and from California or assailed by the seizure of their vessels in a foreign port? To deny this power is to render the Navy in a great degree useless for the protection of the lives and property of American citizens in countries where neither protection nor redress can be otherwise obtained.

The Thirty-fifth Congress terminated on the 3d of March, 1859, without having passed the "act making appropriations for the service of the

Post-Office Department during the fiscal year ending the 30th of June, 1860.'' This act also contained an appropriation ''to supply deficiencies in the revenue of the Post-Office Department for the year ending 30th June, 1859.'' I believe this is the first instance since the origin of the Federal Government, now more than seventy years ago, when any Congress went out of existence without having passed all the general appropriation bills necessary to carry on the Government until the regular period for the meeting of a new Congress. This event imposed on the Executive a grave responsibility. It presented a choice of evils.

Had this omission of duty occurred at the first session of the last Congress, the remedy would have been plain. I might then have instantly recalled them to complete their work, and this without expense to the Government. But on the 4th of March last there were fifteen of the thirty-three States which had not elected any Representatives to the present Congress. Had Congress been called together immediately, these States would have been virtually disfranchised. If an intermediate period had been selected, several of the States would have been compelled to hold extra sessions of their legislatures, at great inconvenience and expense, to provide for elections at an earlier day than that previously fixed by law. In the regular course ten of these States would not elect until after the beginning of August, and five of these ten not until October and November.

On the other hand, when I came to examine carefully the condition of the Post-Office Department, I did not meet as many or as great difficulties as I had apprehended. Had the bill which failed been confined to appropriations for the fiscal year ending on the 30th June next, there would have been no reason of pressing importance for the call of an extra session. Nothing would become due on contracts (those with railroad companies only excepted) for carrying the mail for the first quarter of the present fiscal year, commencing on the 1st of July, until the 1st of December—less than one week before the meeting of the present Congress. The reason is that the mail contractors for this and the current year did not complete their first quarter's service until the 30th September last, and by the terms of their contracts sixty days more are allowed for the settlement of their accounts before the Department could be called upon for payment.

The great difficulty and the great hardship consisted in the failure to provide for the payment of the deficiency in the fiscal year ending the 30th June, 1859. The Department had entered into contracts, in obedience to existing laws, for the service of that fiscal year, and the contractors were fairly entitled to their compensation as it became due. The deficiency as stated in the bill amounted to $3,838,728, but after a careful settlement of all these accounts it has been ascertained that it amounts to $4,296,009. With the scanty means at his command the Postmaster-General has managed to pay that portion of this deficiency which occurred in the first two quarters of the past fiscal year, ending on the 31st

December last. In the meantime the contractors themselves, under these trying circumstances, have behaved in a manner worthy of all commendation. They had one resource in the midst of their embarrassments. After the amount due to each of them had been ascertained and finally settled according to law, this became a specific debt of record against the United States, which enabled them to borrow money on this unquestionable security. Still, they were obliged to pay interest in consequence of the default of Congress, and on every principle of justice ought to receive interest from the Government. This interest should commence from the date when a warrant would have issued for the payment of the principal had an appropriation been made for this purpose. Calculated up to the 1st December, it will not exceed $96,660—a sum not to be taken into account when contrasted with the great difficulties and embarrassments of a public and private character, both to the people and the States, which would have resulted from convening and holding a special session of Congress.

For these reasons I recommend the passage of a bill at as early a day as may be practicable to provide for the payment of the amount, with interest, due to these last-mentioned contractors, as well as to make the necessary appropriations for the service of the Post-Office Department for the current fiscal year.

The failure to pass the Post-Office bill necessarily gives birth to serious reflections. Congress, by refusing to pass the general appropriation bills necessary to carry on the Government, may not only arrest its action, but might even destroy its existence. The Army, the Navy, the judiciary, in short, every department of the Government, can no longer perform their functions if Congress refuse the money necessary for their support. If this failure should teach the country the necessity of electing a full Congress in sufficient time to enable the President to convene them in any emergency, even immediately after the old Congress has expired, it will have been productive of great good. In a time of sudden and alarming danger, foreign or domestic, which all nations must expect to encounter in their progress, the very salvation of our institutions may be staked upon the assembling of Congress without delay. If under such circumstances the President should find himself in the condition in which he was placed at the close of the last Congress, with nearly half the States of the Union destitute of representatives, the consequences might be disastrous. I therefore recommend to Congress to carry into effect the provisions of the Constitution on this subject, and to pass a law appointing some day previous to the 4th March in each year of odd number for the election of Representatives throughout all the States. They have already appointed a day for the election of electors for President and Vice-President, and this measure has been approved by the country.

I would again express a most decided opinion in favor of the construction of a Pacific railroad, for the reasons stated in my two last annual messages. When I reflect upon what would be the defenseless condition of our States and Territories west of the Rocky Mountains in case of a war with a naval power sufficiently strong to interrupt all intercourse with them by the routes across the Isthmus, I am still more convinced than ever of the vast importance of this railroad. I have never doubted the constitutional competency of Congress to provide for its construction, but this exclusively under the war-making power. Besides, the Constitution expressly requires as an imperative duty that "the United States shall protect each of them [the States] against invasion." I am at a loss to conceive how this protection can be afforded to California and Oregon against such a naval power by any other means. I repeat the opinion contained in my last annual message that it would be inexpedient for the Government to undertake this great work by agents of its own appointment and under its direct and exclusive control. This would increase the patronage of the Executive to a dangerous extent and would foster a system of jobbing and corruption which no vigilance on the part of Federal officials could prevent. The construction of this road ought, therefore, to be intrusted to incorporated companies or other agencies who would exercise that active and vigilant supervision over it which can be inspired alone by a sense of corporate and individual interest. I venture to assert that the additional cost of transporting troops, munitions of war, and necessary supplies for the Army across the vast intervening plains to our possessions on the Pacific Coast would be greater in such a war than the whole amount required to construct the road. And yet this resort would after all be inadequate for their defense and protection.

We have yet scarcely recovered from the habits of extravagant expenditure produced by our overflowing Treasury during several years prior to the commencement of my Administration. The financial reverses which we have since experienced ought to teach us all to scrutinize our expenditures with the greatest vigilance and to reduce them to the lowest possible point. The Executive Departments of the Government have devoted themselves to the accomplishment of this object with considerable success, as will appear from their different reports and estimates. To these I invite the scrutiny of Congress, for the purpose of reducing them still lower, if this be practicable consistent with the great public interests of the country. In aid of the policy of retrenchment, I pledge myself to examine closely the bills appropriating lands or money, so that if any of these should inadvertently pass both Houses, as must sometimes be the case, I may afford them an opportunity for reconsideration. At the same time, we ought never to forget that true public economy consists not in withholding the means necessary to accomplish important national objects confided to us by the Constitution, but in taking care that the money appropriated for these purposes shall be faithfully and frugally expended.

It will appear from the report of the Secretary of the Treasury that it is extremely doubtful, to say the least, whether we shall be able to pass through the present and the next fiscal year without providing additional revenue. This can only be accomplished by strictly confining the appropriations within the estimates of the different Departments, without making an allowance for any additional expenditures which Congress may think proper, in their discretion, to authorize, and without providing for the redemption of any portion of the $20,000,000 of Treasury notes which have been already issued. In the event of a deficiency, which I consider probable, this ought never to be supplied by a resort to additional loans. It would be a ruinous practice in the days of peace and prosperity to go on increasing the national debt to meet the ordinary expenses of the Government. This policy would cripple our resources and impair our credit in case the existence of war should render it necessary to borrow money. Should such a deficiency occur as I apprehend, I would recommend that the necessary revenue be raised by an increase of our present duties on imports. I need not repeat the opinions expressed in my last annual message as to the best mode and manner of accomplishing this object, and shall now merely observe that these have since undergone no change.

The report of the Secretary of the Treasury will explain in detail the operations of that Department of the Government.

The receipts into the Treasury from all sources during the fiscal year ending June 30, 1859, including the loan authorized by the act of June 14, 1858, and the issues of Treasury notes authorized by existing laws, were $81,692,471.01, which sum, with the balance of $6,398,316.10 remaining in the Treasury at the commencement of that fiscal year, made an aggregate for the service of the year of $88,090,787.11.

The public expenditures during the fiscal year ending June 30, 1859, amounted to $83,751,511.57. Of this sum $17,405,285.44 were applied to the payment of interest on the public debt and the redemption of the issues of Treasury notes. The expenditures for all other branches of the public service during that fiscal year were therefore $66,346,226.13.

The balance remaining in the Treasury on the 1st July, 1859, being the commencement of the present fiscal year, was $4,339,275.54.

The receipts into the Treasury during the first quarter of the present fiscal year, commencing July 1, 1859, were $20,618,865.85. Of this amount $3,821,300 was received on account of the loan and the issue of Treasury notes, the amount of $16,797,565.85 having been received during the quarter from the ordinary sources of public revenue. The estimated receipts for the remaining three quarters of the present fiscal year, to June 30, 1860, are $50,426,400. Of this amount it is estimated that $5,756,400 will be received for Treasury notes which may be reissued under the fifth section of the act of 3d March last, and $1,170,000 on account of the loan authorized by the act of June 14, 1858, making $6,926,400 from these extraordinary sources, and $43,500,000 from the ordinary sources of the public revenue, making an aggregate, with the balance in the Treasury on the 1st July, 1859, of $75,384,541.89 for the estimated means of the present fiscal year, ending June 30, 1860.

The expenditures during the first quarter of the present fiscal year were $20,007,174.76. Four million six hundred and sixty-four thousand three hundred and sixty-six dollars and seventy-six cents of this sum were applied to the payment of interest on the public debt and the redemption of the issues of Treasury notes, and the remainder, being $15,342,808, were applied to ordinary expenditures during the quarter. The estimated expenditures during the remaining three quarters, to June 30, 1860, are $40,995,558.23, of which sum $2,886,621.34 are estimated for the interest on the public debt. The ascertained and estimated expenditures for the fiscal year ending June 30, 1860, on account of the public debt are accordingly $7,550,988.10, and for the ordinary expenditures of the Government $53,451,744.89, making an aggregate of $61,-002,732.99, leaving an estimated balance in the Treasury on June 30, 1860, of $14,381,808.40.

The estimated receipts during the next fiscal year, ending June 30, 1861, are $66,225,000, which, with the balance estimated, as before stated, as remaining in the Treasury on the 30th June, 1860, will make an aggregate for the service of the next fiscal year of $80,606,808.40.

The estimated expenditures during the next fiscal year, ending 30th June, 1861, are $66,714,928.79. Of this amount $3,386,621.34 will be required to pay the interest on the public debt, leaving the sum of $63,328,307.45 for the estimated ordinary expenditures during the fiscal year ending 30th June, 1861. Upon these estimates a balance will be left in the Treasury on the 30th June, 1861, of $13,891,879.61.

But this balance, as well as that estimated to remain in the Treasury on the 1st July, 1860, will be reduced by such appropriations as shall be made by law to carry into effect certain Indian treaties during the present fiscal year, asked for by the Secretary of the Interior, to the amount of $539,350; and upon the estimates of the Postmaster-General for the service of his Department the last fiscal year, ending 30th June, 1859, amounting to $4,296,009, together with the further estimate of that officer for the service of the present fiscal year, ending 30th June, 1860, being $5,526,324, making an aggregate of $10,361,683.

Should these appropriations be made as requested by the proper Departments, the balance in the Treasury on the 30th June, 1861, will not, it is estimated, exceed $3,530,196.61.

I transmit herewith the reports of the Secretaries of War, of the Navy, of the Interior, and of the Postmaster-General. They each contain valuable information and important recommendations well worthy of the serious consideration of Congress.

It will appear from the report of the Secretary of War that the Army expenditures have been materially reduced by a system of rigid economy, which in his opinion offers every guaranty that the reduction will be permanent. The estimates of the Department for the next have been reduced nearly $2,000,000 below the estimates for the present fiscal year and $500,000 below the amount granted for this year at the last session of Congress.

The expenditures of the Post-Office Department during the past fiscal year, ending on the 30th June, 1859, exclusive of payments for mail service specially provided for by Congress out of the general Treasury, amounted to $14,964,493.33 and its receipts to $7,968,484.07, showing a deficiency to be supplied from the Treasury of $6,996,009.26, against $5,235,677.15 for the year ending 30th June, 1858. The increased cost of transportation, growing out of the expansion of the service required by Congress, explains this rapid augmentation of the expenditures. It is gratifying, however, to observe an increase of receipts for the year ending on the 30th of June, 1859, equal to $481,691.21 compared with those in the year ending on the 30th June, 1858.

It is estimated that the deficiency for the current fiscal year will be $5,988,424.04, but that for the year ending 30th June, 1861, it will not exceed $1,342,473.90 should Congress adopt the measures of reform proposed and urged by the Postmaster-General. Since the month of March retrenchments have been made in the expenditures amounting to $1,826,471 annually, which, however, did not take effect until after the commencement of the present fiscal year. The period seems to have arrived for determining the question whether this Department shall become a permanent and ever-increasing charge upon the Treasury, or shall be permitted to resume the self-sustaining policy which had so long controlled its administration. The course of legislation recommended by the Postmaster-General for the relief of the Department from its present embarrassments and for restoring it to its original independence is deserving of your early and earnest consideration.

In conclusion I would again commend to the just liberality of Congress the local interests of the District of Columbia. Surely the city bearing the name of Washington, and destined, I trust, for ages to be the capital of our united, free, and prosperous Confederacy, has strong claims on our favorable regard.

JAMES BUCHANAN.

SPECIAL MESSAGES.

WASHINGTON, *December 7, 1859.*

To the Senate of the United States:

I transmit to the Senate a report from the Secretary of State and the papers referred to therein, in answer to the resolution of the Senate of the 21st of December last, in relation to the suspension of diplomatic relations with Mexico by the United States legation in that country.

JAMES BUCHANAN.

WASHINGTON, *December 16, 1859.*

To the Senate of the United States:

Having ratified the treaty between the United States and the Empire of China, pursuant to the advice and consent of the Senate as expressed in their resolution of the 15th of December last, I lost no time in forwarding my ratification thither, in the hope that it might reach that country in season to be exchanged for the ratification of the Emperor within the time limited for that purpose. Unforeseen circumstances, however, retarded the exchange until the 16th of August last. I consequently submit the instrument anew to the Senate, in order that they may declare their assent to the postponement of the exchange of the ratifications in such way as they may deem most expedient.

JAMES BUCHANAN.

WASHINGTON, *December 19, 1859.*

To the Senate of the United States:

I transmit to the Senate, with a view to ratification, a treaty of friendship, commerce, and navigation concluded at Asuncion on the 4th of February last between the plenipotentiaries of the United States and Paraguay.

JAMES BUCHANAN.

WASHINGTON, *December 19, 1859.*

To the Senate of the United States:

I transmit to the Senate, for consideration with a view to ratification, a treaty of friendship and commerce between the United States and Nicaragua, signed by their respective plenipotentiaries at Managua on the 16th March last, together with papers explanatory of the same, of which a list is herewith furnished.

I invite attention especially to the last document accompanying the treaty, being a translation of a note of 26th September ultimo from Mr. Molina, chargé d'affaires *ad interim* of Nicaragua, to the Secretary of State, together with the translation of the ratification of the treaty by the Nicaraguan Government, thereto annexed.

The amendment stipulated in the second article of the decree of ratification by Nicaragua is in conformity with the views of this Government, to which the omitted clause was obnoxious, as will be seen by reference to the note of the Secretary of State to Mr. Trisarri of 26th May, 1859, a copy of which is among the documents referred to.

JAMES BUCHANAN.

WASHINGTON, *December 19, 1859.*

To the Senate of the United States:

I transmit to the Senate, with a view to ratification, the special convention concluded at Asuncion on the 4th of February last between the plenipotentiaries of the United States and Paraguay, providing for the settlement of the claims of the United States and Paraguay Navigation Company.   JAMES BUCHANAN.

WASHINGTON, *January 4, 1860.*

To the Senate of the United States:

I transmit to the Senate, for consideration with a view to ratification, a "treaty of transits and commerce between the United States of America and the Mexican Republic," and also a "convention to enforce treaty stipulations" between the same parties, both of which were signed by the plenipotentiaries of the respective Governments at Vera Cruz on the 14th December ultimo.

I also transmit a copy of a dispatch of the minister of the United States accredited to the Mexican Government to the Secretary of State, relative to these instruments.   JAMES BUCHANAN.

WASHINGTON, *January 10, 1860.*

To the Senate of the United States:

I transmit herewith, for your constitutional action thereon, articles of agreement and convention made and concluded on the 5th day of October, 1859, with the Kansas, and recommend that the same be ratified.

JAMES BUCHANAN.

WASHINGTON, *January 10, 1860.*

To the Senate of the United States:

I transmit herewith, for your constitutional action thereon, articles of agreement and convention made and concluded on the 1st day of October, 1859, with the Sacs and Foxes of the Mississippi, and recommend that the same be ratified.   JAMES BUCHANAN.

WASHINGTON, *January 10, 1860.*

To the Senate of the United States:

I transmit herewith, for your constitutional action thereon, articles of agreement and convention made and concluded on the 15th day of April, 1859, with the Winnebagoes, and recommend that the same be ratified.

JAMES BUCHANAN.

WASHINGTON, *January 12, 1860.*

To the Senate of the United States:

In compliance with the resolution of the Senate in executive session of the 10th instant, I transmit herewith the report of the Secretary of State and the papers accompanying it, relating to the treaties lately negotiated by Mr. McLane and to the condition of the existing Government of Mexico.

It will be observed from the report that these papers are originals, and that it is indispensable they should be restored to the files of the Department when the subject to which they relate shall have been disposed of.

JAMES BUCHANAN.

WASHINGTON, January 20, 1860.

To the Senate of the United States:

I transmit herewith, for your constitutional action, articles of agreement and convention made and concluded on the 16th day of July, 1859, with the Chippewas of Swan Creek and Black River and the Christian Indians, and recommend that the same be ratified.

JAMES BUCHANAN.

WASHINGTON, January 23, 1860.

To the Senate of the United States:

In answer to the resolution of the Senate of the 12th instant, requesting information respecting an alleged outrage upon an American family at Perugia, in the Pontifical States, I transmit a report from the Secretary of State and the documents by which it is accompanied.

JAMES BUCHANAN.

WASHINGTON, January 25, 1860.

To the Senate of the United States:

In compliance with the resolution of the Senate of the 11th June, 1858, requesting the President of the United States, if in his judgment compatible with the public interests, to communicate to that body "such information as the Executive Departments may afford of the contracts, agreements, and arrangements which have been made and of proposals which have been received for heating and ventilating the Capitol extension, the Post-Office, and other public buildings in course of construction under the management of Captain Meigs, and of the action of the Secretary of War and Captain Meigs thereon," I transmit herewith all the papers called for by the resolution.

JAMES BUCHANAN.

WASHINGTON, January 30, 1860.

To the Senate of the United States:

I transmit herewith a report of the Secretary of War, with accompanying papers, in answer to the resolution of the 9th instant, requesting the President "to communicate to the Senate the official correspondence of Lieutenant-General Winfield Scott in reference to the island of San Juan, and of Brigadier-General William S. Harney, in command of the Department of Oregon."

JAMES BUCHANAN.

WASHINGTON, *February 6, 1860.*

To the Senate and House of Representatives:

I transmit a copy of a letter of the 22d of April last from the chargé d'affaires *ad interim* of the United States in China, and of the regulations for consular courts which accompanied it, for such revision thereof as Congress may deem expedient, pursuant to the sixth section of the act approved the 11th of August, 1848.   JAMES BUCHANAN.

WASHINGTON, *February 9, 1860.*

To the Senate of the United States:

I transmit for the approval of the Senate an informal convention with the Republic of Venezuela for the adjustment of claims of citizens of the United States on the Government of that Republic growing out of their forcible expulsion by Venezuelan authorities from the guano island of Aves, in the Caribbean Sea.   Usually it is not deemed necessary to consult the Senate in regard to similar instruments relating to private claims of small amount when the aggrieved parties are satisfied with their terms. In this instance, however, although the convention was negotiated under the authority of the Venezuelan Executive and has been approved by the National Convention of that Republic, there is some reason to apprehend that, owing to the frequent changes in that Government, the payments for which it provides may be refused or delayed upon the pretext that the instrument has not received the constitutional sanction of this Government.   It is understood that if the payments adverted to shall be made as stipulated the convention will be acceptable to the claimants.

JAMES BUCHANAN.

WASHINGTON, *February 9, 1860.*

To the Senate of the United States:

I transmit to the Senate, for its consideration with a view to ratification, a treaty of peace, friendship, commerce, and navigation between the United States and the Republic of Bolivia, signed by their respective plenipotentiaries at La Paz on the 13th of May, 1858.

JAMES BUCHANAN.

WASHINGTON, *February 20, 1860.*

To the Senate and House of Representatives of the United States:

Eight memorials numerously signed by our fellow-citizens, "residents for the most part within the territorial limits of Kansas and Nebraska at and near the eastern slope of the Rocky Mountains," have been presented to me, containing the request that I would submit the condition of the memorialists to the two Houses of Congress in a special message. Accordingly, I transmit four of these memorials to the Senate and four to the House of Representatives.

These memorialists invoke the interposition of Congress and of the Executive "for the early extinguishment of the Indian title, a consequent survey and sale of the public land, and the establishment of an assay office in the immediate and daily reach of the citizens of that region." They also urge "the erection of a new Territory from contiguous portions of New Mexico, Utah, Kansas, and Nebraska," with the boundaries set forth in their memorial. They further state, if this request should not be granted, "that (inasmuch as during this year a census is to be taken) an enabling act be passed with provision upon condition that if on the 1st day of July, 1860, 30,000 resident inhabitants be found within the limits of the mineral region, then a Territorial government is constituted by Executive proclamation; or if on the 1st day of September, 1860, 150,000 shall be returned, then a State organization to occur."

In transmitting these memorials to Congress I recommend that such provision may be made for the protection and prosperity of our fellow-citizens at and near the eastern slope of the Rocky Mountains as their distance and the exigencies of their condition may require for their government.

JAMES BUCHANAN.

WASHINGTON, *February 25, 1860.*

To the House of Representatives:

In compliance with the resolution of the House of Representatives of the 16th instant, requesting a copy of a letter of the Emperor of France upon the subject of commerce and free trade, I transmit a report from the Secretary of State, to whom the resolution was referred.

JAMES BUCHANAN.

WASHINGTON, *February 29, 1860.*

To the Senate of the United States:

In answer to the resolution of the Senate of yesterday, requesting information with regard to the present condition of the work of marking the boundary pursuant to the first article of the treaty between the United States and Great Britain of the 15th of June, 1846, I transmit a report from the Secretary of State and the papers by which it was accompanied.

JAMES BUCHANAN.

WASHINGTON, *March 1, 1860.*

To the Senate of the United States:

I transmit herewith, in compliance with the resolution of the Senate of the 1st of February, 1860, a report from the Secretary of War, communicating the information desired relative to the payments, agreements, arrangements, etc., in connection with the heating and ventilating of the Capitol and Post-Office extensions.

JAMES BUCHANAN.

WASHINGTON, *March 5, 1860.*

To the Senate of the United States:

In compliance with the resolution of the Senate of the 23d of February, 1860, I transmit to that body a communication* of the Secretary of War, furnishing all the information requested in said resolution.

JAMES BUCHANAN.

WASHINGTON, *March 8, 1860.*

To the Senate of the United States:

I transmit herewith a report from the Secretary of State, together with the papers accompanying it, in answer to the resolution of the Senate in executive session of the 28th ultimo, calling for the instructions to our minister or ministers in Mexico which resulted in the negotiation of the treaty with that country now before the Senate.

JAMES BUCHANAN.

WASHINGTON, *March 12, 1860.*

To the Senate of the United States:

In answer to the resolution of the Senate of the 6th ultimo, requesting copies of the instructions to and dispatches from the late and from the present minister of the United States in China down to the period of the exchange of ratifications of the treaty of Tien-tsin, and also a copy of the instructions from the Department of State of February, 1857, to Mr. Parker, former commissioner in China, I transmit a report from the Secretary of State and the papers by which it was accompanied.

JAMES BUCHANAN.

WASHINGTON, *March 15, 1860.*

To the Senate of the United States:

Referring to my communication of the 5th instant to the Senate, in answer to its resolution of the 23d February, calling for any "communication which may have been received from the governor of Texas, and the documents accompanying it, concerning alleged hostilities now existing on the Rio Grande," I have the honor herewith to submit for the consideration of that body the following papers:

Dispatch from the Secretary of War to the governor of Texas, dated 28th February, 1860.

Dispatch from the governor of Texas to the Secretary of War, dated 8th March, 1860.

Dispatch from Acting Secretary of War to the governor of Texas, dated 14th March, 1860.

JAMES BUCHANAN.

* Relating to disturbances on the Rio Grande between citizens and military authorities of Mexico and Texas.

WASHINGTON, *March 15, 1860.*

To the Senate of the United States:

In compliance with the resolution* of the Senate in executive session on the 12th instant, I transmit a report from the Secretary of State, with the accompanying copies of Mr. Churchwell's correspondence.

JAMES BUCHANAN.

WASHINGTON, *March 16, 1860.*

To the Senate of the United States:

I transmit herewith a report from the Acting Secretary of War, with its accompanying papers, communicating the information called for by the resolution of the Senate of the 9th instant, respecting the marble columns for the Capitol extension. JAMES BUCHANAN.

WASHINGTON, *March 16, 1860.*

To the Senate and House of Representatives:

I transmit a copy of the convention between the United States and the Republic of Paraguay, concluded on the 4th February, 1859, and proclaimed on the 12th instant, and invite the attention of Congress to the expediency of such legislation as may be deemed necessary to carry into effect the stipulations of the convention relative to the organization of the commission provided for therein.

The commissioner on the part of Paraguay is now in this city, and is prepared to enter upon the duties devolved upon the joint commission.

JAMES BUCHANAN.

WASHINGTON, *March 21, 1860.*

To the Senate of the United States:

In compliance with the request of the Senate contained in their resolution of yesterday, the 20th instant, I return to them the resolution of the 16th instant, "that the Senate do not advise and consent to the ratification of the treaty of friendship and commerce between the United States and Nicaragua, signed at Managua on the 16th day of March, 1859." I also return the treaty itself, presuming that the Senate so intended.

JAMES BUCHANAN.

WASHINGTON, *March 22, 1860.*

To the Senate of the United States:

I transmit to the Senate, for its consideration with a view to ratification, a convention concluded on the 21st instant between the United States and His Majesty the King of Sweden and Norway for the mutual surrender of fugitive criminals. JAMES BUCHANAN.

*Calling for the report of the agent sent to Mexico to ascertain the condition of that country.

WASHINGTON, *March 29, 1860.*

To the Senate of the United States:

In compliance with the resolution of the Senate of the 21st of March, 1860, requesting the President of the United States "to inform the Senate, if in his opinion it be not incompatible with the public interest, if any instructions have been given to any of the officers of the Navy of the United States by which, in any event, the naval force of the United States or any part thereof were to take part in the civil war now existing in Mexico, and if the recent capture of two war steamers of Mexico by the naval force of the United States was done in pursuance of orders issued by this Government, and also by what authority those steamers have been taken in possession by the naval force of the United States and the men on board made prisoners," I transmit the inclosed report, with accompanying papers, from the Secretary of the Navy.

JAMES BUCHANAN.

WASHINGTON, *March 29, 1860.*

To the House of Representatives:

I transmit herewith a report of the Secretary of War, with its accompaniments, communicating the information called for by the resolution of the House of Representatives of the 1st instant, concerning the difficulties on the southwestern frontier.

JAMES BUCHANAN.

WASHINGTON, *March 30, 1860.*

To the House of Representatives:

In answer to the resolution of the 26th instant, requesting information touching the imprisonment of an American citizen in the island of Cuba, I transmit a report from the Secretary of State and the documents by which it was accompanied.

JAMES BUCHANAN.

WASHINGTON, *April 2, 1860.*

To the Senate of the United States:

In compliance with the resolution of the Senate of the 28th of February last, relative to the uniform or costume of persons in the diplomatic or consular service, I transmit a report from the Secretary of State and the papers by which it was accompanied.

JAMES BUCHANAN.

WASHINGTON CITY, *April 3, 1860.*

To the Senate of the United States:

I herewith transmit to the Senate a report of the Attorney-General, in answer to a resolution of the Senate of the 21st of March, "that the

President be respectfully requested to communicate to the Senate the correspondence between the judges of Utah and the Attorney-General or the President with reference to the legal proceedings and condition of affairs in the Territory of Utah.''

JAMES BUCHANAN.

WASHINGTON, *April 5, 1860.*

To the Senate of the United States:

I transmit, for the consideration of the Senate with a view to ratification, a treaty of friendship, commerce, and navigation between the United States and the Republic of Honduras, signed by the plenipotentiaries of the parties in this city on the 28th day of last month.

The fourteenth article of this treaty is an exact copy of the supplemental article of the "treaty of friendship, commerce, and navigation between Great Britain and the Republic of Honduras," dated 26th day of August, 1856, with the necessary changes in names and dates. Under this article the Government and people of the United States will enjoy in the fullest and most satisfactory manner the use of the "Honduras Interoceanic Railway," in consideration of which the United States recognizes the rights of sovereignty and property of Honduras over the line of the road and guarantees its neutrality, and, when "the road shall have been completed, equally engages, in conjunction with Honduras, to protect the same from interruption, seizure, or unjust confiscation, from whatever quarter the attempt may proceed."

This treaty is in accordance with the policy inaugurated by the Government of the United States, and in an especial manner by the Senate, in the year 1846, and several treaties have been concluded to carry it into effect. It is simple, and may be embraced in a few words. On the one side a grant of free and uninterrupted transit for the Government and people of the United States over the transit routes across the Isthmus, and on the other a guaranty of the neutrality and protection of these routes, not only for the benefit of the Republics through which they pass, but, in the language of our treaty with New Granada, in order to secure to themselves the tranquil and constant enjoyment of these interoceanic communications.

The first in the series of these treaties is that with New Granada of the 12th December, 1846. This treaty was concluded before our acquisition of California and when our interests on the Pacific Coast were of far less magnitude than at the present day. For years before this period, however, the routes across the Isthmus had attracted the serious attention of this Government.

This treaty, after granting us the right of transit across the Isthmus of Panama in the most ample terms, binds this Government to guarantee to New Granada "the perfect neutrality of the before-mentioned Isthmus, with the view that the free transit from the one to the other sea may not be interrupted or embarrassed in any future time while this treaty exists.''

In one respect it goes further than any of its successors, because it not only guarantees the neutrality of the route itself, but ''the rights of sovereignty and property'' of New Granada over the entire Province of Panama. It is worthy of remark that when it was sent to the Senate it was accompanied by a message of President Polk, dated February 10, 1847, in which the attention of that body was especially called to these important stipulations of the thirty-fifth article, and in which it was stated, moreover, that our chargé d'affaires who negotiated the treaty ''acted in this particular upon his own responsibility and without instructions.'' Under these circumstances the treaty was approved by the Senate and the transit policy to which I have referred was deliberately adopted. A copy of the executive document (confidential), Twenty-ninth Congress, second session, containing this message of President Polk and the papers which accompanied it is hereto annexed.

The next in order of time of these treaties of transit and guaranty is that of the 19th April, 1850, with Great Britain, commonly called the Clayton and Bulwer treaty. This treaty, in affirmation of the policy of the New Granada treaty, established a general principle which has ever since, I believe, guided the proceedings of both Governments. The eighth article of that treaty contains the following stipulations:

The Government of the United States having not only desired in entering into this convention to accomplish a particular object, but also to establish a general principle, they hereby agree to extend their protection by treaty stipulations to any other practicable communications, whether by canal or railway, across the isthmus which connects North and South America, and especially to the interoceanic communications, should the same prove to be practicable, whether by canal or railway, which are now proposed to be established by the way of Tehuantepec or Panama.

And that the said—

Canals or railways shall also be open on like terms to the citizens and subjects of every other state which is willing to grant thereto such protection as the United States and Great Britain propose to afford.

The United States, in a short time after the Clayton and Bulwer treaty was concluded, carried this stipulation in regard to the Tehuantepec route into effect by their treaty with Mexico of the 30th December, 1853. The eighth article of this treaty, after granting to us the transit privileges therein mentioned, stipulates that ''the Mexican Government having agreed to protect with its whole power the prosecution, preservation, and security of the work, the United States may extend its protection as it shall judge wise, to use it when it may feel sanctioned and warranted by the public or international law.''

This is a sweeping grant of power to the United States, which no nation ought to have conceded, but which, it is believed, has been confined within safe limits by our treaty with Mexico now before the Senate.

Such was believed to be the established policy of the Government at the commencement of this Administration, viz, the grant of transits in our favor and the guaranty of our protection as an equivalent. This guaranty can never be dangerous under our form of government, because it can never be carried into execution without the express authority of Congress. Still, standing on the face of treaties, as it does, it deters all evil-disposed parties from interfering with these routes.

Under such circumstances the attention of the Executive was early turned to the Nicaragua route as in many respects the most important and valuable to the citizens of our country. In concluding a treaty to secure our rights of transit over this route I experienced many difficulties, which I need not now enumerate, because they are detailed in different messages to Congress. Finally a treaty was negotiated exactly in accordance with the established policy of the Government and the views of the Executive, and clear from the embarrassments which might arise under the phraseology of previous treaties. The fourteenth article of the treaty contains a full, clear, and specific grant of the right of transit to the United States and their citizens, and is believed to be perfectly unexceptionable. The fifteenth article, instead of leaving one equivalent duty of protection, general and unlimited, as in our treaty with New Granada and in the Clayton and Bulwer treaty, or instead of that general right assured to the Government in the Mexican treaty of extending its protection as it shall itself judge wise, when it may feel sanctioned and warranted by the public or international law, confines the interference conceded within just and specific limits.

Under the sixteenth article of this treaty the Government of the United States has no right to interpose for the protection of the Nicaragua route except with the consent or at the request of the Government of Nicaragua, or of the minister thereof at Washington, or of the competent, legally appointed local authorities, civil or military; and when in the opinion of the Government of Nicaragua the necessity ceases such force shall be immediately withdrawn. Nothing can be more carefully guarded than this provision. No force can be employed unless upon the request of the Government of Nicaragua, and it must be immediately withdrawn whenever in the opinion of that Government the necessity ceases.

When Congress shall come to adopt the measures necessary to carry this provision of the treaty into effect they can guard it from any abuses which may possibly arise.

The general policy contained in these articles, although inaugurated by the United States, has been fully adopted by the Governments of Great Britain and France. The plenipotentiaries of both these Governments have recently negotiated treaties with Nicaragua, which are but transcripts of the treaty between the United States and Nicaragua now before the Senate. The treaty with France has been ratified, it is understood, by both the French and Nicaraguan Governments, and is now in operation. That with Great Britain has been delayed by other negotiations in Nicaragua, but it is believed that these are now concluded and that the ratifications of the British treaty will soon, therefore, be exchanged.

It is presumed that no objection will be made to "the exceptional case" of the sixteenth article, which is only intended to provide for the landing of sailors or marines from our vessels which may happen to be within reach of the point of difficulty, in order to protect the lives and property of citizens of the United States from unforeseen and imminent danger.

The same considerations may be suggested with respect to the fifth article of the treaty with Mexico, which is also pending before the Senate. This article is an exact copy of the sixteenth article, just referred to, of the treaty with Nicaragua.

The treaty with Honduras, which is now submitted to the Senate, follows on this subject the language of the British treaty with that Republic, and is not, therefore, identical in its terms with the Nicaraguan and Mexican treaties. The same policy, however, has been adopted in all of them, and it will not fail, I am persuaded, to receive from the Senate all that consideration which it so eminently deserves. The importance to the United States of securing free and safe transit routes across the American Isthmus can not well be overestimated. These routes are of great interest, of course, to all commercial nations, but they are especially so to us from our geographical and political position as an American State and because they furnish a necessary communication between our Atlantic and Pacific States and Territories.

The Government of the United States can never permit these routes to be permanently interrupted, nor can it safely allow them to pass under the control of other rival nations. While it seeks no exclusive privileges upon them for itself, it can never consent to be made tributary to their use to any European power. It is worthy of consideration, however, whether to some extent it would not necessarily become so if after Great Britain and France have adopted our policy and made treaties with the Isthmian Governments in pursuance of it we should ourselves reconsider it and refuse to pursue it in the treaties of the United States. I might add that the opening of these transit routes can not fail to extend the trade and commerce of the United States with the countries through which they pass; to afford an outlet and a market for our manufactures within their territories; to encourage American citizens to develop their vast stores of mining and mineral wealth for our benefit, and to introduce among them a wholesome American influence calculated to prevent revolutions and to render their governments stable.

JAMES BUCHANAN.

WASHINGTON, *April 10, 1860.*

To the House of Representatives:

I communicate herewith a report from the Secretary of State, in reply to the resolution of the House of Representatives of the 6th instant, respecting the expulsion of American citizens from Mexico and the confiscation of their property by General Miramon.

JAMES BUCHANAN.

WASHINGTON, *April 10, 1860.*

To the House of Representatives:

In compliance with the resolution of the House of Representatives of the 23d of December, 1858, requesting information in regard to the duties on tobacco in foreign countries, I transmit a report from the Secretary of State and the documents by which it was accompanied.

JAMES BUCHANAN.

WASHINGTON, D. C., *April 11, 1860.*

To the House of Representatives of the United States:

In compliance with the resolution of the House of Representatives of March 26, 1860, requesting me "to transmit to the House all information in the possession of the officer in charge of the Coast Survey showing the practicability of making Harlem River navigable for commercial purposes, and the expenses thereof," I herewith transmit a report from the Secretary of the Treasury containing the desired information.

JAMES BUCHANAN.

WASHINGTON, *April 11, 1860.*

To the Senate of the United States:

In compliance with the resolution of the Senate of the 2d February, 1859, requesting information in regard to the compulsory enlistment of citizens of the United States in the army of Prussia, I transmit a report from the Secretary of State and the documents by which it was accompanied.

JAMES BUCHANAN.

WASHINGTON, *April 12, 1860.*

To the Senate of the United States:

In compliance with the resolution of the Senate of the 23d of February last, requesting information in regard to the occupation by American citizens of the island of Navassa, in the West Indies, I transmit a report from the Secretary of State and the documents by which it was accompanied.

JAMES BUCHANAN.

WASHINGTON, *April 12, 1860.*

To the House of Representatives:

I transmit herewith a report of the Secretary of War, with its accompaniments, communicating the information called for by the resolution of the House of Representatives of the 20th ultimo, respecting Indian hostilities in New Mexico.

JAMES BUCHANAN.

WASHINGTON, *April 16, 1860.*

To the Senate of the United States:

In compliance with the resolution of the Senate of the 4th instant, requesting information not heretofore called for relating to the claim of any foreign governments to the military services of naturalized American citizens, I transmit a report from the Secretary of State and the documents by which it was accompanied.

JAMES BUCHANAN.

WASHINGTON, D. C., *April 17, 1860.*

To the Senate of the United States:

I transmit herewith, for the information of the Senate, the Paris Moniteur of the 4th February last, the official journal of the French Government, containing an imperial decree promulgating a treaty of friendship, commerce, and navigation, concluded on the 11th April, 1859, between France and the Republic of Nicaragua. It will be found in all respects similar to the treaty between the United States and Nicaragua now pending in the Senate.

JAMES BUCHANAN.

WASHINGTON, *April 20, 1860.*

To the House of Representatives:

I transmit herewith a report of the Secretary of the Navy, to whom was referred the resolution of the House of Representatives of April 10, 1860, requesting the President to communicate to the House, in addition to the information asked in the resolution adopted in reference to the African slave trade, "the number of officers and men in the service of the United States belonging to the African Squadron who have died in that service since the date of the Ashburton treaty up to the present time."

JAMES BUCHANAN.

WASHINGTON, *April 20, 1860.*

To the House of Representatives:

In answer to the resolution of the House of Representatives "that the President be requested to communicate to the House, if not incompatible with the public service, all such information as he may possess in relation to the existence" of the Territory of Minnesota, he has to state that he possesses no information upon the subject except what has been derived from the acts of Congress and the proceedings of the House itself. Since the date of the act of the 11th of May, 1858, admitting a portion of the Territory of Minnesota as a State into the Union, no act has been performed by the Executive either affirming or denying the existence of such Territory. The question in regard to that portion of the Territory without the limits of the existing State remains for the decision of Congress, and is in the same condition it was when the State was admitted into the Union.   JAMES BUCHANAN.

WASHINGTON, *April 22, 1860.*

To the Senate of the United States:

I return to the Senate the original convention between the United States and the Republic of New Granada, signed on the 10th September, 1857, and ratified by me as amended by the Senate on the 12th March, 1859.

The amendments of the Senate were immediately transmitted to New Granada for acceptance, but they arrived at Bogota three days after the adjournment of the Congress of that Republic, notwithstanding the session had been protracted for twenty days solely with a view to the consideration of the convention after it should have received the sanction of this Government.

At the earliest moment after the assembling of the New Granadian Congress, on the 1st of February last, the convention as amended and ratified was laid before that body, and on the 25th of the same month it was approved with the amendments. Inasmuch, however, as the period had expired within which by the third amendment of the Senate the ratifications should have been exchanged, the Congress of New Granada provided that "the convention should be ratified and the ratification should be exchanged at whatever time the Governments of the two Republics may deem convenient for the purpose, and therefore the period has been extended which the Senate of the United States had fixed."

The expediency of authorizing the exchange of ratifications at such time as may be convenient to the two Governments is consequently submitted to the consideration of the Senate.

JAMES BUCHANAN.

WASHINGTON, *April 23, 1860.*

To the Senate of the United States:

In answer to the resolution of the Senate of the 18th instant, requesting a copy of the instructions from the Department of State to Mr. McLane when appointed minister to China, I transmit a report from the Secretary of State, with the instructions which accompanied it.

JAMES BUCHANAN.

WASHINGTON, *April 24, 1860.*

To the House of Representatives:

In compliance with the resolutions of the House of Representatives of the 2d March, 1859, and of the 26th ultimo, requesting information relative to discriminations in Switzerland against citizens of the United States of the Hebrew persuasion, I transmit a report of the Secretary of State, with the documents by which it was accompanied.

JAMES BUCHANAN.

WASHINGTON, *April 25, 1860.*

To the Senate of the United States:

In compliance with a resolution of the Senate of the 22d ultimo, calling for information concerning the expulsion from Prussia of Eugene Dullye, a naturalized citizen of the United States, I transmit a report from the Secretary of State, dated the 24th instant.

JAMES BUCHANAN.

WASHINGTON, *April 27, 1860.*

To the House of Representatives:

In compliance with the resolution of the House of Representatives of March 26, 1860, requesting "copies of all official correspondence between the civil and military officers stationed in Utah Territory with the heads or bureaus of their respective Departments, or between any of said officers, illustrating or tending to show the condition of affairs in said Territory since the 1st day of October, 1857, and which may not have been heretofore officially published," I transmit reports from the Secretaries of State and War and the documents by which they were accompanied.

JAMES BUCHANAN.

WASHINGTON, *April 30, 1860.*

To the Senate of the United States:

In compliance with the resolution of the Senate of the 2d of February, 1859, requesting information in regard to the compulsory service of citizens of the United States in the army of Prussia, I transmit an additional report from the Secretary of State and the document by which it is accompanied.

JAMES BUCHANAN.

EXECUTIVE MANSION, *May 1, 1860.*

To the Senate:

In compliance with the resolution of the Senate adopted March 19, 1860, calling for the correspondence, etc., in relation to the Mountain Meadow and other massacres in Utah Territory, I have the honor to transmit the report, with the accompanying documents, of the Secretary of the Interior, who was instructed to collect the information.

JAMES BUCHANAN.

To the Senate,

In compliance with the resolution of the Senate, adopted March 20th 1860, calling for the correspondence &c in relation to the Mountain Meadow and other massacres in Utah Territory, I have the honor to transmit the report, with accompanying documents, of the Secretary of the Interior, who was instructed to collect the information.

James Buchanan

Executive Mansion,
May 1st 1860.

PRESIDENT BUCHANAN'S NOTE TO SENATE RELATING TO
UTAH MASSACRES.

WASHINGTON, *May 3, 1860.*

To the Senate of the United States:

I transmit to the Senate, for its consideration with a view to ratification, a convention between the United States and Spain for the settlement of claims, signed at Madrid on the 5th of March last.

JAMES BUCHANAN.

WASHINGTON, *May 19, 1860.*

To the Senate and House of Representatives:

On the 26th day of April last Lieutenant Craven, of the United States steamer *Mohawk*, captured the slaver *Wildfire* on the coast of Cuba, with 507 African negroes on board. The prize was brought into Key West on the 31st April and the negroes were delivered into the custody of Fernando J. Moreno, marshal of the southern district of Florida.

The question which now demands immediate decision is, What disposition shall be made of these Africans? In the annual message to Congress of December 6, 1858, I expressed my opinion in regard to the construction of the act of the 3d March, 1819, "in addition to the acts prohibiting the slave trade," so far as the same is applicable to the present case. From this I make the following extract:

Under the second section of this act the President is "authorized to make such regulations and arrangements as he may deem expedient for the safe-keeping, support, and removal beyond the limits of the United States of all such negroes, mulattoes, or persons of color" captured by vessels of the United States as may be delivered to the marshal of the district into which they are brought, "and to appoint a proper person or persons residing upon the coast of Africa as agent or agents for receiving the negroes, mulattoes, or persons of color delivered from on board vessels seized in the prosecution of the slave trade by commanders of United States armed vessels."

A doubt immediately arose as to the true construction of this act. It is quite clear from its terms that the President was authorized to provide "for the safe-keeping, support, and removal" of these negroes up till the time of their delivery to the agent on the coast of Africa, but no express provision was made for their protection and support after they had reached the place of their destination. Still, an agent was to be appointed to receive them in Africa, and it could not have been supposed that Congress intended he should desert them at the moment they were received and turn them loose on that inhospitable coast to perish for want of food or to become again the victims of the slave trade. Had this been the intention of Congress, the employment of an agent to receive them, who is required to reside on the coast, was unnecessary, and they might have been landed by our vessels anywhere in Africa and left exposed to the sufferings and the fate which would certainly await them.

Mr. Monroe, in his special message of December 17, 1819, at the first session after the act was passed, announced to Congress what in his opinion was its true construction. He believed it to be his duty under it to follow these unfortunates into Africa and make provision for them there until they should be able to provide for themselves. In communicating this interpretation of the act to Congress he stated that some doubt had been entertained as to its true intent and meaning, and he submitted the question to them so that they might, "should it be deemed advisable, amend the same before further proceedings are had under it." Nothing was done by Congress to explain the act, and Mr. Monroe proceeded to carry it into execution according to his own interpretation. This, then, became the practical construction.

Adopting this construction of President Monroe, I entered into an agreement with the Colonization Society, dated 7th September, 1858, to receive the Africans which had been captured on the slaver *Echo* from the agent of the United States in Liberia, to furnish them during the period of one year thereafter with comfortable shelter, clothing, and provisions, and to cause them to be instructed in the arts of civilized life suitable to their condition, at the rate of $150 for each individual. It was believed that within that period they would be prepared to become citizens of Liberia and to take care of themselves.

As Congress was not then in session and as there was no outstanding appropriation applicable to this purpose, the society were obliged to depend for payment on the future action of that body. I recommended this appropriation, and $75,000 were granted by the act of 3d March, 1859 (the consular and diplomatic bill), "to enable the President of the United States to carry into effect the act of Congress of 3d March, 1819, and any subsequent acts now in force for the suppression of the slave trade." Of this appropriation there remains unexpended the sum of $24,350.90, after deducting from it an advance made by the Secretary of the Interior out of the judiciary fund of $11,348.10.

I regret to say that under the mode adopted in regard to the Africans captured on board the *Echo* the expense will be large, but this seems to a great extent to be inevitable without a violation of the laws of humanity. The expenditure upon this scale for those captured on board the *Wildfire* will not be less than $100,000, and may considerably exceed that sum. Still, it ought to be observed that during the period when the Government itself, through its own agents, undertook the task of providing for captured negroes in Africa the cost per head was much greater than that which I agreed to pay the Colonization Society.

But it will not be sufficient for Congress to limit the amount appropriated to the case of the *Wildfire*. It is probable, judging from the increased activity of the slave trade and the vigilance of our cruisers, that several similar captures may be made before the end of the year. An appropriation ought therefore to be granted large enough to cover such contingencies.

The period has arrived when it is indispensable to provide some specific legislation for the guidance of the Executive on this subject. With this view I would suggest that Congress might authorize the President to enter into a general agreement with the Colonization Society binding them to receive on the coast of Africa, from an agent there, all the captured Africans which may be delivered to him, and to maintain them for a limited period, upon such terms and conditions as may combine humanity toward these unfortunates with a just economy. This would obviate the necessity of making a new bargain with every new capture and would prevent delay and avoid expense in the disposition of the captured. The law might then provide that in all cases where this may be practicable the captor should carry the negroes directly to Africa and deliver them to the American agent there, afterwards bringing the captured vessel to the United States for adjudication.

The capturing officer, in case he should bring his prize directly to the United States, ought to be required to land the negroes in some one or more ports, to be designated by Congress, where the prevailing health throughout the year is good. At these ports cheap but permanent accommodations might be provided for the negroes until they could be sent away, without incurring the expense of erecting such accommodations at every port where the capturing officer may think proper to enter. On the present occasion these negroes have been brought to Key West, and, according to the estimate presented by the marshal of the southern district of Florida to the Secretary of the Interior, the cost of providing temporary quarters for them will be $2,500 and the aggregate expenses for the single month of May will amount to $12,000. But this is far from being the worst evil. Within a few weeks the yellow fever will most probably prevail at Key West, and hence the marshal urges their removal from their present quarters at an early day, which must be done, in any event, as soon as practicable. For these reasons I earnestly commend this subject to the immediate attention of Congress. I transmit herewith a copy of the letter and estimate of Fernando J. Moreno, marshal of the southern district of Florida, to the Secretary of the Interior, dated 10th May, 1860, together with a copy of the letter of the Secretary of the Interior to myself, dated 16th May.

It is truly lamentable that Great Britain and the United States should be obliged to expend such a vast amount of blood and treasure for the suppression of the African slave trade, and this when the only portions of the civilized world where it is tolerated and encouraged are the Spanish islands of Cuba and Porto Rico.

JAMES BUCHANAN.

WASHINGTON, *May 22, 1860.*

To the Senate and House of Representatives:

I transmit herewith the copy of a letter, dated yesterday, from the Secretary of the Interior, communicating the copy of a letter addressed to him on the 13th instant by Fernando J. Moreno, marshal of the southern district of Florida. From this it appears that Lieutenant Stanly, of the United States steamer *Wyandotte*, captured the bark *William*, with about 550 African negroes on board, on the south side of Cuba, near the Isle of Pines, and brought her into Key West on the 12th instant. These negroes have doubtless been delivered to the marshal, and with those captured on board the *Wildfire* will make the number in his custody about 1,000. More may be daily expected at Key West, which, both on account of a deficiency of water and provisions and its exposure to yellow fever, is one of the worst spots for an African negro depot which could be found on the coast of the United States.

JAMES BUCHANAN.

WASHINGTON, *May 22, 1860.*

To the House of Representatives:

In answer to the resolution passed on the 26th of March last, calling for a detailed statement of the expenditures from the ''appropriations made during the first session of the Thirty-fourth Congress and the first and second sessions of the Thirty-fifth Congress for legal assistance and other necessary expenditures in the disposal of private land claims in California and for the service of special counsel and other extraordinary expenses of such land claims, amounting in all to $114,000,'' I have the honor to transmit to the House of Representatives a report of the Attorney-General, which, with the accompanying documents, contains the information required.

JAMES BUCHANAN.

WASHINGTON, *May 26, 1860.*

To the House of Representatives:

In compliance with the resolution of the House of Representatives of the 21st instant, requesting any information recently received respecting the Chinese cooly trade which has not been heretofore communicated to Congress, I transmit a report from the Secretary of State, with the documents which accompanied it.

JAMES BUCHANAN.

WASHINGTON, *June 14, 1860.*

To the Senate of the United States:

I submit, for the consideration of the Senate, articles of agreement and convention with the Delaware Indians, concluded May 13, 1860. I concur in the recommendation of the Secretary of the Interior that the treaty should be ratified, with the amendments suggested by the Commissioner of Indian Affairs.

JAMES BUCHANAN.

JUNE 23, 1860.

To the Senate and House of Representatives.

GENTLEMEN: I feel it my duty to communicate to you that it has been found impracticable to conclude a contract for the transportation of the mails between our Atlantic and Pacific ports on the terms authorized by the fourth section of an act entitled ''An act making appropriations for the service of the Post-Office Department during the fiscal year ending

30th June, 1861," approved 15th June, 1860. The Postmaster-General has offered the California mails to the several companies and shipowners engaged in the trade with the Pacific via the Isthmus, but they have all declined carrying them for the postages. They demand a higher rate of compensation, and unless power is given to the Postmaster-General to accede to this demand I am well satisfied that these mails can not be forwarded. It should not be forgotten that, in consequence of the diversion of a large part of the letter mail to the overland route, the postages derived from the California service have been greatly reduced and afford a wholly inadequate remuneration for the ocean transportation. The weight of these mails, averaging from 12 to 15 tons semimonthly, renders it, in view of the climate and character of the road, manifestly impossible to forward them overland without involving an expenditure which no wise administration of the Government would impose upon the Treasury. I therefore earnestly recommend that the act referred to be so modified as to empower the Postmaster-General to provide for carrying the California mails at a rate of compensation which may be deemed reasonable and just.

JAMES BUCHANAN.

WASHINGTON, *June 25, 1860.*

To the House of Representatives:

I have approved and signed the bill entitled "An act making appropriation for sundry civil expenses of the Government for the year ending the 30th of June, 1861."

In notifying the House of my approval of this bill I deem it proper, under the peculiar circumstances of the case, to make a few explanatory observations, so that my course may not hereafter be misunderstood.

Amid a great variety of important appropriations, this bill contains an appropriation "for the completion of the Washington Aqueduct, $500,000, to be expended according to the plans and estimates of Captain Meigs and under his superintendence: *Provided,* That the office of engineer of the Potomac Waterworks is hereby abolished and its duties shall hereafter be discharged by the chief engineer of the Washington Aqueduct." To this appropriation, for a wise and beneficial object, I have not the least objection. It is true I had reason to believe when the last appropriation was made of $800,000 on the 12th of June, 1858, "*for the completion of the Washington Aqueduct,*" this would have been sufficient for the purpose. It is now discovered, however, that it will require half a million more "*for the completion of the Washington Aqueduct,*" and this ought to be granted.

The Captain Meigs to whom the bill refers is Montgomery C. Meigs, a captain in the Corps of Engineers of the Army of the United States, who has superintended this work from its commencement under the authority of the late and present Secretary of War.

Had this appropriation been made in the usual form, no difficulty could have arisen upon it. This bill, however, annexes a declaration to the appropriation that the money is to be expended under the superintendence of Captain Meigs.

The first aspect in which this clause presented itself to my mind was that it interfered with the right of the President to be "Commander in Chief of the Army and Navy of the United States." If this had really been the case, there would have been an end to the question. Upon further examination I deemed it impossible that Congress could have intended to interfere with the clear right of the President to command the Army and to order its officers to any duty he might deem most expedient for the public interest. If they could withdraw an officer from the command of the President and select him for the performance of an executive duty, they might upon the same principle annex to an appropriation to carry on a war a condition requiring it not to be used for the defense of the country unless a particular person of its own selection should command the Army. It was impossible that Congress could have had such an intention, and therefore, according to my construction of the clause in question, it merely designated Captain Meigs as its preference for the work, without intending to deprive the President of the power to order him to any other army duty for the performance of which he might consider him better adapted. Still, whilst this clause may not be, and I believe is not, a violation of the Constitution, yet how destructive it would be to all proper subordination and how demoralizing its effect upon the morale of the Army if it should become a precedent for future legislation! Officers might then be found, instead of performing their appropriate duties, besieging the halls of Congress for the purpose of obtaining special favors and choice places by legislative enactment. Under these circumstances I have deemed it but fair to inform Congress that whilst I do not consider the bill unconstitutional, this is only because, in my opinion, Congress did not intend by the language which they have employed to interfere with my absolute authority to order Captain Meigs to any other service I might deem expedient. My perfect right still remains, notwithstanding the clause, to send him away from Washington to any part of the Union to superintend the erection of a fortification or on any other appropriate duty.

It has been alleged, I think without sufficient cause, that this clause is unconstitutional because it has created a new office and has appointed Captain Meigs to perform its duties. If it had done this, it would have been a clear question, because Congress have no right to appoint to any office, this being specially conferred upon the President and Senate. It is evident that Congress intended nothing more by this clause than to express a decided opinion that Captain Meigs should be continued in the employment to which he had been previously assigned by competent authority.

It is not improbable that another question of grave importance may arise out of this clause. Is the appropriation conditional and will it fall provided I do not deem it proper that it shall be expended under the superintendence of Captain Meigs? This is a question which shall receive serious consideration, because upon its decision may depend whether the completion of the waterworks shall be arrested for another season. It is not probable that Congress could have intended that this great and important work should depend upon the various casualties and vicissitudes incident to the natural or official life of a single officer of the Army. This would be to make the work subordinate to the man, and not the man to the work, and to reverse our great axiomatic rule of "principles, not men." I desire to express no opinion upon the subject. Should the question ever arise, it shall have my serious consideration.

JAMES BUCHANAN.

VETO MESSAGES.*

WASHINGTON CITY, *February 1, 1860.*

To the Senate of the United States:

On the last day of the last Congress a bill, which had passed both Houses, entitled "An act making an appropriation for deepening the channel over the St. Clair flats, in the State of Michigan," was presented to me for approval.

It is scarcely necessary to observe that during the closing hours of a session it is impossible for the President on the instant to examine into the merits or demerits of an important bill, involving, as this does, grave questions both of expediency and of constitutional power, with that care and deliberation demanded by his public duty as well as by the best interests of the country. For this reason the Constitution has in all cases allowed him ten days for deliberation, because if a bill be presented to him within the last ten days of the session he is not required to return it, either with an approval or a veto, but may retain it, "in which case it shall not be a law." Whilst an occasion can rarely occur when so long a period as ten days would be required to enable the President to decide whether he should approve or veto a bill, yet to deny him even two days on important questions before the adjournment of each session for this purpose, as recommended by a former annual message, would not only be unjust to him, but a violation of the spirit of the Constitution. To require him to approve a bill when it is impossible he could examine into its merits would be to deprive him of the exercise of his constitutional discretion and convert him into a mere register of

* The messages of February 1 and February 6, 1860, are pocket vetoes.

the decrees of Congress. I therefore deem it a sufficient reason for having retained the bill in question that it was not presented to me until the last day of the session.

Since the termination of the last Congress I have made a thorough examination of the questions involved in the bill to deepen the channel over the St. Clair flats, and now proceed to express the opinions which I have formed upon the subject; and

1. Even if this had been a mere question of expediency, it was, to say the least, extremely doubtful whether the bill ought to have been approved, because the object which Congress intended to accomplish by the appropriation which it contains of $55,000 had been already substantially accomplished. I do not mean to allege that the work had been completed in the best manner, but it was sufficient for all practical purposes.

The St. Clair flats are formed by the St. Clair River, which empties into the lake of that name by several mouths, and which forms a bar or shoal on which in its natural state there is not more than 6 or 7 feet of water. This shoal is interposed between the mouth of the river and the deep water of the lake, a distance of 6,000 feet, and in its natural condition was a serious obstruction to navigation. The obvious remedy for this was to deepen a channel through these flats by dredging, so as to enable vessels which could navigate the lake and the river to pass through this intermediate channel. This object had been already accomplished by previous appropriations, but without my knowledge, when the bill was presented to me. Captain Whipple, of the Topographical Engineers, to whom the expenditure of the last appropriation of $45,000 for this purpose in 1856 was intrusted, in his annual report of the 1st October, 1858, stated that the dredging was discontinued on the 26th August, 1858, when a channel had been cut averaging 275 feet wide, with a depth varying from 12 to 15½ feet. He says:

So long as the lake retains its present height we may assume that the depth in the channel will be at least 13½ feet.

With this result, highly creditable to Captain Whipple, he observes that if he has been correctly informed ''all the lake navigators are gratified.'' Besides, afterwards, and during the autumn of 1858, the Canadian Government expended $20,000 in deepening and widening the inner end of the channel excavated by the United States. No complaint had been made previous to the passage of the bill of obstructions to the commerce and navigation across the St. Clair flats. What, then, was the object of the appropriation proposed by the bill?

It appears that the surface of the water in Lake St. Clair has been gradually rising, until in 1858 it had attained an elevation of 4 feet above what had been its level in 1841. It is inferred, whether correctly or not it is not for me to say, that the surface of the water may gradually sink to the level of 1841, and in that event the water, which was, when the bill passed, 13½ feet deep in the channel, might sink to 9½ feet, and thus obstruct the passage.

To provide for this contingency, Captain Whipple suggested "the propriety of placing the subject before Congress, with an estimate for excavating a cut through the center of the new channel 150 feet in width and 4½ feet deep, so as to obtain from the river to the lake a depth of 18 feet during seasons of extreme high water and 12 feet at periods of extreme low water." It was not alleged that any present necessity existed for this narrower cut in the bottom of the present channel, but it is inferred that for the reason stated it may hereafter become necessary. Captain Whipple's estimate amounted to $50,000, but Congress by the bill have granted $55,000. Now, if no other objection existed against this measure, it would not seem necessary that the appropriation should have been made for the purpose indicated. The channel was sufficiently deep for all practical purposes; but from natural causes constantly operating in the lake, which I need not explain, this channel is peculiarly liable to fill up. What is really required is that it should at intervals be dredged out, so as to preserve its present depth; and surely the comparatively trifling expense necessary for this purpose ought not to be borne by the United States. After an improvement has been once constructed by appropriations from the Treasury it is not too much to expect that it should be kept in repair by that portion of the commercial and navigating interests which enjoys its peculiar benefits.

The last report made by Captain Whipple, dated on the 13th September last, has been submitted to Congress by the Secretary of War, and to this I would refer for information, which is, upon the whole, favorable, in relation to the present condition of the channel through the St. Clair flats.

2. But the far more important question is, Does Congress possess the power under the Constitution to deepen the channels of rivers and to create and improve harbors for purposes of commerce?

The question of the constitutional power of Congress to construct internal improvements within the States has been so frequently and so elaborately discussed that it would seem useless on this occasion to repeat or to refute at length arguments which have been so often advanced. For my own opinions on this subject I might refer to President Polk's carefully considered message of the 15th December, 1847, addressed to the House of Representatives whilst I was a member of his Cabinet.

The power to pass the bill in question, if it exist at all, must be derived from the power "to regulate commerce with foreign nations and among the several States and with the Indian tribes."

The power "to regulate:" Does this ever embrace the power to create or to construct? To say that it does is to confound the meaning of words of well-known signification. The word "regulate" has several shades of meaning, according to its application to different subjects, but never does it approach the signification of creative power. The regulating power necessarily presupposes the existence of something to be regulated. As applied to commerce, it signifies, according to the lexicographers, "to subject to rules or restrictions, as to regulate trade," etc. The Constitution itself is its own best expounder of the meaning of words employed by its framers. Thus, Congress have the power "to coin money." This is the creative power. Then immediately follows the power "to regulate the value thereof"—that is, of the coined money thus brought into existence. The words "regulate," "regulation," and "regulations" occur several times in the Constitution, but always with this subordinate meaning. Thus, after the creative power "to raise and support armies" and "to provide and maintain a navy" had been conferred upon Congress, then follows the power "to make rules for the government and regulation of the land and naval forces" thus called into being. So the Constitution, acting upon the self-evident fact that "commerce with foreign nations and among the several States and with the Indian tribes" already existed, conferred upon Congress the power "to regulate" this commerce. Thus, according to Chief Justice Marshall, the power to regulate commerce "is the power to prescribe the rule by which commerce is to be governed." And Mr. Madison, in his veto message of the 3d March, 1817, declares that—

"The power to regulate commerce among the several States" can not include a power to construct roads and canals and to improve the navigation of water courses, in order to facilitate, promote, and secure such commerce, without a latitude of construction departing from the ordinary import of the terms, strengthened by the known inconveniences which doubtless led to the grant of this remedial power to Congress.

We know from the history of the Constitution what these inconveniences were. Different States admitted foreign imports at different rates of duty. Those which had prescribed a higher rate of duty for the purpose of increasing their revenue were defeated in this object by the legislation of neighboring States admitting the same foreign articles at lower rates. Hence jealousies and dangerous rivalries had sprung up between the different States. It was chiefly in the desire to provide a remedy for these evils that the Federal Convention originated. The Constitution, for this purpose, conferred upon Congress the power to regulate commerce in such a manner that duties should be uniform in all the States composing the Confederacy, and, moreover, expressly provided that "no preference shall be given by any regulation of commerce or revenue to the ports of one State over those of another." If the construction of a harbor or deepening the channel of a river be a regulation of commerce, as the advocates of this power contend, this would give the ports of the State within which these improvements were made a preference over the ports of other States, and thus be a violation of the Constitution.

It is not too much to assert that no human being in existence when the Constitution was framed entertained the idea or the apprehension that by conferring upon Congress the power to regulate commerce its framers intended to embrace the power of constructing roads and canals and of creating and improving harbors and deepening the channels of rivers throughout our extensive Confederacy. Indeed, one important branch of this very power had been denied to Congress in express terms by the Convention. A proposition was made in the Convention to confer on Congress the power "to provide for the cutting of canals when deemed necessary." This was rejected by the strong majority of eight States to three. Among the reasons given for this rejection was that "the expense in such cases will fall on the United States and the benefits accrue to the places where the canals may be cut."

To say that the simple power of regulating commerce embraces within itself that of constructing harbors, of deepening the channels of rivers— in short, of creating a system of internal improvements for the purpose of facilitating the operations of commerce—would be to adopt a latitude of construction under which all political power might be usurped by the Federal Government. Such a construction would be in conflict with the well-known jealousy against Federal power which actuated the framers of the Constitution. It is certain that the power in question is not enumerated among the express grants to Congress contained in the instrument. In construing the Constitution we must then next inquire, Is its exercise "necessary and proper"?—not whether it may be convenient or useful "for carrying into execution" the power to regulate commerce among the States. But the jealous patriots of that day were not content even with this strict rule of construction. Apprehending that a dangerous latitude of interpretation might be applied in future times to the enumerated grants of power, they procured an amendment to be made to the original instrument, which declares that "the powers not delegated to the United States by the Constitution nor prohibited by it to the States are reserved to the States respectively or to the people."

The distinctive spirit and character which pervades the Constitution is that the powers of the General Government are confined chiefly to our intercourse with foreign nations, to questions of peace and war, and to subjects of common interest to all the States, carefully leaving the internal and domestic concerns of each individual State to be controlled by its own people and legislature. Without specifically enumerating these powers, it must be admitted that this well-marked distinction runs through the whole instrument. In nothing does the wisdom of its framers appear more conspicuously than in the care with which they sought to avoid the danger to our institutions which must necessarily result from the interference of the Federal Government with the local concerns of the States. The jarring and collision which would occur from the exercise by two separate governments of jurisdiction over the same subjects could not fail to produce disastrous consequences. Besides, the corrupting and seducing money influence exerted by the General Government in carrying into effect a system of internal improvements might be perverted to increase and consolidate its own power to the detriment of the rights of the States.

If the power existed in Congress to pass the present bill, then taxes must be imposed and money borrowed to an unlimited extent to carry such a system into execution. Equality among the States is equity. This equality is the very essence of the Constitution. No preference can justly be given to one of the sovereign States over another. According to the best estimate, our immense coast on the Atlantic, the Gulf of Mexico, the Pacific, and the Lakes embraces more than 9,500 miles, and, measuring by its indentations and to the head of tide water on the rivers, the distance is believed to be more than 33,000 miles. This everywhere throughout its vast extent contains numerous rivers and harbors, all of which may become the objects of Congressional appropriation. You can not deny to one State what you have granted to another. Such injustice would produce strife, jealousy, and alarming dissensions among them. Even within the same State improvements may be made in one river or harbor which would essentially injure the commerce and industry of another river or harbor. The truth is that most of these improvements are in a great degree local in their character and for the especial benefit of corporations or individuals in their vicinity, though they may have an odor of nationality on the principle that whatever benefits any part indirectly benefits the whole.

From our past history we may have a small foretaste of the cost of reviving the system of internal improvements.

For more than thirty years after the adoption of the Federal Constitution the power to appropriate money for the construction of internal improvements was neither claimed nor exercised by Congress. After its commencement, in 1820 and 1821, by very small and modest appropriations for surveys, it advanced with such rapid strides that within the brief period of ten years, according to President Polk, "the sum asked for from the Treasury for various projects amounted to more than $200,000,000." The vetoes of General Jackson and several of his successors have impeded the progress of the system and limited its extent, but have not altogether destroyed it. The time has now arrived for a final decision of the question. If the power exists, a general system should be adopted which would make some approach to justice among all the States, if this be possible.

What a vast field would the exercise of this power open for jobbing and corruption! Members of Congress, from an honest desire to promote the interest of their constituents, would struggle for improvements within their own districts, and the body itself must necessarily be converted into an arena where each would endeavor to obtain from the

Treasury as much money as possible for his own locality. The temptation would prove irresistible. A system of *"logrolling"* (I know no word so expressive) would be inaugurated, under which the Treasury would be exhausted and the Federal Government be deprived of the means necessary to execute those great powers clearly confided to it by the Constitution for the purpose of promoting the interests and vindicating the honor of the country.

Whilst the power over internal improvements, it is believed, was "reserved to the States respectively," the framers of the Constitution were not unmindful that it might be proper for the State legislatures to possess the power to impose tonnage duties for the improvement of rivers and harbors within their limits. The self-interest of the different localities would prevent this from being done to such an extent as to injure their trade. The Constitution, therefore, which had in a previous clause provided that all duties should be uniform throughout the United States, subsequently modified the general rule so far as to declare that "no State shall without the consent of Congress levy any duty of tonnage." The inference is therefore irresistible that with the consent of Congress such a duty may be imposed by the States. Thus those directly interested in the improvement may lay a tonnage duty for its construction without imposing a tax for this purpose upon all the people of the United States.

To this provision several of the States resorted until the period when they began to look to the Federal Treasury instead of depending upon their own exertions. Massachusetts, Rhode Island, Pennsylvania, Maryland, Virginia, North Carolina, South Carolina, and Georgia, with the consent of Congress, imposed small tonnage duties on vessels at different periods for clearing and deepening the channels of rivers and improving harbors where such vessels entered. The last of these legislative acts believed to exist is that of Virginia, passed on the 22d February, 1826, levying a tonnage duty on vessels for "improving the navigation of James River from Warwick to Rocketts Landing." The latest act of Congress on this subject was passed on the 24th of February, 1843, giving its consent to the law of the legislature of Maryland laying a tonnage duty on vessels for the improvement of the harbor of Baltimore, and continuing it in force until 1st June, 1850.

Thus a clear constitutional mode exists by which the legislature of Michigan may, in its discretion, raise money to preserve the channel of the St. Clair River at its present depth or to render it deeper. A very insignificant tonnage duty on American vessels using this channel would be sufficient for the purpose; and as the St. Clair River is the boundary line between the United States and the Province of Upper Canada, the provincial British authorities would doubtless be willing to impose a similar tonnage duty on British vessels to aid in the accomplishment of this object. Indeed, the legislature of that Province have already evinced their interest on this subject by having but recently expended $20,000 on the improvement of the St. Clair flats. Even if the Constitution of the United States had conferred upon Congress the power of deepening the channel of the St. Clair River, it would be unjust to impose upon the people of the United States the entire burden, which ought to be borne jointly by the two parties having an equal interest in the work. Whenever the State of Michigan shall cease to depend on the Treasury of the United States, I doubt not that she, in conjunction with Upper Canada, will provide the necessary means for keeping this work in repair in the least expensive and most effective manner and without being burdensome to any interest.

It has been contended in favor of the existence of the power to construct internal improvements that Congress have from the beginning made appropriations for light-houses, and that upon the same principle of construction they possess the power of improving harbors and deepening the channels of rivers. As an original question the authority to erect light-houses under the commercial power might be considered doubtful; but even were it more doubtful than it is I should regard it as settled after an uninterrupted exercise of the power for seventy years. Such a long and uniform practical construction of the Constitution is entitled to the highest respect, and has finally determined the question.

Among the first acts which passed Congress after the Federal Government went into effect was that of August 7, 1789, providing "for the establishment and support of light-houses, beacons, buoys, and public piers." Under this act the expenses for the maintenance of all such erections then in existence were to be paid by the Federal Government and provision was made for the cession of jurisdiction over them by the respective States to the United States. In every case since before a light-house could be built a previous cession of jurisdiction has been required. This practice doubtless originated from that clause of the Constitution authorizing Congress "to exercise exclusive legislation * * * over all places purchased by the consent of the legislature of the State in which the same shall be, for the erection of forts, magazines, arsenals, dockyards, and other *needful buildings*." Among these "*needful buildings*" light-houses must in fact have been included.

The bare statement of these facts is sufficient to prove that no analogy exists between the power to erect a light-house as a "needful building" and that to deepen the channel of a river.

In what I have said I do not mean to intimate a doubt of the power of Congress to construct such internal improvements as may be essentially necessary for defense and protection against the invasion of a foreign enemy. The power to declare war and the obligation to protect each State against invasion clearly cover such cases. It will scarcely be claimed, however, that the improvement of the St. Clair River is within this category. This river is the boundary line between the United States and the British Province of Upper Canada. Any improvement of its navigation, therefore, which we could make for purposes of war would equally inure to the benefit of Great Britain, the only enemy which could possibly confront us in that quarter. War would be a sad calamity for both nations, but should it ever, unhappily, exist, the battles will not be fought on the St. Clair River or on the lakes with which it communicates.

JAMES BUCHANAN.

WASHINGTON, *February 6, 1860.*

To the Senate of the United States:

On the last day of the last session of Congress a resolution, which had passed both Houses, "in relation to removal of obstructions to navigation in the mouth of the Mississippi River" was presented to me for approval. I have retained this resolution because it was presented to me at a period when it was impossible to give the subject that examination to which it appeared to be entitled. I need not repeat the views on this point presented in the introductory portion of my message to the Senate of the 2d [1st] instant.

In addition I would merely observe that although at different periods sums, amounting in the aggregate to $690,000, have been appropriated by Congress for the purpose of removing the bar and obstructions at the mouth of the Mississippi, yet it is now acknowledged that this money has been expended with but little, if any, practical benefit to its navigation.

JAMES BUCHANAN.

WASHINGTON, *April 17, 1860.*

To the Senate of the United States:

I return with my objections to the Senate, for their reconsideration, the bill entitled "An act for the relief of Arthur Edwards and his associates," presented to me on the 10th instant.

This bill directs the Postmaster-General "to audit and settle the accounts of Arthur Edwards and his associates for transporting the United States through mail on their steamers during the years 1849 and 1853 and intervening years" between Cleveland and Detroit, between Sandusky and Detroit, and between Toledo and Detroit, and "to allow and pay them not less than $28.60 for each and every passage of said steamers between said places during the aforementioned time when the mails were on board."

I have caused a statement to be made at the Post-Office Department of the least sum which can be paid to Mr. Edwards and his associates under the bill should it become a law, and from this it appears the amount will be $80,405.23.

Mr. Edwards and his associates, in 1854, a short time after the alleged services had been rendered, presented a claim to the Postmaster-General for $25,180 as compensation for these services. This claim consisted of nine items, setting forth specifically all the services embraced by the present bill. It is fair to presume that the parties best knew the value of their own services and that they would not by an underestimate do themselves injustice. The whole claim of $25,180 was rejected by the Postmaster-General for reasons which it is no part of my present purpose to discuss.

The claimants next presented a petition to the Court of Claims in June, 1855, "for a reasonable compensation" for these services, and "pray the judgment of your honorable court for the actual value of the service rendered by them and received by the United States, which amounts to the sum of $50,000." Thus the estimate which they placed upon their services had nearly doubled between 1854 and 1855—had risen from $25,180 to $50,000. On the ———, after a full hearing, the court decided against the claim, and delivered an opinion in support of this decision which can not, I think, be contested on legal principles. But they state in the conclusion of the opinion that "for any compensation for their services beyond what they have received they must depend upon the discretion of Congress."

This decision of the Court of Claims was reported to Congress on the 1st of April, 1858, and from it the present bill has originated. The amount granted by it is more by upward of $55,000 than the parties themselves demanded from the Postmaster-General in 1854, and is more by upward of $30,000 than they demanded when before the Court of Claims. The enormous difference in their favor between their own original demand and the amount granted by the present bill constitutes my chief objection to it. In presenting this objection I do not propose to enter into the question whether the claimants are entitled in equity to any compensation for their services beyond that which it is alleged they have already received, or, if so, what would be "a reasonable and fair compensation." My sole purpose is to afford Congress an opportunity of reconsidering this case on account of its peculiar circumstances. I transmit to the Senate the reports of Horatio King, Acting Postmaster-General, and of A. N. Zevely, Third Assistant Postmaster-General, both dated on the 14th of April, 1860, on the subject of this claim.

JAMES BUCHANAN.

WASHINGTON, *June 22, 1860.*

To the Senate of the United States:

I return with my objections to the Senate, in which it originated, the bill entitled "An act to secure homesteads to actual settlers on the public domain, and for other purposes," presented to me on the 20th instant.

This bill gives to every citizen of the United States "who is the head of a family," and to every person of foreign birth residing in the country who has declared his intention to become a citizen, though he may not be the head of a family, the privilege of appropriating to himself 160 acres of Government land, of settling and residing upon it for five years; and should his residence continue until the end of this period, he shall then receive a patent on the payment of 25 cents per acre, or one-fifth of the present Government price. During this period the land is protected from all the debts of the settler.

This bill also contains a cession to the States of all the public lands within their respective limits "which have been subject to sale at private entry, and which remain unsold after the lapse of thirty years." This provision embraces a present donation to the States of 12,229,731 acres, and will from time to time transfer to them large bodies of such lands which from peculiar circumstances may not be absorbed by private purchase and settlement.

To the actual settler this bill does not make an absolute donation, but the price is so small that it can scarcely be called a sale. It is nominally 25 cents per acre, but considering this is not to be paid until the end of five years, it is in fact reduced to about 18 cents per acre, or one-seventh of the present minimum price of the public lands. In regard to the States, it is an absolute and unqualified gift.

1. This state of the facts raises the question whether Congress, under the Constitution, has the power to give away the public lands either to States or individuals. On this question I expressed a decided opinion in my message to the House of Representatives of the 24th February, 1859, returning the agricultural-college bill. This opinion remains unchanged. The argument then used applies as a constitutional objection with greater force to the present bill. *There* it had the plea of consideration, growing out of a specific beneficial purpose; *here* it is an absolute gratuity to the States, without the pretext of consideration. I am compelled for want of time in these the last hours of the session to quote largely from this message.

I presume the general proposition will be admitted that Congress does not possess the power to make donations of money already in the Treasury, raised by taxes on the people, either to States or individuals.

But it is contended that the public lands are placed upon a different footing from money raised by taxation and that the proceeds arising from their sale are not subject to the limitations of the Constitution, but may be appropriated or given away by Congress, at its own discretion, to States, corporations, or individuals for any purpose they may deem expedient.

The advocates of this bill attempt to sustain their position upon the language of the second clause of the third section of the fourth article of the Constitution, which declares that "the Congress shall have power to dispose of and make all needful rules and regulations respecting the territory or other property belonging to the United States." They contend that by a fair interpretation of the words "dispose of" in this clause Congress possesses the power to make this gift of public lands to the States for purposes of education.

It would require clear and strong evidence to induce the belief that the framers of the Constitution, after having limited the powers of Congress to certain precise and specific objects, intended by employing the words "dispose of" to give that body unlimited power over the vast public domain. It would be a strange anomaly indeed to have created two funds—the one by taxation, confined to the execution of the enumerated powers delegated to Congress, and the other from the public lands, applicable to all subjects, foreign and domestic, which Congress might designate; that this fund should be "disposed of," not to pay the debts of the United States, nor "to raise and support armies," nor "to provide and maintain a navy," nor to accomplish any one of the other great objects enumerated in the Constitution, but be diverted from them to pay the debts of the States, to educate their people, and to carry into effect any other measure of their domestic policy. This would be to confer upon Congress a vast and irresponsible authority utterly at war with the well-known jealousy of Federal power which prevailed at the formation of the Constitution. The natural intendment would be that as the Constitution confined Congress to well-defined specific powers, the funds placed at their command, whether in land or money, should be appropriated to the performance of the duties corresponding with these powers. If not, a Government has been created with all its other powers carefully limited, but without any limitation in respect to the public lands.

But I can not so read the words "dispose of" as to make them embrace the idea of "giving away." The true meaning of words is always to be ascertained by the subject to which they are applied and the known general intent of the lawgiver. Congress is a trustee under the Constitution for the people of the United States to "dispose of" their public lands, and I think I may venture to assert with confidence that no case can be found in which a trustee in the position of Congress has been authorized to "*dispose of*" property by its owner where it has been held that these words authorized such trustee to give away the fund intrusted to his care. No trustee, when called upon to account for the disposition of the property placed under his management before any judicial tribunal, would venture to present such a plea in his defense. The true meaning of these words is clearly stated by Chief Justice Taney in delivering the opinion of the court (19 Howard, p. 436). He says in reference to this clause of the Constitution: "It begins its enumeration of powers by that of disposing; in other words, making sale of the lands or raising money from them, which, as we have already said, was the main object of the cession (from the States), and which is the first thing provided for in the article." It is unnecessary to refer to the history of the times to establish the known fact that this statement of the Chief Justice is perfectly well founded. That it never was intended by the framers of the Constitution that these lands should be given away by Congress is manifest from the concluding portion of the same clause. By it Congress has power not only "to dispose of" the territory, but of the "other property of the United States." In the language of the Chief Justice (p. 437): "And the same power of making needful rules respecting the territory is in precisely the same language applied to the other property of the United States, associating the power over the territory in this respect with the power over movable or personal property; that is, the ships, arms, or munitions of war, which then belonged in common to the State sovereignties."

The question is still clearer in regard to the public lands in the States and Territories within the Louisiana and Florida purchases. These lands were paid for out of the public Treasury from money raised by taxation. Now if Congress had no power to appropriate the money with which these lands were purchased, is it not clear that the power over the lands is equally limited? The mere conversion of this money into land could not confer upon Congress new power over the disposition of land which they had not possessed over money. If it could, then a trustee, by changing the character of the fund intrusted to his care for special objects from money into land, might give the land away or devote it to any purpose he thought proper, however foreign from the trust. The inference is irresistible that this land partakes of the very same character with the money paid for it, and can be devoted to no objects different from those to which the money could have been devoted. If this were not the case, then by the purchase of a new territory from a foreign government out of the public Treasury Congress could enlarge their own powers and appropriate the proceeds of the sales of the land thus purchased, at their own discretion, to other and far different objects from what they could have applied the purchase money which had been raised by taxation.

2. It will prove unequal and unjust in its operation among the actual settlers themselves.

The first settlers of a new country are a most meritorious class. They brave the dangers of savage warfare, suffer the privations of a frontier life, and with the hand of toil bring the wilderness into cultivation. The ''old settlers,'' as they are everywhere called, are public benefactors. This class have all paid for their lands the Government price, or $1.25 per acre. They have constructed roads, established schools, and laid the foundation of prosperous commonwealths. Is it just, is it equal, that after they have accomplished all this by their labor new settlers should come in among them and receive their farms at the price of 25 or 18 cents per acre? Surely the old settlers, as a class, are entitled to at least equal benefits with the new. If you give the new settlers their land for a comparatively nominal price, upon every principle of equality and justice you will be obliged to refund out of the common Treasury the difference which the old have paid above the new settlers for their land.

3. This bill will do great injustice to the old soldiers who have received land warrants for their services in fighting the battles of their country. It will greatly reduce the market value of these warrants. Already their value has sunk for 160-acre warrants to 67 cents per acre under an apprehension that such a measure as this might become a law. What price would they command when any head of a family may take possession of a quarter section of land and not pay for it until the end of five years, and then at the rate of only 25 cents per acre? The magnitude of the interest to be affected will appear in the fact that there are outstanding unsatisfied land warrants reaching back to the last war with Great Britain, and even Revolutionary times, amounting in round numbers to seven and a half millions of acres.

4. This bill will prove unequal and unjust in its operation, because from its nature it is confined to one class of our people. It is a boon exclusively conferred upon the cultivators of the soil. Whilst it is cheerfully admitted that these are the most numerous and useful class of our fellow-citizens and eminently deserve all the advantages which our laws have already extended to them, yet there should be no new legislation which would operate to the injury or embarrassment of the large body of respectable artisans and laborers. The mechanic who emigrates to the West and pursues his calling must labor long before he can purchase a quarter section of land, whilst the tiller of the soil who accompanies him obtains a farm at once by the bounty of the Government. The

numerous body of mechanics in our large cities can not, even by emigrating to the West, take advantage of the provisions of this bill without entering upon a new occupation for which their habits of life have rendered them unfit.

5. This bill is unjust to the old States of the Union in many respects; and amongst these States, so far as the public lands are concerned, we may enumerate every State east of the Mississippi with the exception of Wisconsin and a portion of Minnesota.

It is a common belief within their limits that the older States of the Confederacy do not derive their proportionate benefit from the public lands. This is not a just opinion. It is doubtful whether they could be rendered more beneficial to these States under any other system than that which at present exists. Their proceeds go into the common Treasury to accomplish the objects of the Government, and in this manner all the States are benefited in just proportion. But to give this common inheritance away would deprive the old States of their just proportion of this revenue without holding out any the least corresponding advantage. Whilst it is our common glory that the new States have become so prosperous and populous, there is no good reason why the old States should offer premiums to their own citizens to emigrate from them to the West. That land of promise presents in itself sufficient allurements to our young and enterprising citizens without any adventitious aid. The offer of free farms would probably have a powerful effect in encouraging emigration, especially from States like Illinois, Tennessee, and Kentucky, to the west of the Mississippi, and could not fail to reduce the price of property within their limits. An individual in States thus situated would not pay its fair value for land when by crossing the Mississippi he could go upon the public lands and obtain a farm almost without money and without price.

6. This bill will open one vast field for speculation. Men will not pay $1.25 for lands when they can purchase them for one-fifth of that price. Large numbers of actual settlers will be carried out by capitalists upon agreements to give them half of the land for the improvement of the other half. This can not be avoided. Secret agreements of this kind will be numerous. In the entry of graduated lands the experience of the Land Office justifies this objection.

7. We ought ever to maintain the most perfect equality between native and naturalized citizens. They are equal, and ought always to remain equal, before the laws. Our laws welcome foreigners to our shores, and their rights will ever be respected. Whilst these are the sentiments on which I have acted through life, it is not, in my opinion, expedient to proclaim to all the nations of the earth that whoever shall arrive in this country from a foreign shore and declare his intention to become a citizen shall receive a farm of 160 acres at a cost of 25 or 20 cents per acre if he will only reside on it and cultivate it. The invitation extends to

all, and if this bill becomes a law we may have numerous actual settlers from China and other Eastern nations enjoying its benefits on the great Pacific Slope. The bill makes a distinction in favor of such persons over native and naturalized citizens. When applied to such citizens, it is confined to such as are the heads of families, but when applicable to persons of foreign birth recently arrived on our shores there is no such restriction. Such persons need not be the heads of families provided they have filed a declaration of intention to become citizens. Perhaps this distinction was an inadvertence, but it is, nevertheless, a part of the bill.

8. The bill creates an unjust distinction between persons claiming the benefit of the preemption laws. Whilst it reduces the price of the land to existing preemptors to 62½ cents per acre and gives them a credit on this sum for two years from the present date, no matter how long they may have hitherto enjoyed the land, future preemptors will be compelled to pay double this price per acre. There is no reason or justice in this discrimination.

9. The effect of this bill on the public revenue must be apparent to all. Should it become a law, the reduction of the price of land to actual settlers to 25 cents per acre, with a credit of five years, and the reduction of its price to existing preemptors to 62½ cents per acre, with a credit of two years, will so diminish the sale of other public lands as to render the expectation of future revenue from that source, beyond the expenses of survey and management, illusory. The Secretary of the Interior estimated the revenue from the public lands for the next fiscal year at $4,000,000, on the presumption that the present land system would remain unchanged. Should this bill become a law, he does not believe that $1,000,000 will be derived from this source.

10. This bill lays the ax at the root of our present admirable land system. The public land is an inheritance of vast value to us and to our descendants. It is a resource to which we can resort in the hour of difficulty and danger. It has been managed heretofore with the greatest wisdom under existing laws. In this management the rights of actual settlers have been conciliated with the interests of the Government. The price to all has been reduced from $2 per acre to $1.25 for fresh lands, and the claims of actual settlers have been secured by our preemption laws. Any man can now acquire a title in fee simple to a homestead of 80 acres, at the minimum price of $1.25 per acre, for $100. Should the present system remain, we shall derive a revenue from the public lands of $10,000,000 per annum, when the bounty-land warrants are satisfied, without oppression to any human being. In time of war, when all other sources of revenue are seriously impaired, this will remain intact. It may become the best security for public loans hereafter, in times of difficulty and danger, as it has been heretofore. Why should we impair or destroy the system at the present moment? What necessity exists for it?

The people of the United States have advanced with steady but rapid strides to their present condition of power and prosperity. They have been guided in their progress by the fixed principle of protecting the equal rights of all, whether they be rich or poor. No agrarian sentiment has ever prevailed among them. The honest poor man, by frugality and industry, can in any part of our country acquire a competence for himself and his family, and in doing this he feels that he eats the bread of independence. He desires no charity, either from the Government or from his neighbors. This bill, which proposes to give him land at an almost nominal price out of the property of the Government, will go far to demoralize the people and repress this noble spirit of independence. It may introduce among us those pernicious social theories which have proved so disastrous in other countries.

JAMES BUCHANAN.

PROTESTS.

WASHINGTON, *March 28, 1860.*

To the House of Representatives:

After a delay which has afforded me ample time for reflection, and after much and careful deliberation, I find myself constrained by an imperious sense of duty, as a coordinate branch of the Federal Government, to protest against the first two clauses of the first resolution adopted by the House of Representatives on the 5th instant, and published in the Congressional Globe on the succeeding day. These clauses are in the following words:

Resolved, That a committee of five members be appointed by the Speaker for the purpose, first, of investigating whether the President of the United States or any other officer of the Government has, by money, patronage, or other improper means, sought to influence the action of Congress or any committee thereof for or against the passage of any law appertaining to the rights of any State or Territory; and, second, also to inquire into and investigate whether any officer or officers of the Government have, by combination or otherwise, prevented or defeated, or attempted to prevent or defeat, the execution of any law or laws now upon the statute book, and whether the President has failed or refused to compel the execution of any law thereof.

I confine myself exclusively to these two branches of the resolution, because the portions of it which follow relate to alleged abuses in post-offices, navy-yards, public buildings, and other public works of the United States. In such cases inquiries are highly proper in themselves and belong equally to the Senate and the House, as incident to their legislative duties and being necessary to enable them to discover and to provide the appropriate legislative remedies for any abuses which may be ascertained. Although the terms of the latter portion of the resolution are extremely vague and general, yet my sole purpose in adverting to them at present is to mark the broad line of distinction between the accusatory and the remedial clauses of this resolution. The House of Representatives possess no power under the Constitution over the first or accusatory portion of the resolution except as an impeaching body, whilst over the last, in common with the Senate, their authority as a legislative body is fully and cheerfully admitted.

It is solely in reference to the first or impeaching power that I propose to make a few observations. Except in this single case, the Constitution has invested the House of Representatives with no power, no jurisdiction, no supremacy whatever over the President. In all other respects he is quite as independent of them as they are of him. As a coordinate branch of the Government he is their equal. Indeed, he is the only direct representative on earth of the people of all and each of the sovereign States. To them, and to them alone, is he responsible whilst acting within the sphere of his constitutional duty, and not in any manner to the House of Representatives. The people have thought proper to invest him with the most honorable, responsible, and dignified office in the world, and the individual, however unworthy, now holding this exalted position, will take care, so far as in him lies, that their rights and prerogatives shall never be violated in his person, but shall pass to his successors unimpaired by the adoption of a dangerous precedent. He will defend them to the last extremity against any unconstitutional attempt, come from what quarter it may, to abridge the constitutional rights of the Executive and render him subservient to any human power except themselves.

The people have not confined the President to the exercise of executive duties. They have also conferred upon him a large measure of legislative discretion. No bill can become a law without his approval, as representing the people of the United States, unless it shall pass after his veto by a majority of two-thirds of both Houses. In his legislative capacity he might, in common with the Senate and the House, institute an inquiry to ascertain any facts which ought to influence his judgment in approving or vetoing any bill.

This participation in the performance of legislative duties between the coordinate branches of the Government ought to inspire the conduct of all of them in their relations toward each other with mutual forbearance and respect. At least each has a right to demand justice from the other. The cause of complaint is that the constitutional rights and immunities of the Executive have been violated in the person of the President.

The trial of an impeachment of the President before the Senate on charges preferred and prosecuted against him by the House of Representatives would be an imposing spectacle for the world. In the result not only his removal from the Presidential office would be involved, but, what is of infinitely greater importance to himself, his character, both in the eyes of the present and of future generations, might possibly be tarnished. The disgrace cast upon him would in some degree be reflected upon the character of the American people, who elected him. Hence the precautions adopted by the Constitution to secure a fair trial. On such a trial it declares that "the Chief Justice shall preside." This was doubtless because the framers of the Constitution believed it to be possible that the Vice-President might be biased by the fact that "in case of the removal of the President from office * * * the same shall devolve on the Vice-President."

The preliminary proceedings in the House in the case of charges which may involve impeachment have been well and wisely settled by long practice upon principles of equal justice both to the accused and to the people. The precedent established in the case of Judge Peck, of Missouri, in 1831, after a careful review of all former precedents, will, I venture to predict, stand the test of time.

In that case Luke Edward Lawless, the accuser, presented a petition to the House, in which he set forth minutely and specifically his causes of complaint. He prayed "that the conduct and proceedings in this behalf of said Judge Peck may be inquired into by your honorable body, and such decision made thereon as to your wisdom and justice shall seem proper." This petition was referred to the Judiciary Committee; such has ever been deemed the appropriate committee to make similar investigations. It is a standing committee, supposed to be appointed without reference to any special case, and at all times is presumed to be composed of the most eminent lawyers in the House from different portions of the Union, whose acquaintance with judicial proceedings and whose habits of investigation qualify them peculiarly for the task. No tribunal, from their position and character, could in the nature of things be more impartial. In the case of Judge Peck the witnesses were selected by the committee itself, with a view to ascertain the truth of the charge. They were cross-examined by him, and everything was conducted in such a manner as to afford him no reasonable cause of complaint. In view of this precedent, and, what is of far greater importance, in view of the Constitution and the principles of eternal justice, in what manner has the President of the United States been treated by the House of Representatives? Mr. John Covode, a Representative from Pennsylvania, is the accuser of the President. Instead of following the wise precedents of former times, and especially that in the case of Judge Peck, and referring the accusation to the Committee on the Judiciary, the House have made my accuser one of my judges.

To make the accuser the judge is a violation of the principles of universal justice, and is condemned by the practice of all civilized nations. Every freeman must revolt at such a spectacle. I am to appear before Mr. Covode, either personally or by a substitute, to cross-examine the witnesses which he may produce before himself to sustain his own accusations against me; and perhaps even this poor boon may be denied to the President.

And what is the nature of the investigation which his resolution proposes to institute? It is as vague and general as the English language affords words in which to make it. The committee is to inquire, not into any specific charge or charges, but whether the President has, by "money, patronage, or other improper means, sought to influence," not the action of any individual member or members of Congress, but "the action" of the entire body "of Congress" itself "or any committee thereof." The President might have had some glimmering of the nature of the offense to be investigated had his accuser pointed to the act or acts of Congress which he sought to pass or to defeat by the employment of "money, patronage, or other improper means." But the accusation is bounded by no such limits. It extends to the whole circle of legislation—to interference "for or against the passage of any law appertaining to the rights of any State or Territory." And what law does not appertain to the rights of some State or Territory? And what law or laws has the President failed to execute? These might easily have been pointed out had any such existed.

Had Mr. Lawless asked an inquiry to be made by the House whether Judge Peck, in general terms, had not violated his judicial duties, without the specification of any particular act, I do not believe there would have been a single vote in that body in favor of the inquiry.

Since the time of the star-chamber and of general warrants there has been no such proceeding in England.

The House of Representatives, the high impeaching power of the country, without consenting to hear a word of explanation, have indorsed this accusation against the President and made it their own act. They even refused to permit a Member to inquire of the President's accuser what were the specific charges against him. Thus, in this preliminary accusation of "high crimes and misdemeanors" against a coordinate branch of the Government, under the impeaching power, the House refused to hear a single suggestion, even in regard to the correct mode of proceeding, but without a moment's delay passed the accusatory resolutions under the pressure of the previous question.

In the institution of a prosecution for any offense against the most humble citizen—and I claim for myself no greater rights than he enjoys—the constitutions of the United States and of the several States require that he shall be informed in the very beginning of the nature and cause of the accusation against him, in order to enable him to prepare for his defense. There are other principles which I might enumerate, not less sacred, presenting an impenetrable shield to protect every citizen falsely charged with a criminal offense. These have been violated in the prosecution instituted by the House of Representatives against the executive branch of the Government. Shall the President alone be deprived of the protection of these great principles which prevail in every land where a ray of liberty penetrates the gloom of despotism? Shall the Executive alone be deprived of rights which all his fellow-citizens enjoy? The whole proceeding against him justifies the fears of those wise and great men who, before the Constitution was adopted by the States, apprehended that the tendency of the Government was to the aggrandizement of the legislative at the expense of the executive and judicial departments.

I again declare emphatically that I make this protest for no reason personal to myself, and I do it with perfect respect for the House of Representatives, in which I had the honor of serving as a member for five successive terms. I have lived long in this goodly land, and have enjoyed all the offices and honors which my country could bestow. Amid all the political storms through which I have passed, the present is the first attempt which has ever been made, to my knowledge, to assail my personal or official integrity; and this as the time is approaching when I shall voluntarily retire from the service of my country. I feel proudly conscious that there is no public act of my life which will not bear the strictest scrutiny. I defy all investigation. Nothing but the basest perjury can sully my good name. I do not fear even this, because I cherish an humble confidence that the gracious Being who has hitherto defended and protected me against the shafts of falsehood and malice will not desert me now when I have become "old and gray headed." I can declare before God and my country that no human being (with an exception scarcely worthy of notice) has at any period of my life dared to approach me with a corrupt or dishonorable proposition, and until recent developments it had never entered into my imagination that any person, even in the storm of exasperated political excitement, would charge me in the most remote degree with having made such a proposition to any human being. I may now, however, exclaim in the language of complaint employed by my first and greatest predecessor, that I have been abused "in such exaggerated and indecent terms as could scarcely be applied to a Nero, to a notorious defaulter, or even to a common pickpocket."

I do therefore, for the reasons stated and in the name of the people of the several States, solemnly protest against these proceedings of the House of Representatives, because they are in violation of the rights of the coordinate executive branch of the Government and subversive of its constitutional independence; because they are calculated to foster a band of interested parasites and informers, ever ready, for their own advantage, to swear before *ex parte* committees to pretended private conversations between the President and themselves, incapable from their nature of being disproved, thus furnishing material for harassing him, degrading him in the eyes of the country, and eventually, should he be a weak or a timid man, rendering him subservient to improper influences in order to avoid such persecutions and annoyances; because they tend to destroy that harmonious action for the common good which ought to be maintained, and which I sincerely desire to cherish, between coordinate branches of the Government; and, finally, because, if unresisted, they would establish a precedent dangerous and embarrassing to all my successors, to whatever political party they might be attached.

JAMES BUCHANAN.

WASHINGTON, *June 22, 1860.*

To the House of Representatives:

In my message to the House of Representatives of the 28th March last I solemnly protested against the creation of a committee, at the head of which was placed my accuser, for the purpose of investigating whether the President had, "by money, patronage, or other improper means, sought to influence the action of Congress or any committee thereof for or against the passage of any law appertaining to the rights of any State or Territory." I protested against this because it was destitute of any specification; because it referred to no particular act to enable the President to prepare for his defense; because it deprived him of the constitutional guards which, in common with every citizen of the United States, he possesses for his protection, and because it assailed his constitutional independence as a coordinate branch of the Government.

There is an enlightened justice, as well as a beautiful symmetry, in every part of the Constitution. This is conspicuously manifested in regard to impeachments. The House of Representatives possesses "the sole power of impeachment," the Senate "the sole power to try all impeachments;" and the impeachable offenses are "treason, bribery, or other high crimes or misdemeanors." The practice of the House from the earliest times had been in accordance with its own dignity, the rights of the accused, and the demands of justice. At the commencement of each judicial investigation which might lead to an impeachment specific charges were always preferred; the accused had an opportunity of cross-examining the witnesses, and he was placed in full possession of the precise nature of the offense which he had to meet. An impartial and elevated standing committee was charged with this investigation, upon which no member inspired with the ancient sense of honor and justice would have served had he ever expressed an opinion against the accused. Until the present occasion it was never deemed proper to transform the accuser into the judge and to confer upon him the selection of his own committee.

The charges made against me in vague and general terms were of such a false and atrocious character that I did not entertain a moment's apprehension for the result. They were abhorrent to every principle instilled into me from my youth and every practice of my life, and I did not believe it possible that the man existed who would so basely perjure himself as to swear to the truth of any such accusations.   In this conviction I am informed I have not been mistaken.

In my former protest, therefore, I truly and emphatically declared that it was made for no reason personal to myself, but because the proceedings of the House were in violation of the rights of the coordinate executive branch of the Government, subversive of its constitutional independence, and if unresisted would establish a precedent dangerous and embarrassing to all my successors.   Notwithstanding all this, if the committee had not transcended the authority conferred upon it by the resolution of the House of Representatives, broad and general as this was, I should have remained silent upon the subject.   What I now charge is that they have acted as though they possessed unlimited power, and, without any warrant whatever in the resolution under which they were appointed, have pursued a course not merely at war with the constitutional rights of the Executive, but tending to degrade the Presidential office itself to such a degree as to render it unworthy of the acceptance of any man of honor or principle.

The resolution of the House, so far as it is accusatory of the President, is confined to an inquiry whether he had used corrupt or improper means to influence the action of Congress or any of its committees on legislative measures pending before them—nothing more, nothing less.   I have not learned through the newspapers or in any other mode that the committee have touched the other accusatory branch of the resolution, charging the President with a violation of duty in failing to execute some law or laws.   This branch of the resolution is therefore out of the question. By what authority, then, have the committee undertaken to investigate the course of the President in regard to the convention which framed the Lecompton constitution?   By what authority have they undertaken to pry into our foreign relations for the purpose of assailing him on account of the instructions given by the Secretary of State to our minister in Mexico relative to the Tehuantepec route?   By what authority have they inquired into the causes of removal from office, and this from the parties themselves removed, with a view to prejudice his character, notwithstanding this power of removal belongs exclusively to the President under the Constitution, was so decided by the First Congress in the year 1789, and has accordingly ever since been exercised?   There is in the resolution no pretext of authority for the committee to investigate the question of the printing of the post-office blanks; nor is it to be supposed that the House, if asked, would have granted such an authority, because this question had been previously committed to two other committees—one in the Senate and the other in the House.   Notwithstanding this absolute want of power, the committee rushed into this investigation in advance of all other subjects.

The committee proceeded for months, from March 22, 1860, to examine *ex parte* and without any notice to myself into every subject which could possibly affect my character. Interested and vindictive witnesses were summoned and examined before them; and the first and only information of their testimony which, in almost every instance, I received was obtained from the publication of such portions of it as could injuriously affect myself in the New York journals. It mattered not that these statements were, so far as I have learned, disproved by the most respectable witnesses who happened to be on the spot. The telegraph was silent respecting these contradictions. It was a secret committee in regard to the testimony in my defense, but it was public in regard to all the testimony which could by possibility reflect on my character. The poison was left to produce its effect upon the public mind, whilst the antidote was carefully withheld.

In their examinations the committee violated the most sacred and honorable confidences existing among men. Private correspondence, which a truly honorable man would never even entertain a distant thought of divulging, was dragged to light. Different persons in official and confidential relations with myself, and with whom it was supposed I might have held conversations the revelation of which would do me injury, were examined. Even members of the Senate and members of my own Cabinet, both my constitutional advisers, were called upon to testify, for the purpose of discovering something, if possible, to my discredit.

The distribution of the patronage of the Government is by far the most disagreeable duty of the President. Applicants are so numerous and their applications are pressed with such eagerness by their friends, both in and out of Congress, that the selection of one for any desirable office gives offense to many. Disappointed applicants, removed officers, and those who for any cause, real or imaginary, had become hostile to the Administration presented themselves or were invited by a summons to appear before the committee. These are the most dangerous witnesses. Even with the best intentions they are so influenced by prejudice and disappointment that they almost inevitably discolor truth. They swear to their own version of private conversations with the President without the possibility of contradiction. His lips are sealed, and he is left at their mercy. He can not, as a coordinate branch of the Government, appear before a committee of investigation to contradict the oaths of such witnesses. Every coward knows that he can employ insulting language against the President with impunity, and every false or prejudiced witness can attempt to swear away his character before such a committee without the fear of contradiction.

Thus for months, whilst doing my best at one end of the Avenue to perform my high and responsible duties to the country, has there been a committee of the House of Representatives in session at the other end of the Avenue spreading a drag net, without the shadow of authority from the House, over the whole Union, to catch any disappointed man willing to malign my character; and all this in secret conclave. The lion's mouth at Venice, into which secret denunciations were dropped, is an apt illustration of the Covode committee. The star-chamber, tyrannical and odious as it was, never proceeded in such a manner. For centuries there has been nothing like it in any civilized country, except the revolutionary tribunal of France in the days of Robespierre. Now I undertake to state and to prove that should the proceedings of the committee be sanctioned by the House and become a precedent for future times the balance of the Constitution will be entirely upset, and there will no longer remain the three coordinate and independent branches of the Government—legislative, executive, and judicial. The worst fears of the patriots and statesmen who framed the Constitution in regard to the usurpations of the legislative on the executive and judicial branches will then be realized. In the language of Mr. Madison, speaking on this very subject in the forty-eighth number of the Federalist:

In a representative republic, where the executive magistracy is carefully limited, both in the extent and duration of its power, and where the legislative power is exercised by an assembly which is inspired, by a supposed influence over the people, with an intrepid confidence in its own strength, which is sufficiently numerous to feel all the passions which actuate a multitude, yet not so numerous as to be incapable of pursuing the objects of its passions by means which reason prescribes, it is against the enterprising ambition of this department that the people ought to indulge all their jealousy and exhaust all their precautions.

And in the expressive and pointed language of Mr. Jefferson, when speaking of the tendency of the legislative branch of Government to usurp the rights of the weaker branches:

The concentrating these in the same hands is precisely the definition of despotic government. It will be no alleviation that these powers will be exercised by a plurality of hands, and not by a single one. One hundred and seventy-three despots would surely be as oppressive as one. Let those who doubt it turn their eyes on the Republic of Venice. As little will it avail us that they are chosen by ourselves. An elective despotism was not the government we fought for, but one which should not only be founded on free principles, but in which the powers of government should be so divided and balanced among several bodies of magistracy as that no one could transcend their legal limits without being effectually checked and controlled by the others.

Should the proceedings of the Covode committee become a precedent, both the letter and spirit of the Constitution will be violated. One of the three massive columns on which the whole superstructure rests will be broken down. Instead of the Executive being a coordinate it will become a subordinate branch of the Government. The Presidential office will be dragged into the dust. The House of Representatives will then have rendered the Executive almost necessarily subservient to its wishes, instead of being independent. How is it possible that two powers in the State can be coordinate and independent of each other if the one claims and exercises the power to reprove and to censure all the official acts and all the private conversations of the other, and this upon *ex parte* testimony before a secret inquisitorial committee in short, to assume a general censorship over the other? The idea is as absurd in public as it would be in private life. Should the President attempt to assert and maintain his own independence, future Covode committees may dragoon him into submission by collecting the hosts of disappointed office hunters, removed officers, and those who desire to live upon the public Treasury, which must follow in the wake of every Administration, and they in secret conclave will swear away his reputation. Under such circumstances he must be a very bold man should he not surrender at discretion and consent to exercise his authority according to the will of those invested with this terrific power. The sovereign people of the several States have elected him to the highest and most honorable office in the world. He is their only direct representative in the Government. By their Constitution they have made him Commander in Chief of their Army and Navy. He represents them in their intercourse with foreign nations. Clothed with their dignity and authority, he occupies a proud position before all nations, civilized and savage. With the consent of the Senate, he appoints all the important officers of the Government. He exercises the veto power, and to that extent controls the legislation of Congress. For the performance of these high duties he is responsible to the people of the several States, and not in any degree to the House of Representatives.

Shall he surrender these high powers, conferred upon him as the representative of the American people for their benefit, to the House to be exercised under their overshadowing influence and control? Shall he alone of all the citizens of the United States be denied a fair trial? Shall he alone not be "informed of the nature and cause of the accusation" against him? Shall he alone not "be confronted with the witnesses" against him? Shall the House of Representatives, usurping the powers of the Senate, proceed to try the President through the agency of a secret committee of the body, where it is impossible he can make any defense, and then, without affording him an opportunity of being heard, pronounce a judgment of censure against him? The very same rule might be applied for the very same reason to every judge of every court of the United States. From what part of the Constitution is this terrible secret inquisitorial power derived? No such express power exists. From which of the enumerated powers can it be inferred? It is true the House can not pronounce the formal judgment against him of "removal from office," but they can by their judgment of censure asperse his reputation, and thus to the extent of their influence render the office contemptible. An example is at hand of the reckless manner in which this power of censure can be employed in high party times. The House on a recent occasion have attempted to degrade the President by adopting the resolution of Mr. John Sherman declaring that he, in conjunction with the Secretary of the Navy, " by receiving and considering the party relations of bidders for contracts and the effect of awarding contracts upon pending elections, have set an example dangerous to the public safety and deserving the reproof of this House."

It will scarcely be credited that the sole pretext for this vote of censure was the simple fact that in disposing of the numerous letters of every imaginable character which I daily receive I had in the usual course of business referred a letter from Colonel Patterson, of Philadelphia, in relation to a contract, to the attention of the Secretary of the Navy, the head of the appropriate Department, without expressing or intimating any opinion whatever on the subject; and to make the matter if possible still plainer, the Secretary had informed the committee that "*the President did not in any manner interfere in this case, nor has he in any other case of contract since I have been in the Department.*" The absence of all proof to sustain this attempt to degrade the President, whilst it manifests the venom of the shaft aimed at him, has destroyed the vigor of the bow.

To return after this digression: Should the House, by the institution of Covode committees, votes of censure, and other devices to harass the President, reduce him to subservience to their will and render him their creature, then the well-balanced Government which our fathers framed will be annihilated. This conflict has already been commenced in earnest by the House against the Executive. A bad precedent rarely, if ever, dies. It will, I fear, be pursued in the time of my successors, no matter what may be their political character. Should secret committees be appointed with unlimited authority to range over all the words and actions, and, if possible, the very thoughts, of the President with a view to discover something in his past life prejudicial to his character from parasites and informers, this would be an ordeal which scarcely any mere man since the fall could endure. It would be to subject him to a reign of terror from which the stoutest and purest heart might shrink. I have passed triumphantly through this ordeal. My vindication is complete. The committee have reported no resolution looking to an impeachment against me; no resolution of censure; not even a resolution pointing out any abuses in any of the Executive Departments of the Government to be corrected by legislation. This is the highest commendation which could be bestowed on the heads of these Departments. The sovereign people of the States will, however, I trust, save my successors, whoever they may be, from any such ordeal. They are frank, bold, and honest. They detest delators and informers. I therefore, in the name and as the representative of this great people, and standing upon the ramparts of the Constitution which they "have ordained and established," do solemnly protest against these unprecedented and unconstitutional proceedings.

There was still another committee raised by the House on the 6th March last, on motion of Mr. Hoard, to which I had not the slightest objection. The resolution creating it was confined to specific charges, which I have ever since been ready and willing to meet. I have at all times invited and defied fair investigation upon constitutional principles. I have received no notice that this committee have ever proceeded to the investigation.

Why should the House of Representatives desire to encroach on the other departments of the Government? Their rightful powers are ample for every legitimate purpose. They are the impeaching body. In their legislative capacity it is their most wise and wholesome prerogative to institute rigid examinations into the manner in which all departments of the Government are conducted, with a view to reform abuses, to promote economy, and to improve every branch of administration. Should they find reason to believe in the course of their examinations that any grave offense had been committed by the President or any officer of the Government rendering it proper, in their judgment, to resort to impeachment, their course would be plain. They would then transfer the question from their legislative to their accusatory jurisdiction, and take care that in all the preliminary judicial proceedings preparatory to the vote of articles of impeachment the accused should enjoy the benefit of cross-examining the witnesses and all the other safeguards with which the Constitution surrounds every American citizen.

If in a legislative investigation it should appear that the public interest required the removal of any officer of the Government, no President has ever existed who, after giving him a fair hearing, would hesitate to apply the remedy.

This I take to be the ancient and well-established practice. An adherence to it will best promote the harmony and the dignity of the intercourse between the coordinate branches of the Government and render us all more respectable both in the eyes of our own countrymen and of foreign nations.

JAMES BUCHANAN.

PROCLAMATION.

BY THE PRESIDENT OF THE UNITED STATES OF AMERICA.

A PROCLAMATION.

Whereas an extraordinary occasion has occurred rendering it necessary and proper that the Senate of the United States shall be convened to receive and act upon such communications as have been or may be made to it on the part of the Executive:

Now, therefore, I, James Buchanan, President of the United States, do issue this my proclamation, declaring that an extraordinary occasion requires the Senate of the United States to convene for the transaction of business at the Capitol, in the city of Washington, on the 26th day of

June instant, at 12 o'clock at noon of that day, of which all who shall then be entitled to act as members of that body are hereby required to take notice.

　　Given under my hand and the seal of the United States, at Washington, this 25th day of June, A. D. 1860, and of the Independence of the United States the eighty-fourth.

[SEAL.]

JAMES BUCHANAN.

　By the President:
　　LEWIS CASS,
　　　Secretary of State.

FOURTH ANNUAL MESSAGE.

WASHINGTON CITY, *December 3, 1860.*

Fellow-Citizens of the Senate and House of Representatives:

　Throughout the year since our last meeting the country has been eminently prosperous in all its material interests. The general health has been excellent, our harvests have been abundant, and plenty smiles throughout the land. Our commerce and manufactures have been prosecuted with energy and industry, and have yielded fair and ample returns. In short, no nation in the tide of time has ever presented a spectacle of greater material prosperity than we have done until within a very recent period.

　Why is it, then, that discontent now so extensively prevails, and the Union of the States, which is the source of all these blessings, is threatened with destruction?

　The long-continued and intemperate interference of the Northern people with the question of slavery in the Southern States has at length produced its natural effects. The different sections of the Union are now arrayed against each other, and the time has arrived, so much dreaded by the Father of his Country, when hostile geographical parties have been formed.

　I have long foreseen and often forewarned my countrymen of the now impending danger. This does not proceed solely from the claim on the part of Congress or the Territorial legislatures to exclude slavery from the Territories, nor from the efforts of different States to defeat the execution of the fugitive-slave law. All or any of these evils might have been endured by the South without danger to the Union (as others have been) in the hope that time and reflection might apply the remedy. The immediate peril arises not so much from these causes as from the fact that the incessant and violent agitation of the slavery question throughout the North for the last quarter of a century has at length produced its malign influence on the slaves and inspired them with vague notions of freedom. Hence a sense of security no longer exists around the family altar. This feeling of peace at home has given place to apprehensions of servile insurrections. Many a matron throughout the South retires at night in dread of what may befall herself and children before the morning. Should this apprehension of domestic danger, whether real or imaginary, extend and intensify itself until it shall pervade the masses of the Southern people, then disunion will become inevitable. Self-preservation is the first law of nature, and has been implanted in the heart of man by his Creator for the wisest purpose; and no political union, however fraught with blessings and benefits in all other respects, can long continue if the necessary consequence be to render the homes and the firesides of nearly half the parties to it habitually and hopelessly insecure. Sooner or later the bonds of such a union must be severed. It is my conviction that this fatal period has not yet arrived, and my prayer to God is that He would preserve the Constitution and the Union throughout all generations.

But let us take warning in time and remove the cause of danger. It can not be denied that for five and twenty years the agitation at the North against slavery has been incessant. In 1835 pictorial handbills and inflammatory appeals were circulated extensively throughout the South of a character to excite the passions of the slaves, and, in the language of General Jackson, "to stimulate them to insurrection and produce all the horrors of a servile war." This agitation has ever since been continued by the public press, by the proceedings of State and county conventions and by abolition sermons and lectures. The time of Congress has been occupied in violent speeches on this never-ending subject, and appeals, in pamphlet and other forms, indorsed by distinguished names, have been sent forth from this central point and spread broadcast over the Union.

How easy would it be for the American people to settle the slavery question forever and to restore peace and harmony to this distracted country! They, and they alone, can do it. All that is necessary to accomplish the object, and all for which the slave States have ever contended, is to be let alone and permitted to manage their domestic institutions in their own way. As sovereign States, they, and they alone, are responsible before God and the world for the slavery existing among them. For this the people of the North are not more responsible and have no more right to interfere than with similar institutions in Russia or in Brazil.

Upon their good sense and patriotic forbearance I confess I still greatly rely. Without their aid it is beyond the power of any President, no matter what may be his own political proclivities, to restore peace and harmony among the States. Wisely limited and restrained as is his power under our Constitution and laws, he alone can accomplish but little for good or for evil on such a momentous question.

And this brings me to observe that the election of any one of our fellow-citizens to the office of President does not of itself afford just cause for dissolving the Union. This is more especially true if his election has been effected by a mere plurality, and not a majority of the people, and has resulted from transient and temporary causes, which may probably never again occur. In order to justify a resort to revolutionary resistance, the Federal Government must be guilty of "a deliberate, palpable, and dangerous exercise" of powers not granted by the Constitution. The late Presidential election, however, has been held in strict conformity with its express provisions. How, then, can the result justify a revolution to destroy this very Constitution? Reason, justice, a regard for the Constitution, all require that we shall wait for some overt and dangerous act on the part of the President elect before resorting to such a remedy. It is said, however, that the antecedents of the President elect have been sufficient to justify the fears of the South that he will attempt to invade their constitutional rights. But are such apprehensions of contingent danger in the future sufficient to justify the immediate destruction of the noblest system of government ever devised by mortals? From the very nature of his office and its high responsibilities he must necessarily be conservative. The stern duty of administering the vast and complicated concerns of this Government affords in itself a guaranty that he will not attempt any violation of a clear constitutional right.

After all, he is no more than the chief executive officer of the Government. His province is not to make but to execute the laws. And it is a remarkable fact in our history that, notwithstanding the repeated efforts of the antislavery party, no single act has ever passed Congress, unless we may possibly except the Missouri compromise, impairing in the slightest degree the rights of the South to their property in slaves; and it may also be observed, judging from present indications, that no probability exists of the passage of such an act by a majority of both Houses, either in the present or the next Congress. Surely under these circumstances we ought to be restrained from present action by the precept of Him who spake as man never spoke, that "sufficient unto the day is the evil thereof." The day of evil may never come unless we shall rashly bring it upon ourselves.

It is alleged as one cause for immediate secession that the Southern States are denied equal rights with the other States in the common Territories. But by what authority are these denied? Not by Congress, which has never passed, and I believe never will pass, any act to exclude slavery from these Territories; and certainly not by the Supreme Court, which has solemnly decided that slaves are property, and, like all other property, their owners have a right to take them into the common Territories and hold them there under the protection of the Constitution.

So far then, as Congress is concerned, the objection is not to anything they have already done, but to what they may do hereafter. It will surely be admitted that this apprehension of future danger is no good reason for an immediate dissolution of the Union. It is true that the Territorial legislature of Kansas, on the 23d February, 1860, passed in great haste an act over the veto of the governor declaring that slavery "is and shall be forever prohibited in this Territory." Such an act, however, plainly violating the rights of property secured by the Constitution, will surely be declared void by the judiciary whenever it shall be presented in a legal form.

Only three days after my inauguration the Supreme Court of the United States solemnly adjudged that this power did not exist in a Territorial legislature. Yet such has been the factious temper of the times that the correctness of this decision has been extensively impugned before the people, and the question has given rise to angry political conflicts throughout the country. Those who have appealed from this judgment of our highest constitutional tribunal to popular assemblies would, if they could, invest a Territorial legislature with power to annul the sacred rights of property. This power Congress is expressly forbidden by the Federal Constitution to exercise. Every State legislature in the Union is forbidden by its own constitution to exercise it. It can not be exercised in any State except by the people in their highest sovereign capacity, when framing or amending their State constitution. In like manner it can only be exercised by the people of a Territory represented in a convention of delegates for the purpose of framing a constitution preparatory to admission as a State into the Union. Then, and not until then, are they invested with power to decide the question whether slavery shall or shall not exist within their limits. This is an act of sovereign authority, and not of subordinate Territorial legislation. Were it otherwise, then indeed would the equality of the States in the Territories be destroyed, and the rights of property in slaves would depend not upon the guaranties of the Constitution, but upon the shifting majorities of an irresponsible Territorial legislature. Such a doctrine, from its intrinsic unsoundness, can not long influence any considerable portion of our people, much less can it afford a good reason for a dissolution of the Union.

The most palpable violations of constitutional duty which have yet been committed consist in the acts of different State legislatures to defeat the execution of the fugitive-slave law. It ought to be remembered, however, that for these acts neither Congress nor any President can justly be held responsible. Having been passed in violation of the Federal Constitution, they are therefore null and void. All the courts, both State and national, before whom the question has arisen have from the beginning declared the fugitive-slave law to be constitutional. The single exception is that of a State court in Wisconsin, and this has not only been reversed by the proper appellate tribunal, but has met with such universal reprobation that there can be no danger from it as a precedent. The validity of this law has been established over and over again by the Supreme Court of the United States with perfect unanimity. It is founded upon an express provision of the Constitution, requiring that fugitive slaves who escape from service in one State to another shall be "delivered up" to their masters. Without this provision it is a well-known historical fact that the Constitution itself could never have been adopted by the Convention. In one form or other, under the acts of 1793 and 1850, both being substantially the same, the fugitive-slave law has been the law of the land from the days of Washington until the present moment. Here, then, a clear case is presented in which it will be the duty of the next President, as it has been my own, to act with vigor in executing this supreme law against the conflicting enactments of State legislatures. Should he fail in the performance of this high duty, he will then have manifested a disregard of the Constitution and laws, to the great injury of the people of nearly one-half of the States of the Union. But are we to presume in advance that he will thus violate his duty? This would be at war with every principle of justice and of Christian charity. Let us wait for the overt act. The fugitive-slave law has been carried into execution in every contested case since the commencement of the present Administration, though often, it is to be regretted, with great loss and inconvenience to the master and with considerable expense to the Government. Let us trust that the State legislatures will repeal their unconstitutional and obnoxious enactments. Unless this shall be done without unnecessary delay, it is impossible for any human power to save the Union.

The Southern States, standing on the basis of the Constitution, have a right to demand this act of justice from the States of the North. Should it be refused, then the Constitution, to which all the States are parties, will have been willfully violated by one portion of them in a provision essential to the domestic security and happiness of the remainder. In that event the injured States, after having first used all peaceful and constitutional means to obtain redress, would be justified in revolutionary resistance to the Government of the Union.

I have purposely confined my remarks to revolutionary resistance, because it has been claimed within the last few years that any State, whenever this shall be its sovereign will and pleasure, may secede from the Union in accordance with the Constitution and without any violation of the constitutional rights of the other members of the Confederacy; that as each became parties to the Union by the vote of its own people assembled in convention, so any one of them may retire from the Union in a similar manner by the vote of such a convention.

In order to justify secession as a constitutional remedy, it must be on the principle that the Federal Government is a mere voluntary association of States, to be dissolved at pleasure by any one of the contracting

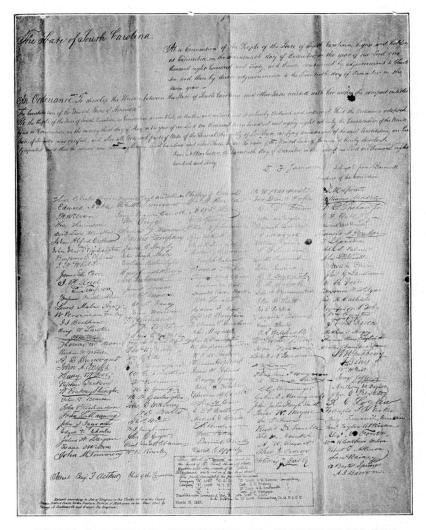

SOUTH CAROLINA'S ORDINANCE TO SECEDE FROM THE
UNION, DECEMBER 20, 1860, DURING BUCHANAN'S
ADMINISTRATION.

parties. If this be so, the Confederacy is a rope of sand, to be penetrated and dissolved by the first adverse wave of public opinion in any of the States. In this manner our thirty-three States may resolve themselves into as many petty, jarring, and hostile republics, each one retiring from the Union without responsibility whenever any sudden excitement might impel them to such a course. By this process a Union might be entirely broken into fragments in a few weeks which cost our forefathers many years of toil, privation, and blood to establish.

Such a principle is wholly inconsistent with the history as well as the character of the Federal Constitution. After it was framed with the greatest deliberation and care it was submitted to conventions of the people of the several States for ratification. Its provisions were discussed at length in these bodies, composed of the first men of the country. Its opponents contended that it conferred powers upon the Federal Government dangerous to the rights of the States, whilst its advocates maintained that under a fair construction of the instrument there was no foundation for such apprehensions. In that mighty struggle between the first intellects of this or any other country it never occurred to any individual, either among its opponents or advocates, to assert or even to intimate that their efforts were all vain labor, because the moment that any State felt herself aggrieved she might secede from the Union. What a crushing argument would this have proved against those who dreaded that the rights of the States would be endangered by the Constitution! The truth is that it was not until many years after the origin of the Federal Government that such a proposition was first advanced. It was then met and refuted by the conclusive arguments of General Jackson, who in his message of the 16th of January, 1833, transmitting the nullifying ordinance of South Carolina to Congress, employs the following language:

The right of the people of a single State to absolve themselves at will and without the consent of the other States from their most solemn obligations, and hazard the liberties and happiness of the millions composing this Union, can not be acknowledged. Such authority is believed to be utterly repugnant both to the principles upon which the General Government is constituted and to the objects which it is expressly formed to attain.

It is not pretended that any clause in the Constitution gives countenance to such a theory. It is altogether founded upon inference; not from any language contained in the instrument itself, but from the sovereign character of the several States by which it was ratified. But is it beyond the power of a State, like an individual, to yield a portion of its sovereign rights to secure the remainder? In the language of Mr. Madison, who has been called the father of the Constitution—

It was formed by the States; that is, by the people in each of the States acting in their highest sovereign capacity, and formed, consequently, by the same authority which formed the State constitutions. * * * Nor is the Government of the United States, created by the Constitution, less a government, in the strict sense of the term, within the sphere of its powers than the governments created by the constitutions of the States are within their several spheres. It is, like them, organized into legislative, executive, and judiciary departments. It operates, like them, directly on persons and things, and, like them, it has at command a physical force for executing the powers committed to it.

It was intended to be perpetual, and not to be annulled at the pleasure of any one of the contracting parties. The old Articles of Confederation were entitled "Articles of Confederation and Perpetual Union between the States," and by the thirteenth article it is expressly declared that "the articles of this Confederation shall be inviolably observed by every State, and the Union shall be perpetual." The preamble to the Constitution of the United States, having express reference to the Articles of Confederation, recites that it was established "in order to form a more perfect union." And yet it is contended that this "more perfect union" does not include the essential attribute of perpetuity.

But that the Union was designed to be perpetual appears conclusively from the nature and extent of the powers conferred by the Constitution on the Federal Government. These powers embrace the very highest attributes of national sovereignty. They place both the sword and the purse under its control. Congress has power to make war and to make peace, to raise and support armies and navies, and to conclude treaties with foreign governments. It is invested with the power to coin money and to regulate the value thereof, and to regulate commerce with foreign nations and among the several States. It is not necessary to enumerate the other high powers which have been conferred upon the Federal Government. In order to carry the enumerated powers into effect, Congress possesses the exclusive right to lay and collect duties on imports, and, in common with the States, to lay and collect all other taxes.

But the Constitution has not only conferred these high powers upon Congress, but it has adopted effectual means to restrain the States from interfering with their exercise. For that purpose it has in strong prohibitory language expressly declared that—

No State shall enter into any treaty, alliance, or confederation; grant letters of marque and reprisal; coin money; emit bills of credit; make anything but gold and silver coin a tender in payment of debts; pass any bill of attainder, *ex post facto* law, or law impairing the obligation of contracts.

Moreover—

No State shall without the consent of the Congress lay any imposts or duties on imports or exports, except what may be absolutely necessary for executing its inspection laws.

And if they exceed this amount the excess shall belong to the United States. And—

No State shall without the consent of Congress lay any duty of tonnage, keep troops or ships of war in time of peace, enter into any agreement or compact with another State or with a foreign power, or engage in war, unless actually invaded or in such imminent danger as will not admit of delay.

In order still further to secure the uninterrupted exercise of these high powers against State interposition, it is provided that—

This Constitution and the laws of the United States which shall be made in pursuance thereof, and all treaties made or which shall be made under the authority of the United States, shall be the supreme law of the land, and the judges in every State shall be bound thereby, anything in the constitution or laws of any State to the contrary notwithstanding.

The solemn sanction of religion has been superadded to the obligations of official duty, and all Senators and Representatives of the United States, all members of State legislatures, and all executive and judicial officers, "both of the United States and of the several States, shall be bound by oath or affirmation to support this Constitution."

In order to carry into effect these powers, the Constitution has established a perfect Government in all its forms—legislative, executive, and judicial; and this Government to the extent of its powers acts directly upon the individual citizens of every State, and executes its own decrees by the agency of its own officers. In this respect it differs entirely from the Government under the old Confederation, which was confined to making requisitions on the States in their sovereign character. This left it in the discretion of each whether to obey or to refuse, and they often declined to comply with such requisitions. It thus became necessary for the purpose of removing this barrier and "in order to form a more perfect union" to establish a Government which could act directly upon the people and execute its own laws without the intermediate agency of the States. This has been accomplished by the Constitution of the United States. In short, the Government created by the Constitution, and deriving its authority from the sovereign people of each of the several States, has precisely the same right to exercise its power over the people of all these States in the enumerated cases that each one of them possesses over subjects not delegated to the United States, but "reserved to the States respectively or to the people."

To the extent of the delegated powers the Constitution of the United States is as much a part of the constitution of each State and is as binding upon its people as though it had been textually inserted therein.

This Government, therefore, is a great and powerful Government, invested with all the attributes of sovereignty over the special subjects to which its authority extends. Its framers never intended to implant in its bosom the seeds of its own destruction, nor were they at its creation guilty of the absurdity of providing for its own dissolution. It was not intended by its framers to be the baseless fabric of a vision, which at the touch of the enchanter would vanish into thin air, but a substantial and mighty fabric, capable of resisting the slow decay of time and of defying the storms of ages. Indeed, well may the jealous patriots of that day have indulged fears that a Government of such high powers might violate the reserved rights of the States, and wisely did they adopt the rule of a strict construction of these powers to prevent the danger. But they did not fear, nor had they any reason to imagine, that the Constitution would ever be so interpreted as to enable any State by her own act, and without the consent of her sister States, to discharge her people from all or any of their federal obligations.

It may be asked, then, Are the people of the States without redress against the tyranny and oppression of the Federal Government? By no means. The right of resistance on the part of the governed against the oppression of their governments can not be denied. It exists independently of all constitutions, and has been exercised at all periods of the world's history. Under it old governments have been destroyed and new ones have taken their place. It is embodied in strong and express language in our own Declaration of Independence. But the distinction must ever be observed that this is revolution against an established government, and not a voluntary secession from it by virtue of an inherent constitutional right. In short, let us look the danger fairly in the face. Secession is neither more nor less than revolution. It may or it may not be a justifiable revolution, but still it is revolution.

What, in the meantime, is the responsibility and true position of the Executive? He is bound by solemn oath, before God and the country, "to take care that the laws be faithfully executed," and from this obligation he can not be absolved by any human power. But what if the performance of this duty, in whole or in part, has been rendered impracticable by events over which he could have exercised no control? Such at the present moment is the case throughout the State of South Carolina so far as the laws of the United States to secure the administration of justice by means of the Federal judiciary are concerned. All the Federal officers within its limits through whose agency alone these laws can be carried into execution have already resigned. We no longer have a district judge, a district attorney, or a marshal in South Carolina. In fact, the whole machinery of the Federal Government necessary for the distribution of remedial justice among the people has been demolished, and it would be difficult, if not impossible, to replace it.

The only acts of Congress on the statute book bearing upon this subject are those of February 28, 1795, and March 3, 1807. These authorize the President, after he shall have ascertained that the marshal, with his *posse comitatus*, is unable to execute civil or criminal process in any particular case, to call forth the militia and employ the Army and Navy to aid him in performing this service, having first by proclamation commanded the insurgents "to disperse and retire peaceably to their respective abodes within a limited time." This duty can not by possibility be performed in a State where no judicial authority exists to issue process, and where there is no marshal to execute it, and where, even if there were such an officer, the entire population would constitute one solid combination to resist him.

The bare enumeration of these provisions proves how inadequate they are without further legislation to overcome a united opposition in a single State, not to speak of other States who may place themselves in a similar attitude. Congress alone has power to decide whether the present laws can or can not be amended so as to carry out more effectually the objects of the Constitution.

The same insuperable obstacles do not lie in the way of executing the laws for the collection of the customs. The revenue still continues to be collected as heretofore at the custom-house in Charleston; and should the collector unfortunately resign a successor may be appointed to perform this duty.

Then, in regard to the property of the United States in South Carolina. This has been purchased for a fair equivalent, "by the consent of the legislature of the State," "for the erection of forts, magazines, arsenals," etc., and over these the authority "to exercise exclusive legislation" has been expressly granted by the Constitution to Congress. It is not believed that any attempt will be made to expel the United States from this property by force; but if in this I should prove to be mistaken, the officer in command of the forts has received orders to act strictly on the defensive. In such a contingency the responsibility for consequences would rightfully rest upon the heads of the assailants.

Apart from the execution of the laws, so far as this may be practicable, the Executive has no authority to decide what shall be the relations between the Federal Government and South Carolina. He has been invested with no such discretion. He possesses no power to change the relations heretofore existing between them, much less to acknowledge the independence of that State. This would be to invest a mere executive officer with the power of recognizing the dissolution of the confederacy among our thirty-three sovereign States. It bears no resemblance to the recognition of a foreign *de facto* government, involving no such responsibility. Any attempt to do this would, on his part, be a naked act of usurpation. It is therefore my duty to submit to Congress the whole question in all its bearings. The course of events is so rapidly hastening forward that the emergency may soon arise when you may be called upon to decide the momentous question whether you possess the power by force of arms to compel a State to remain in the Union. I should feel myself recreant to my duty were I not to express an opinion on this important subject.

The question fairly stated is, Has the Constitution delegated to Congress the power to coerce a State into submission which is attempting to withdraw or has actually withdrawn from the Confederacy? If answered in the affirmative, it must be on the principle that the power has been conferred upon Congress to declare and to make war against a State. After much serious reflection I have arrived at the conclusion that no such power has been delegated to Congress or to any other department of the Federal Government. It is manifest upon an inspection of the Constitution that this is not among the specific and enumerated powers granted to Congress, and it is equally apparent that its exercise is not "necessary and proper for carrying into execution" any one of these powers. So far from this power having been delegated to Congress, it was expressly refused by the Convention which framed the Constitution.

It appears from the proceedings of that body that on the 31st May, 1787, the clause "*authorizing an exertion of the force of the whole against a delinquent State*" came up for consideration. Mr. Madison opposed it in a brief but powerful speech, from which I shall extract but a single sentence. He observed:

The use of force against a State would look more like a declaration of war than an infliction of punishment, and would probably be considered by the party attacked as a dissolution of all previous compacts by which it might be bound.

Upon his motion the clause was unanimously postponed, and was never, I believe, again presented. Soon afterwards, on the 8th June, 1787, when incidentally adverting to the subject, he said: "Any government for the United States formed on the supposed practicability of using force against the unconstitutional proceedings of the States would prove as visionary and fallacious as the government of Congress," evidently meaning the then existing Congress of the old Confederation.

Without descending to particulars, it may be safely asserted that the power to make war against a State is at variance with the whole spirit and intent of the Constitution. Suppose such a war should result in the conquest of a State; how are we to govern it afterwards? Shall we hold it as a province and govern it by despotic power? In the nature of things, we could not by physical force control the will of the people and compel them to elect Senators and Representatives to Congress and to perform all the other duties depending upon their own volition and required from the free citizens of a free State as a constituent member of the Confederacy.

But if we possessed this power, would it be wise to exercise it under existing circumstances? The object would doubtless be to preserve the Union. War would not only present the most effectual means of destroying it, but would vanish all hope of its peaceable reconstruction. Besides, in the fraternal conflict a vast amount of blood and treasure would be expended, rendering future reconciliation between the States impossible. In the meantime, who can foretell what would be the sufferings and privations of the people during its existence?

The fact is that our Union rests upon public opinion, and can never be cemented by the blood of its citizens shed in civil war. If it can not live in the affections of the people, it must one day perish. Congress possesses many means of preserving it by conciliation, but the sword was not placed in their hand to preserve it by force.

But may I be permitted solemnly to invoke my countrymen to pause and deliberate before they determine to destroy this the grandest temple which has ever been dedicated to human freedom since the world began? It has been consecrated by the blood of our fathers, by the glories of the past, and by the hopes of the future. The Union has already made us the most prosperous, and ere long will, if preserved, render us the most powerful, nation on the face of the earth. In every foreign region of the globe the title of American citizen is held in the highest respect, and when pronounced in a foreign land it causes the hearts of our countrymen to swell with honest pride. Surely when we reach the brink of the yawning abyss we shall recoil with horror from the last fatal plunge.

By such a dread catastrophe the hopes of the friends of freedom throughout the world would be destroyed, and a long night of leaden despotism would enshroud the nations. Our example for more than eighty years would not only be lost, but it would be quoted as a conclusive proof that man is unfit for self-government.

It is not every wrong—nay, it is not every grievous wrong—which can justify a resort to such a fearful alternative. This ought to be the last desperate remedy of a despairing people, after every other constitutional means of conciliation had been exhausted. We should reflect that under this free Government there is an incessant ebb and flow in public opinion. The slavery question, like everything human, will have its day. I firmly believe that it has reached and passed the culminating point. But if in the midst of the existing excitement the Union shall perish, the evil may then become irreparable.

Congress can contribute much to avert it by proposing and recommending to the legislatures of the several States the remedy for existing evils which the Constitution has itself provided for its own preservation. This has been tried at different critical periods of our history, and always with eminent success. It is to be found in the fifth article, providing for its own amendment. Under this article amendments have been proposed by two-thirds of both Houses of Congress, and have been "ratified by the legislatures of three-fourths of the several States," and have consequently become parts of the Constitution. To this process the country is indebted for the clause prohibiting Congress from passing any law respecting an establishment of religion or abridging the freedom of speech or of the press or of the right of petition. To this we are also indebted for the bill of rights which secures the people against any abuse of power by the Federal Government. Such were the apprehensions justly entertained by the friends of State rights at that period as to have rendered it extremely doubtful whether the Constitution could have long survived without those amendments.

Again the Constitution was amended by the same process, after the election of President Jefferson by the House of Representatives, in February, 1803. This amendment was rendered necessary to prevent a recurrence of the dangers which had seriously threatened the existence of the Government during the pendency of that election. The article for its own amendment was intended to secure the amicable adjustment of conflicting constitutional questions like the present which might arise between the governments of the States and that of the United States. This appears from contemporaneous history. In this connection I shall merely call attention to a few sentences in Mr. Madison's justly celebrated report, in 1799, to the legislature of Virginia. In this he ably and conclusively defended the resolutions of the preceding legislature against the strictures of several other State legislatures. These were mainly founded upon the protest of the Virginia legislature against the "alien and sedition acts," as "palpable and alarming infractions of the Constitution." In pointing out the peaceful and constitutional remedies—and he referred to none other—to which the States were authorized to resort on such occasions, he concludes by saying that—

The legislatures of the States might have made a direct representation to Congress with a view to obtain a rescinding of the two offensive acts, or they might have represented to their respective Senators in Congress their wish that two-thirds thereof would propose an explanatory amendment to the Constitution; or two-thirds of themselves, if such had been their option, might by an application to Congress have obtained a convention for the same object.

This is the very course which I earnestly recommend in order to obtain an "explanatory amendment" of the Constitution on the subject of slavery. This might originate with Congress or the State legislatures, as may be deemed most advisable to attain the object. The explanatory amendment might be confined to the final settlement of the true construction of the Constitution on three special points:

1. An express recognition of the right of property in slaves in the States where it now exists or may hereafter exist.

2. The duty of protecting this right in all the common Territories throughout their Territorial existence, and until they shall be admitted as States into the Union, with or without slavery, as their constitutions may prescribe.

3. A like recognition of the right of the master to have his slave who has escaped from one State to another restored and "delivered up" to him, and of the validity of the fugitive-slave law enacted for this purpose, together with a declaration that all State laws impairing or defeating this right are violations of the Constitution, and are consequently null and void. It may be objected that this construction of the Constitution has already been settled by the Supreme Court of the United States, and what more ought to be required? The answer is that a very large proportion of the people of the United States still contest the correctness of this decision, and never will cease from agitation and admit its binding force until clearly established by the people of the several States in their sovereign character. Such an explanatory amendment would, it is believed, forever terminate the existing dissensions, and restore peace and harmony among the States.

It ought not to be doubted that such an appeal to the arbitrament established by the Constitution itself would be received with favor by all the States of the Confederacy. In any event, it ought to be tried in a spirit of conciliation before any of these States shall separate themselves from the Union.

When I entered upon the duties of the Presidential office, the aspect neither of our foreign nor domestic affairs was at all satisfactory. We were involved in dangerous complications with several nations, and two of our Territories were in a state of revolution against the Government. A restoration of the African slave trade had numerous and powerful advocates. Unlawful military expeditions were countenanced by many of our citizens, and were suffered, in defiance of the efforts of the Government, to escape from our shores for the purpose of making war upon the unoffending people of neighboring republics with whom we were at peace. In addition to these and other difficulties, we experienced a revulsion in monetary affairs soon after my advent to power of unexampled severity and of ruinous consequences to all the great interests of the country. When we take a retrospect of what was then our condition and contrast this with its material prosperity at the time of the late Presidential election, we have abundant reason to return our grateful thanks to that merciful Providence which has never forsaken us as a nation in all our past trials.

Our relations with Great Britain are of the most friendly character. Since the commencement of my Administration the two dangerous questions arising from the Clayton and Bulwer treaty and from the right of search claimed by the British Government have been amicably and honorably adjusted.

The discordant constructions of the Clayton and Bulwer treaty between the two Governments, which at different periods of the discussion bore a threatening aspect, have resulted in a final settlement entirely satisfactory to this Government. In my last annual message I informed Congress that the British Government had not then "completed treaty arrangements with the Republics of Honduras and Nicaragua in pursuance of the understanding between the two Governments. It is, nevertheless, confidently expected that this good work will ere long be accomplished." This confident expectation has since been fulfilled. Her Britannic Majesty concluded a treaty with Honduras on the 28th November, 1859, and with Nicaragua on the 28th August, 1860, relinquishing the Mosquito protectorate. Besides, by the former the Bay Islands are recognized as a part of the Republic of Honduras. It may be observed that the stipulations of these treaties conform in every important particular to the amendments adopted by the Senate of the United States to the treaty concluded at London on the 17th October, 1856, between the two Governments. It will be recollected that this treaty was rejected by the British Government because of its objection to the just and important amendment of the Senate to the article relating to Ruatan and the other islands in the Bay of Honduras.

It must be a source of sincere satisfaction to all classes of our fellow-citizens, and especially to those engaged in foreign commerce, that the claim on the part of Great Britain forcibly to visit and search American merchant vessels on the high seas in time of peace has been abandoned. This was by far the most dangerous question to the peace of the two countries which has existed since the War of 1812. Whilst it remained open they might at any moment have been precipitated into a war. This was rendered manifest by the exasperated state of public feeling throughout our entire country produced by the forcible search of American merchant vessels by British cruisers on the coast of Cuba in the spring of 1858. The American people hailed with general acclaim the orders of the Secretary of the Navy to our naval force in the Gulf of Mexico "to protect all vessels of the United States on the high seas from search or detention by the vessels of war of any other nation." These orders might have produced an immediate collision between the naval forces of the two countries. This was most fortunately prevented by an appeal to the justice of Great Britain and to the law of nations as expounded by her own most eminent jurists.

The only question of any importance which still remains open is the disputed title between the two Governments to the island of San Juan, in the vicinity of Washington Territory. As this question is still under negotiation, it is not deemed advisable at the present moment to make any other allusion to the subject.

The recent visit of the Prince of Wales, in a private character, to the people of this country has proved to be a most auspicious event. In its consequences it can not fail to increase the kindred and kindly feelings which I trust may ever actuate the Government and people of both countries in their political and social intercourse with each other.

With France, our ancient and powerful ally, our relations continue to be of the most friendly character. A decision has recently been made by a French judicial tribunal, with the approbation of the Imperial Government, which can not fail to foster the sentiments of mutual regard that have so long existed between the two countries. Under the French law no person can serve in the armies of France unless he be a French citizen. The law of France recognizing the natural right of expatriation, it follows as a necessary consequence that a Frenchman by the fact of having become a citizen of the United States has changed his allegiance and has lost his native character. He can not therefore be compelled to serve in the French armies in case he should return to his native country. These principles were announced in 1852 by the French minister of war, and in two late cases have been confirmed by the French judiciary. In these, two natives of France have been discharged from the French army because they had become American citizens. To employ the language of our present minister to France, who has rendered good service on this occasion, "I do not think our French naturalized fellow-citizens will hereafter experience much annoyance on this subject."

I venture to predict that the time is not far distant when the other continental powers will adopt the same wise and just policy which has done so much honor to the enlightened Government of the Emperor. In any event, our Government is bound to protect the rights of our naturalized citizens everywhere to the same extent as though they had drawn their first breath in this country. We can recognize no distinction between our native and naturalized citizens.

Between the great Empire of Russia and the United States the mutual friendship and regard which has so long existed still continues to prevail, and if possible to increase. Indeed, our relations with that Empire are all that we could desire. Our relations with Spain are now of a more complicated, though less dangerous, character than they have been for many years. Our citizens have long held and continue to hold numerous claims against the Spanish Government. These had been ably urged for a series of years by our successive diplomatic representatives at Madrid, but without obtaining redress. The Spanish Government finally agreed to institute a joint commission for the adjustment of these claims, and on the 5th day of March, 1860, concluded a convention for this purpose with our present minister at Madrid.

Under this convention what have been denominated the "Cuban claims," amounting to $128,635.54, in which more than 100 of our fellow-citizens are interested, were recognized, and the Spanish Government agreed to pay $100,000 of this amount "within three months following the exchange of ratifications." The payment of the remaining $28,635.54 was to await the decision of the commissioners for or against the *Amistad* claim; but in any event the balance was to be paid to the claimants either by Spain or the United States. These terms, I have every reason to know, are highly satisfactory to the holders of the Cuban claims. Indeed, they have made a formal offer authorizing the State Department to settle these claims and to deduct the amount of the *Amistad* claim from the sums which they are entitled to receive from Spain. This offer, of course, can not be accepted. All other claims of citizens of the United States against Spain, or the subjects of the Queen of Spain against the United States, including the *Amistad* claim, were by this convention referred to a board of commissioners in the usual form. Neither the validity of the *Amistad* claim nor of any other claim against either party, with the single exception of the Cuban claims, was recognized by the convention. Indeed, the Spanish Government did not insist that the validity of the *Amistad* claim should be thus recognized, notwithstanding its payment had been recommended to Congress by two of my predecessors, as well as by myself, and an appropriation for that purpose had passed the Senate of the United States.

They were content that it should be submitted to the board for examination and decision like the other claims. Both Governments were bound respectively to pay the amounts awarded to the several claimants "at such times and places as may be fixed by and according to the tenor of said awards."

I transmitted this convention to the Senate for their constitutional action on the 3d of May, 1860, and on the 27th of the succeeding June they determined that they would "not advise and consent" to its ratification.

These proceedings place our relations with Spain in an awkward and embarrassing position. It is more than probable that the final adjustment of these claims will devolve upon my successor.

I reiterate the recommendation contained in my annual message of December, 1858, and repeated in that of December, 1859, in favor of the acquisition of Cuba from Spain by fair purchase. I firmly believe that such an acquisition would contribute essentially to the well-being and prosperity of both countries in all future time, as well as prove the certain means of immediately abolishing the African slave trade throughout the world. I would not repeat this recommendation upon the present occasion if I believed that the transfer of Cuba to the United States upon conditions highly favorable to Spain could justly tarnish the national honor of the proud and ancient Spanish monarchy. Surely no person ever attributed to the first Napoleon a disregard of the national honor of France for transferring Louisiana to the United States for a fair equivalent, both in money and commercial advantages.

With the Emperor of Austria and the remaining continental powers of Europe, including that of the Sultan, our relations continue to be of the most friendly character.

The friendly and peaceful policy pursued by the Government of the United States toward the Empire of China has produced the most satisfactory results. The treaty of Tien-tsin of the 18th June, 1858, has been faithfully observed by the Chinese authorities. The convention of the 8th November, 1858, supplementary to this treaty, for the adjustment and satisfaction of the claims of our citizens on China referred to in my last annual message, has been already carried into effect so far as this was practicable. Under this convention the sum of 500,000 taels, equal to about $700,000, was stipulated to be paid in satisfaction of the claims of American citizens out of the one-fifth of the receipts for tonnage, import, and export duties on American vessels at the ports of Canton, Shanghai, and Fuchau, and it was "agreed that this amount shall be in full liquidation of all claims of American citizens at the various ports to this date." Debentures for this amount, to wit, 300,000 taels for Canton, 100,000 for Shanghai, and 100,000 for Fuchau, were delivered, according to the terms of the convention, by the respective Chinese collectors of the customs of these ports to the agent selected by our minister to receive the same. Since that time the claims of our citizens have been adjusted by the board of commissioners appointed for that purpose under the act of March 3, 1859, and their awards, which proved satisfactory to the claimants, have been approved by our minister. In the aggregate they amount to the sum of $498,694.78. The claimants have already received a large proportion of the sums awarded to them out of the fund provided, and it is confidently expected that the remainder will ere long be entirely paid. After the awards shall have been satisfied there will remain a surplus of more than $200,000 at the disposition of Congress. As this will, in equity, belong to the Chinese Government, would not justice require its appropriation to some benevolent object in which the Chinese may be specially interested?

Our minister to China, in obedience to his instructions, has remained perfectly neutral in the war between Great Britain and France and the Chinese Empire, although, in conjunction with the Russian minister, he was ever ready and willing, had the opportunity offered, to employ his good offices in restoring peace between the parties. It is but an act of simple justice, both to our present minister and his predecessor, to state that they have proved fully equal to the delicate, trying, and responsible positions in which they have on different occasions been placed.

The ratifications of the treaty with Japan concluded at Yeddo on the 29th July, 1858, were exchanged at Washington on the 22d May last, and the treaty itself was proclaimed on the succeeding day. There is good reason to expect that under its protection and influence our trade and intercourse with that distant and interesting people will rapidly increase.

The ratifications of the treaty were exchanged with unusual solemnity. For this purpose the Tycoon had accredited three of his most distinguished subjects as envoys extraordinary and ministers plenipotentiary, who were received and treated with marked distinction and kindness, both by the Government and people of the United States. There is every reason to believe that they have returned to their native land entirely satisfied with their visit and inspired by the most friendly feelings for our country. Let us ardently hope, in the language of the treaty itself, that ''there shall henceforward be perpetual peace and friendship between the United States of America and His Majesty the Tycoon of Japan and his successors.''

With the wise, conservative, and liberal Government of the Empire of Brazil our relations continue to be of the most amicable character.

The exchange of the ratifications of the convention with the Republic of New Granada signed at Washington on the 10th of September, 1857, has been long delayed from accidental causes for which neither party is censurable. These ratifications were duly exchanged in this city on the 5th of November last. Thus has a controversy been amicably terminated which had become so serious at the period of my inauguration as to require me, on the 17th of April, 1857, to direct our minister to demand his passports and return to the United States.

Under this convention the Government of New Granada has specially acknowledged itself to be responsible to our citizens "for damages which were caused by the riot at Panama on the 15th April, 1856." These claims, together with other claims of our citizens which had been long urged in vain, are referred for adjustment to a board of commissioners. I submit a copy of the convention to Congress, and recommend the legislation necessary to carry it into effect.

Persevering efforts have been made for the adjustment of the claims of American citizens against the Government of Costa Rica, and I am happy to inform you that these have finally prevailed. A convention was signed at the city of San Jose on the 2d July last, between the minister resident of the United States in Costa Rica and the plenipotentiaries of that Republic, referring these claims to a board of commissioners and providing for the payment of their awards. This convention will be submitted immediately to the Senate for their constitutional action.

The claims of our citizens upon the Republic of Nicaragua have not yet been provided for by treaty, although diligent efforts for this purpose have been made by our minister resident to that Republic. These are still continued, with a fair prospect of success.

Our relations with Mexico remain in a most unsatisfactory condition. In my last two annual messages I discussed extensively the subject of these relations, and do not now propose to repeat at length the facts and arguments then presented. They proved conclusively that our citizens residing in Mexico and our merchants trading thereto had suffered a series of wrongs and outrages such as we have never patiently borne from any other nation. For these our successive ministers, invoking the faith of treaties, had in the name of their country persistently demanded redress and indemnification, but without the slightest effect. Indeed, so confident had the Mexican authorities become of our patient endurance that they universally believed they might commit these outrages upon American citizens with absolute impunity. Thus wrote our minister in 1856, and expressed the opinion that "nothing but a manifestation of the power of the Government and of its purpose to punish these wrongs will avail."

Afterwards, in 1857, came the adoption of a new constitution for Mexico, the election of a President and Congress under its provisions, and the inauguration of the President. Within one short month, however, this President was expelled from the capital by a rebellion in the army, and the supreme power of the Republic was assigned to General Zuloaga. This usurper was in his turn soon compelled to retire and give place to General Miramon.

Under the constitution which had thus been adopted Señor Juarez, as chief justice of the supreme court, became the lawful President of the

Republic, and it was for the maintenance of the constitution and his authority derived from it that the civil war commenced and still continues to be prosecuted.

Throughout the year 1858 the constitutional party grew stronger and stronger. In the previous history of Mexico a successful military revolution at the capital had almost universally been the signal for submission throughout the Republic. Not so on the present occasion. A majority of the citizens persistently sustained the constitutional Government. When this was recognized, in April, 1859, by the Government of the United States, its authority extended over a large majority of the Mexican States and people, including Vera Cruz and all the other important seaports of the Republic. From that period our commerce with Mexico began to revive, and the constitutional Government has afforded it all the protection in its power.

Meanwhile the Government of Miramon still held sway at the capital and over the surrounding country, and continued its outrages against the few American citizens who still had the courage to remain within its power. To cap the climax, after the battle of Tacubaya, in April, 1859, General Marquez ordered three citizens of the United States, two of them physicians, to be seized in the hospital at that place, taken out and shot, without crime and without trial. This was done, notwithstanding our unfortunate countrymen were at the moment engaged in the holy cause of affording relief to the soldiers of both parties who had been wounded in the battle, without making any distinction between them.

The time had arrived, in my opinion, when this Government was bound to exert its power to avenge and redress the wrongs of our citizens and to afford them protection in Mexico. The interposing obstacle was that the portion of the country under the sway of Miramon could not be reached without passing over territory under the jurisdiction of the constitutional Government. Under these circumstances I deemed it my duty to recommend to Congress in my last annual message the employment of a sufficient military force to penetrate into the interior, where the Government of Miramon was to be found, with or, if need be, without the consent of the Juarez Government, though it was not doubted that this consent could be obtained. Never have I had a clearer conviction on any subject than of the justice as well as wisdom of such a policy. No other alternative was left except the entire abandonment of our fellow-citizens who had gone to Mexico under the faith of treaties to the systematic injustice, cruelty, and oppression of Miramon's Government. Besides, it is almost certain that the simple authority to employ this force would of itself have accomplished all our objects without striking a single blow. The constitutional Government would then ere this have been established at the City of Mexico, and would have been ready and willing to the extent of its ability to do us justice.

In addition—and I deem this a most important consideration—European Governments would have been deprived of all pretext to interfere in the territorial and domestic concerns of Mexico. We should thus have been relieved from the obligation of resisting, even by force should this become necessary, any attempt by these Governments to deprive our neighboring Republic of portions of her territory—a duty from which we could not shrink without abandoning the traditional and established policy of the American people. I am happy to observe that, firmly relying upon the justice and good faith of these Governments, there is no present danger that such a contingency will happen.

Having discovered that my recommendations would not be sustained by Congress, the next alternative was to accomplish in some degree, if possible, the same objects by treaty stipulations with the constitutional Government. Such treaties were accordingly concluded by our late able and excellent minister to Mexico, and on the 4th of January last were submitted to the Senate for ratification. As these have not yet received the final action of that body, it would be improper for me to present a detailed statement of their provisions. Still, I may be permitted to express the opinion in advance that they are calculated to promote the agricultural, manufacturing, and commercial interests of the country and to secure our just influence with an adjoining Republic as to whose fortunes and fate we can never feel indifferent, whilst at the same time they provide for the payment of a considerable amount toward the satisfaction of the claims of our injured fellow-citizens.

At the period of my inauguration I was confronted in Kansas by a revolutionary government existing under what is called the ''Topeka constitution.'' Its avowed object was to subdue the Territorial government by force and to inaugurate what was called the ''Topeka government'' in its stead. To accomplish this object an extensive military organization was formed, and its command intrusted to the most violent revolutionary leaders. Under these circumstances it became my imperative duty to exert the whole constitutional power of the Executive to prevent the flames of civil war from again raging in Kansas, which in the excited state of the public mind, both North and South, might have extended into the neighboring States. The hostile parties in Kansas had been inflamed against each other by emissaries both from the North and the South to a degree of malignity without parallel in our history. To prevent actual collision and to assist the civil magistrates in enforcing the laws, a strong detachment of the Army was stationed in the Territory, ready to aid the marshal and his deputies when lawfully called upon as a *posse comitatus* in the execution of civil and criminal process. Still, the troubles in Kansas could not have been permanently settled without an election by the people.

The ballot box is the surest arbiter of disputes among freemen. Under this conviction every proper effort was employed to induce the hostile parties to vote at the election of delegates to frame a State constitution, and afterwards at the election to decide whether Kansas should be a slave or free State.

The insurgent party refused to vote at either, lest this might be considered a recognition on their part of the Territorial government established by Congress. A better spirit, however, seemed soon after to prevail, and the two parties met face to face at the third election, held on the first Monday of January, 1858, for members of the legislature and State officers under the Lecompton constitution. The result was the triumph of the antislavery party at the polls. This decision of the ballot box proved clearly that this party were in the majority, and removed the danger of civil war. From that time we have heard little or nothing of the Topeka government, and all serious danger of revolutionary troubles in Kansas was then at an end.

The Lecompton constitution, which had been thus recognized at this State election by the votes of both political parties in Kansas, was transmitted to me with the request that I should present it to Congress. This I could not have refused to do without violating my clearest and strongest convictions of duty. The constitution and all the proceedings which preceded and followed its formation were fair and regular on their face. I then believed, and experience has proved, that the interests of the people of Kansas would have been best consulted by its admission as a State into the Union, especially as the majority within a brief period could have amended the constitution according to their will and pleasure. If fraud existed in all or any of these proceedings, it was not for the President but for Congress to investigate and determine the question of fraud and what ought to be its consequences. If at the first two elections the majority refused to vote, it can not be pretended that this refusal to exercise the elective franchise could invalidate an election fairly held under lawful authority, even if they had not subsequently voted at the third election. It is true that the whole constitution had not been submitted to the people, as I always desired; but the precedents are numerous of the admission of States into the Union without such submission. It would not comport with my present purpose to review the proceedings of Congress upon the Lecompton constitution. It is sufficient to observe that their final action has removed the last vestige of serious revolutionary troubles. The desperate band recently assembled under a notorious outlaw in the southern portion of the Territory to resist the execution of the laws and to plunder peaceful citizens will, I doubt not, be speedily subdued and brought to justice.

Had I treated the Lecompton constitution as a nullity and refused to transmit it to Congress, it is not difficult to imagine, whilst recalling the position of the country at that moment, what would have been the disastrous consequences, both in and out of the Territory, from such a dereliction of duty on the part of the Executive,

Peace has also been restored within the Territory of Utah, which at the commencement of my Administration was in a state of open rebellion. This was the more dangerous, as the people, animated by a fanatical spirit and intrenched within their distant mountain fastnesses, might have made a long and formidable resistance. Cost what it might, it was necessary to bring them into subjection to the Constitution and the laws. Sound policy, therefore, as well as humanity, required that this object should if possible be accomplished without the effusion of blood. This could only be effected by sending a military force into the Territory sufficiently strong to convince the people that resistance would be hopeless, and at the same time to offer them a pardon for past offenses on condition of immediate submission to the Government. This policy was pursued with eminent success, and the only cause for regret is the heavy expenditure required to march a large detachment of the Army to that remote region and to furnish it subsistence.

Utah is now comparatively peaceful and quiet, and the military force has been withdrawn, except that portion of it necessary to keep the Indians in check and to protect the emigrant trains on their way to our Pacific possessions.

In my first annual message I promised to employ my best exertions in cooperation with Congress to reduce the expenditures of the Government within the limits of a wise and judicious economy. An overflowing Treasury had produced habits of prodigality and extravagance which could only be gradually corrected. The work required both time and patience. I applied myself diligently to this task from the beginning and was aided by the able and energetic efforts of the heads of the different Executive Departments. The result of our labors in this good cause did not appear in the sum total of our expenditures for the first two years, mainly in consequence of the extraordinary expenditure necessarily incurred in the Utah expedition and the very large amount of the contingent expenses of Congress during this period. These greatly exceeded the pay and mileage of the members. For the year ending June 30, 1858, whilst the pay and mileage amounted to $1,490,214, the contingent expenses rose to $2,093,309.79; and for the year ending June 30, 1859, whilst the pay and mileage amounted to $859,093.66, the contingent expenses amounted to $1,431,565.78. I am happy, however, to be able to inform you that during the last fiscal year, ending June 30, 1860, the total expenditures of the Government in all its branches—legislative, executive, and judicial—exclusive of the public debt, were reduced to the sum of $55,402,-465.46. This conclusively appears from the books of the Treasury. In the year ending June 30, 1858, the total expenditure, exclusive of the public debt, amounted to $71,901,129.77, and that for the year ending June 30, 1859, to $66,346,226.13. Whilst the books of the Treasury show an actual expenditure of $59,848,474.72 for the year ending June 30, 1860, including $1,040,667.71 for the contingent expenses of Congress, there must be deducted from this amount the sum of $4,296,009.26, with the interest upon it of $150,000, appropriated by the act of February 15, 1860, "for the purpose of supplying the deficiency in the revenues and defraying the expenses of the Post-Office Department for the year ending June 30, 1859." This sum, therefore, justly chargeable to the year 1859, must be deducted from the sum of $59,848,474.72 in order to ascertain the expenditure for the year ending June 30, 1860, which leaves a balance for the expenditures of that year of $55,402,465.46. The interest on the public debt, including Treasury notes, for the same fiscal year, ending June 30, 1860, amounted to $3,177,314.62, which, added to the above sum of $55,402,465.46, makes the aggregate of $58,579,780.08.

It ought in justice to be observed that several of the estimates from the Departments for the year ending June 30, 1860, were reduced by Congress below what was and still is deemed compatible with the public interest. Allowing a liberal margin of $2,500,000 for this reduction and for other causes, it may be safely asserted that the sum of $61,000,000, or, at the most, $62,000,000, is amply sufficient to administer the Government and to pay the interest on the public debt, unless contingent events should hereafter render extraordinary expenditures necessary.

This result has been attained in a considerable degree by the care exercised by the appropriate Departments in entering into public contracts. I have myself never interfered with the award of any such contract, except in a single case, with the Colonization Society, deeming it advisable to cast the whole responsibility in each case on the proper head of the Department, with the general instruction that these contracts should always be given to the lowest and best bidder. It has ever been my opinion that public contracts are not a legitimate source of patronage to be conferred upon personal or political favorites, but that in all such cases a public officer is bound to act for the Government as a prudent individual would act for himself.

It is with great satisfaction I communicate the fact that since the date of my last annual message not a single slave has been imported into the United States in violation of the laws prohibiting the African slave trade. This statement is founded upon a thorough examination and investigation of the subject. Indeed, the spirit which prevailed some time since among a portion of our fellow-citizens in favor of this trade seems to have entirely subsided.

I also congratulate you upon the public sentiment which now exists against the crime of setting on foot military expeditions within the limits of the United States to proceed from thence and make war upon the people of unoffending States with whom we are at peace. In this respect a happy change has been effected since the commencement of my Administration. It surely ought to be the prayer of every Christian and patriot that such expeditions may never again receive countenance in our country or depart from our shores.

It would be a useless repetition to do more than refer with earnest commendation to my former recommendations in favor of the Pacific railroad; of the grant of power to the President to employ the naval force in the vicinity for the protection of the lives and property of our fellow-citizens passing in transit over the different Central American routes against sudden and lawless outbreaks and depredations, and also to protect American merchant vessels, their crews and cargoes, against violent and unlawful seizure and confiscation in the ports of Mexico and the South American Republics when these may be in a disturbed and revolutionary condition. It is my settled conviction that without such a power we do not afford that protection to those engaged in the commerce of the country which they have a right to demand.

I again recommend to Congress the passage of a law, in pursuance of the provisions of the Constitution, appointing a day certain previous to the 4th March in each year of an odd number for the election of Representatives throughout all the States. A similar power has already been exercised, with general approbation, in the appointment of the same day throughout the Union for holding the election of electors for President and Vice-President of the United States. My attention was earnestly directed to this subject from the fact that the Thirty-fifth Congress terminated on the 3d March, 1859, without making the necessary appropriation for the service of the Post-Office Department. I was then forced to consider the best remedy for this omission, and an immediate call of the present Congress was the natural resort. Upon inquiry, however, 1 ascertained that fifteen out of the thirty-three States composing the Confederacy were without Representatives, and that consequently these fifteen States would be disfranchised by such a call. These fifteen States will be in the same condition on the 4th March next. Ten of them can not elect Representatives, according to existing State laws, until different periods, extending from the beginning of August next until the months of October and November. In my last message I gave warning that in a time of sudden and alarming danger the salvation of our institutions might depend upon the power of the President immediately to assemble a full Congress to meet the emergency.

It is now quite evident that the financial necessities of the Government will require a modification of the tariff during your present session for the purpose of increasing the revenue. In this aspect, I desire to reiterate the recommendation contained in my last two annual messages in favor of imposing specific instead of *ad valorem* duties on all imported articles to which these can be properly applied. From long observation and experience I am convinced that specific duties are necessary, both to protect the revenue and to secure to our manufacturing interests that amount of incidental encouragement which unavoidably results from a revenue tariff.

As an abstract proposition it may be admitted that *ad valorem* duties would in theory be the most just and equal. But if the experience of this and of all other commercial nations has demonstrated that such duties can not be assessed and collected without great frauds upon the revenue, then it is the part of wisdom to resort to specific duties. Indeed, from the very nature of an *ad valorem* duty this must be the result. Under it the inevitable consequence is that foreign goods will be entered at less than their true value. The Treasury will therefore lose the duty on the difference between their real and fictitious value, and to this extent we are defrauded.

The temptations which *ad valorem* duties present to a dishonest importer are irresistible. His object is to pass his goods through the custom-house at the very lowest valuation necessary to save them from confiscation. In this he too often succeeds in spite of the vigilance of the revenue officers. Hence the resort to false invoices, one for the purchaser and another for the custom-house, and to other expedients to defraud the Government. The honest importer produces his invoice to the collector, stating the actual price at which he purchased the articles abroad. Not so the dishonest importer and the agent of the foreign manufacturer. And here it may be observed that a very large proportion of the manufactures imported from abroad are consigned for sale to commission merchants, who are mere agents employed by the manufacturers. In such cases no actual sale has been made to fix their value. The foreign manufacturer, if he be dishonest, prepares an invoice of the goods, not at their actual value, but at the very lowest rate necessary to escape detection. In this manner the dishonest importer and the foreign manufacturer enjoy a decided advantage over the honest merchant. They are thus enabled to undersell the fair trader and drive him from the market. In fact the operation of this system has already driven from the pursuits of honorable commerce many of that class of regular and conscientious merchants whose character throughout the world is the pride of our country.

The remedy for these evils is to be found in specific duties, so far as this may be practicable. They dispense with any inquiry at the custom-house into the actual cost or value of the article, and it pays the precise amount of duty previously fixed by law. They present no temptations to the appraisers of foreign goods, who receive but small salaries, and might by undervaluation in a few cases render themselves independent.

Besides, specific duties best conform to the requisition in the Constitution that "no preference shall be given by any regulation of commerce or revenue to the ports of one State over those of another." Under our *ad valorem* system such preferences are to some extent inevitable, and complaints have often been made that the spirit of this provision has been violated by a lower appraisement of the same articles at one port than at another.

An impression strangely enough prevails to some extent that specific duties are necessarily protective duties. Nothing can be more fallacious. Great Britain glories in free trade, and yet her whole revenue from imports is at the present moment collected under a system of specific duties. It is a striking fact in this connection that in the commercial treaty of January 23, 1860, between France and England one of the articles provides that the *ad valorem* duties which it imposes shall be converted into specific duties within six months from its date, and these are to be ascertained by making an average of the prices for six months previous to that time. The reverse of the propositions would be nearer to the truth, because a much larger amount of revenue would be collected by merely converting the *ad valorem* duties of a tariff into equivalent specific duties. To this extent the revenue would be increased, and in the same proportion the specific duty might be diminished.

Specific duties would secure to the American manufacturer the incidental protection to which he is fairly entitled under a revenue tariff, and to this surely no person would object. The framers of the existing tariff have gone further, and in a liberal spirit have discriminated in favor of large and useful branches of our manufactures, not by raising the rate of duty upon the importation of similar articles from abroad, but, what is the same in effect, by admitting articles free of duty which enter into the composition of their fabrics.

Under the present system it has been often truly remarked that this incidental protection decreases when the manufacturer needs it most and increases when he needs it least, and constitutes a sliding scale which always operates against him. The revenues of the country are subject to similar fluctuations. Instead of approaching a steady standard, as would be the case under a system of specific duties, they sink and rise with the sinking and rising prices of articles in foreign countries. It would not be difficult for Congress to arrange a system of specific duties which would afford additional stability both to our revenue and our manufactures and without injury or injustice to any interest of the country. This might be accomplished by ascertaining the average value of any given article for a series of years at the place of exportation and by simply converting the rate of *ad valorem* duty upon it which might be deemed necessary for revenue purposes into the form of a specific duty. Such an arrangement could not injure the consumer. If he should pay a greater amount of duty one year, this would be counterbalanced by a lesser amount the next, and in the end the aggregate would be the same.

I desire to call your immediate attention to the present condition of the Treasury, so ably and clearly presented by the Secretary in his report to

Congress, and to recommend that measures be promptly adopted to enable it to discharge its pressing obligations. The other recommendations of the report are well worthy of your favorable consideration.

I herewith transmit to Congress the reports of the Secretaries of War, of the Navy, of the Interior, and of the Postmaster-General. The recommendations and suggestions which they contain are highly valuable and deserve your careful attention.

The report of the Postmaster-General details the circumstances under which Cornelius Vanderbilt, on my request, agreed in the month of July last to carry the ocean mails between our Atlantic and Pacific coasts. Had he not thus acted this important intercommunication must have been suspended, at least for a season. The Postmaster-General had no power to make him any other compensation than the postages on the mail matter which he might carry. It was known at the time that these postages would fall far short of an adequate compensation, as well as of the sum which the same service had previously cost the Government. Mr. Vanderbilt, in a commendable spirit, was willing to rely upon the justice of Congress to make up the deficiency, and I therefore recommend that an appropriation may be granted for this purpose.

I should do great injustice to the Attorney-General were I to omit the mention of his distinguished services in the measures adopted and prosecuted by him for the defense of the Government against numerous and unfounded claims to land in California purporting to have been made by the Mexican Government previous to the treaty of cession. The successful opposition to these claims has saved the United States public property worth many millions of dollars and to individuals holding title under them to at least an equal amount.

It has been represented to me from sources which I deem reliable that the inhabitants in several portions of Kansas have been reduced nearly to a state of starvation on account of the almost total failure of their crops, whilst the harvests in every other portion of the country have been abundant. The prospect before them for the approaching winter is well calculated to enlist the sympathies of every heart. The destitution appears to be so general that it can not be relieved by private contributions, and they are in such indigent circumstances as to be unable to purchase the necessaries of life for themselves. I refer the subject to Congress. If any constitutional measure for their relief can be devised, I would recommend its adoption.

I cordially commend to your favorable regard the interests of the people of this District. They are eminently entitled to your consideration, especially since, unlike the people of the States, they can appeal to no government except that of the Union.

JAMES BUCHANAN.

SPECIAL MESSAGES.

WASHINGTON, *December 5, 1860.*

To the Senate of the United States:

I transmit, for the consideration of the Senate with a view to ratification, a convention for the adjustment of claims of citizens of the United States against the Government of the Republic of Costa Rica, signed by the plenipotentiaries of the contracting parties at San Jose on the 2d day of July last.

JAMES BUCHANAN.

WASHINGTON, *December 5, 1860.*

To the House of Representatives:

In answer to the resolution of the House of Representatives of the 9th of April last, requesting information concerning the African slave trade, I transmit a report from the Secretary of State and the documents by which it was accompanied.

JAMES BUCHANAN.

WASHINGTON, *January 2, 1861.*

To the Senate of the United States:

I transmit to the Senate, for its consideration with a view to ratification, a treaty of amity, commerce, and navigation, and for the surrender of fugitive criminals, between the United States and the Republic of Venezuela, signed at Caracas on the 27th of August last.

A similar treaty was concluded on the 10th July, 1856, was submitted to the Senate, and was by a resolution of that body approved, with an amendment, on the 10th March, 1857. Before this amendment could be laid before the Government of Venezuela for acceptance a new minister of the United States was accredited to that Government. Meantime the attention of this Government had been drawn to the disadvantage which would result to our citizens residing in Venezuela if the second article of the treaty of 1856 were permitted to go into effect, the "pecuniary equivalent" for exemption from military duty being an arbitrary and generally an excessive sum. In view of this fact it was deemed preferable to instruct our new minister to negotiate a new treaty which should omit the objectionable second article and also the few words of the twenty-eighth article which had been stricken out by the Senate.

With these changes, and with the addition of the last clause to the twenty-seventh article, the treaty is the same as that already approved by the Senate.

JAMES BUCHANAN.

WASHINGTON CITY, *January 8, 1861.*

To the Senate and House of Representatives:

At the opening of your present session I called your attention to the dangers which threatened the existence of the Union. I expressed my opinion freely concerning the original causes of those dangers, and recommended such measures as I believed would have the effect of tranquilizing the country and saving it from the peril in which it had been needlessly and most unfortunately involved. Those opinions and recommendations I do not propose now to repeat. My own convictions upon the whole subject remain unchanged.

The fact that a great calamity was impending over the nation was even at that time acknowledged by every intelligent citizen. It had already made itself felt throughout the length and breadth of the land. The necessary consequences of the alarm thus produced were most deplorable. The imports fell off with a rapidity never known before, except in time of war, in the history of our foreign commerce; the Treasury was unexpectedly left without the means which it had reasonably counted upon to meet the public engagements; trade was paralyzed; manufactures were stopped; the best public securities suddenly sunk in the market; every species of property depreciated more or less, and thousands of poor men who depended upon their daily labor for their daily bread were turned out of employment.

I deeply regret that I am not able to give you any information upon the state of the Union which is more satisfactory than what I was then obliged to communicate. On the contrary, matters are still worse at present than they then were. When Congress met, a stronge hope pervaded the whole public mind that some amicable adjustment of the subject would speedily be made by the representatives of the States and of the people which might restore peace between the conflicting sections of the country. That hope has been diminished by every hour of delay, and as the prospect of a bloodless settlement fades away the public distress becomes more and more aggravated. As evidence of this it is only necessary to say that the Treasury notes authorized by the act of 17th of December last were advertised according to the law and that no responsible bidder offered to take any considerable sum at par at a lower rate of interest than 12 per cent. From these facts it appears that in a government organized like ours domestic strife, or even a well-grounded fear of civil hostilities, is more destructive to our public and private interests than the most formidable foreign war.

In my annual message I expressed the conviction, which I have long deliberately held, and which recent reflection has only tended to deepen and confirm, that no State has a right by its own act to secede from the Union or throw off its federal obligations at pleasure. I also declared my opinion to be that even if that right existed and should be exercised by any State of the Confederacy the executive department of this Government had no authority under the Constitution to recognize its validity by acknowledging the independence of such State. This left me no alternative, as the chief executive officer under the Constitution of the United States, but to collect the public revenues and to protect the public property so far as this might be practicable under existing laws. This is still my purpose. My province is to execute and not to make the laws. It belongs to Congress exclusively to repeal, to modify, or to enlarge their provisions to meet exigencies as they may occur. I possess no dispensing power.

I certainly had no right to make aggressive war upon any State, and I am perfectly satisfied that the Constitution has wisely withheld that power even from Congress. But the right and the duty to use military force defensively against those who resist the Federal officers in the execution of their legal functions and against those who assail the property of the Federal Government is clear and undeniable.

But the dangerous and hostile attitude of the States toward each other has already far transcended and cast in the shade the ordinary executive duties already provided for by law, and has assumed such vast and alarming proportions as to place the subject entirely above and beyond Executive control. The fact can not be disguised that we are in the midst of a great revolution. In all its various bearings, therefore, I commend the question to Congress as the only human tribunal under Providence possessing the power to meet the existing emergency. To them exclusively belongs the power to declare war or to authorize the employment of military force in all cases contemplated by the Constitution, and they alone possess the power to remove grievances which might lead to war and to secure peace and union to this distracted country. On them, and on them alone, rests the responsibility.

The Union is a sacred trust left by our Revolutionary fathers to their descendants, and never did any other people inherit so rich a legacy. It has rendered us prosperous in peace and triumphant in war. The national flag has floated in glory over every sea. Under its shadow American citizens have found protection and respect in all lands beneath the sun. If we descend to considerations of purely material interest, when in the history of all time has a confederacy been bound together by such strong ties of mutual interest? Each portion of it is dependent on all and all upon each portion for prosperity and domestic security. Free trade throughout the whole supplies the wants of one portion from the productions of another and scatters wealth everywhere. The great planting and farming States require the aid of the commercial and navigating States to send their productions to domestic and foreign markets and to furnish the naval power to render their transportation secure against all hostile attacks.

Should the Union perish in the midst of the present excitement, we have already had a sad foretaste of the universal suffering which would result from its destruction. The calamity would be severe in every portion of the Union and would be quite as great, to say the least, in the Southern as in the Northern States. The greatest aggravation of the evil, and that which would place us in the most unfavorable light both before the world and posterity, is, as I am firmly convinced, that the secession movement has been chiefly based upon a misapprehension at the South of the sentiments of the majority in several of the Northern States. Let the question be transferred from political assemblies to the ballot box, and the people themselves would speedily redress the serious grievances which the South have suffered. But, in Heaven's name, let the trial be made before we plunge into armed conflict upon the mere assumption that there is no other alternative. Time is a great conservative power. Let us pause at this momentous point and afford the people, both North and South, an opportunity for reflection. Would that South Carolina had been convinced of this truth before her precipitate action! I therefore appeal through you to the people of the country to declare in their might that the Union must and shall be preserved by all constitutional means. I most earnestly recommend that you devote yourselves exclusively to the question how this can be accomplished in peace. All other questions, when compared to this, sink into insignificance. The present is no time for palliations. Action, prompt action, is required. A delay in Congress to prescribe or to recommend a distinct and practical proposition for conciliation may drive us to a point from which it will be almost impossible to recede.

A common ground on which conciliation and harmony can be produced is surely not unattainable. The proposition to compromise by letting the North have exclusive control of the territory above a certain line and to give Southern institutions protection below that line ought to receive universal approbation. In itself, indeed, it may not be entirely satisfactory, but when the alternative is between a reasonable concession on both sides and a destruction of the Union it is an imputation upon the patriotism of Congress to assert that its members will hesitate for a moment.

Even now the danger is upon us. In several of the States which have not yet seceded the forts, arsenals, and magazines of the United States have been seized. This is by far the most serious step which has been taken since the commencement of the troubles. This public property has long been left without garrisons and troops for its protection, because no person doubted its security under the flag of the country in any State of the Union. Besides, our small Army has scarcely been sufficient to guard our remote frontiers against Indian incursions. The seizure of this property, from all appearances, has been purely aggressive, and not in resistance to any attempt to coerce a State or States to remain in the Union.

At the beginning of these unhappy troubles I determined that no act of mine should increase the excitement in either section of the country. If the political conflict were to end in a civil war, it was my determined purpose not to commence it nor even to furnish an excuse for it by any act of this Government. My opinion remains unchanged that justice as well as sound policy requires us still to seek a peaceful solution of the questions at issue between the North and the South. Entertaining this conviction, I refrained even from sending reenforcements to Major Anderson, who commanded the forts in Charleston Harbor, until an absolute necessity for doing so should make itself apparent, lest it might unjustly be regarded as a menace of military coercion, and thus furnish, if not a provocation, at least a pretext for an outbreak on the part of South Carolina. No necessity for these reenforcements seemed to exist. I was assured by distinguished and upright gentlemen of South Carolina that no attack upon Major Anderson was intended, but that, on the contrary, it was the desire of the State authorities as much as it was my own to avoid the fatal consequences which must eventually follow a military collision.

And here I deem it proper to submit for your information copies of a communication, dated December 28, 1860, addressed to me by R. W. Barnwell, J. H. Adams, and James L. Orr, "commissioners" from South Carolina, with the accompanying documents, and copies of my answer thereto, dated December 31.

In further explanation of Major Anderson's removal from Fort Moultrie to Fort Sumter, it is proper to state that after my answer to the South Carolina "commissioners" the War Department received a letter from that gallant officer, dated on the 27th of December, 1860, the day after this movement, from which the following is an extract:

> I will add as my opinion that many things convinced me that the authorities of the State designed to proceed to a hostile act.

Evidently referring to the orders, dated December 11, of the late Secretary of War.

> Under this impression I could not hesitate that it was my solemn duty to move my command from a fort which we could not probably have held longer than forty-eight or sixty hours to this one, where my power of resistance is increased to a very great degree.

It will be recollected that the concluding part of these orders was in the following terms:

> The smallness of your force will not permit you, perhaps, to occupy more than one of the three forts, but an attack on or attempt to take possession of either one of them will be regarded as an act of hostility, and you may then put your command into either of them which you may deem most proper to increase its power of resistance. You are also authorized to take similar defensive steps whenever you have tangible evidence of a design to proceed to a hostile act.

It is said that serious apprehensions are to some extent entertained (in which I do not share) that the peace of this District may be disturbed before the 4th of March next. In any event, it will be my duty to preserve it, and this duty shall be performed.

In conclusion it may be permitted to me to remark that I have often warned my countrymen of the dangers which now surround us. This may be the last time I shall refer to the subject officially. I feel that my duty has been faithfully, though it may be imperfectly, performed, and, whatever the result may be, I shall carry to my grave the consciousness that I at least meant well for my country.

JAMES BUCHANAN.

WASHINGTON, *January 15, 1861.*

To the Senate of the United States:

In compliance with the resolution of the Senate passed on the 10th instant, requesting me to inform that body, if not incompatible with the public interest, "whether John B. Floyd, whose appointment as Secretary of War was confirmed by the Senate on the 6th of March, 1857, still continues to hold said office, and, if not, when and how said office became vacant; and, further, to inform the Senate how and by whom the duties of said office are now discharged, and, if an appointment of an acting or provisional Secretary of War has been made, how, when, and by what authority it was so made, and why the fact of said appointment has not been communicated to the Senate," I have to inform the Senate that John B. Floyd, the late Secretary of the War Department, resigned that office on the 29th day of December last, and that on the 1st day of January instant Joseph Holt was authorized by me to perform the duties of the said office until a successor should be appointed or the vacancy filled. Under this authority the duties of the War Department have been performed by Mr. Holt from the day last mentioned to the present time.

The power to carry on the business of the Government by means of a provisional appointment when a vacancy occurs is expressly given by the act of February 13, 1795, which enacts—

That in case of vacancy in the office of Secretary of State, Secretary of the Treasury, or of the Secretary of the Department of War, or of any officer of either of the said Departments whose appointment is not in the head thereof, whereby they can not perform the duties of their respective offices, it shall be lawful for the President of the United States, in case he shall think it necessary, to authorize any person or persons, at his discretion, to perform the duties of the said respective offices until a successor be appointed or such vacancy be filled: *Provided,* That no one vacancy shall be supplied in manner aforesaid for a longer period than six months.

It is manifest that if the power which this law gives had been withheld the public interest would frequently suffer very serious detriment. Vacancies may occur at any time in the most important offices which can not be immediately and permanently filled in a manner satisfactory to the appointing power. It was wise to make a provision which would enable the President to avoid a total suspension of business in the interval, and equally wise so to limit the Executive discretion as to prevent any serious abuse of it. This is what the framers of the act of 1795 did, and neither the policy nor the constitutional validity of their law has been questioned for sixty-five years.

The practice of making such appointments, whether in a vacation or during the session of Congress, has been constantly followed during every Administration from the earliest period of the Government, and its perfect lawfulness has never to my knowledge been questioned or denied. Without going back further than the year 1829, and without taking into the calculation any but the chief officers of the several Departments, it will be found that provisional appointments to fill vacancies were made to the number of 179 from the commencement of General Jackson's Administration to the close of General Pierce's. This number would probably be greatly increased if all the cases which occurred in the subordinate offices and bureaus were added to the count. Some of them were made while the Senate was in session; some which were made in vacation were continued in force long after the Senate assembled. Sometimes the temporary officer was the commissioned head of another Department, sometimes a subordinate in the same Department. Sometimes the affairs of the Navy Department have been directed *ad interim* by a commodore and those of the War Department by a general. In most, if not all, of the cases which occurred previous to 1852 it is believed that the compensation provided by law for the officer regularly commissioned was paid to the person who discharged the duties *ad interim*. To give the Senate a more detailed and satisfactory view of the subject, I send the accompanying tabular statement, certified by the Secretary of State, in which the instances are all set forth in which provisional as well as permanent appointments were made to the highest executive offices from 1829 nearly to the present time, with their respective dates.

It must be allowed that these precedents, so numerous and so long continued, are entitled to great respect, since we can scarcely suppose that the wise and eminent men by whom they were made could have been mistaken on a point which was brought to their attention so often. Still less can it be supposed that any of them willfully violated the law or the Constitution.

The lawfulness of the practice rests upon the exigencies of the public service, which require that the movements of the Government shall not be arrested by an accidental vacancy in one of the Departments; upon an act of Congress expressly and plainly giving and regulating the power, and upon long and uninterrupted usage of the Executive, which has never been challenged as illegal by Congress.

This answers the inquiry of the Senate so far as it is necessary to show "how and by whom the duties of said office are now discharged." Nor is it necessary to explain further than I have done "how, when, and by what authority" the provisional appointment has been made; but the resolution makes the additional inquiry "*why* the fact of said appointment has not been communicated to the Senate."

I take it for granted that the Senate did not mean to call for the reasons upon which I acted in performing an Executive duty nor to demand an account of the motives which governed me in an act which the law and the Constitution left to my own discretion. It is sufficient, therefore, for that part of the resolution to say that a provisional or temporary appointment like that in question is not required by law to be communicated to the Senate, and that there is no instance on record where such communication ever has been made. JAMES BUCHANAN.

WASHINGTON, *January 22, 1861.*

To the House of Representatives:

I herewith transmit to the House of Representatives a communication from the Secretary of the Navy, with accompanying reports, of the persons who were sent to the Isthmus of Chiriqui to make the examinations required by the fifth section of the act making appropriations for the naval service, approved June 22, 1860.

JAMES BUCHANAN.

WASHINGTON, *January 24, 1861.*

To the Senate of the United States:

In compliance with the resolution of the Senate of the 19th instant, requesting a copy of correspondence between the Department of State and ministers of foreign powers at Washington in regard to foreign vessels in Charleston, I transmit a report from the Secretary of State and the documents by which it was accompanied.

JAMES BUCHANAN.

WASHINGTON CITY, *January 28, 1861.*

To the Senate and House of Representatives of the United States:

I deem it my duty to submit to Congress a series of resolutions adopted by the legislature of Virginia on the 19th instant, having in view a peaceful settlement of the exciting questions which now threaten the Union. They were delivered to me on Thursday, the 24th instant, by ex-President Tyler, who has left his dignified and honored retirement in the hope that he may render service to his country in this its hour of peril. These resolutions, it will be perceived, extend an invitation "to all such States, whether slaveholding or nonslaveholding, as are willing to unite with Virginia in an earnest effort to adjust the present unhappy controversies in the spirit in which the Constitution was originally formed, and consistently with its principles, so as to afford to the people of the slaveholding States adequate guaranties for the securities of their rights, to appoint commissioners to meet, on the 4th day of February next, in the city of Washington, similar commissioners appointed by Virginia, to consider and, if practicable, agree upon some suitable adjustment.''

I confess I hail this movement on the part of Virginia with great satisfaction. From the past history of this ancient and renowned Commonwealth we have the fullest assurance that what she has undertaken she will accomplish if it can be done by able, enlightened, and persevering efforts. It is highly gratifying to know that other patriotic States have appointed and are appointing commissioners to meet those of Virginia in council. When assembled, they will constitute a body entitled in an eminent degree to the confidence of the country.

The general assembly of Virginia have also resolved—

That ex-President John Tyler is hereby appointed, by the concurrent vote of each branch of the general assembly, a commissioner to the President of the United States, and Judge John Robertson is hereby appointed, by a like vote, a commissioner to the State of South Carolina and the other States that have seceded or shall secede, with instructions respectfully to request the President of the United States and the authorities of such States to agree to abstain, pending the proceedings contemplated by the action of this general assembly, from any and all acts calculated to produce a collision of arms between the States and the Government of the United States.

However strong may be my desire to enter into such an agreement, I am convinced that I do not possess the power. Congress, and Congress alone, under the war-making power, can exercise the discretion of agreeing to abstain ''from any and all acts calculated to produce a collision of arms'' between this and any other government. It would therefore be a usurpation for the Executive to attempt to restrain their hands by an agreement in regard to matters over which he has no constitutional control. If he were thus to act, they might pass laws which he should be bound to obey, though in conflict with his agreement.

Under existing circumstances, my present actual power is confined within narrow limits. It is my duty at all times to defend and protect the public property within the seceding States so far as this may be practicable, and especially to employ all constitutional means to protect the property of the United States and to preserve the public peace at this the seat of the Federal Government. If the seceding States abstain ''from any and all acts calculated to produce a collision of arms,'' then the danger so much to be deprecated will no longer exist. Defense, and not aggression, has been the policy of the Administration from the beginning.

But whilst I can enter into no engagement such as that proposed, I cordially commend to Congress, with much confidence that it will meet their approbation, to abstain from passing any law calculated to produce a collision of arms pending the proceedings contemplated by the action of the general assembly of Virginia. I am one of those who will never despair of the Republic. I yet cherish the belief that the American people will perpetuate the Union of the States on some terms just and honorable for all sections of the country. I trust that the mediation of Virginia may be the destined means, under Providence, of accomplishing this inestimable benefit. Glorious as are the memories of her past history, such an achievement, both in relation to her own fame and the welfare of the whole country, would surpass them all.

JAMES BUCHANAN.

WASHINGTON, *January 30, 1861.*

To the Senate of the United States:

I have received the resolution of the Senate of the 24th instant, requesting the return to that body of the convention between the United States and the Republic of Venezuela on the subject of the Aves Island. That instrument is consequently herewith returned. It was approved by the Senate on the 24th June last with the following amendment:

> Article III: Strike out this article, in the following words:
> In consideration of the above agreement and indemnification, the Government of the United States and the individuals in whose behalf they have been made agree to desist from all further reclamation respecting the island of Aves, abandoning to the Republic of Venezuela whatever rights might pertain to them.

The amendment does not seem necessary to secure any right either of the United States or of any American citizen claiming under them. Neither the Government nor the citizens in whose behalf the convention has been concluded have any further claims upon the island of Aves. Nor is it known or believed that there are any claims against the Government of Venezuela having any connection with that island other than those provided for in this convention. I therefore recommend the reconsideration of the subject.

No steps have yet been taken toward making known to the Venezuelan Government the conditional approval of the convention by the Senate. This might have been necessary if the instrument had stipulated for a ratification in the usual form and it had been ratified accordingly. Inasmuch, however, as the convention contains no such stipulation, and as some of the installments had been paid according to its terms, it has been deemed preferable to suspend further proceedings in regard to it, especially as it was not deemed improbable that the Senate might request it to be returned. This anticipation has been realized.

JAMES BUCHANAN.

WASHINGTON, *February 5, 1861.*

To the Senate and House of Representatives:

I have received from the governor of Kentucky certain resolutions adopted by the general assembly of that Commonwealth, containing an application to Congress for the call of a convention for proposing amendments to the Constitution of the United States, with a request that I should immediately place the same before that body. It affords me great satisfaction to perform this duty, and I feel quite confident that Congress will bestow upon these resolutions the careful consideration to which they are eminently entitled on account of the distinguished and patriotic source from which they proceed, as well as the great importance of the subject which they involve.

JAMES BUCHANAN.

WASHINGTON, *February 8, 1861.*

To the Senate and House of Representatives:

I deemed it a duty to transmit to Congress with my message of the 8th of January the correspondence which occurred in December last between the "commissioners" of South Carolina and myself.

Since that period, on the 14th of January, Colonel Isaac W. Hayne, the attorney-general of South Carolina, called and informed me that he was the bearer of a letter from Governor Pickens to myself which he would deliver the next day. He was, however, induced by the interposition of Hon. Jefferson Davis and nine other Senators from the seceded and seceding States not to deliver it on the day appointed, nor was it communicated to me until the 31st of January, with his letter of that date. Their letter to him urging this delay bears date January 15, and was the commencement of a correspondence, the whole of which in my possession I now submit to Congress. A reference to each letter of the series in proper order accompanies this message.

JAMES BUCHANAN.

WASHINGTON CITY, *February 12, 1861.*

To the Senate of the United States:

I herewith submit to the Senate, for their advice, the proceedings and award of the commissioners under the convention between the United States of America and the Republic of Paraguay, proclaimed by the President on the 12th of March, 1860. It is decided by the award of these commissioners that "the United States and Paraguay Navigation Company have not proved or established any right to damages upon their said claim against the Government of the Republic of Paraguay, and that upon the proofs aforesaid the said Government is not responsible to the said company in any damages or pecuniary compensation whatever in all the premises.

The question arises, Had the commissioners authority under the convention to make such an award, or were they not confined to the assessment of damages which the company had sustained from the Government of Paraguay?

Our relations with that Republic had for years been of a most unsatisfactory character. They had been investigated by the preceding and by the present Administration. The latter came to the conclusion that both the interest and honor of the country required that our rights against that Government for their attack on the *Water Witch* and for the injuries they had inflicted on this company should, if necessary, be enforced. Accordingly, the President in his annual message of December, 1857, called the attention of Congress to the subject in the following language:

A demand for these purposes will be made in a firm but conciliatory spirit. This will the more probably be granted if the Executive shall have authority to use other means in the event of a refusal. This is accordingly recommended.

After due deliberation, Congress, on the 2d of June, 1858, authorized the President "to adopt such measures and use such force as in his judgment may be necessary and advisable" in the premises. A commissioner was accordingly appointed and a force fitted out and dispatched to Paraguay for the purpose, if necessary, of enforcing atonement for these wrongs.

The expedition appeared in the waters of the La Plata and our commissioner succeeded in concluding a treaty and convention embracing both branches of our demand. The convention of indemnity was signed on the 4th of February, 1859. The preamble of this convention refers to the interruption for a time of the good understanding and harmony between the two nations which has rendered that distant armament necessary. By the first article the Government of Paraguay "binds itself for the responsibility in favor of the United States and Paraguay Navigation Company which may result from the decree of commissioners" to be appointed in the manner provided by article 2. This was in accordance with the instructions to our commissioner, who was told that an indispensable preliminary to the negotiation would, "of course, be an acknowledgment on the part of the Paraguayan Government of its liability to the company." The first paragraph of this second article clearly specifies the object of the convention. This was not to ascertain whether the claim was just, to enforce which we had sent a fleet to Paraguay, but to constitute a commission to "determine," not the existence, but "the amount, of said reclamations." The final paragraph provides that "the two commissioners named in the said manner shall meet in the city of Washington to investigate, adjust, and *determine the amount* of the claims of the abovementioned company upon sufficient proofs of the charges and defenses of the contending parties." By the fifth article the Government of Paraguay "binds itself to pay to the Government of the United States of America, in the city of Assumption, Paraguay, thirty days after presentation to the Government of the Republic, the draft which that of the United States of America shall issue for the amount for which the two commissioners concurring, or by the umpire, shall declare it responsible to the said company."

The act of Congress of May 16, 1860, employs the same language that is used in the convention, "to investigate, adjust, and determine the amount" of the claims against Paraguay. Congress, not doubting that an award would be made in favor of the company for some certain amount of damages, in the sixth section of the act referred to provides that the money paid out of the Treasury for the expenses of the commission "shall be retained by the United States out of the money" (not any money) "that may, pursuant to the terms of said convention, be received from Paraguay."

After all this had been done, after we had fitted out a warlike expedition in part to obtain satisfaction for this very claim, after these solemn acts had been performed by the two Republics, the commissioners have felt themselves competent to decide that they could go behind the action of the legislative and executive branches of this Government and determine that there was no justice in the original claim. A commissioner of Paraguay might have been a proper person to act merely in assessing the amount of damages when an arbiter had been provided to decide between him and the commissioner on the part of the United States, but to have authorized him to decide upon the original justice of the claim against his own Government would have been a novelty. The American commissioner is as pure and honest a man as I have ever known, but I think he took a wrong view of his powers under the convention.

The principle of the liability of Paraguay having been established by the highest political acts of the United States and that Republic in their sovereign capacity, the commissioners, who would seem to have misapprehended their powers, have investigated and undertaken to decide whether the Government of the United States was right or wrong in the authority which they gave to make war if necessary to secure the indemnity. Governments may be, and doubtless often have been, wrong in going to war to enforce claims; but after this has been done, and the inquiry which led to the reclamations has been acknowledged by the Government that inflicted it, it does not appear to me to be competent for commissioners authorized to ascertain the indemnity for the injury to go behind their authority and decide upon the original merits of the claim for which the war was made. If a commissioner were appointed under a convention to ascertain the damage sustained by an American citizen in consequence of the capture of a vessel admitted by the foreign government to be illegal, and he should go behind the convention and decide that the original capture was a lawful prize, it would certainly be regarded as an extraordinary assumption of authority.

The present appears to me to be a case of this character, and for these reasons I have deemed it advisable to submit the whole subject for the consideration of the Senate.

JAMES BUCHANAN.

WASHINGTON, *February 21, 1861.*

To the Senate of the United States:

The treaty concluded between Great Britain and the United States on the 15th of June, 1846, provided in its first article that the line of bound-

ary between the territories of Her Britannic Majesty and those of the
United States from the point on the forty-ninth parallel of north latitude up to which it had already been ascertained should be continued
westward along the said parallel "to the middle of the channel which
separates the continent from Vancouvers Island, and thence southerly
through the middle of said channel and of Fucas Straits to the Pacific
Ocean." When the commissioners appointed by the two Governments
to mark the boundary line came to that point of it which is required to
run southerly through the channel which divides the continent from Vancouvers Island, they differed entirely in their opinions, not only concerning the true point of deflection from the forty-ninth parallel, but also as
to the channel intended to be designated in the treaty. After a long-
continued and very able discussion of the subject, which produced no
result, they reported their disagreement to their respective Governments.
Since that time the two Governments, through their ministers here and
at London, have had a voluminous correspondence on the point in controversy, each sustaining the view of its own commissioner and neither
yielding in any degree to the claims of the other. In the meantime
the unsettled condition of this affair has produced some serious local
disturbances, and on one occasion at least has threatened to destroy the
harmonious relations existing between Great Britain and the United
States. The island of San Juan will fall to the United States if our construction of the treaty be right, while if the British interpretation be
adopted it will be on their side of the line. That island is an important
possession to this country, and valuable for agricultural as well as military purposes. I am convinced that it is ours by the treaty fairly and
impartially construed. But argument has been exhausted on both sides
without increasing the probability of final adjustment. On the contrary,
each party seems now to be more convinced than at first of the justice of
its own demands. There is but one mode left of settling the dispute, and
that is by submitting it to the arbitration of some friendly and impartial
power. Unless this be done, the two countries are exposed to the constant danger of a collision which may end in war.

It is under these circumstances that the British Government, through
its minister here, has proposed the reference of the matter in controversy
to the King of Sweden and Norway, the King of the Netherlands, or to
the Republic of the Swiss Confederation. Before accepting this proposition I have thought it right to take the advice of the Senate.

The precise questions which I submit are these: Will the Senate approve
a treaty referring to either of the sovereign powers above named the dispute now existing between the Governments of the United States and
Great Britain concerning the boundary line between Vancouvers Island
and the American continent? In case the referee shall find himself
unable to decide where the line is by the description of it in the treaty of
15th June, 1846, shall he be authorized to establish a line according to

the treaty as nearly as possible? Which of the three powers named by Great Britain as an arbiter shall be chosen by the United States?

All important papers bearing on the questions are herewith communicated in the originals. Their return to the Department of State is requested when the Senate shall have disposed of the subject.

JAMES BUCHANAN.

WASHINGTON, *February 23, 1861.*

To the Senate of the United States:

In compliance with the resolutions of the Senate of the 17th and 18th February, 1858, requesting information upon the subject of the Aves Island, I transmit a report from the Secretary of State and the documents which accompanied it.

JAMES BUCHANAN.

WASHINGTON, *February 23, 1861.*

Hon. JOHN C. BRECKINRIDGE,
President of the Senate.

SIR: Herewith I inclose, for constitutional action of the Senate thereon should it approve the same, supplemental articles of agreement made and concluded with the authorities of the Delaware Indians on the 21st July last, with a view to the abrogation of the sixth article of the treaty of May 30, 1860.

JAMES BUCHANAN.

WASHINGTON, *February 23, 1861.*

To the House of Representatives of the United States:

In answer to a resolution of the House of Representatives adopted on the 11th instant, respecting the seizure of the mint at New Orleans, with a large amount of money therein, by the authorities of the State of Louisiana, the refusal of the branch mint to pay drafts of the United States, etc., I have to state that all the information within my possession or power on these subjects was communicated to the House by the Secretary of the Treasury on the 21st instant, and was prepared under the resolution above referred to and a resolution of the same date addressed to himself.

JAMES BUCHANAN.

WASHINGTON, *February 26, 1861.*

To the Senate of the United States:

In answer to the resolution of the Senate of the 25th instant, requesting information relative to the extradition of one Anderson, a man of color, charged with the commission of murder in the State of Missouri,

I transmit a report from the Secretary of State and the documents by which it was accompanied. The dispatch of Mr. Dallas being in the original, its return to the Department of State is requested.

JAMES BUCHANAN.

WASHINGTON, *March 1, 1861.*

To the House of Representatives:

In answer to their resolution of the 11th instant [ultimo], "that the President of the United States furnish to the House, if not incompatible with the public service, the reasons that have induced him to assemble so large a number of troops in this city, and why they are kept here; and whether he has any information of a conspiracy upon the part of any portion of the citizens of this country to seize upon the capital and prevent the inauguration of the President elect," the President submits that the number of troops assembled in this city is not large, as the resolution presupposes, its total amount being 653 men exclusive of the marines, who are, of course, at the navy-yard as their appropriate station. These troops were ordered here to act as a *posse comitatus*, in strict subordination to the civil authority, for the purpose of preserving peace and order in the city of Washington should this be necessary before or at the period of the inauguration of the President elect.

Since the date of the resolution Hon. Mr. Howard, from the select committee, has made a report to the House on this subject. It was thoroughly investigated by the committee, and although they have expressed the opinion that the evidence before them does not prove the existence of a secret organization here or elsewhere hostile to the Government that has for its object, upon its own responsibility, an attack upon the capital or any of the public property here, or an interruption of any of the functions of the Government, yet the House laid upon the table by a very large majority a resolution expressing the opinion "that the regular troops now in this city ought to be forthwith removed therefrom." This of itself was a sufficient reason for not withdrawing the troops.

But what was the duty of the President at the time the troops were ordered to this city? Ought he to have waited before this precautionary measure was adopted until he could obtain proof that a secret organization existed to seize the capital? In the language of the select committee, this was "in a time of high excitement consequent upon revolutionary events transpiring all around us, the very air filled with rumors and individuals indulging in the most extravagant expressions of fears and threats." Under these and other circumstances, which I need not detail, but which appear in the testimony before the select committee, I was convinced that I ought to act. The safety of the immense amount of public property in this city and that of the archives of the Government, in which all the States, and especially the new States in which the public lands are situated, have a deep interest; the peace and order of the city itself and the security of the inauguration of the President elect, were objects of such vast importance to the whole country that I could not hesitate to adopt precautionary defensive measures. At the present moment, when all is quiet, it is difficult to realize the state of alarm which prevailed when the troops were first ordered to this city. This almost instantly subsided after the arrival of the first company, and a feeling of comparative peace and security has since existed both in Washington and throughout the country. Had I refused to adopt this precautionary measure, and evil consequences, which many good men at the time apprehended, had followed, I should never have forgiven myself.

JAMES BUCHANAN.

WASHINGTON, *March 2, 1861.*

To the Senate of the United States:

I deem it proper to invite the attention of the Senate to the fact that with this day expires the limitation of time for the exchange of the ratifications of the treaty with Costa Rica of 2d July, 1860.

The minister of that Republic is disappointed in not having received the copy intended for exchange, and the period will lapse without the possibility of carrying out the provisions of the convention in this respect.

I submit, therefore, the expediency of the passage of a resolution authorizing the exchange of ratifications at such time as may be convenient, the limitations of the ninth article to the contrary notwithstanding.

JAMES BUCHANAN.

VETO MESSAGE.

WASHINGTON CITY, *January 25, 1861.*

To the House of Representatives of the United States:

I return with my objections to the House, in which it originated, the bill entitled "An act for the relief of Hockaday & Leggit," presented to me on the 15th instant.

This bill appropriates $59,576 "to Hockaday & Leggit, in full payment for damages sustained by them in reduction of pay for carrying the mails on route No. 8911; and that said amount be paid to William Leggit for and on account of Hockaday & Leggit, and for their benefit."

A bill containing the same language, with the single exception that the sum appropriated therein was $40,000 instead of $59,576, passed both Houses of Congress at their last session; but it was presented to me at so late a period of the session that I could not examine its merits before the time fixed for the adjournment, and it therefore, under the Constitution, failed to become a law. The increase of the sum appropriated in the present bill over that in the bill of the last session, being within a fraction of $20,000, has induced me to examine the question with some attention, and I find that the bill involves an important principle, which if established by Congress may take large sums out of the Treasury.

It appears that on the 1st day of April, 1858, John M. Hockaday entered into a contract with the Postmaster-General for transporting the mail on route No. 8911, from St. Joseph, Mo., by Fort Kearney, Nebraska Territory, and Fort Leavenworth, to Salt Lake City, for the sum of $190,000 per annum for a weekly service. The service was to commence on the 1st day of May, 1858, and to terminate on the 30th November, 1860. By this contract the Postmaster-General reserved to himself the right "to reduce the service to semimonthly whenever the necessities of the public and the condition of affairs in the Territory of Utah may not require it more frequently." And again:

That the Postmaster-General may discontinue or curtail the service, in whole or in part, in order to place on the route a greater degree of service, or whenever the public interests require such discontinuance for any other cause, he allowing one month's extra pay on the amount of service dispensed with.

On the 11th April, 1859, the Postmaster-General curtailed the service, which he had a clear right to do under the contract, to semimonthly, with an annual deduction of $65,000, leaving the compensation $125,000 for twenty-four trips per year instead of $190,000 for fifty-two trips. This curtailment was not to take effect till the 1st of July, 1859.

At the time the contract was made it was expected that the army in Utah might be engaged in active operations, and hence the necessity of frequent communications between the War Department and that Territory. The reservation of the power to curtail the service to semimonthly trips itself proves that the parties had in view the contingency of such curtailment "whenever the necessities of the public and the condition of affairs in the Territory of Utah may not require it more frequently."

Before the Postmaster-General ordered this curtailment he had an interview with the Secretary of War upon the subject, in the course of which the Secretary agreed that a weekly mail to St. Joseph and Salt Lake City was no longer needed for the purposes of the Government— this, evidently, because the trouble in Utah had ended.

Mr. Hockaday faithfully complied with his contract, and the full compensation was paid, at the rate of $190,000 per annum, up to the 1st July, 1859, and "one month's extra pay on the amount of service dispensed with," according to the contract.

Previous to that date, as has been already stated, on the 14th of April, 1859, the Postmaster-General curtailed the service to twice per month, and on the 11th May, 1859, Messrs. Hockaday & Co. assigned the contract to Jones, Russell & Co. for a bonus of $50,000. Their property connected with the route was to be appraised, which was effected, and they received on this account about $94,000, making the whole amount about $144,000.

There is no doubt that the contractors have sustained considerable loss in the whole transaction. The amount I shall not pretend to decide, whether $40,000 or $59,576, or any other sum.

It will be for Congress to consider whether the precedent established by this bill will not in effect annul all restrictions contained in the mail contracts enabling the Postmaster-General to reduce or curtail the postal service according to the public exigencies as they may arise. I have no other solicitude upon the subject. I am informed that there are many cases in the Post-Office Department depending upon the same principle.

JAMES BUCHANAN.

PROCLAMATION.

BY THE PRESIDENT OF THE UNITED STATES OF AMERICA.

A PROCLAMATION.

Whereas objects of interest to the United States require that the Senate should be convened at 12 o'clock on the 4th of March next to receive and act upon such communications as may be made to it on the part of the Executive:

Now, therefore, I, James Buchanan, President of the United States, have considered it to be my duty to issue this my proclamation, declaring that an extraordinary occasion requires the Senate of the United States to convene for the transaction of business at the Capitol, in the city of Washington, on the 4th day of March next, at 12 o'clock at noon on that day, of which all who shall at that time be entitled to act as members of that body are hereby required to take notice.

Given under my hand and the seal of the United States, at Washing-

[SEAL.]   ton, the 11th day of February, A. D. 1861, and of the Independence of the United States the eighty-fifth.

JAMES BUCHANAN.

By the President:

> J. S. BLACK,
>   *Secretary of State.*